RAkc
4/89

NEW YORK INTELLECT

Toward an Urban Vision (1975)

Community and Social Change in America (1978)

The Making of American Society (co-author, 1978)

Editor:
Democracy in America, by Alexis deTocqueville (1981)

NEW YORK
INTELLECT

A History of Intellectual Life in New York City,

from 1750 to the Beginnings of Our Own Time

THOMAS BENDER

THE JOHNS HOPKINS UNIVERSITY PRESS

BALTIMORE

Originally published in 1987 as a Borzoi Book by Alfred A. Knopf, Inc.
Johns Hopkins Paperbacks edition, 1988, published by arrangement with
Alfred A. Knopf, Inc.

The Johns Hopkins University Press
701 West 40th Street, Baltimore, Maryland 21211

The paper used in this publication meets the minimum requirements
of American National Standard for Information Sciences—Permanence
of Paper for Printed Library Materials,
ANSI Z39.48-1984.

Library of Congress Cataloging-in-Publication Data

Bender, Thomas
New York intellect.

Bibliography: p.
Includes index.
1. New York (N.Y.)—Intellectual life.   I. Title.
[F128.3.B46   1988]   947.7'1   87-31123
ISBN 0-8018-3639-5 (pbk.)

FOR

Gwendolyn

New Yorker by Choice

AND

David and Sophia

New Yorkers by Birth

There has always been in American literature a New York tradition as well as a New England one, but it has never been so much talked about precisely because it is less provincial. The New Yorkers, all facing, as it were, in the direction of the mouth of the Hudson, have more easily passed out into the larger world, and the great city in which they have all sojourned has been cosmopolitan and always changing. The New Englanders of the classical generation did derive a certain strength from their relation to small strongly-rooted communities . . . but they suffered from the crampedness of these places. The New Yorkers . . . are all men or women of the world in a way that no New Englander is, and they have, most of them, a sense of the country as a whole such as few New Englanders have had.

—EDMUND WILSON (1947)

CONTENTS

ACKNOWLEDGMENTS

A book so many years in the making and so broad in its range incurs many debts. Some of these debts are of the material sort, and I am deeply appreciative of the John Simon Guggenheim Memorial Foundation for a fellowship in the 1980–81 academic year. The gift of time that it provided at the beginning of the project enabled me to think out the larger framework of the book, and a second fellowship from the Rockefeller Foundation in 1984–85 enabled me to complete the first full draft.

I have a different obligation to John C. Sawhill, president of NYU at the time I began this project. By so publicly displaying his faith in me and by recognizing the importance of my subject, he encouraged me to persist. I am also indebted to him for his support of Richard Sennett's dream of a center for the humanities in New York that would be of as well as in the city. The New York Institute for the Humanities—which began in a basement at NYU, with Sennett and me as the first two fellows —has, with its diverse group of academic and non-academic fellows, taught me much about the urban intellect.

Most of my research was conducted in the magnificent collections of the New York Public Library and at the New-York Historical Society Library. Other libraries were also important to me, particularly Butler Library at Columbia University and Bobst Library at NYU. Bayrd Still, the grand old man of New York's historical studies, continually encouraged my interest in New York's history, and in his capacity as director of the NYU Archives was quite helpful, as was Tom Frusciano. Sara Vos of Central Filing at Columbia University was equally generous with her assistance.

Various parts of this book were originally presented as lectures. I learned much from my audiences at the American Historical Association, Harvard University, Princeton University, the Dallas Public Library, the New York Public Library, Georgia State University, Columbia University, Rockefeller University, the University of Michigan, Grey Art Gallery at NYU, and the Hungarian Academy of Sciences.

Many other people have helped—by talking over parts of my story with me, by reading and commenting on parts of the manuscript, and by directing me to information. Almost everyone I talked to over the past several years contributed something, but—without implicating them at all in any of the book's shortcomings—let me specifically acknowledge the help of Quentin Anderson, Iver Bernstein, Patricia Bonomi, Lynn Garafola, the late Herbert G. Gutman, David Hollinger, Margaret Hunt, Elizabeth Kendall, Pauline Maier, Barbara Tischler, Wilson Smith, the late John William Ward, and Sean Wilentz. Two graduate students at NYU helped with the tedious task of checking footnotes: Barbara Balliet and James Strandberg. Adam Gopnik at Alfred A. Knopf, always gracious, suggested important improvements as he guided the book through production.

John Higham, Eric McKitrick, and William R. Taylor not only encouraged me over the years but were always willing to write letters in support of my fellowship applications. I was just beginning this project when I met Carl E. Schorske. Over the years since then, he has been continually and invaluably supportive of me and my work, if not always in agreement with me or with it. More than that, however, his own work and his sense of scholarly vocation have been an inspiration to me.

Ever since my son, David, was old enough to know what a book is, he has had to live with his father's book as well as with his father. As the book finally neared completion, in his eighth year, he left a note on my typewriter: "Get your book don fast." Such a note could be worrisome, but the worry turned into a special pleasure when he followed it with an oral command the next morning: "And when you finish the book, I'm going to write another note telling you to start another book fast." Gwendolyn, who married me, along with the book and David, two and a half years ago, has not only buoyed me with her faith but gotten me through many a trouble spot with her splendid historical intelligence and her feel for the grace that can be achieved in the written word. Gwendolyn, David, and little Sophia, who is yet too young to know what a book is, all encourage my commitment to intellect and books, but they also sustain in me an appreciation of much more that life has to offer.

Finally, let me thank Maxine Groffsky and Robert Gottlieb. At a time when only a small portion of the book was written, they both grasped its importance and embraced it. To work with Gottlieb is a special experience, known only to a privileged group of writers among whom I can—happily—now count myself.

T.B.

PREFACE

When New York City was finally recognized after World War II as an international cultural metropolis, few realized how long, how complex, how thorough, if irregular, its foreground of preparation had been. As a milieu for art and intellect, New York City was neither comfortable nor convenient, but it supplied, as the characteristic if unique example of Walt Whitman testifies, the means for making democratic culture under modern conditions.

Anyone who longs for the ideals, institutions, and traditions characteristic of European intellectual life will be disappointed with New York. Neither the ideas nor the actual social organization of European intellectual life has been successfully transplanted in New York; Manhattan schist never allowed Old World culture to root itself in New York. Many of the city's most celebrated intellectuals today have been embarrassed by the city's divergence from European patterns. Such cultural provincialism, most recently evident in a symposium on intellectuals in America published in a special issue of the quite serious and highly regarded quarterly *Salmagundi*, has made it difficult to recognize our own culture.

One must be precise on this matter. The presence of Europe is fundamentally important to the culture and society of New York. The city of New York has been the historic point of entry not only for European immigrants but also for European ideas and cultural ideals. Neither European immigrants nor European ideas have made New York over in their own image, but neither were they simply assimilated into a fixed native society and culture. What is interesting in both cases is the play of experiences and cultures. The way in which the continuing aspiration for European patterns of intellectual life and the actual life of the city found resolution produced in New York a distinctive cultural formation.

So long as we remain unable to identify the intellectual traditions of our own capital city, we shall be vulnerable to the myth of Europe, displaying our provincialism and even our foolishness as we seek to establish the terms of our intellectual life. We cannot understand ourselves as intellectuals, as Americans, until we grasp the special character of New York—both its possibilities and its limitations—as a place of intellect.*

One must begin by accommodating the obvious: New York is not a European city, even if it is the most European of American cities. It is not a capital city in the manner of Paris, but it is in its own way the American metropolis. European cultural models have played a crucial role in the cultural aspirations of New York, but cultural ideals and social history interacted to produce neither a replica of Europe nor a failure, but rather a distinctive cultural milieu. If the coherence of Parisian intellectual life derives from a long-standing pattern of institutional centralization and Cartesianism, the rich complexity of intellect in New York is the product of a polycentric society and the cultural diversity of a city of immigrants. One cannot, in other words, begin to understand the life of the mind in New York or America without beginning, as Alexis de Tocqueville long ago demonstrated, with the distinctive social conditions of the city. The most fruitful comparative orientation, then, is not one of lamentation. We must appreciate instead the interplay of European models and local historical and sociological conditions in New York. It is worth the effort: to understand the evolution of various configurations of cultural aspiration and their realization in New York is to go far toward grasping the relationship of intellect, democracy, and society in modern times.

So little of the history of the men and women who sought a place for the mind in the American capital of commerce has been written that my research has been a voyage into the unknown. When I began the study, I assumed that the proper starting point would be the late nineteenth century. As the study progressed, however, the roots of New York's qualities as a setting for intellectuals turned out to extend farther into the city's past, back to the middle of the eighteenth century. And the relationship to Europe turned out to be more complicated than I had anticipated.

For the culturally ambitious of New York there was not one Europe, but three. Different groups and generations of New Yorkers of intellectual aspiration looked to different European models for their intellectual charters. The earliest model was based upon Edinburgh, an extraordinary city of the Enlightenment, the city of David Hume and Adam Smith, a city where a cluster of cultural institutions brought together men of letters, professionals, and men of affairs. By the 1840s the New York patrician culture built upon this model, appallingly vacuous and thus vulnerable to the challenge of Jacksonian democracy, had been routed.

* Here and elsewhere I resort to the general term "intellect" to avoid an anachronistic use of "intellectuals," a word that came into use, as we shall see, in the 1890s and 1900s.

New York's intellectual orientation became more explicitly literary, leaving the orbit of the Edinburgh of Hume and even of Walter Scott for that of Paris, where, it seemed, the writer was properly honored and where the atmosphere of the city was electric with literary ideas. After the Civil War, particularly in the 1880s, a sense of failure, a sense that authoritative intellect was being lost in the marketplace of culture that was New York, prompted cultural reformers to look toward the model of the German research university. Here, they thought, intellectual discourse would be purified and the authority of intellect justified.

These distinct cultures of intellectual life succeeded each other, the perceived failure of one prompting the next, but they also coexisted with each other and interacted with each other.* I use "Civic Culture," "Literary Culture," and "Academic Culture" as typological terms, and as such they provide the structure for the three main parts of the book. Although the order in which these programmatic intellectual charters appear in my narrative represents the order in which they assume a dominant position in the intellectual culture of the city, their triumphs are never complete. While earlier models are eclipsed or subordinated by later ones, prior ones persist as ideals and as practice, thus giving a potentially vital tension to the city's intellectual life.

We have inherited these three structures of intellect; they lie deep in the life of the city. Even after the archaeological work undertaken in this book, however, they remain barely visible. Yet these different intellectual charters continue to orient the life of the mind. Even though none has been fully realized, their continuity and interplay account for the complexity, depth, and texture of the city's intellectual culture.

New York City constitutes one of the most complicated and contentious of human environments. In politics, in the economy, and in its intellectual life, the appearance of disorder and confusion has prompted attempts to rationalize and control experience. There have been, as we shall see, repeated attempts to reform the city's culture, to tighten intellectual life and its sustaining institutions. Again and again, reformers tried to establish authoritative institutions, like those of Edinburgh, Paris, Berlin, even Boston. Again and again, the city proved to be the solvent of their dreams.

Historical description here becomes prescription: those who claim to represent authoritative intellect and legitimate tradition must relentlessly

---

* My use of the phrase "cultures of intellectual life," or elsewhere "intellectual culture," is intended to convey my realization that intellectual life constitutes only a part of what is represented by the word "culture," even in a restricted usage of the word. A full cultural history would embrace more than I attempt here. Also, at the point when science develops its own language and publication system, it drops out of my notion of intellectual culture for reasons that will, I hope, become clear.

continue seeking to consolidate that authority, but they must as certainly be successfully challenged, forcing them to accommodate themselves to new voices. It is this contentious process of mixing that makes New York unique in America. What is so impressive about New York City—from either a general American or a European perspective—is the battle-ground quality of its intellectual life. The uncentered but not utterly formless character of intellectual culture in New York is its special, though not always welcome, gift to the life of the mind. Only in New York might one find so many and such distinct points of intellectual energy, each with a chance of momentarily flourishing as a center, even if on the periphery. Such a milieu protects intellectuals, if they have the wit to want such protection, from incorporation into any one coterie. Upon this can be built the intellectual's most important birthright: inde-pendence.

The forces of authority and the forces of the new (whether new ideas or new groups, including, recently, groups and ideas of non-European origin) have repeatedly fought each other to creative standoffs. But not all groups, one must insist. Catholics, whether of older immigrant stock or newer Hispanic immigrants, blacks, Asians, and women have not claimed so large a domain in the city's civic, literary, and academic cul-tures as have male WASPs and, in the mid-twentieth century, Jews. In-justices there have been and are. Yet New York is more open than any other cultural capital in history. While dominant groups repeatedly try to consolidate their authority against challenging groups, they just as repeatedly fail to do so successfully. But neither can they be pushed entirely aside. The tension is fruitful; the result is an unmatched vitality and, even, a basis for democratic culture, though not necessarily and not yet the thing itself.

At its best, at its most democratic, as in the case of Randolph Bourne or Walt Whitman, intellect in New York relished the notion of a polyglot culture; at its most nervous, New York's intellectual elite has sought to protect itself from democracy and heterogeneity (immigration). One may, as I do, embrace the vision of Bourne and Whitman, but that is not really what is demanded in New York, past or present. We must simply appreciate, not evade, the contested quality of the city's public culture, the tension between democracy and standards, between groups and classes.

For two hundred years intellectual life in New York has been inspired by and haunted by the idea of a democratic intellect. Is democratic dis-tinction possible? It is a hard question, not fully answered in our time. Yet it is helpful as we think about the city's past to realize that many proposals offered as a defense of standards have been in fact acts of exclusion. The record is rich in generous democratic visions as well as in transparently self-interested defenses of privileged intellect against democracy.

The notion of democratic culture is a capacious one, and it means many things in this narrative. But there is a consistent cluster of meanings, with different emphases and patterns of emphasis for different people at different historical moments. Sometimes it is social equality that is most salient, or political access, or engagement with the diversity and changes of urban life, or an assault on established institutions and restrictive policies, or a broad commitment to justice—and more. If the democratic idea of inclusion is an inspiring beacon, a democratic culture is an ongoing historical creation. It is this historical process of creating, not the particular battles, visions, and evasions recorded here, that constitutes our legacy as we continue the task of finding intellect's place in the world's most modern and democratic city.

What follows is a long essay—or, more accurately, three longish and interrelated essays—focused on the changing definitions and social configurations of intellectual life in New York City. I have striven for an essayistic quality in this work to avoid the looming danger in a study of such scope of falling into a vast catalogue of names, dates, and thumbnail ideas that might constitute an encyclopedia (or telephone book) of New York intellectual life. Adopting a narrative form, I have stressed selected analytical and interpretive themes. I have concentrated my attention on a large but limited number of individual thinkers and structures of intellectual life that most interestingly illuminate my themes. My hope is that the reader, when he or she finishes the book, will have a richer sense of the city and familiarity with the men and women of ideas for whom the city was a working environment, ever present in their work.

Beyond the desire to tell an important story that has not yet been told, two sets of concerns have motivated this work, one professional, the other civic. When I completed my graduate training in 1971, American historical writing was divided by a great schism. Social history and intellectual history, for decades partners in extending the territory of history, had become rivals. A vigorous new social history challenged the very legitimacy of intellectual history. If it made me nervous to see how easily some practitioners of the new social history dismissed the importance of subjective perceptions and cultural meanings, I had to acknowledge the validity of much of what they said about the sins of intellectual history, which presumed much more than it demonstrated. It was not enough to trace ideas; they had to be located in social as well as in intellectual contexts, in social institutions and in discourses. One had to understand the discourse of intellectuals not only as a part of a particular social world but also in relation to the larger social world within which that smaller world was located. By the late 1970s, it had occurred to me that by locating men and women thinking in a particular place, in a great city, and by conceiving of them in relation to urban society and a public culture, it might be possible to reunify and revive social and intellectual history.[1]

My interest in locating the understandings of culture held by intellectuals within the actual social history of the city was only in part a methodological matter. It also derived from civic concern. When I began this work, New York City was under the cloud of a catastrophic political event known as the "fiscal crisis" of 1975. The more I followed (and lived through) the unfolding of that event, the more I felt that its meaning was far wider than the political and economic commentary on it suggested. It was, I thought, just as much a cultural and intellectual crisis. What struck me about the sea of journalism and scholarship that surrounded the crisis was the inability of New York's intellectuals to generate compelling general ideas about New York as a democratic city. No one seemed to know how to initiate—within the context of a local, urban culture—a serious and general discourse about the most important city in the world.[2] The city, it seemed, was a mere incident in various discourses of organized, professionalized interest groups, some local, some not, but all sectoral in orientation, whether their project was classical music, social services, or office space. It seemed that such a silence was a "cultural event" that must have a history and a cause. I now realize that I was looking for a sort of centered, coherent, even totalizing discourse that one errs in seeking in New York. Yet I have been confirmed in my initial belief that the civic possibilities of the city exceed what was achieved in 1975 and that the work of a historian might forward the cause of civic revitalization.[3]

My specific aims in this book are fivefold, and they can be stated with great concision. First, I wanted to make an analytical point about the structure of intellectual life. I have sought to show—and I have done this in the very structure of the book—that three distinct cultures of intellectual life have both succeeded one another and coexisted with each other over the course of the past two centuries. Second, I wanted to illuminate the complex, tangled, but enormously consequential relations among democracy, culture, and the city. My third intention flows directly from the second. I want to insist upon and demonstrate the existence of a continuous discussion, or discourse, or conversation in New York about the relation of intellect to democracy and society. Because traditional culture was always vulnerable in diverse and contentious New York, this discussion began earlier and was pursued with greater intensity in New York than in any other American or, for that matter, European city. To track this discussion amounts, of course, to a history of the meaning of learned culture in New York City, a history with profound moral and political implications. Fourth, I want to insist upon the importance of the city as a context for intellectual life. In the process of elaborating the metropolitan milieu, I have attended to the social and physical development of the city. And I have drawn into my story many figures important in their own time but since forgotten, thereby providing a new context for the well-known, whom I have thus sought to associate with the cultural tradition of the city and its changing social and intellectual milieu. Finally, by making democracy and public culture my guiding concerns, I hope to enhance the prospect for strengthening the public and democratic possibilities of city culture in our own time.

NEW YORK INTELLECT

New York City and the Condition of Intellect

New York is, to paraphrase Charles Dickens from another context, the best of cities and the worst of cities. Intellectuals must acknowledge both cities, understanding that New York is a place where one finds life at its most highly accomplished levels of mind, art, and technique, and where life is confronted, daily, at its most elemental, as a matter of sheer survival. Such is the moral context and practical challenge of intellect in our time.

Alexis de Tocqueville's New York, that of the 1820s and 1830s, witnessed the spread of the egalitarian spirit and the unbridled celebration of democracy. This period, whether one thinks of the Mechanics Institute, the founding of New York University, the *Democratic Review,* or much else, seems to have represented a special and plastic moment of democratic promise. But realization then eluded New York, except perhaps for the belated, surprising, and not fully understood appearance of *Leaves of Grass* in 1855. Yet the promise did not evaporate with the passing of that generation. There has always been, from 1750 to our own time, an undercurrent of democratic possibility, admittedly ebbing and flowing, associated with the dream of a modern and metropolitan culture in New York.

Equally persistent, however, has been the aspiration of intellectuals to distinguish themselves from the common life of the metropolis. No, more than that. They have sought to establish themselves as authoritative in matters of culture and, often, politics. In the eighteenth century such claims were grounded on the basis of social position, while in the nineteenth and twentieth centuries position or class has been masked somewhat by assertions that culture or expertise conferred not only honor but authority and power as well. If the final outlines of a modern and democratic culture are not yet clear, one can fairly say that all conceptions of intellect that withdraw it from the public realm—whether under cover of art or of expertise—cannot but compromise the ideal. Intellect cannot be dissociated from everyday life; it must be in energetic collision with the city in all of its experiential richness.

The civic culture of eighteenth-century Edinburgh and New York seems far from us in part because within the culture of those cities there were no boundaries between public life and intellectual life. Both the literary culture and the academic culture that developed subsequently and are more familiar to us can ill afford to lose touch entirely with that earlier civic definition of intellect. Not only hindsight makes this apparent. The prescient Adam Ferguson, a contemporary and friend of David Hume and Adam Smith, offered us advance warning in his too little remembered *Essay on the History of Civil Society* (1766). Ferguson grasped, even before Smith, the prospective division of labor in modern societies and economies, and he worried more than did Smith about its implications—for intellectual as well as social life. "Thinking itself," Ferguson observed, "may become a peculiar craft." While this may seem to "contribute to the forward progress of the arts," Ferguson worried that it would do more to divide society into classes. And it would isolate men of ideas from common life, from society. "Men at a distance from the objects of knowledge," he cautioned, "could produce only the jargon of a technical language and accumulate the impertinence of academical forms." Such "separation" threatened "in some measure to break the bands of society, to substitute mere forms and rules of art in place of ingenuity, and to withdraw individuals from the common scene of occupation, on which the sentiments of the heart, and the mind, are most happily employed."[1]

Though it is, of course, impossible, Ferguson seems to have anticipated the academicization of knowledge and art in our time: the academic novel, grounded in theory rather than in experience and such a worrisome index of the limited social worlds, real and fictive, of too many writers today; current literary criticism, with its methodological virtuosity and obscurantism; and academic social science that can, as it recently did at Harvard University, explicitly dismiss scholarship that engages deeply felt issues in the common life in the public and accessible language of that life.[2]

The problem of the vast increase in the cultural territory captured by the university in the past generation has been widely recognized. Yet so serious and deeply ingrained is this academicization that would-be reformers have tended to look exclusively to the university to solve it. Yet the university, increasingly the home of the arts—writing, painting, music, dance—as well as scholarship, is itself the problem. General cultural reform must establish itself beyond and outside the bounds of the academy. A revitalized public culture requires the stimulation of other, non-academic, modes of intellectual life—particularly serious literary journalism and community-based adult education, the traditional vehicles of literary and civic culture—in order to challenge, even reverse, the danger of a deadening academic hegemony. Such competition may, moreover, prompt much-needed reform within the academy, while providing a wider venue for those scholars within the academy who want on occasion to move out into the public culture of their time.

The great and indispensable value of New York City in the national culture is as a staging area for such cultural renovation. Only in New York are there the traditions and resources to reconstruct a vital and democratic public culture, one that includes the cultures of esoteric art and the academy, even while it challenges them both.

The problem of our culture today is not a lack of consensus, a lack of unity, but rather the absence of an adequate social or intellectual basis for contact and conflict among its parts. At its best a great city supplies just this, and New York City, when it has worked, has been such a place. One need not be either nostalgic or hopelessly idealistic in embracing such a role for the city. Life and intellect in New York are not held together by a single idea, and they never have been. Many ideas, many dreams, many disappointments meet in New York. What holds people and ideas together, what brings them into contact in a way that does not happen elsewhere, is simply the glamour and excitement of it all. Not a noble basis for a common life and a public culture, certainly not the bond of justice that, for Aristotle, bound men together in the polis, but it is real. It works, and it can work for all classes of people.

The plurality of voices and values in the city is not merely a manifestation of academic hegemony in our time; it is a mark of modern consciousness, itself a product of the metropolitan transformations of the past century. To ask for a return to a unified culture is simply reactionary. Yet to the degree that thought and imagination lose contact with the subjective experience of the metropolis, to the degree that intellect suburbanizes itself, whether into the artistic or ideological coterie or into the university, our civic life and our ordinary life suffer.

If the metropolis offers us an intensity and range of experience that is so overwhelming that it cannot easily be shut out of the life of the mind, we need still more from New York. In addition to being a place of experience, it must also be a milieu for initiating a conversation out of a multiplicity of experiences and discourses that threaten to become self-contained and self-referring. A great city is a profound challenge to the impulse to make one's own interpretation of reality universal, whether by enforcing it on others in totalitarian fashion or by withdrawing into ever smaller worlds of shared opinion. A conversation does not imply a unified culture, nor even a common or universal language. Communication cannot, need not, be perfect, but metropolitan life provides both the example and the context for some real, if limited, conversation in public over a myriad of differences.

Modern intellectual life and the modern city are adventures that require a diversity of voices in public. They are democratic insofar as there are no certification requirements for participation, other than the ability to contribute to the conversation, to take part in the adventure. The modern metropolis not only creates the need for such conversation; it also provides the means for conducting it. New York has been and is itself a many-voiced conversation of unparalleled complexity.[3]

The New York story is significant in its own terms. But it is, I would argue, more general in its implications. It was in New York—not in Europe, not in Boston, not in Chicago, not in Los Angeles—that advanced culture and learning first confronted modern urban conditions. Before their counterparts in any of the great European capitals, men and women of learning in New York had to confront the ideology and practice of democracy and unprecedented social heterogeneity. These elements of modernity changed the terms of the relation of intellect to society, and we seek still to understand more fully the possibilities of intellect in modern times.

What we can learn from New York thus has more than parochial significance. For two hundred years New York lived with, talked about, even fought about, cultural issues that all modern urban intellectuals must confront. At the least we should recall Edmund Wilson's remark that nineteenth-century New Yorkers were more representatively American than their New England contemporaries, more cosmopolitan, and more engaged with the world. But Wilson still claims too little, I think. The history of intellect in New York anticipates the conditions of modern intellectual life. New York is not Paris or London in preparation; rather it marks the modern condition toward which they, too, are moving. Paris and London, in fact, have yet to catch up with New York. And coming late has for them severe disadvantages. Their full confrontation with modernity, with democracy and social diversity, will occur not in the context of growth and power, as was New York's good fortune, but in the midst of their own post-imperial tensions and decline. Whatever New York's substantial problems, it is still our best hope for a place and an example of democratic culture.

PART I

CIVIC CULTURE

CHAPTER 1

The Emergence of City Culture in New York

The eighteenth-century Republic of Letters was proudly cosmopolitan. Yet this republic was not, to adapt an eighteenth-century political term, a consolidated one. It was organized in cities and was a federation of individual, even fiercely independent and competitive, local centers of culture. The Enlightenment was city culture; its major figures "flourished in the city,"[1] whether we speak of the two capitals of the Enlightenment, Paris and London, or of the great arc of provincial cities, embracing Edinburgh, Philadelphia, and Bordeaux. Even Rousseau, the *philosophe* most hostile to cities and towns, took the occasion of a contest sponsored by the local academy at Dijon to make his reservations about cities and advanced culture known in his famous *Discourse* on the arts and sciences.[2] David Hume, referring in his autobiography to his own move to Edinburgh in 1751, spoke for his fellow *philosophes:* "I removed from the country to the town, the true scene for a man of letters."[3] William Johnson, an ambitious young man in New York City during the 1790s, had neither the genius of Hume nor the intellectual resources of Edinburgh at hand, yet he echoed Hume when he wrote to the dramatist and painter William Dunlap, who had left the city for rural New Jersey: "You had better leave a dull uninteresting country scene & join us. The Town is the only place for rational beings."[4]

The urban orientation of eighteenth-century learning reflects important shifts in the sociology of intellectual life. The professional and bourgeois classes of cities and towns succeeded, in rough chronological order, such predecessor sponsors of learning as monasteries, medieval universities, aristocrats, and monarchical courts and learned institutions. Indeed, as Daniel Roche has shown in respect to France, provincial societies of arts and science, established as part of the same centralizing and rationalizing impulse of the absolute monarchy that produced the Royal Academy in 1666, took on in the eighteenth century a different, more distinctly urban and locally independent character, expressing the formation of local urban elites.[5] In eighteenth-century England, the voluntary character of dissenting churches and dissenting academies, a product of the political and religious settlement of 1689, known as the Glorious Revolution, provided a model for conducting intellectual life outside of the established church and universities, from which dissenters were excluded. Hence the deep involvement of dissenting ministers and laymen in local learned societies. Throughout Europe, as Margaret Jacob has recently discovered, there was a locally based but international fraternity of Masons. Both the local and international networks and associations they formed, particularly in England, France, and the Netherlands, nourished a serious discourse on the arts, science, politics, and religion. These societies, she argues rather persuasively, sustained a thread of radical enlightenment thought that ran all the way to freethinking, with all the political and religious subversion such thought implied in the eighteenth century.[6]

While the formal and formidable Royal Society (1662) loomed large on the cultural landscape of the English-speaking world in the middle of the eighteenth century, serious intellectual life was sustained in both London and Edinburgh—the two European Enlightenment cities best known by New Yorkers with intellectual aspirations—by small and often quite informal groups. Johnson and his circle, which included Garrick, Reynolds, Burke, Gibbon, and Joseph Banks (who, not so incidentally, was president of the Royal Society), met in a London coffeehouse, while David Hume, Adam Smith, Lord Kames, Adam Ferguson, William Robertson, and the other Scottish luminaries dined together in Edinburgh and also found each other at meetings of such formally organized clubs as the "Select Society" and "The Poker." This pattern of intellectual life was not simply urban in the sociology of its sustaining institutions; it strove as well for urbanity as an intellectual style. It was aggressive, secular, polished in a way that found its most typical expression in the essay, of which Hume was the acknowledged master. It acquired a distinctive metropolitan character by the conjunction of literary and practical affairs. This quality was especially evident in the less populous provincial cities. In Edinburgh or, as we shall see, New York, the small and intimate scale of elite society precluded much differentiation and specialization, with the result that men of intellect and men of power were unavoidably associated; more often than not, in fact, they were the same men. Urban elites were not cultural patrons; they were practitioners.[7]

The eighteenth century marks one of those periodic swings in social and geographic perception that sharpen the distinction between city and country. The city rather aggressively became the home of a noticeable surplus of wealth in Western Europe, and a new bourgeois elite associated with this wealth socialized it in the form of public edifices—whether churches, exchanges, or government buildings—and public culture defined by an expanded realm of social space and constituted by new patterns of leisure, learning, and social etiquette. These changes were apparent in England's provincial cities as early as 1700, and they appeared in Edinburgh in the years following the Act of Union (1707). In France, as Daniel Roche shows, this new urban self-consciousness emerged only slightly later.[8]

Such developments in the history of cities are rarely identified with a single year, or even a decade. But it is possible to identify the 1750s as the moment when New York City assumed self-consciousness as an eighteenth-century provincial city. Indeed, the year 1754 alone was a remarkable one in the formation of urban culture in New York. That year witnessed the founding of King's College and the New York Society Library. It was also the year in which the Royal Exchange, perhaps the city's most notable pre-Revolutionary public architecture, was completed, and it was in this year that New Yorkers witnessed "the first really memorable season of theatricals."[9] Two years before, the Walton House, New York's most distinguished colonial mansion, was built on Pearl Street, while in 1768 the New York Chamber of Commerce was chartered. The public "Pest-House," authorized in 1754, was opened in 1758, while the New York Hospital was organized in 1771. Trinity Church had been enlarged and "beautified" in 1737, and in 1766 the same Anglican elite undertook to build the still standing St. Paul's Chapel, which when completed was one of the most sophisticated buildings in the colonies and surely colonial America's "grandest church."[10]

These developments—as well as the changes in intellectual life that will be our theme—were the work of an elite that had formed itself by the middle third of the eighteenth century. Major New York families, now in their second and third generations, had consolidated their power and their wealth through the development of their vast landed estates on the Hudson River. But they were not simply a rural gentry, or even agrarian capitalists. Some, like the De Lanceys, began in the city, while others made their presence increasingly felt in the city, which at that time had a population of about 13,000. Commerce was fundamental, even for the landed families, and by midcentury they had recognized the advantage of having at least one son educated and trained in the law. A group of wellborn and bright young lawyers, who found the city sadly wanting in respect not only to professional standards but to liberal culture generally, became the first to make the case for city culture in New York. With support from some elite members of the medical profession and a few merchants, these professionalizing lawyers set out to reform, or given their dim view of existing conditions, to implant in New York the sort of enlightened culture nourished in the cities of Europe. They sought to bring their city more clearly into association with the metropolitan culture of London and Edinburgh. Or, put differently, they sought to reconstitute English culture but under American conditions, and this implied an embrace of Enlightenment rather than traditional ideas, civic rather than traditional institutions. For all of them, the promise of city culture was a new and secular hierarchy of learning, one which would reward and honor their individual talents, while advancing the prestige of the local milieu that gave significance to their lives.

Like the eighteenth-century Edinburgh lawyers who orchestrated an intellectual life second only to Paris, the ambitious young men of the New York Bar were aware of being on the periphery of a greater world. Although they relished Bishop Berkeley's prophecy about the westward movement of empire and learning, they knew that in their own lifetimes they would remain provincials. Unable to realize for themselves the level of cultural accomplishment evident in European capitals, they nonetheless sought to raise New York to the level of a provincial city, one that participated in the movement of ideas centered in Europe. And they were determined to erase the common (and probably accurate) colonial perception that New York, while commercially more successful than Boston and Philadelphia, had far less commitment to the arts and sciences.

The charge that New Yorkers sacrificed learning at the altar of commerce was an old one. While religion had been central to the founding and initial definition of community purpose at Boston and Philadelphia, New Amsterdam had never pretended to represent anything higher than the promise of trade. It was founded purely and simply as a commercial enterprise, and an enormously successful one it turned out to be. But by the time its succcess was assured in the eighteenth century, some commentators began to demand more of the city that in 1665 had become New York. John Sharpe, "Chaplaine to her Majestys Garrisons in the Province of New York," a man remembered for first proposing a "publick library" to "advance learning and piety" in New York and for leaving a collection of books for such a library, observed in 1713: "The City is so conveniently Situated for Trade and the Genius of the people so inclined to merchandise . . . that letters must be in a manner forced upon them not only without their seeking, but against their consent."[11] Writing nearly a half century later, William Smith, one of New York's earliest historians and one of the improving lawyers of the 1750s, charged New Yorkers with "a long shameful neglect of all the arts and sciences."[12] A writer in the *New York Weekly Journal* lamented in 1749: "This *Province*, above any other, has felt the Miseries of Ignorance, and they still remain our sorest Afflictions. A sordid thirst after Money, sways the Lives of our People."[13] While declension was the preoccupation of intellectual leaders in Boston, the absence of an original lofty vision among New York's founders produced there a different and perhaps more activist rhetoric —that of failure to achieve full potential.

The passage of two centuries provides no cause for softening contemporary judgments. Remarkably few individuals of note in America's pre-Revolutionary intellectual history were New Yorkers. The experience of one of the few New Yorkers regularly found in surveys of colonial intellectual history tends to confirm the weakness of intellectual culture in New York. Cadwallader Colden, a physician educated in Edinburgh and London, came to New York in 1718 and served for many years as lieutenant governor. Colden is remembered in the history of science for his work in botany and physics; his *History of the Five Indian Nations* (1727) was and is recognized as a major work in history and ethnography. But it is in connection with Colden's most ambitious work—the project apparently dearest to him, but one in which New World residence offered no advantage—that the undeveloped character of New York's intellectual culture becomes apparent. Newton's great unanswered question concerned the cause of gravity, and Colden sought in two books, *First Causes of Action in Matter and the Cause of Gravitation* (1746) and *The Principles of Action in Matter* (1751), to provide an answer. The books were and are considered failures. More important, however, they were largely incomprehensible to the European—and American—scientists to whom Colden sent copies. It is all too easy, perhaps, in explaining his failure to exaggerate the limiting environment and neglect the importance of the peculiar bent of his mind, more rationalistic and non-experimental than the Anglo-American scientific world in which he sought to find a place. Yet it seems undeniable, as historians of colonial American science Brooke Hindle and Raymond Stearns affirm, that the character and quality of the books were significantly, if not completely, shaped by his isolation from an immediate context of learned discourse, whether within formal institutions or in an informal circle.[14] These circumstances made him vulnerable and liable to idiosyncrasy.

To be sure, equally confused books were published in Europe by aspiring Newtons. But Colden was not someone on the fringes of intellectual life in New York, and he was, for his time, exceptionally well educated. But to be at the center of New York intellectual life was, in a very important sense, to be nowhere. Colden, moreover, recognized his isolation and his need for the discipline of an intellectual community. In this spirit he proposed in 1728 the establishment of a learned society in America on the model of the Royal Society in London.[15] This suggestion, later communicated through John Bartram to Benjamin Franklin, earned him credit as godfather, if not actual founder, of the American Philosophical Society. But for Colden and for New York it is more important to remark that when the society was organized in 1743, its home was Philadelphia, not New York. Whatever the eventual fate of his suggestion, Colden's personal circumstance was that of a poignant and provincial isolation. Sending some of his scientific work to a London correspondent in 1742, Colden expressed his intellectual loneliness. He was, he declared, pleased "to communicate some thoughts in natural philosophy which have remained many years with me undigested, for we scarcely have a man in this country that takes any pleasure in such kinds of speculations."[16] Yet if little had been accomplished in the arts and sciences, Andrew Burnaby, a Scottish traveler who visited New York in 1759, was correct in noting that "everyone seems zealous to promote learning."[17]

PROFESSIONALISM AND LEARNING

Easily the most significant figure in the midcentury effort to reform the professions and intellectual life generally was William Livingston.[18] Literally to the Albany manor born in 1723, Livingston was the scion of one of the colony's wealthiest and most powerful families. His father sent him to Yale, and he became part of a generation, New York's first, of nonministerial college graduates. At Yale, Livingston had been introduced, even if in a limited way, to a world of Enlightenment ideas and to the notion of a community of scholars, and he missed such a culture of learning when he arrived in New York to study law in 1742. At first he simply wished he were back at Yale as a tutor or a fellow, but sought to overcome his sense of isolation by initiating a correspondence with Noah Welles of Yale. For nearly twenty years this correspondence and regular journeys to New Haven for Yale's annual commencement allowed Livingston to maintain a private and public connection to the world of learning.

If he was slow to relinquish his fondness and nostalgia for his alma mater, he rather quickly threw himself into the intellectual and political life of the city. The elite of New York became acquainted with this third-generation Livingston in a rush, when he arrived in the city to study law with two of the city's most distinguished and learned lawyers, James Alexander, who had come to New York from Edinburgh in 1715, and William Smith, Sr. What they saw was a tall, thin, young man, often slovenly in appearance. In time he became a formidable lawyer; still later he would be one of General Washington's aides and wartime governor of New Jersey. But the gift that first became publicly known in New York City was his facility with a pen. Combined with his personal impulse toward invective, this talent made him a savage and much-feared polemicist.

To say that Livingston was committed to Enlightenment ideas is insufficient, for there was not one Enlightenment but many. Or put differently, there was a spectrum of Enlightenment ideas one might hold, some actually bolstering established authority, others gently corrosive, and still others profoundly radical and subversive. Livingston is best characterized as a liberal, dissenting Whig, leaning toward but well short of the so-called radical Enlightenment. He leaned enough in that direction, however, to challenge, as we shall see, the comfortable Anglican Enlightenment in New York City.

Key words in Livingston's vocabulary were "reason," "nature," "common sense." He believed that the "Liberal Sciences" would make one "Wise and Virtuous." He praised conduct conforming to "rules of reason and virtue," and he believed that reason was the foundation for the character essential to "publick communities." [19] Hostile to notions of royal prerogative, he was a natural-rights republican in politics. He was a Christian, but he was also a latitudinarian who considered religion a private matter. It was among the "unalienable rights of Man to Examine himself in matters religious." [20] Anticlerical to the core, he raged against "Priestcraft" and organized religion, insisting that "a man may be a good Christian tho' he be of no Sect in Christendom." [21] Reason, he believed, was an essential counter to both the "enthusiasm" of the extreme elements of the Great Awakening and the "superstition" of the Catholic and Anglican churches. [22]

From his privileged position—with his inherited wealth and status and his superior liberal and professional education—he found his supposed counterparts in the city wanting. The legal profession was not, it appeared to Livingston, a few practitioners like his teachers perhaps excepted, a genuinely learned profession. More generally, he feared that the urban elite he was joining was made up of libertines and dunces. "It is indeed prodigious," he wrote to Noah Welles, "that in so populous a City so few Gentlemen have any relish for learning. Sensuality has devoured all greatness of soul and scarce one in a thousand is even disposed to talk serious." [23] He wished to reform the "Young Gentry," his own and successor generations in the city. While not a complete democrat or an unambiguous proponent of merit, he insisted that social honor and power should not be associated only with wealth. He complained that in New York City "a poor man of the most shining accomplishments can never emerge out of his Obscurity; while every wealthy Dunce is loaded with Honours." [24] A revaluation of learning in New York City would, he thought, overcome this wrong.

Livingston found like-minded colleagues in William Smith, Jr., the son

of his mentor, and John Morin Scott, young lawyers with whom he became acquainted during his legal apprenticeship. The three, known as
the "triumvirate," sought to raise the whole profession to their standard,
denying the professional legitimacy of many practitioners in the process.
It was one of those generational ambitions of talented youth that are at
once idealistic and ungenerous, necessary and unrealistic. It could not
fully succeed. Yet there was over the next generation a remarkable improvement in the status and quality of the legal profession in New York.[25]

The elevation of the legal profession had broad consequences in the
city. Following the lead of the triumvirate, the legal profession assumed
a special place in the task of raising the general level of intellectual life in
the city. In 1765, for example, Cadwallader Colden observed that "few
men except in the profession of the Law, have any kind of literature."[26]
Colden may have slighted his own medical profession, since under the
leadership of John Bard and, later, John's son Samuel, a similar project
of improvement stressing better training, higher and more formal standards of certification, and general cultural leadership was getting under-
way. It is clear, however, that in the 1750s Livingston and his two friends
dominated the cultural life of the city. Milton Klein, the best student of
Livingston's activities during these years, notes of the triumvirate that
"there was scarcely a single project of cultural improvement in mid-
eighteenth century New York in which they were not active."[27]

"New York," William Smith, Jr., observed in 1757, "is one of the most
social places on the continent. The men collect themselves into weekly
evening clubs."[28] Two of these clubs were more than social; they deserve
to be remembered for their intellectual aspirations. One, organized by
John Bard about 1750, was referred to as a "weekly society" of "professional gentlemen." Though its membership was drawn largely from the
physicians of the city, they met as cognoscenti rather than in their strict
professional character as medical men. The society was organized much
like Benjamin Franklin's famous Junto in Philadelphia. In fact, before
migrating to New York, John Bard had as a young man participated in
the Junto, and when Franklin visited New York he often attended meetings of Bard's group.[29] It is difficult to specify any concrete products of
this association in the 1750s, but there is no doubt that it had a formative
influence on Bard's son, Samuel, who during the last third of the eighteenth century, as we shall see, dramatically reformed and improved
medical training and assumed responsibility for the well-being of several
key general cultural institutions in New York City.

The other group was made up largely but not exclusively of lawyers.
Again, its purposes were general. Begun in 1749 by Livingston and his

friends, with advisory roles for James Alexander and William Smith, Sr., it was an attempt to re-create the sense of an intellectual coterie such as Livingston had known at Yale. The group was, as Livingston wrote to a Yale friend, a "Society for Improving themselves in Useful Knowledge."[30] This association of men quickly became identified as a center of Enlightenment speculation in the city, and it was soon tagged as radical. Referring to the Society as a "republican cabal," custodians of official English culture in the city attacked Livingston and his friends as Freemasons, atheists, and political factionalists.*[31]

Livingston, with the help particularly of Smith Jr., sought to extend the improving and the political ambitions of the circle through the publication of a weekly magazine. Initially speaking of Addison and Steele's *Spectator* as a model, they seem to have been also influenced by the *Independent Whig*, published by Trenchard and Gordon in London. The new journal, the *Independent Reflector*, combined natural-rights Whig politics with a program of cultural elevation, the urbanity that Addison had earlier brought to English readers. Both aims depended upon the creation of a public sphere, an arena of public culture, such as Addison had helped to develop and sustain in London.[32]

Acutely aware, perhaps too much so, of their own exceptional ability, the triumvirate demanded more of their city. They wanted the institutions and circles of learned discourse characteristic of European city culture to provide sustenance and accompaniment to their own ambitions. William Livingston, in particular, lamented the "want of liberal Education" in New York, and he observed that if New Yorkers were to establish a college their children would feel themselves to have been born "in a more enlightened age than their fathers."[33] He justified a social investment in an intellectual elite, something that could be interpreted as serving a rather small class, by insisting that "the Advantages flowing from the Rise and Improvement of Literature, are not to be confined to a Set of Men: they are to extend their chearful Influence thro' Society in general."[34]

Livingston envisioned a New York regarded for its cultural accomplishment as much as for its devotion to wealth. In proposing the establishment of a college in New York, he welcomed the opportunity it would provide for the cultivation of "polite" culture in New York.[35] But, in common with nearly all American proponents of the Enlightenment, Livingston understood learning or knowledge to be useful as well as polite. Writing in the *Independent Reflector* in 1753, he insisted that "whatever literary Acquirement cannot be reduced to Practice, or exerted to

* Although Livingston held many ideas common to the international fraternity of Masons associated with the radical and popular dimensions of the Enlightenment, there is no evidence of his actually being a Mason, though other Livingstons were.

the Benefit of Mankind, may perhaps procure its Possessor the Name of a Scholar, but is in Reality no more than a specious Kind of Ignorance."[36]

KING'S COLLEGE

The year 1754 saw the establishment of the first formal "literary" institutions in New York City—the New York Society Library and King's College. William Livingston was deeply involved with the founding of both, and in the debate he initiated with respect to King's College he articulated a vision of culture that associated it with place and made it urban in a way that was unprecedented in colonial America.[37]

In the course of an evening's conversation, William Livingston, William Smith, Jr., John Morin Scott, Philip Livingston, Robert Livingston, and William Alexander set the library project afoot. Their intention, as William Smith later remembered it, was to promote "a spirit of inquiry among the people."[38] This small group expanded its number, and the project was presented to the public under the auspices of twelve founders drawn from "a variety of lines of activity," who, in the words of the library's historian, represented the "best that the province afforded in position, cultivation, attainments, native ability and character."[39] The library quickly found subscribers among the public; after a search for books with "an established Reputation among the learned," it opened in quarters provided by the municipal authorities. When the library opened in City Hall in 1754, Hugh Gaine, editor of the *New York Mercury* and a leading figure in the city's cultural life, declared that it "will take off that Reflection cast on us by the neighbouring Colonies, of being an ignorant People."[40]

When we think of this library—which still exists on New York's Upper East Side—we may not appreciate the cultural ambition it implied. It was to be more than a repository of books. Like Franklin's Library Company of Philadelphia, the New York Society Library was to combine the function of museum and research institute with that of making books available to readers. Recalling the intentions of the founders, William Smith explained that "the remote object of the projectors was an incorporation by royal charter, and the erection of an edifice at some future day, for a museum and observatory, as well as a library."[41] The triumvirate and their colleagues envisioned a local institution that would encourage and provide a focal point for learning. The project derived from a general desire for cultural improvement, and it aimed toward the stimulation of a city culture, by being inclusive in its clientele and comprehensive in the range of its intellectual concerns. Its ambition is evident in the bookplate designed by William Livingston for the library, which clearly identifies New York as the modern Athens.[42]

Though modern New Yorkers are sometimes put off by the name of the New York *Society* Library, this use of the word "society" suggested the library's commitment to nourishing a public, albeit, of course, elite, culture in the city. The word "society" had not yet taken on the connotations of exclusivity and private ambition that it would assume in the nineteenth century. It referred to the whole civil community; by calling it the Society Library its founders communicated the fact that it was a private corporation with a public purpose.

Within a year of its founding, the Society Library was embroiled in controversy. The first annual election of officers in 1755 turned out to be a hotly contested and bitter affair, pitting a largely Anglican slate against a Presbyterian one.[43] This struggle for control of the library reveals how deeply it was embedded in the social and political life of the city, and it also had profound implications for the definition of learned culture in New York. Would learned culture be locally comprehensive or would it be mapped along intercolonial religious fault lines? The library elections between 1755 and 1757 revolved on this question, but the focus of this debate was elsewhere, and we can best pursue it there, remembering that much that was said in connection with the controversy over the founding of King's College was said as well in the Society Library elections.

As early as 1704, three years after the founding of Yale College, there had been public discussion of establishing a college in New York. It was not until 1746, however, that any action was taken. In that year, the colonial assembly authorized a public lottery "for the advancement of learning and towards the founding of a college."[44] Funds accumulated rather quickly for what the *New York Evening Post* characterized as an "ornamental and useful" institution, and in 1751 a board of trustees for the projected King's College was created.[45] That board had to confront two questions, both more controversial than anyone had anticipated. Little attention had been given to the probable location of the college. Most probably assumed it would be located in the city, but there developed a rather extended discussion of the relative value of an urban as opposed to a rural location. The question of control and organization of the new college turned out to be even more explosive, pitting the triumvirate against the Anglican clerics who hoped to establish in New York an Anglican college that would compete with the Presbyterian college recently established (1746) in Newark, New Jersey (later Princeton), and the older Congregational colleges at New Haven and Cambridge.[46] For our purposes, these two debates can be said to be about the nature of learned culture in the city—the first concerning the existence and worth of city culture, the second its definition.

Of course, it is easy to interpret the controversy over the location of the college in terms of the politics of local interests. Certainly this staple of American political life was apparent in the case of King's College. But there was also a genuine debate about city culture. Opponents recognized the existence of city culture—the immediacy of issues, the range of knowledge, the intensity of intellectual and social engagement that was possible only in an urban context. They at once feared its temptations to vice and recognized that it offered something essential to the college's task of creating gentlemen.

Perhaps the most important proponent of a rural location was Cadwallader Colden. In a letter to Benjamin Franklin he outlined his argument for a rural location, not only for King's but also for Franklin's proposed College of Philadelphia. Arguing that agriculture should be taught because "it is truly the foundation of the Wealth and wellfare of the Country and it may be personally usefull to a greater number than any of the other Sciences," it followed, he explained, that a location near farms and farmers was appropriate. But his argument went further into the character of city culture itself, and his inability to mount a fully anti-urban argument largely explains why the college ended up in the city. At a country college, Colden observed, "Schollars will be freed from many temptations to idleness and some worse vices that they must meet with in the city." Yet he admitted a certain and crucial advantage to the city. "The chief objection to the College's being in the Country I think is that the schollars cannot acquire that advantage of behaviour and address which they would acquire by a more general conversation with Gentlemen." He thought that something might be done within the curriculum of a country college to achieve what city living produced in its regular course. The students, he speculated, might be obliged "to use the same good manners towards one another with a proper regard to their several ranks as is used among well bred Gentlemen." He is not, however, fully satisfied with this solution, and a passing remark stimulated by his unease gives away everything. The city is indispensable after all in the education of gentlemen: "And as no doubt they [the students] must be allow'd to go to the City [sometimes] I am of the opinion the advantages from the Country are [no?] less than what may arise [from] the College's being in or near the town."[47]

Colden conceded so much to the city as virtually to nullify his argument for a rural location. Three years later, in 1752, William Smith (not William Smith, Jr., the lawyer, but an Anglican to be ordained a year later and shortly thereafter to be chosen to head the College of Philadelphia) asked in *Some Thoughts on Education: with Reasons for Erecting a College in this Province and Fixing the Same at the City of New-York* whether it made sense to "send our Youth into the Depths of Woods, to perform their

Collegiate exercises, in the unambitious Presence of inanimate Trees?" If the students are to "unite the Scholar with the Gentleman," then let them associate with "Men and the World" during their college years. Only in the city can they be guided by the "polished and learned Part of the Province" as they "learn *Belles Lettres*, Breeding, and some knowledge of Men and Things."[48]

The trustees named in 1751 were strongly identified with the city. Eight of the ten were members of the city's merchant and legal elite. For them, there was no question about the location of the college. It was to be an urban institution and a civic ornament. When they made this decision in 1753, they did not feel compelled to explain their preference for an urban location, and the two rural representatives on the board apparently did not even take part in the decision. It must have seemed to the board, as it did to William Livingston, who was one of their number, that "the most superficial Thinker" should realize that "the College ought to be plac'd in or near this City."[49]

Livingston's impatience with the controversy over location was related to his desire to initiate discussion over the matter of control. If the college was in the city, was it to represent the city itself, or was the city to be merely the location of a church or "Party" college? Such was the question that Livingston and his friend Smith forced into public discussion, and by August of 1754 William Smith could observe that "all the town was alive" with the controversy over the college.[50]

The governing board of King's was heavily Anglican, two-thirds of its membership being communicants of that church. Yet the case could perhaps be made that this proportion was reasonably representative of the religious affiliations of New York's wealthiest and most powerful in the 1750s. And non-Anglican groups, like the Presbyterian Livingstons, were represented on the board. But when Trinity Church, the nominally established Anglican church and without question the wealthiest and most powerful church in the city, offered land to endow King's, assuming it would be Anglican in character, Livingston was moved to speak out. Writing to an old Yale friend, he declared: "Our future College . . . is like to fall without a vigorous opposition, under the sole management of Churchmen. The Consequence of which will be universal Priestcraft and Bigotry in less than half a Century."[51] In the *Independent Reflector* Livingston insisted that to allow "the Government of the College to be delivered out of the Hands of the Public to a Party," particularly one he identified with the darkness of the established church, was of enormous consequence to local culture, for it was the college, by forming the elite, that would henceforth shape the political and intellectual culture of New York.[52]

The Anglican clerics who were promoting King's College as a denominational institution understood neither the intensity nor the substance of Livingston's argument. The Anglicans knew that they had not proposed anything unusual; they were not innovators. They were doing only what they assumed the established church, as the official custodian of English learned culture, ought to do. In proposing that King's be essentially a denominational college they were, moreover, only seeking to replicate what was already common in other colonies. All of the existing colleges were associated with one or another denomination, and intercolonial cultural relations were interpreted in terms of the lineaments provided by religious denominations.[53] Hence they thought Livingston was being unfair in attacking them; all they could see in his argument was a Presbyterian claim against an Anglican one. Since the Presbyterians already had Princeton just across the river at Newark, and the Congregationalists had Yale in New Haven and Harvard at Cambridge, the Anglicans thought it only just that they have a college in New York.

The Anglican clerics, particularly Samuel Johnson, who would become the first president of King's College, were not narrow sectarians. Rather they assumed the responsibilities and prerogatives of a legally established church, however shaky that establishment may in reality have been. They envisioned, in a surprisingly unproblematic way, a case in which the college of the established church would be both Anglican and nonsectarian. They assumed it was possible to embrace the whole community in an Anglican institution.[54] This confidence explains why the first offer of land by Trinity Church on March 5, 1752, contained no provisions protecting Anglican control of the college. Only after the Anglicans recognized the lack of a consensus on the authoritative place of the Anglican church in the city did they add the notorious provision that the head of the college must forever be an Anglican.[55]

The aim of the Anglican clerics was to secure official English culture, which was by definition Anglican, within authoritative institutions. In this way they aimed to protect it from the emerging challenge of enlightened freethinkers and New Light religious enthusiasts spawned by the Great Awakening.[56] They did not believe in natural rights, nor did they believe in the separation of church and state. While toleration was acceptable to them, it did not, for them, imply an impartial attitude toward the various sects in New York. It was essential and obvious to them that a distinction be made between the authority of the established church and the status of other religious groups. Livingston attacked the "church college" from a natural-rights position, insisting that civil magistrates derived their power from their constituents, not from God. He argued, moreover, that religious belief was a private matter, beyond the power of the state, and he advocated a "free" college that would be governed by the people of New York in their public, not religious, character and through public authorities.[57] It was not a matter of opposing governance by one sect or religious faction. No sect should govern it.[58] "While the Government of the College is in the Hands of the People, or their Guardians," Livingston explained in the *Independent Reflector,* "its Design cannot be perverted."

> Our College therefore, if it be incorporated by Act of Assembly, instead of opening a Door to universal Bigotry and Establishment in Church, and Tyranny and Oppression in the State, will secure us in the Enjoyment of our respective Privileges both civil and religious. For as we are split into a great Variety of Opinions and Professions; had each Individual his Share in the Government of the Academy, the Jealousy of all Parties combating each other, would inevitably produce a perfect Freedom for each particular Party.[59]

The Anglicans never grasped Livingston's innovating vision of learned culture in New York City. What they could understand was denominational rivalry, and they repeatedly tried to force the controversy into these familiar terms. The most important defense of the Anglican position, the pamphlet *A Brief Vindication of the Proceedings of the Trustees Relating to the College* (1754) by Benjamin Nicoll, a lawyer and college trustee, could make sense of Livingston's opposition only by portraying him as a representative of Presbyterian interests. What Livingston intended, Nicoll charged, was to retard the development of a college in New York until the college recently established in New Jersey by Presbyterians, "one agreeable to his own sentiments, . . . might take Root."[60]

Livingston's essays in the *Independent Reflector* and elsewhere during the controversy articulated the outlines of a learned culture in which the college would be pluralistic like the city itself, secular though Protestant in orientation, and in the custody of a politically representative body rather than of a church or any other private party. In the process of making these arguments he anticipated the formulation of the notion of freedom based on diversity that James Madison later developed in the fifty-first of the *Federalist* papers. William Livingston was comfortable with this vision of learned culture based on reason and political representation rather than upon authoritative institutions and religion. For Samuel Johnson, however, it was a frightening prospect. He feared that Livingston's proposals would make the college "a sort of free-thinking latitudinarian seminary."[61]

Though Livingston, Smith, and their friends brought their battle to the colonial legislature and the governor, they were unable to secure the establishment of a non-denominational college controlled by the legislature. Nor did they quite succeed in blocking the charter for what they called, always, the "church college." Livingston interpreted the result as a defeat. Writing to Noah Welles, he reflected on his failed effort: "We stood as long as our legs would support us, & I may add, even fought for some time on our stumps, but . . . we were vanquished."[62]

Yet the resolution was in fact more complicated. In recognition of the opposition that Livingston had organized to prevent the public lottery money from going to the "church college," the legislature divided the money in half, giving half to King's College, but diverting the other half to the municipal government of New York City to be used for public purposes, primarily, as it turned out, for the establishment of a "Pest-House" and for the erection of a "publick Gaol."[63] While these public uses are, to our sensibilities, hardly elevating and improving in the way a college is, they are an acknowledgment of the urban orientation and purposes of Livingston and his allies.

More can be said to qualify Livingston's negative judgment. The actual operation of the college during its first decade or so reveals that the ministers lost much, perhaps even more than did Livingston.[64] The urban elite, the laymen who dominated the Trinity vestry and the King's College board of trustees, was more urban than it was Anglican. While accepting the proviso for an Anglican president, they gave the president of King's less authority than any other American college president. The board was lay rather than clerical, and it was never exclusively Anglican, while the charter opened the college to non-Anglicans on an equal basis.[65] The college was run by the city's elite for the young men of their class, whom they wished to prepare for the professions and polite society generally.* Although Livingston seems to have envisioned a somewhat wider spectrum of the city's class structure being served directly by the college (for this reason he opposed the classical curriculum),[67] the college that emerged aspired to embrace and serve the whole elite of the city regardless of religion.

Although the college fell short of exemplifying Livingston's ideal of city culture, King's, along with the College of Philadelphia, represented an unprecedented urbanity in American higher education. King's quickly assumed an urban character as the city grew up around it, while Princeton's Nassau Hall (1757) was set in a large greensward, America's first campus. More important, the debate over control of the college constituted the broadest and most clearly focused discussion of the definition of learned and city culture conducted in eighteenth-century America.[68] Livingston presented a view of culture that rooted it locally and generalized it beyond any established religious group, something that had not been achieved, or even imagined, by Harvard, Yale, or Princeton. Those who opposed the Anglican college in New York spoke in terms of com-

* One-half of the students during the first six years were sons or nephews of board members.[66]

petition between whole communities rather than dividing the cultural world along intercolonial denominational lines. Ultimately, a pattern of pluralism and competition within the city won out over the impulse to consolidate resources under a unified community leadership, but that came much later. In the 1750s, Livingston, Smith, and their followers fought for a radically new definition of culture that was unique to the cities of the middle colonies, Philadelphia and New York.

During the last third of the eighteenth century Samuel Bard exemplified and worked to extend the pattern of city culture that had begun to emerge with Livingston's efforts at midcentury. Like Livingston, Bard came to his profession, in this case medicine, with all the privileges, and he found his colleagues wanting. The son of John Bard, one of the city's most eminent practitioners, Samuel studied medicine at the University of Edinburgh, then the most distinguished medical school in the world. Returning to New York in 1765, he found the city, in the words of his most famous student, Samuel L. Mitchill, in "a season when there was a call for hands to improve and decorate the social fabric." And he "was not sparing of his exertions."[69]

Along with Peter Middleton, also trained at Edinburgh, and Samuel Clossy, Bard sought to reform medical education and credentials in New York. Clossy had begun lectures on anatomy at King's College in 1763, and when Bard returned from Edinburgh they formed a medical school in conjunction with King's College. It was their hope that the M.D. degree would serve as a license to practice. Then in 1769 Bard delivered a notable address proposing that a hospital be founded and that it be affiliated with the medical school. In 1771, the hospital (today's Cornell Medical Center–New York Hospital) was granted a royal charter, having relied upon the political management of William Smith, Livingston's associate many years earlier in founding the New York Society Library, a founder of the New York Bar, and a member of the hospital's first board of governors. A fire and then the Revolutionary War delayed the effective organization of the hospital until 1791, but it was clearly a product of the midcentury improving spirit.

In undertaking to reform the medical profession, a goal which included creating the medical school, the hospital, and a medical society, all on the Edinburgh model, Bard and his colleagues had their provincial eyes trained upon the metropolitan standards of Europe. When they turned west, however, their ambition took on a different coloration, for New York developments were then viewed through the lenses of city rivalry. They anxiously watched developments in Philadelphia, where John Morgan, Bard's fellow student at Edinburgh, preceded the New

Yorker in establishing a medical school and hospital. One cannot understand early city culture in New York unless one appreciates this combination of provincial inferiority and ebullient intercity rivalry for
American leadership.

For Bard the hospital was as much a civic as a scientific institution. In
fact, he tended to merge these two ways of thinking about the hospital
and the profession of medicine. He insisted that medical education could
be pursued properly only in a city, and he suggested that each city ought
to have its own medical institutions. While acknowledging that medical
theory was universal, practice, he explained, must be localized. "Every
country," he observed in his *Discourse upon the Duties of a Physician* (1769),
"has its particular Diseases; the Varieties of Climate, Exposure, Soil, Situation, Trades, Arts, Manufactures, and even the Character of a People,
all pave the Way to new Complaints, and vary the Appearance of those,
with which we are already acquainted."[70]

In order to understand better the configuration of intellectual life in
late-eighteenth-century New York, it may be helpful to inquire a bit more
into Bard's sense of city culture and his notion of professionalism. One
errs to assume, as is often done, that Bard in linking the university and
the hospital anticipated "the modern structure of academic medicine."[71]
While it is true that Bard enunciated an ambitious professional ideal for
medicine in New York, there is a profound difference between his
professionalism and that dating from the founding of the Johns Hopkins
Medical School late in the nineteenth century. Bard's professional and
civic activities reveal the urban orientation of intellectual culture at the
end of the eighteenth century, rather than the autonomous scientific
professionalism to which William H. Welch, the founder of the Hopkins
medical school, was committed.[72]

Members of the eighteenth-century learned professions were commu-
nity-oriented. Their introduction to professional life was usually under
the sponsorship of their elite families or friends in the local community.
The status of a member of the learned professions was not unaffected by
the quality of their education and performance, but their character,
known through personal experience, was the basis of their authority.
Only later, in the anonymous society of the twentieth century, would the
formalized and abstract standards Abraham Flexner formulated for the
medical profession in 1910 seem necessary and appropriate. While eighteenth-century professionals were somewhat specialized and definitely
cosmopolitan, they did not identify with professional disciplines. They
identified with local communities. Indeed, as Bard's rivalry with John
Morgan of Philadelphia reveals, their cosmopolitanism often took the
form of city-boosting. Like his father, Samuel Bard could easily think of
himself as a medical professional and as a member of the city's general

cultural elite. His contemporaries were as likely to characterize him as a leading citizen of the city as they were to think of him as a preeminent professional.[73] He was active in the effort to rebuild Trinity Church after it was damaged in the Revolutionary War, he was a leader in the successful effort to transform King's College into Columbia, he was instrumental in revitalizing the New York Society Library in 1772, he was a founder of the New-York Historical Society, and he was the projector of the New York Society for Promoting Useful Knowledge, which he hoped, only to be disappointed, would rival Philadelphia's more successful American Philosophical Society. His advocacy of a hospital, then, was linked to his efforts in behalf of a whole network of civic institutions, and city culture to him was the sum of these interconnected elite institutions.

THE FRIENDLY CLUB

When George Washington arrived in New York City in 1789 to assume the presidency of the newly established national government, the cultural landscape of New York looked far different than it had in 1750. Livingston and Bard had substantially raised the general prestige of their respective professions, and they had probably raised the level of technical competence as well. But it is also clear that many inferior and inadequately trained doctors and lawyers continued to offer their services to New Yorkers.[74] The establishment of the library and the college were essential first steps in the creation of a serious general intellectual culture in New York City, but they fell far short of the impact imagined by their projectors. One cannot dispute the sardonic judgment of the French traveler Brissot de Warville in 1788 that "this city does not abound in men of learning," though he noted that a good deal of intellectual excitement could be found "at the moment" because "the presence of Congress attracts the most celebrated persons from the various parts of the United States."[75] When the capital—and the federal establishment—was moved to Philadelphia, intellectual life in New York suffered the loss of, among others, Thomas Jefferson, James Madison, and John Adams.

After the excitement of having been, however briefly, the political and cultural capital of the nation, the city was thrown upon its own meager resources. The great hopes of the 1750s had come to painfully little. The prediction of Edward Antill, in 1759 in a letter to Samuel Johnson, president of King's College, had turned out to be distressingly wide of the mark. He had expressed his confidence that one result of the establishment of the college would be the coming, rather soon, to New York of the day when there would be "a Taste for learning rearing its head, learned Men courted, Invited, encouraged & revered."[76]

In 1788, Noah Webster halfheartedly tried to defend New York against the charges in William Smith's *History of the Province of New-York* that the city in the 1750s had neglected improvements of the mind. He pointed out that the city was then young—and still was. So much can be excused. Even so, he had to conclude that New York was deficient in those "societies for the encouragement of science, arts, manufactures, etc.," so characteristic of the improving spirit of the Enlightenment.[77] Yet it is clear that the successful conclusion of the war for American independence and the excitement of establishing a new government under the Constitution stimulated optimism about cultural life in the new nation. The brief residence of the federal establishment in New York raised expectations, and the removal of the cultural and political giants associated with it left the sort of vacuum that seems to have encouraged the aspirations of ambitious young intellectuals.

Between the end of the war and the end of the century, a large number of learned circles, of varying degrees of formality and pretention, were established in New York. These included two formal (and unsuccessful) organizations on the model of the American Philosophical Society: the Society for Encouraging Useful Knowledge (1784) and the New York Society for Promoting Agriculture, Arts, and Manufactures (1791). Smaller and less ambitious clubs included the Calliopean Society (1788), the Uranian Society (n.d.), Horanian Society (1796), Belles Lettres Club (1799), while professionally oriented or specialized societies included the American Mineralogical Society (1798), Law Society (n.d.), the Medical Society (1782?), and the Philological Society (1786).[78] The most important intellectual association, however, was more of a coterie than a society. Called the Friendly Club (1793–98), it represented the first fruitful attempt to form a group for literary discussion and criticism in behalf of the production of serious work. Henry May, in his recent account of the Enlightenment in America, appraises the group as "perhaps the most brilliant of all the organizations of earnest and enlightened young men" in America.[79]

Because it reveals late-eighteenth-century New York's intellectual life at its best, the Friendly Club deserves somewhat extended discussion. It also illustrates two sharp differences between eighteenth-century and twentieth-century patterns of intellectual life: first, in the relative unimportance of the academy (Columbia College), and second, in the rather close association of men of letters, professionals, and businessmen. While May has emphasized that in general American intellectual life in this era was dominated by religion and, more often than not, by clerics, New York is an exception. Although the religious radicalism of the Friendly

Club is easily exaggerated (and is by May, in fact), it reflects the exceptionally secular character of New York intellectual life.

The guiding force for the club was supplied by Elihu Hubbard Smith, a young (b. 1771) Yale graduate and physician who arrived in New York in 1793. He shared lodgings with another man from Connecticut, William Woolsey, then twenty-six years of age and destined to become a prominent corporation president (of a fire insurance company, a bank, and a railroad) and the father of Theodore D. Woolsey, president of Yale College (1844–71). They quickly met another young man residing in their quarter of the city, William Dunlap, twenty-seven years old in 1793, who had come to the city from New Jersey and who would eventually achieve note as a painter, as a historian of the arts, and as the founder of the professional theater in America. This talented trio quickly expanded their acquaintance to include other young and ambitious New Yorkers, and sometime in late 1793 they organized themselves into the Friendly Club. In his partly autobiographical *History of the Rise and Progress of the Arts of Design in the United States*, William Dunlap recalled that he became "a member of a literary society formed by young men for mutual instruction and improvement." The result, he observed, was "a more regular course of study than I had ever known. I sought assiduously to gain knowledge, but unfortunately could not be content without exposing my ignorance by writing and publishing."[80] In fact, one of the most valuable services these aspiring intellectuals found in one another was sympathetic but rigorous criticism for the work in progress that they circulated among themselves. Fortunately for the historian, the activities of the club and an account of their collective quest for intellectual improvement are recorded in the massive diary of Elihu Smith. Here we learn not only who participated but what kinds of things they talked about—and how they felt about themselves as men of intellect in New York.

On September 6, 1795, Smith recorded in his diary the original members of the Friendly Club: William Dunlap, William Woolsey, G. M. Woolsey, Horace Johnson, Seth Johnson, William Johnson, Elihu Smith, Prosper Wetmore, Lynde Catlin, and Thomas Mumford. Mumford, Catlin, and Wetmore left the club early, while James Kent joined the group soon after it was organized, and Charles Brockden Brown was counted a member when he was in New York. Four others were associated with the group, but they apparently were not "members" of the club: Samuel Lathrop Mitchill, Anthony Bleecker, John Wells, and Samuel Miller. As in all such associations, some members were more conscientious about attendance than others. Smith's diary shows that Smith, Dunlap, William Johnson, and William Woolsey never missed a weekly meeting if they were in town.

Some idea of the level of the talent collected in this small association may be indicated by recounting the later achievements of the leading members of the group. Smith, though he died tragically young in the yellow-fever epidemic of 1798, had already secured a place in history for himself by co-founding, with Samuel L. Mitchill, the first medical journal (and the first magazine of any kind to last more than eight years) in the United States, *The Medical Repository* (1797–1824). He had also been appointed staff doctor at the New York Hospital, along with Mitchill, Bard, and John Rodgers, the leaders of the profession. Chancellor James Kent, most commonly known by his title, was the most important American legal scholar before Holmes, author of the famous *Commentaries on the American Law* (1826–30). William Johnson became controller of Trinity Church and a Columbia College trustee as well as the nation's most noted legal reporter—noted in part as the reporter of Kent's decisions as Chancellor. Dunlap as playwright and manager almost singlehandedly established the professional theater in America, wrote the most important early drama criticism, and authored histories of the theater and the arts of design that are still indispensable. He was also an active painter and collaborated with Samuel F. B. Morse in organizing the National Academy of Design. Woolsey, as has been noted, became a wealthy and successful businessman. Samuel Miller authored *A Brief Retrospect of the Eighteenth Century* before leaving New York to become the first professor and longtime head of the theological school at Princeton. Samuel L. Mitchill, scientist and Jeffersonian politician, was the most versatile intellectual in turn-of-the-century New York. He could have filled any chair at Columbia; in fact he was "Professor of Natural History, Chemistry, Agriculture, and other Arts Depending Thereon." Member of more than fifty national and international learned societies, founder of the New York Lyceum of Natural History (today's New York Academy of Sciences), he was aptly characterized by Henry Adams as "a universal genius, a chemist, botanist, naturalist, physicist, and politician."[81] Anthony Bleecker was a successful lawyer, prolific writer, a man whose literary judgment Washington Irving valued above all others', and a patron of the arts and civic leader. Finally, John Wells, with George Washington Strong (father of the famous New York diarist George Templeton Strong), founded what remains today the oldest and most prestigious legal firm in the city.

The membership of the group always included businessmen and professionals. Men of affairs and men of ideas formed a single circle, ensuring a broad spectrum of experience and special knowledge at their meetings. There was, quite obviously, the possibility then of a common language of serious discourse despite this diversity.

The Friendly Club was their way of participating, as Smith put it, in the "republic of intellect."[82] It also provided them with a concrete means to self-improvement, through prolonged discussion of ideas. We still give lip service to this notion of learning, though most professionals and businessmen are simply too busy to devote the time and attention that the Friendly Club did. The group met weekly in the home of one of the members. The host had the obligation (or the opportunity) to initiate the discussion by introducing the topic of his choice. The topics recorded in Smith's diary include the novel, Hume on parties and religion, Mary Wollstonecraft, St. Pierre's theory of the tides, veracity and sincerity, Godwin's *Political Justice*, comparisons of the styles of Hume, Robertson, and Gibbon, the distribution of justice, crime, and punishment. Politics was a residual topic of discussion. As is common in meetings of general associations of cognoscenti, when discussion of learned topics exhausted itself, the club turned to political discussion. At some meetings they discussed each other's work, though such discussions generally were not part of club meetings. Mutual criticism usually occurred during their many contacts between meetings of the club. By Smith's diary, it appears that a day seldom passed without at least three or four members of the club talking singly or together either at a tavern or in each other's rooms.

What strikes the reader of Smith's diary is the seriousness of these efforts at intellectual improvement as well as their ever-present awareness of the special political promise of their time and place. The stakes are high. There is little of the sort of spontaneous, freewheeling drift of discussion we might expect in conversations. Rather there is a programmatic determination to reap the maximum harvest from discussion. There was, as the editor of Smith's diary notes, a certain grimness in their approach to literary affairs.[83] Smith judged the worth of almost every meeting; sometimes conversation was "agreeable" or "somewhat ingenious." But he also recorded his disappointment, condemning one conversation as "pitifully rambling & uninstructive." After the conversation thus described, Smith confided to his diary: "I can not but regret that we do not give a higher & more efficient character to this little association, which certainly is not wanting in capacity & information, & ought to be devoted to something better than mere amusements."[84]

Smith may have been the most demanding of the group. After the young doctor's death in 1798, Charles Brockden Brown described him as "a man whose whole ambition was to increase his intellectual powers, with a view of devoting them to his fellow men."[85] Throughout the diary—which is a sort of intellectual's Pilgrim's Progress in pursuit not of salvation but of knowledge, particularly politically and socially useful knowledge—Smith assesses his progress to date and urges himself to greater effort. In large part we are indeed dealing here with specific personal qualities, but much the same quality is evident in several others in the group, including Mitchill, Kent, and Dunlap.

Beyond the personal cultivation and assimilation of knowledge, Smith and his colleagues sought to diffuse it. In a letter to Joseph Dennie, remembered as the editor of one of the era's most notable magazines *(The Farmer's Weekly Museum)*, Smith pointed out that "the great object of all our labors must be to enlighten our fellow-men & render them more happy. The more complete the information conveyed to them, the better. Nor can I conceive it of any importance whether they receive it from you, me, or another."[86] The ideological divisions of the 1790s do not seem to have qualified the faith of Smith and his circle in the objectivity of knowledge, including social and political knowledge. Though Smith and most of his friends were Jeffersonians, he understood the knowledge to be diffused among the people by himself and by the Federalist Dennie to be essentially the same.

The gathering of information and its distribution was a preoccupation of Smith and his circle, and in this they were being, by their own lights, both scientific and republican. In referring to his editorship of *The Medical Repository* (the name itself is revealing), he characterized the role of himself and Mitchill as "the mere conduit-pipes, in conveying . . . information to the public."[87] To extend the learning of their circle over a wider expanse, they became associated with the *New York Magazine*. This magazine, published by Thomas and James Swords and edited initially by Noah Webster, was published from 1790 to 1797, and as such it was the longest-lived eighteenth-century American magazine.[88] After the third volume most of the original articles were supplied by members of the Friendly Club, for this purpose referred to as the Drone Club.

It seems to have been characteristic of this period, at least for successful magazines, to be linked to a definite literary group that supplied original articles and editorial assistance. In this respect, the relationship of the Drones to the *New York Magazine* was similar to that of the Anthology Club to Boston's *Monthly Anthology* and of the Tuesday Club to Philadelphia's *PortFolio*. The *New York Magazine* was essentially a New York magazine, written by New Yorkers and relying upon New York subscribers, who were artisans as well as patricians. In thus exemplifying city culture, it again reflected more general American conditions. Frank Luther Mott, in his history of American magazines, notes that there was no successful national magazine or review before 1825; all were restricted to readers and writers within a fifty-mile radius.[89]

The original announcement of objectives published by the Swords brothers articulated an understanding of the purposes of a magazine that was shared by Smith and his circle. The magazine was not undertaken, they averred, out of any "pecuniary motives," nor was the motive the "ambition of acquiring literary reputation," for, as they explained, "it will be our studied endeavor to remain unknown." "We plead," they wrote, "the cause of Science." The pursuit of science, by which they meant the disciplined pursuit of general cultural interests, would, they reflected, give to their minds and to the minds of their readers "a certain refinement and delicacy of character." And they hoped to advance the cause of intellectual life in New York: "A well conducted magazine, we conceive must . . . contribute greatly to diffuse knowledge throughout a community and to create in that community a taste for literature."[90]

In 1797, the year the magazine ceased publication, Smith, in one of the many appraisals of his progress that he entered into his diary, emphasized this public role over any personal achievement. While acknowledging that he had achieved "some respectability" in science, he refused to flatter himself "with the expectation of fame as a great discoverer or great scholar." He hoped, rather, to stimulate others and to "do some good by increasing a spirit of attention to other objects than the mere pursuit of wealth."[91]

There was among this group of young *philosophes* a recurrent fear that learning—and progress—might be threatened by the pursuit of wealth. At times Smith was optimistic, but running through his diary is a constant refrain that the taste for commerce and for politics in the narrow sense seemed to grow faster than the taste for learning. It had been assumed by Smith's generation of aspiring intellect that political liberty, economic growth, and cultural progress would all flow from the Revolution in a mutually reinforcing manner.[92] But developments seemed more regressive than progressive in the 1790s.

If newspapers once carried literary items, if they formerly "abounded with serious & profound disquisitions, in polity, morals, & letters," things had changed. In the past two years, he wrote in 1795, "elegant & useful communications have been wholly banished." Politics had turned newspapers into records of "the history of public contests & private intrigues." They served only the "politician," not the "man of literary leisure."[93] Characteristically, he tried to be optimistic. "The change in the nature of our News-Papers . . . will deserve to be regarded as fortunate, rather than a subject of regret, if a successful establishment can be effected, of a Journal of an opposite character: if an equal circulation can be given to a Paper wholly devoted to literary & scientific entertainment, as to a Paper entirely occupied in detailing the news of the day."[94] Such a newspaper, needless to say, never made its appearance in New York, and these young men of intellectual ambition seemed increasingly unable to orient themselves to the emerging party politics in the city and the nation. Unable to become party ideologues, neither could they establish themselves as free intellectuals and general cultural critics.

The experience of James Kent as professor of law at Columbia College was also profoundly disturbing to Smith. In recognition of Kent's scholarship and recognizing as well the shallowness of legal learning in the city, Columbia's trustees appointed Kent to a professorship of law in 1794. In the fall of 1795, only two students attended Kent's lectures. With thirty clerks in the State Supreme Court and many lawyers with students in their offices, Smith was convinced there should have been far more auditors. Explaining the problem to himself, in the privacy of his diary, Smith complained that New York lawyers wanted "practice," not science. "The history of the City of New York," he wrote, "is the history of the eager cultivation & rapid increase of the arts of gain, & the neglect of elegant & useful science, the art of genius, taste, & society." Unless, he warned, "some arm is found . . . to arrest the fatal progress of the demon of Speculation," he doubted that any "permanent Institution, friendly to literature & useful knowledge," would meet any fate save "a speedy dissolution."[95] In New York, it seemed to Smith, "Commerce, News, & pleasure are the giddy vortices which absorb the whole attention of our people." Other cities, perhaps, might offer a home for literature, but in New York, he worried, "the mass of inhabitants are too ignorant; & all, are too busy."[96]

The intellectual resources that Smith and his colleagues found in New York, beyond themselves, were quite meager. Perhaps that is why they clove so tightly to each other. At just this time, Jedidiah Morse, father of Samuel F. B. Morse, acknowledged in his American Geography (1792) that in New York "a literary and scientific spirit is evidently increasing," but he also found little of the institutional infrastructure of a vigorous intellectual life. One may, he observed, "ask the citizens for their societies for the encouragement of sciences, arts, manufactures, etc. Such enquiries might be made with propriety, but could not, at present, be answered satisfactorily."[97] The Society Library, for which William Livingston and William Smith had had such high hopes as the center of city culture in New York City, is never mentioned by the members of the Friendly Club, and except for reference to it as a location when visiting Samuel Mitchill in "his rooms" there, Columbia does not figure much in the intellectual life of this brilliant circle. Smith recorded his complaints about the absence of sustaining intellectual institutions in his diary in 1796: "How infinitely superior are the opportunities of acquiring extensive information in most parts of Europe, to those with which we are provided in America! I sicken at the thought of it. To gain a smattering of learning, such as will answer for the ordinary purposes of life, is easy—& easier here, perhaps, than there; but for all beyond, there is no provision. No Museums, Libraries, Collections—not even learned men."[98] Smith's own circle refuted the last point, but the others cannot be denied. Columbia provided the tools, the classical authors and moral philosophy, central to the sort of mutual pursuit of learning important to Smith, but it was not itself an ongoing auxiliary to that process. If there was any one indispensable institution in the intellectual life of New York in the 1790s, it was the bookshop tended by the French immigrant Hocquet Caritat. His bookshop brought European learning to New York; he imported the Enlightenment. His contribution to "the literary life of New York," Gilbert Chinard has rightly observed, "can hardly be over-emphasized."[99]

For all its shortcomings, however, New York did sustain a remarkable group of young men of wit and brilliance. Smith could not, finally, forget or fail to appreciate this. He knew how much better off he was than his fellow aspirants for knowledge, those who were in "scattered situations, which deny them the means of procuring the implements of science & the benefits of frequent communication."[100] In 1798 Smith wrote a letter to John Aiken, editor of London's *Monthly Magazine*. The letter deserves rather extensive quotation for two reasons: it is a good description and evaluation of the Friendly Club, and it represents the first assertion of a role that would later become central to the definition of New York intellectuals in the nation—the assumption of the authority to speak for America to Europe. (With Caritat's bookshop, the city was already beginning to assume the complementary role of bringing European learning to America.)

There exists in this city [Smith wrote], a small association of men, who are connected by mutual esteem, & habits of unrestricted communication. They are of different professions & occupations; of various religious or moral opinions; & tho' they coincide in the great outlines of political faith, they estimate very variously many of the political transactions of the men who have, from time to time directed the councils of the nation. This diversity of sentiment, however, as it has never affected their friendship, has made them more active in investigation; & tho' they may have formed different judgments concerning facts, has led them to a general concurrence in the facts themselves. Natives of America, & of remote parts of the Union,

they are in habits of constant communication with the several States,
& are well informed of the state of letters, science, & opinions in
these States, with some few exceptions.[101]

Five months after he wrote this letter, Smith died suddenly, at the age of
twenty-seven, as a consequence of treating a friend in the yellow-fever
epidemic of 1798. Since he was the leader who kept the group going, his
death was fatal to the group, though it was endangered in other ways as
well. Their very brilliance ensured success for the members of the group,
and their businesses and professions took more and more time. The
intense association that held the young men together was difficult to
sustain as they married and pursued their careers. Brown returned to
Philadelphia to edit a magazine, and Kent, appointed justice (1798) and
then chief justice (1804) in the State Supreme Court, left the city. Dunlap,
too, rusticated himself to New Jersey, first to flee the yellow fever, then
to reduce expenses. Caritat tried to re-create the group in 1801, when he
established a "Literary Assembly" in the reading room he organized at
the City Hall in association with his bookshop. He hoped it would become
a "chief center of literature," a place where writers, lawyers, scientists,
doctors, and clergymen would meet and discuss books and ideas as the
Friendly Club had. When it failed to attract enough people, he even took,
in 1803, the innovating step of inviting women to join the men at the
room. But it was a reading room, not a salon, and especially not a coterie.
It was too public, too general, and it did not have the leadership of a
Smith and a specific meeting hour. Literary life needs more structure
than is provided by the existence merely of a place to drop in for talk. It
needs a formula, such as the Friendly Club had, for initiating discussion
around a serious topic. Caritat apparently misread the source of the
Friendly Club's success, but one also senses that in the decade after
Smith's death the young migrants to the city were unwilling or unable to
devote themselves to intellectual improvement as had the ambitious
young men who formed the Friendly Club.[102]

CONFIGURATION AND ACHIEVEMENT

Having traced the key episodes in the late-eighteenth-century efforts to
implant learned culture in New York City, we can now ask what defined
or distinguished the intellectual culture of New York in this period. As
in other cities of the Enlightenment, the cultural reformers of New York
embraced values of cosmopolitanism (along with civic and national
pride), humanism, and classicism. The general concern of intellect was
moral, but its mode was not theological, but scientific, literary, and political discourse. And the many agencies of cultural transmission they estab-

lished or sought to establish were intended to induct ever larger numbers into an enlightened world of knowledge and progress.

The intellectual culture of New York was the product of the city's general intellectual elite, with lawyers and physicians most prominent. The extensive involvement of businessmen, notable and quite surprising from the perspective of our own time, is simply a reflection of the unified character of the city's leadership class. The clergy, however, are not very prominent in organizing the city's intellectual life. The contrast with Boston is thus striking, but it is not that much different from the secular pattern of Franklin's Philadelphia, or of Dr. Johnson's famous Literary Club in London, which included no clergymen. The learned circle of New York developed out of a social experience of familiar fraternity at the upper levels of society. Livingston's group in the 1750s and Smith's Friendly Club members in the 1790s met almost daily and shared a whole class-based social network.

The differentiation between doers and thinkers was slight. The tired saying of our time about those doing who can do, and those teaching who cannot, would have made no sense in eighteenth-century New York. Advanced learned circles included doers. Practical men of affairs and the literati were intimate; often, indeed, they were the same individuals. As Merle Curti once observed, "conditions in the colonies"—this seems to hold as well for other provincial cultures, even in Europe—"not only stimulated intellectuals to take up practical pursuits, but also stimulated practical men to cultivate intellectual interests." [103] It is this sociological fact that largely explains another quality of eighteenth-century city culture: it was not oppositional or anti-bourgeois. The withdrawal of the alienated intellectual from bourgeois society is a later development, associated with political democracy, expansive capitalism, unprecedented urban growth, and romantic notions of genius.

The phrase "man of letters" was rather more inclusive in the eighteenth century than it would become later; it embraced anyone who was fond of literature, not only makers of literature. Such a non-writer might join a literary circle in order to be an active consumer, in personal touch with the writer. After the middle of the nineteenth century, such associations of literary life evaporated, and the writer produced for an anonymous consuming public. But in eighteenth-century New York there was no literary market. Nowhere in America, as Charles Brockden Brown noted in 1799, was there a "set or class of persons, denominated authors." [104] Doctors, lawyers, and merchants supplied the literary men of New York, though Smith's circle in the 1790s included two individuals who at least anticipated later patterns of intellectual life. Samuel L. Mitchill earned his living as a Columbia professor while pursuing his scientific and literary and political ambitions, and William Dunlap as a professional theater manager earned his living in a field related to his work as a playwright, critic, and painter.

Continual references to men has been intentional. Women were not involved in the learned culture of New York. Some women were subscribers to the New York Society Library; a widow is even listed on the royal charter obtained in 1771, but, as we have already noted, the library did not fulfill its promise as a focus for advanced learning. No women, of course, were educated at Columbia. None of the early magazines published in New York seem to have relied upon female contributors, though the first issue of the *New York Magazine* contained a communication, apparently from a woman, expressing her hope that the new journal would provide a "place in which to deposit our [referring to women] sentiments."[105] Except for the invitation from Hocquet Caritat to join his failing Literary Assembly in 1803, women were not part of the social circles devoted to literary discussion that occupied the evenings of men in New York. No evidence has survived of anything like the Gleaning Society, a mutual improvement society much like the Friendly Club, organized in Boston in 1805 by and for women.[106] The two women of most notable intellectual accomplishment in New York serve to emphasize their exclusion from the male-oriented, public, learned culture of the city. While talented women in Paris found opportunity in the context of the semi-public world of the salon,[107] in New York such extraordinarily talented women as Susan Colden, with her study of natural history at the beginning of our period, and Theodosia Burr, a woman of wide learning and cultivation, at the end, were protégées of their extremely solicitous and talented fathers, Cadwallader Colden and Aaron Burr. But their intellectual experience was largely confined within the family—indeed, even in a more restricted dyadic relationship with their fathers.

The framework of intellectual discourse was classical and moral; this was the common language of the literati. And it was to supply this basic language that King's, later Columbia, College was devoted. With this universal language men addressed local and concrete matters in a pragmatic spirit.

Knowledge was valued for its use. In a pamphlet outlining a plan for the proposed college, William Smith insisted that "a great stock of learning, without knowing how to make it useful in the conduct of life, is of little significancy."[108] William Livingston, as we have seen, stigmatized learning that cannot be "exerted for the Benefit of Mankind" as a "specious Kind of Ignorance."[109]

This utilitarian notion of knowledge was part of a larger and multifaceted culture of improvement. Knowledge did not stand alone, as an independent vehicle of improvement. Rather material and intellectual developments were associated in social advance. It was no different in principle to cultivate better crops than to cultivate classical learning. It was perfectly natural in such a context for New Yorkers to name an organization for cultural improvement the New York Society for Promoting Agriculture, Arts, and Manufactures (1791). Again, we find William Livingston expressing the view of his time and place when he incorporated art and learning into a broad agenda of improvement to be encouraged by the provincial legislature: the "Rise of Arts, the Improvement of Husbandry, the Increase of Trade, the Advancement of Knowledge in Law, Physic, Morality, Policy, and the Rules of Justice and civil Government," were to him of a piece.[110]

The man of knowledge was thought to be encyclopedic, a notion that acknowledges the existence of special fields (if not full nineteenth-century specialization), but which contains as well an aspiration to embrace them all. Or, to put it differently and literally precisely, to have a speaking acquaintance with them all.

Intellectual life was founded on conversation. Perhaps this pattern of secular intellectual discourse was founded upon an earlier Protestant tradition of Bible study. Whatever its origin, however, its difference from the modern pattern is striking. Contemporary intellectual life is carried, almost exclusively, by means of the printed word. By contrast, in eighteenth-century New York books were valued, but conversation was the medium of intellectual growth. We might think, as foundations seem to today, that such a pattern of intellectual life is wasteful—new insights and new knowledge are not preserved and packaged for consumption. An important source, if not the sole cause, of our discomfort with talk and the eighteenth-century acceptance of it is that they did not have our industrial notion of the production of knowledge. They were interested in self-improvement and cultivation, which, after all, means growth. They sought to acquire, not create, learning. After assimilating it, they endeavored to diffuse it, either through further conversation or by means of publication. The magazines they published were, in effect, an extension of their talk.

In the early nineteenth century, the public lecture would become a vehicle for diffusion perhaps even more important than print. But both patterns of intellectual life, in contrast to our own, emphasized cultivation rather than the creation of new knowledge. No one stated the essentials of the eighteenth-century New York ideal so concisely as did Cadwallader Colden in a guide for the "study of Phylosophy" that he wrote in 1760 for the use of his grandchildren:

The gentleman, who proposes to be generally useful in society, ought not to fix his thoughts singly on any one branch of science, but to have a competent knowledge of the principles of every branch, which he may obtain without fatiguing his imagination, by too continued an application. While he reads and thinks by turns, he should, in the intervals, cultivate his intellectual faculties by general conversation, where he may obtain more useful knowledge, than can be learned from Books. The mere Scholar, the mere Physician, the mere Lawyer, Musician, or painter, take them out of their own way, and they are often more insipid, than the mere plowman.[111]

While I have stressed the close associations, even identity, of practical men and men of ideas, and denied the existence of an eighteenth-century intellectual in the modern oppositional sense, there were contradictions and ill omens for men of intellect living in a business society. During the 1790s, serious men of letters, men like Elihu Smith, Charles Brockden Brown, and William Dunlap, were disturbed by the tensions between commerce and learning, but they did not then assume an explicit and self-defining anti-bourgeois stance.

These men who had come of age in the heady atmosphere of a successful revolution imagined that freedom, commerce, and literature would all flourish in republican soil and would, because they were inevitably intertwined, vitalize one another. Joseph Ellis, in his sensitive and insightful book *After the Revolution,* explains that for such young men of ideas "there was no presumed tension between artistic values on the one hand and public opinion or the values of the marketplace on the other."[112] Indeed, such was the ideal to which the Friendly Club subscribed. It underlay their dream of a flourishing American culture. Yet this hope was being nudged aside by increasingly worrisome contrary experience.

The hope of post-Revolutionary Americans was articulated in an editorial statement printed in the first volume of the *New York Magazine* (1790). The editors noted that "while the active spirit of their country expands the sail of Commerce in every clime, its pervading genius will, we trust, lead them to explore each region of Science."[113] Five years later, in a preface affixed to the sixth volume of the magazine, the editors were less optimistic. In the United States, and in New York in particular, there is "a disregard of any objects but those attached to the active scene of business." It seemed "impossible to arrest the attention of those attached to the active scene of business," the editors concluded.[114] Yet the hope was still deeply embedded in the minds of New York's ambitious young men. In a mischievous comment in 1797 on Mandeville's argument that national prosperity depends upon individual vice, William Dunlap linked "commerce, luxury, & the fine arts" as united in their essential character and all "incompatible with virtue."[115]

Quotes of the optimistic and pessimistic sort could be multiplied. One could count them up, and decide quantitatively what the general attitude was—or one could perhaps trace a shift over time. But such a strategy would miss the point. Intellect in the 1790s was genuinely of two minds. These men believed in their patriotic dreams, and they were genuinely fearful that letters might be crushed by dollars.[116] One thing can perhaps be said, however. Those who were actually writers were more worried than those who were friends of letters. Since the next chapter will be devoted primarily to cultural philanthropists, men for whom the dream was everything, it seems fitting here to give the last word to the writers.

The first volume of the *Monthly Magazine* (1799) carried an article "On the State of American Literature." Though unsigned, it was probably written by Charles Brockden Brown. It expresses ideas that he elsewhere articulated, and these ideas were voiced at one time or another by all the Friendly Club circle. It is a patriotic article, expressing admiration for free government and the "more equal distribution of property" in the United States. "The American character . . . ranks with the most respectable and dignified on the globe," but Brown reveals as well that his "pleasure in contemplating our national character is not without alloy." The "most obvious of the defects," he claims, is the "superficial" nature of the nation's "literary character." While the general diffusion of knowledge is impressive, he agrees with foreign criticism that insists that "what is called a *liberal education* in this country, commonly includes a degree of information and intellectual polish much less accurate and extensive than is called by the same name in any other country." He suggests a variety of causes, including defective college curricula, the absence of a critical mass of literary men against which to match oneself, the sparseness of monetary reward for literary work, and the scarcity of books. But his fundamental explanation is "the love of gain" that was "very prevalent" before the war and which has increased rather than decreased since, making the United States an almost unprecedented "theatre for *speculation*."[117]

For men of intellect, then, the promise of the Revolution evolved into paradox as it unraveled itself. Expecting both literature and commerce to flourish in an environment of freedom, they found commerce not only embedded in richer soil but somehow leaching the soil in which the arts and literature were planted. Out of this paradox the modern intellectual would emerge. But in 1799, this nineteenth-century creation had at most been seeded. It would not take root and blossom for many years.

. . .

Five years later, just barely into the new century, the Swords brothers, Thomas and James, published a remarkable book in two volumes with the ambitious title *A Brief Retrospect of the Eighteenth Century . . . containing a Sketch of the Revolutions and Improvements in Science, Arts, and Literature During that Period.** It was written by Samuel Miller, the young (b. 1769) minister at the Brick Presbyterian Church in New York. Miller's remarkable essay at appraising the eighteenth-century achievement is, as Gilbert Chinard long ago remarked, "one of the earliest and most important contributions to American cultural history."[118] Miller and his book also provide a way of locating the intellectual life of eighteenth-century New York in two larger contexts, that of the Western European Enlightenment and that of the emerging American national culture.

During the 1790s and 1800s, Miller thrived in the city. Though not actually a member of the Friendly Club, he was a close associate of its members and often attended its meetings. In fact, without a coterie of learned colleagues such as the club supplied for him, it is doubtful that anyone Miller's age (or any age) could have written such a wide-ranging book. Miller also took an active part in the city's political life as a staunch Jeffersonian, often being called upon by the Tammany Society to give orations on various celebratory occasions. And he was active in the city's formal cultural organizations, being one of the founders of the New-York Historical Society and, from 1806 to 1813, a trustee of Columbia College.

When he left New York in 1813 to found the Princeton Theological Seminary, where he remained a professor until his retirement in 1849, Miller entered a different intellectual world: a Presbyterian, denominational world. The standards were high, but it was a religious rather than an urban culture. At Princeton, he repented the New York Jeffersonianism of his youth, calling it an "error."[119] More revealing of his transformation from an urban to a denominational intellectual, he now disparaged the urban intellectual life he had led in New York, criticizing it (and himself) for partaking of too much diversion and not hewing enough to his ministerial calling.[120]

Two points must be made here. Miller could not have written the great book he wrote without the diversions of urban culture. But when he went to Princeton he entered a world that shaped nineteenth-century American intellectual life perhaps more than did the urbanity of New York. Princeton Presbyterianism was the headquarters of what Henry May calls the "didactic Enlightenment," which constituted the last chapter of the Enlightenment in America and assimilated it to what became nineteenth-

---

* Its publication date is given on the title page as 1803, but the printed volumes were not actually ready until January 1804.

century Victorianism.[121] What was best in Victorian intellectual life was carried in the great denominational reviews, particularly those controlled by Princeton Presbyterians and by Harvard and Andover Unitarians. That intellectual culture was pervasive and vital for Americans outside of New York. Indeed, its national cultural force is one way of measuring the weakness of New York as the nation's cultural capital during the first half of the nineteenth century. It is perhaps worth commenting here that both American urban and denominational cultures were deeply influenced by the Scottish Enlightenment. The Presbyterian denominational tradition implanted at Princeton and elsewhere was largely the work of two Scottish ministers who were longtime presidents of Princeton, first John Witherspoon (1768–94) and then James McCosh (1868–94); while the secular, urban culture of New York owed much to the model of Edinburgh, where many of the cultural leaders of eighteenth-century New York had been educated.

In time New York would eclipse this provincial, religious culture sustained by regional denominational institutions and reviews. By the end of the 1870s, in fact, non-denominational Union Theological Seminary in New York, whose urban origins and character are clear, would intellectually surpass the old denominational network of theological schools. But that is in the future. When Miller left New York, its city culture and its pretensions to national leadership were embryonic at best, and his move to Princeton turned out to be a move into the American mainstream.

But before abandoning the city, he produced a work that sums up the cultural achievements of eighteenth-century New York. His retrospect of the eighteenth century provides an opportunity for reflection on the intellectual community that gave it birth, for it is the finest product of eighteenth-century New York's most notable learned circle.

It was a compendium of eighteenth-century knowledge. A listing of the chapter headings may be tedious, but it is the most economical way to indicate the character of the book: Mechanical Philosophy, Chemical Philosophy, Natural History, Medicine, Geography, Mathematics, Navigation, Agriculture, Mechanic Arts, Fine Arts, Physiognomy, Philosophy of the Human Mind, Classic Literature, Oriental Literature, Modern Languages, Philosophy of Language, History, Biography, Romance and Novels, Poetry, Literary Journals, Literary and Scientific Associations, Encyclopedias, Education, and Nations Lately Become Literary. He did more than summarize the state of knowledge in each of these fields, though that is one thing he did. Throughout the book runs an important argument; he is responding to Condorcet's theory of progress as argued in *Outlines of an Historical View of the Progress of the Human Mind* (1794). Progress of the intellectual and material sort does not, Miller insisted, lead to perfectibility. One cannot equate such progress with moral progress. The idea that "education has a kind of intellectual and moral *omnipotence*" that will enable human nature to "reach a state of absolute perfection in this world, or at least go on to a state of unlimited improvement," he rejected. It is *"contrary to the nature and condition of man."* Acknowledging that every generation may make progress over its predecessors in respect to "literary and scientific acquisitions," he argued that this is "by no means the case with regard to intellectual discipline and moral qualities." Each individual must anew acquire knowledge and moral discipline. Finally, he asked his readers whether the "most learned and scientific nations" are the "most virtuous." "It is presumed that no reflecting mind will answer these questions in the affirmative."[122] Here he is already speaking the language of Princeton Presbyterianism. Though his fellow New Yorkers were not so naïve as to answer his question in the affirmative, they hoped more than he did that the answer might be yes.

Miller also included a rather extensive discussion of the foundations of eighteenth-century intellectual life. Learned societies, not colleges, were the key institutions. Noting that the Royal Society and Royal Academy both dated from the seventeenth century, he declared that "the eighteenth century is pre-eminently remarkable for multiplying these associations"; few cities of any aspiration in France and Italy lack one. These learned societies, he concluded, "may be reckoned among the principal causes of the [advance of the] moderns over the ancients." They unify the "republic of letters," and they increase "intercourse and connections among the learned" thus making them "among the most important sources of modern improvements in science."[123]

In his final chapter, a discussion of nations recently become literary, he assessed the progress and condition of science and letters in the United States. He dated the beginnings of intellectual life in New York from the 1750s, with the establishment of the New York Society Library and King's College. "From this period," he wrote, "we may date the rise of a literary spirit in the province of New York. It is true, this spirit was possessed, for a long time afterwards, by comparatively few individuals, and produced effects by no means so general or important as the friends of knowledge would wish: but from this time the advantages of liberal education were more frequently enjoyed in the province." And in New York, as in other parts of the United States, "literary institutions of various kinds were multiplied with astonishing rapidity," while the "rewards of literary labour, though still too small, were considerably augmented."[124]

Like others in the orbit of the Friendly Club, Miller tempered his hopeful vision with worries. He listed the usual collection of "causes which have hitherto impeded the progress of American literature." The colleges were "defective," not enough books were available, there was no leisure class and not enough patronage, and, most insistently expressed, there was the problem that "the spirit of our people is *commercial.*" Yet he concluded that New York was a young city and the United States a young country. He thought that perhaps these difficulties were "declining" as factors and that "the literary prospects of our country are brightening every day."[125] For Miller, and others among his New York associates, a retrospect on developments since 1750 allowed one to be prudently optimistic about intellectual culture, even in a city of commerce.

CHAPTER 2

Patricians and
Artisans

The origins of the Society of St. Tammany are shrouded in mystery. Apparently it existed in at least embryonic form in New York as early as 1786. The first public celebration held under its auspices occurred in 1787, and by 1789, the year when the new government of the Constitution was organized in New York City, Tammany held its second celebration. From that year onward there is a public history of Tammany, and in its early years one finds Tammany linked to projects of cultural reform, both through individuals associated with it and through its own programs. According to the historian of the society, the "guiding influence" in the establishment of Tammany was a young merchant named John Pintard, who was, it seemed, "a member of every society and a participant in every movement of importance in New York."[1]

Tammany before 1795 does not conform to the accepted mythology of the institution. It was not in its first decade of existence identified as a partisan organization. Many Federalists like Pintard were active in it until 1795, and only after the demise of the Democratic Society did Tammany become overtly partisan.[2] Tammany in those early years is perhaps best described as a nationalist or patriotic improving society. In a letter to Jeremy Belknap in 1790, Pintard described Tammany as "a political institution founded upon a strong republican basis, whose democratic principles will serve in some measure to correct the aristocracy of our city." Although some have suggested that it was thus organized to counter the aristocratic Society of Cincinnati, it is difficult to sustain this position in view of the friendly relations between the two organizations, including

significant levels of dual membership and friendly toasts offered by the
Tammany Society for the Cincinnati at its celebrations.³

What Pintard seems to have had in mind is an organization that comprehended both the mechanic and merchant classes. One cannot but be
struck with the degree to which the general membership of the society
and its officeholders actually reflected this aim. William Pitt Smith of
Columbia College declared in 1790 that Tammany united "in one patriotic band, the opulent and industrious—the learned and unlearned,
the dignified servants of the people and the respectable plebian, however
distinguished by name, by sentiment, or by occupation." Although mechanics were more numerous in the rank and file than in the leadership
of the organization, the first Grand Sachem was William Mooney, an
upholsterer, paperhanger, and furniture dealer. Other sachems were
also mechanics; one-half of the officers between 1789 and 1795 were
mechanics and small tradesmen.⁴ It represented the dream of a harmonious and unified republican culture and polity.

Pintard's very special hope for Tammany, however, was the creation of
a museum. As he wrote in another letter to Belknap, "I engrafted an
antiquarian scheme upon it."⁵ In a letter to Thomas Jefferson, Pintard
described his rather ambitious aims for the Tammany Museum: "To
collect and preserve whatever relates to our country in art or nature, as
well as every material which may serve to perpetuate the Memorial of
national events and history."⁶ A newspaper announcement in the *New
York Journal* in 1791 indicated that the museum had been established "for
the purpose of collecting and preserving everything relating to the history of America, likewise every American production of nature or art."⁷
The museum format, as developed by Charles Willson Peale in Philadelphia, from whom Pintard apparently got the idea, was intended (in
Peale's words) to "form a school of useful knowledge" and "to diffuse it
to every class" in the community. It was thus a vehicle of democratic
culture; it was also intended by both Pintard and Peale to make their
respective cities and museums the center of a national network of museums and historical societies advancing knowledge and encouraging national patriotism.⁸

The museum was funded by the Tammany Society, and it sponsored
free exhibitions open to public view in a room in the old Royal Exchange
on Tuesday and Friday afternoons. In 1795, when Tammany began to
assume its later partisan character, the society discontinued its support
and turned the museum over to Gardiner Baker, the keeper, who con-
verted it into a commercial enterprise. From him it passed in 1798 into
the hands of John Scudder, and it was as Scudder's Museum that it
became in 1841 the core collection for P. T. Barnum's famous museum
on Broadway.

Barnum's Museum was not the only long-term cultural asset the city derived from this little-known episode in the history of the Society of St. Tammany. In the course of his association with the Tammany project, Pintard formed a close friendship with De Witt Clinton, a recent (1786) graduate of Columbia College. This friendship, stimulated initially by their joint interest in the Tammany Society during its non-partisan period and nourished particularly by their mutual enthusiasm for the museum, evolved over the next three decades into an extraordinary partnership devoted to improving the material and cultural life of New York City. To this task they brought both confidence and determination, qualities evident in Pintard's response to Jedidiah Morse's comments on the limited progress of the arts and sciences in New York and particularly the absence of learned and improving societies. "Tell our friend Morse," he wrote to Belknap, "that by the next edition of his Geography our city will offer a better picture of the *progress of civil society* than in his last."[9]

The longtime friendship of Pintard and Clinton was a multifaceted enterprise of improvement that included the initiation of the Erie Canal project and the founding of the Literary and Philosophical Society of New York. They believed deeply in the cultural premises underlying Bishop Berkeley's famous "Verses on the Prospect of Planting Arts and Learning in America." That poem not only predicted a western movement but also offered in its imagery a cultural theory that associated economic and cultural success. Berkeley spoke of "the rise of empire and the arts"—thus assuming a link between economic and political development on the one hand and intellectual and artistic progress on the other.[10] It was an assumption central to the careers in civic improvement pursued by Pintard and Clinton, and, as we have seen, an assumption already problematical for the most sophisticated young men of intellect in the city.

The quest for city culture begun with this assumption in 1750, with William Livingston and his fellow reformers, achieved fulfillment in the urban institutions founded by Pintard and Clinton in the first quarter of the nineteenth century. At the same time, however, one finds clear indications by 1830 of the enervation of the ideal of civic culture and premonitions of the literary and academic cultures that would succeed it.

PATRICIAN IMPROVERS

In 1784, eight years after his graduation from Princeton, Pintard wrote to his college friend Elias Boudinot about his hopes for himself. His ambition, he acknowledged, was to become "one of the first characters" of New York.[11] He was well on his way toward that goal when he met Clinton.[12] Born in New Rochelle in 1759, of French Huguenot parents, Pintard was orphaned at the age of one year and raised by his uncle, Lewis Pintard, a prosperous New York merchant. By the 1780s, he was a prominent and rising merchant in New York, plying the East India trade. He had already served as a city alderman when he was elected in 1791 to the State Assembly, having been nominated by the city's mechanics.

Early in the 1790s, however, he became associated with the notorious William Duer, co-signing notes for a variety of the latter's speculations. When Duer's financial schemes collapsed in 1792, he carried Pintard, who was unable to meet the obligations he had assumed, down with him. It is unclear to what degree Pintard was cognizant of the nature of his associate's machinations. But even if we grant—as some of his biographers insist—that he was unaware of Duer's improprieties, it is clear that his own ambition seriously beclouded his good judgment, even if it did not tarnish his honesty. (In his later career it is evident that he had learned a lesson: he never again assumed the role of entrepreneur, and there is a constant, though muted, refrain in his letters expressing disapproval of the atmosphere of speculation and entrepreneurial risk that characterized New York's economic life.)

Pintard fled to Newark, New Jersey, in the hope of escaping the suits of his creditors, and he spent eight years in exile there. One of those creditors, however, pursued him across the river, and this resulted in his spending a year (1797–98) in the Newark debtors' prison. During this humiliating period, when he dated his letters "Newark, *in carcere*," he used his time well, reading widely though, characteristically, not deeply. In 1800, he returned briefly to New York, then he traveled to New Orleans in search of opportunity. After unsuccessfully appealing to the Jefferson administration for a place, perhaps one that might take advantage of his French connections and of his newly acquired knowledge of the Louisiana Territory, he returned to New York and began reconstructing a successful life.

In his second New York City life he earned his living from salaries rather than from mercantile investment. In 1804, his friend Mayor Clinton bestowed upon him the position of City Inspector, a job that Pintard held until 1809, when he moved from a reliance on municipal salaries to corporate managerial ones, becoming secretary of the Mutual Insurance Company, a successor company, incidentally, to the Mutual Assurance Company, of which he had been secretary from 1787 until 1792. This position not only provided him with a salary; it supplied him with residential quarters above the office at 52 Wall Street. He held this position for twenty years, following it with nearly twenty more years' service as a director of the company. In 1817, in a letter to his daughter,* he indicated that he held four salaried offices: secretary of the Mutual Insurance Company, director of the Brooklyn Steamboat Company, clerk of the Corporation of Sailor's Snug Harbor, recording secretary of the board of managers of the American Bible Society.[13]

Between 1801, when he returned to New York, and the late 1830s, when he began reducing his activities, Pintard assumed active roles in such a large number of civic institutions that to list them strains credibility. But he had extraordinary energy, and in many of these organizations his maintaining and nurturing activity kept them going. Letters to his daughter record meeting upon meeting, obligation upon obligation. Besides the organizations already named, he was founder and secretary of the New-York Historical Society, founder of the New York Institution of Learned and Scientific Establishments, treasurer of the American Academy of Fine Arts, trustee of the New York Society Library, curator of the Literary and Philosophical Society, secretary of the Chamber of Commerce, trustee of the Free School Society, manager of the Society for the Prevention of Pauperism, vice-president of the Society for the Encouragement of Faithful Domestic Servants, trustee of the General Theological Seminary, vestryman of the French Protestant Church, a manager of the House of Refuge, an officer of the New York Fire Insurance Company, a founder and eventually president of the city's first savings bank, board member of the Fuel Saving Fund, a board member of the Society for the Relief of Distressed Debtors (after 1800 called the Humane Society), and secretary of the Erie Canal Celebration Committee. At least one biographer, moreover, gives him credit for taking an active and decisive role in inducing the legislature to approve the 1811 plan that established Manhattan's gridiron with its numbered streets and avenues north of Houston Street.[14] This extraordinary spectrum of activities —cultural, charitable, financial—shows the breadth of Pintard's vision of civic improvement. No wonder he could observe in 1816: "What a field our large city presents for active exertions & useful improvements."[15]

Though he never achieved the kind of distinction he might have won had not his mercantile career crashed in the 1790s, he reconciled himself to his still impressive position a cut below the highest circle of society. In reflecting on his life, he emphasized his usefulness and appreciated the recognition that his activities won for him "with the intellectual & worthy part of the community." As he assured his daughter in 1817: "I do not want a reasonable share of respect." Forty years later in a collective biography of the city's great merchants, it could be said of him: "There never

* These letters to his daughter—beginning in 1816, when she married a New Orleans physician, and continuing almost weekly until her death in 1833—provide an extraordinary "diary" of Pintard's life and of life in New York.

lived that man in the city who could start great measures as John Pintard could do." [16]

Unlike Elihu Smith and his circle, or even Livingston, Pintard was not a man of ideas. Although he enjoyed reading the serious literature of his time (excepting, curiously, science, which seldom turns up in his notes on his reading), he had none of the intensity of the intellectually serious. He enjoyed acquaintance with books and ideas commonly discussed in intellectual circles. But his comments on books seldom show much insight or engagement, and he was more interested in the maintenance and administration of the learned societies he organized than in taking advantage of what they offered him in the way of personal intellectual improvement. Pintard knew his limitations. "Altho' I possess considerable book reading," he confided to his daughter, "I dare not call it learning; for want of intercourse & collision, my stores are not always at my ready command. Professional men are always going over their well cultivated fields of learning, while a poor layman can only cull a flower here & there from his scanty parterre." [17] He understood his place as that of one who provided the material means for others; he found his satisfaction in a supportive rather than a leading role. "It falls to my lot," he reflected to a friend in 1815, "to plant that acorn which is to produce the tree under whose shade future Academicians are to repose." [18]

De Witt Clinton was not so comfortable in the background. For a generation—as mayor of the city and governor of the state—Clinton was the most visible and controversial public figure in New York. As the biographer of one of Clinton's rivals observes, "It is hardly an overstatement to say that from 1800 to his death in 1828 Clinton was the major issue in New York State politics." [19] Clinton's place in the intellectual life of the city was equally a subject of attention and contention.

De Witt Clinton was born in 1769 in Orange County, New York. [20] In this rural county nestled in the corner west of the Hudson River where New York and New Jersey share a land border, he was educated and prepared for college. His family intended that he attend Princeton, but on his way to Princeton he stopped in New York. While in the city he became aware of the recently completed reorganization of King's College into Columbia College and its imminent opening. He stayed, entered the college, and became the first person to graduate from Columbia College in 1786. After graduation he studied law, being admitted to the New York Bar in 1788. Two years later, he became private secretary to his uncle, George Clinton, governor of the state since 1777. Given his privileged access to the higher reaches of New York's political elite, it is not surprising to see him succeed quickly in his quest for political office, winning a seat in the State Assembly and then becoming a state senator. In 1802, he was elected to the U.S. Senate, but in the next year he resigned to accept appointment as mayor of New York City. He was mayor of the city from 1803 until 1815, with the exception of two terms, 1807–8 and 1810–11. In 1817 he was elected governor, being reelected twice and defeated once before his death in office in 1828.

While pursuing this active and enormously successful public career, he was deeply involved in the civic culture of New York City. The year after graduation, he joined the Uranian Society and soon thereafter the Tammany Society. He was a director of the Manhattan Company (the water company that has become the Chase Manhattan Bank) and of the New York Hospital. He was one of the founding members of the New-York Historical Society, the Literary and Philosophical Society, and the American Bible Society. As president of the American Academy of Fine Arts in 1816, he revitalized, at least briefly, an organization that was fated to expire in the 1820s. The Free School Society, a private charitable school system that became the foundation of the New York public school system, was Clinton's work. His greatest work, pursued in and out of office, was the massive public-works project that more than any other single thing consolidated New York's position as the commercial and financial metropolis of the nation. It is for good reason that the Erie Canal was once referred to as "Clinton's Ditch."

The lives of men like Clinton, men who are too important to be ignored yet not really great, typically suffer the fate of being remembered by a phrase in our textbooks and encyclopedias. For Clinton, the phrase is "the father of the spoils system."[21] While certainly he did make innovations in appointment policies, he fell far short of the revolution in politics that eventuated in the Jacksonian party system. This later development, which linked systematic patronage to party organization, was largely the work of other, younger New Yorkers whom Clinton never fully understood: Martin Van Buren and Thurlow Weed. Clinton deserves to be remembered in a somewhat different context. Theodore Roosevelt was correct in insisting that while Clinton's political practices deserve to be remembered, so do his indefatigable civic efforts for "philanthropic, scientific, and industrial improvements" in New York.[22]

Clinton was very proud of his intellectual accomplishments. Indeed, he even had the boldness to describe himself in print under the cover (very slight) of a pseudonym:

Mr. Clinton, amidst his other great qualifications, is distinguished for a marked devotion to science:—few men have read more, and few men can claim more various and extensive knowledge. And the bounties of nature have been improved, by persevering and unintermitted industry. It was natural that such men should have high rank in literary institutions; and he was accordingly elected the first President of the Literary and Philosophical Society of New York.[23]

Although one cannot accuse the author of these remarks of being modest, he nonetheless neglected to add here that he was simultaneously president of the American Academy of Fine Arts and vice-president of the New-York Historical Society. Certainly Clinton was a presence in the intellectual culture of New York. One easily gets the impression, moreover, that Clinton wanted to be known as New York's Thomas Jefferson —and indeed hoped to follow James Madison in the Jeffersonian line of presidential succession. But he was not Jefferson. Clinton brought much learning to intellectual discourse, but he had a tendency, as Dixon Ryan Fox put it, toward "vain pomposity and parade of erudition."[24]

In natural science his reputation was more solid than in belles lettres.* It is surely not insignificant that his first two biographers were scientists who knew and admired him. David Hosack, botanist, physician, and Fellow of the Royal Society, described him as "one of those few active and gifted men, who unite the elevated pursuits of science and letters, with the fullest occupation of his professional and public duties." Hosack claimed, in addition, to know "no man in the United States so well qualified to discharge the duties appertaining to a professorship of natural history in any of our Universities." James Renwick, professor of natural and experimental philosophy at Columbia College, ranked him "far beyond the head of amateur *savans* [sic]"; he belonged "in the rank of professional naturalist."[25] Yet younger scientists, more professionally oriented ones, did not accept Clinton as a colleague. Indeed, as we shall see, they rejected his name twice for membership in the Lyceum of Natural History before granting him an honorary membership and thus additional kudos.

Whether in politics or letters, Clinton evoked strong reactions, either positive or negative. Much of this is directly attributable to his personality, but there is as well a historical issue. Clinton seems to have been a transitional figure. In politics, he was not so fastidious as Washington, but neither was he the new sort of party politician that Van Buren was becoming at the time of Clinton's death.[26] In intellectual life, he was not primarily a scientist or scholar; learning was an avocation to be indulged in during his leisure hours. To the degree that younger men began to see the possibility of thinking of themselves as scientists or writers, whatever their means of earning a living, Clinton represented a pattern of intellectual life they wished to escape. Yet all men of intellect recognized, as they

* Some of his critics among literary men charged him—probably accurately—with resorting to conventional compendia of classical phrases to ornament his orations.

had to, that in Clinton, the cultivator of knowledge and friend of learning, they had an ally of unprecedented value. Here was a man of power
willing to use that power to advance the cause of learning, both at the
higher levels and at the level of the general population. In time, even
those who treated him most roughly, Gulian Verplanck among writers
and the young men aspiring to a new model of professionalism in the
Lyceum of Natural History, gave him his due.[27]

The inauguration of George Washington in New York City portended a
transformation of the city. Even if locating the new national government
in New York City was understood to be temporary, many thought it could
be made permanent. And such permanence implied a process of social
concentration that would make New York a capital city in the way that
Paris and London were. Here power, fashion, wealth, and intellect would
meet and shape the new nation's political and cultural life. Nothing better
illuminates these possibilities—and their realization even in the short
compass of a year—than the guest list of Mrs. John Jay, wife of the first
Chief Justice. On that list one finds a remarkable array of talent and
power.[28] During New York's brief career as national capital the city
seemed on its way to becoming the crucible out of which a national elite
could be forged.

But that was not the America many, including Thomas Jefferson, envisioned. For Jefferson and his followers, the republican promise was
associated with decentralization and equality, not consolidation. It was
not that Jefferson did not appreciate the cultural possibilities of great
capital cities; it was rather that he feared more the political consequences
of the gross inequalities of wealth and hierarchies of power in them.
Feeling himself forced to choose—in America—between advanced culture or political virtue, he chose the latter. When New York's Alexander
Hamilton, who revealed a surprising lack of interest in science and letters,
offered to accept the Jeffersonian cultural vision in exchange for his own
version of the concentration of wealth and power, a swamp along the
Potomac was selected as the future site of the national capital.

During the 1790s, in the interim before the government moved to the
new District of Columbia, Philadelphia served as the nation's capital. To
the extent that the United States had an "intellectual centre" in 1800, it
was, as Henry Adams observed, Philadelphia.[29] Here for a brief moment
power, intellect, and society converged in a way that suggested national
capitals in Europe. Unlike New York, however, Philadelphia could not
sustain an ambition to be a cultural capital without the political capital,
especially after New York in the third decade of the nineteenth century
surpassed Philadelphia as the financial center of the nation.

When New York ceased to be the national capital, the United States lost what could easily have become in the nineteenth century its natural center. But this fact was not so evident in the 1790s as it would be later. For New York itself, however, the loss was immediately and traumatically felt. It produced a momentary loss of confidence, but engendered as well a rather quick compensatory response. The result was the strengthening of an elite civic consciousness, a sense of the city fundamentally localistic and based on the complementarity of commerce and culture.

It was as if, having been shunned as being unsuitable for the nation's capital, New York City decided to go it alone. New York would not be America. It would be New York, the most important economic and cultural center in the United States. This point is difficult but important to make. New York did not claim that its economic and cultural achievements were national achievements. Spokesmen for the city were remarkably forthright in justifying their ambitions in civic rather than national terms. Whether Clinton spoke of the Literary and Philosophical Society or the Erie Canal, he was not hesitant to say that the one would place New York next to European centers of culture, while the other would make all the United States a suburb or tributary of New York. He did not think it important, even rhetorically, to claim that New York was contributing to the greatness of the national culture or economy. This contrasts with the ambition of the Society of St. Tammany in 1790; when New York was the national capital, Tammany presented itself as a national improvement society. To make the point differently, we can compare Clinton's "Introductory Discourse" before the Literary and Philosophical Society in 1814 with that delivered by Stephen Elliott before the Literary and Philosophical Society in Charleston, South Carolina, in the same year. While Clinton made great claims for New York's greatness without alluding to the society's contribution to national greatness, Elliott—in this era of South Carolina's staunch nationalism and New York's limited nationalism—emphasized that the cultural progress to be nourished by learned societies was national, not local or parochial.[30]

Out of the disappointment of losing the national capital, New York defined a version of cultural improvement that was distinctly local and civic rather than general and national. Here we have the origins of that special quality of New York as a cultural capital. Rejected as a fit home for the national capital, the city has remained uncomfortable in the nation—as the nation has remained uncomfortable with New York. New York's cultural leadership thus cannot be assumed, it must be proclaimed. New York stands semi-detached, shunned but indispensable.

Since New York City's metropolitan status was founded upon the practical fact of economic ascendancy rather than upon political leadership, New Yorkers were inclined to interpret culture as proceeding directly from commerce. Commerce and culture were seen as twin facets in a general project of improvement, an association not unique to New York thinking but pointedly apt. In time intellectuals would question the civilizing effect of commerce, but in the seventeenth and eighteenth centuries, as Albert Hirschman has revealed, it was a common association.[31] Pintard and Clinton had not a glimmer of doubt. Indeed, it is revealing to the point of being explanatory that the two most effective proponents of the Erie Canal, one the most famous and the other the least well known, were these two cultural improvers. And it is more than simply one of those lucky historical coincidences that the earliest known proposal for a canal was made in 1724 by Cadwallader Colden, a man who has already appeared in our story as a cultural improver.[32]

When, in 1807, Samuel L. Mitchill published the first guidebook to New York City, it was routine to call the city "the commercial metropolis of North America."[33] Though probably true, this claim was vulnerable to revision until the completion of the Erie Canal solidified the city's centrality in national interregional trade and in international trade.[34]

De Witt Clinton proposed that such economic and financial dominance constituted the foundation for cultural achievement. Two public statements iterated this point. First, speaking before a Committee of a Meeting of Citizens of New York in 1824, Clinton prophesied that the "City will in the course of time become the Granary of the western world, the emporium of commerce, the seat of manufacture, the focus of great moneyed operations, and the concentrating point of vast, disposable and accumulating capital which will stimulate, enliven, extend, reward the exertions of human labor and ingenuity." The canal would be the instrument for this civic glory. The revenue from the canal, moreover, would not only "defray the expenses of the government but it will in time realize a vast fund applicable to all the objects of human improvement, upon intellectual and moral cultivation."[35] To an audience of Columbia College alumni, Clinton predicted that the wealth the canal would produce for New York would bring together there "men of science and ingenious artists." "Whoever wealth can tempt, knowledge allure, or the delights of polished and refined society attract, will occasionally visit or permanently reside in this great emporium."[36] We have direct evidence that at least one significant artist was thinking along the same line. Samuel F. B. Morse decided in 1823 to move to New York, anticipating that the canal would result in patronage for the arts and the development of an artistic community in New York.[37]

The year 1817 marks the beginning of the Erie Canal. It also is the year when the firm of Harper & Brothers was established. A coincidence yes, but one with some historical content. That Harper's was the greatest New York (and American) publisher by the 1850s was attributable directly to the canal. With the canal dramatically reducing transportation costs, economies of scale enabled Harper's to undersell local and regional publishers in their own territories, especially in the lucrative school book and religious book markets.[38] Thus not only were culture and commerce associated; in New York culture itself was commerce. Pintard recognized, at least part of the time, that culture was a business. This is worth noting because, as things turned out, the distinctive quality of New York City as a cultural center has not been as the home of writers and artists but rather as the place where their books are published, their plays produced, their paintings sold. The business side of intellectual life made New York a cultural metropolis.[39]

The chosen vehicle of improvement for Pintard and Clinton was the special-purpose institution, as the list of their activities amply reveals. In this respect, they typified the activities of the culturally ambitious between the 1780s and 1820. The cultural news during this period, as John Bach McMaster long ago noted, was not significant writing or scientific work but rather the repeated efforts at founding the kinds of institutions that it was thought would call such significant work into existence, whether they were academies of art, learned societies, or magazines.[40] Here, interestingly, we have a parallel between American strategies of this period in cultural life and economic life. By the development of the transportation infrastructure through public and private cooperation—most notably, as Carter Goodrich has pointed out, in the case of canals—private economic activity in the market was greatly stimulated.[41] But while this approach was remarkably successful in stimulating American capitalism, it seems to have been much less effective in cultural life.

What Clinton and Pintard had in mind were not voluntary associations, at least not in the narrow definition that implies an alternative to governmental institutions. Neither had any hesitation in mixing public resources and private energies, whether one speaks of Pintard's request of Mayor Clinton for the assignment of free city rooms for various cultural organizations or Governor Clinton's readiness to use state funds for the Erie Canal project.

If the vision of improvement articulated by Pintard and Clinton rather confidently based itself on commerce and assumed a link between commerce and culture, they were moved as well by the ideology of popular learning and improvement associated with the international movement of Freemasonry. Long ago Bernard Fäy observed that "almost all of the learned societies which flourished in the second half of the eighteenth century were imbued with the spirit of Masonry and often worked in close cooperation with the local lodges." More recently, and in a far more sophisticated study, Margaret Jacob has established the close association of Masonry with republicanism and popular enlightenment thought in the Anglo-Dutch world. And in the new American nation, as Dorothy Lipson has shown, Freemasonry was deeply involved in movements for education, charity, and the inculcation of a secular social morality compatible with republicanism.[42] These generalizations find specific realization in the cultural history of New York.

Not only were Pintard and Clinton leading Masons (both were masters of Holland Lodge; Clinton was later grand master of New York State Masonry for fourteen years), so were many of their collaborators. The Holland Lodge alone, besides Pintard and Clinton, claimed as members Henry Brevoort (a writer associated with Washington Irving), Cadwallader Colden Jr., William Dunlap, William Delafield (a member of the Lyceum of Natural History and a founder of NYU), William Irving (brother of Washington), Charles King (president of Columbia), Edward Livingston (brother of William and a major legal theorist and jurist), Robert R. Livingston (another brother, diplomat, purchaser of Louisiana), Morgan Lewis (a founder of NYU), Samuel L. Mitchill, William Wheaton (a founder of the New York Atheneum), and William Wilcocks (a founder of the Mechanics Institute). To some extent, what we have here is simply a pattern of the interlocking patterns of memberships characteristic of a society with a multifunctional elite. But there is more to be said about the connection between Masonry and the diffusion of knowledge. At least in respect to cultural ambition and education, it is difficult to distinguish the ideology of Masonry from that of republicanism. It was self-consciously identified with enlightenment, with the progress of mind and diffusion of knowledge that "dispelled the gloom of ignorance and barbarism."[43]

The defining characteristics of early American Freemasonry as a cultural orientation can be denoted by emphasizing its secular, dissenting, latitudinarian, cosmopolitan, charitable, and self-educating qualities. Masonic educational programs included all branches of "polite learning" as well as popularizing science. The Masonic study groups established to transmit the arcana of the order were also used for broader purposes, especially instruction in science. The lodges, then, were social and intellectual bodies, offering both companionship and learning.[44]

Masons of New York saw themselves as members of an improving organization located within a society specially favored with possibilities for improvement. They aimed particularly at encouraging morality and the "propagation of knowledge."[45] One Masonic historian of the order, in fact, referred to the common school, which in New York City dates its institutional history from the Public School Society founded by De Witt Clinton, "as the purest exemplification of Freemasonry."[46] Though Freemasonry, like the Republic of Letters, was international, it was rooted in local institutions and sought to contribute to the shaping of a local society by selecting and giving intellectual and moral direction to men of likely influence in that society. James Hardie, a prominent Mason and author of one of the first guidebooks to New York City, explained that "within the walls of a lodge, no one should be admitted, unless he have made himself conspicuous by the rectitude of his conduct, and his improvement in those arts and sciences, which tend to refine our morals, and render us more worthy and upright members of society." Hardie insisted that the "cultivation" of the "liberal arts and sciences" was necessary if one wished to arrive at "distinction" among the Masons.[47] These values carried within the culture of Masonry were brought by Clinton, Pintard, and others in New York into the general culture of the city in those years following 1790 when the extraordinary performance of New York City's economy sustained an ebullient spirit of improvement.[48]

De Witt Clinton's first published oration was the address he gave at his installation as master of Holland Lodge on December 24, 1793. In that address he defined Masonry in terms that would characterize his own activities as a civic improver. Masonry developed out of the desire of "scientists and ingenious men" to assemble together "to improve the arts and sciences, and to cultivate a pure and sublime system of morality." Clinton insisted that the whole meaning of Masonry, the secrecy of the rituals notwithstanding, was the democratization of knowledge. When Masonry began its career, "knowledge . . . was restricted to the chosen few," but with the advent of printing new possibilities arose and "the generous cultivators of Masonry communicated with cheerfulness to the world, those secrets of the arts and sciences." Self-improvement, Clinton added, was as important as benevolence. It was the duty of every Mason "to enrich his mind with knowledge," devoting to mental improvement those hours remaining "after pursuing the ordinary concerns of life."[49]

For Clinton the ideal Mason was represented in the person of the Grand Master of New York State Masonry, Chancellor Robert R. Livingston, whom Clinton described as "the scholar, the gentleman, and the statesman."[50] In time, of course, Clinton would similarly be described. His death provided a special—and stressful—occasion for such a description, for when Clinton died in 1828, New York Masonry was in crisis. The disappearance of William Morgan, an upstate New York Mason who had allegedly threatened to reveal the secrets of the sect, brought it under a cloud. Indeed, Masonry is best remembered by American historians for this incident, which spawned a political party—the Anti-Masonic Party—that was instrumental in the realignment of electoral allegiances which produced the so-called second or Jacksonian party system. What has been forgotten was Masonry's earlier centrality to our cultural and intellectual history. Samuel Knapp, in the course of memorializing Clinton's life, tried to affirm and fix this meaning of Masonry at the onset of the anti-Masonic surge that, from today's vantage, drove Masonry underground, to emerge eventually with the image of a Midwestern fraternal lodge. Clinton represented the enlightened and republican ideals of Masonry. "He early saw," Knapp avowed, "that Masonry was a great moral engine which might be used, in the hands of enlightened men, in forming the minds, and in directing the energies of the young and enterprising men of this youthful republic."[51] *

The crisis of Masonry produced by the Morgan incident exposed a very troubling contradiction in the movement: How could an organization that was dedicated, as Clinton said it was, to science, merit, equality, philanthropy, and natural religion, be equally dedicated to rituals of secrecy? While Samuel Miller had recognized this difficulty and warned his fellow Masons about it in 1795, Clinton and most other Masons never confronted the dilemma. In part, this was because they saw the secrecy and exclusivity of the order as essential to its proper functioning. Adopting a rather sophisticated pedagogical assumption, Masons argued that the secrecy and solidarity of the lodge captivated the imagination and intensified the members' engagement with learning. They understood the value of a certain exclusivity and intensified group experience as aids to learning and as promoters of intellectual commitment—something we too recognize, if we do not always acknowledge it, in our institutes, disciplinary associations, and departments.[52]

The literature of Masonry repeats a single predictable metaphor, but its obviousness makes it no less apt. The usefulness of Masonry to society, it was said, is that it builds foundations. Certainly Pintard and Clinton in their institution-founding saw themselves as building foundations for a republican culture.

If Masonry seems to have united the cultural improvers of early republican New York, party loyalty seems not to have divided them. No organization seems to have been exclusively the product of a Federalist or anti-Federalist elite. Even later, when Democratic-Republican opposition to Federalism had developed, one finds no party division in the various

---

* Note the association with national progress in this statement, something not seen in Clinton's New York orations. It is noteworthy, therefore, that Knapp delivered this address in Washington, D.C.

cultural and benevolent societies, with the important distinction that anti-slavery organizations seem to have lacked significant Democratic-Republican representation. The religious backgrounds of cultural reformers were also diverse. Columbia College, it is true, had become an intensely Episcopalian institution in the first decade of the nineteenth century, but it had by then so isolated itself from the life of the city that it was not really a civic institution and so is not a real exception. All of the learned societies and organizations for cultural improvement were free of association with any particular religious persuasion.

Historians of various urban educational and welfare institutions have in recent years stressed their origins in fear of new forms of urban poverty and disorder, and they have been described as institutions of elite social control.[53] Others have emphasized the transformation of Protestant theology and the development of a new and militant Christian benevolence.[54] Still others, assuming a somewhat different angle, stress the active role of the lower classes in the process of social formation; they were not passive victims of the elite.[55] While all of these ways of looking at social innovation bear upon developments after 1820, they seem to offer very little guidance in explaining the efforts of Pintard and Clinton. Reading their public and private statements, one senses immediately that they were Christians, but their religion lay lightly on them. I would characterize them both as tolerantly or generously Christian. Pintard, for example, worried about urban vice, but thought that keeping the theaters open constituted a perfectly Christian solution to the problem of providing "proper direction to young minds."[56] He looked not for perfection. The internalization of the notion of voluntary sin and Christian stewardship that underlay the militancy of a later New Yorker like abolitionist Arthur Tappan was not part of the Christianity of Pintard and Clinton.

Considering their attitude toward social change in the city, one is more struck by their optimism than by their fear. Again and again, they speak of wonderful improvement—economic, social, cultural. Even when Pintard expected some disorder during the citywide celebrations of the opening of the Erie Canal, he could not help remarking "on the progressive improvement in the moral character of this city." Not only was New York relatively free of riot and disorder during the celebration; Pintard noted that even with "multitudes . . . collected in the Battery & thro' our Streets," it was possible for "Ladies & children" to pass "unoffended by any indelicate expressions." All of this, he thought, did great honor to the city. "What have we not to expect from the rising generation favoured with so many advantages of education. . . . I am confirmed in the belief that the world is growing better."[57]

Although by nature Pintard seems to have been tolerant and unthreatened, his comfort with his city was rather characteristic of his generation.

It was after 1825, the year of the canal celebration, that one begins to see evidence of the kinds of concerns and fears that were translated into a working-class self-awareness and a quest for elite social control. Later, in the 1840s, when New York's elite was beginning to feel threatened by social crisis and when culture had come to be defined as a special realm distinct from society, the most conscientious of New Yorkers began to worry about having to choose between a commitment to society and one to culture. And under such circumstances, they wondered whether one could choose culture in such an atmosphere of injustice and danger. To read the diary of George Templeton Strong is to see a man of wide cultural appreciation, attentive to, if not actively concerned for, the unfortunate of the city, struggle with the emerging conflict between social improvement and cultural improvement. Fearful of poverty, he asks whether it is right for his class to pursue and enjoy "liberal pursuits" while hundreds, even thousands, of their fellow citizens lacked the bare necessities of life.[58]

All of this, however, postdates the seemingly less complicated years of Pintard and Clinton, when such choices were neither necessary nor conceptually present. It is their understanding of the relation of culture to society that I wish to stress here. Yet I would not like to be misunderstood as suggesting that Pintard and Clinton were in some sense more liberal in any modern sense. They were both quite conservative and no more sympathetic to the working classes than later elite reformers of the social-control sort and probably less sympathetic than Strong.

TO MAKE A CENTER

As the WPA arts projects demonstrated in the 1930s, successful government cultural patronage can be triggered by events utterly unrelated to the arts. Municipal patronage of the arts and sciences in early-nineteenth-century New York provides another such case. This patronage was a direct result of the loss of the national capital. When the federal government moved out of the City Hall that had been remodeled for its use, there was a good deal of excess municipal space available in the city, and it was given over to cultural uses. This building thus became the first home of the American Academy of Fine Arts (founded 1801) and of the New-York Historical Society (1804). When, however, the new (that is, the present) City Hall neared completion in 1811, it was determined that the old one should be demolished. The cultural organizations that had found a place there were about to become homeless.

Pintard, who was active in both of these organizations, wrote a letter to his friend Mayor Clinton in August 1812 asking for municipal patronage in the form of free space. In seeking municipal support for the arts and sciences, he specifically excluded from his request "Colleges and Seminaries of learning." He had in mind the learned associations that, as we have seen, defined the city's intellectual culture. He spoke not only for the two institutions threatened with homelessness but also for organizations not housed in the old City Hall (e.g., Scudder's Museum and the New York Society Library) and for "some other institutions that ought to be established & promoted." He told Clinton that "several gentlemen of taste & literature" seek to "combine within one establishment, if possible, all that at present exists in this city" relating to the encouragement of the arts and sciences, assuming that "by concentrating all our resources we may give a greater impulse and elevation to our intellectual character." What was needed, he explained, was a "Building sufficiently central & suitable for all these purposes." It would be a contribution to "intellectual improvement & rational amusement" in the city. Although Pintard assumed that since "every citizen has an equal interest in the benefit," there could be no opposition to such municipal patronage, Clinton did not immediately bring the suggestion before the Common Council. On the back of the letter is a notation by Clinton's secretary: "The request was too imprudent to be submitted for consideration."[59]

Two months later, Pintard's letter to Clinton was followed by a formal memorial to the Common Council from the New York Society Library, the Academy of Fine Arts, and the Historical Society. This petition, doubtless the work of Pintard, proposed the establishment of an institution for the "promotion of Arts and Sciences" that would include a museum of natural history, an academy of fine arts, "means of Instruction in useful and liberal Sciences, such as Chemistry, Mechanical Philosophy, Agriculture, and Botany," a society for the encouragement of arts, manufactures, and commerce, a public library, and a public reading room or Atheneum.[60] By the time this memorial was received, New York's and the nation's attention was turning increasingly to the war that had been declared against Great Britain the previous June, and Clinton, the most powerful municipal official and the most likely friend of the proposal, was busy seeking to establish himself as an antiwar candidate and to unseat President James Madison.

After the conclusion of the war, however, Clinton, his presidential ambitions dashed and even his political future in New York a bit clouded, returned to Pintard's proposal. Political reverses seem often to have stimulated Clinton's cultural interests, and in April 1815 he sent a message to the Common Council suggesting that "the return of peace and its attendant blessings, has enabled you by patronizing the arts and sciences & encouraging the cultivation of the human mind, to elevate still more the character of this great community, and to erect imperishable monuments of public utility."[61]

In June, the Common Council voted thirteen to four to provide the support requested by Pintard. Stressing the prior establishment of the economic foundations for cultural achievement in New York, the council, in a rather overdone but perhaps apt horticultural metaphor, saw a special opportunity for shifting resources from war to peace. "Now that the war is over and there exists no longer any necessity to provide for the tented field, would not a *garden spot* in which young plants of science would be cultivated, be a suitable & delectable first fruit offering to the *Goddess* of Peace. Many have presumed . . . that our soil [New York's] is sterile and unfit for such culture. But fortunately your petitioners have with great talent and perseverance proven them to be indigenous. . . . With considerable success they have already planted & nourished several and if the cultivation is only moistened with your friendly dew, these young trees will ere long exhibit a luxuriance and spread into a grove of science under the shade of which your men of genius may securely repose."

If the council perceived commerce to be not only compatible with culture but its lifeblood, they remained sensitive to the old charge that New York neglected learning in its pursuit of the dollar. "The Citizens of New York," they commented, "have too long been stigmatized as phlegmatic, money making & plodding—Our Sister Cities deny we possess any taste for the sciences." The council saw in Pintard's petition an opportunity to "speedily retrieve the reputation of our City" and to establish "its title to literary fame." In so doing, New York would be following in the steps of Edinburgh, London, Paris, Amsterdam, and Leyden—cities that have achieved "celebrity" as homes of learning by providing "municipal aid" to their literary institutions.[62]

The report closed by offering a resolution that "the spacious building in the rear of the City Hall belonging to this City" be appropriated for the use of the associated learned societies. The unnamed building was in fact the old Almshouse, recently become surplus with the completion of new facilities for the poor at Bellevue. Fitz-Greene Halleck, a popular poet and wit of the period, could not resist comment on this change in tenants. In his widely read poem *Fanny* (1819), a satire on New York political and cultural life, he quipped:

> It remains
> To bless the hour the Corporation took it
> Into Their heads to give the rich in brains,
> The worn-out mansion of the poor in pocket.[63]

In the following summer the New York Institution of Learned and Scientific Establishments, usually referred to simply as the New York Institution, was organized with seven affiliates, each holding leases from the city government that called for the payment of one peppercorn per year as rent. The constituent organizatons were the New York Society Library (though it later declined the space, being unable to dispose favorably of the building it owned), the New-York Historical Society, the Academy of Fine Arts, John Scudder's Museum, the U.S. Military and Philosophical Society, John Griscom's Chemistry Laboratory, and the Literary and Philosophical Society of New York. In March 1817, the United Society of Journeymen Shipwrights and Caulkers obtained a room to display model ships in the interest of sustaining and encouraging New York's distinction in naval architecture. Also within the first year, Griscom gave up part of his space for the use of the Bible Society. In 1818, the Society for the Instruction of the Deaf and Dumb was granted rooms, the Savings Bank founded by Pintard was given space in the basement in 1819, and in 1820 the Lyceum of Natural History was given the space originally held by the already dormant U.S. Military and Philosophical Society.[64] Many organizations petitioned for space but did not obtain it, including the College of Physicians and Surgeons, the County Medical Society, the State Medical Society, Columbia College, and the Grand Lodge of New York Masons. The defining organizations, the organizations that were most closely intertwined in the minds of the founders and, so far as one can tell from mention in public sources, in public opinion, were the original petitioners, excepting the library (Scudder's Museum, the Academy of Fine Arts, the Historical Society) and two associations organized after the petition was sent, the Literary and Philosophical Society and the Lyceum of Natural History.

The promise of the New York Institution was to consolidate and concentrate the existing elements of the city's intellectual culture in the interest of invigorating it and giving it more social force. Pintard and others had no doubt that they were thus taking the first steps toward the creation of the cultural density that they identified with European capitals and the major learned societies in them.[65]

Each of the organizations was broad in its definition of purpose. For example, the New-York Historical Society's original charter pledged it to preserve "whatever may relate to the natural, civil, literary, and ecclesiastical history" of the city, state, and nation. It claimed to be "an association for the purposes of general knowledge," and the committee structure that had developed by 1818 validates this claim.[66] Its six committees were (1) zoology; (2) botany and vegetable physiology; (3) mineralogy and fossils; (4) coins and medals; (5) manuscripts; (6) books. The society had established a natural-history cabinet in 1816, which it maintained until 1829, when it was turned over to the Lyceum of Natural History. The museum that John Scudder superintended was a commercial enterprise that was also devoted to the cultivation of natural history. It was, in the words of John Pintard, "eminently calculated to cultivate and diffuse the knowledge of Natural History besides affording a pleasing field for gratifying innocent & laudable curiosity."[67]

Two points ought to be made about these constituent institutions. The first is that many of the boundaries that we accept as properly dividing up the intellectual world were not respected in the civic culture—or learned society—configuration we are describing. Neither disciplinary boundaries nor the distinction between high and low, learned and general culture was recognized in anything like the manner and degree that would mark the period at the end of the nineteenth century. Nor was there any notion in this endeavor that the pursuit of knowledge or culture and its proper diffusion were antithetical to commercial values. No one was at all bothered or uncertain about the propriety of Scudder's commercializing his cabinet. Only later would the presentation of culture become sacred and non-commercial, the project of elite-dominated non-profit organizations.

The second point concerns the membership of these organizations. The leadership of the various organizations I have named as the defining ones came largely from a single group, and often the same individuals. It was New York's elite, with merchants somewhat underrepresented and professionals, especially physicians, somewhat overrepresented. Patrons of learning as well as doers were from this class, and they came together here on terms that were, for perhaps the last moment in the city's intellectual history, comfortable. What we have here is a revealing case of interlocking directorates at the top. The New York Institution thus embodied, in the words of Brooke Hindle, "a strong sense of the interrelationships of cultural and learned societies, and it promoted them."[68]

The Literary and Philosophical Society, founded almost in conjunction with the New York Institution, best represents the particular aspiration of the institution and, by extension, of New York's civic culture in the first quarter of the nineteenth century. It was founded in 1814 by Clinton, Pintard, Hugh Williamson, a statesman and scientist, and Dr. David Hosack, a student of Bard, founder of the Elgin Botanical Garden, professor of medicine, and a man at the center of much of the city's cultural activity—though remembered, for example by Alexis de Tocqueville, more for his table (sustained by what contemporaries called a good marriage) and his conversational brilliance than for any real intellectual accomplishment.

In late January 1814, several prominent gentlemen in New York City received a printed circular signed by Williamson. It invited them to a meeting for the purpose of organizing an association that would "pro-

mote the literary character of this great state and increasing city."[69] At
the consequent organizational meeting, chaired by Clinton, the role of
literary institutions in stimulating city culture in Europe was invoked as a
reason for doing the same in New York.[70] At a second meeting a constitution was approved, one that established four "classes" of inquiry:

1. Belles Lettres, Civil History, Antiquities, Moral and Political
   Economy;
2. Medicine, Chemistry, Natural Philosophy & Natural History;
3. Mathematics, Astronomy, Navigation, and Geography;
4. Husbandry, Manufactures, and the Useful Arts.

Thus the breadth of culture as conceived by this generation. Fittingly,
the assignments of individuals in the various classes showed much overlap. That is, a single individual was often listed as participating in more
than one class. Moreover, the classes were not homogeneous in their
membership. Although doctors predominated in class 2, it was not theirs
exclusively. (Most diverse in membership, as one might expect, were classes
1 and 4.)[71] The membership of the society was broadly representative of
the city's elite. Doctors, lawyers, and Columbia College professors in
nearly equal numbers predominated, but merchants, politicians, and one
clergyman were also among the original thirty-five members.[72] While we
are thus talking about a circle of amateurs, the papers read were serious
and often by leading figures, particularly in the field of natural history,
where American science was strongest. Samuel L. Mitchill and Constan-
tine Rafinesque presented papers that were demanding enough to make
the society more than the institutionalization of honor and fashion,
though certainly it was that.

De Witt Clinton was the first president of the society. The "Introductory Discourse" that he delivered upon his installation provides his generation's interpretation of the history of intellectual life in New York.
When Clinton went before his audience in December 1814, the political
and cultural life of New York seemed to have its center in him. Not only
the state's most prominent political figure and mayor of the city, Clinton
was also president of the American Academy of Fine Arts and vice-
president of the New-York Historical Society. No one could speak with
such authority or legitimacy about learned culture in New York.

As Jefferson had felt compelled to do a generation earlier, Clinton first
addressed the criticisms of Comte Georges Louis Leclerc de Buffon and
William Robertson, both of whom had suggested a lack of energy and
vitality in America—evident, they said, in the natural history as well as
the civil history of the New World. Clinton insisted that America was not
a mistake and that there is nothing in "our climate, our soil, our government, our religion, our manners, or morals" that prevents "the cultivation

of literature." He acknowledged that "generally speaking we are far behind our European brethren in the pursuits of literature." But this, he explained, had to do with the youth of America; it was not a chronic condition. American preoccupation with politics and accumulation of wealth had been a necessary preliminary to cultural progress. Colonial New York had lacked the concentration of talent in a single place that is necessary for the pursuit of "truth and genuine knowledge." More important was the very condition of being a colony, with a government, therefore, that was "derivative and dependent." No colony, Clinton insisted, can fully promote literature and learning, for "the benumbing effects" of a "provincial and dependent position" operate with great force "upon the efforts of genius."[73]

Drawing upon Hume's essay on the "Progress of Arts & Sciences," Clinton argued that progress in these fields follows the establishment of free government. Countering the oft-repeated charge of New York's excessive commercialism, Clinton insisted that "there is nothing in the commercial spirit which is hostile to literature. On the contrary, the wealth it produces furnishes both incentives and rewards."[74] The causes of whatever retardation one might find in New York's intellectual progress were, he thought, removable and might soon cease to operate. Partisan politics, he reflected, draws too much energy; the medical profession, which should provide intellectual leadership, is expending itself in factional warfare; and lawyers are too narrow, concentrating on Coke's rules rather than Bacon's example. Instead of using wealth to advance knowledge, wealth is too much cherished for its own sake. But such circumstances can be reformed.

Clinton looked toward learned societies to enhance the level of intellectual life in the city. While there is, he says, a "vast mass of knowledge" in New York and America, it is, "generally speaking, of the common kind; all know the elementary parts of instruction, but few know the higher branches of science." Learned societies in cities, in New York in particular, promise to concentrate and elevate learning. They "are productive of great individual and collective effort; they stimulate the mind to exertion, produce emulation, and form habits of observing with accuracy and of reading with attention; they elicit powers that would otherwise lie dormant, and collect knowlege that would otherwise be scattered." In brief, they were to do what we now allocate to the university system, with its professionalized disciplines. And Clinton saw evidence that since the Revolution New York had been taking appropriate steps in this direction; he listed the various learned societies organized or attempted since the conclusion of the war, including the three organizations he currently represented as an officer.[75] These were signs that the will was there, that New York was beginning to concern itself with literary progress.

But for Clinton genuine progress would be a product of the development of the city itself, an organic product of the city's economic ascent.
Cultural progress and economic development were two sides of the same
process. If one rejects the aspersions of Buffon and Robertson, Clinton
insisted, one must assume that letters will be cultivated in the United
States. And this implied a further point: "It cannot be doubted that this
city is the proper site for a great literary and scientific institution. When
we view the magnitude of its population, the extent of its commerce, the
number of its manufactures, and the greatness of its opulence; when we
contemplate its position near the Atlantic, its numerous channels of communication by land and by water with every part of the United States,
and the constant and easy intercourse it can maintain with all parts of the
civilized world; when we consider the vast fund of talent, information,
enterprise, and industry which it contains; and when we take a prospective view of the rank which it is destined to occupy as the greatest commercial emporium in the world, we must acknowledge that no position
could be selected better adapted for acquiring information, concentrating
knowledge, improving literature, and extending science." It was this
urban achievement he foresaw for New York that enabled Clinton to
believe in its cultural importance. To bolster his point, he quoted the
comment of Bishop Sprat, when he had reflected on the propriety of
London as the site of the Royal Society: "A city where all the noises and
business of the world do meet."[76]

Neither Clinton's personal aspiration to intellectual eminence in the city
nor his hopes for the Literary and Philosophical Society nor his vision of
New York as the American metropolis were to be fulfilled. Indeed, his
"Introductory Discourse" was immediately attacked in the press by a
younger generation of writers, led by Gulian Verplanck, the wellborn
lawyer, politician, and writer who later became the first president of the
Century Club. Clinton's discourse relied heavily upon the writings of
Bacon, Swift, Johnson, and others; rather quickly he was charged in the
public press with plagiarism.[77] He was also held up to ridicule by Verplanck for his parade of erudition, which in fact, as Verplanck's friend
William Cullen Bryant observed, relied upon "compends which are in
everybody's hands."[78] Verplanck savaged both Clinton and the learned
societies to which he belonged. While acknowledging that the societies
included "gentlemen who would do honour to any literary institution in
the world," Verplanck charged that "the genius of literary imposture, or
to speak without metaphor, Mr. Clinton's management . . . finally succeeded in getting the entire control of these bodies." Men of learning
have undermined themselves by allowing fakes into their societies, in-

deed by allowing Europeans to think that Clinton is New York's "first man of science." Verplanck brought up a subject of great sensitivity when he went on to remark that "the only scientific society in this city which has pursued its avowed objects steadily, vigorously, successfully, and honourably, is the Lyceum of Natural History, an institution which has never for a moment permitted this spirit to show [itself] . . . and where the Governor himself was more than once blackballed."[79]

Verplanck's attack and the Lyceum's vote in 1817 against making Clinton a member (though he was elected to honorary membership in 1818) are usually attributed to politics, to partisanship simply overflowing the boundaries of electoral politics into the arena of cultural discourse.[80] Certainly there is truth in this, but the language of the controversy suggests that there is more fueling it: generational conflict is finding expression in alternative notions of intellectual life in the city.

The personal conflict between Verplanck and Clinton dated from 1811, when Clinton was mayor and the young Verplanck, recently graduated from Columbia College, was charged with inciting a riot at the college's commencement exercises. Political partisanship surrounded the riot, from its genesis to the denouement. A graduating student proposed to deliver a commencement oration that was considered by the Federalist faculty to be pro-Jeffersonian, and they informed him before the commencement that unless he altered it, he would not be given his degree. He at first agreed to the revision, but changed his mind before the ceremony and read the original version, whereupon he was denied his degree. Hugh Maxwell, who was in the audience during the commencement, held in Trinity Church, raised his voice in support of the student. There was some confusion, and Verplanck mounted the stage demanding that the provost of the college justify the action. Upon hearing the explanation, Verplanck turned to the audience: "The reasons, sir, are not satisfactory." He was arrested and hauled into the municipal court, where Clinton, as mayor, presided. Clinton, who was then seeking Federalist support for his presidential aspirations, dealt harshly with Verplanck, and Verplanck, recognizing the political considerations motivating Clinton's instructions to the jury, was furious.

But Clinton was not motivated simply by politics. Some years later, in replying to Verplanck's attack on the "Introductory Discourse," Clinton characterized Verplanck as a young man whose "first grand exhibition in life was that of a rioter in a church." Clinton was also distressed, as he put it in his charge to the jury, at the sight of a "young man of his age" having "the boldness, with matchless intrepidity of face, to mount the stage, and insolently demand of the provost the causes of his conduct."[81] The idea that Maxwell and Verplanck would appeal to a general audience, including even women and children, to pass judgment on the actions of a college faculty was to Clinton beyond belief. Again in his response to Verplanck, Clinton refers to the younger man as a "literary stripling" who, with his friends, dashes "venom in the faces of their superiors." Defending himself and the Literary and Philosophical Society, Clinton declared that "an institution established on the broad basis of public utility, by honourable and high-minded men, for the purpose of extending the empire of science, can never . . . be destroyed by *puppies.*"[82]

Linked to this generational conflict was a difference in the proper definition of intellectual life. Clinton prided himself on his amateur status. As he observed in his address to the Linnaean Society of New York in 1824, and as he had said in his early address to the Holland Lodge, his intellectual endeavors were leisure pursuits. "Many of the hours which I could spare from the pursuits of an active life, and from studies immediately connected with my public avocations, have been devoted to natural science."[83] He was disturbed by the indications he perceived in Verplanck and his friends of a group of writers who saw themselves primarily as writers, even if it was not yet possible to earn a living by one's pen alone. His harshest words for Verplanck were that this rioter "has finally settled down into a magazine writer for money."[84] Speaking more generally, Clinton complained that in almost "every other place men write for amusement or for fame—but here there are authors by profession, who make it a business and a living."[85]

Clinton's problems with the Lyceum were analogous. The members of the Lyceum were incipient professionals. With the exception of Mitchill, the founder, most of the members were recent graduates of Columbia College or the College of Physicians and Surgeons.[86] Pintard recognized that the Lyceum represented a younger generation with a rather strong professional orientation. With his usual tolerance, he rather calmly phrased his recognition of the challenge they presented to his generation. "The zeal of these aspiring youths," he wrote his daughter, "will eclipse the old Societies if we do not take care."[87]

The Lyceum was for practitioners, not mere appreciators of science. Only three merchants were counted among the original thirty-one members, and it is proper to call these particular businessmen practitioners. Take, for example, William Redfield, a self-made businessman internationally recognized for his meteorological research and the first president of the American Association for the Advancement of Science when it was organized in 1848. The rules emphasized its proto-professional ethos: within twelve months of their election, members had to present a formal scientific paper. The *American Monthly Magazine* aptly characterized the Lyceum as a group of "young, active and zealous cultivators of the Natural Sciences" whose "sittings are frequent" and whose communications "are numerous and important."[88] It is worth recalling that it was at the

Lyceum that Asa Gray got his first training in natural history, under the guidance of John Torrey. Gray, in fact, held the position of curator there in 1836–37, and this job has been characterized by one historian of science as the first paid scientific position in America.[89]

The Lyceum is proto-modern in two important respects that differentiate it from its companion organizations at the New York Institution. Unlike Scudder's Museum, another center of natural-history knowledge, the Lyceum was neither commercial nor a public amusement. And, unlike the New-York Historical Society, it was specialized rather than eclectic in its membership and intellectual concerns. The Lyceum was in fact far more specialized than other organizations in the New York Institution.[90] Science in the beginning of the second quarter of the nineteenth century was beginning to separate itself from the general culture, developing its own institutions and publication system, and the Lyceum of Natural History represented New York's participation in this general movement.[91]

In the context of such developments, there was less and less room for the De Witt Clintons who had flourished earlier. At the Lyceum of Natural History one finds in embryo the forms of identity with one's intellectual work that would eventually be incorporated into the professional ethos.[92] A politician who devoted his spare hours to reading natural history was not a natural historian to this younger generation. Clinton understood himself in the same way, but to him it was a compliment rather than a fatal flaw. He saw himself as a statesman with intellectual interests. The younger generation at the Lyceum saw themselves as natural scientists, whatever their means of earning a living. This new identity enabled them to challenge Clinton's credentials and his legitimacy as an intellectual leader. Though not yet there, these young men were pointing toward the professional legitimacy that would come later in the century. Already, however, they had lost sympathy with the attitude expressed by Pintard that it was "indecorous" that "a personage so elevated in civil society and who fills such distinguished offices in the scientific and other institutions of our State" should be judged in so impersonal a way by a "juvenile Society."[93]

A final point on this conflict concerns the difference between Clinton and Samuel L. Mitchill. Superficially Mitchill appears much like Clinton, combining political and intellectual work. Yet he was a member, indeed a founder of the Lyceum. What differentiates the two men? If Mitchill was a professor, politician, and a scientist, he thought of himself first of all as a literary and scientific man, who happened to be earning his living at Columbia and who found pleasure and value in participating in public life, rather than the other way around.

. . .

The emergence of professional aspiration represents one challenge to the patrician culture of Pintard and Clinton; changes in the local social geography and life style of the elite also undermined the ideal. The experience of the New York Atheneum is illuminating on this point. Its establishment in 1824 might be taken as the final fulfillment of the cluster of civic cultural institutions outlined by Pintard in his letter to Mayor Clinton in 1812. He had suggested among the new institutions that might appropriately be developed in the city an Atheneum or public reading room, which he described as a "genteel place of resort."[94] Instead, the brief history of the Atheneum reveals the dimensions of the failure of Pintard's dream.

The model for New York's Atheneum was the Liverpool Atheneum, established in 1798, and imitated in Boston (1807) and Philadelphia (1814). In 1820, Pintard suggested that such a reading room be attached to the New-York Historical Society. His idea seems instead to have stimulated the establishment of the Apprentices Library and the Mercantile Library, and it was not until early 1824 that a movement to organize an Atheneum in New York took shape. In March a meeting was held in the City Hotel, the participants of which included the "wealthiest and most learned" in the city.[95] William Gracie, one of the gentlemen in attendance, then drafted a report, signed by, among others, Pintard, stressing the lack of adequate libraries and collections of the periodical press in New York, and proposing a public reading room with a collection of non-circulating books and magazines.[96] While the Atheneum that emerged did in fact have a pleasant reading room—one that Alexis de Tocqueville and Gustave Beaumont used almost daily during their visit in New York as a place to relax and read English, French, and American newspapers —it aspired to more.[97] It aimed as its main business to organize public lectures, to be held in the chapel of Columbia College, then located downtown at College Place, just west of City Hall. It was thought that such lectures would "excite a more intense and lively interest" than "books or private instruction."[98] Learning was to be a social event, even at the risk of superficiality.

The organizational form of the Atheneum followed its function. There were two kinds of members. Subscribers served as financial patrons and the audience for the lectures, while a Board of Associates, operating like a faculty or program board, designated topics and lecturers. Most of the time the lecturers were selected from the Board of Associates. Two distinct types of lectures were specified in the bylaws, "public discourses" that considered the "progress of those branches of literature and science . . . most intimately connected with their [the lecturers'] individual pursuits," and "popular lectures," which were seen as diversions from the "cares of domestic life, the dissipation of the fashionable world, and the turmoil of business." Because of the character of the popular lectures, women were invited to attend.[99]

No matter how carefully the organizers distinguished between the two sorts of lectures, the minutes of the board and the lectures announced seem to be of only one type, all addressed to a wide audience. In 1824, twenty-seven different lecturers offered instruction on a wide range of topics: Verplanck on political economy; John McVickar of Columbia College on the history of the philosophy of mind; James Renwick, also of Columbia, on applied mechanics; the Reverend Dr. Wainwright on oratory; and Dr. F. King on phrenology. The next year, Professor Anthon of Columbia lectured on Roman literature; Samuel F. B. Morse on painting; and Isaac Hone, Jr., on the history of commerce. But as early as 1827, the minutes of the board started expressing two kinds of concern: audiences were declining and it was getting very difficult to obtain lecturers. In December 1828, the lectures were abolished, and a few months later one finds the last entry in the minutes. The Atheneum had ceased to have any business, though it continued as a reading room until 1839, when it was absorbed by the New York Society Library.[100]

It is difficult to understand why an institution that began with such high hopes should evaporate so quickly, disappearing with hardly a whimper, let alone a bang. One discovers a partial cause by considering the spatial dimension of class and cultural formation. The Atheneum was an upper-class institution—this quality is clear from the elite status of the founding committee and from reports describing the audience as "distinguished for fashion, beauty, and accomplishments."[101] It seems to have been conceived as a sort of social club in the residential precinct of the city's elite, that area of New York which included Barclay and Murray streets, Church Street and College Place, and Chambers Street west of Broadway.

However, in the 1820s the elite left this downtown quarter near City Hall and moved uptown. As they reestablished themselves in new prestigious neighborhoods, the social geography of the upper class became more diverse, for there were now several such neighborhoods.[102] This geographical dispersion reflected the growing scale and heterogeneity of the city's upper class. Without a unified and geographically concentrated urban elite, such a fashionable place of resort for intellectual diversion could not survive. It was too far to return downtown from Bond Street or LeRoy Place or Greenwich Village to evening lectures. Distance made it far more difficult in particular for elite women to attend. The result was that the Atheneum became a morning reading room for men commuting downtown from their newly suburbanized residences. The original idea of the centering role of the Atheneum, a role that would have it bring together the city's wealthy, powerful, and fashionable, male and female, around literary concerns, lost its constituency and with it its vital moral and financial support.[103] No one cared anymore, and it quietly faded away. For Pintard's model of intellectual culture to work, the elite had to be unified and it had to care. As it became physically dispersed, this class would require much more than the literary institutions proposed by Pintard and Clinton to sustain their cultural commitment and legitimate their cultural hegemony.

Just when Pintard and Clinton seemed to be on the verge of fulfilling a dream of city culture dating from the 1750s, the taste of the fruits of their efforts turned out to be unexpectedly bitter. Patrician culture did not become established—the sort of Brahmin class that developed in Boston failed to take root in New York.[104] Nor could New York claim, on any other basis, significant intellectual accomplishment. However edifying the city's literary institutions may have been to their founders and supporters, they had not produced the means for countering the famous cultural condemnation of Sydney Smith in the pages of the *Edinburgh Review* in 1820. It is perhaps worthwhile, given our concern with the definition of culture in relation to commerce, to recall that Smith's attack was as broad and inclusive as was the cultural ambition of Pintard and Clinton. He not only wrote: "Who reads an American book? or goes to an American play? or looks at an American picture or statue?" He asked, as well, whether American science, medicine, or manufacturing had contributed anything to civilization worth noting. Who "wears American coats or gowns, or sleeps in American blankets?"[105] New York's elite simply failed; they were not up to the challenge they had assumed.

Gouverneur Morris, one of the early republic's most notable statesmen, recognized the substantial element of fantasy in his fellow New Yorkers' ambitions for the Literary and Philosophical Society. Although he became one of the original members, he was more aware of its limited possibilities than the founders, Williamson, Hosack, Clinton, and Pintard. It so happened that on the evening the founders met to organize the society, Morris was to have dinner at Hosack's home. When Hosack arrived late to greet his guests, he apologized, saying by way of explanation: "Mr. Morris, I have been detained with some friends, who together this evening have founded a Philosophical Society." To which Morris tellingly replied: "Well, well, that's no difficult matter, but pray, Doctor, where are the philosophers?"[106]

Instead of philosophers, the learned societies of early-nineteenth-century New York, with the partial exception of the Lyceum of Natural History, nourished pretenders. Verplanck had been correct, and so was George Templeton Strong when he criticized the Historical Society forty years later. "The Historical Society," he wrote in his famous diary, "owns some nice books. My life membership is not absolutely valueless." But it prospers because of its "loud braying." As for the "lectures and 'papers' it generates so abundantly, I set down as equal to zero: an estimate more charitable than accurate, for they are properly affected with a negative sign, as gaseous secretions of vanity and dilettantism." [107]

It need not have turned out as it did. Let us compare another provincial learned society, the Manchester Literary and Philosophical Society. Between its founding in 1781 and the establishment of Owen College (now the University of Manchester) in 1851, it provided the institutional base for a succession of major British scientific figures as well as nourishing the development of statistics and the social sciences in Victorian England. Such a comparison insists that New York is here being judged by its own standards, not by later ones. The learned-society model was not as a form inadequate to the progressive intellectual tendencies of the age, and New York failed on its own terms, not simply from the later perspective of university-based science and scholarship. [108]

The failure of elite and fashionable society to justify its intellectual pretensions partially explains the withdrawal of municipal patronage from the New York Institution in 1830. As early as 1827, the city refused to renew leases for the New York Institution, except for short terms, saying that it was likely that the expanding city government would need the space. Finally, in 1831, it acted and turned the cultural organizations out of the Almshouse, converting the space for use by the courts and municipal offices. Not only had the learned societies not produced, but by 1830, with the egalitarian ideology identified with the age of Jackson increasingly filling the air and with class division being articulated in public for the first time, it seemed not entirely proper to have the whole public support the cultural activities of an elite that was no longer fully accepted as speaking for the whole culture.* Councilman James Roosevelt was the strongest opponent of the New York Institution, and in the report he presented for action by the Common Council, he opposed renewal of the leases on these grounds. As he put it: "The great length of time during which so large an amount of public property has been suffered to be applied, without any material equivalent, almost exclu-

---

* It should be noted, perhaps, that the first public criticism of municipal support for this interlocking elite came in 1818, but it seems to have been grounded more in elite rivalry than in anything suggesting class tensions. [109]

sively to private uses, has been a subject of frequent and, it must be admitted, of just animadversion."[110]

The withdrawal of support has been interpreted, both by the patriciate at the time and by historical commentators since, as a backward step, something not progressive, something illiberal, as an anti-intellectual attack on learning and culture. It might be interpreted that way, but when one recognizes the growing cultural division in the city and the widely expressed cultural ambitions of the artisans and mechanics in the 1820s and 1830s, it appears that some political choices about culture were being forced onto the municipal agenda: either stop subsidizing the culture of the elite or subsidize equally the competing artisanal culture as well.

As was often the case in Jacksonian America, the emergence of competing interests resulted in a policy of avoiding choice, of public withdrawal. The elite had earlier been able to get the city to underwrite their own class-based cultural pretensions. But by 1830 they had been unable to show substantial accomplishment that would thrust New York into the select circle of cities noted at the founding of the New York Institution. Nor had they been able to show that they in fact represented the culture of New York City. What the elite had seen as a public service was perceived by others as a private privilege sustained by public resources.[111]

Within three years of the withdrawal of municipal support, the Literary and Philosophical Society dissolved, while the American Academy of Fine Arts lingered on for ten years. Only the New-York Historical Society and the Lyceum of Natural History (since 1876 the New York Academy of Sciences) survived without municipal patronage and continue to this day. And here it is interesting that the Lyceum was differently conceived than the other organizations, and the New-York Historical Society survived in part by limiting its range of intellectual interests and moderating its pretensions.

The attack on the New York Institution represents the first formal challenge to elite cultural hegemony. Until about 1830, what William Charvat wrote of critical thought in the period applies to the whole spectrum of cultural life: "a practically homogeneous upper class . . . felt itself competent to legislate culturally, for other classes." These men (and they were all men) spoke with the authority of "a class or an organization, rather than of an individual." Culture was dominated by the economic and professional elite of the city. In no other period, Charvat remarks, "has our culture been so completely and directly dominated" by this elite; "concomitantly, in no other period has the economically dominant class exhibited such an interest in the arts."[112] The significance of Roosevelt's report and the withdrawal of patronage is that this elite did not simply withdraw; its legitimacy in cultural affairs was directly challenged in the

1830s. They were to a degree pushed from the position they had assumed as of right. Much of the subsequent history of the professions and of intellectual life is a quest for reestablishing such cultural authority on terms a formally democratic society would accept.

LEARNED MECHANICS

In eighteenth-century New York, artisans and mechanics, the largest part of the city's population, accepted the elite's self-definition of themselves as custodians of culture and learning. Though historians are debating the degree to which they conceded political leadership, there seem to have been no contests over cultural leadership.[113] No mechanics or artisans were members of the cultural organizations we have so far discussed, unless one insists upon Tammany during the brief period it included a museum and the little-noticed Shipwrights and Caulkers room in the New York Institution. This pattern of exclusion may suggest more elite domination of cultural institutions and discourse than in some other cities. Recall that Franklin's Junto included leather-apron boys as well as such a professional as John Bard, though in a place like Charleston, South Carolina, intellectual life was exclusively patrician—and remained so much longer. Equally significant, I have not found evidence in New York of separate institutions before 1820 for mechanics and artisans, whether shadow institutions or alternative ones. During the 1820s, however, they do emerge, though, as we shall see, their development has roots in the late-eighteenth-century aftermath of the Revolution. These developments in the relation of class and culture constitute an unnoticed but major event in the social and intellectual history of the city.

The institutionalization of a learned culture among New York mechanics and artisans begins with the founding of the General Society of Mechanics and Tradesmen. Organized in 1785 as an unincorporated benevolent society, it did not initially have the qualities of an improvement society. It met traditional needs for security. Even so, the efforts of the mechanics to obtain a state charter for the society became a major issue in city politics. The merchants, fearing that a strong artisanal organization might give mechanics and artisans the power to increase wages and perhaps even enable them to achieve a dominant rather than subordinate role in government, successfully opposed their application for a state charter until 1792. Incorporation was then achieved, the way having been eased by the creation of a separate Assembly slate endorsed by artisans and mechanics for the 1791 election, a slate that included the name of John Pintard.[114]

When it was initially organized in 1785, the society represented specific trades already organized in the city. It did not have general members or individual members. It was a federated center of the various craft organizations, reflecting the continuing legacy of medieval traditions in the city. But already in 1792, when the society was incorporated, membership was on an individual basis. The charter lists names of individuals without naming any trade association that they might have represented. They now represented themselves.[115] The organization had close relations with Tammany, but it was not really partisan. Between 1800 and 1810, for example, it continuously had a president and vice-president from opposing political parties.[116] Nor is there much evidence of religious division. In this respect, the General Society of Mechanics and Tradesmen was like the elite civic cultural institutions we have discussed.

In this period to call someone a mechanic was not necessarily to designate him as being near the bottom of the distribution of wealth. There were among mechanics some men of substantial wealth, even social and political prominence as aldermen or assistant aldermen. The General Society consisted primarily of the city's more prosperous craftsmen and manufacturer mechanics, the elite of the mechanical and tradesmen population of the community. They were masters, employers rather than employees, but, as Howard Rock has recently written, they nonetheless "represented the entire artisan community's aspiration for stature, economic opportunity, and dignity."[117]

In 1810, the orientation of the society began to change from security to improvement. Ambitious master mechanics, confronted with the opportunities of more extensive markets, increasingly needed credit. They found that merchant-dominated banks were not inclined to take their business or, if they did, to treat them with respect. Under these circumstances, the General Society of Mechanics and Tradesmen sponsored the organization of a Mechanics' Bank with the hope that it would meet the special needs of mechanics without having to respond to the demands or interests of merchants.* To ensure this, the charter provisions included a stated preference to mechanics in the purchase of stock and a requirement that seven of the sixteen directors be members of the General Society of Mechanics and Tradesmen as well as making the president of the society an ex officio member of the board of directors.

This new departure coincided with a decision by the society to expand membership, largely for financial reasons. The bank and the new membership policy together produced unanticipated and unwanted results. The leaders of the society, by deciding not to be "overscrupulous" about the requirement that one really be a mechanic or tradesman to be eligible for membership, opened themselves up to an invasion by merchants.

---

* The founders asked John Pintard to be cashier, but he declined, instead becoming president of the Savings Bank of New York.

They had assumed that if they admitted merchants who had some vague connection in the past with mechanical or trades occupations, the merchants would increase the treasury with their fees and, given their wealth, would seldom draw pensions from the society's reserve. What happened, however, was that many of the men who applied for membership were merchants who wanted to gain a privileged relationship to the bank. Such men, with greater banking and financial experience, quickly took over the bank and turned it to mercantile and speculative purposes. The society, in disgust and anger, sold 5,000 of its 6,000 shares in the bank.* The whole episode eroded mechanic trust in the General Society, and it was largely dormant from 1811 until 1820, when it was revived under the leadership of Thomas Mercein, who in the latter year had been elected president of the society. Mercein was a wealthy baker who had served as an alderman (Federalist) in 1811–12, and he was on his way to becoming a prominent figure in the city's commercial life. He transformed the society, opening an Apprentices Library in 1820, followed two years later by the organization of a Mechanics' Institute.[119]

These shifts in direction by the General Society of Mechanics and Tradesmen reveal changes in the city's artisanal culture. In the 1790s, what the artisans—masters as well as journeymen and apprentices—wanted most, in the context of a stable and traditional pattern of economic expectations and technology, was security. During the first decade of the nineteenth century, a period when the first possibilities of larger markets became apparent and the first impulses of what we now call economic modernization became evident, the most ambitious masters needed capital for expansion, to become capitalists. Capital was a way of adapting to change; hence the bank. Then, by the 1820s, knowledge, the acquisition of new knowledge in particular, seemed increasingly important to artisans for its practical value and for maintaining the respectability of the artisanal class. We have here, first of all, the earliest indication of what would be identified after World War II by Daniel Bell as the "knowledge society." Second, for New York's artisans in the 1820s and 1830s, to acquire knowledge, to participate in such a society, did not require leaving their class. They did not have to cease being mechanics and tradesmen to embrace learning. Education or knowledge was a device of group or, if you will, class self-improvement, not a vehicle of mobility out of the class into which one was born. Neither was it—as it would become—a means of denying the existence of permanent class divisions in the city. In the 1820s and 1830s, New York artisans and workingmen had great faith in knowledge—a popular Baconian trust in

* The bank, after a series of mergers, became a part of the Chase Bank and is thus an ancestor of today's Chase Manhattan Bank.

objective facts, whether presented in newspapers or popular lectures or museums. And this knowledge had for them, as Dan Schiller has revealed, a political value: objective fact was embraced by them as protection against the cultural hegemony, the power to interpret, claimed by the mercantile elite.[120]

At the moment when the artisans made their move to advance learning, the cultural monopoly of the elite had lost much of its legitimacy. In time, the place of knowledge in society would be reestablished on elite terms—through the university and the professionalized disciplines. That reorganization of culture would erode the cultural legitimacy of the learned mechanic, but in the 1820s and 1830s there seemed to be other possibilities.

Before proceeding further with our discussion of the learned mechanic and the culture of the artisanal classes in New York, it is necessary to say something about evidence. Did the General Society of Mechanics and Tradesmen in the 1820s truly represent the artisans, or was it by then simply an employers' organization? Can one still make the distinction between capitalists denominated mechanics and those called merchants? It appears that there was indeed a subjective experience of difference, even though changes in the social relations of production were already creating new categories, a class of employers and a class of wage employees. In respect to specific economic and political questions, a wealthy mechanic like Mercein might have and pursue a common interest with employer merchants; but in the realm of general values and social identity, he felt himself part of an artisanal culture.

Sean Wilentz has shown that as late as 1825, during the Erie Canal celebration, craft identity overrode the distinction between employer and employee in this more general realm of culture and values. In Wilentz's reading of this urban ritual of the 1820s, "the employees and employers in each craft formed a symbolic body." He ventures further to suggest that throughout the 1820s in New York City "the trades seemed to celebrate an artisan system of production and distribution quite unlike the divided, entrepreneurial, accumulation-oriented regime that had begun to emerge in the city's workshops." Only in the 1830s does the emergence of capitalist social relations find expression in public language and ritual.[121] It seems reasonable, therefore, to take the public statements of members of the General Society of Mechanics and Tradesmen, men who were employers, often on a capitalist model, as expressions of a general cultural ideal embraced by ordinary artisans in the city.

. . .

It is unclear just how the Apprentices Library came to be organized under the auspices of the General Society of Mechanics and Tradesmen. Commonly such devices for working-class improvement in nineteenth-century cities were sponsored by the elite—hence their identification with social control in historical discussions of them. In this instance, the project apparently received its initial push from such an elite group. In a letter to his daughter in February 1820, Pintard mentions that at a meeting of the trustees of the Society for the Prevention of Pauperism, the idea of an apprentices library was raised. Pintard noted that he much liked the idea—as did others—but that instead of themselves proposing to organize it, they communicated the idea to the "Mechanic Society."[122] Thomas Mercein, the current president of the society and a man whose economic success doubtlessly made him familiar to the patrician elite, took the idea and quickly brought the library into existence. It should be noted that, as with the New York Institution, there was some municipal assistance, less but still significant. The Common Council granted the General Society of Mechanics and Tradesmen five years' free ground rent for the library.[123] At about this time the society also established a school.

The changing aims of the society were reflected in the revisions of the society's charter that were proposed in 1821. The organization had previously been limited to using funds for the "support of indigent members . . . or widows and children of any person having been a member." They now sought authorization "to appropriate a part of their funds to the support of a School for the gratuitous education of children of deceased or indigent members of the said Society, and also to the establishment of an Apprentices Library, for the use of the Apprentices of Mechanics in the City of New York." A few years later, when the second charter expired, another amendment was written into the new charter creating a committee and a special fund "for promoting and disseminating Literary and Scientific Knowledge."[124]

In an address at the opening of the Apprentices Library, Mercein defined the meaning and place of learning in the city's artisanal culture. While as an employer he had his own interest in stressing social fixity and harmony, his expression of the cultural ideals of the artisanal community seems, as we have indicated, to have been largely accepted by that community for its symbolic if not necessarily social truth. He accepted as a fact of urban life "artificial divisions and distinctions." He observed that "different pursuits and various occupations naturally designate distinct departments in our social order." And culture, he thought, should serve not as a bridge between classes but rather as a means of fostering the internal cohesion and unity of each class. "While these lines of discrimination remain, there must be a common bond, and a mutual sympathy, between those who fall under the same distinction. Common interests, and similar vocations, create ties and attachments, that are interwoven with the strongest feelings of the heart." This community of culture within the larger society must be, he assumed, autonomous. Improvement must be made within this context; individual learning or economic advancement must not predicate removal from the society of mechanics. He proposed that the mechanics develop their own culture, including advanced learning. "There seems," he declared, "to be a moral propriety in each class superintending the immediate concerns of the members of its distinct profession and pursuit." All the means that the General Society of Mechanics and Tradesmen have initiated to improve and strengthen the economic, moral, and intellectual well-being of mechanics—charity, bank, school, library—"should be zealously attended by this Society."[125]

The opening ceremonies included a "reply" by an apprentice. This reveals perhaps even more clearly the expectation that the acquisition of knowledge would mean improvement within the artisanal culture rather than being, as it is today thought to be, a means of mobility out of it. "We aim," he declared, "not at the higher walks of literature," presumably meaning the classics that set the professionals from Columbia off from the remainder of society. "We aspire not to the embellishments of refinement. Our lot of labour will ever stifle a hope so vain. The extent of our desires will be satisfied with that simple mental food, which imparts contents to the mind and health to the morals." The library would, as the *Mechanic's Gazette* put it, enhance the "respect" and increase the "usefulness" of the city's "mechanical" class.[126]

Finally, two years later, in an address at the laying of the cornerstone for the Mechanics' Institute, Mercein articulated a vision of the autonomous social and intellectual condition—and the improvement of the city's artisanal population. "The Mechanics of the City of New York," he declared, "constitute a body of men, who do much in sustaining the prosperity of this Metropolis: They form one of the strongest, firmest pillars in our social Edifice. Industry and enterprize belong to their ranks, and in order to assume that respectability and that influence which are due to their numbers, and to their wealth; the streams of knowledge and intelligence must be infused among them."[127]

The Mechanic and Scientific Institution, with its building on Chambers Street, was organized "to foster the Mechanic and useful Arts, and to enlighten the minds and stimulate the genius of those who practise them." Its major means of accomplishing this was to be annual courses of "popular lectures." It was expected that such an institution, by nurturing the learned mechanic, would advance the class economically and morally. Such a society, the founders claimed, "can hardly fail in its general operation to elevate the prospects of this highly important class of our fellow citizens, to excite useful emulation, and to awaken that genius which, without such a beneficial excitement, might have slumbered for ever."[128]

It is important to stress—as the founders did—that this organization was not the product of elite philanthropy.* They claimed that it was the first Mechanics Institution "founded in any part of the world, almost exclusively by Mechanics, and for the express purpose of diffusing the benefits of science throughout the various mechanical professions."[130] Even before it was incorporated, the institution sponsored its first series of lectures. The topic was "mechanical philosophy and chemistry," and they were delivered by John Griscom. The second "professor" appointed by the institution was Dr. Samuel Akerly, who lectured on the "terminology and the diseases incident to mechanics." Both of these men were part of New York elite culture and both were professionals. Griscom was one of the tenants of the New York Institution, while Akerly was a prominent member of the Historical Society. What can we learn here about the nature of elite involvement in artisanal cultural institutions? Is what we can learn fatal to the ideal of an autonomous culture of learned mechanics?

Very little is known about Akerly, but with Griscom, a noted Quaker educator and philanthropist, we can pursue these questions. It is clear that he lacked the drive for cultural domination one might look for in assessing any version of social control or Gramscian hegemony. He was, in fact, not entirely comfortable with the city's cultural elite, and in 1826 he lost some of his space in the New York Institution to the Lyceum of National History.[131]

John Griscom began his career in the city as a schoolkeeper in 1807, after having migrated to New York City from Burlington, Vermont. While in Burlington, he had given lectures and demonstrations, and in 1808 he introduced "experimental chemistry as the object of popular instruction in New York." This instruction was given, he observed, "independent of any corporate body." A few years later, it is true, he became one of the incorporators of the Literary and Philosophical Society, but his lectures were not sponsored by that group, and his laboratory in the New York Institution was his alone. It belonged to no group. In 1817, he inaugurated a series of lectures on natural philosophy for females; these having been a success, "special audiences" of merchants, mechanics, apprentices, and professional men were "gotten up" for other lectures. It was within this context of independent educational work that he came to discuss with Stephen Allen and a few of the city's master mechanics the

---

* Compare the Franklin Institute of Philadelphia, founded in 1824. It was initiated by the merchant class, and it differed too in seeking to provide opportunity for *individual* mechanics as opposed to *class* improvement.[129]

possibility of a "systematic course of popular lectures, adapted to their peculiar wants." Such a course, he thought, offered the possibility of a "more elevated standing and estimation in general society . . . [for] working mechanics."[132]

In his inaugural lecture as professor of mechanical and chemical philosophy in the New York Mechanic and Scientific Institution, the only formal "professorial" affiliation he ever held, he declared that the mechanics of the city needed education that would develop their "judgment, knowledge, and science." In this lecture, which was intended, at least in its printed version, to be noticed by patricians as well as mechanics, Griscom rejected any principle that made learning "a thing of patrician acquirement." Rather, he observed, the American political system required "universality of instruction." The diffusion of learning "throughout all ranks of the people" would, he reflected, advance the "useful arts, the progress of manufactures, the extension of commerce." For the mechanics of New York, he proposed an advanced education "of a nature appropriate to their stations, as their time and duties will admit." Such education would prepare them not only for their trades but for public stations in which they will be called to serve. "There is not, I conceive, any class of the community better entitled to the fostering care of those, who have it in their power to patronize education, than Mechanics. They constitute in every city, town and village, a numerous portion of our population. There is included among them, and ever must be included, persons endowed by nature, with genius and talents of the first order."[133]

Most important of all, however, was the way in which the mechanics used elite learning for their own purposes. Lacking professionals among their own class, they asked members of the learned professions to speak on topics of concern specifically to mechanics. Lectures on chemistry and natural philosophy were important to improvers among the mechanics. M. M. Noah, for example, advocated the study of chemistry before an audience of mechanics. It is, he explained, "a hand-maid of the arts." It is "not alone sufficient" for a mechanic "to know how to complete a piece of work, it is proper to know the causes that lead to its completion."[134] And Akerly spoke, not on medicine, but specifically on what we would call occupational health issues of concern to mechanics. So even these two men who bridged the two cultures in the intellectual life of the city did so as much on the terms of the mechanics as upon the terms of their own class.

Examination of the incorporators and original board of managers of the Mechanic and Scientific Institution sustains the claim that it was the product of the city's mechanics. The thirteen incorporators included the proprietor of a leather store, a stone works manager, two soap manufacturers, a rigger, a baker, a painter, a watchmaker, a brass and iron founder, an architect, a leather and hide tanner, a bookbinder, a builder, and Griscom and Akerly. It is important to recognize that these leaders represented the most successful and well-to-do of the city's mechanics. They were as wealthy as many who belonged to the mercantile or professional classes. To take one of the most prosperous, the leather and hide tanner, for an example: Jacob Lorillard was born into a prosperous artisanal family, and by the age of forty-one he owned three houses and two leather stores, as well as forty acres of Manhattan land. In 1815, his wealth was estimated at $90,000. He served as president of the Mechanics' Bank, and he had been elected assemblyman in 1812–13 and had served in 1815 as an assistant alderman. Yet he retained his identity as a mechanic and proudly affiliated with the city's organized mechanics rather than seeking to move into the merchant class.[135]

Even more interesting is the case of Stephen Allen, first president of the Mechanic and Scientific Institution. Turning to the 1822 city directory, one cannot help but be surprised to find him listed as the city's mayor. So much, it would seem, for the self-confident mechanics and their culture; obviously, they had sought a member of the traditional elite to assume symbolic leadership of the institution. When one looks more closely at Allen's life, however, there emerges a very different and very interesting story of success within the artisanal culture.

Allen, whose father was a carpenter, was born in New York in 1767. He lost his father when he was ten or eleven, and after only the most basic of schooling he was apprenticed by his mother to a sailmaker, joining his brother, who had been earlier apprenticed. Stephen Allen quickly showed skill in the work, and before the specified conclusion of his apprenticeship, he went into business for himself, forming several partnerships over the years. Reading widely and taking an enthusiastic interest in politics—first as a Jeffersonian and then as a Jacksonian—he achieved prominence as well as wealth. After joining Tammany, he was elected alderman, serving from 1812 to 1821, and he held the office of Grand Sachem of Tammany in 1814. Over the years, he became involved in a number of improving societies in New York, though, interestingly, there is very little overlap with Pintard's affiliations. He was president of the General Society of Mechanics and Tradesmen, president of the Mechanic and Scientific Institution, a founder of the House of Refuge, a governor of the New York Hospital and the New York Eye Infirmary, a director of the American Bible Society, the New York Tract Society, and the American Prison Discipline Society. His business associations included serving as a director of the Mechanics' Bank, the Fulton Insurance Company, and the Firemen's Insurance Company. His most important public offices were that of mayor from 1821 to 1824 and, during the 1830s and

1840s, commissioner of the Croton Water Works. His financial and civic standing was given public expression in 1835, when he took up residence at 1 Washington Square North, the first house in the magnificent Greek Revival row usually identified exclusively with the city's merchant princes. He retired from active business in 1825, at the age of fifty-nine, but he lived until 1852, when he was killed in the explosion of the riverboat *Henry Clay.*

In retirement he wrote an autobiography in the form of a series of letters, perhaps never sent or even intended to be sent. From those letters, however, one realizes that for all his worldly success, he remained till his death a mechanic, never seeking the status or culture of the merchant/professional elite of the city. Referring to his appointment as mayor (New York's mayors were not elected until 1834), Allen insisted that he told the Council of Appointments in Albany, which was considering his appointment, that he did not wish the post. When he was nonetheless tendered an appointment, he decided to accept. His reason for accepting is important here as an affirmation of the culture of the learned mechanic. He accepted, he explained, because of "a belief that I ought to make good the declaration I had frequently made that any man of ordinary talents not bred to the law, as all our former Mayors were, might perform the duties of the station with credit to himself and benefit to the city." A few years later, in a different situation, he affirmed again his identification with the mechanics of the city. The Mechanics Institution of 1822, which had expired in the late 1820s, was replaced in the 1830s by a second Mechanics Institution, organized in 1831 and chartered in 1833, which in turn was assimilated into the American Institute, an organization devoted to holding annual fairs to honor and advance the development of American industry. With this development, Allen dissociated himself from the organization, declaring that it had fallen "into the hands of the manufacturers of cotton and woolen cloths, and is now used by them under the appellation of the American Institute to increase the duty on importation and by a high tariff . . . to oppress the people and by that means enrich themselves."[136]

Allen's pride in the collective achievements of the city's mechanics and tradesmen and the prickly, even aggressive, self-defense of their dignity and interest were central to the artisanal culture of the 1820s—and it was the motive for the vision of the learned mechanic. At the time the American Institute had in the 1830s become a vehicle of capitalist self-interest, the working-class social experience was beginning to find expression in a labor radicalism that signaled the end of the employer/employee ideological or symbolic unity within the crafts.[137] It also called into serious question any vision of a unified culture in the city.

. . .

By 1830, the reality of civic culture had fallen well short of Pintard's and Clinton's dreams. It was not creating philosophers, and it was less legitimate in 1830 as the official culture of the city than it had been at the beginning of the century. The cultural elite of the city sought to encourage a practical and useful knowledge, without the practical knowledge itself, which in 1830 still resided in the heads and hands of mechanics. The intellectual life of the city was divided into those who thought learning and culture were founded on the classics and those whose knowledge was more practical and closer to the daily life of the city's work. Could a civic culture be forged in the increasingly divided city? Or would knowledge frankly dissociate itself from the city and the civic impulse, becoming its own justification and universe of discourse?

CHAPTER 3

A University of
the City

The extraordinary success of the Erie Canal, surpassing even the most
sanguine hopes of Clinton, transformed New York, both in its relation to
the nation and in its internal understanding of itself. With the new canal
emptying the agricultural produce of the West into the port of New York,
even the least visionary of New Yorkers (and non–New Yorkers) could
imagine the day not very far off when the city would be the great economic and financial center of an integrated national economy. This progress of commerce reinvigorated the ambition that New York be
institutionalized as the capital of the national culture. Identifying culture
with commerce, with appropriate references to Venice, a group of civic
leaders who proposed to establish a University of the City of New York
insisted that the "commercial metropolis of the land" owed it "to the
nation which is enriching it with its commerce . . . to make knowledge
and science keep pace with our wealth." Soon, it was assumed, New York
"will exert that sway over the public mind, which the great cities of Europe have so long enjoyed." [1]

Although these university founders talked of organizing in New York
a "National Literary and Scientific Society" somewhat on the model of
the French Academy, what is striking about the thinking in New York as
the 1820s became the 1830s is the assumption that the proper means for
organizing culture within the city and for establishing one's claims for
national cultural leadership lay in the organization of a great urban university. In their sense that the eighteenth-century learned societies no
longer adequately provided the means of city culture, New Yorkers were
participating in an international rethinking of the foundations of intellec-

tual life. By the time the University of the City of New York was established in 1831, new universities had been established in Europe's great cities, most notably London and Berlin.

In New York, according to James M. Mathews, one of the founders of the new university and its first chancellor, the city's "various literary associations" were either languishing or failing to "reach the distinction they both deserved and desired." But with the university, he assured the community, they will be brought together into "close alliance and mutual support" and, presumably, achieve their original purpose of stimulating city culture in New York.[2]

It was as if the cultural leaders in the great cities suddenly recognized what apparently had long been assumed in such exceptionally distinguished provincial cities as Edinburgh and Geneva, that the arms and legs of city culture (the learned societies) lacked a directing intelligence and nervous system that could be supplied best by a civic university. New Yorkers, receiving direct stimulus from the example of London, where the University of London was organized in 1826, decided it was time for them to act, their city being "in comparative populousness, in enterprise, and the extent of commercial connections, and in intellectual resources" the place "in our Western Hemisphere . . . assigned to London in the Old World."[3]

THE UNIVERSITY AND THE CLASS SYSTEM

The movement for the university may have been part of a larger shift in the configuration of Western urban intellectual life, but the discussion and plans for it that emerged responded as well to the particularity of New York's social and intellectual history. While the canal put New York on its way to metropolitan domination of the national economy and fueled ambitions for national cultural leadership, it also complicated life within the city. As new ambitions were spawned for some, many others found traditional expectations dashed. For some mechanics, there was a promise of prosperity such as no mechanic had ever before dreamed. Others, however, a far larger number, were threatened with proletarianization, with the likelihood of being reduced to permanent and undignified wage-earning status by merchants and by more clever entrepreneurial mechanics. The fault lines in the social and cultural life of the city were sharpened and intensified at every level of income and class. What had formerly been differentiations threatened to become social divisions. In the 1830s, for the first time, the patriciate realized that they could no longer command the deferential respect of the masses. Traditional forms of class authority had evaporated.[4]

While the most obvious civic concerns flowing from these developments in the 1820s and 1830s were political and economic, they also informed discussions of city culture. Put into simple and dichotomous terms, it was a question of one culture or two. The dream of a widely accepted civic culture under patrician auspices was crumbling into two partial cultures. One was identified with the mercantile and professional elite, with the New York Institution and Columbia College; while the other found a focus in the learned mechanics and their Mechanics Institution and Apprentices Library.* One culture or two? On what terms could one culture be sustained? If two, what would be the terms of contact. These concerns—and they are central to cultural definition—were at the heart of the discussions leading to the founding of the University of the City of New York, today's New York University.

The university was expected to assume a vital civic role at a crucial moment in the city's history. Chancellor James Mathews, in his inaugural address in 1832, declared that the "most casual observer" must recognize that New York has arrived at a "crisis in its history." Like the youth on the eve of adulthood, the city has in its recent past absorbed the ingredients that must be formed into its permanent character and culture. The city "has shot up with a rapidity that defies calculation, numbering in its population, multitudes from every quarter of our globe which are not yet assimilated into a common character or animated by a common spirit." New York's "intellectual character is yet, in a great degree, to be formed; our community is yet in that plastic state in which it cannot remain long, but must soon become set either to our honor or dishonor." Almost two years earlier, when the new university was just being organized, John Pintard looked upon it as a vehicle for giving New York the cultural distinction that had so far eluded it. "Our contemplated university," he wrote to his daughter, "will in the course of a few years work wonders in rearing up a new generation whose superior education must change the present, in a degree, grovelling character of N. Yorkers."[5]

During the 1820s, when New Yorkers were redefining city culture in a way that needed a new kind of service from an institution of higher education, Columbia College was profoundly unprepared to respond. Indeed, it was hardly fulfilling its traditional role as one of many auxiliary institutions, let alone being ready to assume a directing role. From the 1790s until after the Civil War, Columbia seems to have lost its sense of urban identity, of its place in the city. Turning inward on itself, the college in the 1820s was aristocratic in social attitude and resolutely classical in its curriculum. In the phrase of John Pintard, an Episcopalian and generally a friend of the institution, Columbia was so "Episcopalized"

---

* A more radical version of artisanal learning at this time was the Hall of Sciences (1829–31) established by Fanny Wright and Robert Dale Owen in an abandoned church on Broome Street, near the Bowery.

as to isolate it from the mainstream, even of the city's elite culture. Nor was it among the nation's leaders of higher learning. When in 1819 Joseph Green Cogswell, one of the first Americans educated in a German graduate faculty and later the founding librarian of the Astor Library, named America's major institutions of learning, he listed Harvard, Yale, and Princeton, leaving Columbia unmentioned. Columbia, in the words of a recent historian, "appeared to founder for a purpose." Enrollment was low and in this long period of quiescence the trustees devoted most of their energies to property management.[6] Well endowed, it asked nothing of the city—and it gave nothing.* Unlike the new university, which in its charter styled itself the University *of* the City, the charter that transformed King's College into Columbia specified "the college *within* the City of New York, heretofore called King's College [shall] be forever hereafter called and known by the name of Columbia College" [my italics].

An anonymous communication printed in the *New York American* in 1819 suggested the sort of obligations toward civic culture New Yorkers wanted the college to undertake. It was proposed that Columbia expand its role in the city by doing two things. First, it should assume the leadership in a movement to combine and consolidate all the city's literary institutions; second, it should offer a "Public Course," including lectures on such modern subjects as political economy, chemistry, architecture, public and commercial law, literature, and criticism.[8] Columbia was not stirred from its slumber by the item, but the newspaper did outline what would soon be proposed for the new university. A university of the city would assume a directing role in uniting the intellectual resources of the city, and its curriculum was expected to extend over the full range of knowledge inherent in the life and work of the city.

The first recorded meeting of the group who became the founders of the University of the City of New York was held on December 16, 1829.[9] Nine men attended the meeting: the Reverend James M. Mathews, the Reverend Jonathan Mayhew Wainwright, Dr. J. Augustine Smith, Dr. Valentine Mott, John Delafield, Joseph Delafield, Hugh Maxwell, Isaac S. Hone, and Myndert Van Schaick. The diversity of their backgrounds and the predominance of secular occupations reflects the established pattern of cultural leadership in New York. Two were clergymen (Mathews and Wainwright), two were physicians (Smith and Mott), two were merchants (Hone and Van Schaick), one a lawyer, currently the district attor-

---

* It neither solicited nor received private donations during these years. Between 1787 and 1850, Columbia received only one gift, in 1843. Its last state grant was in 1819.[7]

ney (Maxwell), one was a banker and active leader of the New-York Historical Society (John Delafield), and the last, Joseph Delafield, was a gentleman of leisure noted for his devotion to science and in 1829 president of the Lyceum of Natural History.

In succeeding meetings, these nine men invited the city's existing literary organizations to join in their endeavor and they made up a list of cultural leaders to be invited to a public meeting on January 6, 1830. The man elected chair of the meeting had come without being invited, a remarkable oversight. Morgan Lewis, who assumed the chair and remained a major figure in the effort to create the university, was the former governor, president of the New-York Historical Society, and grand master of the New York Masons. Since the death of Clinton two years earlier, Lewis had partially if not entirely taken upon himself the broad role of cultural leadership that Clinton had for so long assumed. All leaders at the meeting were not, however, representative of continuity with Clinton. Certainly the secretary of the meeting was not a stand-in for Clinton, for he was Hugh Maxwell, who had in 1811 been before Clinton as a co-defendant with Gulian Verplanck, both having been charged with inciting the Columbia commencement "riot." Such is the stuff of which college founders are made!

The meeting unanimously resolved "that it is highly desirable and expedient to establish in the city of New-York, a University, on a liberal foundation, which shall correspond with the spirit and wants of our age and country, which shall be commensurate with our great and growing population, and which shall enlarge the opportunities of education for such of our youth as shall be found qualified to improve them."[10] There was obviously enthusiasm for some kind of distinctively urban university. But what would its precise character be?

A second result of the meeting was the publication of a rather detailed prospectus for the university. This statement, *Considerations Upon the Expediency and Means of Establishing a University in the City of New York,* was probably written by Wainwright. The grandson of Jonathan Mayhew and a graduate of Harvard, Wainwright in 1830 was rector of Grace Church; twenty years later he became Episcopal bishop of New York. The pamphlet he published contained his own ideas and those of the nine men who had been discussing the university during the weeks preceding the public meeting, but it is clear that he incorporated parts of the discussion from that meeting into his statement.[11] Hence we can take this statement as a synthesis of opinion on what the university was to be.

Arguing for innovation, Wainwright insisted that universities, like any other institutions, must respond to the social and intellectual movements that surround them. But universities—especially universities—are often loath to change. Columbia College was like other American colleges in this respect. It has not, he complained, represented the growth of the city and its way of life either in its enrollment, which has remained stable in spite of a massive population increase, or in its curriculum. Colleges have restricted themselves to preparing "young men for what are termed learned professions," and Columbia is "decidedly" such a "preparatory school." As such, Columbia opens itself to the charge that it is "conducted in an exclusive spirit," providing education "for a privileged class." It is open only to those prepared for and desiring to pursue a classical education. Acknowledging that "no one can be esteemed an accomplished scholar who has not undergone a thorough classical discipline," Wainwright observed that not all want "to be accomplished scholars." Yet these same students, while not potential scholars, may desire instruction in the "higher departments of knowledge" that may better "suit their capacity or their intended profession or occupation in life." [12]

Higher education, he proclaimed, must open itself to the life of the city, particularly a city that is likely to become the metropolis of the New World. A city like New York is "the grand point and focus" of "wisdom." "There is," he averred, "an exalted and liberalizing influence in the commercial activity of the place." A place managing half the commerce of the United States cannot "fail likewise to promote mental intercourse, and diffuse the various branches of human knowledge." [13]

The university he described was to be of the city and responsive to its life. The ancient universities of England and, for that matter, the less ancient American colleges, by their charter privileges and endowments, were able to remain cloistered from the life of the city. Wainwright, however, noted the contrasting case of the recently established University of London, an urban university descending in an identifiably direct lineage from Geneva and Edinburgh. [14] While the universities of Geneva and Edinburgh were governed directly by the City Republic and by the City Council respectively, London's and the proposed New York university were non-governmental, albeit intended to represent civic purposes. Wainwright proposed—and this was how the university was initially organized—that donors become shareholders in a joint stock company. The governing council, as in any corporation, was elected by shareholders.

But governance was only part of the matter. The curriculum was really at the heart of the enterprise. The traditional curriculum at Columbia did not, Wainwright claimed, "meet the literary needs of the city." A "literary and scientific education" adequate to the needs of New York City had to be broad and modern. It must not be restricted to the needs of the "young man designed to be a lawyer, physician, or clergyman." It must also respond to the educational wants of "young persons designed to be merchants, mechanics, farmers, manufacturers, architects, civil engineers," and it must be institutionalized in a way that such students may attend "with equal privileges and equal advantages, and pursue those studies respectively, which will aid them in their future occupations." [15]

A very important part of Wainwright's *Considerations* was concerned to associate the new university with the institutions of civic culture that we have already discussed. He proposed that the university bring existing learned associations under its protective wing to facilitate their "harmonious co-operation." The institutions he had in mind were, for the most part, constituent members of the New York Institution, and Wainwright proposed that the old Almshouse become the home of the university along with its current tenants. Considering the "common benefit" the city would derive by its patronage of the university, certainly there could be, in Wainwright's view, no objection to providing this space gratis. For its part, the university would make higher education available to all religions and all classes. And it would allow the city to designate a number of outstanding students for free tuition at the university. For those who felt that the literary life of the city had lacked both rigor and effect, consolidation under the aegis of the university would enhance the quality and impact of these many diverse institutions. By being thus "concentrated," the "literary means" of the city would be made "more imposing." In the spirit of consolidation, Wainwright even offered to incorporate Columbia College into the university. Professing no hostility to Columbia—it performed its limited task well—he proposed that it be "modified" to become a "constituent part of the university." [16]

With the exception of Columbia, the city's cultural institutions welcomed the founders' invitation to join the movement for a university. The New-York Historical Society, the Lyceum of Natural History, and the Mercantile Library Association all responded favorably, though one major institution, the New York Society Library, declined, saying it was "inexpedient at this time." [17] The Lyceum and the Historical Society agreed to allow the university to use their library and collections, and until the university's new building on Washington Square was completed classes were held in the Mercantile Library Association's Clinton Hall, at the southwest corner of Nassau and Beekman streets.

These invitations and responses were not, however, restricted to patrician institutions. The Mechanics Institution enthusiastically allied itself with the university, allowing it to hold classes from 1833 to 1835 in Mechanic's Hall, on Chambers Street, across City Hall Park from Clinton Hall. Mechanics who opposed the New York Institution as an example of public assistance for "private benefit" of the elite, supported municipal aid to the proposed university because "the advantages of a university on the liberal and large scale proposed will extend to and benefit the community at large."[18] During these years there was much discussion within the General Society of Mechanics and Tradesmen concerning ways of "promoting and disseminating literary and scientific knowledge"; in February 1830, the society went on record supporting the new university and appropriated $1,000 for it. "Respectable mechanics and trades people," William Cullen Bryant observed, "are all for a university."[19] Indeed, Thomas Mercein of the society and of the Mechanics Institution was an active member of the standing committee and the executive committee through which the preliminary organization of the university was managed. His name even appears on one of the draft slates for the first council of the university, though it was not on the official slate sent out to those subscribers qualified to vote.*

I wish to emphasize the interest and activity of the mechanics, for we are inclined to underestimate the pressure artisans and the larger working-class public put on the New York City elite to democratize and extend learning on a ground acceptable to them. Artisanal pride in the contribution of their class to the progress of civilization and culture was substantial and evident in ceremonial addresses of the period.[20] This pride, mixed with a combative defensiveness, led to practical results in the realm of cultural innovation. It was pressure from below, for example, that in the 1830s produced the ideal of objectivity and the cult of facticity in the city's largest disseminators of knowledge, the penny press.[21]

Although two of the founders of the new university were trustees of Columbia, Columbia did not view the new venture as a friendly gesture. A committee sent to confer with Columbia returned to tell their colleagues that the new university ought to proceed on its own. If Columbia declined the offer to join the new venture, it was nonetheless roused, momentarily, from its somnolence. Fearing a rival, Columbia sought to undercut the proposed university and prevent its establishment. To the City Council, Columbia proposed that in return for city patronage, including donation of the old Almshouse, Columbia would become the "City College," and it would allow the municipal authorities to name one trustee for every $20,000 in money or real estate donated until the city held one-half of the seats on the Columbia board. By this means, Columbia informed the mayor, "all *citizens*, merchants, mechanics, working men as well as professional men," would have a voice in the running of Columbia. Nothing came of this proposal, however, and neither institution succeeded in obtaining municipal patronage.[22]

But Columbia sought as well to counter the curricular innovations of the new university. It created a "scientific and literary course" that required no classics and promised a series of "Public Lectureships" on a

* The minutes of the preliminary meetings do not reveal why his name was deleted.

variety of topics, ranging from English literature to mechanics and machines, to political economy, to constitutional law. These lectures were to be "open to all persons who may choose to attend."*²³

The new university had announced that it would provide free tuition to a dozen selected students, with two per year named by the corporation of the City of New York, the High School, the Public Library Society, the Clinton Hall Association, the Mechanic and Scientific Institution, and the General Society of Mechanics and Tradesmen. In addition, each denomination in the city might send one ministerial student to the university free of charge. Columbia adopted the same policy, insisting that with this act, Columbia has met the objection "that it is not identified with the interests of the community."²⁴

Columbia coupled its positive response to the claims of the city with a cynical and negative argument. If the public were to support the movement for a university and bring it into being, then Columbia, its trustees warned, would be driven into the arms of the Episcopal Church. By rejecting the new university, "the citizens of New-York have now an opportunity to prevent forever Columbia College from being . . . devoted to sectarian purposes, and to make her emphatically a city college."²⁵

Rivalry, ambition, and cynicism, as one might expect, surrounded the whole enterprise. Yet through the fights and intrigues, a central dilemma about the definition of city culture continued to be of utmost importance. This had to do with the participation of the mechanics and their organizations in the university movement. It found focus in the relative merits of classical and non-classical curricula. This controversy, though generally treated as part of a wide-ranging discourse on pedagogy—disciplining the mind, traditionalists versus progressives, etc.—was, as are most educational issues, fundamentally a social and cultural problem of some consequence. And it was recognized as such.

For the proponents of the university, what the city wanted and what the university was expected to be was an institution devoted to both the advancement and the diffusion of knowledge. It was understood that the debate between defenders of the classical curriculum and the utilitarian proponents of modern subjects bore directly upon the question of diffusion and, therefore, upon the very definition of city culture.

This curricular debate in New York, which occurred at a crucial moment in the formation of the city's class-structure and cultural configuration, gave focus to a larger national discourse on the place of classical

---

* The literary and scientific course was discontinued in 1843, after NYU was no longer a threat. The public lectures rather quickly evaporated as well.

learning in America and the place of advanced learning in a democracy.[26] Just two years before, in 1828, the faculty of Yale College had issued its famous *Reports on the Course of Instruction*. That document is remembered for its defense and justification of the classical curriculum at Yale. While it has been common for moderns to see the Yale Report as simply reactionary, a fair reading reveals a rather open-minded document. In fact, there is no difficulty in finding justification for the proposed New York university at several points in the Yale Report, though, perhaps predictably, defenders of Columbia thought the report sufficient to dissuade right-thinking New Yorkers from proceeding with their innovative university.[27] What was overlooked by the defenders of the classical curriculum as well as by its opponents was the insistence of the Yale professors that they were prescribing only for Yale. Other places, particularly larger cities with greater resources, intellectual and financial, were wished well with an alternative and more comprehensive academic plan. In this respect they specifically noted the proposed University of London, which was to be so influential two years later in the plans for the University of the City of New York.[28]

The Yale Report repeatedly acknowledged that a classical college education was only a part of a "finished education," whether one went on to study the "higher branches, became a professional, or pursued any other occupation in business or agriculture." There are, the professors pointed out, different institutions for different purposes, and it is this whole configuration of educational opportunities that must be appraised rather than focusing on a single institution within it. They saw no reason for advocating the development at New Haven of a comprehensive institution embracing all of them, including practical experience in business and agriculture. Yet they did not preclude it for other institutions in larger cities and with generous endowments. If one could thus cite the Yale Report in favor of the plans of the urban progressives in New York, the Yale professors recoiled from the crucial and most radical points in the New York proposal. They resisted the idea of making other courses of study equal to the classical one, and they were distinctly uncomfortable with the prospect of the indiscriminate or promiscuous student body that would populate a comprehensive institution.[29]

The question of how best to effect the advancement and diffusion of knowledge in the context of American democratic culture was to be agitated a few years later when Congress weighed the possible forms for the institution to be created out of the £100,000 bequest of James Smithson. After considering the establishment of a national university, Congress created the Smithsonian Institution. As shaped by Joseph Henry, the Smithsonian committed itself to the patronage of professional—or professionalizing—science in America. Although coming after the great debate over the university for New York, it represented another attempt to resolve the same problem of the advancement and diffusion of knowledge (the criteria of Smithson's bequest). Henry's solution was, as we shall see, anticipatory of the future, but it was not nearly so "democratic" as that proposed by the most important supporter of the new university.[30]

Albert Gallatin was the most accomplished and distinguished of New York's citizens in 1830. He had been born into one of the aristocratic families of Geneva in 1761. Educated at the Academy there, he left in 1780, pursuing adventure in America. He sought his adventure—and his fortune—in the West, settling in western Pennsylvania. By the early 1790s, he had become active and prominent in political affairs, ultimately becoming a notable Jeffersonian, serving as Secretary of the Treasury under Thomas Jefferson and James Madison, and in that position easily rivaling the accomplishments of his predecessor from New York, Alexander Hamilton.

Gallatin's theoretical position on cities was not unlike Jefferson's, but he, far more than Jefferson (who did envy, one must remember, those who lived in Paris), found himself drawn to the seaport cities of the United States, particularly to New York. Through marrying into the Nicholson family, a prominent Republican enclave in New York City, he became, in the words of Henry Adams, "attached . . . by connection and interest to the active intellectual movement of a great city." After serving as a member of the commission which negotiated the Treaty of Ghent, ending the War of 1812, and then as minister to France (1816–23) and England (1826–27), Gallatin made New York City his home, becoming president of the National Bank of New York City. However distinguished his public career, Gallatin, again like his friend Jefferson, had a wide range of other talents. Henry Adams felt that Gallatin's work as a scientist —principally his work on American Indian languages which established him as the founder of American ethnology*—would alone have sufficed to secure him permanent fame. Even as a statesman and as a New York banker, Gallatin, who understood public finance and banking better than any other American of his time, displayed the fineness of his mind. His state papers, like those of John Quincy Adams, repay reading as literature as well as political economy.[31]

It is uncertain just when Gallatin interested himself in the university. The first time his name appears in relation to the university is on a subscription list dated September 8, 1830. Just over a month later, Octo-

---

* Gallatin was founder, in 1842, of the American Ethnological Society; his principal work was his *Synopsis of the Indian Tribes . . . of North America* (1836).

ber 18, 1830, he was elected first president of the governing council of the university.[32] And just two days after taking this office, he found himself addressing a convention of distinguished "Literary and Scientific Gentlemen" from all over the country who were assembled in the Common Council Chamber of New York's City Hall in order to discuss and make suggestions for the organization of the new university.

Gallatin began his address by observing that "two objects are contemplated." One is to "elevate the standard of learning" in the city, to "assimilate the University to the most celebrated establishments abroad." The other is "to diffuse knowledge, and to render it more accessible to the community at large." The first of these objects seemed to Gallatin to face no very great obstacles. It is merely a matter of means to establish an "upper department" in "science and letters" or, as it is called in Europe, a "philosophical faculty." But the aim of "diffusing knowledge more generally, and of extending the blessings of education to that numerous class which as yet has not had the opportunity of enjoying them, is still more important, and is attended with considerable difficulty." Though more difficult, this second mission was essential in a democratic polity and society.

Universities, Gallatin explained, were founded well before the era of democracy, prior to the Reformation. They were at that time "well adapted to the existing state of society." With one possible exception, there was then no European nation with a national literature. Latin and Greek authors contained most of the world's knowledge and served as models of "style, taste, and eloquence." Latin provided an international language among the small class of readers and men of learning. But all of this has changed. Printing called into existence national literatures and new readers. New knowledge in "every science, natural, moral, or mathematical, has made immense progress" and surpassed the ancients. Every man of science or letters today writes in "his vernacular tongue." The argument that the study of classical languages better forms the mind than any other inquiry, he found unpersuasive. "Every branch of knowledge," Gallatin insisted, "properly taught, will unfold and exercise the faculties."

The point Gallatin pressed most forcefully, however, is a larger one. The privileged place of the classics, he argued, distorts the whole educational system and thereby the culture. While the "learned languages" are admittedly useful for those "designed for one of the learned professions," the absolute insistence on requiring them for all advanced learning "must be considered the greatest impediment to the general diffusion of knowledge." No boy lacking the family resources, the time, or even the inclination to devote years to the study of these languages has any opportunity for college-level instruction. Even the high school or, as it was properly called, the grammar school (which stands above the elementary school system) devotes most of its energies to instruction in these ancient languages so that students may continue on to college. This distorts and skews the whole educational system above the elementary level. The result is not simply that collegiate education is closed to the masses, but that the intermediate level of the educational system is also largely closed to those unable or unwilling to study Latin and Greek.

The problem, Gallatin observed, is that "a few only" are destined to become professionals. But in an age of science and democracy, many more are in need of—and desire—"practical and useful knowledge," something denied them by the "absolute requisite" of classical learning. This "great evil" can be removed only by "substituting a more rational system of education, and [one] better fitted to the situation, pursuits, and wants of the community." To accomplish this, Gallatin proposed the establishment of an "English college" within the university. He insisted that there must not be "an invidious distinction" between the student who pursues the English course and the one who pursues the classical one.* The new university must demonstrate that "no superiority is claimed for any branch of learning." In "the republic of letters, every science has a right to claim equality." So long as we reserve the appellation of educated man for those of classical learning, "there is but little hope of any essential improvement in our system of education, and none whatever to make this generally popular." [34]

With an English college in New York, Gallatin observed in a subsequent letter to Josiah Quincy, president of Harvard College, the whole local educational system would be reoriented. A system of preparatory schools emphasizing more useful subjects would replace Latin grammar schools, and the means of access to scientific knowledge would be vastly broadened. It would all result, Gallatin hoped, in the diffusion, "more widely than is done at present amongst all those who are not destined for the liberal professions, [of] some share of elementary mathematical, natural and historical knowledge, as well as that of their own language and of its literature." [35]

Although there had been earlier statements of Gallatin's position in New York—in the middle of the eighteenth century Cadwallader Colden had supported Benjamin Franklin's ideas for an English education in Philadelphia, and William Livingston preferred more useful knowledge to a classical curriculum at King's College—classical languages had for the most part been defended as demarcations in the culture. They established patrician gentility and superiority. "Classical learning," Samuel

---

* After reflecting on this point for several weeks, Gallatin wondered whether even this plan of two colleges within the university might permit the distinction to continue. Perhaps, he wrote Harvard's Josiah Quincy, it would be best to leave classical learning to existing colleges and make the university entirely an English college. [33]

Bard observed in 1819, marks off those destined for "any employment above those of the mechanical arts."[36] The point was to preserve the invidious distinction.[37] While Gallatin sought to remove such distinctions, he did not imagine a unitary culture. He sought only—though this is a great deal—to "raise the standard of *general* education and the mind of the laboring classes nearer to a level of those born under more favorable circumstances."[38]

Gallatin's was not the only approach to educational reform to be discussed in New York. Some well-meaning patricians thought that the best way to improve the education of mechanics was to teach them Latin so that they could then cross the traditional barrier distinguishing the educated from the uneducated.* This approach to educational advancement would devalue the general culture of the city's mechanics, while allowing certain individuals to escape it. It is a familiar pattern in aristocratic societies, such as England, where the talented youth is sent off to Oxford or Cambridge as a scholarship boy to be transported out of his community, his class, and his culture. This devaluation of inherited culture— rather than its enhancement—is at the heart of much of the pain involved in education-sponsored social mobility in modern society.[40]

Gallatin had something quite different in mind. He assumed that one need not cease being a mechanic to be educated.† He sought to connect the intellectual aspirations of the learned mechanic *as mechanic* with those branches of higher learning that would be of practical use. This is not vulgar utilitarianism. It is important to remember that the great intellectual achievements of the nineteenth century were not the study of the classical languages (though there was notable achievement there), but rather in the scientific, literary, and historical scholarship that Gallatin wanted to make part of non-professional education in the city. Gallatin had a vision of a two-culture (and, let it be said, two-class) city. But he sought to reduce sharply the invidious distinctions of a bifurcated culture by allowing all access on their own terms to the whole range of higher learning available at the collegiate level.

The ideal Gallatin and his associates had for the new university and new culture of the city was most concisely stated in the petition they submitted to the legislature seeking a charter for the new university:

* Professor Anthon of Columbia did this when in 1840 he promised annually to take six scholars from the school of the General Society of Mechanics and Tradesmen into the Columbia Grammar School at no charge.[39]

† Although neither Gallatin nor anyone else engaged in the New York debate seems to have realized it, much of this debate had been rehearsed some five years before by the board of Philadelphia's Franklin Institute. Although they discussed the need for a college that would make no invidious distinction between modern, technical, and classical education, no practical proposal emerged.[41]

Knowledge in this country is chiefly sought for and appreciated in reference to its subserviency to the actual pursuits of life. And whilst the University will provide means of instruction for those who devote themselves exclusively to scientific or literary pursuits, one of its prominent and essential purposes is to afford to all classes of the public the education best fitted to aid them in their pursuits, whether intended for the learned professions, commerce, or the mechanical and useful arts. . . . A person may as suitably graduate upon his attainments in the sciences and modern languages or without any other than his native tongue as with the acquisition of Greek or Latin. . . . The mechanic can thus obtain for his son who is destined to continue his calling, the most complete English education and an opportunity of learning all that the sciences have discovered in aid of his business.[42]

The opening of the new university in the fall of 1832 was not auspicious. Albert Gallatin had already resigned from the council and its presidency. Publicly, he cited reasons of health, but in private he complained that "the clergy had obtained control," the original "liberal principles" had been abandoned, and the whole seemed now to be little more than a conventional college. Under such circumstances, he decided that it was not worth his effort.[43]

The opening ceremonies were held in the midst of a devastating cholera epidemic; more than five thousand persons had died in the city during the three months preceding the inaugural ceremonies. The opening address by the Reverend Dr. James Milnor of St. George's Church and acting president of the council virtually announced the abandonment of Gallatin's dream, insisting upon the distinction and superiority of the classical course option over that of the scientific and literary program also being offered. He described three levels of distinction. Lowest was the non-classical. For those with "more extensive" talents and expectations, the university offered the traditional classical education. And for a select few, there would be advanced or graduate study as at "Seats of Learning in the transatlantic world."[44] The two-class system—with invidious distinction—was established, and the university proceeded to deny the B.A. degree to all save those who completed the classical course.*[45] Gallatin's successor as president of the council was James Tallmadge, who rhetorically supported Gallatin's idea, but in fact strongly backed the chancellor's

* It should, perhaps, be noted here that four years earlier Union College had begun offering a B.A. degree to its students who pursued its scientific course rather than its classical one. So by the time NYU began graduating students, it was not even innovative in New York State.

revision of the original ideals.* He supported Mathews when, in the aftermath of the devastating depression of 1837, which nearly caused the university to go under, he fired eight professors who resisted Mathews's leadership, at least in part on the basis of their belief in Gallatin's original vision.[46] After 1838, it was clear that the effort to reform the culture of the city with the university established on Washington Square had failed.

The failure of the new university was costly to the ideal of the learned mechanic. But there were other important losers as well. The merchants of the city very much wanted and needed a collegiate institution that would concentrate on modern and commercial subjects. Old methods of recruitment to and training for a mercantile life were transparently inadequate in the context of New York's dynamic economy and complex social life. At the end of the 1830s, once NYU's failure was evident to all, the Mercantile Library Association lamented the circumstance in which the city found itself. The association even discussed turning itself into a "collegiate institution," since no other institution seemed able or willing to train merchants, both in technical commercial subjects and in the liberal arts needed to form merchants as public men.[47]

The abandonment by the University of the City of New York of the effort to establish collegiate education on a broader definition of learned culture did not extinguish either the idea or the desire for it. The next important effort came in the 1840s. The impetus here came not from the merchant elite but rather from certain elements within the Working Men's Party and the radical Locofoco faction of the Democratic Party, who kept the issue before the public until the late 1840s, when the idea was realized with the founding of the Free Academy (1847).†

The promise of the Free Academy, according to William Cullen Bryant, editor of the Democratic *Evening Post,* was that it would "give us intelligent mechanics." The Free Academy came into being largely because of the vision and commitment of a self-made merchant and Democratic politician named Townsend Harris. Born in Washington County in 1804, Harris was apprenticed in a New York dry-goods store at the age of thirteen. He became a successful importer. Regretting his limited education, he read constantly. When he was elected president of the Board of Education in 1846, he set for his goal the establishment of a Free Academy. Neither Columbia nor New York University, he felt, was

---

* It is worth noting that Tallmadge was also president of the American Institute, which, as Stephen Allen complained, used the rhetoric of common interest with the mechanical classes to advance merchant interests.

† The Free Academy became City College in 1866, and in 1961 a part of the massive City University of New York.

relevant to the needs of the city, a fact reflected by their small student bodies in the midst of a burgeoning city. He proposed a college with "especial reference to the active duties of operative life, [rather] than those more particularly regarded as necessary for the Pulpit, Bar, or the Medical Profession." Harris did not completely dismiss the possibility of a classical curriculum, but he clearly reduced it to an *"adjunct,* rather than a *primary* object of the academy." A modern and "practical" curriculum was "best calculated" to advance in their "calling" those youths destined to "follow what are termed the *productive pursuits of life."* Such an institution, he thought, offered much to the city and its mechanics; it would raise "up a class of mechanics and artists, well skilled in their several pursuits, and eminently qualified to infuse into their fellow-workmen a spirit that would add dignity to labor" and make the laboring classes better appreciate and value "republican institutions."[48] Again, this was not a strategy of individual mobility out of the laboring classes; it was a means of assimilating advanced learning into the artisanal culture in the interest of enhancing its dignity and the quality of general and technical knowledge available to mechanics. Whig opposition to the Free Academy was based on a different understanding of the relation of higher education and the emerging American class system. They feared that such education would disrupt the labor market, inducing rising expectations and fueling the ambition of upward mobility. Though the Whig perception would prove truer in the long run, the initial impulse of the Democrats was to enhance the industrial class rather than provide the means of escaping it. Only later, as Sherry Gorelick has shown, did City College in fact become the mechanism for mobility that has been so much discussed in recent years.[49]

Just as the University of the City of New York lost Gallatin and abandoned its ideals, so the Free Academy lost Harris—and some of its ideals. In January 1848, Harris resigned the presidency of the Board of Education. His reasons were personal: his mother, with whom he was extremely close, had died, leaving him too depressed to work. He left the city, traveling in the Far East, where he ultimately achieved fame as the American consul who won the affection of the Japanese and opened Japan to the West. Whether Harris's continued leadership would have produced the sort of curriculum he and Gallatin envisioned is, of course, impossible to determine. But the Free Academy, like the University of the City of New York, very quickly took on most of the trappings of a conventional college. Although most of its students were middle-class and native-born during its first decade, the working classes were fairly represented in its student body. The lowest quartile of the city's socioeconomic scale was completely absent, however, and the children of the merchant class were overrepresented by a factor of three. If not fully representative, the Free

Academy was clearly less exclusive than Columbia or New York University in the 1850s.[50] The Free Academy seems to have facilitated some working-class mobility (or, more precisely, upgrading of skills) that resulted in employment in the newly developed clerical sector. Boys from the top of the working classes were moved into low-level and probably dead-end white-collar jobs in the expanding business organizations of the city. Others, especially women educated at Hunter College (established for women in 1886 as a normal school), moved into teaching. Seven graduates in the first decade of the Free Academy became engineers, an occupational choice that might be seen as an expansion and enhancement of opportunity within the working classes.[51]

During the 1850s, John W. Draper, New York University's most distinguished nineteenth-century professor, tried, one last time, to define the university's association with the version of civic culture articulated by Gallatin—that is, one inclusive of the aspirations of the city's mechanics. Draper was a man of many and diverse accomplishments. Founder of the university's medical school and the American Chemical Society, he may also have been the first person to photograph the human face, and he was a prolific historian, writing on the American Civil War and authoring the first intellectual history of Europe written by an American. He came to New York University in 1839, after the original plans had been abandoned. But he knew of them and made an effort, even at the risk of being anachronistic, to restate and recover them. A distinguished university, Draper insisted, is essential for any city that wishes to be more than a commercial emporium. If it aspires to recognition as "the Metropolis of America," New York must support "costly establishments for the culture of science." New York, Draper complained in an address to the alumni, has "not comprehended her University." New Yorkers do not understand, for example, that the work of only two of its professors has already paid for the university many times over. He referred to Morse's telegraph, which, among other things, made possible the national organization of business that allowed New York to dominate the nation's economy, and to his own discovery of the means of photographing the human face, which had brought pleasure to vast numbers and provided employment—particularly, he noted, to women, who thereby escaped a dependent position in society.[52]

But Draper's words were directed to the university even more than to the city. The university must be "put in relation with the City." And this meant something other than providing a classical education for sixty students in a city with a population of three-quarters of a million people. Clearly, Draper reflected, "we are offering what the City does not want."

There must, he explained, "be an affinity between the wants of the city and the nature of its institutions." The education of ministers, physicians, and literary men has been and is being accomplished, but they "constitute only a small portion of the community." Besides, the literary and classical education they receive is not really appropriate to the nineteenth century. "Mere literary acumen is becoming utterly powerless against profound scientific attainment." Is science or literature, he asked, "shaping the thought of the world?" His prescience deserves remark. The most important fact about science in the nineteenth century was its progressive isolation from the gentleman scholar, and, as Stow Persons has observed, the great failure of "gentry culture" was its incapacity to incorporate science. "Ultimately," he writes, "it was the scientist as investigator," both in natural science and in the social sciences, "who displaced the gentleman as scholar." [53]

The middle of the nineteenth century, Draper explained, requires new learning and new learners. A modern curriculum would enable the university to meet "the great task of dealing with the true strength of New-York—its commercial classes, manufacturers, engineers, and mechanics." Here is the great mass in need of higher learning; their education is central to the role of the university in the culture of the city. The business of the university is "that class, which in some places is the terror . . . but which here, if submitted to the influence of science and letters, will surely form the guard of the public order." What Draper looked forward to was the day "when we shall see the New-York Mechanic passing up the steps of the University, and depositing the tools he has been using, behind the lecture-room door." [54] Draper assumed, in a way reminiscent of Gallatin and Harris, that the mechanic would retrieve his tools after class, that advanced learning would be incorporated into the culture of the city's artisans. But his was a nostalgic vision. The class of artisans that had prompted Gallatin's proposal was by the 1850s undermined by economic change, and replaced by an increasingly immigrant working class. Such altered circumstances encouraged and fostered a narrowing, if also an elevation, of the anticipated role of the metropolitan university.*

METROPOLITANISM AND UNIVERSITY LEARNING

The main thrust of cultural reform in the 1850s lost touch with Gallatin's democratic hope; instead reformers devoted their energies to that aspect of university reform that Gallatin had called easy. The linkage between

* Within a decade, Draper, too, would shift his emphasis, developing out of his commitment to science the program of expert leadership evident in his book *Thoughts on the Future Civil Polity of America* (1865).

university learning and metropolitan culture proposed in the 1850s was reminiscent of the 1830s, but it also pointed forward to the modern research university, with its capacity for securing intellectual authority and status within the general culture. The plans of the 1850s conceived of the university as a vehicle for elite cultural hegemony in the city. This movement was manifold, but it was given its most important and compelling expression by Henry P. Tappan, one of the original professors at the University of the City of New York and one of those fired during the crisis of 1838.

The university Tappan proposed to create was to be of the city as well as in it, and it was to consolidate existing learned institutions. The intellectual life of mechanics was not something that concerned him. Yet Tappan's proposal was still an extraordinary articulation of metropolitan culture in New York, and he worked hard for its realization. Tappan established, as had never been done before, a vision of the university as the keystone of a great metropolitan home for the learned of the United States.

The failure of his approach exhausted for a generation the drive for an urban university in New York. Not until the late 1880s would the ideal of a university-based learned and civic culture reemerge in New York City. In the 1890s, when Seth Low resurrected this New York civic tradition at Columbia, he found that the development of disciplines had produced a very real—though he hoped fruitful—tension in intellectual life between local civic culture and translocal academic or disciplinary cultures. In 1850, the centrifugal power of disciplines was not a significant concern. Seeking to bring order to the confusion and superficiality of intellectual life, urban cultural reformers defined a new role for the university. Instead of being one of many cultural institutions held together by a widely acknowledged interlocking elite leadership, they wanted the college, now transformed into a university, to institutionalize cultural authority by assuming a coordinating and directing role at the center. Urban culture would be defined in terms of the university and, perhaps even more important, the university itself would be defined in terms of the city rather than as the agglomeration of disciplines it later became.

The whole point of a metropolis, as James Bryce reminded Americans in the process of telling them that they lacked one, is that it concentrates the nation's cultural resources and thus makes them more powerful. "The conjunction of the forces of rank, wealth, knowledge, intellect . . . makes such a city a sort of foundry." There "opinion is melted and cast." Then it "can be easily and swiftly propagated and diffused through the whole country," with the special authority of the symbolic center, the metropolis.[55] New Yorkers had long recognized that they had failed to achieve this kind of cultural authority in the nation, and they understood, correctly, that in part this was because they had been unable to draw together the various strands of intellect and power in the city. In *The Great American Metropolis* (1837), Samuel Knapp, one of Clinton's memorialists, commented that "in some communities, the intellectual powers of the place, like galvanic batteries, grow powerful by becoming connected in a pile." Such was not the case in New York, where he found, to understate the case, "no extraordinary harmony in any profession or among bodies of men."[56]

In 1840, Joseph Green Cogswell surveyed the condition of intellect in America, and he complained that the inefficiency and ineffectiveness of American "higher literary institutions" resulted from the absence of a real university in the metropolis. A university is needed, he explained, so "that men of science may be brought together, and act upon each other, and act collectively upon the community." With "at least one point of centralization" to set a standard of performance and an object of ambition, "all our existing literary institutions would be exceedingly advanced."[57] Such had been the ambition of the University of the City of New York as it had been earlier for the New York Institution, and it was very much Tappan's aim in the 1850s.

By the 1850s it appeared that there were in New York several men with the means to endow such an institution. This sense of possibility is revealed in an entry that George Templeton Strong made in his diary in 1850. Strong, who was sensitive to the weakness of city culture in New York and to Columbia's unwillingness or inability to help, was also aware of the vast amounts of wealth that might be applied to the problem. He recorded his fantastic reverie of a New York filled with richly endowed cultural institutions:

> What churches I would build and what charities I would endow if I was poor W. B. Astor! How art would flourish after I'd founded my Gallery of Paintings. . . . My "conservatoire" would . . . [provide] the highest order to classical music performed by an orchestra permanently established. . . . The erection of Columbia College with six sister institutions into a university . . . with its richly endowed observatory, its three hundred resident fellows and professors, and its fourteen hundred free scholarships.[58]

Strong, alas, was no such capitalist. It was a dream; he had no such money. Moreover, he was by nature an observer, not a leader. It fell, not to him, but to Tappan to try to persuade Astor (and others) that they ought to use a few of their millions to endow a great university in New York to consolidate and give authority to the city's intellect.

· · ·

There is no little irony in Tappan's ambition for himself and for New York City. The most compelling spokesman of his generation for the value of a university in shaping the metropolitan role of New York City, he had fifteen years earlier been dismissed from a professorship at New York University, an institution founded with precisely the same cultural ambitions. Even more, he is remembered in the history of higher education for making the beginnings of the modern university in a small Midwestern town as president of the University of Michigan.[59]

Henry Tappan had been born into an old Dutch family (he was a third cousin of De Witt Clinton) in Rhinebeck, New York, a hundred miles up the Hudson from the city. He graduated from Union College in Schenectady in 1825 and from there went to the Theological Seminary at Auburn. He began his ministerial career in 1827, but the strain on his voice that preaching caused combined with growing intellectual interests to turn him toward an academic career. In 1832, he accepted the chair of Moral and Intellectual Philosophy at the newly established University of the City of New York. Moving to the city, he responded to city life with eagerness and a catholicity of spirit. After six years at the university he was dismissed, along with seven other professors who publicly expressed a lack of confidence in the administration of the university. But he had gained much in those years. "He was," his biographer notes, "no longer the inexperienced youth" who had come to the city in 1832. "Six years in the metropolis had done much to mature him in mind and personality." Wishing to stay in the city, he assumed the administration of a fashionable private school at elegant LeRoy Place, as Bleecker Street between Greene and Mercer was then called. For the next decade he read widely in theology, philosophy, and education. Then, in 1851, he made his first journey to Europe. It was in the nature of a pilgrimage; for him Europe became the "embodiment of civilization."[60] While there he established friendships with various European writers, most notably Victor Cousin. More important in connection with his dreams for New York, he saw at first hand the German university system that he had studied so much in books. In Germany he was confirmed in his belief that the United States had no university and that no college could become a university. A university was a thing in itself, not a superior or improved college. The Prussian example also encouraged in him the conviction that a university could be generated through a single great act.[61] Though there was no one in America with the absolute authority that had created the University of Berlin, there were, especially in New York, men of great wealth who might provide democracy with a university.

In 1851, on the eve of his European trip, Tappan published *University Education;* four years later, after two trips to Paris and Berlin, and after accepting the presidency of the University of Michigan in 1852, Tappan delivered an address to the New York Geographical Society that reasserted the possibilities of an American university. In both, but especially in the latter, he insisted that the lesson of Berlin was the inextricable association of civic institutions and the university in forming a metropolitan culture. It was this connection that made Berlin so special.[62]

Tappan's proposed university was to be an urban institution. He stressed the historic association of learning with cities, particularly commercial cities, and he declared that New York had reached a stage in its historical development that demanded achievements of a higher order than bricks, banks, and water systems.[63] In *University Education,* he articulated the way in which New York as a commercial metropolis might work also as a cultural metropolis.

> New York is really the metropolitan city of our country. The centre of commercial activity, the vast reservoir of wealth, it takes the lead in the elegancies and splendor of life, in the arts of luxury and amusement. It is also the great emporium of books and the fine arts. Here resort the professors of music and of the arts of design. Here literary men are taking up their abode. Here literary institutions of various kinds and grades have already come into being. . . . Commerce, wealth, and elegance invite, nay, demand the invigorating life, the counterbalancing power and activity of intellectual cultivation. Whatever is requisite for a great Institution of Learning can here be most readily collected. . . . By adding to the natural attractions of a metropolitan city the attractions of literature, science, and art, as embodied in a great University, students from every part of the Union would be naturally drawn together. We should thus have a fully appointed national Institution where the bonds of our nationality would be strengthened by the loftiest form of education, the sympathy of scholars, and the noblest productions of literature.[64]

The city itself was indispensable to his definition of the university. In insisting upon the university's metropolitan location, he had in mind both the psychology of urban life and the auxiliary institutions to be found there. Cities, he thought, produced a "wonderful influence" that encouraged accomplishment in art, science, and literature. "It is," he observed, "the influence of words, of looks, of manners." When men with a "common stock of information and ideas" talk daily, they "keep each other's minds at work." He admitted that there is often in great cities too much excitement—"too much talking, hearing, and seeing, going about, and not enough still thought; but, nevertheless, here, more than in any other form of life, men are sharpening each other's wits."[65]

He carefully distinguished between a major institution located in the city—as the Royal Society was in London—and a civic institution that was of as well as in the city. His model for New York was Berlin, where the university stood first among a diverse cluster of distinguished cultural institutions. A city of learned societies, he declared, needs a university as its core.[66]

Tappan offered the university as an instrument of reform in a city whose cultural life seemed confused and diffuse. "A great institution would collect together all that is now scattered and isolated among us, be the home of scholars, the nurse of scholarlike endeavors, the regulating and harmonizing center of thought and investigation." Like other cultural critics of his time, Tappan worried about the "hosts of mere expert empirics, who without learning succeed in gaining a reputation for learning and . . . invade the most sacred offices of society." A great university, he suggested, would restore intellectual authority to those who deserve it. It would enable the public to "begin to comprehend what scholarship means" and it would demarcate advanced scholarship as the special province of "a few men of great and cultivated powers." The university would thereby provide a base for a "learned class" in the city, so that the "population would feel the plastic power of intellectual development and progress" through "public lectures under the direction of an elite corporation."[67]

The details of his plan reveal the directing and consolidating role Tappan envisioned for the university. Columbia, New York University, and the Free Academy would be reduced to *gymnasia* within an educational system capped by the university. The various scientific and literary societies in the city, including the city's theological seminaries, the newly established Astor Library, and the projected Cooper Union, would be coordinated under the aegis of the university. Thus all the city's "Institutions of learning would grow into a harmonious whole."

Unlike later versions of the university, Tappan's did not distinguish sharply between the learned discourse of the university and the general elite culture of the city. His proposal was clearly within the tradition of civic culture; one sees very little of the later university in his outline. Professors would, in his plan, participate in the city's culture, and the city's finest non-academic minds would be associated in various ways with the university. Professors would be "required to give popular courses to the public" in addition to their lectures in a prescribed field to "Academical Members of the University." This wider audience of elite and educated adults would share in the consolidated resources of the university. "The result," he observed, "would be that the libraries, cabinets, laboratories, and lecture rooms of the University would become the resort of students of every grade; it would thus become the great centre of intellectual activity."[68]

Tappan's dream of reform was supported by the leaders of the American scientific community, the so-called Lazzaroni. Alexander Dallas Bache, echoing a privately circulated plan developed by Benjamin Peirce of Harvard, proposed for New York City "a great University of the arts and sciences, in which the practical man may meet on equal terms with the scholar." He suggested that scholars from all over the nation be brought to New York to assume lectureships of a five-year duration at the university. Here they would be at the center of a cluster of urban institutions even more diverse than Tappan had imagined: the Chamber of Commerce was as prominent as the Astor Library on Bache's list. With the university providing direction and clear standards of excellence, intellectual life in the city would unite "men of progress, scholars, practical men, mechanics, artists."[69]

During the 1850s there was much discussion of the place of a university in reforming the culture of New York and establishing its metropolitan status. The subject repeatedly occupied the trustees of Columbia, while Draper tried to urge reform on New York University. The Lazzaroni were publicly and privately trying to advance the cause, though they were less securely tied to New York City. Peter Cooper had announced his intention to found and substantially endow an institution for the advancement of science and art, and there was the proposal of Fernando Wood, that curious mayor of the city, so often the scoundrel and epitome of the urban boss, who was drawn to Tappan's idea and proposed in 1856 the creation of a university under municipal patronage.[70] There was, as well, the Astor fortune: the library had just been endowed, and it could be expanded into a university, if the Astors were willing.

William B. Astor, son of John Jacob Astor and inheritor of the bulk of the Astor fortune, seemed to offer the best prospects. Wood's proposal was not favorably received by the Board of Aldermen, and Peter Cooper's intentions were difficult to interpret, though Tappan sensed (accurately) that, whatever Cooper intended, it was not quite what Tappan had in mind. So Tappan worked on Astor. He reminded him that his father's will had indicated that surplus funds at the Astor Library could be used to sponsor lectures. Here was already the basis for a university. It would not take much more.

After a meeting with Astor that produced neither clear encouragement nor clear discouragement, Tappan placed all of his hopes on a long letter to Astor. Writing from Ann Arbor, he first sought to establish the need for a university, then he aimed to assure Astor that what he had in mind would succeed. A university, he explained, was needed to complete the system of education in the city and the nation. It would "furnish us with scientific and literary men of the highest grade," while affording a "true standard of general culture" and diffusing "a taste for it." Columbia, he explained, "has never extended itself to meet the wants of the city" and it is no university. Nor has the university at Washington Square been a university, for it has "failed through mismanagement."

Astor worried, quite legitimately, that the small number of students at Columbia and New York University suggested a lack of interest in higher learning in America. To this Tappan responded simply that "there never yet was a true university established that did not succeed." "Give New York a true university," he predicted, "and a want of students is the last thing we need to fear."

European example, according to Tappan, demonstrated the centrality of the university to both the material and the cultural welfare of great cities. "To remove from Paris, Berlin, and Munich their Universities and dependent institutions would be as fatal to their elevation and prosperity, as to plan such institutions among us would be auspicious to ours." At Michigan, he explained, he headed a "respectable institution" but "it cannot realize my idea." In New York, with its wealth and talent, with its many literary institutions, most centrally the Astor Library, the promise is of a different order. "No city in the world is of so much promise as New York. It is naturally the seat of a great university. It demands it for its social & intellectual elevation, and for its political security."[71]

Astor was not persuaded. He decided, instead, to expand the library without changing its essential character. With this failure—and with the regents of the University of Michigan beginning to wonder whether their new president was not devoting too much attention to affairs in New York—Tappan abandoned the project in 1857.[72]

There is a final irony in this story. Tappan could not understand why Peter Cooper did not embrace the opportunity he was being offered to create in New York what the King of Prussia had created in Berlin. Tappan's vision of organizing elite culture simply did not appeal to the millionaire who identified himself on the legal papers that created the Cooper Union as "a mechanic of New York" and who originally intended to name his institution "The People's Union." Thirty years of effort to create a well-endowed institution for the advancement and diffusion of modern, non-classical learning had culminated in Cooper's establishment of a "workingman's institute" designed to "improve and elevate the working classes of the city." Cooper, whose grandfather had been one of the first vice-presidents of the General Society of Mechanics and Tradesmen, wished to provide free to the laboring classes of both sexes training in the arts and sciences. Nothing could have been farther from Tappan's dream.[73]

When F. A. P. Barnard, president of Columbia College, sought in 1868 to establish an affiliation between the two institutions, making Cooper

Union a university-based technical school, Cooper resisted. Abram Hewitt, Cooper's business partner, son-in-law, and a graduate of Columbia, was infuriated by Cooper's refusal to acknowledge and embrace the superiority of elite culture as represented by Columbia. We will have, he sputtered, an institution for the working classes, but it will have "no reputation" for science.[74] Others among the city's elite, however, were more sympathetic to Cooper, most notably Frederick Law Olmsted, then a young literary man and later to distinguish himself as the designer of Central Park. Hearing of Cooper's plans in the context of his own growing interest in urban reform, Olmsted confided to a friend: "Hurrah for Peter Cooper and Hurrah for the Reds."[75]

Cooper's plans were based upon his own memories of decisive educational experiences as he grew up in New York as a mechanic. He had never attended any regular or formal instruction, and he saw no need for such in his Union, though in a subordinate place he was willing to have it. His enthusiasm was for a large museum, having had his mind when he was a young man stimulated and his imagination provoked by his visits to Scudder's Museum and, later, to Barnum's. He also wanted a cosmorama, depicting foreign lands, historical events, and eminent persons. A regular lecture-goer as a young man, he also planned a large lecture hall. But with the mechanic's belief in mutual learning, he proposed as well a large number of smaller rooms where young men would meet and discuss topics of mutual interest.

Abram Hewitt, whose Columbia education had enabled him to escape the class of his mechanic father and, for that matter, his father-in-law, was, in the words of his biographer, Allan Nevins, driven to "despair" by these ideas. He gradually persuaded the reluctant Cooper to modify his plans, making formal instruction a central part of the Union. The lecture hall was retained—and it still serves the city as the Great Hall—but the rooms for mutual discussion were transformed into classrooms. The museum was replaced by a library and reading room. (The stuffed whale that Cooper had already purchased for the museum was given to another museum.) Cooper went along with this, but he never fully accepted the compromises. He was often heard to say: "Sometimes I think my first plan was best."[76]

The Cooper Union for the Advancement of Science and Art opened in 1859, and it quickly evolved into one of the most remarkable institutions in the city. To this day, it remains America's only tuition-free private institution of higher learning. Well into the twentieth century, on New York's Lower East Side, Peter Cooper's remarkable benefaction stands as a beacon of opportunity and learning for the boys and girls of the city's poor.

From the start it was both an academy and a college, offering formal courses of instruction in the liberal arts and sciences. But it had as well what was called "the free night college for the working classes," providing higher education for young women, mechanics, and apprentices. The public lectures, which continue to this day in the Great Hall, were given by major political figures (for example, Lincoln's Cooper Union address in 1860 was perhaps the most important of his presidential campaign) as well as speakers on a variety of liberal subjects, from languages and literature to radical reform, to telegraphy, design, and engineering. There was a public reading room, a museum displaying rare inventions, and an art gallery.

New York had in Cooper Union an institution that was indeed of the city, but not in the way Tappan might have imagined, though Gallatin and others in the 1830s might have. At the inaugural ceremonies in 1859, Draper, whose address to the NYU alumni four years earlier surely must have appealed to Peter Cooper, delivered the major address. So far as I can tell, Tappan was not invited to attend.

A century of institution-building in the tradition of civic culture had come to disappointingly little in New York City. If it was ironic, it was nonetheless not much of an indication of success that the most well-endowed and secure institution of advanced learning founded so far in the nineteenth century was established outside the learned culture of the elite, founded by a mechanic for the education of other mechanics. Elite efforts to organize intellectual culture, first on the learned-society model and then on the civic-university model, came to very little. New York seemed to be failing as a city culture; it was not becoming a cultural metropolis, at least not on a *civic-culture* model. It would be a new generation of writers, a generation distinguished from the earlier professional and classically educated elite, who would as literary men and women establish New York's metropolitan claims in the nation's intellectual life.

PART II

LITERARY CULTURE

CHAPTER 4

Toward a Metropolitan Sensibility

On the eve of the completion of the Erie Canal, the painter Samuel F. B. Morse and the poet William Cullen Bryant, two New Englanders who would become fast friends in New York City, decided to try their luck in Gotham, in the hope of finding patronage for their respective arts.* Both had a clear sense that the city's economic promise might offer opportunity to young and ambitious writers and artists. The city in time rewarded each of them with financial success and every civic honor, but not in the ways they had hoped in their youth. Their glory did not derive from their poetry and painting; Bryant's came to him as the crusading editor of the *Evening Post*, while Morse's came to him as inventor of the telegraph.

Bryant, a young lawyer unhappy with the practice of law in Great Barrington, Massachusetts, began to think in the early 1820s of migrating to New York City under the sponsorship of the wealthy and powerful Sedgwick family. He had already publicly expressed the conviction that "in the history of the world" one could not "point out [any] example of a free, opulent, and flourishing community, which had not encouragements for learning and rewards of genius."[1] And so, in 1825, the year of the great canal celebration, Bryant made his move to New York City.

Morse had an especially acute grasp of the connection between cities and culture, and he thought naturally of metropolitan patterns of cultural development. Between 1815 and 1823, as an itinerant painter, he

* Our understanding of the young Bryant is enhanced by his portrait, now at the National Academy of Design, that Morse painted in the year of his arrival.

explored and speculated upon the prospects of Philadelphia, New York, and Boston as likely centers for the support of American art. Then in 1823, with telling insight, he grasped the likely cultural implications of the Erie Canal. He chose New York as the place to seek an artistic career. Writing to his wife, he remarked that "New York does not yet feel the influx of wealth from the Western canal, but in a year or two she will feel it, and it will be advantageous to me to be identified among her citizens as a painter." Already in this letter Morse was thinking of himself as more than a painter, and of New York as more than a city. He saw New York as a developing metropolis; he knew that leadership of the New York artistic community would translate into national leadership. The letter continued:

> Colonel Trumbull is growing old . . . and there is no artist of education sufficiently prominent to take his place as President of the Academy of Arts. By becoming known to the New York public, and exerting my talents to discover the best methods of promoting the arts, and writing about them, I may be promoted to his place, where I could have a better opportunity of doing something for the Arts in our Country. . . . [2]

Further insight into his sense of the metropolitan as opposed to the merely urban character of New York and its institutions can be gleaned from another letter. Dated Florence, 1831, it was written after Morse had served five years as president of the National Academy of Design. "All of our plans," he wrote, "must be large and liberal, worthy of the great capital of our great and envied country."

> I shall not feel satisfied with a local institution; it must be the great institution of the United States, around which all true artists will rally. . . . Artists must have no local prejudices in favor of particularities. New York is the capital of our country and here artists should have their rallying point.[3]

There seemed to be great promise in New York, and there was. In the short run, however, both Morse and Bryant had doubts. Bryant bitterly complained in 1827, after the failure of the *New York Review and Atheneum Magazine*, which he edited: "nobody cares anything for literature." The man of genius is not the writer or artist but rather "the man who has made himself rich."[4] After less than a year in New York, Morse, who was finding little work, wrote to his wife that he and his fellow artists agreed that "there is little doing in New York. This city seems given wholly to commerce. Everyman is driving at one object, the *making of money*, not the spending of it." And a few years later, writing to the novelist James Fenimore Cooper, Morse made almost the same point: "there is nothing new in New York; everybody is driving after money as usual."[5] While Morse and Bryant were making a familiar complaint, Morse, at least, was making it from a somewhat new position, from an emerging understanding of the artist and writer familiar to us but unknown to the eighteenth century.

ECHOES AND PREMONITIONS

The life of Samuel Finley Breese Morse in New York City represents at once the most substantial accomplishment of patrician civic culture and its rejection. A representative of civic culture as an inventor and scientist, he anticipated later literary and academic cultures as a painter and ideologist for the arts in America.

Morse lived through the juncture that separates the cultural history of the eighteenth century from that of the nineteenth. In the eighteenth century, as we have seen, culture did not imply some special realm. Culture and society were not sharply distinguished. In the nineteenth century and in our own they have been torn asunder. Indeed, contention and conflict came to define their relations—art and culture became oppositional to society.

In the eighteenth century it was still difficult to distinguish conceptually the artist and artisan. By the early nineteenth century inclusive understandings of culture, arts, artisans began to break down. The comprehensive "useful arts" became divided into the "mechanical arts" and "Art." Poetry, music, and the visual arts were regrouped as the "fine arts." All of this is associated, as Paul O. Kristeller has observed, with changes in the support of the arts, and it is related to a new secularism. Traditional patrons, committed to classical standards, sought mimesis. God created, while man imitated. As God receded to the background, art assumed a higher office. It became a higher, a sacred realm, and it increasingly assumed God's prerogative. Creative genius was valued more highly than mimetic skill. The new anonymous, bourgeois public, supporting art through a market mechanism, looked for invention, creativity. The new cult of creativity shattered, by necessity, established discourse, with its universal or even common standards. The patron's power eroded; a public replaced the audience, but this new public existed, as T. J. Clark has so insightfully grasped, only in the mind of the artist. It could not be identified in society. While the artist is burdened with the idea of the omnipresent public, he need not listen to its criticism. He is above the language of public culture.[6] He recognizes only his own self-criticism and that of his circle of peers, that is to say, a coterie of like minds. He will not accept the market's judgments or that of the undifferentiated public.

With the collapse of the traditional pattern of patrician patronage and its replacement with the market, the critic emerged in literary culture. But the critic, one must understand, represents the coterie of the artist, not the public. And the "right of aesthetic pronouncement," as sociologist Levin Schücking has put it, "is regarded as withdrawn from the public."[7] This new aspiration toward the autonomy of literary and artistic work is apparent, as we shall see, in the ideology of the New York artistic community promoted by Morse as president of the National Academy of Design, and it cuts at the core of any notion of civic culture.

The echoes of the past and the premonitions of the future of intellectual life in New York City are particularly clear in the career of Morse. It is possible to give an account of Morse's New York experience that exemplifies the highest ideals of patrician civic culture. But it is equally easy to show him as the first American intellectual to separate art and intellect from the general culture. It is not so much a matter of choosing between these two partial portraits, but rather to recognize that in Morse one captures a decisive moment in the reconfiguration of intellectual culture in New York City.

When Morse arrived in New York, he brought with him substantial social assets.[8] Born into the American gentry, he was the son of Jedidiah Morse of Connecticut, one of New England's most notable ministers and the author of the widely admired *American Geography* (1789). Young Finley (as his family called him) arrived in New York City at the age of thirty-two, coming with the advantages of a liberal education at Yale and artistic training at the Royal Academy in London. Class, education, travel, and his literary inclinations gave him a place among the patrician cultural elite of the city. Indeed, he rather quickly became one of the most prominent of the city's gentlemen of culture. He was from the beginning of his residence in New York engaged in the elite social life of the city; he was no isolated artist. A widower young, in 1825, Morse nonetheless participated fully in the social life of the city, and even as a single man entertained regularly at his house on Canal Street in the late 1820s.

Morse early formed friendships with James Fenimore Cooper, William Cullen Bryant, and Gulian Verplanck, the most notable writers living in the city in the 1820s, and he was invited to join their lunch club, called Bread and Cheese.* Bread and Cheese, when Morse joined it, was a fairly small group of writers, artists, lawyers, merchants, and doctors, and it was a self-consciously exclusive group. Morse rejoiced over his membership, pointing out to his parents that "many respectable literary charac-

---

* Washington Irving was in Europe from 1815 to 1832. The club's name derived from its balloting system for the election of new members: a bit of bread favored election, a piece of cheese denied membership.

ters of the city have been denied admittance."[9] Morse and Bryant were also leaders of a circle of artists and writers who met regularly as the Sketch Club, which in 1846 was expanded and reorganized to become the Century Club. Later Morse was one of the twelve members of the quite patrician Club of Gentlemen or, as it was usually denominated, simply the Club.[10]

In New York of the 1820s and early 1830s, then, Morse (as well as other artists and writers) had both formal and informal contact with the merchant elite of the city who played the indispensable role of patrons. Some of these men, unlike their post–Civil War counterparts, were acknowledged for their taste and their support of American artists. Luman Reed, Jonathan Sturges, and Philip Hone, for example, were welcomed into the organizations formed by and for artists. Patronage in America has been shamefully little studied—presumably on the assumption that there was none. But certain antebellum New York merchants stand out as supporters of American artists. One thinks of *Kindred Spirits* (1849), Asher Durand's striking celebration of the friendship of the poet William Cullen Bryant and the painter Thomas Cole that now hangs on the third floor of the New York Public Library, just outside the doorway of the main catalogue and reading rooms. It was commissioned after Cole's death by Jonathan Sturges, a friend of Durand, Cole, and Bryant. Or consider Luman Reed, the business partner of Sturges, who commissioned Cole's most famous series of paintings, the allegorical "Course of Empire" (1836), which now hangs in the New-York Historical Society. We depend, in fact, on Cole's explanation of his intentions in his correspondence with Reed in order to interpret these panels.[11]

To return to Morse, we should note that Morse's extended trip to France (where he painted his famous "Gallery of the Louvre") and Italy from 1829 to 1832 was financed by twenty-one of the city's leading merchants and professional men. They commissioned Morse (paying in advance) either to copy masters or, much better and in fact more common, to dispose of the commission as Morse saw fit. Philip Hone, retired merchant and former mayor, contributed a hundred dollars "to be disposed of in such way as may be most agreeable to Mr. Morse." He specified only that the picture be no larger than twenty-five by thirty inches. Together, the commissions of the merchants provided Morse with an advance of three thousand dollars.[12] Earlier, the city's elite, under the vehicle of municipal patronage, provided Morse with the opportunity to execute his best painting, the portrait of Lafayette (1825–26) that they commissioned for the City Hall.

Morse's most important association with the city's patrician culture, however, came through the New York Atheneum. The Atheneum, as we have seen, represented a brief episode in the history of New York's patrician culture. But it was vitally important to Morse, who was deeply involved with it. (What we know of the Atheneum comes from the minutes deposited at the New-York Historical Society, written in the fine hand of its secretary, Samuel F. B. Morse.) The first series of lectures at the Atheneum in 1826 included one on the arts by Morse and one on poetry by William Cullen Bryant, then editor of the *New York Review and Atheneum Magazine,* which was, in the language of today's cultural organizations, the Atheneum's publication program.[13] As befitted the aims of the sponsoring organization, Morse prepared his lectures for a general audience, as opposed to a professional audience of fellow artists.[14]

Professor James Freeman Dana of Columbia College and his wife attended Morse's course of lectures. Morse, in turn, listened to Dana's popular lectures on electromagnetism delivered at the Atheneum early in 1827. Although Morse had been well educated at Yale—and had attended the scientific lectures of Professor Benjamin Silliman there—it was at Dana's lectures that Morse acquired the scientific base for his later experiments in telegraphy.*[15]

This is not the place to go into the exceedingly complex history of the invention of the telegraph. Our concern here is only to show that the stimulus and much of the technical information for its development came from the institutions of New York's civic culture.[16] The experiments themselves were carried out in Morse's rooms at the newly founded University of the City of New York, where Morse had been appointed to the nation's first professorship in the history and literature of the arts of design. His colleague and collaborator there, Leonard Gale, as well as Alfred Vail, a recent graduate of the university who became Morse's partner, both had been members of the New York Mechanics Institution.

Morse the inventor worked in and depended upon a pattern of civic culture that insisted that the arts and sciences were part of a single, general discourse that comprehended the common life of the city. The intellectual culture that nourished his creativity was in no sense separated from the commerce or common culture of New York City. Learning was not—as it was to become—a series of closed and mutually exclusive languages, motives, and meanings. Nor did science or its pursuit have any special moral superiority or significance for Morse.[17] Science was for him utilitarian, as it had been for Benjamin Franklin a generation (or two)

---

* Morse, incidentally, was not the only person later involved with the invention of the telegraph who attended. Unknown to each other, not only Morse, but Leonard Gale, later one of Morse's assistants, and Joseph Henry, the nineteenth century's most notable American-educated physicist, were among Dana's auditors. Dana died tragically young, on April 14, 1827; otherwise he might have had a continuing influence in the development of the telegraph.

earlier, and as it had been for his fellow New York painter and inventor Robert Fulton. Morse did not insist upon the purity or autonomy of science. Indeed, neither Morse nor anyone else could clearly distinguish his scientific from his business success.

One must resist the temptation to say: Of course. That is the way science (as opposed to art) is. But it is not so simple. By the time Morse in 1844 sent his famous message from Washington to Alfred Vail in Baltimore ("What hath God wrought?"), science had changed. By then the word "scientist" had been coined and come into use in England and America. Science was developing its own esoteric language and a separate system of publication.[18] Empiricism was being replaced by theory, amateurs by professionals. The ideology of professionalism in science was beginning to insist upon the purity and moral aura of scientific inquiry in an effort to separate science from the common life and commercial values of the city. Men like Morse would drop by the wayside, as would so notable a New York scientific figure as Morse's friend James Renwick, the primary science professor at Columbia for most of the first half of the nineteenth century. As the professionalizing impulse of American scientists gathered momentum at midcentury, as the emphasis on scientific theory discredited a simple empiricism and utilitarianism, Renwick became vulnerable. And he was ousted from his Columbia chair in 1853.[19]

A brief comparison with Joseph Henry, only six years younger than Morse, suggests something of the shift in American intellectual life that we are discussing. Henry's experiments in electromagnetism, experiments that put him into an international race for priority with James Forbes of Edinburgh and Michael Faraday in Manchester, were, as Morse acknowledged, essential to Morse's achievement. Henry also provided direct assistance.* But they represented profoundly different versions of science. Henry, in contrast to Morse, was anxious to remove science from the general public. He ridiculed "ingenious but illiterate mechanics,"[20] and he insisted that American scientific institutions be exclusive rather than inclusive in their membership, allowing only professionals. Discussing the establishment of an American equivalent to the British Association for the Advancement of Science, Henry wrote to a fellow scientist that "a promiscuous assembly of those who call themselves men of science in this country would end only in our disgrace."[21] He had a strong fear that without quite restrictive definitions of science and scientists the coun-

* Henry and Morse were later estranged. One could argue that the basis of their future rift had to do, at least in part, with the differences being outlined here, but the precipitating incident was a published account of the invention of the telegraph by Morse's partner Alfred Vail which omitted mention of Henry. Instead of a quick apology, Morse hesitated and then defended his hesitation with an attack on Henry, and Henry returned the compliment.

try would be "over-run . . . with charlatanism."[22] If Morse could not distinguish between science and the general culture, if he could not distinguish between himself as a scientist and as a businessman, Henry could. Over the course of his thirty-two years as head of the Smithsonian Institution (1846–78), Henry devoted himself to the legitimation of the purity and autonomy of science, to the creation of non-localized professional scientific institutions and identities.[23]

The irony is that the first argument for this sort of withdrawal from public culture was made not for science but for art.* And the most comprehensive and important statement for the autonomy of art was made by Samuel F. B. Morse, in his address to the public as the first president of the National Academy of Design. The definition of the relation of art to society that Morse articulated is best understood in the context of the history and failure of the patrician American Academy of Fine Arts and the founding of the National Academy of Design by a group of New York artists.

The American Academy of Fine Arts, founded in New York in 1801, was revitalized and reorganized in 1816, when De Witt Clinton became its president and it joined with several other institutions to form the New York Institution of Learned and Scientific Establishments. The patrician elite who established these organizations sought to improve the general level of taste and culture in the city. Art for them was not a special realm of sensibility and insight, so their support was not sharply distinguished from other efforts in human and civic improvement. There were no presumed conflicts between artistic values and those of ordinary life in the city—neither business values nor political ones. Art, commerce, power were part of a single moral equation. De Witt Clinton, after all, a lawyer by training and a politician by instinct, could with perfect plausibility be at once mayor (later governor), president of the American Academy of Fine Arts, president of the Literary and Philosophical Society, and vice-president of the New-York Historical Society.

What Morse would argue is that art or Culture, with a capital C, is not of a piece with ordinary life. Whatever a general elite's right to social and political leadership, to judge questions of politics, business, or social good, they had no legitimacy as promoters or judges of art.

The first sign of this new attitude came in 1818, in an article in the *National Advocate*, published by Mordecai M. Noah, later a famous New York Jacksonian. The paper was anti-Clinton in politics, and the article

---

* In this connection, it is worth noting that the professionalized, specialized, and academic model of the German university, imported in part into the United States in the late nineteenth century, began not, as is commonly assumed, with the sciences, but rather in the humanities, with classical philology.[24]

is clearly politically motivated. Its authorship is undetermined; it may
have been Noah or it may have been Clinton's bitter political enemy of
these years, Gulian Verplanck. But however unclear the authorship, the
point of the article is clear. It attacked the interlocking directorate that
dominated the city's cultural life. "One set of men govern and direct all
the literary and scientific institutions in this city." For some of these
institutions, the writer allowed, this was acceptable, but not in respect to
the Academy of Fine Arts. "The gentlemen who are directors of the
academy are profound physicians, able lawyers, men of science and talents, but are very poor judges of the value or merit of pictures, and,
consequently, are not well calculated to advance the character of the Arts
in this City." How can a physician presume to judge pictures? Such judgments "are the peculiar duties incumbent on artists."[25]

We must understand the precise character of the American Academy
of Fine Arts. It was not an association of artists. Its aim was not the
training of artists, but the promotion of an appreciation of the arts in
New York, with the clear intention of raising the prestige of the city. It
was organized as a joint-stock company, with membership—and the right
to vote—purchasable for twenty-five dollars. While this was a reasonable
fee for wealthy merchants and professional men, it was beyond the reach
of artists. When it was reorganized in 1816, artists were given twenty
places in the academy, but still no votes. Particularly galling was the
language of the regulations for exhibits, which "invited" stockholders to
hang pictures while "permitting" only the "most distinguished artists" to
do so.[26]

The revolt of the developing professional community of artists came
when John Trumbull, an old and established artist who succeeded Clinton as president of the academy, denied young artists access to the academy, where they wished to practice their drawing. Instead he gave them
a lecture about the "gentlemen" who, as stockholders, owned the pictures
and casts. This little talk at the door of the academy concluded with
Trumbull's homily: "They [the artists] must remember that beggars are
not to be choosers." William Dunlap, a close friend of Morse and one of
the artists shut out that morning, remarks of this statement in his *History
of the Rise and Progress of the Arts of Design in the United States:* "We may
consider this as the condemnatory sentence of the American Academy of
Fine Arts."[27]

Late in 1825, Morse and several other artists of his generation formed
the New York Drawing Association. Continued hostility by Trumbull,
combined with a rapidly developing sense of professional ambition and
consciousness among the dissidents, led in the next year to the transformation of the Drawing Association into the National Academy of

Design, with Morse as president, an office he held for twenty years.* If the American Academy of Arts had little concern with the practicing artist, seeking, in Dunlap's words, to raise "the character of their countrymen, by increasing their knowledge and taste," the National Academy represented and sought to advance the development of artists.[28] While the earlier academy spoke of the advancement of the arts in America, the newer one insisted that such was only half the task. The preface of the catalogue for the first exhibition of the National Academy made this point. The academicians, one reads, "have no object in view but the advancement of the Arts *and the benefit of the artists.*"[29] Creation, not simply appreciation, concerned the National Academy of Design.

The aims of the National Academy of Design were reflected in its structure of governance. Instead of investing suffrage in a class of gentlemen shareholders, the National Academy was controlled strictly by professional artists. A complex voting system devised by Morse ensured that professional artists, not amateurs, would constitute the academy. Each member of the New York community of artists, broadly defined to include professionals, amateurs, and students, was asked to submit a ballot with the names of fifteen persons he considered to be professional artists of the highest distinction. The top fifteen so named then elected another fifteen, and these thirty professionals constituted a self-perpetuating academy.[30]

In order to explain and justify such self-governance, Morse delivered and published a lecture on the history of academies. They went back, he insisted, to 1345, in Venice. But it was the academy established in sixteenth-century Florence by Vasari for the mutual education of artists that most appealed to Morse. In thus turning to the Italian Renaissance academies as his model, Morse was taking part in a broader contemporary movement in Europe, where younger artists were rebelling against hierarchical, mechanical state academies and returning to the earlier Italian pattern of artistic association.[31] Morse explained to New Yorkers that the essentials of the earlier academies were four in number. First, artists founded and governed them. Second, they had schools for students. Third, they offered premiums for excellence. And, finally, they organized exhibitions of the work of living artists.

Although the structure and programs of the National Academy of Design, especially when contrasted with the American Academy of Fine Arts, suggest the direction of Morse's thought, Morse, unlike most artists, was comfortable with words—and he gave precise verbal expression to

---

* It might be noted that this revolt is almost exactly contemporary with the somewhat more ambiguous but related contretemps already discussed regarding the election of De Witt Clinton to the Lyceum of Natural History.

his conception of the proper organization of the artistic enterprise. He once observed in a letter to James Fenimore Cooper that he had "quite as much" to do with his "pen for the arts as the pencil." If his writings could "so enlighten the public mind as to make the way easier for those that come after me," he would thereby do far more than he could by "painting pictures which might be appreciated one hundred years after I am gone."[32] Certainly, his role in publicly shaping the ideology of the National Academy of Design justified this reflection.

Morse addressed the public in characteristically felicitous prose: "The National Academy of the Arts of Design is founded on the commonsense principle, that every profession in a society knows what measures are necessary for its own improvement."[33] However easy it reads to our eyes, or sounds to our ears, this is a momentous statement. It rejects the past and establishes a whole new premise for art and intellect in New York.*

Morse denies the earlier patrician assumption that art is of a piece with politics, business, and other affairs of ordinary life. Equally important, Morse is protecting the artistic enterprise from the emerging egalitarianism in intellectual and political life that was already as he spoke being identified as Jacksonian democracy. When Alexis de Tocqueville visited the United States in 1831, he took note of the egalitarian impulse in American intellectual life: "Everyone . . . attempts to be his own sufficient guide and makes it his boast to form his own opinions on all subjects."[35]

The impulse toward the separation of literary and artistic discourse from the common life and language of democratic society was expressed with force and clarity by James Fenimore Cooper, one of Morse's closest friends. In a letter to a mutual friend, the sculptor Horatio Greenough, Cooper lamented: "You are in a country in which every man swaggers and talks; knowledge or no knowledge; brains or no brains; taste or no taste. They are all ex nato connoisseurs . . . and everyman's equal." Greenough must, Cooper warned, expect his art and ideas to be "estimated by the same rules, as they estimate pork, rum, cotton."[36] Cooper, who in Paris with Morse had come to appreciate the status of the European writer and artist, regretted that in America the writer was expected to be one of the democratic multitude. In Europe a known writer "enjoys

---

* Two letters printed in the *New York Evening Post* in 1827 defended Morse's position in general terms. At the time they were thought by many to be written by Morse, but the more likely author is William Cullen Bryant, Morse's friend and professor of mythology at the National Academy of Design. Bryant was then assistant editor of the *Evening Post* and soon to become editor (1829). "Just as far as the arts are of public importance—just so far as it is proper that their direction should be under the control of those who best understand them. Courts of Justice are not placed under the control of physicians; medical degrees are not conferred by lawyers, nor the chamber of Commerce composed of artists. Why, then, should the concerns of the Artists be thought in better hands than in their own."[34]

immense advantages," but, as he explained it to fellow writer William Gilmore Simms of Charleston, the United States "is not yet sufficiently civilized for this." [37]

Morse offered artists and writers a way of surviving in a democratic and commercial society. Using an argument to which we now give the names "peer review" and "meritocracy," he limited the play of market values in estimating artistic worth. The same device at once freed artists from the paternalism of the patrician elite, while simultaneously avoiding a fall into the clutches of an aggressive democracy bent on denying the existence of privilege or distinction, whether economic or intellectual. Morse insisted, especially in a commercial society, upon the autonomy of artistic discourse. It is not a part of the same moral equation as other aspects of social life; no longer a contribution to the general culture, the arts thus become a culture in themselves, a culture that belongs to a higher and better realm. The artist, in this clearly romantic definition, must be free of public opinion and free to express inner artistic genius. Morse thus took a large step toward modernity, toward the day when artistic and other professional creation would be expected to express some inward (or specially trained) capacity independent of the general community. His defense of the artist's prerogatives pointed toward the day when the slogan "art for art's sake" would, ironically, be difficult to distinguish from the ideology of an interest group, similar to the insistence on self-regulation by the medical profession or multinational corporations.

GENTRY

When James Fenimore Cooper died in 1851, the leading citizens of New York City organized a memorial meeting. Washington Irving served as chairman of the committee, and William Cullen Bryant delivered the eulogy. Of this triptych of writers who stood before the world as the first generation of New York's literary culture, Cooper was the first to die. In their youth these three, along with a supporting cast of lesser writers, most notably Fitz-Greene Halleck, Gulian Verplanck, James Kirke Paulding, Joseph Rodman Drake, and Robert Sands, exemplified the literary culture of a soon-to-be-challenged urban gentry.

All these writers, save Cooper, were lawyers or had received legal training, and Cooper himself was an amateur lawyer who personally litigated his many libel suits. The law, as Robert A. Ferguson has recently argued, provided a social foundation and an intellectual orientation for much early-nineteenth-century literary culture. The legal profession, at least at its best, as represented by New York's Chancellor James Kent, sustained a commitment to literary breadth and elegance, to classical forms, and to civic republicanism. With the culture of the law and that of literature thus nearly fused, literature inherited the law's commitment to neoclassical order and responsibility in letters and in life. It was against this profoundly conservative practice of letters, a literary practice that would by midcentury lose touch with the dynamics and the very principles of American social experience, that the generation of Whitman and Melville rebelled. Similarly, as legal practice became more technical, instrumental, and case-specific, law and letters diverged, becoming distinct, both socially and intellectually. New literary commitments, pressed on writers by the influence of romanticism and the ideal of democracy, further subverted the early-nineteenth-century legal-literary culture of the gentry.[38]

Knickerbocker writing, which dates, perhaps, from the publication of the first number of the *Salmagundi* papers in 1807, has been characterized as "town literature."[39] That is to say, much of its interest depended upon the social world out of which it emerged and to which it directed itself. The natural habitat of the Knickerbocker writer was the world of gay conversation in clubs, the relaxed style of sociability in city taverns, particularly the Shakespeare Tavern at Fulton and Nassau streets, and the round of dinners and parties of New York society, where, in the words of Washington Irving's nephew and first biographer, "the literati and men of wit and intellect entered" in a way that was unlikely fifty, even twenty, years later.[40] Writing came without angst; authorship rested lightly on the shoulders of the young gentry who sought to amuse themselves as much as their readers. One might even say that much of this writing was a translation of conversation into print. As in conversation in society, readers and writers were assumed to belong to the same homogeneous upper class. The Knickerbockers were gentlemen who wrote, not writers. One is reminded of the story of Voltaire's visit to the famous English dramatist William Congreve. When he indicated that Congreve's fame as a writer inspired his visit, Congreve astonished Voltaire by insisting that he was not primarily an author but a gentleman.

The pattern of literary life Knickerbocker New York embraced owed much to the ways of the literary gentlemen of Edinburgh who belonged to the circle of Walter Scott and Francis Jeffrey, editor of the *Edinburgh Review*, founded in 1802. In Edinburgh, as in New York, literary life was managed by a group of gentlemen, mostly trained in the law, who were deeply involved in a male social world of urban clubs, taverns, and dinners. Many of the Knickerbockers were personally acquainted with their Edinburgh counterparts. Washington Irving, in particular, was a personal protégé of Scott and a critical favorite of Jeffrey. Indeed, Jeffrey, a critic who began a review of Wordsworth's *Excursion* with the now notorious words "this will not do," honored Irving for the classicism of his style and the sentimentality of his sensibility. Irving, he claimed, was one of the three living writers he approved.[41] And Cooper, of course, was often called the American Scott.

Washington Irving (born 1783), like Bryant, Verplanck, and Sands, was trained in the law but declined to pursue it as a profession. Irving preferred society, writing, and travel. Fortunately for him, his brothers, Peter and William, recognized and appreciated his talents and desires. They gave him a one-fifth share of their joint business on the expectation that he would not assume an active role. Rather, he was expected "to devote himself to literature."[42] Irving's career as a writer was launched under these generous circumstances, and the arrangement lasted until 1818, when the family business went into bankruptcy. Thereafter Irving supported himself with government offices in the diplomatic corps and by the earnings of his pen, which have been estimated at $200,000. Yet, no matter how much Irving earned as an author, it is hard to think of him as a professional writer. He identified with his class rather than his profession. He was always a gentleman who wrote; after 1832, when he established himself at Sunnyside Manor near Tarrytown, thirty miles up the Hudson, he wrote as a country squire.

The success of Irving's *Salmagundi* papers (written in collaboration with his brother William and James Kirke Paulding) and his *Knickerbocker's History of New York* reflected the city's literary culture and provided a model for it. The contrast with Boston is striking. Instead of ethics, philosophy, and theology—instead of thought—we have light, sophisticated wit, satire, and burlesque. As Irving and Paulding wrote in the first number of *Salmagundi*, "we are laughing philosophers, and clearly of the opinion, that wisdom, true wisdom, is a plump, jolly dame." Considering neither money nor fame, they went on, "we write for no other earthly purpose but to please ourselves." Irving accurately characterized his avocation in a letter to Henry Brevoort, a cultivated New York lawyer and his closest friend. "I have attempted no lofty theme," he acknowledged, "nor sought to look wise and learned." His intention had been to address himself "to the feeling and fancy of the reader, more than to his judgment; my writings, therefore may appear light and trifling in our country of philosophers and politicians."[43]

To Cooper, who, besides finding joy in constructing romances, sought to instruct his countrymen as a philosopher and political commentator, Irving's work did indeed have a certain insubstantiality. With a vigor of mind—and of body—alien to Irving, and a boldness bordering on the rawness of two later New York writers, Whitman and Melville, he was put off by Irving's polite, sophisticated style; there was something too soft, too detached, in his fellow author. Cooper missed evidence of a moral and political stance, and neither he nor anyone else could fail to recognize, though no one in New York publicly said it, that Irving barely confronted American society. In his writing style as in his residence, Irving was very little a New Yorker, even very little an American.[44]

The judgment of the modern Anglo-American critic Martin Green is harsh, but it is difficult to call it unjust. Irving, Green says, "showed how the American writer could be a national hero. But he showed even more vividly how he could also be an imaginative failure, an intellectual fraud." What Irving did was discover and offer to Americans a "formula that combined as much as possible of what was harmless in the new romanticism with an essentially conservative sensibility, and to serve up the result with such obtrusive grace and suavity that the American reader could feel culturally flattered."[45]

Both Cooper and Bryant were gentlemen as well. Cooper, as much as was possible at that time and place, was raised in an atmosphere of manorial life, while Bryant's family had been professionals for generations, ministers and then, in the three generations preceding him, physicians. In 1825, Bryant publicly argued that writers should not pursue literature as a trade. "Let the avocation of literature be a recreation of an opposite character of one's business or profession." Cooper, writing to William Dunlap a few years later, bemoaning the abuse American critics were directing toward him, insisted: "I cannot forget that I was born an American gentleman."[46]

With Cooper and Bryant, however, the writer's vision and experience are much broadened. For Irving politics meant patronage positions; Cooper and Bryant engaged the political life of the city and the nation. They articulated and debated political principles, and they addressed much of their writing to the formation of public opinion, Bryant as editor of the *Evening Post* and Cooper in several social novels as well as in books of direct political commentary, most notably *The American Democrat*. It might even be argued that Cooper more than anyone else of his generation struggled with the problem of democratic culture and the place of the intellectual in it. While he yearned to be free of its standards, his commitment to a writer's career tied him irrevocably to society. He was unwilling to withdraw entirely from society. He was the first New York intellectual to worry about what has become the vocation of the modern intellectual, the formation of public opinion. No American of his time pondered more often and more passionately the problem of public opinion in a democracy.[47]

Both Bryant and Cooper voted Democratic, but neither was a complete democrat. Cooper must be characterized as a conservative republican, while Bryant, though he was a supporter of the principles of the "radical" equal-rights wing of the Jacksonian democracy, had curious lacunae. His rather generous humanitarian concern never reached into the pathos of lower-class life in New York City. One looks in vain for discussion of the problems of poverty and immigration in his editorials. Evading confrontation with the city and the complexity of his relation to it, Bryant achieved success and serenity rather than insight, something costly to him as a poet and as an intellect.[48]

By 1868, when he assumed the presidency of the Century Association, Bryant was truly, in the words of Allan Nevins, the "most distinguished resident of the city, referred to and honored as its first citizen."[49] On public occasions, he stood consistently at the head. He was chosen to commemorate the lives of Thomas Cole, James Fenimore Cooper, Washington Irving, Gulian Verplanck, and Fitz-Greene Halleck, and he was the main speaker at the dedication of the Morse, Shakespeare, Scott, Goethe, and Mazzini monuments in Central Park. He was also chairman of the committee that organized the Metropolitan Museum of Art. Cooper, by contrast, gradually withdrew from the city. Although he had relished life in the city in the 1820s, when at the rather late age of thirty he embarked on a career of writing, he was never able to reestablish himself in the city after his long stay in Europe, particularly Paris, from 1826 to 1833. In 1836, he left the city, moving his family upstate to Otsego Hall, the remodeled old family manor. Though he continued to visit the city, Cooper had gone into a sort of internal exile. Only in the last years of his life, when he began to work on a history of the city, the surviving fragments of which reveal his affection for the place, did Cooper seem to be moving toward a reconciliation and reinvigoration of his associations with New York.[50]

When Cooper returned to New York in 1833, the association of literary gentlemen he had so enjoyed a decade before could not be reconstructed. Literary life after the fashion of Edinburgh had vanished. The newer pattern of literary culture he had seen and appreciated in Paris was not —or at least not yet—available for him in New York. He felt a great distance from the city that had once meant so much to him as a writer.

Soon after moving into the city from Westchester County in 1822, Cooper had organized the Bread and Cheese Club.[51] It was, we recall, a lunch group that, according to John W. Francis, litterateur and physician, included, besides himself, "a large number of the most conspicuous professional men, statesmen, lawyers, and physicians."[52] The club met weekly, at the Washington Hotel. Cooper later recalled his founding of the club as "one of the acts of my life . . . in which I take great pride." The writers Bryant, Halleck, Verplanck, and Sands were members, as were the artists Morse, Asher B. Durand, William Dunlap, John Wesley Jarvis, and

Thomas Cole. Science and scholarship were represented by several members of the Columbia faculty, while the legal profession contributed the very paragon of American scholarship, Chancellor James Kent.[53] Other lawyers included Henry Brevoort, Anthony Bleecker, John and William Duer, and Hugh Maxwell. Philip Hone, William Gracie, Isaac Hone, and Charles A. Davis represented the city's mercantile elite. Cooper's powerful personality dominated the group, and he relished the role. He had created in New York just the sort of comradeship among writers, artists, professionals, and merchants for which New Yorkers had long envied Edinburgh.

When Cooper left New York in June 1826 for a European residence of undetermined length, his absence proved fatal to the club. With his embracing energy, interests, and personal force gone, divisions within the group came rather quickly to the surface, and it broke up. The nature of these divisions can be grasped by taking note of the way in which the club life of the city's gentlemen was subsequently restructured. The collapse of Bread and Cheese seems to have stimulated Morse, Bryant, and other writers and artists to form the Sketch Club (1829).[54] Although generalizations here cannot be absolute, it appears that those members of Bread and Cheese who were artists and writers and Democratic in their political inclinations went into the Sketch Club, after the more conservative merchant and professional gentlemen formed the exclusive Literary Club (1827). Only three men—Morse, Halleck, and Verplanck—were able to bridge this division. The unifying elements that had comprised the Bread and Cheese Club were by now unstable, and one recognizes all the more both Cooper's achievement and the impact of his departure on the structure of intellectual life in New York.

In time, however, this schism would be partially repaired, and the symbol of that reconciliation—as well as of much else in this period of the city's history—was Gulian Verplanck. Artists and writers once again came together with statesmen, professionals, and merchants when the Sketch Club was expanded and reorganized into the Century Club in 1846, with Gulian Verplanck, who had been chairman of the organizing committee, as president, an office he held until 1864. But the Century did not really recover the qualities of Cooper's literary lunch, and surely it did not advance serious literary culture in New York City. It was, as it still is, a male club, a sanctuary for the city's artistic, political, and economic elite.

If ever an official head of an organization epitomized its character, then Verplanck of the Century Association was such an individual.[55] Gulian Crommelin Verplanck was born in New York City, on August 6, 1786.[56] He grew up in the shadow of Federal Hall, and as a small child probably watched George Washington's inauguration there. Wall Street was at that time the city's most fashionable residential thoroughfare, and Verplanck's family was one of the city's most notable. His affection for the city and his identification with it were almost boundless. The dedication page of one of his books reads:

To His Native City
To Which he is Bound by Every Tie
of
Affection and Gratitude

His fascination with and love for the history, the growth, the tumult of New York emerges in a series of essays published in collaboration with William Cullen Bryant in *The Talisman,* an annual which they edited with Robert Sands from 1828 to 1830. These essays, published under the general rubric "Reminiscences of New York," capture both his longing for the city into which he was born and his enthusiasm for the dynamism, energy, and transformation of New York under the impact of the opening of the Erie Canal.

As one might have expected of so New York and so Episcopalian a family as Verplanck's, Gulian was prepared for Columbia. He entered at the age of eleven, and he graduated in 1801, at the age of fourteen, the youngest person ever to get a degree from the college. Although he studied law with two of the most distinguished practitioners in the city (J. O. Hoffman and Edward Livingston), he never took a client after being admitted to the bar in 1807.

Politics and literature captured his imagination. Though born into a staunch Federalist family, Verplanck was himself to become something of a maverick. Entering politics as a Federalist, he soon established himself as one of the city's leading anti-Clintonians. He served in the New York State Assembly from 1820 to 1824, moving in the latter year to the U.S. House of Representatives. In Congress he established himself as an anti-tariff Jacksonian Democrat, but when he declined to support Jackson on the bank charter in 1832, he was denied renomination by the New York Democracy. Switching parties over the bank issue, he ran for mayor of the city as a Whig, losing by a narrow margin to Cornelius Lawrence. Later, from 1838 to 1841, he served in the New York State Senate. While in Congress, he was chairman of the Ways and Means Committee during the Nullification Crisis, and it was to his committee that Henry Clay submitted the bill that became the compromise Tariff of 1833. Verplanck was also instrumental in securing a revision of the copyright laws while in Congress, a service to the literary community for which he was thanked in the form of a public dinner in 1831, organized by the literati of New York.

To judge his political career is to judge much, but not all, of his life.

While it is an impressive career, it also shows Verplanck to be an anachronism. Although he had to work within the Jacksonian party system, which was the creation of a new breed of professional politicians who found in it a vehicle for their ambition, Verplanck remained an amateur, motivated, apparently, by an eighteenth-century sense of civic responsibility. The longer he lived, the more he seemed to belong to an earlier time. As Edward K. Spann observes, he "had adjusted well to a world that was passing away."[57] He lost the presidency of the Century Club in 1864 because the overwhelmingly Republican and pro-Union membership of the club was embarrassed by his Copperhead, pro-slavery, anti-Lincoln stance.

The range and number of Verplanck's activities in the city strain credibility. As Bryant put it in his eulogy, Verplanck "was connected in so many ways with our literature, our legislation, our jurisprudence, our public education, and public charities."[58] Although Verplanck apparently never donated funds to any cause or philanthropy, he gave his time and talents to a vast array of civic enterprises. For fifty years he served as a trustee of the New York Society Library, for twenty-six years a Trinity Church vestryman, for forty-four years he was a regent of the University of the State of New York and a trustee of Columbia College over the same period. He was a governor of the New York Hospital, a trustee of the Public School Society, and vice-president of the American Academy of Fine Arts and the New-York Historical Society. From 1846 to 1864 he was president of the Century Club, and from 1848 until his death in 1870 president of the Board of Emigration.

His writing ranged from political satire, mostly directed against De Witt Clinton, to a study of the *Evidences of Revealed Religion* (1824), one of the first American works influenced by Scottish commonsense philosophy; to a treatise, *The Doctrine of Contracts* (1825), where he argued against the notion of *caveat emptor* on the grounds that imposing greater moral responsibility on the seller would make a better society without significantly harming the economy. Much later, in 1847, he published *Shakespeare's Plays: With His Life*. He was best known for his public addresses, many of which were collected in his *Discourses and Addresses on Subjects of American History, Arts, and Literature* (1833).

Surely Henry W. Bellows captured an essential truth when he remarked—at the memorial proceedings for Verplanck held at the Century —that he "was a singular illustration of the union of the scholar and thinker with the man of affairs."[59] Many years before, in a commencement address at Union College in 1836, Verplanck himself had sketched out such a conception of the American scholar. This most notable of his addresses, "The Advantages and the Dangers of the American Scholar," was intended as a prescription for the country's educated youth, but it

was to assume by the time of Verplanck's death the character of a pre-
monitory autobiography. Distinguishing America from Europe, Verplanck declared not only that there was no learned class in America, no
class devoted exclusively to scholarship, but that this circumstance was a
cultural asset rather than a deficit. It meant that American men of learning ought to be and would be involved in all aspects of life. Intellectual
isolation allows the scholar's mind to "brood undisturbed over its own
little stock of favorite thoughts." Better, Verplanck argued, was the
stimulation of the tumult of American life, where the man of intellect is
"forced to sympathize with the living world around, to enter into the
concerns of others and of the public." Unless science, particularly the
science of politics, economics, and ethics, becomes "familiar and popular," then science "must remain a barren theory, dry and useless." Ad-
mitting that in a commercial society without a learned class "some
laborious arts of refinement requiring for their successful cultivation . . .
silent abstraction and unremitting, undivided labor for years" may be lost
"amid the strife and bustle," he avows his willingness, if necessary and
with regret, to lose them. "Such acquirements of accomplishments cannot
flourish here, because they require the devotion of the whole man to
their service, whilst the American man of letters is incessantly called off
from any single inquiry, and allured or compelled to try his ability in
every variety of human occupation." Though he warned at the end of his
address against the danger of falling into a "smattering superficiality in
consequence of that very universality of occupation and inquiry which
seems, in other respects, so propitious to the formation of a sound, comprehensive understanding," he seems in the years following the address
to have succumbed to precisely this danger.[60]

Edgar Allan Poe is not noted for the fairness of his appraisals of fellow
writers, but his sketch of Verplanck in "The Literati of New York City"
contained a brutal truth. "Mr. Verplanck," Poe wrote, "has acquired reputation—at least his literary reputation—less from what he has done than
from what he has given indication of ability to do." Then followed the
sort of thrust that made Poe so notorious, but which here is surely apt:
"many of his friends go so far as to accuse him of indolence." Indeed,
one finds in Verplanck more versatility than vitality. Bryant noted that
his friend preferred the convivial atmosphere of the club to the discipline
of the study, loathing even the physical act of writing, usually dictating at
the Century, with Bryant and others acting as his amanuenses. Almost
always working well within a framework of accepted, even dated, ideas,
Verplanck as a man of letters merely exploited them for society's and his
own pleasure. He was, as his modern biographer concludes, too involved
with "amusing trivia and sterile scholarship."[61]

There is so much that is attractive in the outward accomplishments and activities of Verplanck as a metropolitan intellect that one hesitates to acknowlege the truth of the inner void. It is with much the same emotion —and for the same reason—that one approaches the history of the institution that he founded, led, and epitomized, the Century Association.

The aim of the Century Association was to bring together in a single club distinguished men "belonging to all guilds. Artists, Literary Men, Scientists, Physicians, Officers of the Army and Navy, members of the Bench and Bar, Engineers, Clergymen, Representatives of the Press, Merchants and men of leisure." [62] This was to be accomplished within the framework of the first section of the club's constitution: "It shall be composed of authors, artists, and amateurs of Letters and the Fine Arts, residents of the city of New York and its vicinity: its objects the cultivation of a taste for Letters and the Arts and social enjoyment." When it was founded, more than a third of its members were artists and writers, in large part because twenty-three of the original forty-two members had been in its predecessor organization, the Sketch Club. [63] By the time Verplanck died, however, the complexion of the club had changed. The phrase "amateurs of Letters and the Fine Arts" evidently was generously applied and the aim of "social enjoyment" was especially emphasized. Of the 571 members in 1871, only 117 were classified as artists, authors, professors, or journalists, while there were 141 lawyers, 122 merchants, 58 men of leisure, 30 physicians, 26 bankers, and 12 railroad and insurance officials. [64]

Expressing a midcentury wish rather than reality, Henry W. Bellows, the prominent Unitarian minister and a member of the Century, compared the club to the French Academy. [65] While the Century may well have been comparable in its stuffiness and in the hierarchical and conservative social and cultural opinions of its members, it is ludicrous to class it in importance or intellectual seriousness with the French Academy. Rather, the Century was the headquarters for a clubbish, genteel culture, a culture identified in the 1840s and 1850s with the *Knickerbocker Magazine,* whose editor, Lewis Gaylord Clark, was a founder, and after the Civil War with the poets and litterateurs on whom both Whitman and George Santayana bestowed the epithet "genteel." [*][66] The tone established by Verplanck made the Century a comfortable place after the war for New York writers of the genteel tradition, such as Thomas Bailey Aldrich, Bayard Taylor, Richard Stoddard, and Edmund Clarence Stedman. [67] By any account, the writers outside of the Century were far more serious, far more important, than those who were in: Whit-

---

* Whitman: "Do you call those genteel little creatures American poets?"

man and Melville in the 1850s (and beyond) and Howells and Twain in the 1880s.*

The problem of the Century is captured in an anecdote dating from the removal of the club to its present location at 7 West Forty-third Street. When they moved into that magnificent Italian Renaissance building by McKim, Mead and White in 1891, admission fees and annual dues were substantially increased. Some worried that the cost of membership might work a hardship on artists and writers, thus excluding them. The Century's most effective response, articulated by Edmund Clarence Stedman, the Wall Street poet, was that any writer or artist fit to be in the Century had the necessary cash. In some awful sense Stedman was, I fear, correct.[68]

DEMOCRACY

The literary excitement of New York in the era of the raven and the whale, pursuing the quest for a national and democratic literature, was, as Perry Miller has so brilliantly and amusingly recounted, played out in the shadow of Lewis Gaylord Clark's *Knickerbocker Magazine,* which opposed nearly all of the developments we now appreciate. Taking its name from one of Washington Irving's most popular literary creations, the *Knickerbocker* (which published a series of Irving's Geoffrey Crayon sketches beginning in 1839) represented his sort of urbane wit, burlesque, elegance of style, and conservatism in matters social, religious, and political.[69]

The *Knickerbocker* presented itself as the ultimate in metropolitan sophistication. This was particularly true of the "Editor's Table" section at the back, which grew until it amounted to more than a third of each issue by the 1850s—much like *The New Yorker*'s "Talk of the Town" a century later. Readers were offered a supposed peek into the world of Clark and his gentleman authors. The magazine communicated an appreciation, even an exaggerated respect, for literature, but it emanated, more importantly, an unquenchable love of literary gossip. When Clark bought the magazine in 1834, a year after Samuel Langtree had founded it, there were only 500 subscribers. Within three years, the subscription list had grown to 5,000, and the *Knickerbocker* was, in Frank Luther Mott's phrase, at the "forefront" of American magazines.[70]

Reading through issue after issue today, one finds it hard to see why it was so popular. Unlike the *Democratic Review,* the *Broadway Journal,* or *Putnam's Monthly,* which we will also consider here, the *Knickerbocker* stimulates no excitement in the modern reader. While it published most of

---

* Howells finally became a member in 1897, when he was sixty years old, more interesting then for his reminiscences than for his current work.

the notable writers of the time, the magazine as a whole lacks something. One cannot help but concur in Poe's judgment that the *Knickerbocker* was without a "precise character," that it exhibited "no determinateness, no distinctiveness, no saliency or point."[71]

Neither Poe nor Melville belonged (nor would they ever belong) to the circle of Lewis Gaylord Clark. Rather, they adhered to another literary confederacy, which styled itself "Young America," and the differences between the groups are both striking and significant. The second group was devoted to literary nationalism and, for the most part, to the radical Locofoco wing of the Democratic Party. While the *Knickerbocker* circle stood for the ideal of the gentleman litterateur, Young America, by contrast, represented the first generation of American free intellectuals, men and women from a variety of social backgrounds who assumed a new and self-conscious social identity as writers, even as an intelligentsia.[72]

Although the origins of this movement, both social and intellectual, were diverse and complex, one can say that it first took form in 1835 or 1836 on Bleecker Street, in the home of Evert A. Duyckinck.[73] The Duyckincks were in no sense a patrician family, but they could trace their family line back to the founders of New Amsterdam, and Evert's generation was able to live off family money instead of working. Evert Duyckinck was born in New York in 1816, the son of a bookseller of the same name, a bookseller who, in fact, had given the Harper brothers their first order for printing a book. Evert attended Columbia College, graduating in 1835. He read for the law and was admitted to the bar in 1837, though he too never practiced. In 1838–39 he traveled in Europe, prizing the monuments of culture he found there, particularly in Paris. In 1840, after marrying, Duyckinck moved to 20 Clinton Place (today's East Eighth Street, near University Place), where he surrounded himself with literary friends and with his large library (estimated at half the size of the New York Society Library when it was donated to the Lenox Library upon his death in 1878). Although one does not sense in Duyckinck a person of great animation or vigor, he won the affection of men of greater vitality. Herman Melville, a neighbor, living a few blocks away on Fourth Avenue, found in him both a literary admirer and a fine drinking companion.[74]

One might not expect such a reclusive man, a man "not fond of crowds," to be a lover of the city, but Duyckinck was.[75] After Duyckinck's death, William A. Butler, a poet and the son of Benjamin Butler, Martin Van Buren's law partner, recalled that the older man "loved the city, its nearness to his quiet nook of study, the concourse of its streets, its public libraries and exhibitions of art, its repositories of books and engravings, its strong and busy life." Duyckinck willingly assumed several civic obligations, including service as a trustee of Columbia College and the New

York Society Library and as corresponding secretary of the New-York Historical Society. But the most remarkable evidence of the quality of his attachment to the city was his simple refusal to leave it, even during those sultry Augusts that take such a toll on the souls of New Yorkers. Butler, again, recalls that "he was never willingly away from it. A day's ramble in the country now and then sufficed for out-of-town enjoyments. . . . He kept to the city, and shunned a change even in mid-summer heats." Nathaniel Hawthorne, another of Duyckinck's circle, though at a New England distance, knew his correspondent well when he wrote Duyckinck a charming letter about the plans he and Melville had for "making an excursion" in the summer from the Berkshires to New York. "I have nearly come to the conclusion," Hawthorne observed, "that summer is the worst time to live in the country, it being so inhospitable to ramble about in the hot sun; whereas, in cities, there is always the shady side of the well-watered street, and awnings on the sunny side; not to speak of ice creams and all kind of iced liquors, which are greatly preferable to the luke-warm basin of a Brook, with its tadpoles and insects mingling in your draught."[76]

Young America began when Duyckinck and three fellow writers started to meet in his library to discuss the possibilities and future of American literature. Besides Duyckinck, there was Cornelius Mathews, a prominent writer of moderate talent and an ego of monumental proportions; William Alfred Jones, a fine critic who was excommunicated from the literary world in 1848 because of an impropriety with Duyckinck's niece and who then became, quietly and unobtrusively, the librarian of Columbia College; and, finally, Jedidiah Auld, a writer little known in his time and in ours. At this stage the circle was, as Auld described it, "the society of educated, well-bred and polished gentlemen."[77]

But the Tetracty's Club, as it was then called, aimed for much more: its members sought to make a case for literary nationalism, and they meant to make an impact in the public world. Duyckinck, their leader, took two routes to the public life of literary New York. He became an advisory editor to Charles Wiley and George Putnam, editing their "American Library" and their "Library of Choice Readings." With Mathews and Jones, he also established a literary review, *Arcturus*. In these two capacities—and in his later editorship of the *Literary World* (1847–53)—he did more, according to Perry Miller, "than any man in his time to get authors published and books reviewed; he was midwife to much of the best writing" and a good deal of competent writing.[78] Duyckinck, who like Cooper worried whether the American democracy would be civilized, did not follow Cooper into despair. He refused to believe that America would never get beyond "buying and selling, sowing and reaping." He looked forward to an appreciation in America of "that higher life which the poet teaches us to live."[79] *Arcturus* would, he hoped, do its part, preparing the new, mass public for literature in an age of equality, thus preparing the way for, perhaps even helping create, the great American poet.

Arcturus had a certain brilliance, but it shone briefly, running to only eighteen monthly issues between December 1840 and May 1842. Besides reviews, poetry, and fiction, this combination of a magazine and a review covered the fine arts and the theater in New York. In a rather general monthly feature, "The City Article," it surveyed life in the city, its politics, society, and culture. In the first number Cornelius Mathews called for a national literature, something done for generations, but this prophecy had a new, distinctively urban twist. While Mathews talked about the celebration of America's special relation to nature, the usual point of such calls, he saw American democracy as well in the sorts of material that would later come vividly into literary life with Whitman's poetic genius. In his preface to *The Politicians*, an unperformed play written at this time, Mathews expressed the ambition of the *Arcturus* program, directing the American writer to "the crowded life of cities, the customs, habitudes, and actions of men dwelling in contact, or falling off into peculiar and individual modes of conduct, amalgamated together into a close but motley society, with religions, trades, politics, professions, and pursuits, shooting athwart the whole live mass, and forming a web infinitely diversified."[80]

For all its virtues, however, *Arcturus* could not establish a compelling public presence. When Duyckinck sent a copy to George Templeton Strong, the broadly cultured lawyer politely acknowledged the gift. But in the privacy of his diary he raged:

> Literature pursued as an end, for its own sake and not for the truths of which it may be made the vehicle, is a worthless affair, and those who cultivate it for itself alone are always unreal, and unless they have ability and originality far above their fellows, are pretty sure to degenerate into puppyism and pedantry. Where such a litterateur is feeble himself and is dealing with and laboriously commenting on and striving to magnify the writings of people like himself, his productions are apt to be among the most pitiful specimens of human infatuation that are to be found anywhere. And Mr. Duyckinck and Mr. Mathews, criticizing and comparing and weighing with the nicest accuracy the relative merits and demerits of the small fry of authors, authors, foreign and domestic, exhibit and illustrate in their own persons the ridiculous side of humanity and with painful force and clearness.[81]

When *Arcturus* expired early in 1842, Duyckinck, Jones, and Mathews placed their hopes in a magazine for which they had already, upon occasion, written, the *United States Magazine and Democratic Review.* The *Democratic Review,* as it was usually known, aimed for the appeal of a magazine and the intellectual force of a review.* While it sought a wide audience, it proclaimed a belief that the public could reach "a few higher rungs" on the "intellectual ladder" than *Godey's* or *Graham's* required.[82] Duyckinck registered the ambition of the *Democratic Review* when he insisted, not entirely with justice, that "what are called lady's magazines, with plates of fashion, do not generally . . . enter into an estimate of the national literature."[83]

Unlike the rather precious *Arcturus,* the *Democratic Review,* with its close ties to the Van Burenite or reform wing of the Democratic Party and its vigorous political commentary, together with literature of real excellence, established itself solidly in the public culture of the city. George Templeton Strong and others among the city's Whig elite had to notice it, even if its doctrines gave them a jolt. Before long, in fact, the New York Whigs paid the *Democratic Review* the ultimate compliment; in 1845 they established their own conservative version, the *American Review: A Whig Journal of Politics, Literature, Art and Science.*

The editor and informing spirit of the *Democratic Review* was John L. O'Sullivan, an Irish-American political intellectual. His life has mostly been lost to history, save for that fame which rests upon his having coined a phrase—"Manifest Destiny"—that seemed to justify continental, even hemispheric, American imperialism. O'Sullivan, who was surely one of the most romantic figures in all of New York's intellectual history, deserves to be remembered. Julia Ward Howe, who as a young girl knew him as a visitor to her father's mansion on Bond Street, was much later "irresistibly reminded of O'Sullivan" in 1903 when she met W. B. Yeats, perhaps the most romantic writer in all of modern literature.[84]

Even a brief account of O'Sullivan's life strains the imagination.[85] His father, also John O'Sullivan, a sometime American consul "to the Barbary states," was in Gibraltar with his family in 1812. When a plague broke out, the kindly captain of a British man-of-war took the family on board, and the Irish-American John L. O'Sullivan was born on an enemy ship during the War of 1812. His father seems to have drifted from brief consular assignments in obscure places to stretches of varying lengths as a supercargo on merchant ships trading mostly in Latin America, to what seem surely to have been occasional lapses into piracy, carrying his family all over the world. Nonetheless, John seems to have spent enough time in England and France to receive a good preparation for college. He

---

* Its circulation during the period 1837–46 ran from about 3,500 in its best years to a low in 1845 of 2,000.

entered Columbia in 1828, graduating three years later. He then read law and established a law practice at 63 Cedar Street in New York City.

The years when he edited the *Democratic Review* and, during the same period, the *New York Morning News* were clearly the good years of his life. There were many obscure periods, and many bad years, when one wonders how he earned a living. In his few surviving letters, mostly to Duyckinck and to Samuel J. Tilden, a leading New York Democrat, one finds telling references to small loans negotiated and paid—loans for living, not for investment. After he lost control of the *Democratic Review* in 1846, he became increasingly erratic in his politics and his activities. Perhaps believing too much in his own rhetoric of Manifest Destiny, O'Sullivan became involved with various filibustering projects directed at Cuba and other parts of Latin America. Writing Tilden in 1850, he expressed his support for the "liberation of Cuba."[86] Apparently words proceeded to action. A year later he was arrested in the port of New York for having armed a vessel with the intention of attacking Cuba. Fortunately for him, the trial ended in a hung jury. Notwithstanding this scandal, Franklin Pierce in 1853 appointed O'Sullivan United States minister to Portugal, where he served for six years. With the outbreak of the Civil War, he stayed in Europe, astonishing his former colleagues on the *Democratic Review*, who had evolved into Free-Soil Democrats and then into Republicans, by speaking in favor of slavery and supporting the South. He returned to New York in the 1870s, a convinced spiritualist. There is no evidence that he went back to politics or renewed old political friendships. There is a story, however, repeated in several sources, that he reappeared briefly in public life on October 26, 1886, when the New York Democrats needed someone who could speak French at the dedication of the Statue of Liberty. But no evidence of his participation shows up in the newspaper accounts of that event, and he died in obscurity in 1893, the resident of a small hotel on East Eleventh Street that was demolished a few years later. He died without a will and without the assets that would recommend one.

O'Sullivan was a dreamer. "He was," according to Nathaniel Hawthorne's son, Julian, "always full of grand and world-embracing schemes, which seemed to him, and which he made to appear to others, vastly practicable and alluring, but which invariably miscarried by reason of some oversight which had escaped notice for the very reason that it was so fundamental a one."[87] Most of his schemes, needless to say, came to naught. But the *Democratic Review* flourished, becoming the most brilliant periodical of its time. Even a hundred years later, as Perry Miller remarked, "it is exciting to turn over its pages."[88]

The conjunction of needs and opportunities that went into the founding of the journal shows all the marks of O'Sullivan's remarkable talents and of the special way fortune entered his life. While working in Washington as a journalist, he dreamed of a magazine that would "strike the hitherto silent string of the democratic genius of the country." [89] His sister had just married Samuel D. Langtree, who had four years earlier founded the *Knickerbocker Magazine*. When O'Sullivan and Langtree approached Van Buren and his close associate Attorney General Benjamin F. Butler about their proposed *Democratic Review*, the idea was well received, and the two political leaders persuaded Andrew Jackson to become the first subscriber. Butler, himself a sometime poet who would in the next year found the law school at New York University, gave five hundred dollars to the venture and tried to find other Democratic money for it. [90] But what really made it all possible seems to have been a stroke of Irish luck: Back in 1823, O'Sullivan's father had been falsely prosecuted for piracy by the United States government. In 1836, Mary O'Sullivan, his widow, was awarded nearly $20,000. It seems to be without doubt this payment from the United States Treasury that made the *Democratic Review* happen. [91] It was established in Washington in 1837; three years later O'Sullivan moved it to New York.

O'Sullivan thought of the Democratic Party as both an instrument of democratic politics and an agent of cultural advance. Apparently many American writers agreed; the list of contributors to the *Democratic Review* is stunning. Hawthorne, a close friend of O'Sullivan, published more tales in the *Democratic Review* than in any other magazine, but there were many others: Bryant, Whittier, Lowell, Greenough, Thoreau, Longfellow, Simms, Bancroft, Brownson, Poe. The point is not simply the list of notables, for the *Knickerbocker* had a similar list. Rather it was that O'Sullivan managed to achieve in the pages of the *Democratic Review*, as William Alfred Jones put it, "a prevailing tone of sentiment and a unanimity of spirit between all the writers for it." [92]

The Democratic Party in the 1840s is not often seen as intellectually interesting. Knowing that Lincoln and the Civil War were looming on the horizon, historians have been more concerned with the rise of the Republican ideology. Yet the man who essentially wrote the first Republican platform in 1856, Parke Godwin, developed his ideas and style as a political writer while contributing to O'Sullivan's *Democratic Review*. [93] More broadly, recognizing that new technology and new business methods had made New York the center of American publishing and communication, O'Sullivan and his circle thought of the city as a base for national political and cultural influence. [94] What they established in the emerging metropolis during these years was the first formation of New York intellectuals as a group allied with the radical wing of the New York City and the national Democratic Party, which was, after all, dominated in their time by the President from New York, Martin Van Buren.

The election of 1840, so often spoken of as an election without principle, an election won with a campaign of log-cabin symbolism and hard-cider refreshments, looks different in the pages of the *Democratic Review*. Certainly, 1840 represents the maturation of many "modern" campaign techniques. But historians err badly in accounting for the record high turnout of voters of that year by making reference *only* to campaign hoopla. Principles were also at stake. When Edwin Forrest, the actor so popular with the workers of New York, whether on the stage of the Bowery Theater or on the Democratic hustings, delivered a Fourth of July oration in New York in 1838, he spoke of a democratic revolution, begun by Jefferson, advanced by Jackson, now in grave danger from forces of counterrevolution. In an article on "Mr. Forrest's Oration," the *Democratic Review* picked up the theme: "The money power is the militant power which is now waging war upon the democracy, with a fierceness of attack almost unprecedented in the annals of party strife."[95] The campaign of 1840 was hard fought, at least in part, because the ideological stakes were thought to be high.

The ideological patron saint of the *Democratic Review* and of radical or Locofoco Democracy in New York was William Leggett. Though he died in 1839, his *Political Writings,* edited by Theodore Sedgwick, Jr., were published in 1840, for use in the campaign. These essays, developing the Locofoco (Equal Rights Party) doctrine that equal rights and open competition were the standard for judging legislation, had first been published in Bryant's *Evening Post* in the early 1830s.* On Leggett's death in 1839, Bryant published a moving poem to his memory in the *Democratic Review,* testifying to his continuing influence in these lines:

> The words of fire, that from his pen
> Were flung upon the lucid page,
> Still move, still shake the hearts of men,
> Amid a cold and coward age.[96]

Without question, his legacy lived through the 1840s. Reviewing Leggett's political writings, the *Democratic Review* commended a "mind original and bold." Although the essays first appeared in the "daily print," readers were assured that they addressed fundamental, not "transient topics." Leggett raised "questions of the highest moment," questions "destined" to be discussed "for many years."[97]

* Even though Bryant found it necessary in 1836 to remove Leggett from the *Evening Post,* because Leggett's radicalism was costing him too many subscribers, the two men remained personally close.

Leggett was born in New York City in 1801.[98] He attended Georgetown College, but left when his father died. Then, in 1819, the whole family moved to Illinois, where Leggett wrote for the local Edwardsville press. He entered the Navy in 1823, but left soon, court-martialed, and in 1827 obtained a job with the *New York Mirror*, writing theater criticism. Soon he was writing about literature generally and other topics. Riding this success, he established *The Critic*, which he apparently wrote almost entirely by himself. It was a critical success, but a financial disaster. With the collapse of his own magazine, he got a job as Bryant's assistant on the *Evening Post* in 1829. At first he did no political writing, for he seems to have had few political interests. But from somewhere, if only from looking about the city, or perhaps from observing its radical workingmen's groups, he developed a profound awareness of the class disparities in the city. It seems likely that it was from Bryant and Sedgwick that he learned of the radical implications of Adam Smith's doctrine of competition. Stressing equal rights and the competitive side of Adam Smith's vision of capitalism, he examined all of the issues of the 1830s, from chartered privileges in banks to those of literary institutions, both of which he opposed because they represented privileged advantage for established incorporators. At the core of his politics was the assertion that "if we analyze the nature and essence of free governments, we shall find that they are more or less free in proportion to the absence of monopolies." [99]

Leggett was resolute in applying the logic of equal rights and competition, a trait that in the confused politics of the era brought him into a pattern of political conflicts that threatened to isolate him. Yet he remained a personal and moral inspiration to all progressives. Walt Whitman, an avid disciple, compared him with Thomas Jefferson. Even Whig publications, like the *Knickerbocker* and the *New York Review,* expressed great affection and respect for the person, if not his doctrine.

After leaving the *Evening Post,* he returned to writing fiction for leading magazines, and in 1836 he established another magazine, the *Plaindealer,* which had the same fate as his earlier *Critic.* For a few years he seems to have been in desperate straits, impoverished and seriously ill, living off the charity of his friend Edwin Forrest. Then in 1839, Martin Van Buren offered him a diplomatic post in Central America, where, it was hoped, the warm weather might improve his health. Unfortunately, before he could take up the post, he died at the age of thirty-eight.

Committed to Leggett's equal-rights doctrine, the *Democratic Review* proposed the logic that democracy would equalize wealth, that such redistribution would increase leisure and comfort among the masses, thus increasing their taste for "elevated and refined enjoyment." The final result would be a worthy democratic literature and art. "The Spirit of literature and the Spirit of Democracy are one." [100]

Neither wealth nor learning, they insisted, conferred any special rights. While learning tended to represent class, true intelligence, they maintained, was widely distributed in the masses. This mass intelligence may not be able to express itself well in language, but does so instead "primarily in action." And that action represented "God, acting through the People." Acknowledging—insisting—that even in a democracy men of learning are necessary, they declared that intellectuals must associate themselves with the masses. They must not presume a privileged place in society. The many were advised to "avail themselves of the services of educated individuals," but they must "not trust in them." [101]

For the writers in the *Democratic Review*, literature stood *above* all in the hierarchy of social values, but it was not *before* all. Material needs were primary; the reformer must not offer poetry to the indigent. William A. Jones made the point clearly: "To render a man physically comfortable, and to give him sufficient occupation, of whatever sort circumstances demand, is the primary duty of society; but, immediately next to that, to seek to elevate and refine, deepen and expand, the characters of all men. . . ." [102] Literature was not, however, a mere add-on. What Martin Duberman writes of James Russell Lowell, who was in New York in 1843 and closely associated with the group, is true of them all. They regarded literature as action, and the writer was a person who could shape perception, individual and political. [103] Yet after this is said, it was still assumed that political democracy would generate the social reform that would nourish democratic literature, rather than the other way around.

The mixture of politics and literature in the *Democratic Review* raises a question that bedeviled American intellectuals during the middle third of the twentieth century as it did in the nineteenth century: Should political standards be used to judge literature? In a famous and angry statement Longfellow claimed that this was happening in New York: "The *Locofocos*," he wrote, "are organizing a new politico-literary system. They shout Hosannas to every locofoco authorling, and speak coolly of, if they do not abuse, every other." Even Emerson, more sympathetic to radical Democracy, complained to Margaret Fuller, one of the New York group, that O'Sullivan sees "Washington" in everything; he is a "politico-literary and has too close an eye to immediate objects." [104] In fact, most of the writers of the age deserving praise were Democrats. Reading the reviews, one is surprised by how infrequently an outright political standard is used, though reminded again of how often petty personal animosities affect the judgments of New York intellectuals. [105] It is possible that political sympathy resulted in the overpraise of some authors, but I doubt that it caused the denial of recognition to anyone deserving it.*

The two volumes published in 1843 marked the high point of the *Democratic Review*. They included five stories by Hawthorne, as well as Horatio Greenough's two famous essays on American art and architecture. Other contributors included Orestes Brownson, John Greenleaf Whittier, and Parke Godwin. There was, in addition, a translation of Balzac, registering the growing French influence on New York's literary culture. But the most portentous essay was by William Alfred Jones, one of the most reliable New York critics. In "Poetry for the People," Jones gave vivid expression to Young America's dream of a "Homer of this Mass," who would become a "world-renowned bard." Echoing O'Sullivan's hope in founding the magazine, Jones declared that the "master passions of the age" must be captured in poetry, as earlier poetry gave expression to the character of the "patriarchal period" in which it was written. In keeping with democratic times the American Shakespeare, Jones explained, ought to deal with the "necessity and dignity of labor," celebrate the "native nobility of an honest and brave heart," and condemn "conventional distinctions of rank and wealth." Above all, this poet must affirm the "brotherhood and equality of man." [107]

Even as Jones wrote, larger developments in the nation were threatening the cohesion in political and literary culture that had made those issues of the *Democratic Review* of 1843 so remarkable. Within three years O'Sullivan lost control of the magazine. There were growing divisions within the Democratic Party, mostly over the emerging issue of slavery, which could not be banished from national politics, try as Democrats might to remove it. If the New York intellectuals wished to speak as a national intelligentsia, they must be vulnerable to the fault lines in the nation's politics and culture. Even in 1843, O'Sullivan realized that the magazine was in a "somewhat cramped financial condition." After trying without success to get more Democratic Party help, and after trying to get Duyckinck to buy in, again without success, O'Sullivan in 1846 was forced to sell the magazine to Thomas Prentice Kettell. [108] Under Kettell, there was no more Locofocoism and much less literature. Kettell's magazine supported expansion abroad and temporized on the explosive domestic issues; it represented the disastrous cautiousness of the Democratic Party in the 1850s. Parke Godwin, a regular contributor to the *Democratic Review*, suggested a new start in 1844, proposing a new magazine, *Young America*, which would be "in politics" and "in literature . . . bold and independent." [109] He was unable to follow through on

---

* Later, after 1852, well after O'Sullivan left the *Democratic Review*, George Sanders became editor and its character substantially changed. The tendency toward political judgments of literature then became distinctly more pronounced. [106]

this idea, though he would find a new opportunity in 1853, when as co-editor of *Putnam's Monthly* he took direct aim at the crumbling Democratic Party, their policy of expansion, and their solicitude toward slavery. O'Sullivan, too, hoped he might leap from the *Democratic Review* to a new, national political paper that would "represent Northern Democracy." The paper would, he wrote to Tilden, "be a terror to evil doers and a centre of the organization of the honest part of the Democracy of both Congress and the country."[110] But nothing came of this plan.

In the wake of the collapse of O'Sullivan's magazine, one might say his literary circle's dreams of a democratic culture were unrealistic, a sad example of easy rhetoric. But of course that would be a momentous error. All of this discussion of democracy, nationalism, and literature, mostly by men lost to historical memory, established the terms of intellectual life for Herman Melville and Walt Whitman, who were both democrats and Democrats. And in the 1850s, when the movement had passed, when no one was around to fully recognize it, they produced the works Jones and others had called for in the pages of the *Democratic Review*. While *Moby Dick* (1851) and *Leaves of Grass* (1855) were both the product of unique genius, they must forever be associated with the vision of literary democracy promoted by Young America and O'Sullivan's *Democratic Review*.

Melville and Whitman embraced the cultural program of Young America, as they self-consciously rejected the literary culture of the legal gentry. While the lawyers, including Melville's father-in-law, Lemuel Shaw, one of the leading jurists of the era, unsuccessfully tried to hold together a society careening toward civil war, Whitman and Melville rejected the authority and the literature of their predecessors.* Melville, ever ready to confront the darkness of the cosmos, refused to be responsible; he would be subversive in his incessant questioning. Whitman, no more amenable to the conventional ethic of responsibility, would address the problems of literature and social cohesion with a poetic imagination more complex than the neoclassical lawyers could even begin to grasp—insisting at once upon the full play of ego, of "personalism" and the claims of "ensemble." With their self-proclaimed barbarism and their deep commitments to literature, Melville and Whitman were America's most democratic writers.[111]

Herman Melville's literary apprenticeship was quite late and quite short. He was involved in the literary culture of New York for only ten years before he lapsed into silence, and all of this was after O'Sullivan

---

* One cannot but note, however, that in the 1860s Abraham Lincoln, the lawyer and President, in his two greatest speeches, the Gettysburg Address and his second Inaugural, renovated, enriched, and democratized the legal literary tradition before it was completely eclipsed.

had lost the *Democratic Review*. Yet the discussions of literature and democracy that were stimulated by Young America and swirled around
Duyckinck were decisively important to Melville's development. Melville
took his stand with New York, with the aspirations of the urban literary
culture we have been discussing. After hearing Emerson lecture in Boston in 1849, Melville, writing to Duyckinck, associated himself with the
messiness, the concreteness, even the barbaric honesty of life in New
York. Not for him Boston's high ethics and purified transcendentalism.
Melville, who had just discovered Shakespeare, was annoyed to see the
great bard in the hands of "snobs." "I would to God Shakespeare had
lived later, & promenaded in Broadway." While he did not necessarily
look forward to "the pleasure of leaving my card for him at the Astor" or
even making "merry with him over a bowl of Duyckinck punch," he
suggested that the experience of democracy and the city would have
nourished an even greater Shakespeare. "That muzzle which all men
wore on their soul in the Elizabethan day, might not have intercepted
Shakespeare's full articulations. For I hold it a verity, that even Shakespeare, was not a frank man to the uttermost." Melville meant to explain,
not condemn. "Who in this intolerant Universe is [frank], or can be?" But
in an affirmation of the promise of American democratic culture, Melville
concluded: "the Declaration of Independence makes a difference." [112]

Melville absorbed the ideals of intellectual life promoted by Young
America, but he differed from most of them in an important way. They
were so anxious to celebrate the literature of democracy that they forgot
what Melville did not: a metropolitan intellectual must be a critic as well
as a celebrant of American literature and democracy. Evert Duyckinck
well understood his friend Melville when he observed, in reviewing
Mardi, that the American writer must occasionally lift his voice, "boldly
to tell the truth to his country people." [113]

Emerson, in the famous letter of praise he sent to Whitman upon reading
Leaves of Grass, remarked that the work "must have had a long foreground somewhere." Emerson was correct. Whitman's preparation was
complex and irregular as well as long. If, as recent critics have shown,
the popular theater and the opera were fundamental to Whitman's aesthetics and to his development as a poet, his general understanding of
culture and democracy, which deeply influenced his poetry as well as his
critical commentary on literature and literary life, was the product of a
long preparation in the milieu of O'Sullivan's *Democratic Review.* [114]

When, at the age of twenty-two, Whitman moved for the first time
from Brooklyn to New York to begin his experience in the city's literary
culture, it was in the orbit of the *Democratic Review.* A notebook of the

time records: "went to New York in May 1841, and wrote for the *Democratic Review,* worked at printing business in *New World* office, boarded at Mrs. Chipman's." The *Democratic Review,* he recalled some years later, was then much praised, "especially by the young men." [115] He also published several Hawthorne-like tales in the *Democratic Review* over the name of Walter Whitman, and in retirement at Camden, New Jersey, Whitman recalled the magazine in his conversations with Horace Traubel: "The Democratic Review was quite famous in those days —started . . . by a young man—Sullivan, I think was his name. I knew him well—a handsome, generous fellow. He treated me well." [116]

During the 1840s, according to Whitman's biographer Gay Wilson Allen, he "was almost constantly influenced" by the literary group around the *Democratic Review.* He later "seldom mentioned" it, and "he failed to appreciate [it] because the influence extended over many years." [117] The first notebook out of which *Leaves of Grass* eventually emerged began with a statement about the democratic nature of America that rehearsed the language of O'Sullivan's *Democratic Review.** [118] But Whitman was not only aware of Young America's many discussions of literature and democracy; he somehow absorbed them and by some mysterious alchemy transmuted them into the great poem they dreamed about. The result not only surpassed the hopes of Young America; it reached toward the urban poem that was Charles Baudelaire's ambition. "Who among us," Baudelaire asked, "has not dreamt, in moments of ambition, of the miracle of a poetic prose, musical without rhythm and without rhyme, supple and staccato enough to adapt to the undulations of dreams, and the sudden leaps of consciousness." Such a poem, Baudelaire recognized and insisted, "is above all a child of the experience of giant cities, of the intersections of their myriad relations." [119]

It is important to establish the way in which Democratic politics and literature, as well as the city itself, provided a framework for the transmutation of Walter Whitman into Walt Whitman. He was born into an artisan/farming family in Huntington, Long Island, in 1819 (the same year Herman Melville was born on Pearl Street, thirty miles away). His father was a Locofoco Democrat, and like the son an admirer of William Leggett and Fanny Wright. His associations with both literature and politics in New York City from 1841 until he returned to Brooklyn in 1845 were fully within the radical wing associated with the *Democratic Review.* When he returned to Brooklyn to edit the *Brooklyn Eagle,* his ties to the party machinery were close and strong, and he was in most years a party official of one sort or another. When he wrote on cultural and political

---

* It was in the *Democratic Review* that Whitman, announcing "an American bard at last," published the first of several anonymous reviews of his own *Leaves of Grass.*

topics, he echoed the *Democratic Review,* and he supported many local reforms, ranging from parks and hospitals to criticism of police harassment of prostitutes and the poor and, especially, the advancement of education.[120]

It is, perhaps, easiest to grasp the importance of Young America's message for Whitman by taking note of the advice he received from Lewis Gaylord Clark's rather genteel circle. In 1836, the year before the *Democratic Review* was founded, the *Knickerbocker* published an article titled "Prospects of American Poetry." There Whitman might have read: "The poet who would be the literary redeemer of the land, must not only dissever himself from the base associations of the day, but he must kindle new altars, at which his innermost soul may worship."[121] Whitman, of course, relished those associations that the *Knickerbocker* would call base.*

When Moncure Conway and Henry David Thoreau visited Whitman in New York in 1855, soon after the publication of *Leaves of Grass,* both reported to Emerson, whose emissaries they were, that Whitman greeted as friends many of the working class. "He says," Conway informed Emerson, that "he is one of that class by choice, that he is personally dear to some thousands of such . . . who love him but cannot make head or tail of his book."[123] The paradox of a people's poet who could not be understood by the people bothered Whitman, more than it bothered others who have presumed to represent democratic art. But he never lost faith in the mass; he never turned against them because his hopes were unfulfilled.†

In time, however, Whitman did diverge in an important way from the political and cultural principles of the *Democratic Review.* As we have noted, Young America believed that political reform, especially equal rights, represented the fundamental reform, the one that would bring social improvement and the flowering of a democratic culture. Whitman

---

* Curiously, the conservative George Templeton Strong, who knew and continuously pondered the city, revealed, as well, in 1855, that he grasped, at least for a moment, its poetic possibilities. In the privacy of his diary and with no apparent knowledge of either Whitman or the kind of poetry Whitman was about to bring into the public life of the city, Strong reflected that a poet of "true feeling" must "venture to deal with . . . the men and women and things of 1855. . . . There is poetry enough latent in the South Street merchant and the Wall Street financier; in Stewart's snobby clerk chaffering over ribbons and laces; in the omnibus driver that conveys them all from the day's work and the night's relaxation and repose; in the brutified denizen of the Points and the Hook; in the sumptuous courtesan of Mercer Street thinking sadly of her village home; in the Fifth Avenue ballroom; in the Grace Church contrast of eternal vanity and new bonnets; in the dancers at Lewis Jones's and Mr. Schiff's, and in the future of each and all."[122]

† The connection of artisan and artist still existed in the person of Whitman. The printing of the first edition of *Leaves of Grass* was supervised by Whitman, who in fact set much of the type. The fine art of poetry and the practical art of printing were joined in this truly democratic book.

eventually rejected that vision, believing, increasingly, that cultural reform, not politics, would be the path to a fulfilled American democracy.

The same collapse of the parties that carried down O'Sullivan's *Democratic Review* made Whitman reconsider conventional politics. Increasingly disillusioned with party politics, he began to think of artists as an avant-garde for general improvement. In a lecture before the Brooklyn Art Union in 1851, he referred to artists as a "close phalanx, ardent, radical, progressive."[124] By the time he published *Democratic Vistas* in 1871, he had resolved an ambiguity in his own thought about the relation of politics and culture. Literature and aesthetics, Whitman finally concluded, promised the new America of his dreams.*

Democratic Vistas originated in a commission to write an article on democracy for *Galaxy* magazine in New York. The immediate occasion was Thomas Carlyle's charge—put forth in "Shooting Niagara: And After?" —that democracy would destroy civilization. Whitman set out to refute him, but in the course of writing realized that there was much to worry about in American democracy. Much improvement was needed, and he came to a sense of democracy as a process which would constantly advance individuals and society. What would make the process move? He concluded that a democratic art must precede and prepare the way for a democratic society. Literature, for Whitman, then, was not a report on the state of society, rather it was formative.[125] In *Democratic Vistas,* as he told a correspondent a year after it was published, Whitman sought "to make patent the appalling vacuum in our times & here . . . and to suggest & prophesy such a Literature as the only vital means of sustaining & perpetuating such a people."[126] Poets would supplant politicians in forming and reforming a democratic America.†

"Our fundamental want to-day in the United States," Whitman told his readers, "is of a class, and the clear idea of a class, of native authors . . . sacerdotal, modern, fit to cope with our occasions, lands, permeating the whole mass of American mentality, taste, belief, breathing into it a new breath of life, giving it decision, affecting politics far more than the popular superficial suffrage, with results inside and underneath the elections of Presidents or Congresses. . . . " Whether or not Americans realized it, Whitman instructed them that "a few first-class poets, philosophs, and authors, have substantially settled and given status to the entire religion, education, law, sociology, etc. of the hitherto civilized world . . .

---

* It should be noted that this position is distinctly different from Morse's view of the role of art. Morse wished to elevate the artist in order to secure the artist's autonomy and advancement. Whitman's elevation of art does not remove it from society; rather, it asks the artist to assume responsibility for general social improvement. Whitman is to be distinguished as well from later avant-garde movements which tend to forget the origin of the term and become self-enclosing instead of society's advance regiment.

† He had, by the way, read Shelley's *Defence of Poetry*.

such must also stamp, the interior and real democratic construction of this American continent." Whitman, as he himself recognized, is here on difficult ground for a democrat. "We find ourselves," he notes, "in close quarters with the enemy, this word Culture." How will Whitman's democratic literary class—and their culture—be characterized? Troubled by the word "culture," but not wanting to disown it, he insists upon "a programme of culture, drawn out, not for a single class alone, or for the parlors or lecture rooms, but with an eye to practical life also of the middle and working strata." Culture "must have for its spinal meaning the formation of a typical personality . . . and *not* restricted by conditions ineligible to the masses." [127]

URBANITY

By the middle of the nineteenth century, New York City, which in Gulian Verplanck's youth could have been grasped in a single view from the steeples of Trinity Church or St. Paul's, which could be covered in a single walk, had grown too large to be grasped in traditional ways. The city had become multiple environments, unknown to each other and, perhaps, unknowable through direct or personal experience. The city as a shared experience was no longer immediate; it was now mediated, even created, by the cheap, new large-circulation newspapers. Awareness of the various worlds of the city was now acquired through the press. [128]

Between 1840 and 1860, printing and publishing was the fastest-growing industry in the city; by 1860, in fact, it had become New York's leading industry. [129] Newspaper costs dropped; local and national newspaper and magazine circulation increased with the advent of the steam press in the 1830s and the Hoe rotary press in 1846, and this enabled the editors to assume prominent places in the city's public culture and in the nation.

At midcentury, the city's two best-known and most respected private citizens were newspaper editors; their occupation made Horace Greeley and William Cullen Bryant public figures, a circumstance made official by the municipal authorities when they established Greeley Square and Bryant Park. The city's most identifiable business structures were the great newspaper buildings on Park Row; the architecture of these buildings was in a very important sense public architecture, not business architecture. If the Park Row area was already called Printing House Square, before long individual newspapers would give their own, private names to major public squares in the city: Herald Square (1895) and Times Square (1904).

The development and centralization of the newspaper and magazine press strengthened New York's metropolitan claims. New York newspapers and magazines, following established lines of commerce, acquired increasingly national circulations, which gave them a larger role in the intellectual and political life of the nation.[130] It was not bothersome that the political capital of the nation was elsewhere. "The seat of commerce," a writer in the *Literary World* reflected in 1847, is necessarily "the centre of literary power."[131] Just as New Yorkers knew and admired Greeley and Bryant, so did Americans hundreds of miles into the city's national hinterland. Out of all these changes emerged a new kind of urban writer, the serious literary or political journalist.

Cooper's libel suits against the Whig editors who, in his opinion and in that of the courts, went beyond the proper bounds of a literary review to heap personal abuse on him, prompted literary New York to consider the place of the newspaper press in the city's intellectual life. A writer in the very serious and very Whig *New York Review* contrasted the newspapers of New York with those of Paris. Parisian newspapers, with their better-paid writers, their more demanding readers, and their distribution through *cabinets de lecture,* where they were read, rather than through newsboys, showed the potential of a newspaper. They proved what a newspaper could be. If the American public asks only for "politics, business, and news," one cannot expect editors to supply "the elegant feuilleton and other pleasant appendages of a Paris newspaper."[132]

An essay titled "Journalism" in the *Democratic Review* favorably noticed the increasing importance of newspaper and magazine journalism. With Leggett in mind as the ideal, the writer called for "intellectual men" in the profession, "firm and independent men" with "power of thought and facility of expression." The responsibility of journalism was great, and so were its possibilities, because the journalist, more than any other writer, establishes "immediate contact with the public mind." It was, the writer exclaimed, a matter for rejoicing "that young men of education and talent, who have been accustomed to crowd the professions of law, medicine, theology are many of them directing their energies to the business of editorship and popular instruction."[133]

Poe, who liked to call himself a "magazinist" rather than a journalist, insisted that the increase in magazines was not a sign of "a downward tendency in American taste or letters." Magazines, he explained, are "but a sign of the times, an indication of an era in which men are forced upon the curt, the condensed, the well-digested in place of the voluminous— in a word, upon journalism in lieu of dissertation."[134]

The old notion of a "literary republic" was transformed with the rise of metropolitan journalism. Instead of an international commitment to letters and science, bound together by intellectual correspondence, the literary republic became a local society of writers and journalists, what is now in careerist circles called a "network." Frederick Law Olmsted had this meaning in mind when he wrote to his father proposing that he become a partner in and an editor with *Putnam's Monthly Magazine.* "There is," he explained to his merchant father, "a sort of literary republic which it is not merely pleasant and gratifying to my ambition to be recognized in, but also profitable. It would, for example, if I am so recognized & considered, be easy for me, in the case of the non-success of this partnership, to get employment in the newspaper offices or other literary enterprises at good wages." The connections he established as a literary man proved more important than he could imagine. It was a friendship established in this literary republic that provided a decisive endorsement that won him his first appointment as superintendent of Central Park, which led in turn to his extraordinary career as an urban theorist and designer.[135]

In the 1840s, literary journalism in New York, which had until then consisted all too often of "mere hasty notices" of books, was sudddenly supplied with new and very high standards.[136] In 1844 both Edgar Allan Poe and Margaret Fuller joined the ranks of New York's journalistic corps.

More than any other American journalists of their time, Poe and Fuller developed and elaborated the critical theories that guided their work. They were professionals. But this is about all they had in common: their differences are more interesting and important for our purposes. They represented the two possible extremes in critical approaches to literature. Poe, like the Southern "New Critics" who would come North a century later, was a formalist, rather uninterested in the moral meaning or historical context of literary texts, while Fuller approached literature with historical concerns not unlike the so-called New York Intellectuals of a century later.[137]

Margaret Fuller (born 1810) left transcendental New England to accept Horace Greeley's offer to write for the *New York Tribune,* becoming the first full-time book reviewer on an American newspaper. Emerson and her friends associated with *The Dial* thought it rather unbecoming, even improper, that someone of Fuller's intellect, one of their own circle, should soil her hands with the ink of a metropolitan daily.[138] But she knew what she was doing. Besides, she appreciated, even admired Greeley as a democrat and a "man of the people." Greeley, in turn, encouraged her growing interest in political and social topics that had seemed too concrete for Boston. One of her first acts after establishing herself in the city was to visit "the most unfortunate of her sex" at the female asylum on Blackwells Island (now Roosevelt Island). This led her to survey poverty and philanthropy in the city, and to write about it.[139] In fact, addressing the whole range of cultural life—contemporary, historical life—in New York City for the paper with the city's largest circulation made her a better writer. It concentrated and toughened her style, and it vastly broadened the range of her literary, moral, and political judgments.

Fuller found in New York more time to write than she had ever had and, more important to her, a means of moving from the tight circle of personal influence to a public life.[140] The desire to establish herself in the public culture, which was, after all, male-dominated, was fundamental to the transaction between Fuller and Greeley. Not long before she left Boston, her friend Emerson, her family, and her circle of women with whom she had conducted her famous "conversations," she told her brother that she wanted more. "A noble career is yet before me," she wrote to him. "I have given almost all of my young energies to personal relations; but, at present, I feel inclined to impel the general stream of thought." Knowing that a woman's grasping for something new and better for herself might be interpreted as desertion by others to whom she meant so much, she added: "Let my dearest friends also wish that I should take a share in public life."[141]

For Fuller, as for Goethe, whom she admired, and for Edmund Wilson and Lionel Trilling in the twentieth century, literature—and thus criticism—was "a medium for viewing all humanity, a core around which all knowledge, all experience, all science, all the ideal as well as the practical in our nature" can be examined.[142] Fuller was generously inclusive in her definition of literature, and she moved naturally to larger social and moral questions. Literary questions, she understood, do not all point to God, or even to classical models; they as well point to the world around, the great city which so multiplied life and experience. "The eye of man," as she put it, "is fitted to range all around no less than to be lifted." She was sensitive as a critic, as was Whitman, to the matter of class in literary life. "Literature," she believed, "may be regarded as the great mutual system of interpretation between all kinds and classes of men." Her sense of the place of literature in forming a common, democratic culture remains moving: "It is an epistolary correspondence between brethren of one family, subject to many and wide separations, and anxious to remain in spiritual presence of one another."[143] And in all of this she was an intellectual cosmopolitan in the best New York tradition. It was "one great object of her life," she wrote, to bring the work of Europe's "great geniuses" to New York so that they might provide America's young writers "a higher standard" than that supplied by their own time and place. Out of the interplay, mingling, she said, she anticipated the development of an American literature.[144]

Just before she left New York for Europe in 1846, after twenty months on the *Tribune,* she appraised the literary consequences of newspapers. Having grown as a person and as a writer in New York, she sought to justify her journalistic career. Writers, she warned, must recognize that "the life of intellect" is going to be carried more and more in "the weekly and daily papers." They hold the promise of "great excellence," particularly for the "condensed essay, narrative, criticism." As a means of "diffusing knowledge and sowing the seeds of thought," the newspaper "cannot be too highly prized by the discerning and the benevolent." Much of the nation's intellectual class, she observed, will remain "indisposed to this kind of writing," but "he who labors to the benefit of others . . . may be content to use an unhonored servant to the grand purposes of Destiny, to work in such a way at the Pantheon which the ages shall complete, on which his name may not be inscribed, but which will breathe the life of his soul."[145]

While Fuller came to literature infused with the spirit of a reformer, Poe, a man who, admittedly, led an indescribably miserable life, despaired of human improvement. Writing to James Russell Lowell, who was at the time probably more deeply involved in reform, specifically abolitionism, than any other major writer of his time, Poe declared that he "had no faith in human perfectibility." He was determined that "human exertion will have no appreciable effect upon humanity." The idea—even the possibility—of progress meant nothing to him. "Man is now only more active—not more happy—nor more wise, than he was 6000 years ago."[146]

Poe sought to establish literary authority (or reestablish it in modern times), and he carried a dream of creating a great literary review to this end as he moved from the South to Philadelphia and, finally, to New York.[147] His literary review would not, however, involve itself with broad cultural or political questions, not even with the opinions in the literature reviewed. For Poe poetry and criticism constituted a separate realm; they belonged to neither time nor place. The poet, as he wrote in a review of Fitz-Greene Halleck's poems, is a "citizen of a higher country."[148]

An essay published by Cornelius Mathews in *Arcturus* stimulated Poe to define his formalist critical theory. Mathews had defined the territory of criticism broadly, saying that it was not particularly concerned with grammar and rhyme but did include history, philosophy, and the "broadest views of statesmanship." Poe's response defined criticism as a "science," insisting that the practice of criticism should not be carried on in the form of the general essay. The exclusive concern of criticism was the literary quality of the work. Literary judgments were, Poe believed, based upon scientific standards that come from or represent an analysis of human nature. For this reason, criticism is a universal science. "The laws of man's heart and intellect," Poe explained, "cannot vary." The critic should not be concerned with the truth or falsity of a book or poem; his function is "simply to decide upon *the mode* in which these opinions are brought to bear." The literary concerns in a work of literature inhere in the rules of grammar and rhyme, and in such errors as mixed metaphors. "Criticism is not," Poe declared, "an essay, not a sermon, nor an oration, nor a chapter in history, nor a philosophical speculation, nor a prose-poem, nor an art-novel, nor a dialogue. In fact, it *can be* nothing in the world but criticism." [149]

Poe's formalism and his universalism made it difficult for him to insert himself into the particularity of the culture of New York City and to exploit it in a literary way.* The difference between Poe's capacity to respond to and use the city and that of someone deeply attuned to urban culture may be seen in Poe's association with the *Broadway Journal*. That journal, which published only two volumes, is remembered by literary historians because of Poe's association with it, and his sole editorship of the second volume. Since Poe wrote almost the whole of the second volume, that is the more interesting one to students of American litera-ture, but to the student of urban culture it is the first volume that draws attention. The informing intelligence on this first volume was Charles F. Briggs, the founder of the magazine. Briggs wanted a magazine of wit, urbanity, and sophistication. New York, he was determined, would not be a provincial town, but instead a metropolis, an American Paris. Defin-ing the character of his magazine on the first page of the first number, dated January 4, 1845, in a way that his friend Maria White Lowell, wife of James Russell Lowell of Boston, thought too "cockney," he declared:

> Broadway is confessedly the finest street in the first city of the New World. It is the great artery through which flows the best blood of our system. All the elegance of our continent permeates through it . . . the most elegant shops in the City line its sides; the finest build-ings are found there, and all fashions exhibit their first gloss upon its sidewalks. . . . Wall Street passes its wealth into its broad channel, and all the dealers in intellectual works are here centered; every exhibition of art is found here, and the largest caravanseries in the world border upon it. Its pavement has been trod upon by every distinguished man that has visited our continent. . . . It terminates at one end in the first square in the city [Union Square], doubtless in the Union, and at the other in the Battery, unrivalled for its entire beauty, by any marine parade in the world. . . . New York is fast becoming, if she be not already, America, in spite of South Carolina and Boston. [150]

* Interestingly, Poe's great urban story "The Man in the Crowd"—a story much admired by those two great communicators on urban modernism Charles Baudelaire and Walter Benjamin—was set in London, a city Poe had not seen since he was ten or eleven years old, when he was brought there by the Allan family.

The magazine, under Briggs, reviewed books, the first—and the choice is revealing—being *Mind Amongst the Spindles,* a collection of stories written by the women who worked in the textile mills of Lowell, Massachusetts. But in addition to reviews, the magazine had page after lively page covering the cultural life of the city—what was going on in the worlds of art, architecture, music, and literature. But most revealing of all was the invitation to readers to enjoy the city. There was a regular column describing "Places Worth Visiting." While the discussion of the city often raised touchy questions about poverty, it was more concerned with pleasure. When Poe, whom Briggs had hired as an assistant, forced Briggs out and took over the magazine himself, most of these features were abandoned, and the magazine became narrowly and relentlessly literary.

Obscurity and misfortune have been Briggs' fate. Even in his own time he was better known by the name Harry Franco, the name of a fictional character he created. By any name, he slipped through the memory screen of history, except in biographies of Poe and Lowell, men with whom he was for a period of each's life importantly involved. He was not rediscovered until Perry Miller presented a fascinating, though indeterminate, portrait of him in *The Raven and the Whale.* In his acknowledgments, Miller remarked that if the story he presented "inspires further disclosure of him, I shall not have worked in vain." [151] We still know too little of this man who was, as his friend Lowell knew, a better man than anything he wrote. [152]

Born in Nantucket in 1804, Charles Francis Briggs was the son of a China trader. His father failed when during the War of 1812 the British seized his vessel, and the downwardly mobile Briggs took to the sea as a common sailor when he came of age. Briggs, like Melville, who had a similar experience as a youth, never forgot. He was always sensitive to—even actually angry about—poverty and economic injustice. There is always an edge to his writing, prompted by a commitment not to forget the unfairness of American life.

His name first appears in the New York city directory for 1838, where he is listed as a wholesale merchant on Water Street. He was not particularly successful in business, but neither was he so unsuccessful as he later implied. Authorship came late to this ex-sailor, even later than to Melville. When Briggs was thirty-five, he published *The Adventures of Harry Franco,* a tale of the Panic of 1837. This very successful fiction was followed by *The Haunted Merchant* and *Working a Passage.* In 1847, after the failure of the *Broadway Journal,* he published *The Trippings of Tom Pepper,* which, like Balzac's great urban novels, provides glimpses of a vast array of urban types and classes. A brief burlesque of the literati of New York is savage, but it is so true that even today one can identify his targets. [153]

He chose to identify himself as a journalist. Literary men were, he believed, too inclined to dismiss such workaday fellows as himself, and he argued that they should recognize journalists as within their fraternity, for "they are the real writers of this country who are, at least, the Exponents of National Thought, if they are not directors of it."[154] He drifted from one journalistic position to another after the failure of the *Broadway Journal*. He worked on *Holden's Dollar Magazine*, then *Putnam's Monthly* (1853–57), where, as we shall see, he edited the era's most notable magazine. After he left *Putnam's* he took work as assistant editor of the *New York Times*, returning briefly as editor of the revived *Putnam's Magazine* (1868–70). The last few years of his life, until his death in 1877, were spent on the *Brooklyn Union* and the *Independent*.

The ex-sailor from Nantucket was a New Yorker by affirmation. Sometimes, as is often the case of New Yorkers by choice, he was too strenuous in his metropolitanism. James Russell Lowell complained: "You Gothamites strain hard to attain a metropolitan character, but I think if you *felt* very metropolitan you would not be showing it on all occasions."[155] *The Adventures of Harry Franco* and *The Trippings of Tom Pepper*, whatever their substantial weaknesses, are the closest New York came to a Dickensian or Balzacian urban novel.

Briggs was particularly interested in the growth and architecture of the city; his architectural writings, scattered through several journals and in a book, *The Architect* (1849), are so intelligent and informed as to warrant recovery. In his own day his urban interests and knowledge were first recognized when the commissioners of Central Park appointed him to a consulting board in 1856, charged with helping to devise guidelines for the plan for Central Park, which provided the basis for the brilliant design submitted by Frederick Law Olmsted and Calvert Vaux. Then from 1853 to 1877 fell to him the task or opportunity of writing the introduction to the annual edition of *Trow's City Directory*. In these brief but deeply affectionate essays, Briggs allies himself with the thrill and excitement of the growth and future of the city, while recovering and relishing its past.

A slightly built man, Briggs had a thin face and a sharp chin. He looked always as if he had "weathered harsh experience."[156] His life truly was hard. He was a man of talent, a man who grasped the idea of metropolitan culture better than any of his contemporaries and who, in the founding of the *Broadway Journal* and *Putnam's Monthly*, showed his willingness to gamble everything for it—and both times he lost. While editing *Putnam's* he wrote to Lowell: "If it were not for the variety and exacting nature of my employments, suicide or insanity would be my lot, I am certain."[157]

As an editor Briggs valued independence above all. He objected to the *Democratic Review* and the *Whig Review* because their political associations narrowed their possibilities. Reform movements, too, he found limiting, though he himself supported most of the reforms of the day, except feminism. He was a reformer who recognized the blindness of reformers. Writing to Lowell, his abolitionist friend in Boston, he remarked caustically and characteristically that "Mass. keeps her slaves in So. Carolina and Georgia." [158] While editing the *Broadway Journal*, he offended abolitionists by refusing to allow it to become an anti-slavery magazine. His anti-slavery sympathies were evident in the journal, but it was to be a metropolitan magazine, not a movement one. What the metropolis, urbanity, offered him was an open, always changing, always provocative pattern of possibilities as a writer and an editor.

Putnam's Monthly was, Frank Luther Mott writes in his multivolumed history of American magazines, "the first genuinely civilized magazine in America." It bore comparison with its best European counterparts; William Makepeace Thackeray pronounced it the best magazine in the world. [159] It is one of those wonderful ironies of intellectual life in America that Charles Briggs, who created a magazine of such quality and urbanity, was wont, as was Melville, to identify himself as an urban barbarian.*

Almost as much as libraries, restaurants are central institutions in New York City's intellectual life, and *Putnam's*, like so much else in the city, began in a restaurant. Briggs, who was at the time employed at the New York Customs House, dined at Windust's Restaurant on Park Row in June 1852 with George William Curtis. A young writer (born 1824) from Rhode Island who had resided at Brook Farm for a period, Curtis was a perfect foil for Briggs. The son of a banker, he was personally acquainted with leading figures in Boston and, to a lesser extent, New York. Briggs and Curtis discussed the creation of an independent magazine, using only original contributions. At a time when *Harper's Monthly* had achieved an unprecedented circulation by reprinting (pirating) English writers, Briggs and Curtis had in mind a magazine for American writers, paying them generously. [161]

They found a sympathetic backer in George Palmer Putnam, the publisher who had supported Duyckinck's American Library and who had been one of the original sponsors of the *Literary World* (1847–53). There was a second dinner in early fall, hosted by Putnam at his home off fashionable Stuyvesant Square, at 92 East Sixteenth Street. This dinner turned out to be the first of what became regular Tuesday-evening literary receptions at the Putnam home. [162] At Putnam's suggestion, Parke Godwin was added to the enterprise.

Godwin, born in Paterson, New Jersey, in 1816 and educated at Prince-

---

* Briggs once described himself in a letter to Lowell as a "Clod of earth," obviously unfit for the purity of Boston's culture. [160]

ton, had been trained for the law but did not practice, "not thinking the law an honest profession."[163] He met Bryant in a New York City boardinghouse, and in 1837 Bryant asked him to become his assistant. Five years later he married Bryant's eldest daughter, and the public and private lives of the two men were thereafter intertwined. In 1839, Godwin became a regular contributor to O'Sullivan's *Democratic Review,* and in the 1840s, he became one of the major English-language explicators of Charles Fourier, publishing *Democracy: Constructive and Pacific* (1844) and *A Popular View of the Doctrines of Charles Fourier* (1844).[164] With the addition of Godwin, the editorial arrangements of *Putnam's Monthly* were established with Briggs as editor, Curtis as assistant editor responsible for social and literary topics, and Godwin responsible for political affairs.

George Putnam wrote to the nation's most notable literary figures, informing them of the planned monthly and asking them to contribute. The publication would, he explained, "combine the popular character of a magazine, with the higher & graver aims of a Quarterly review."[165] The list of writers who responded and wrote for the magazine during its four-year existence is impressive; it also indicates something of its character as a magazine. The list includes both New York and Boston writers, suggesting the formation of a particular Northeastern axis.* It is also notable how many of its contributors were drawn from Briggs's world of metropolitan journalism,† something that doubtless helped the magazine to escape sentimentality and encouraged urban realism. This combination gave *Putnam's* tight-printed, double-columned pages a character of authoritativeness and lightness, instruction and amusement. "A popular magazine," Briggs wrote in the introductory statement, "must amuse, interest, and instruct."[166] As befitted the leading magazine in New York, *Putnam's,* to a degree unmatched in its time, attended to the literatures of Europe, not just England but also, even especially, France and Germany.

Putnam's oriented itself to be at once a national force and a New York magazine. It localized itself in New York, and it spoke with a New York voice as the nation's intellectual capital. Briggs assumed that the nation's readers wanted to read about "life in New York" as well as the work of American writers.[167] A large portion of the non-fiction articles in *Putnam's* (as well as the engravings) offered an enthusiastic celebration of the American metropolis. What Briggs did with *Putnam's* was to create a panoply of visual icons and social forms that represented the city to itself and to the nation.

---

* These writers included: Melville, Lowell, Longfellow, Thoreau, Bryant, Henry James, Charles Dudley Warner, Charles Eliot Norton, Richard Grant White.

† Besides Briggs and Godwin, these included Greeley, C. A. Dana, George Ripley, Clarence Cook, William Henry Hurlbert.

Here Briggs's interest in architecture served the magazine well. New York at midcentury was beginning to understand that its claims to metropolitan stature rested in part upon and could be projected by means of a new kind of public architecture—Central Park, the Crystal Palace, the elegant Gothic churches built on Broadway and Fifth Avenue by James Renwick and Richard Upjohn, the department stores, newspaper offices, hotels, and more. New York, Clarence Cook wrote in the second issue of *Putnam's*, "has successfully commenced the work of lining her streets with structures of stone and marble worthy of her pretensions as the metropolis of the Union."[168]

One finds in *Putnam's*, too, numerous articles describing the development of the physical city and its key social institutions. *Putnam's* was projecting images of the metropolis to the nation, thus associating the nation with the metropolis, particularly with its iconography at a time when such visual images had more impact, not yet being devalued by omnipresence.* The most important of these articles was a series called "New York Daguerreotyped," but there were other articles, such as "Church Architecture in New York," "Places of Public Amusement," and, making a social point, "The St. Nicholas [Hotel] and the Five Points," as well as long essays on benevolent and educational institutions in the city. After Briggs left the editorship in 1856, there was less emphasis on the physical city, but this loss was made up by a new department at the back of each issue, "The World of New York," a commentary on political, social, and cultural affairs in the city.

Putnam's was a force in national politics. Although Briggs had been hesitant to identify the *Broadway Journal* with the anti-slavery movement and even rejected (very regretfully) one of Melville's stories out of fear it would turn religious opinion against the magazine, he supported the strong political essays written by Godwin, perhaps because they were attached to a set of principles that were independent of any existing parties.[169] Godwin began his series, which were later collected into a book, *Political Essays* (1856), with "Our New President," a savage attack on the lack of principle and the crass dealing out of offices that seemed to characterize the Pierce administration. The essays covered annexation, the crisis of the parties, slavery, among other topics. The most notable was titled "American Despotisms." Here Godwin attacked the party system, the slave South, and "ecclesiastical organizations" for trying to stifle free political dissent. It was a daring article, one which established the intellectual and moral position of *Putnam's*. "A feeling of surprise has sometimes been expressed" that *Putnam's Monthly* has so often mingled

---

* One might argue that the distribution of visual icons among the national population is an index of the cultural hegemony of a modern metropolis.

"with our lighter entertainments grave and thoughtful considerations of the leading political, social, scientific, and religious topics of the day." Anyone so puzzled, Godwin pointed out, must not understand "the proper aims and duties of a first-class periodical." Then he struck out at the softness of so much of the literary and general culture of the time.

It was never our intention to issue a monthly exclusively for the milliners; we had no ambition to institute a monopoly manufacture of love-tales and sing-song verses . . . No! we had other conceptions of the variety, the dignity, and the destiny of literature. Our thought, in establishing this enterprise, was, and it still is, that literature is the full and free expression of the nation's mind, not in *belles-lettres* alone, nor in art alone, nor in science alone, but in all these, combined with politics and religion. It seemed to us, that the cultivated men, the literary men of the nation, are among its best instructors, and that they feebly discharge their function, if they are not free to utter their wisest thought, their most beautiful inspirations, on every subject which concerns the interests, the sensibilities, and the hopes of our humanity.[170]

Godwin's essays had an enormous impact, and to a very large degree *Putnam's* provided the medium for the development of the cluster of political principles that gradually defined Northern political opinion, the ideology of the Republican Party, whose first platform was, as we have already noted, drafted by Godwin, using much of the very language of his *Putnam's* articles. While the *Democratic Review*, attached to a very unstable and collapsing Democratic Party, moved toward the sort of decentralization of opinion and practice that finally found its best expression in the notion of "popular sovereignty" promoted by Stephen A. Douglas, *Putnam's*, free of the incubus of the collapsing Democratic Party or any other party that needed to be protected from principle, assumed and promoted metropolitan-based national standards. By the end of the decade, after *Putnam's* had ceased publication, anti-slavery opinion would find an extraordinary voice in Abraham Lincoln and an institutional home in the sectional but nationalistic Republican Party.

If metropolitanism meant the articulation of national principles, it also meant a particular kind of intellectual life within the metropolis, a pattern that itself made a contribution to the national role of a metropolis. Since all the various partial elements that are the material of a national culture find expression in a nation's central city, the metropolis is a crucible within which a public culture can be forged. "The tone of such a capital," an editorial in *Putnam's* explained, "must tend toward common sense and impartiality." In Paris and New York the "exaggerated estimate which men are quite as apt to form of their parties, their pursuits, and their professions, as of their personal qualities and merits, will always be sagely chastised by metropolitan criticism."[171]

The career of *Putnam's* was brilliant but brief. Was the problem literary or financial? What evidence there is suggests the latter. Circulation was substantial, ranging between 12,000 and 20,000.[172] This could not compare with the figures for *Harper's,* a far less serious magazine, but it was enough for the magazine to pay its way. The magazine seems twice to have been victim of financial crises unrelated to itself. In 1856, George P. Putnam, whose publishing company was in difficulties, feared bringing *Putnam's Monthly* down with him if he fell. So he sold it to another publishing company, Dix & Edwards.[173] Although Briggs was a casualty of this transaction, the magazine was effectively edited after the transfer, with Frederick Law Olmsted as what we would call managing editor and George William Curtis, in secrecy, making the editorial decisions. The magazine continued to pay its way, but Dix & Edwards failed in the business depression of 1857, and they did what Putnam had sought to avoid: they pulled the profitable *Putnam's* down with them.[174]

History is not chronology. Yet the historian cannot but notice the special significance of certain dates. *Putnam's* failed in New York in 1857, while in that year the *Atlantic Monthly* was established in Boston. This death and birth of literary magazines does, I think, signify something in American intellectual history, the relative gain Boston made over New York as a publishing center during the late 1850s, the 1860s, and part of the 1870s. While before 1857, many Boston writers were published by New York houses, after that date one finds New York writers for the first time being published in Boston. New York would recover its leadership by the late 1870s and would overwhelm Boston by the end of the 1880s, but this temporary shift is important for assessing the shape of American literary life in the third quarter of the nineteenth century. Boston and New York were—and are—very different places. The shift from New York to Boston, from a dynamic metropolis to a college town, was a shift from the concreteness, toughness, and diversity of New York's urbanity to the evocation of a state of mind, a mind of cultivation and rectitude, but in the realm of the ideal rather than of the reality of the city. The best New York magazine writing of the 1860s and 1870s sought to assimilate these many different qualities into a new kind of intellectual journalism, generated in the metropolis but proposing a national standard for public life and morality.

CHAPTER 5

The Metropolitan Gentry: Culture Against Politics

During the third quarter of the nineteenth century, New York transformed itself into a metropolis that could be compared, at last, with Paris and London. New York's population, drawn from all parts of the world as well as from the American provinces, surged past the one million mark, and the city assumed a commanding and never again challenged position in the nation's economic and cultural life. Even in politics, this metropolis that was not a national capital was nonetheless a dominating force. Both the politics of the city and the political opinion of its journalists loomed large, decisively so, in national political affairs, in part because the New York Customs House was the primary source of federal revenue.

The city's aspirations toward metropolitan grandeur were increasingly realized in its architecture and thus visible to anyone who walked the city's streets or subscribed to the proliferating illustrated magazines that so often published pictures of New York. There were, for example, the rows upon rows of bourgeois brownstones extending north from Washington Square, the new Central Park, the enormous (for its time) Grand Central Depot on Forty-second Street, A. T. Stewart's grand department store at Broadway and Ninth Street or his marble mansion (the city's first) at Thirty-fourth Street and Fifth Avenue, the large and luxurious hotels that lined Broadway from Canal Street to Madison Square, where the elegant Fifth Avenue Hotel (built in 1859 and boasting the world's first hotel elevator) served as a New York home for visiting foreign dignitaries and for the American political elite.

The metropolitan quality of the city was reflected, as well, in the elaboration of economic, cultural, and philanthropic institutions on a new scale. Financial and communications industries led the way in business, organizing corporate headquarters from which they administered their national enterprises. Any walker in the city could immediately recognize the Broadway buildings that housed and symbolized, for example, the Equitable Life Assurance Society and the Western Union Company.

Private philanthropy, often with municipal assistance, now began to reform and consolidate both social welfare agencies and institutions of elite culture. The Association for Improving the Condition of the Poor (founded 1843) and the Charity Organization Society (founded 1882), for example, sought to coordinate the myriad of social welfare agencies serving the city's growing class of unfortunates, while the Children's Aid Society, founded in 1853, quickly established itself as the nation's most innovative urban philanthropy.

Some of the cultural philanthropies of this period still stand as major institutions. The scholarly, wealthy James Lenox endowed a great library (later combined with the Astor Library and Tilden Trust to form the New York Public Library). Lenox commissioned Richard Morris Hunt, the first American trained at the Ecole des Beaux Arts, to design a magnificent home for his library at Fifth Avenue and Seventy-first Street, while Peter B. Wight designed a new and impressive home for the National Academy of Design, a much-praised Venetian Gothic building located at Fourth Avenue and Twenty-third Street. Two privately organized and privately controlled not-for-profit corporations collaborated with the municipality to establish the Metropolitan Museum of Art and the American Museum of Natural History. In no other American city did civic leaders dare give such titles to local institutions. Only in New York did such use of "metropolitan" and "American" seem natural.

Such metropolitan progress was, of course, heartening to the men and women who concerned themselves with the city's cultural life. But political and social problems kept intruding onto the terrain of high culture, even with the last two institutions named. In order to obtain the charters necessary to incorporate the Museum of Natural History and the Metropolitan Museum, elite cultural reformers had to engage the political skills of William Marcy Tweed, "Boss Tweed." Their errand to Tweed presented them with something of a conundrum: How could their definition of culture relate to the diverse cultures of the city? It was difficult, all the more so because distaste for the city's working people—all of those who sustained Tweed in power—so easily overcame the rhetoric of uplift. Until the 1890s, when pressure from Tammany Hall forced a change, the private board that ran the Metropolitan Museum often talked about democratic culture but declined to open on Sunday, the only day when men and women of the city's working classes might, if they should so desire, take the time during the day to look at the pictures and sculpture in the museum.

If we allow it to, this little story about the museum points toward the underlying circumstance and the constant preoccupation of intellectual life in New York City in the second half of the nineteenth century. Before all is the overwhelming fact of inequality. Perhaps in no other great city, whether European or American, was social inequality so extreme.[1] By 1876, 50 percent of the city's population lived in tenements, many scandalously unhealthy; the residents of these tenements accounted for 65 percent of the city's deaths and an appalling 90 percent of the deaths of children under five years of age. Here we have the defining circumstance of life in Gilded Age New York.

The problem for intellectuals was to establish a place for themselves in a city whose politics and culture were conditioned by this troubling fact. What, they asked themselves, are the prerogatives of the cultivated in the politics of a city in which Tammany thrived as a link between a new and very rich class of crude capitalists and the ignorant masses? Was there, they worried, any place for learning, for the cultivated ideals that they so valued? What, they had to ask, is the role of elite culture in the larger culture of the city? Should they—could they—reach out to the masses, or was recoil in self-righteousness not only easier but more appropriate? They were troubled about the possibilities and implications of both extension and withdrawal. Perhaps they could redefine public life—or culture —in ways more congenial to themselves. What, after all, was their rightful authority? Their social responsibility? Their complicity in the social inequality of the city? These were the fundamental questions in Boss Tweed's New York. For the learned, these questions coalesced into a larger worry about whether either culture or democracy could survive the new conditions of metropolitan life in New York City. Because New York had become the center of American journalism and, thus, opinion making, these local concerns and worries informed the culture of the middle classes emerging in the cities and towns of the nation.

THE AUTHORITY OF CULTURE

Certain words, those Raymond Williams has designated "keywords," gather into themselves and represent the structure of meaning and feeling that informs the social life and imagination of a historical period.[2] Neither the meaning nor the social salience of these words is fixed; they may change meaning over time, and they may move from the center to the periphery of discourse and back again. To track these changes in meaning and significance is to get very close to some basic facts of intellectual life—facts with considerable ideological significance.

Culture is a keyword, and its meaning was quite different, with profoundly different implications, in 1770 and 1870. We cannot trace the slow process of change, but one point is fundamental. The word was redefined in the context of emerging political democracy and expansive capitalism, and it came to distinguish itself from these developments. If for Clinton and Pintard culture meant improvement of all sorts, practical and intellectual, it now came to represent something higher, more refined, than ordinary life. Ideality, it was assumed, ought to dominate practice in economic and political life. For the individuals who embraced culture (and its cognates, cultivation, education, civilization), the prize was, it was presumed, special authority and, perhaps, responsibility. Something of Samuel Taylor Coleridge's dream of a national clerisy thus got involved with the notion of culture, and this association, though not formally acknowledged, colored American usage.[3]

The post–Civil War writers and reformers in New York City of concern here, those I call the metropolitan gentry, took up a notion of culture that had its American origins in New England. It was largely derived from Ralph Waldo Emerson, though later the direct Anglo-French influence of Matthew Arnold would somewhat obscure this New England background.[4] The reforming ambitions of the metropolitan gentry were inspired by Emerson's observation that men could be turned away from their narrow pursuit of money and power only "by the gradual domestication of the idea of culture." Here, perhaps, Emerson had in mind self-culture rather than a model of social leadership, but he elsewhere translated his idea of culture into a justification for gentry leadership. He explained that every society "wants to be officered by a best class, who shall be masters instructed in all the great arts of life; shall be wise, temperate, brave, public men, adorned with dignity and accomplishments."[5]

Emerson's distaste for New York was great and his contacts there few, but Charles Eliot Norton, who by the 1880s had become Harvard's and Boston's "apostle of culture," extended Boston's influence through lines of friendship and an active, mentor-like correspondence with the rising generation of New York gentry.[6] Norton, who imbibed Emerson's ideas and combined them with a profoundly conservative concern for bolstering the leadership position of his class in the nation, forged a strong postwar link between Boston and New York. His *Considerations on Some Recent Social Theories*, published anonymously in 1853, was the definitive statement of Brahmin elitism, and by the time of the Civil War, Norton believed that the moment had come for the cultivated class to "seize control of society and give it practical direction."[7] Whatever the origins of these ideas, it was in New York that they got their test. New England's highly refined ideas came out of doors in New York and confronted American life in all its democratic complexity.

The culture of Emerson and Norton was exclusive; it separated or distinguished the elite more than it unified the masses. At the other extreme was Walt Whitman, whose *Democratic Vistas* we have already discussed. It is worth recalling, however, that in his plea for democratic culture, Whitman nervously acknowledged the tension between democracy and culture. With this word, he observed, we are in close quarters with the enemy, but he insisted upon an understanding of culture that was not divisive, not a basis for exclusion and class privilege.

As Whitman wrote, however, a new generation of New Yorkers, a metropolitan gentry, responding to broad changes that redefined the social position and weakened the intellectual authority of the traditional learned classes in America, embraced culture for precisely the reasons that worried Whitman. In the claims of culture they found the basis for reasserting gentry leadership outside of the traditional professions. Not yet glimpsing the authority that academic and disciplinary professions would later confer, they imagined themselves appointed to assume social leadership because of their cultivation, all in the interest of civilization.

The New Yorkers were not, however, so confident as their Boston counterparts that a commitment to culture elided the problem of democracy. Here we can compare Thomas Wentworth Higginson's complacent "A Plea for Culture," which he published in Boston's *Atlantic* in 1867, with an essay by Charles Dudley Warner, one of New York's circle of intellect, published in New York's *Scribner's Monthly* in 1872. The very title of Warner's essay, "What Is Your Culture to Me?," shows the greater complexity of the issues surrounding the term in New York. While Warner was not Whitman, neither was he so smugly confident as Higginson of the claims of culture. Educated men, he warned, must do more than plead with society to embrace and respect the moral authority of cultivation. They must stand ready to explain themselves, to justify themselves to the less privileged.[8] It is this awareness of the contested claims of culture in New York that makes so rewarding an examination of the literary men and women who embraced it as a vehicle to power, influence, and responsibility.

The elevation of culture (and of the cultivated) implied a restriction of the realm of the political. While the new gentry all acknowledged democracy, some embracing it, they limited its possibilities by insisting upon the special claims of the opinions of the educated. This made democracy conditional. So long as the "lower kinds" of people, whether workers, immigrants, blacks, or women, accepted the leadership of the cultivated and the imperatives of the definition of culture, all was well. When they showed ambitions and aims of their own, the whole business of democracy became problematical.*

The New York intellectual elite had a difficult problem. Their relation to society and politics was more complicated than that faced by their European counterparts. American political democracy, for all of its limitations on the rights of women, blacks, Indians, was a fundamental fact that presented an unprecedented, troubling, and distinctively American problem for the midcentury literary generation that sought power in New York and the nation. New York had the largest urban electorate in the world. Americans turned to political parties and machines, not to intellectuals, to make the system work.[9]

In a comparative view, it was a structural condition that facilitated the elevation of Tweed over the intellectuals. In England, the serious reading public reached by the English men of letters was almost exactly congruent with the political nation, even in the years immediately following the Reform Act of 1867.[10] The problem of intellect in New York was the radical difference between the reading public and the political public. Their readers constituted a distinct political minority, and this had enormous consequences for the self-perception and public role of intellect. It encouraged both self-pity and arrogant claims for the authority of the cultivated in public affairs.

Literary men had a proclivity for bypassing electoral politics. Henry Bellows, the New York Unitarian minister and reputedly the best conversationalist in the Century Club, went beyond the bounds of what was publicly acceptable when, during the Civil War crisis, he proposed in a private letter to Norton the creation of a voluntary council of "men of standing, moral weight, and courage" to replace the politicians in giving direction to the country.[11] Toned down, this impulse found wide public expression and had substantial success in empowering various forms of private or appointed (as opposed to elected) authority—whether we speak of the Metropolitan Museum of Art, the Central Park Commission, the Metropolitan Police Commission, or the Metropolitan Board of Health. And it was behind the gentry's passion for Civil Service Reform.

In the realm of culture, as well, they looked for freedom from the disorderly marketplace of ideas. Especially opposed to the sort of commercial culture represented by P. T. Barnum, they proposed purer alternatives, whether Central Park or the Metropolitan Museum of Art.[12] More narrowly, in the realm of learned culture alone, they sought both

---

* They claimed a special role for cultivation, not expertise. Hence, though the issues bear some relation to the twentieth-century problem of professional expertise in a democracy, there is a difference. Culture is not a claim of technical knowledge. It is a general claim, even a claim of superior character. There is not even the pretense of defining the line that might separate the technical from the political.

purity of discourse and institutional support for their intellectual authority in a variety of proposed and established academies, institutes, associations, and, finally, the university.[13]

The men and women who concern me in this chapter constitute a new
gentry, new because it was more open to the claims of intellect alone than
the older gentry of the rich and wellborn. Frederick Law Olmsted, one
of the leaders of the metropolitan gentry, defined the group in a letter
of 1862. His immediate purpose in the letter was to set out his ideas about
who ought to be in the Union League Club, then being founded in New
York. Of course, loyalty to the Union and a commitment to freedom for
the slaves were obvious criteria dating back to the Republican ideas articulated in *Putnam's Monthly* before the war; but more important, and less
fully realized in the Union League Club as it developed, was a second
point. Members, Olmsted insisted, must be loyal to the democratic idea.
He realized the complexity of the problem of leadership and culture in a
democracy, but he would reject for membership anyone who ruled out
the possibility of democratic excellence, who lamented the absence of a
European social structure and culture in the city.

Finally, and this is what specifically defines the people we will discuss,
Olmsted dissociated the notion of "standing" from wealth. While arguing
for the inclusion of men of family, wealth, character, and prominence,
especially in the legal field, he defined a second group of "clever men,
especially of letters, wits, and artists who have made their mark." He
argued that dues should be moderate and the quarters modest; this
would be necessary and appropriate if the club were to embrace the
second group, "who must live on their pay & all who must live carefully
& feel every dollar."[14] Thus the metropolitan gentry, a group of New
Yorkers, perhaps the first in the city's history, who supported themselves
entirely from the pay they earned off their ideas.

The writers among this gentry were largely the product of a revolution
in publishing, particularly the emergence of several great national magazines in New York City after the Civil War. These journalists were, as
William Dean Howells later observed, the first Americans able to pursue
literature as a lifetime "business." The reformers among them, like
Olmsted, were also the first generation to create careers and earn livings
simply as urban professionals, addressing the problems and opportunities of modern city life.[15]

Formed by literary culture but reaching beyond it, the metropolitan
gentry took various paths toward public life—as publicists, as social reformers. While they shared much—including personal association with
each other and a sense of themselves as a distinctive group in the city and
in the nation—this group was diverse. While the publicists emphasized
the privilege culture ought to confer in a democracy, the importance of

the cultivated in the making of political opinion, for the reformers cultivation implied responsibility and culture itself presented ameliorative
and unifying possibilities. Neither publicist nor reformer, however, ever
realized how limited was the bourgeois culture to which they were committed. Nor, except for E. L. Godkin, did they have any sense that the
claims they made for their culture in a vast metropolis, riven by class
division and marked by unprecedented cultural diversity, profoundly
qualified the democratic ideal.

METROPOLITAN JOURNALISM AND POLITICAL OPINION

The metropolitan gentry came of age during the crisis of Union, and it
was in the crucible of the Civil War that they forged a generational
identity. Edmund Wilson and George Fredrickson have shown us how
important the war was in shaping intellect and intellectual institutions in
the United States.[16] One could go further, however, to suggest that much
of the meaning of the war derived from its close and perhaps peculiar
association with cities, especially New York City. The consolidation of the
Union—on terms articulated largely by New York's political journalists
—established the metropolitan gentry as a national political force and
established their political language, a language deriving from the conditions of metropolitan life, as a national political language.

The U.S. Sanitary Commission illuminates this process. This legendary
vehicle of Northern philanthropic spirit during the war symbolizes, as
Fredrickson has demonstrated, the new pattern of elite authority, but he
errs in associating the ideological and institutional forms it represents
entirely with the war. It was an elaboration of ideas of authority and
responsibility that had earlier been developed in the gentry's confrontation with urban poverty in New York City.[17] What it in fact represents is
the nationalization of a cluster of social understandings defined in New
York. Now the emergent metropolitan gentry were ready to reconstruct
the South and the nation as they had begun to reconstruct the city. Such
activism, they anticipated, would not only save society, but would as well
win for them the authority to which they aspired and which they thought
was owed to them. If they did not act, they feared, men of their sort
would vanish completely from public life.

The metropolitan gentry responded to a broad and long-term transformation of politics and society. The process was accelerated (and sharpened in their perception) by the Civil War, but it was not caused by the
war.[18] These ambitious young men looked to a strengthened national
state as the means of reforming Southern society, Northern cities, and
for providing an arena for cultivated intelligence in politics. So they
pressed for federal intervention in the South, they applauded the Su-

preme Court's decision in *Gelpcke* v. *Dubuque* (1863), which represented a federal restraint on fiscal irresponsibility in cities, and they hoped that the war to defend the authority of the national government would strengthen institutions generally. It would have the effect, at least indirectly, of bolstering the "best men," as many of them styled themselves.[19]

This cluster of concerns was intertwined with Radical Republicanism, which the metropolitan gentry had helped to define. But within a very few years, no later than the early 1870s, the very same concerns motivated a rejection of national power in the South and of the whole notion of positive government. The metropolitan gentry abandoned their sympathy for Radical Republicanism and formulated in its stead the laissez-faire Liberalism associated with the New York *Nation* in the 1870s and 1880s. The story of this reversal is at once complex and fascinating. It reveals not only a subtle interplay of national and local concerns in a metropolis but as well the way in which developments in the city's social and political life pressed a frightened intellectual elite to recast its thought, with serious costs for the blacks abandoned in the South as well as for the workers, immigrants, and women in the city who had hoped to enlist the state in their interests.

The two men who best represent the metropolitan gentry in national affairs—George William Curtis and E. L. Godkin—together created the career of political journalist in New York and America. More than any previous generation of American writers and editors, they grasped that public opinion, the product of political journalism, would be a fundamental fact of modern government. Godkin, for that matter, deserves credit as the first serious American student of public opinion.[20] For nearly forty years these two pursued their weekly calling, Curtis in *Harper's Weekly* and Godkin in *The Nation*, as the country's most widely and attentively read publicists, providing reliable guidance to their middle-class audiences on art, manners, and, especially, politics. They were read, at least in part, because they pioneered a lighter but still serious type of writing that was characteristic of New York journalism—and a contrast to that of Boston's heavier *Atlantic* or *North American Review*.[21]

The two were, as we shall see, very different men. Curtis held weekly conversations in print with his readers, and they seem to have loved him. Godkin sought to intimidate his readers, and they respected him. Curtis had a bit of transcendental idealism and softness in his character (he had lived for a while at Brook Farm instead of going to college) and plenty of decency, while Godkin had more than a little ruthlessness and even unscrupulousness. Curtis believed more in human capacity for good, and he had an abiding faith, too generous no doubt, in improvement and democracy. Godkin had a low opinion of human nature and of democracy. Yet on the big issues of their time, Curtis and Godkin tended to come out on the same side. On only one major issue, women's suffrage, did they disagree, with Curtis consistently and strongly supporting it, while Godkin moved from tepid support to opposition.

Curtis, who had started his literary career as a writer of romantic novels and gentle, but telling, satires on New York's fashionable society and metropolitan foibles, received a political education through his association with *Putnam's Monthly*. On the magazine, men like Charles F. Briggs, Parke Godwin, and, later, Frederick Law Olmsted drew him toward public affairs. So did a change in personal circumstances, when his marriage to Anna Shaw brought him within the orbit and influence of a family of New England abolitionists, transplanted to Staten Island. Finally, there was a series of disturbing national events, most notably the spectacle of Bloody Kansas and the caning of Charles Sumner in the Senate chamber by a slaveholding congressman. On August 5, 1856, Curtis gave his first political oration, "The Duty of the American Scholar to Politics and the Times." This address, delivered at Wesleyan University by the thirty-two-year-old Curtis, was published in the *New York Weekly Tribune*. Horace Greeley's *Tribune*, performing well as a metropolitan newspaper with a national edition circulation of 173,000 copies, enabled Curtis to become overnight a leader of Northern opinion.

Curtis's address was eloquent and unambiguous. Respectful though he was of learning for its own sake, he insisted upon more. While studying "Greek roots" had its value, there are, he insisted, "American topics and times" that must be addressed. He wanted scholars to do more than accumulate learning; they must be "wise" and, like John Milton, bring this wisdom into the course of human affairs. The calling of the scholar is that of a "public conscience by which public measures may be tested." In a republic, Curtis explained, a scholar assumes the obligation to "have an opinion on great public measures" and issues. In the present instance, he declared, the great issue was "human slavery" and the "great fight of Freedom."[22]

His oration announced his support for John C. Frémont and Republicanism in 1856. Four years later, Curtis was a delegate to the Republican convention that nominated Abraham Lincoln. In 1863, having already assumed a regular column in *Harper's Monthly*, where for forty years he would comment on literature, metropolitan life, and the arts, he became political editor of *Harper's Weekly*, which had a circulation in excess of 100,000, rising above 200,000 in the 1870s. By the 1880s, such was Curtis's stature in the nation's literary life that he, not Mark Twain, nor even William Dean Howells, was identified by the Harvard *Crimson* as the favorite American writer of Harvard's students.[23]

Remaining always a literary man, he redefined his literary vocation. He abandoned fiction to commit himself to influencing public life as a lecturer and writer. Though he ran for office three times—and was seriously considered for the presidency in 1872—he never became a politician; he was always a literary man in politics.[24] In time, he became one of the city's and the nation's most revered citizens. After the death of William Cullen Bryant, whose eulogy Curtis delivered, Curtis was summoned as the city's chosen spokesman for formal literary and civic occasions of celebration and commemoration. To a rapidly expanding national middle class, he served, in Vernon Parrington's phrase, "as volunteer political mentor and critic." When Curtis died in 1892, he was memorialized as "a great citizen" and "one of our few really influential critics of public events."[25]

The weekly "Journal of Civilization" that the brothers Harper established in New York in 1857 had been initially Democratic and hostile to Lincoln in 1860. But it moved into the Republican camp as the war proceeded. From 1863 onward, when Curtis became editor, its Protestant, educated, middle-class readers received a verbal and visual presentation of the Republican meaning of the war in the editorials of Curtis and in Thomas Nast's powerful drawings. After the war, Curtis used the pages of *Harper's* to argue the case of national responsibility for black citizenship in the South.[26]

By 1870, Curtis had begun in his column to express deep misgivings about the direction of politics in New York. Tammany Democracy, it seemed, involved no less a threat to republican (and Republican) principles than did the slaveholding Democracy of the South.[27] Tammany in his view had "subverted" popular government and had established an "imperialism" sustained by "plebiscite."[28] When Curtis in words and Nast in pictures turned on Tammany in 1870, Boss Tweed responded by throwing Harper textbooks out of the city's schools. But Fletcher Harper stood with his principled journalists, while circulation tripled.[29] So the campaign continued until Tweed was toppled, to Curtis's immense pleasure, in November 1871.[30]

Although both Nast and Curtis believed deeply in Republican principles and were offended by Tweed's corruption of democratic government, there was always an uncomfortable tension between them. They were two very different kinds of men, using two very different kinds of media. Curtis's "graceful and forceful" editorials embodied a personal and intellectual style quite distinct from the "sledge-hammer cartoons" drawn by Nast.[31] The scrappy immigrant Nast took note of the difference between himself and the refined, gentlemanly Curtis. When Curtis "attacks a man with his pen," Nast reflected, "it seems as if he were apologizing for the act. I try to hit the enemy between the eyes and knock him down."[32]

Both his medium and his style allowed Nast to reach beyond Curtis's cultivated constituency to a wider, if not quite a mass, audience. It was, therefore, Nast, not Curtis, who drew the wrath of Boss Tweed: "I don't care a straw for your newspaper articles, my constituents don't know how to read, but they can't help seeing those damned pictures."[33] However democratic his sympathies, Curtis, who isolated himself on Staten Island after his marriage, never had a feel for the hopes, conflicts, hatreds of the ordinary working people of the city, and he did not know how to communicate with them. They were not part of his democratic city, even though in an abstract way he cared for them. In this respect, too, he was successor to the kind and gentle Bryant.

Curtis, who was drawn into public life by the moral appeal of a political party identified with the great cause of anti-slavery, saw in New York's Tweedism and in the patronage-driven politics emerging in Washington a denial of the kind of party that had won his allegiance. He talked of the corruption of parties and government, and by that he meant something quite specific. Parties, he felt, had ceased to be "an agency of the people." Instead of parties identified with a public purpose and sustained by principle, he saw in their stead a "machine" that had "no public purpose" beyond its own perpetuation.[34] Like most of the metropolitan gentry, he became a Mugwump, one of those independents who took their ground above both parties. But to say that he became a Mugwump out of anti-party feeling would misread Curtis. He left the Republican Party because it had deserted not only its founding principles but the very conception of principled parties. Without such parties there was, of course, little need for the literary man in politics that Curtis had called for and become in 1856.

Out of these concerns Curtis turned to Civil Service Reform, a movement exceptionally closely associated with the cultivated elite of New York, who supplied its leadership.[35] Curtis became the movement's most authoritative spokesman. Opponents of Civil Service Reform claimed that it was merely the cry of the "outs," and historians since have interpreted it as an elite attack on democracy. In a very broad sense both of these charges are true, but it is also true that Curtis claimed that the movement sought a restoration of democracy, of principled, responsible government.[36] Close attention to what was said and done reveals some specific meanings, for democracy and politics were at issue. So was the place of intellect.

Curtis and his fellow literary men had an interest in a politics based, as they would put it, on intelligence rather than on spoils. If parties divided over issues rather than on spoils, then, as Stephen Showronek has recently remarked, "men with skills in the formulation of great issues" and in the formation of "national opinion" would become a potent political force in the cities and in the nation.[37] And this, as Curtis saw it, was a move toward the restoration of democracy. The spoils system, he argued, had corrupted the true purpose of parties and emasculated the authority of the executive. Under the spoils system, he argued, a "selfish class interest in politics is created" and this severely incapacitated government. When the object of government becomes the protection of this interest, which seems to have been the case in Tweed's Tammany, the public interest dissolves. A movement to end the corruption of parties and government was, thus, a "people's reform."[38]

There is something very appealing in Curtis, something even noble. Yet one feels his isolation from the stuff of life and politics. Theodore Roosevelt, who also supported Civil Service Reform, understood, as Curtis did not, how really limited the reform was, how inadequate to the real issues of Gilded Age New York and America. Too many Civil Service Reformers, Roosevelt recalled in his autobiography, "proved tepidly indifferent or actively hostile to reforms that were of profound and far-reaching social and industrial consequence."[39]

If Curtis had little feel for the social and industrial issues, the class issues, at stake in New York and the nation, his fellow publicist E. L. Godkin was intensely attuned to them. But instead of lending support to an active governmental response to such problems, he made the New York *Nation* a national oracle of laissez-faire liberalism.

During and immediately after the Civil War the idea of a unified, powerful nation, with a single set of metropolitan standards in politics and culture, took hold of New York's metropolitan gentry. Some sort of publication was needed, national in its reach but based in New York, if the gentry of the metropolis was to establish and sustain such a standard. The project of a "weekly paper" that was "independent of mere party politics, and upholding sound principles of loyalty and nationality" originated with Frederick Law Olmsted, and he formally proposed it to a group of writers and potential financial backers at the Union League Club in June 1863.[40] Soon after the close of the war, in July 1865, the idea was realized with the founding of *The Nation*, with E. L. Godkin as editor. Godkin had not been the first choice for the editorship, but he so quickly and so thoroughly gave the paper the stamp of his authority that any other editor was and is unimaginable. Godkin and *The Nation* became interchangeable, the interchangeability being furthered by his policy of having no signed articles.

But if Godkin thus represented New York in the nation's culture and politics, he was never fully a New Yorker. *The Nation* betrayed this, for it always conveyed a suggestion of Boston Brahmin culture trying to cope with the overwhelming reality of New York. Godkin was always drawn to Boston; he did not like the wide-open culture of New York, where swarms of "quack poets, quack novelists, and quack historians . . . enjoy the greatest consideration." Nor did he like most New Yorkers. But after moving his residence to Boston in the late 1870s, he found the cultivated calm more than he could take. The energy and vitality of New York—which had, after all, given him his chance—looked better from Boston.[41] New York was irresistible, and the basic orientation of the magazine was metropolitan. Like *Harper's Weekly*, it assumed that the whole nation should be interested in and familiar with the city's ways and institutions. New York topics, as befitted a metropolis, were the staple of New York and, for that matter, provincial magazines.[42]

Edwin Lawrence Godkin was born in Ireland in 1831, of a Protestant family that claimed English descent.[43] His father was a fairly well-known Dissenting minister and journalist. The younger Godkin was sent to Queens College, Belfast, where he was schooled in the classical political economy of David Ricardo and James Mill. After graduating in 1851, he took up a career in journalism, serving as a correspondent for the London *Daily News* covering the Crimean War. In 1856, he emigrated to the United States. Supporting himself by free-lance journalism, Godkin studied law and was admitted to the New York Bar in 1858. But he had little interest in the law, preferring a literary career. In this aspiration he was the beneficiary of a fortuitous friendship. Because Charles Loring Brace, a New York writer and reformer we shall discuss later in this chapter, had in 1854 married Letitia Neill of Belfast, whose family was well known to Godkin, the ambitious immigrant had on arrival a valuable contact in the city's literary world, and it was one he effectively used.

Through Brace, Godkin came to know Olmsted, who in turn sustained him during the rocky beginnings of *The Nation*. The magazine's original investors had been abolitionists concerned about the fate of the freedmen. For them, equality before the law was a national issue, and their overriding concern was the removal of "all artificial distinctions" between blacks and the "rest of the population."[44] Godkin, however, was neither fully committed to this ideal nor completely frank about his reservations. The first issue of *The Nation* forced the matter into the open. The front-page column, "The Week," contained a remark that everyone "is heartily tired of discussing his [the freedman's] condition and his rights, and little else is talked about."[45] The furor was immediate, and it almost cost Godkin the magazine. It was an unseemly beginning, but Godkin was saved, it seems, by the steadfast support of Boston's Charles Eliot Norton and by the willingness of Frederick Law Olmsted to evidence his public confidence in his friend Godkin.[46]

The Nation, as Godkin conceived it, represented an "experiment" to "see whether the best writers in America can get a fair hearing from the American public on questions of politics, art, and literature through a newspaper."[47] Intuitively grasping the journalistic opportunities of modern culture and politics, Godkin defined a central role for *The Nation*. In "modern democracies," Godkin asserted, newspapers have "taken the place in the formation of public opinion which was filled in ancient ones by the habit of assembling in the Agora."[48] Not much at home in the promiscuous crowds implied by the image of the agora, Godkin preferred metropolitan journalism, with its remove to the medium of print and the extended influence that could be achieved by a New York publication. His community of discourse would not include the ordinary folk, and he would not have to mix with them on the "democratic plan," something he felt was quite "disagreeable."[49] Rather his truncated public would be nearer his social sympathies—writers, editors, professors, the cultivated generally. Godkin, the publisher Henry Holt recalled, was "an authority with authorities."[50]

Opinion for him was neither the product nor the possession of the whole social body. It belonged to a disciplined and cultured minority. His reform of public life would be a movement from above, comprehending, as he explained to Carl Schurz, "thoughtful, educated, high-minded men —gentlemen in short."[51] *The Nation* was written by gentlemen for gentlemen; its readership, which was usually around 6,000 and never exceeded 12,000, thought of themselves as being "linked by bonds of intellectual and moral congeniality."[52] Godkin's purpose was not the extension of democracy, but rather its purification. No wonder Charles Eliot Norton declared that *The Nation* stood with "Harvard and Yale Colleges" as "almost the only solid barriers against the invasion of modern barbarism and vulgarity."[53]

When *The Nation* commenced, Henry James, then a young New York writer, welcomed it because "it made no secret of a literary leaning," and he was pleased to publish his early criticism in it. Many years later, when Godkin died, William James testified that to his "generation" Godkin "was certainly the towering influence in all thought concerning public affairs," determining "the whole current of discussion."[54] How does one account for Godkin's enormous influence? He assumed a supreme sense of superiority, condemning the shallowness and absence of moral and mental discipline about him.[55] By treating himself as an institution, he became one. If not original, he was always clever and forceful. "He was," recalled Brander Matthews, the theater critic and Columbia professor, "clear-headed, but he was never open-minded."[56] By the late 1880s, some of the narrowness and prejudice of his journalism had become apparent; Godkin had brought Liberalism to a shrill negation, always choosing pessimism over tolerance. But until then, *The Nation* under his direction offered its readers a way of placing the events of the day within the context of a compelling interpretation of historical tendencies.

In 1865, the year *The Nation* was founded and two years after Curtis became the editor of *Harper's,* New York opinion was broadcast weekly to the rest of the country. This metropolitan opinion was both identifiable and influential; to a considerable extent, it was also unified. Hostile to Democratic localism, these organs of New York political journalism stood for nationalism and positive government. The central issue for both magazines, if not the exclusive one, was the nationalization of civil rights. Committed to metropolitan standards of citizenship, these Republican publicists, believing the war marked "an epoch by the consolidation of nationality under democratic forms," wanted the national government to guarantee the voting rights of freedmen in the South.[57]

Within a decade, however, all of this changed. New York's political journalists moved from Radical Republicanism, which implied a general commitment to use positive government to realize a democratic society, and instead took up the notion of limited government based upon a Liberal celebration of economic man. From the defense of the freedmen, the New York political journalists moved to a defense of market capitalism. The withdrawal of national support for black rights in the South was intimately connected to urban developments in the North that seemed to require a defense of the market against political intervention.

It is often said that New York's Republican reformers simply tired of the problem of the freedmen and abandoned them.[58] In fact, the story is far more complicated than that. The rise of economic man, limited government, and the abandonment of national responsibility for the freedmen were different aspects of the same phenomenon, one rooted in the social history of Northern cities, particularly New York. There was, close examination reveals, an important class issue underneath it all. The intellectual elite, fearful that various subordinate groups might capture the democratic government to advance their own special interests, redefined the role of government in a way that would, they hoped, preclude such an active use of the government to address social and economic problems.

This change is witnessed most easily in the pages of *The Nation.* By paying particular attention to the timing and context of change there, one can see how the political and social history of the city and the nation between 1865 and 1875 became intertwined and played into the process of ideological reversal. The conjuncture of rather specific social, political, and intellectual developments was not, as we shall see, merely fortuitous; it was causal.

Godkin's democratic commitments had never been deep; he had long believed that democratic citizenship did not automatically confer the vote, and he regularly suggested restricting suffrage in the city, either to those who passed a literacy test or to taxpayers.[59] It was relatively easy for him, therefore, when provoked, to retreat from Radical Republicanism. And he was provoked by the labor movement's postwar agitation for legislative enactment of the eight-hour day. When Congress enacted legislation in 1868 establishing the eight-hour day for federal contract work, Godkin and Curtis began to rethink the relations of politics, economics, and government. Almost singlehandedly, they redefined (narrowed) for their readers the legitimate universe of political discourse in the United States.

In October 1865, *The Nation* ran the first of many articles on the eight-hour movement. In common with others that would follow, it was first of all an attack on the very notion of working-class politics. Class relations, it explained, were beyond the reach of government. One cannot interfere with the "natural law of supply and demand." If workers want more of the good life, they should help increase production; but they not only should not but could not alter distribution by political means. To accept the demands of the working people, *The Nation* announced, would bring the country and the city very quickly to the time "when all things will be in common and grass will grow in Broadway."[60] Knowing full well that the working classes had numbers on their side in an electoral democracy, Godkin ruled out politics as a means of addressing economic issues. He sought to keep these issues in the realm of opinion, where the cultured minority he represented had considerable resources, including the moral support of the upwardly mobile middle classes.

While acknowledging, even insisting upon, the special political authority that went with the acquisition of culture, Godkin did not worry overmuch about denying the working classes, through long hours, the opportunity to acquire such culture for themselves. Physically overtaxing labor, he acknowledged, might legitimately be regulated in a way compatible with natural laws, but one could not interfere with these laws in behalf of culture. Besides, he self-righteously explained to those who might sympathize with the workers, he knew businessmen and lawyers who also suffered from "want of time for self-culture."[61]

Curtis entered the discussion at this point, with what he called "A Saturday Sermon." He explained, again, that an eight-hour law amounted to legislating "against the attraction of gravity." Capital will flee; the economy will collapse. But the more sympathetic Curtis went on to ruminate about the cultural implications of this position. He could not but respond to the claim of workers, made now for several generations, that they wanted time to pursue cultural interests. "Must the laborer," Curtis worried, "be forever a mere drudge . . . hopelessly debarred from intellectual expansion, the delights of art, and of intelligent leisure, which we call mental culture?" The question was apt and put with feeling. The answer, however, left the realm of social analysis and escaped into a world of quasi-religious hopefulness, where utopian fantasy had the effect of denying the legitimacy of labor politics and culture. "Surely not," he wrote, "unless the world is a total failure and the deepest human faith a lie. But there are no short cuts to happiness." He hoped that education and invention would solve the problem, the one overcoming selfishness, the other increasing production. In time, he anticipated, the competition between labor and capital would be replaced by the "spirit of fraternity and cooperation."[62]

It was at this point, already worried about the labor movement, that Curtis and Godkin took notice of Tweed, who had taken over the city of New York. While they detested Tweed because of his financial corruption, that was not the issue. Godkin in particular saw in Tweed (and, for that matter, Fernando Wood, his predecessor) the specter of a class politics.

Godkin denied that local majorities had any moral force. Virtue and intelligence, he contended, surely had a greater claim than the ignorant, degraded majorities mobilized by Tweed. The democratic majority, Godkin insisted, does not have the right "to mismanage its affairs."[63] But what sort of mismanagement worried Godkin? The answer came in a rush two months later. An article titled "Classes in Politics" explained to the readers of The Nation just why they should be worried. Before the war there had been no noticeable class division in New York or America; now, however, a "wide social gulf" had emerged in New York, with the eight-hour movement a predictable result. The problem with democratic politics, and particularly with universal manhood suffrage, was that both parties were "bidding for the support" of the toiling masses. The Democrats, moreover, were creating as well an ethnic politics, appealing to the Irish Fenian Party. At the same time Radicals were trying to organize "a distinct negro party at the South." Godkin's problem is now apparent: these three classes (and potentially more, if the principle were to be accepted) were looking after themselves in politics. They were not accepting the definition of the best interests of the whole offered by the metropolitan gentry, by the journalistic makers of opinion. To Godkin and Curtis this looked like a choice between class government and principled government. The immediate prospect, it seemed, was the formation of a "workingman's party," an "Irish party," and a "black party," each "bent on the promotion of their own interests, at whatever cost."

Worst of all, each would be "putting up their votes for sale at every great election"—and finding buyers.[64]

Godkin did not have to look far for other threatening groups. Beyond labor, ethnic, and black interests, he worried about Greenbackers and feminists.[65] Collectively they presented the specter of a coalition of subordinate groups seeking to use the government to advance their interests. Susan B. Anthony and Elizabeth Cady Stanton, for example, committed their feminist paper, *The Revolution,* to Greenbackism, eight-hour legislation, protection of black rights in the South, and an active government generally. Although Stanton occasionally lapsed into Godkinesque statements quite contemptuous of blacks and immigrants, preferring educated women voters to "ignorant manhood," and even though the feminist alliance with labor had dissolved by the early 1870s, Godkin and Curtis had been frightened by this potential coalition of positive government advocates, all seeking a redistributive government.[66]

It was Tweed, however, who lay nearest the center of their fears. His threat to the metropolitan gentry was concrete, specific, and painful. Culture and intelligent opinion had too little authority in Tweed's New York, while ignorant voters had too much. Tweed's politics of spoils not only challenged the gentry's status, it left them without a public function: no one needed their special literary skills and no one wanted their ideas. The prospect of a politically mobilized working class threatened their interests, and they feared that Tweedism might bring such a politics into practice. So the danger was multiple, covering class, status, and role. A move to narrow the range of electoral politics, especially in the city, and a move to depoliticize economic issues offered at least a partial solution to these problems.

By 1871, this logic had begun to play itself out, with emerging city fears getting translated into a revised Southern strategy. In *The Nation* it was proposed that the vote in cities be restricted to taxpayers and that Reconstruction, obviously a failure, be abandoned as a national project, leaving the local Southern elite to work out their own solution.[67] Godkin's effort to establish the authority of culture in politics, placing its judgments beyond the reach of electoral politics, had led him to deny that the city had a political character at all. If Godkin's theory of municipal law was indeed incorporated into the legal doctrine of Gilded Age America, in the Dillon Rule, it was rejected by the groups that worried him.[68]

These issues, still amorphous in 1871, were crystallized and joined in a dramatic way in the tense atmosphere of the Tompkins Square Riot of January 1874. A downturn in the economy brought demands for public employment from the city's workers. In the past such demands had evoked both sympathy and an official, if inadequate, response. But 1873 was different. The city had changed since the war; the distance, both physical and social, between the working and middle classes was greater. Middle-class New York, moreover, could not easily forget the working-class and immigrant participation in the Draft Riots of 1864 and the more recent Orange Riot (1871), nor could they help but be apprehensive about socialism in the wake of the Paris Commune. The city refused the workers, Mayor Havenmeyer objecting that public works meant higher taxes and thus the "confiscation of property."[69]

Godkin and Curtis defined the issue for the middle classes in the city and the nation. The demands of labor were a clear case of just what they feared: a politics of parochial interest rather than of their own comprehensive ideals. Worried about a working-class takeover in New York, hostile to the idea of an active state for that very reason, they treated the demand for work as something beyond the legitimate realm of politics and political rights.

It was true that the Spring Street "International," a local, non-Marxist, Greenbacker radical group recently expelled from the socialist International Workingmen's Association, frankly embraced such interest politics. The government, they argued, passed legislation for the rich, so now it was time to pass some for the workers. The legitimacy of even *making* this demand was denied. When workers tried to hold a rally at Tompkins Square on January 13, 1874, the police charged and dispersed the meeting. Put differently, the police prevented workers from holding a public meeting in the largest public space on the Lower East Side. The incident, as Herbert G. Gutman has observed, was an instance of the forcible denial of political rights to workers. It was not seen in this light, however, by the educated classes of the city. *Harper's Weekly* praised the police, thanking them for suppressing such an un-American project, so reminiscent of the Paris Commune.[70]

Godkin pondered the whole event, and his response came three months later, in an article aptly titled "The Real Nature of the Coming Struggle." The danger, he asserted, was not revolution. Rather, it was the prospect that the working class would come to power through the vote.

Tweedism, he explained, was the development that made such a political result possible. And it was the product of a larger social and political problem. The growth of manufacturing, itself the product of an "artificial stimulus" supplied by the tariff and immigration, created a dependent class, a class of wage earners completely "different in tone and mind and mode of life" from that envisioned by the founders of the Republic. These working-class voters and, for that matter, "southern negroes" as well were inclined to "take the short view of things." Hostile, perhaps understandably, to the capitalist class, workers tended, with less justification, to "distrust" the "educated class," who "as the keepers of the record of the human experience" must point out "the futility of all plans for the promotion of prosperity which do not rest on the capacity of the people for self-denial." When intellectuals "honestly" fulfill this "obligation" to society, he self-righteously lamented, they make themselves "odious" to the working classes. Even if the working people did not appreciate his efforts, Godkin would instruct them—and, more important, those of the middle classes who might otherwise sympathize with workers.

During the war, he explained, there was a "great increase in the powers of the Government." But that development should not be misunderstood. It was not intended that various groups would turn to the government to "make money cheap" or even to "stimulate industry." The problem with Tweedism, as Godkin saw it, was that it encouraged precisely this sort of parochial shortsightedness. Invented in New York City, "owing to unusually favorable local circumstances," Tweed's system was a device for "the transfer of power to the ignorant and the poor, and the use of Government to carry out the poor and ignorant man's view of the nature of society." Godkin presented this contest over power, influence, and material goods as a "conflict . . . between civilization and barbarism." There was, he had written two years earlier, no surer way to fall "down into barbarism" than to elevate equality to the "highest political good." It would, he was covinced, "prove fatal to art, to science, to literature, and to law."[71]

A political crisis in a national metropolis always has national implications. In New York during the 1860s and 1870s, the metropolitan gentry, responding to their local circumstances, redefined the domain of political discourse, greatly reducing its territory. Writing for the nation's middle classes as well as for those of their own city, New York's political journalists were able to propagate a liberal opinion that advanced their own interest, as a class and as intellectuals, while denying the legitimacy of any other interests.

By the centennial year of 1876, *The Nation* had come to represent, in Godkin's word, "Liberalism," a political standard thought to be higher than and better than either party. It stood for laissez-faire policies and a role for the educated in politics. The problem was no longer to guarantee the freedmen their rights, but rather, in the words of the political scientist Alan Grimes, "to hold the ground of morality and orthodoxy against the increasing assaults by 'the people.' "[72]

This Liberalism pointed rather directly to Civil Service Reform and to the American Social Science Association. Founded in Boston in 1865 and dominated by Boston and New York gentry, the ASSA gathered into itself, according to member Whitelaw Reid, "a large amount of college respectability."[73] It was not a gathering of university professors, something its name might suggest today. Rather it preceded the university and comprehended educated gentlemen and some women from all the learned occupations. It was at once a humanitarian organization and an institutional vehicle for increasing the political force of gentry opinion. While some urban reformers and feminists embraced its humanitarian possibilities, for Godkin and other Liberals, those who participated in politics from the privacy of their studies, it conferred institutional authority on their opinion.[74]

Godkin wanted political influence for himself and his class without having much to do with political life. Unlike Theodore Roosevelt, Godkin did not like politics. Roosevelt's affectionate portrayal in his autobiography of his introduction to politics at the Twenty-first District Republican Association, which met above a saloon, is inconceivable for Godkin; so, too, is the friendship begun there with Joe Murray. Roosevelt had Godkin's type in mind when he urged educated men not to "shrink from contact with the rough people who do the world's work."[75] Godkin, however, had a different sense of the place of the educated in America; he wanted broad influence in public life that was independent of electoral politics.

The American Social Science Association would, Godkin assumed, show the public that some opinions, like some men, were better than others.[76] Godkin and his circle were concerned to establish their opinion in public; they were not interested in a public or political sphere that served as an arena of competing ideas and interests. Sound opinion, as they conceived it, would not emerge from the give-and-take of political life. Rather it was assumed that it was possible for men of their class and education to discover the laws of society rather directly. The authoritative knowledge gained by the educated would, it was hoped, nullify the disturbing political competition of interest groups, and social science would thus justify the neutral state.[77] Since they imagined that problems, particularly those of political economy, could, at least in principle, be resolved by discovering the natural harmony of society, there would be no contradictions, no trade-offs.[78] Without the stuff of politics, there would be no need for politics at all. Politicians would be unnecessary, while the educated would be indispensable.

Things did not work out so neatly. Yet Godkin and Curtis, situated in the nation's metropolis, communicating with the nation's educated and middle classes, had an enormous impact on the definition of the terrain of politics in the United States. These literary men, perhaps in a fitting exercise of their special skills, deserve considerable credit—or blame— for setting new and rather constricting boundaries on the language of American politics.

By separating the discourse of politics from that of economics—at a crucial moment in the history of American capitalism—they immunized the market economy from the challenge of politics, whether in theory or in practice. For the most part, in fact, American social inquiry since Godkin has been distinctive in the degree to which politics and economics have been analyzed separately, as autonomous realms.[79] Changes in the social and political geography of the city limited the capacity of the working class to challenge this constriction of the language of politics. The separation of work and residence and the local organization of politics into a pattern of ethnic competition made it difficult to bring the relations of labor and capital into political discourse. And what Godkin and Curtis wrote comforted the newly created middle classes, mostly entrepreneurial, enabling them to resist the sporadic demands of those who claimed that something was profoundly wrong.[80]

"CIVIC MURDER"

By the 1880s, Godkin was becoming more predictable and more shrill. Eighteen-eighty-six, in particular, was a trying year. In Henry George, labor found a strong candidate for the mayoralty of New York. The issue was clear for Godkin; the supporters of George, he wrote, aim "by a large vote to undo what has been done for law and order," for they know that city officials will "placate anybody who can command votes."[81] Almost merging in his and Curtis's perception with the George threat was the shocking news from Chicago: while the police were breaking up an anarchist meeting (May 4, 1886), a bomb exploded. Seeing only political insurrection and working-class and immigrant barbarism in the Haymarket tragedy, *The Nation* and *Harper's Weekly* rushed to judgment, blaming the anarchists, even in the absence of evidence. When death sentences were handed down for the accused anarchists a year later, respectable opinion accepted the judgment.[82]

But one notable refused. William Dean Howells, literally in the process of transforming himself from a Boston writer to a New York one, declined to sacrifice liberty to the cultivated but plainly reactionary standard of civilization preached by Godkin and Curtis. Howells, now one of the nation's most celebrated writers, had as a youth been deeply affected by Curtis's oration on the scholar in politics.[83] He began his career as a professional journalist in New York, as a writer for *The Nation* in 1865, before establishing his long association with Boston's *Atlantic*. Later, after Curtis died, he took over Curtis's column in *Harper's Monthly*. Howells's opposition must, therefore, have surprised Godkin and Curtis; one even senses that at times it surprised Howells himself. The key issue, however, was clear to him. Howells understood that workingmen, radicals in this case, were not being allowed to present their ideas in public. The universe of political discourse had been so narrowed as to deny political legitimacy to their ideas, and in the name of an optimistic and complacent middle-class civilization they were being denied their civil rights. To Howells it was "civic murder." The Chicago anarchists died in *"the freest Republic the world has ever known, for their opinions' sake."*[84]

Howells was an unlikely defender of the Chicago anarchists. Early in 1886, before Haymarket, he had proposed in a review of Dostoevsky an American realism that concerned itself "with the smiling aspects of life, which are more American."[85] He was at this time no reformer; he was not even in any strict sense a political man. But Haymarket became a national issue just when he was abandoning Boston for New York, just when, at the age of fifty, he was exploring and learning about metropolitan life, about the social and industrial conditions of his time. Unlike Curtis or Godkin, he came to know the city by walking its streets and neighborhoods, and he let the life of the city touch him. Coming to know the city, Howells recognized the terrible narrowness of laissez-faire orthodoxy. His sense of justice outgrew his capacity to believe in Godkin's natural laws of economy.

After 1881, Howells, who had resigned the editorship of the *Atlantic*, spent more and more time in New York, although he did not officially move there until the end of the decade. Literature and literary culture in Boston and New York were quite different. In Boston, there was a spiritual quality to literature that kept it above ordinary life, not at all implicated in its affairs, particularly not in economic affairs. But in New York literature was a business, and the material reality of its life was overwhelming.[86]

Howells came to favor New York. Explaining his feelings to John W. De Forest in 1887, Howells remarked that "there is little or nothing left for me in Boston." In New York, he told his father, "there is more for me to see and learn."[87] Like his character Basil March, who made the same transition in *A Hazard of New Fortunes*, Howells had come to feel that the "intellectual refinement" of Boston "was not life—it was death-in-life."[88] By 1888, he was telling Henry James that he expected New York to become his home; "at the bottom of our wicked hearts we all like New York." He hoped, moreover, "to use some of its vast, gay, shapeless life" in his fiction. To a Boston friend, he reported that "there are lots of interesting young painting and writing fellows, and the place is lordly free, with foreign touches of all kinds . . . Boston seems of another planet."[89]

While exploring and learning from New York, Howells was trying to get Curtis to write an editorial in *Harper's Weekly* supporting a commutation of the death sentence for the anarchists. Curtis, who had already committed the magazine against the victims, refused. When Curtis declined even to allow a strong letter by Howells to appear in *Harper's*, Howells turned to Whitelaw Reid, who vigorously opposed the position but nonetheless published the letter in the *Tribune* in deference to How-ells's stature.[90] The executions were carried out in spite of his efforts. But Howells resolved someday "to do justice" to those "irreparably wronged men."[91]

A Hazard of New Fortunes (1890) was his response to New York and to Haymarket. As he wrote in a preface of 1909, it was the "first fruit of my New York life." He also thought it the "most vital of my fictions," having been motivated by a "quickened interest in the life about me" that "had been symbolized by the bombs and scaffolds of Chicago."[92] He began the novel in October 1888, writing most of it in a house overlooking Stuyves-ant Square in New York, a quiet and elegant neighborhood that was, nonetheless, a short walk from the Lower East Side.

Still angry about the executions, having just finished Tolstoy's *War and Peace,* and worried about the contradiction of his enjoyment of private comfort and his public sympathy with socialism, he tried to embrace a larger canvas and nobler issues than the "love-affairs common to fic-tion."[93] To Henry James he wrote: "I'm not in very good humor with 'America' myself. . . . I should hardly like to trust to pen and ink with all the audacity of my social ideas." For fifty years, he reflected, he had been optimistically "content with 'civilization' and its ability to come out all right in the end." Yet "I now abhor it," feeling "it is coming out all wrong in the end, unless it bases itself anew on a real equality."[94]

By no means a great novel, *A Hazard of New Fortunes* is an ambitious and admirable one. It was the first novel to bring New York "fully into fiction."[95] It is about a magazine, *Every Other Week,* edited by Basil March, a transplanted Bostonian, and about a streetcar strike (based on an actual strike going on in the city while Howells wrote). Within this framework of Basil March's introduction to New York, the business and editorial side of the magazine, and the strike, Howells is able to explore the city, bringing together intellectuals, capitalists, philanthropists, radicals, im-migrants, and the working class. Clearly giving no credence to Godkin's economic laws, the novel presses a vague kind of socialism on the reader. But it is more importantly a commentary on the relation of business and art, of money and culture within a magazine and within society generally. Howells's accomplishment is considerable; he forces the intellectual to acknowledge his or her complicity in the social and economic world about him. Realizing even that the artist's inclination to see the city aesthetically limits the humanitarian impulse and political implications of what he sees. Howells forces March, as he forced himself, to respond to New York "as life," not as a "spectacle."[96]

If Godkin identified laissez-faire with the cause of civilization, Howells, deeply disturbed by the inequality of life in America, saw in the labor movement and in state intervention the only hope for civilization. Rejecting the whole implication of Godkin's thrust, Howells protested a narrowing of the political realm that denied to working people the right to seek "more power, more ease, more freedom." [97]

Howells continued to write on social and political issues, but after 1897, when a long period of prosperity began, "the old vehemence had left him." [98] If he was less interesting for what he wrote himself, Howells, now known as the Dean of American Letters, vastly enriched and expanded the sensibilities of literary New York. More than any other writer of his generation, he broadened the world of fiction to encompass the life of immigrant New York. He welcomed younger writers who knew that life better than he, most notably Stephen Crane, who got his "artistic education" on "the Bowery." [99] He even invited some of those born into the immigrant experience of the Lower East Side, like Abraham Cahan, into respectable literary companionship.*

URBAN REFORM

The isolation of Howells in 1886 reveals how far the Liberal journalism of Curtis and Godkin had strayed from the high hopes for democracy and metropolitan culture that had informed *Putnam's Monthly* in the 1850s. But if one turns from national political commentators to men and women more closely associated with the city, those who sought to influence national practice by local example, another legacy is evident, one proceeding more consistently from the metropolitan and democratic ambition that had infused the literary culture of midcentury New York. If Godkin and Curtis withdrew from the city under the cover of culture, others brought culture into the city.

No less concerned with the authority and civilizing potential of culture, they were more confident of its power to embrace and inform a wider spectrum of the city's population. More responsive to the actual experience of life in the city for the less well-off, economically and culturally, and less willing to acquiesce in Godkin's stark economic determinism, they enlisted both public and private resources to intervene and elevate the social and cultural circumstances of the mass of the population. Their urban Liberalism, while still rooted in the limitations of time and place, pointed away from laissez-faire and toward Progressivism and the New Deal welfare state.

This tradition of urban reform, no less than Godkin's and Curtis's political journalism, germinated in the fertile soil of the city's literary

---

* Cahan was born in Lithuania, near Vilna, in 1860. He came to New York in 1882. He edited the Yiddish and socialist *Jewish Daily Forward,* and he was the author of several fictions, including a remarkable novel of Jewish assimilation, *The Rise of David Levinsky* (1917).

culture. Frederick Law Olmsted was, as we have seen, an editorial associate of Curtis at *Putnam's* and of Godkin at *The Nation,* while Charles
Loring Brace, whose article "The Benevolent Institutions of New York"
appeared in the first volume of *Putnam's,* was the man who introduced
Godkin to literary New York.

Olmsted and Brace responded to the needs of the new city and its opportunities by creating a new kind of intellectual career. They made careers
out of the theory and practice of reform. They expressed their ideas not
only in books and articles but in institutions and, in Olmsted's case, in the
physical form of the city itself. Finding the traditional learned professions
inadequate to both the times and their own ambitions, they created new
ones. In so doing, they represented a phenomenon of their era. Speaking
to a group of Harvard students in 1854, Ralph Waldo Emerson, referring
specifically to Brace, remarked that "all men of power and originality
nowadays make their own profession." [100]

When these two young men from Hartford, Connecticut, arrived in
the city, neither had a clear vocational idea. Having a generational sense
of themselves as men of "plans and theories and *aims,*" they resolved, in
Olmsted's words in a letter to Brace, to "give our thoughts a practical
turn," for "there's a great work [that] wants doing in our generation." [101]
They sought to influence other men, and they wrote to achieve this influence. Brace began with religious newspapers, a notable essay on Emerson
published in the *Knickerbocker* in 1850, books on the failed revolution in
Hungary and on home life in Germany, and a series of articles, "Walks
Among the New York Poor," in the *New York Times.* Olmsted started with
articles on apples, pears, and parks in the *Horticulturalist,* on the rights of
sailors in the *American Whig Review,* a book on England, *Walks and Talks
of an American Farmer in England* (1852), and his famous articles on the
South. Published in the *New York Times,* they became the basis for his
three classic books on the South.

The two ambitious writers also became participants in the Saturday-
evening literary gatherings at the home of Anne Charlotte Lynch, a
young teacher and poet. Soon after her arrival in 1846 with little money
and few connections in the city, this witty, attractive woman who had the
gift of prompting serious conversation assumed a position at the center
of the city's literary life. [102] Hers was, perhaps, the first intellectual circle
in the city's history that included both men and women on what seem to
have been equal terms.* The salon, off Washington Square, moved to

* She was a strong advocate of women's education. She later endowed a prize in the
French Academy to honor works on the education of women. After a few years, claiming a
lack of interest in the subject, the Academy absorbed the fund into its general endowment.

West Thirty-seventh Street in 1855, after her marriage to the NYU professor of Italian literature Vincenzo Botta. During the late 1840s and 1850s, literary New York came to her home for tea, cookies, and *conversazioni*. Poe, who first read "The Raven" at one of her meetings, was a regular, as were Greeley, Curtis, Bryant, Fuller, Briggs, Lydia M. Child, Grace Greenwood, Catherine Sedgwick, and Helen Hunt. Godwin recalled that it "came closer to forming a salon as we read of in France than any we had before her."[103] Olmsted had known Lynch from his boyhood days in Hartford, and he resumed the acquaintance in the city. He intended, he wrote his father, to cultivate her friendship, even though her verses were "dull." The reason, he allowed, was that "she is acquainted with all the distinguished people and her taste is highly cultivated."[104]

At the suggestion of Brace, Henry Raymond, the founding editor of the *New York Times*, commissioned Olmsted to write a series of letters on the South and slavery. The letters were enormously influential, becoming the most important authority, as Eric Foner has remarked, for a central element of a developing free-labor ideology of the new Republican Party.[105] They established Olmsted, and for the first time the possibility of a literary career seemed real for him. He expressed confidence to his father that he "might hereafter make a decent living by writing."[106] Not long afterward, in the spring of 1855, he became managing editor of *Putnam's Monthly*. Feeling he had no talent at all for business, he had "an oppressive and desperate desire to make a success of his literary career."[107] Asking his father for a loan to help finance the advertising of his first book on slavery, he explained that he expected with it "to take & keep a position as a recognized litterateur, as a man of influence in literary matters." Not only would such success be "gratifying" to him, it would open other "literary enterprises" to him.[108]

Events, however, dashed this particular dream. *Putnam's Monthly* went under, leaving Olmsted and Curtis with substantial debts. But fortune brought Olmsted another opportunity, the superintendency of the proposed Central Park and, a year later, the chance, with Calvert Vaux, to design it. Unlike some of the metropolitan gentry, Olmsted tried to establish himself as at once both a literary and a practical man. He always, in fact, attributed his appointment to his literary reputation, particularly to the literary connections that enabled him to get the endorsement of Washington Irving.[109] All through his career there is a tension between the literary and active, the impractical and practical. Though extremely active and practical in the world, Olmsted never ceased being a literary man, something evidenced in the subtitle of the stinging pamphlet he published in 1881, when he finally left New York for the peacefulness of Boston, *Spoils of the Park: With a Few Leaves from the Deep-laden Note-books of "A Wholly Unpractical Man."* He used his literary connections and his writing to advance his notion of the park, while seeking to educate and influence the aesthetic understanding of the cultivated classes with his parks.[110]

Brace had come to New York to study theology at Union Theological Seminary, with the intention of a career of writing and preaching. But compared to the life of the city—the *"flood* of humanity" that "sweeps along" Broadway—theology seemed tame and ineffectual.[111] His disillusionment with cloistered intellect was advanced when he spent the winter of 1850–51 in Berlin. There he came to appreciate American practicality, finding the "literary class" of Berlin highly cultivated but preoccupied with "a sort of vapor with shadows on it" rather than with the "solidity and stuff" of life. He returned to New York having decided to undertake "some course of work for the unfortunate in our city."[112]

Brace became associated with various philanthropic groups in the city, while continuing to pursue his studies and his literary work. As a student at Yale a few years before, he had worried that his "heart is wrong and my tastes are all set against sympathizing with the low and vulgar." He had so little "practical knowledge" that he thought he would have no skill for associating with "men of the lower class." Once in New York, however, he seems to have developed a genuine sympathy for poor people. He was particularly moved by an experience in 1849, when he preached one Sunday in the Almshouse Chapel on Blackwells Island to an audience of paupers, vagrants, and "diseased prostitutes." It was, he wrote to his father, "one of the most exciting and interesting days I ever spent." It moved him deeply; "never had my whole nature so stirred up within me."[113]

Still, if Brace had pretty much decided to devote himself to helping the poor and unfortunate, it was not yet clear that practical philanthropy, rather than literature, would become his vehicle. In 1852, after the success of Harriet Beecher Stowe's *Uncle Tom's Cabin,* he dreamed of writing a "grand work" of literature that would "do for the mechanics" what Stowe had done for the slaves.[114] Within a year, however, he and a group of philanthropic New Yorkers had organized the Children's Aid Society. He anticipated that after a year or so he would move on to "some wider and more intellectual field," but in fact he stayed with it for forty years, continuing always to write and using his literary connections, as did Olmsted in respect to the park, to advance the interest of the Children's Aid Society.[115] Indeed, working at the intersection of literary life and practical reform allowed or enabled Brace to become, in the words of Paul Boyer, "an incisive, original social thinker," a genuinely "innovative force in urban moral reform."[116]

What remains most vital in Brace's thought and work is his articulation of an alternative to institutional care for deviant and dependent children, an idea that—because of him—was identified specifically with New York City in the nineteenth century.* Here I want to explore his sense of the city as a place of rich and poor, a place where, in his view, a shared moral, if not learned, culture was possible.

Brace, like others of the new gentry, worried about the growth of a lower class in New York; indeed, his most important book, published in 1872, was titled *The Dangerous Classes of New York*. This report of Brace's twenty years' work with them was sympathetic to the poor, even while acknowledging their threat. His readers thus found both cause for worry and the basis for hope. There was something that could be done, even if there was in New York "just the same explosive social elements" as in Paris.[117] The important point for Brace throughout his career was that "the crowd of poor" in New York was "made of up *individuals* debased by their own fault or made wretched by circumstances, *who can be influenced*."[118] Rejecting the common image of the poor as simply an ignorant mass, he saw individuals. He responded with considerable respect for their intelligence and possibilities. He sought "to so change their material circumstances, and draw them under the influence of the moral and fortunate classes, that they shall grow up as useful producers and members of society, able and inclined to aid it in its progress."[119]

With a great faith in the advantages that the impersonality of a great metropolis offered individuals seeking to improve their lives, Brace, who was related to Asa Gray and was a friend of Charles Darwin, spoke in Darwinian imagery of the struggle for survival. Unlike Godkin, however, he proposed to help the poor in this struggle, using public and private financial resources and the voluntary work of middle-class men and women. He felt that if "children of the streets" were trained "to the habits of industry and self-control and neatness," if they were given "the rudiments of a moral and mental education," they would have a real chance for respectable lives.[120] The Industrial and Evening Schools run by the Children's Aid Society were devised to accomplish this.

Brace's vision for these schools went beyond formal educational goals. It was his hope that in these schools, which were staffed largely by volunteers, the two ends of society would come "nearer together in human sympathy." In his *Second Annual Report* (1855), he observed that "it is a great evil of our city life that classes become so separated. Union Square or the Avenues know as little of Water Street or Cherry Street, as if they were different cities." With the rich and poor becoming "almost castes," he wanted the schools to "make one link between them."[121]

* I have dealt with this aspect of his work in my *Toward an Urban Vision*, chap. 6.

This bond may have been edifying to the better-off, like Theodore Roosevelt's father, who was a regular volunteer, but for the poor, as Brace saw it, it offered an invitation to civilization. One cannot but be struck by Brace's confidence that he—and others of his class—could indeed transcend their differences with the poor and share enough of a common culture to make the effort worthwhile.[122] He had no doubt, moreover, that personal association would produce an "unconscious influence" by which the less fortunate would come to share the civilized values of their betters.[123]

Of course, there is a certain naïveté here. There is, as well, something not only simplistic but perhaps even morally suspect about a vision of complete assimilation to the bourgeois values that Brace represented. Yet his dream is more appealing than the acquiescence in the permanent division of society so common among theorists and welfare professionals in our century. Considering the way Godkin and many of his readers walled themselves off from the city's other half, one can appreciate the heartfelt praise that Jacob Riis, who with his camera later strove to reunite the halves of society, had for Brace and the Children's Aid Society.[124]

Frederick Law Olmsted had a somewhat more complex vision that at once affirmed the possibility of a shared public culture *and* recognized the permanence of social and cultural differences based on class, ethnicity, and gender. Olmsted's extraordinary understanding of the urbanistic function of parks and suburbs is, as a whole, beyond the scope of this discussion;* here, however, two themes concern me. First, his commitment to intervention in behalf of extending culture to the whole people, and, second, the shape that the resulting and presumptively democratic culture would take.

In 1846, before he came to New York City, the twenty-four-year-old Olmsted reflected on the problem of having an "influence" on the "popular mind" in a democratic era, in a time when the traditional learned professions had lost their authority as makers of "public opinion."[125] Once in New York, he continued to pursue this theme, wondering whether a "democraticizing" of "knowledge, intellectual & moral culture, and esthetic culture" was possible.[126] Not until he went to the South, however, reporting as a New York writer on the region and its institutions, did he begin to define the dimensions of a democratic vision of metropolitan culture. Rather early on in his Southern journey, in December 1853, he spent two days in Nashville, Tennessee, with Samuel Perkins Allison, a former Yale classmate of his brother's and a slaveholder. De-

---

* I have discussed these themes in my *Toward an Urban Vision*, chap. 7.

fending slavery, Allison pointed to the poverty and misery in Northern cities, especially New York. Shaken by this direct attack on his assumption of Northern and urban superiority, Olmsted wrote a long letter to Brace, who had just asked Olmsted whether he should turn his energies to the Children's Aid Society. The advice to Brace is advice to himself; the reflections on his own self-understandings are intended to guide Brace.

Olmsted confessed that their friend Allison's challenge compelled him to choose; he must either forget democracy and become an "Aristocrat or more of a Democrat than I have been—a Socialist Democrat." He acknowledged that "our state of society" in the North is not "sufficiently Democratic . . . or likely to be by mere *laissez aller.*" Unlike Godkin, Olmsted never abandoned this vision of positive government. But for him the realm of culture, not the economy, was the proper locale for this activism. "We need institutions," he wrote Brace, "that shall more directly *assist* the poor and degraded to elevate themselves. Our educational principle must be enlarged and made to include more than these miserable common schools. The poor & wicked need more than to be let alone." Democracy, as he understood it, was more than a political process; he was "inclined to believe that Government should have in view the encouragement of a democratic condition of society as well as of government—that the two need to go together." Again, however, he was referring less to the redistribution of economic resources than to the extension of cultural ones. "The poor," he declared, "need an education to refinement and taste and the mental & moral capital of gentlemen." Proposing among other things a weekly magazine of opinion, the first inkling of the idea that later became *The Nation,* he urged Brace toward practical philanthropy. "The moral of this damnedly drawn out letter," he concluded, is "go ahead with the Children's Aid and get up parks, gardens, music, dancing schools, reunions which will be so attractive as to force into contact the good & bad, the gentlemanly and the rowdy." [127]

These private concerns and conclusions found public expression in his dispatch to the *New York Times,* printed January 12, 1854. While he complimented the cities of the North, stressing the superiority of a free society over a slave one, Olmsted insisted that much remained to be done. "Democratic Government" must do more than devote itself to providing "protection to capital." The "aesthetic faculties need to be educated—drawn out"; "taste and refinement," he added, "need to be encouraged as well as the useful arts." But he called especially (and prophetically, not then knowing that he would be New York's great park maker) for "places and time for *re-unions,* which shall be so attractive to the nature of all but the most depraved of men, that the rich and the poor, the cultivated and well-bred, and the sturdy and self-made people shall be attracted together and encouraged to assimilate." And he saw no reason why the aid of the "State" should not be given to organizations devoted to such cultural integration.

Four years later, after he had begun work on the park, Olmsted shared his hopes for the project with Parke Godwin. Central Park, he was convinced, was "a democratic development of the highest significance." Upon the "success" of the park depended "much of the progress of art & esthetic culture in this country."[128]

Deeply committed to democracy as well as to culture, Olmsted always had difficulty bringing the two into proper relation to each other. Democratic culture was not, for him, the product of interclass collaboration. It was a matter of the extension of his own notion of culture. He was not, however, cooperating, except in the broadest sense, in an elite's imposition of its culture on the rest of society. In fact, Olmsted always resisted the notion that he was a servant or instrument of elite purposes. He wanted to reform the elite as much as the lower classes. Much like Morse a generation before, but with a different purpose, he assumed the special prerogatives of art to secure intellectual independence from the dominant classes. Taking the "title of artist," he informed the park commissioners that the "design must be almost exclusively in my imagination. No one but myself can feel . . . the true value or purpose of much that is done on the park." The "chief value" of his services to the city, he argued, "rests upon a sort of artistic perception of what is necessary," something "dependent" upon his "personal ideal."[129]

Inherent in his position was a clear conflict between democratic culture and democratic politics. In time that conflict drove him from the park—and from New York. It was the misfit between culture and politics (culture defined by him, politics by Tammany) that was the theme of his angry but perceptive summation of his frustration with New York, *Spoils of the Park* (1881). Olmsted's lament was taken by some, at the time and since, as a plea for Civil Service Reform, but it was in reality a plea for artistic freedom, the freedom to give the people what the artist knew would advance their aesthetic pleasure and education.

What made this aesthetic experience democratic for Olmsted was its commonality. Art, in the form of the park, would provide a shared cultural experience that would overcome the divisions and competitions of urban society. The park, therefore, would have a "distinct and harmonizing influence" in the city.[130] It offered an "opportunity for people to come together for the single purpose of enjoyment, unembarrassed by the limitations with which they are surrounded at home, or in the pursuit of their daily avocations."[131]

It is easy to overlook, but there is in this notion of the park a brilliant insight into the possibilities of a shared culture distinctive to the kind of metropolis that New York was and is. He defined a version of public culture under modern, pluralistic conditions. Recognizing the ineradicable social and economic structures that divided the population of the metropolis, he insisted, however, that it was possible in a great urban park to create moments of transcendence, moments of a shared metropolitan culture that both acknowledged and overcame the profound cultural and economic differences that marked life in New York City.

First of all, he insisted that the park be open to all. He rejected any "cowardly conservatism," any worries about a presumed rowdyism that would make the park unsafe for the respectable. Such threats, if real, would make interclass culture impossible, even for a moment. It was possible, he argued, to develop park regulations, enforced by a special park police, that would make the park a place where rich and poor, young and old, vicious and virtuous, would enjoy themselves "without infringing upon the rights of the others." [132]

Second, he understood that sharing the common culture, even on the essentially bourgeois terms he proposed, did not require participants to cease being who they were. Speaking to the American Social Science Association meeting in 1870, Olmsted explained that in Central Park one found a public culture made up of many different cultures. In the park, he reported, "you may . . . often see vast numbers of persons brought closely together, poor and rich, young and old, Jew and Gentile. I have seen a hundred thousand thus congregated." He remarked on their evident "glee in the prospect of coming together, all classes largely represented . . . each individual adding by his mere presence to the pleasures of all others." [133]

Olmsted surely overstates the pleasure and social unity that his park brought to the city, but he has, as well, articulated a very complex notion of metropolitan culture. Without ceasing to be what they were, without severing their lives from structures of culture smaller than the public culture of the city, all citizens could participate in the common experience of being a public in a public space. The people in the park represented a diverse, interclass, and interethnic democratic culture, while remaining, Olmsted realistically understood, rooted in more limited and homogeneous separate worlds constrained by class, gender, ethnicity, and geography—all of which gave a distinctive meaning to their being in public.

The final point to be made about this vision is its exclusive focus, as I have already suggested, on the cultural realm, the non-working, non-economic side of city life. Indeed, as is probably well known, Olmsted defined the park as the opposite of the architecture, social constraints, and economic activities of the city. For him, modern life came in two parts, one part commerce, the "other occupied in such a manner as will relieve the effect of the special activities, strains, and restraints of the first." Accepting the urban economy as a fixed fact, Olmsted devoted all his efforts for the advancement of "civilization" to the cultural realm.[134] In special enactments of a common culture, not in social structure, democracy would be found.

This strategy of responding in the cultural realm to the consequences of an economy that was allowed to manufacture inequality points in important ways to our own consumer society. And it has, of course, rather obvious limits. Olmsted, however, seems not to have grasped them. Nor did Brace and the many well-meaning men and women who devoted themselves to social philanthropy. Almost alone among her colleagues, Josephine Shaw Lowell, one of the leaders of organized charity in the second half of the nineteenth century, penetrated this problem. She grasped the economic complicity as well as the philanthropic and cultural responsibilities of the elite. The Consumer's League, which she founded, did not solve the problem, but it edged toward a confrontation with the economic basis of the cultural gap that divided the working class and the middle class.

Born into a wealthy and abolitionist family, Josephine Shaw was drawn as well into the literary and political world of George William Curtis, who married her older sister, Anna. At the beginning of the Civil War, Josephine married Charles Russell Lowell, whose idealism in leading black troops into battle made him one of the war's great martyrs when he was killed, widowing his young wife, who dressed in black for more than forty years and devoted herself to the cause of the poor, unfortunate, and oppressed. After the war, she became a leader in American social philanthropy, writing prolifically on the theory of philanthropy, organizing the Charity Organization Society of New York in 1882, and successfully leading the campaign to establish a separate women's prison in New York State. Like Brace, she won the respect of Jacob Riis, for whom she represented "civic conscience."[135] More than many of her associates among the metropolitan elite, she had a tolerance for democracy and its ways. "Republics," she reflected, "are ungrateful and stupid, but I think, in the end, they usually understand right from wrong."[136]

Her great insight, which came rather late in her career, was to grasp, better than any of her philanthropic contemporaries, the difference between charity and reform. For her, as for other feminists, the new social sciences proposed by the ASSA represented, not authority, but an understanding of society that emphasized social interdependence and social wholes.[137] When charity was examined in such a broader theoretical context, it seemed a limited, if not an actually futile, response. By the late 1880s, she acted upon this growing perception, withdrawing from most of her charitable activities. "If working people had all they ought to have," she wrote to Anna Shaw Curtis, "we should not have the paupers and criminals." "Common charity," she increasingly feared, was "wicked," not in intention, but in result. What the "poor want is fair wages and not little doles of food." [138]

In 1886, the year of Haymarket and the George campaign, Lowell had begun meeting with a group of working women on the Lower East Side. Out of these meetings emerged the Working Women's Society. At the first public meeting of the society, February 2, 1888, Lowell rejected Godkin's political economy and accepted Howells's notion of social complicity. She insisted that her class acknowledge its partial responsibility for the condition of the working classes. She argued for state intervention to ensure adequate health and safety standards and to regulate maximum hours and minimum wages. [139]

Two years later, after studying the problem of salesgirls, Lowell and her organizing committee called a mass meeting in May 1890 in Chickering Hall, at Fifth Avenue and Eighteenth Street. At this meeting the Working Women's Society was transformed into the Consumer's League. Seeking a collaboration between middle-class and working-class women, she insisted that consumers have the "power to secure just and human conditions of labor if they would only use it." [140] But they must value justice as much as they value cheapness. "Most decent people," she observed, "object to buying stolen goods, even though they get them very cheap." The problem, however, is that they apparently do not recognize "that it is almost as bad to buy goods which are cheap because part of the time and strength of the people who made them have been virtually stolen, even though under the forms of law." [141] With that time and human energy restored, the working people would be better able to share the cultural possibilities of the city.

As with Howells, Lowell's radical moment of insight was forgotten. Howells was fated to be remembered—or pilloried—as the man who called, before Haymarket, for a realism emphasizing the "smiling aspects" of American life. For Lowell, a category already existed for distorting her memory. Americans have long had a means of blunting the unsettling ideas and example of women who challenge our pieties: we canonize them and elevate them above us all. We revere them as we ignore the point of their lives. This happened to Jane Addams in Chicago, and it happened to Josephine Shaw Lowell in New York.

After her death in 1905, a group of Lowell's friends and admirers memorialized her with a fountain in Bryant Park. Few New Yorkers today know either the fountain or the woman it commemorates. Even fewer know how the city later falsified her memory, her historical significance, to mask the challenge to social complicity that she represented by the end of her life. Municipal officials transformed a critic into a saint.

When the memorial fountain designed by her friend Charles Platt was dedicated on May 12, 1912, with a presentation address by another friend, Seth Low, former mayor and former president of Columbia University, a memorial tablet was placed at the fountain. Her life and her work, the tablet read, were dedicated to "quickening the finer nature alike of the oppressor and the oppressed." [142] After the park was reconstructed and redesigned to accommodate the construction of the IND subway in the 1930s, the fountain was moved to its present location at the Sixth Avenue entrance. In the process, however, the original tablet was removed. It was replaced with the present inscription praising her "beautiful character" and her "inspiriting" and "consecrated labors." The language of oppressors and oppressed, which so well captured her disturbing challenge to the gentry culture of her time and the complacency of our own time, is obliterated.

CHAPTER 6

The Modern Literary Intellectual

The bohemian writers and artists who in the decade before World War I shared with Italian immigrants the red-brick precincts surrounding Washington Square referred to the city's bourgeoisie as "brownstone-fronters." If one silently adds the limestone fronts that were beginning to show themselves on the Upper West Side, the characterization is apt. When, in the 1850s, the city's bourgeoisie began to move north of Washington Square, the red-brick city turned into row upon row of brownstone. The shift remains inscribed in the streets crossing lower Fifth Avenue. Walking north from about Tenth Street, one notices red-brick houses, with their striking white Greek Revival detailing, giving way to darker tones and Italianate details.

This architectural transformation coincides with and represents the consolidation of bourgeois New York. The red-brick Greek Revival houses of lower Manhattan, still characteristic of much of today's Greenwich Village, had in the early nineteenth century housed both patricians and artisans, the only difference being that of relative size and elegance. With the emergence of a modern capitalist economy and a class structure in which artisans disappeared, sinking into a newly formed working class or rising into an emerging capitalist class, housing styles assumed a class identity. Those who worked with their hands, now working class rather than artisans, did not live in brownstones; they lived in tenements. The Victorian brownstone was exclusively bourgeois, and it became the center of bourgeois life and culture.

· · ·

The culture of Brownstone New York, in its public and private dimensions, was the target of Edith Wharton's quiet but terribly corrosive New York novels, and it was the culture forever stigmatized by George Santayana's epithet of 1911, "the genteel tradition." Attempting to deny the commercial basis of bourgeois life and culture, refusing to acknowledge the commercialization of value that marked the Gilded Age, Brownstone New York worshipped at the altar of the ideal. At the core of this culture, as Henry F. May long ago outlined it, was a faith in the universality of moral values and the inevitability of progress. It demanded an absolute commitment to the importance and value of Anglo-American literary culture.[1]

What is too ironic to miss in all of this, however, is the commercial basis for New York's claims to national intellectual leadership. Unlike antebellum Concord, it was not as the home of great writers nor was it as the home of a great university that New York in the 1880s could ground its cultural claims in the nation. Rather, it was as the home of the practical or business side of intellectual life, the work of editing and publishing, that the city achieved recognition as a literary center. New York was the home of the largest publishing houses and the great monthly magazines that provided the financial basis for the emergence of the American writer as a professional.

It was in this period, moreover, that women were brought into the professional literary community. If Margaret Fuller, a generation before, had been a lone pioneer in New York journalism, by the 1880s one finds many widely recognized women writing for the New York monthlies. Having defined their magazines as "family magazines," the editors of the monthlies assumed that having women as writers made as much sense as having them as readers. At the prestigious *Century,* for example, Mariana Griswold Van Rensselaer wrote regularly on architecture, and Helen Hunt Jackson wrote both fiction and her searing classic on American treatment of the Indians, *Century of Dishonor* (1881). Mary Booth edited *Harper's Bazaar* for more than twenty years, wrote the first comprehensive history of New York City, and was the center of an important literary salon in the city. Jane Croly, a career journalist and important feminist, founded Sorosis in New York City in 1868, the first club for professional women.

If, then, literary culture opened its doors, at least a bit, to women, does this mean, as some have suggested, that the culture of New York was thus feminized?[2] The honor these magazines repeatedly bestowed on Theodore Roosevelt, the practical idealist who was born in a New York brownstone in 1858, suggests otherwise. Surely here was a man who expressed, even exaggerated, Victorian masculinity. But there is, of course, more depth to the question than such a response acknowledges. The next generation of writers, in fact, worried that the genteel culture of New York, from which they wanted to distinguish themselves, was too domestic, too tied to home and not enough engaged with the tough and unsavory aspects of American life, particularly the nation's politics and business. As Lincoln Steffens noted when he arrived in New York in 1892, science, philosophy, books in general, all "seemed tame" in contrast to the life of the city. "New York was real," he concluded. "Literature and the arts did not show it as it was." Theodore Dreiser, arriving at about the same time, experienced an equal difficulty connecting New York literature to New York life, and for Joseph Freeman, born in Russia, growing up on the Lower East Side, the English of the schools and magazines seemed to deny the life and language of the street, a language he did not see in literature until Hemingway.[3]

Critics as diverse as George Santayana, in his *Character and Opinion in the United States* (1920), Harold Stearns, in *Civilization in the United States* (1922), and Sinclair Lewis, in his Nobel speech (1930), charged that the genteel culture of the magazine era was feminine in its motives and sensibility, too much like Aunt Polly, not enough like Huck Finn (or Walt Whitman). While the problem with genteel culture is captured in this contrast, the association with feminization is, I think, misleading, at best a partial truth. Sex roles were too diverse and changing to represent in themselves such cultural tendencies. The configuration of Brownstone culture has far more to do with the problem of bourgeois class formation under provincial conditions than it has to do with sex roles.

This culture reached its peak in the 1880s and early 1890s, and then, as we shall see, survived past its time into the twentieth century, setting the stage for an exceptionally intense drama of generational conflict. At its best and in its own time, however, it was centered at the publishing house of Charles Scribner's Sons, where William Crary Brownell, in the role of literary adviser, represented the finest (save for the expatriated Henry James) New York literary intelligence, and in the finely printed and beautifully illustrated pages of *The Century* magazine, edited by Richard Watson Gilder.

Brownell and Gilder, the nation's premier book and magazine editors, were the gatekeepers for the Brownstone culture of New York; by their decisions, they defined its public existence. They saw themselves as part of and representatives of Brownstone New York, and they sought to shape the literary expression of that class's ideals. The modern literary intellectuals, who emerged in New York as the nineteenth century turned into the twentieth, defined themselves in opposition to this culture. They attacked Brownell and Gilder by name, but more importantly they rejected the Victorian definition of the relation of intellect to the class system. If Brownell and Gilder, in proper Arnoldian fashion, conceived of the man of letters as a member of, to repeat a term Randolph Bourne used in reference to Brownell, the "significant" class, and if they thought of intellectual culture as the finest representation of the possibilities of that class, the new literary intellectuals of the early twentieth century, the first Americans to call themselves intellectuals, rejected such class affiliation.

Our modern distaste for the form, the content, even the hypocrisy of the genteel tradition should not obscure for us the extraordinary significance of this shift in the intellectual culture of the city and the nation. It represents an abandonment of the ideal of a cultured minority committed to public life, extending itself out into society. In time, by the 1920s, intellectuals embraced an alternative vision of a minority culture, or even minority cultures, marked by very uncertain relations, if any, to the public.[4]

THE ARNOLDIAN IMPULSE

When William Crary Brownell died in 1929, Edith Wharton wrote that the "most discerning literary critic of our day is dead." At the time she stated it, the compliment was clearly false. But when, many years before as a young writer, she had first offered her work to the editor, it was doubtless true. Edmund Wilson, who probably *was* the best critic in 1929, acknowledged Brownell's influence and observed that while Brownell may have been less "emancipated" than the younger generation, he "possessed a sounder culture than we."[5]

Like Matthew Arnold before him and T. S. Eliot after, Brownell found in France a literary tradition, a sense of discipline and of center, a quality of urbanity and liveliness, that he wanted to bring into the Anglo-American literary tradition that he loved and in which he worked. If Emerson complained once that France did not allow its writers enough individuality ("you would think all the novels and all the criticism were written by one and the same man"), Brownell worried that American individualism, unrestrained by the context of a literary milieu in New York City, would produce a "characterless" literature, more like "noise" than "music."[6]

Brownell was born in 1851, on Twelfth Street, just off Fifth Avenue, into one of the city's comfortable Episcopalian families. He was carried across Fifth Avenue to be baptized at the brownstone Church of the Ascension, erected ten years earlier to Richard Upjohn's Gothic Revival

designs and notable as Fifth Avenue's first church.* After graduating
from Amherst College in 1871, Brownell returned to New York, taking
up work as a journalist, first for the *New York World* and then, from 1879
to 1881, at *The Nation*. Later, at Scribner's, he was noted for his wit, his
elegant dress, his love of books, and his loyalty to the firm. His opinions
on manuscripts, in a very small, even cramped script, were in fact critical
essays, comparing the aspiring author with authors of the past. His task
as editor and critic was to distinguish—with the guidance of tradition—
the "good and the beautiful from the false and ugly."[7]

In 1881, Brownell left *The Nation* and traveled in France for three
years. They were important years. In France, Brownell experienced a
society that in its most fundamental social principles seemed to invert
those of his native land. After returning to the United States to resume
his journalism and, then, to begin his Scribner's career in 1888, Brownell
published his reflections on France and America. *French Traits* (1889) is a
remarkable essay in comparative culture, one of the best ever written by
an American, and one that in its penetration to the fundamentals evokes
the earlier analysis, going the other way, of Alexis de Tocqueville. What
Brownell learned in France and clarified in the process of writing *French
Traits* established the principles that shaped his later social and cultural
criticism, most notably *Standards* (1917) and *Democratic Distinction in America* (1927), but also *Victorian Prose Masters* (1901), *American Prose Masters*
(1909), and *French Art* (1892).

For Brownell the key to French history and society was the "social
instinct." By this he meant essentially what Emile Durkheim a decade
later would call a "social fact." They both understood that in France the
"true center" of the moral self was outside oneself. Institutions of public
life, formal and informal, imposed constraints on the individual. Coming
from an America that celebrated untrammeled individualism, Brownell
observed that in France "individuals are of less import than the relations
between them," and the result is an environment that cherishes disciplined and public artifice, both as manners and as art. Again and again,
he remarked upon and praised the "impersonal," public quality of
French manners and intellect. The existence of an external, impersonal
culture was, he thought, the basis for the clear prose of French writers.
Whitman's "defiance of culture," he charged, only masked the "essential
elementariness" of our individualistic and amateur literary life.

Paris is the "apotheosis of intellect," he explained, because there is a
"common ground" of belief in the worth and power of intellectual dis-

* Further evidence of the culture and class represented by the church is supplied by the
story of its interior reconstruction between 1885 and 1889, following the designs of Stanford
White. At that time, the present altar murals and stained glass by John La Farge and the
altar relief by Augustus Saint-Gaudens were done.

course. There is a public culture accessible to all, and this produces a "mental exhilaration" and a "universal vivacity." With such public culture, magazines can concentrate on ideas instead of, as in America, personalities. French writers, more than their American counterparts, can venture beyond their special subjects to generalizations that show "the relations as well as the character" of particular subjects. "No where," but in Paris, he wrote, "is there so much activity; no where so little chaos."[8]

A man with a fine eye for art and architecture,* Brownell found the strength of Paris's public culture clearly expressed in its architecture. "The entire city is a composition, the principle of fitness in whose lines and masses, tones and local tints secures elegance in the ensemble." Arriving home at the West Side piers in 1884, Brownell received a jolt; never had Paris looked so lovely "as it now appears in memory." Having gotten used to an order of life and activities into which one "fitted so perfectly," even if a stranger, that one is only "half-conscious of its existence," Brownell discovered that such urbanity was constructed by the culture of Paris; it was not "merely normal, wholly a matter of course." Emerging into West Street one met chaos. "There is," he reflected, "no palpable New York in the sense in which there is a Paris, a Vienna, a Milan. You can touch it at no point. It is not even ocular. There is instead a Fifth Avenue, a Broadway, a Central Park, a Chatham Square." But what was most striking of all was the impoverishment of public culture in New York, its screaming and discordant privatism. Living a block from the "overwhelming" Osborne apartment building at Fifty-seventh Street when it was constructed in 1885, he observed that it was similar in its dimensions to the Arc de Triomphe, but the cultural meaning was profoundly different. "One," he explained, is "a private enterprise and the other a public monument." Considering "the obvious suggestions of each," he continued, they "furnish a not misleading illustration of the spectacular and moral contrast between New York and Paris."[9]

While Paris made people into Parisians, he feared that New York simply absorbed people, resulting in a "characterless individualism." New York offered "noisy diversity" without any "effect of ensemble." While it is true that the "brownstone regions" of the city provided "reposeful and rational prospects," in the ordinary operation of the city there was an absence of "that salutary constraint and conformity without which the most acutely sensitive individuality inevitably declines to a lower level of form and taste." New York and America produced individuals, but "in giving us the man it has robbed us of the milieu." Without this milieu, the spirit of individualism in criticism "fairly runs amuck"; any opinion

* His closest friend at this time was Montgomery Schuyler, New York's first great architecture critic, the first in the line that proceeds to Lewis Mumford and Ada Louise Huxtable.

on Shakespeare seemed possible.[10] The standards that he so much wanted in America were, or would be, he realized, the "products not of philosophy but of culture." And what he meant by culture was something shared, held in common, by the artist and the public.[11] Though he was a disciple of Arnold, Brownell was less impressed with the importance of formal academies.[12] More in the spirit of Eliot,* he looked to tradition, to the critic, and to the milieu to restrain personal eccentricities, to achieve objectivity, distance, and coherence in literature.

Conservative in his defense of cultural standards, Brownell was a political liberal who admired Jefferson and believed in Lincoln's "lofty maxim" about "government of the people, for the people, and by the people." He was skeptical of those, like Godkin, who transformed the last phrase into "the best people."[13] He understood that the "interests of the people in general" are not those of the cultural elite; this, he further understood, made elite rule of the Godkin sort both unacceptable and probably impossible. Speaking in tones that would have horrified Godkin, Brownell even suggested that the growing claims of "wealth and intelligence" in the realm of politics threatened American democracy.[14]

Expansive claims of the Arnoldian "remnant" in the realm of culture were not only acceptable but indispensable to the improvement of literature and even of society itself. In a democracy the remnant must reach out, extend itself. Brownell could not but have agreed with the point made by Matthew Arnold in a lecture in New York (in 1884, when Brownell was still in France) that the remnant can save civilization only if its numbers increase. Brownell criticized those intellectuals who were contemptuous of their "poor relations" and whose social contacts were so restricted that they could not "extend" the remnant. The only justification of the "remnant" is "that it is constantly enlarging its confines in the direction of ceasing to be one."[15]

All of this could be egalitarian and democratic in implication. To the extent that "distinction" cannot be made general in a democracy, to the extent it appears to require special class privilege, then, according to Brownell, the program of the remnant has failed. "The men of culture," as Arnold had put it, "are the true apostles of equality." The "great men" are those who have a "passion for diffusing, for making prevail, for carrying from one end of the society to the other, the best knowledge, the best ideas of their time . . . to humanize it, to make it efficient outside the clique of the cultivated and learned, yet still remaining the *best* knowledge and thought of the time."[16] Insofar as Arnold—and Brownell—understood this as a process and not as a mere matter of absolutes to be acquired, something which both men at times understood, then, as Ray-

* I have in mind Eliot's "Tradition and the Individual Talent" (1919).

mond Williams has argued, this Arnoldian program has within it the seeds of genuinely democratic social criticism.[17]

Despite the complexity and essentially progressive character of Brownell's cultural and political ideas, he is often—and erroneously—lumped together with the outright reactionary New Humanists Irving Babbitt and Paul Elmer More.[18] Why? Partly this is Brownell's own fault. He became identified with a general resistance to modernism. Although he remained, for example, cordial with and continued to publish the books of James Gibbons Huneker, since the 1890s the New York advance man for European modernism, Brownell began to worry deeply about the way modernists claimed simply to reject tradition. After World War I, or, for Brownell, after Post-Impressionists Paul Cézanne, Henry Matisse, and Pablo Picasso, modern art and literature seemed to go crazy. Artists claimed to reject the notion of a public, individualism was celebrated, representation was abandoned. *Standards,* published in 1917, was Brownell's worst book. It was shrill and defensive, yet happily endorsed and used by many simple reactionaries. It is important to remember, however, the other side of his postwar legacy. Brownell published and encouraged the young Max Eastman, and the successor he trained at Scribner's, Maxwell Perkins, published in the 1920s, with Brownell's blessing, Ernest Hemingway, F. Scott Fitzgerald, and others of our pantheon of twentieth-century novelists.

For all of his appreciation of the public life of cities and intellect, Brownell was himself a private man. Not so Richard Watson Gilder. From his base at *The Century* offices on Fourteenth Street and, even more so, from the salon he and his wife, the artist Helena de Kay, presided over in the former stable on Fifteenth Street that their friend Stanford White redesigned for them, Gilder played a prominent role in the political and cultural life of New York. Curiously enough, however, with the reclusive Brownell one gets a sense of savoir faire, while with the more public and activist Gilder one's impression is of a sincere but hopelessly naïve idealist. There is no sense of depth, tension, struggle. Form and didacticism were always more important than substance or inquiry.[19] To the extent that Gilder became the American custodian of the Arnoldian impulse— it was at his salon that Arnold was a guest when he came to New York— much of its democratic thrust was lost. Arnold's active and processual notion of culture was reduced in Gilder's presentation of it to an emblem, an insignia of the significant classes.

Born in Bordentown, New Jersey, the son of a minister, Gilder did not go to college. After the Civil War, he took a job as a journalist with the *Newark Daily Advertiser,* and he began writing poetry. He continued to write verse, publishing a volume every five years or so, calling himself the "squire of poesy."[20] In 1870, he moved to New York as the assistant editor of *Scribner's Magazine*; under his editorship the magazine became independent of the Scribner firm in 1880, changing its name at that time to *The Century*. Quickly, Gilder became involved in the city's literary and artistic circles, where he met Helena de Kay, granddaughter of Joseph Rodman Drake, a poet in the circle of Bryant and Verplanck. After their marriage in 1874, their home became a center of literary and artistic life; their Friday evenings included writers, artists, and theater people. Their best friends included John La Farge, Augustus Saint-Gaudens, Stanford White, and the actor Joseph Jefferson. The great Eleonora Duse was a regular visitor to their home. There was a distinctly *fin de siècle* quality to their social life, not quite decadent, but with at least a suggestion of extravagant aesthetic delight.

Yet in his public role as custodian of genteel culure, Gilder's moral and aesthetic standards were prim and prissy. The contradiction is striking. Unwilling to print any of Whitman's poetry in *The Century*, Gilder was—by his own and Whitman's account—hospitable to the poet when Brownstone New York would have nothing to do with him.[21] Gilder took pride in having expurgated the serial version of *Huckleberry Finn* that he ran in *The Century*, and many years later he told Max Eastman (whose work Brownell praised and published) that he would not even read his essay on "Morals of *Leaves of Grass*" because *The Century* was a family magazine.[22]

Without, as Gilder put it, any "appeal downward," *The Century* achieved a circulation in the mid-1880s of 250,000, and it had a reputation as possibly the best-edited magazine in the world.[23] He conceived of *The Century* as a New York magazine with a national responsibility. It was, he thought, "a national factor of no little importance," particularly in restoring "mutual respect and sympathy" between North and South, something he furthered through the famous series of Civil War memoirs that he published. More generally, he sought with *The Century* "to make our multitudinous American communities feel and appreciate their national unity and destiny."[24] It was, in short, to be a metropolitan force in American life, a force that would consolidate a national middle class, exposing it to traditional culture and values in the interest of higher public standards of morality, literature, and graciousness.

Gilder was an activist in the cultural and political life of the city. Both the Author's Club and the Society of American Artists were founded at his home. The Author's Club, founded in 1882, with Brownell one of the original members, provided a fellowship for writers in the city. Once or twice even Herman Melville, then living a few blocks north of the Gilders, dropped in on the meetings.[25] Out of this group emerged the American

Copyright League and, by a somewhat circuitous route, the National Institute of Arts and Letters. The Society of American Artists represented the rebellion of "younger" artists—La Farge, Saint-Gaudens, and the younger Albert Pinkham Ryder—against the stodgy National Academy of Design. Today's Art Students League is the legacy of this rebellion on Fifteenth Street.

In the 1890s, Gilder became increasingly involved in city politics and reform. He fought Tammany Hall, taking an active role in Seth Low's 1897 mayoralty campaign; he led the efforts to save City Hall from destruction and to open the Metropolitan Museum on Sundays; he raised the money to erect the Washington Arch in Washington Square Park; and he served as president of the Public Art League. He published the work of social reformers—Washington Gladden, Albert Shaw, and Richard Ely—all of whom argued for greater municipal provision of social services. He became president of the New York Kindergarten Association, campaigning for free kindergartens, and in 1894 he served as chairman of the New York Tenement House Commission. His work on the commission resulted in the transformation of Mulberry Bend, made infamous by Jacob Riis, into a city park. His idealism was affronted by what he learned of Trinity Church, and he publicly exposed the church as one of the city's slumlords. Through it all, he was, in the words of a *Tribune* editorial, "a reformer, but also a gentleman." [26] He seems to have been motivated by a sense that public life could be improved only by the participation of "the idealists, the artists, the poets," and by a deep love of the city. "I have great hope for and belief in this metropolis," he wrote a friend in 1891, "a love for it, I may say, for only in it or near it have I found all that is best in this life." [27]

For all the good he sought to do, there is a narrowness to his approach to the city. Unlike Brownell, Gilder never recognized interest politics. He always assumed he and his fellow idealists knew the "right" way; he had no sense of alternatives, even less of a struggle of interested parties. Immigrant and working-class New York was for him merely an object of philanthropy, a population in need of uplift. He did not believe that they could seriously partake of his culture, the true program of the remnant. More radical possibilities were even more unthinkable. Gilder could not imagine his culture being enriched by interaction with that of the Lower East Side, and it was inconceivable that a later generation of New York intellectuals was growing up on the streets of the Lower East Side—and would retain symbols of that origin. It was in failing to recognize the cultural implications of immigration that Brownstone culture most clearly fell short. It was his grasp of this fact—and his sympathy for it—that made Howells a traitor to the Brownstone class that sponsored and adored him. [28]

UNION SQUARE

The narrow bounds of Gilder's culture are particularly apparent in the context of the Union Square area where he lived and worked. The Square and its precincts, more than any other place in the city in the Gilded Age, represented to the city and to others the cultural complexity and role of the nation's metropolis. Edith Wharton's evocation of upper-class New York, *The Age of Innocence*, described the Academy of Music at the Square. By looking more closely, we see that it was also the home of other institutions of elite culture. Next to the Gilder home on Fifteenth Street was the Century Club, with the Union League Club not far away on another border of the Square. The Metropolitan Museum of Art's first home was on Fourteenth Street, the New-York Historical Society was just to the east on Second Avenue, while the Astor Library, the New York Society Library, and New York University were just to the south. To the west was fashionable Fifth Avenue, and just off the northeast corner was Gramercy Park, the city's most elegant neighborhood.

For Gilder, as he described his neighborhood to his readers, the Square was the home of theaters, hotels, restaurants, department stores, and Broadway.[29] Though he went no farther, the Square was also the place of both work and play for the working and immigrant classes of New York. By the 1880s, the Square had become part of their neighborhood, as the expanding Lower East Side surged toward Fourteenth Street. Men and women worked in the many ancillary music and theater businesses (costumes, sets, printing, musical instruments, etc.) that were concentrated there. Union Square, in fact, was the first home of Tin Pan Alley, and it was the base for the first national booking and theater organizations. Women of the working classes, employed as clerks, met their middle-class counterparts across the sales counters of the department stores, but also, under Josephine Shaw Lowell's leadership, at nearby Chickering Hall, where they established the Consumer's League. The area was the home of a wide range of popular entertainments, ranging from pleasure gardens, equestrian shows, and dime museums to theaters with playbills advertising the day's fare as "A Woman's Adventures in a Turkish Harem." At the theater in Tammany Hall's headquarters on Fourteenth Street, theatrical history was made in 1881 when Tony Pastor took advantage of the interclass, interethnic, and mixed-sex character of the area to create American vaudeville, a form of family entertainment far from *The Century*. It was the remarkable mix of classes and sexes, work and play, high culture and popular culture, that defined the city's public culture as it represented itself at Union Square.[30]

I want to consider, briefly, three cultural formulations that articulate ways of relating art and intellect to the sort of metropolitan public constituted at Union Square. One is that of the *Century* crowd, of Gilder and, especially, his protégé, assistant, and successor, Robert Underwood Johnson. The second is a self-conscious group of bohemians, the circle of James Gibbons Huneker, all deeply immersed in the musical and art culture of the area, all of whom spent much of their time in a series of cafés east of the Square. Finally, there is the People's Choral Union, established by Frank Damrosch a few blocks south of the Square, at Cooper Union.

Brownell once observed that works of classical music, which "vibrate in the memory," offered the most immediate possibility of forming a public in which democracy and distinction, general public and professional, would be reconciled.*[31] One cannot but wonder if he had in mind the extraordinary example of musical democracy proposed and brought to fruition by Frank Damrosch.

The Leopold Damrosch family, which immigrated from Germany in 1871, supplied several generations of musical leadership in New York, and it is well remembered in the city—one need only think of Damrosch Park at Lincoln Center. But mostly it is Leopold's second son, Walter, conductor of the New York Symphony at Carnegie Hall (Carnegie apparently had him in mind when he built it) and, later in the 1930s, as a conductor of the NBC "Musical Appreciation Hour," who is remembered for his work of "genteel musical uplift."[32] If Leopold's other son, Frank, was less of a celebrity, if, unlike his brother, he was not elected to the National Academy of Arts and Letters, he made a novel and a deeply moving, if largely forgotten, contribution to the promise of democratic culture in New York.

While directing the chorus at the Metropolitan Opera in the 1880s, Frank, under the influence of Felix Adler, organized free concerts at the Working-Men's School of Adler's Ethical Culture Society. He also started giving talks on music instruction to teachers in the public schools.† But when the opera interior burned in 1892, Frank was dismissed. For Damrosch this misfortune was an opportunity, as he wanted to engage the wider society of the city. The settlement workers he met at Adler's had told him about life on the Lower East Side, and now Damrosch went to them with a proposal. Realizing that music was part of all immigrant cultures, he hoped to build upon those interests to make music the center

---

* In making this argument, Brownell interestingly anticipates the key idea of Nobel laureate Eugenio Montale's classic essay, "The Second Life of Art," originally published in Italian in 1949.

† Frank Damrosch is usually remembered for his work in music education. He founded the school that eventually became today's Juilliard School of Music.

of a larger, collective experience.³³ He wanted to make classical music and serious musical training a part of working-class life. So far, the idea looked like typical uplift, but Damrosch did not have the usual charitable relation in mind. He did not intend to ask the rich ladies of musical New York to pay for it. With the advice of a Lower East Side labor leader, Edward King, Damrosch envisioned the project as being self-supporting, with no "odor of charity." Believing that the poor cherished "higher interests," he insisted they would be willing to pay.³⁴ A handbill addressed to "The Working People of New York" was distributed. Damrosch announced his intention to "open a course of lessons in reading music and choral singing." He explained, further, that he hoped "to form from the members of these classes a grand People's Chorus that shall be able to sing the greatest works of the greatest masters."³⁵

The first meeting was to be held at Cooper Union, in the Great Hall, which could accommodate seven hundred persons. When Damrosch arrived at the appointed time, he saw hundreds of people jamming around the building. Thinking at first that by some mix-up the doors had not been opened, he discovered that more than two thousand men and women of the Lower East Side—Germans, Russian Jews, Irish, Italians, Poles, and others—had come to the People's Singing Classes. It was chaos, but at this meeting the assembled crowd voted, after he told them he could get the necessary funds from philanthropists, for independence and a fee of ten cents per lesson. They also voted, at a subsequent meeting, to learn classical rather than popular music.

Damrosch treated his classes and the chorus as fellow musicians, not as objects of philanthropy. When the People's Choral Union appeared in Carnegie Hall a year later, critics evaluated the concert as a musical performance, not a charitable one. Within three years, the success of the People's Choral Union, self-sufficient and self-managed, was assured. Its membership, with strong support from Damrosch and some resistance from labor leaders, was broadened beyond the working classes to comprise as well a portion of the middle classes, young men and women who worked in banks, bookstores, insurance companies, and law offices. To Damrosch, like Felix Adler, who at this time changed his Working-Men's School into a general school of the Ethical Culture Society, interclass organizations had a democratic character. Singing together had civic value.³⁶

At the same time, Damrosch pursued another ambition, the creation of the Musical Art Society. It was a professional group to study and perform sixteenth-century works in *a capella* style. With this ambitious project for achieving the best in choral music, he did go to his wealthy friends for support. He also arranged with these philanthropists to provide four hundred seats at each performance of the Musical Art Society to be available free to members of the People's Singing Classes and People's Choral Union.[37]

Damrosch's extraordinary accomplishment of the 1890s, then, was to contain, within the range of his own musical activities, both art for the people and art for its own sake, both cultivation of the best and the extension of the remnant. Like the parent who cannot say which child he loves most, Damrosch could never choose between the People's Choral Union and the Musical Art Society, only both.[38]

Damrosch's faith in the collaborative quality of democracy and distinction was not at all representative of cultural leadership in the 1890s. Instead of seeking to extend the remnant, the city's literary and artistic elite, having rather exaggerated notions of their own importance, sought to bolster and defend it by turning inward, by institutionalizing it in an academy. In 1898 the genteel writers of New York organized the National Institute of Arts and Letters.[39] A few years later, in 1904, in Gilder's office at *The Century*, Edmund Clarence Stedman, Robert Underwood Johnson, and Edward McDowell conceived the idea of an even more exclusive body, the American Academy of Arts and Letters, whose members would be chosen from the larger National Institute.

At the most obvious level, of course, the aim was simply social—to bring together, at regular dinners, the leaders in literature, art, and music. More formally, they embraced and repeated Matthew Arnold's justification of an academy as a national center for establishing, in Stedman's words, a "high correct standard in intellectual matters."[40] But there is more to it than these "official" statements. As one reads the letters and autobiographies of some of the most active members, it is clear that another, less elevated motivation fed into the founding and life of the institute and the academy. Many of these men* were united by a commitment to Anglo-Saxonism in literature and life; they were deeply worried about democracy, immigration, and modernism. It was fitting that the first public function of the academy was a four-day celebration of James Russell Lowell. For Johnson and Columbia's president, Nicholas Murray Butler, who came to dominate the academy, the central issue of intellectual life seemed to be the threat, from immigrants and modernism, to the purity of the English language. There was no greater danger to mind in America than the bastardization of English. Johnson, who did sit-ups every morning, even at age seventy, filled his autobiography with tirades against modern "degeneration."[41]

* I use "men" advisedly, for Julia Ward Howe was the only woman elected to the institute for its first nineteen years, and the only woman elected to the academy in its first twenty-two years.

Parading as a public representation of art and intellect, the institute and the academy represented in fact complacent withdrawal. When Ellen Glasgow in her autobiography remembered meeting, at the Author's Club in New York, the writers "who would soon become, by self-selection, the Forty Immortals of the American Academy," she remarked that the "trouble was that I thought of them as old gentlemen, and they thought of themselves as old masters."[42] William James caught the nub of it in his letter of 1905 declining election to the academy and resigning from the institute. "I am not informed," he wrote, "that this Academy has any definite work cut out for it of the sort in which I could play a useful part; and it suggests *tant soit peu* the notion of an organization for the mere purpose of distinguishing certain individuals (with their own connivance) and enabling them to say to the world at large 'we are in and you are out.' "[43] Whatever its occasional rhetorical claims, the creation of the institute and the academy represented the loss of faith in the Arnoldian remnant and a democratic public.

Bohemian New York, anathema to the Immortals, also lost faith in the public, and—somewhat more forthrightly—said so. Since the time of Henry Clapp's circle, which included Ada Clare and, sometimes, Walt Whitman, at Pfaff's saloon on Broadway, the area north of Houston from Broadway east had been hospitable to various bohemian groups. In the 1890s, James Gibbons Huneker was the central figure of a bohemia headquartered in the café society of Union Square and the saloons of the immigrant neighborhood of Tompkins Square.

Born in Philadelphia, the son of a prosperous housepainter who loved music, Huneker studied piano (and much else) in Paris, and then in 1886, at the age of twenty-nine, moved permanently to New York, where he gravitated to Union Square.[44] Though not a great pianist, he was a well-trained one; when he gave up the dream of performing, he became an excellent teacher at the National Conservatory on Irving Place, teaching with such distinguished colleagues as Victor Herbert and Anton Dvořák. He began writing criticism, first of music, then of all the arts.

During the 1890s, Huneker formed a close friendship with fellow journalist Vance Thompson, the son of a Presbyterian minister who got a Heidelberg Ph.D. after graduating from Princeton in 1883. The two young men indulged their considerable aesthetic sensibilities, drank enormous quantities of beer, and complained about the tameness of New York's magazines. They dreamed of the *fin de siècle* magazines of Paris and London, even of Chicago's *Chapbook* and *The Lark* in San Francisco. In 1895, they published their own *M'lle New York,* a magazine printed on buff-colored paper, with pink and black graphics. The first cover displayed a seductive woman, with elaborate headgear, posed near beer drinkers in a café. Inside the covers, one found a series of lightly dressed women and leering men, elegantly and finely drawn. The writing, nearly all by Thompson and Huneker, was vaguely imitative of the decadent French writer J.-K. Huysmans, with a suggestion of Nietzsche, though in general, the writing was inferior to the art. Looking at the magazine today, one gets a sense of highly cultivated if somewhat spoiled aesthetes at work.

The foreword in the first issue, however, was a bold attack on the assumptions of genteel culture. Attacking Howells and, especially, Gilder, by name, Thompson and Huneker hailed the "mob" of Shakespeare's time, happy in its ignorance and strong in its instincts, as far superior to the gentility of the readers and writers of *The Century*. Taking aim directly at the heart of the Arnoldian tradition, the two bohemians declared that *M'lle New York* was not concerned with the public. "Her only ambition is to disintegrate some small portion of the public into its original component parts—the aristocracies of birth, wit, learning, and art, and the joyously vulgar mob." The "public," they declared, is a "grotesque aggregation of foolish individuals." In a very different way from their enemies, who three years later would organize the National Institute, they declared the artist beyond society and democracy "bankrupt."[45]

Huneker, by far the more significant of the two editors, was the forerunner of H. L. Mencken. Mencken eagerly read *M'lle New York* as a young man in Baltimore and later acknowledged Huneker's influence, even paying homage by publishing him in the first issue of Mencken's own *American Mercury* (1924). Huneker was, in the words of his biographer, the "first effective opponent" of the genteel tradition. And if he was, as Alfred Kazin puts it, a bit too "Europe struck," it is also true that he introduced New York and American culture to such major European modernists as Ibsen, Shaw, Strindberg, Strauss, Debussy, Schönberg, Cézanne, and Matisse.[46] Even so, we must conclude that, however commendably cosmopolitan in his tastes, Huneker, like Mencken, lacked a genuine grasp of the nature of real or possible relations of art and intellect to society. It was easier, and certainly more fun, simply to ridicule the very idea of a democratic culture. Both men ultimately were nihilists.

Although the gentlemen of the older order did not yet realize it—and would never acknowledge the fact—their order had passed away. With some help from the social transformation of the city that made Anglo-Saxonism a transparently minority and class-specific culture and from the constant attacks of the likes of Huneker, the way was cleared in New York City for the creation in the next generation of the modern literary intellectual.

METROPOLITANISM AND THE INTELLECTUAL

Herbert Croly was the precursor of the modern intellectual in New York. The youngest and most emancipated of the traditionalists, he became the oldest of the emergent young intellectuals. If Brownell began with the public, Croly began with the individual artist or intellectual and his work. Though he is remembered chiefly as a political philosopher—for *The Promise of American Life* (1909)—and as a political journalist—as founding editor of *The New Republic* (1914)—he was most deeply concerned with the place of intellect in democratic society and politics.

Croly believed that the modern American intellectual must be disinterested, thus free of class affiliation. The problem, therefore, was to articulate the nature of the intellectual's connection to society in other terms. Beginning his literary career as an architecture critic, he came to define the task of the intellectual or artist as doing one's work and doing it with a personal and absolute commitment to excellence. Always, however, the artist or intellectual should be alert to the possible connections of his work to wider social experience and cultural tendencies. Genuine success would be found not within the confines of one's special field, but in that hoped-for moment when one's work becomes a public fact. In an example of the striking way that history occasionally imitates and validates literature, Croly experienced precisely this kind of success. Worrying and writing in professional isolation, he suddenly captured the public's imagination with the very book in which he articulated this theory of the role of the American intellectual.

Croly, who in his maturity was a man of moderate height, slight build, and almost pathological shyness, grew up in Manhattan's Greenwich Village. He was born into a journalistic family in 1869; his parents, David Goodman Croly and Jane Cunningham Croly, were reform-minded journalists who believed strongly in the power of reason and fact to change the world. Jane Croly, who often went by the pen name Jennie June, edited *Demorest's Illustrated Monthly* and *Godey's Lady's Book* and loomed large in the city's reform and journalistic world. Between mother and son, however, there was a noticeable tension, and Herbert seems later to have been embarrassed by her literary work. With his father, a man of exceptional integrity and generosity of spirit, Herbert felt extremely close, particularly in the decade or so before the elder Croly's death in

1889, when Herbert was a Harvard undergraduate.[47] Croly's education at Harvard was much interrupted, stretching over eleven years (1886–97), and ending without a degree.* At Harvard, he was drawn mostly to courses in the Philosophy Department, where he studied with George Santayana, Josiah Royce, and William James. After Harvard and a marriage that brought him financial security, he became editor of the *Architectural Record*, a position available to him as the son of David Croly, who had been close to the owner of the journal.

His essays in the *Architectural Record* announced the principal themes of his life work: the problem of intellectual and artistic excellence in a commercial society, the relation of the intellectual to tradition, the necessity of public culture, and the role of a metropolis in giving public force to ideas and ideals. "Public affairs," Edmund Wilson explained at the time of Croly's death, mattered to him "as deeply as our private affairs do to the rest of us."[48] Croly's approach to public affairs was, however, rooted in cultural concerns. For him, as for Walter Lippmann, his colleague at *The New Republic*, social improvement was an intellectual and cultural problem, not a merely political or technical one.†

It was, of course, partly an accident that Croly should express his concerns, at least initially, in the context and language of architecture. But it was both fitting and appropriate to the time. The 1890s and early 1900s were a period when urban elites tried to enhance public culture by achieving greater unity and coherence in the physical form of cities. The most notable of such efforts were the Chicago World's Fair of 1893 and the replanning of Washington, D.C., in 1901. But in New York, too, as the drama critic and Columbia professor-about-town Brander Matthews recalled, architecture was the premier public art of the time.[49] This sensitivity to the relationship of urban design to public culture motivated the founding of the Municipal Art Society in 1892 and the efforts of civic reformers, most notably Manhattan borough president George McAneny, to incorporate a program of city planning and civic art into the function of municipal government.

From his perspective at the *Architectural Record*, Croly doubted that either the "best European models" or popular and indigenous forms in America provided an adequate tradition for American artists and intellectuals. The former were too alien, the latter still too inchoate.[50] Without standards, Croly feared, American intellect was vulnerable. Architects, the immediate object of his concern, might become irresponsible in either

* He was awarded a Harvard B.A. in 1910, after the success of his book *The Promise of American Life*.

† I am referring here to Lippman's *Preface to Politics* (1913) and *Drift and Mastery* (1914).

of two ways: they might become frankly commercial, supplying clients with mere technical competence, or they might turn inward, working in a "language [that] does not carry beyond the studio." What they in fact needed, he explained, was to "become closely united by some dominant and guiding tradition." Was it, he worried, impossible for art in a "modern democratic community" to be "both genuinely popular and thoroughly self-respecting"? Acknowledging that Athens and Florence provided successful examples in the past, he considered them to be unusual in the homogeneous quality of their populations, their intense local spirit, and their apparently natural sense of beauty. American life, by contrast, was "noisy, discordant, and meaningless."[51]

Something different was necessary in modern America. The modern economy being born in the United States at the turn of the century offered, he suspected, an essential clue. "What the United States needs," he reflected, "is a nationalization of their intellectual life comparable to the nationalizing, now under way, of their industry and politics."[52] A few months later he published a remarkable article, "New York as the American Metropolis."

He began by defining a metropolis and metropolitanism. Mere size is not enough; a metropolis is defined by its function in the national culture. A metropolis would not only "mirror typical American ways of thought and action"; but it would also "anticipate, define, and realize national ideals." Most important of all, it would stand for a "conception of metropolitan excellence." New York did not, he admitted, fully serve this role. Nor would it ever become like Paris in France. But it was, he thought, on its way to becoming metropolitan in an American way that recognized the continual contentions of a polycentric society. It was becoming a place where "men will be attracted in proportion as their enterprises, intellectual and practical, are far-reaching and important." In America's agrarian past, such a city and role were impossible, but now, in an age of industry that was centralized on a national scale, a metropolitan role became possible for New York. But before New York could effectively serve as a metropolis, it had to come to stand for more than the making and spending of money; privatism must be subordinated to larger social and aesthetic ideals. The "poverty of public life" in New York had to be overcome by the discovery or invention of an authoritative, "really inclusive and democratic social ideal." Otherwise the concentration of talent in New York would result only in "merely technical" and "academic" work divorced from larger life. He was hopeful, however; Theodore Roosevelt, a New Yorker who represented "the best form of the national idea," in fact might anticipate the future of New York in the nation.[53]

· · ·

The Promise of American Life was motivated by a concern with the conditions and quality of intellectual life in America. More immediately, it was prompted by Croly's reading of a third-rate novel about an idealistic architect—Robert Grant's *Unleavened Bread* (1900). Disturbed by the fate of genuine "individual intellectual effort" in America, Croly set out "to justify the specialized contemporary intellectual discipline and purposes."[54] Although Croly's book has been canonized as a political classic and has even been credited with having profoundly influenced Theodore Roosevelt's New Nationalism and the Progressive Party, it is not a political work. Its concluding chapter does not offer a political program; rather, it is a discussion of the role of intellectuals in establishing the national purpose and ideals that must precede and surround any political movement. It is a call for an "intellectual awakening."[55]

The book represents a resolution to the cultural problem that had been haunting Croly in his *Architectural Record* essays. He had been lamenting with painful regularity the absence of tradition in America, a tradition that would enable the architect to "build better than he knew" while supplying him with the basis for innovation and revolt.[56] There were in his *Record* essays, it is true, occasional glimpses of a non-traditional source of discipline and convention, but only in *The Promise of American Life* does he firmly move beyond his lament for an American yet European-like cultural tradition. Although the first half of the book recounts American history up to about 1880, the second half proceeds largely independently of that history. American history before 1880 belongs in the past; it is not relevant to the new era. Instead of tradition, Croly proposed a creed. The promise of America, he now argued, is "determined by an ideal," not by history. What Americans need is "an idea which must in certain essential respects emancipate them from their past"—"a constructive social ideal" compatible with American history and society but not continuous with it. This ideal, which would be the gift of intellectuals, would supply a principle of coherence for American culture and politics. It would supply what Athens and Florence had enjoyed and, for that matter, what the United States had in the simpler era of Thomas Jefferson. Only with such a "constructive national purpose" might one expect to tame private interest in America.[57]

Once formulated in a compelling way, the ideal would be permanent, though pragmatic solutions to particular problems would be devised "almost every generation."[58] It is important to notice how this concept differs from the popular pragmatic thinking of the time. There are prior ideals for Croly; neither process nor the pragmatic search for solutions is autonomous for him. The national ideal always intervenes into and determines the configuration of the pragmatic resolution. If pragmatism became the charter for the bureaucratic expert, Croly's formulation pointed toward an independent role for the artist and intellectual—the cultured individual who knew the past and dared to dream of a better future.

For Croly, the interests of creative intellect and the public good were one. While the excess of private and commercial interests stunted them both, the intellectual could save the public by saving himself. If artists and intellectuals needed a moral and intellectual atmosphere that respected "disinterested achievement"—and Croly was certain they did—they must themselves take responsibility for bringing such conditions into being. The previous generation, Croly insisted, had been too quick to accept the precepts of the genteel tradition; they had been as defiant as a "milch cow." He called upon intellectuals to emancipate themselves, insisting that intellect "has a discipline, an interest, and a will of its own." Croly was convinced that the pursuit of that interest was in the public interest. By successfully asserting "his own claim to distinction," the individual artist or intellectual "is doing more to revolutionize and reconstruct the American democracy than can a regiment of professional revolutionists and reformers." [59]

In their pursuit of excellence and popularity, artists and intellectuals would give birth to a progressive and public ideal. Croly pariicularly criticized those intellectuals hesitant to engage the public realm. They were too quick, he thought, to blame a philistine public when in fact the intellectuals had not tried hard enough. Croly refused to believe that Americans would fail to respond to excellence. The problem was that intellectuals thought the road should be easy, that they should be "immediately taken" at their "own valuation and loaded with awards and opportunities." Should not the intellectual and artist, he asked, have the obligation of making themselves "interesting to the public"? [60] Doing work of some distinguishing merit, he counseled, will produce talk of it, and this will in turn produce a public for such work. The public will demand more, and demand the same level of excellence. Society will be on the way to reform.

But the individual artist or intellectual must make the first move. "The fact that he is obliged to make a public instead of finding one ready made" is not so bad, Croly assured his readers, for it "will in the long run tend to keep his work vital and human." If it is the true interest of society to nourish the creative individual, it is also in the best interest of that individual to be surrounded by a public culture that demands excellence of him. "He cannot obtain the opportunities, the authority, and the independence which he needs for his own individual fulfillment, unless he builds up a following; and he cannot build up a . . . following without making his performances appeal to some general human interest." [61]

The task of the critic, according to Croly, was fundamental in this circular process. He must discern trends and identify authentic culture as it emerges from diverse works, and he must mediate between the artist and the public, explaining the public significance of distinctive special achievement. He must give form to the "authoritative and edifying" national ideal; he is the custodian of the developing national creed.[62] Croly hoped that *The New Republic,* which he founded in 1914, would perform this task.

The New Republic, located in a yellow-brick house on West Twenty-first Street, in Chelsea, sought to be the voice of a metropolitan intellect. Two of the three founding editors, Croly and Lippmann, were born in New York, and the greater number of contributors were New York writers. It realized Croly's dream of New York "as America's nationalizing metropolitan hub."[63] Like the *Democratic Review* seventy-five years earlier, it symbolized a New York–Washington reformist political axis that would again be prominent in the 1930s and 1960s. Writing to Dorothy and Willard Straight, the wealthy New York patrons who, impressed with *The Promise of American Life,* offered to fund the magazine, Croly explained the role of the critic: it was to "transmute the experience the American people will obtain . . . into socially formative knowledge."[64]

In the first issue, published three months after the war broke out in Europe, *The New Republic* announced itself committed to "sound and disinterested thinking," insisting that ideas were the only force superior to war.[65] Like Godkin's earlier *Nation, The New Republic* readership (15,000 in 1915; 43,000 in 1920) was select and highly educated. But while Godkin saw an undifferentiated cultural elite as his audience, *The New Republic,* responding to a significant restructuring of American society and politics, was particularly concerned to influence a new and emerging class, a strategic elite. To some extent, such a focus, largely the influence of Lippmann, compromised Croly's democratic vision. Inherent in the notion of strategic elites was the temptation to embrace power, to seek direct political influence, and to subordinate ideals to pragmatic practice. Croly and *The New Republic* succumbed in 1916, when they joined Woodrow Wilson's crusade. But that story belongs to a later point in this narrative.

In 1914, *The New Republic* seemed to represent the realization of the vision of national cultural renewal articulated in *The Promise of American Life.* Croly aimed in the magazine to be "thoroughly critical" of the "actual practice of the arts in this country," but, as he explained to a writer he recruited for the magazine, "there must also be a positive impulse behind our criticism."[66] For the next generation, for the self-proclaimed "Young Intellectuals," Croly and his new magazine marked, in the words of

Waldo Frank, "a new critical era." In dedicating *The Re-Discovery of America* (1929) to Croly, Frank gave him credit for laying "the foundation, in modern real terms" for a "democratic nation" that would have a place for artists and intellectuals.[67]

THE YOUNG INTELLECTUALS

The term "intellectual" entered political and cultural discourse in 1898, when the Dreyfusards used it to name themselves and to claim by it a new sort of oppositional moral authority. Within three months, the word appeared in America, in an editorial in *The Nation,* and by 1900 it was being used on New York's Lower East Side, referring to those immigrants who, under settlement-house auspices or in café society, had formed study groups to incorporate into their lives American literature and culture. But it was William James, who had privately identified with the defenders of Dreyfus and embraced the designation in 1898, who seems to have given the word wide public currency in the United States in 1907. One of James's purposes then was to apprise his fellow professors of potential competition. The intellectual, he suggested, would be at home in the literary and magazine world of New York.*[68] If the university had a generation before, when James himself became an academic, held out the promise of intellectual excitement and influence, by 1910 that promise seemed, for many, to have faded. Many of James's best students at Harvard, most notably the brilliant Walter Lippmann, declined to follow him into the academy, going instead to New York, where in Greenwich Village a cultural revolt that would establish the ideal of twentieth-century American intellectual life was being staged.

The story of Greenwich Village has been told many times—in histories, in fiction, in film. The cultural highlights are familiar: a happy collaboration of "revolutionary" writers and artists at the editorial offices of *The Masses* on Greenwich Avenue; the wide-ranging discussion of politics and culture, from syndicalism (with Bill Haywood) to Freudianism (with A. A. Brill), from Isadora Duncan's modern dances to Harlem's jazz, held on Wednesday evenings in Mabel Dodge's living room at 23 Fifth Avenue; the innovative Provincetown Players—Susan Glaspell, George Cram Cook, Eugene O'Neill, and, at one time or another, almost every man or woman of the Village rebellion; Alfred Stieglitz's famous gallery at 291 Fifth Avenue, where Village intellectuals were tutored in modern aesthetics and introduced to Post-Impressionist art; the Armory Show (1913), which in a single dramatic moment forced a larger art public out

---

* It is certainly worth noting that James published his speech in a popular New York magazine.

of its comfortable provincial standards and introduced those of international modernism; the Paterson Strike Pageant at Madison Square Garden, organized by John Reed in support of IWW strikers; the founding of new magazines, always a sign of cultural change—*The Masses, The New Republic,* and *Seven Arts* as well as a group of short-lived but consciously avant-garde and coterie magazines with such names as *Broom, Quill, Glebe, Others, Rogue, Pagan,* and *Rong-Wrong;* meeting places, such as the Liberal Club, Polly's restaurant, Albert Boni's bookstore, and, finally, Petitpas, where the painter John Butler Yeats, who had been a correspondent of Whitman and was the father of the great poet of the Irish renaissance, William Butler Yeats, assured the Young Intellectuals that in America, too, "the fiddles are tuning up."

The emergence of the Greenwich Village intellectuals was an event of multitudinous dimensions, difficult to characterize in general. But from the perspective of our concerns with the structure of intellectual life and its definition, what becomes most salient about the rebellion is its sense of itself as a youth movement, as the *young* intellectuals. Rejecting the class affiliation of Brownell's generation and unable to establish a firm connection to another class, the working class, the Young Intellectuals defined themselves not as a class but as a generation. At this point, generational conflict enters our intellectual life as both a structural fact and a subject of that life.

The Young Intellectuals, whether in the United States or in Europe, were the first generation to come of age within a bourgeois culture that had consolidated itself politically, financially, and culturally. They rejected both the personal values represented by the Victorian family and the public culture of their parents. Whether in London, Paris, Berlin, Rome, or Vienna, the precise pattern of the revolt of the young within and against the "success" of the parents' generation took different forms.[69] But everywhere, with an awareness of the international character of their movement, young men and women searched for a newer and more vital culture.

Traditional culture seemed to be more secure in New York than it in fact was. At *The Century* and the Century Association, at Scribner's, in President Butler's office at Columbia, in those many brownstone parlors, New York must have seemed an invulnerable bastion of traditional culture and a compelling symbol of capitalist progress. In ways not visible from brownstone windows, however, the city offered considerable resources for those who would subvert the culture of the city's "significant classes." One could hardly imagine, in fact, a better place than New York City from which to launch an attack upon traditional culture. Not only was the city moving into closer touch with continental intellectual currents, but its rapidly increasing immigrant districts were giving lie to any

Anglo-Saxon definitions of the city and its culture. To the considerable extent that New York deviated from the Anglo-Saxon norm, the young embraced it. Immigrant New York, somewhat romanticized as in Hutchins Hapgood's *The Spirit of the Ghetto* (1902), captured the imagination of the young. Here was a life more real and authentic than their experience of growing up, whether in the Midwest or in the bourgeois neighborhoods of New York and its suburbs.

As the young gradually became aware of the socialism and Russian fiction discussed by Jewish intellectuals in the café society of the Lower East Side, they discovered a moral intensity that implied a richer, deeper sense of culture than traditional culture seemed to offer. The increasing visibility of poverty and of labor militancy on the Lower East Side—to say nothing of the tragic Triangle Shirtwaist Factory fire of 1911, when 146 Jewish working girls died only a block east of Washington Square— suggested an economy of exploitation as much as one of progress. And Tammany Hall was, of course, a continual affront to genteel notions of politics. In New York, then, it was possible to believe, as Walter Lippmann put it, that his generation was "born into a world in which the foundations of the older order survive only as habits or by default."[70]

The Greenwich Village section of the city, moreover, provided a special kind of sanctuary within the city itself from which to fly the banners of revolt. Surrounded by immigrants, avoided by traffic, situated halfway between the city's two skyscraper districts (what Scott Fitzgerald called Manhattan's two "sugar lumps"), Greenwich Village offered a place where it seemed possible to escape bourgeois values and art. It was, in Floyd Dell's phrase, "a moral-health resort."[71]

Here, in the freer atmosphere of the Village, the Young Intellectuals could in word and deed attack conventional notions of family and sex roles, the foundation of traditional culture. They embraced feminism in this spirit, and they welcomed Elsie Clews Parsons, born into Brownstone New York and still residing there, into the intellectual circles of the Village because her anthropological writings, as she fully understood and intended, took aim at and undermined the traditional family.*[72] What the Village offered to the Young Intellectuals was an opportunity to fuse life and art, the personal and the political, in their effort to reconstruct American culture. "There was," Max Eastman, editor of *The Masses*, recalled, "a sense of universal revolt and regeneration, of the just-before-

---

* During this early period in her career, before withdrawing to fieldwork in the Southwest, Parsons was active in Dodge's salon, published in *The Masses*, played a role in the founding of *The New Republic*, and was part of a discussion group that met at 31 Jones Street which Lewis Mumford recalled as providing the "best sustained conversation" he ever knew.[73]

dawn of a new day in American art and literature and living-of-life as well as in politics."[74]

The politics of the Village revolt, deeply rooted as they were in personal needs, had, as Christopher Lasch and others have noted, limits.[75] Whatever the rhetoric of justice, there seemed always to be a greater concern about *repression* of personal desire and creative talent in America than about class *oppression*. While they believed, as Van Wyck Brooks, the least political of the rebels, put it, that "literary criticism is always impelled sooner or later to become social criticism," what they particularly sought in any "wholesale reconstruction of social life" was a release of the creative spirit and the making of a more secure place for the creative intellectual in America.[76] It was not that they cared less about social justice, but rather that their own needs and ambitions were much more vivid and immediate.

Within the bourgeois city there was, then, a special milieu that nourished the rebellion. It is important to understand the degree to which the revolt was headquartered in New York and the extent to which the resolution in New York has defined the basic terms of intellectual culture in twentieth-century America.[77] One cannot, for example, but be struck by the absence of revolt in Boston, and by the difference between the one in Chicago and that in New York. The slightly earlier Chicago renaissance was unmistakably Midwestern, native American, and aesthetic, with the poet, as has been often remarked, its most characteristic product.[78] The more cosmopolitan atmosphere of New York produced the critic, an intellectual type driven as much by ethics as by aesthetics. The New York intellectual, long before the *Partisan Review,* was characteristically an essayist who ranged widely, assimilating all phenomena to cultural issues. These Young Intellectuals were, as Henry May has pointed out, "equipped to attack the dominant credo and culture on the moral, political, philosophical, and literary fronts all at once."[79]

Most centrally at stake in the revolt of the younger generation was the definition of culture itself. The Young Intellectuals were self-consciously modern, but we must be careful to specify what modern culture meant for them. Under the influence of Lionel Trilling in particular, we have come to identify modernism with a rage against civilization, with irrationality, the breaking of form, and, even, nihilistic futility. Yet there are, as Peter Gay has suggested, other equally legitimate versions of modernism that are more moderate, positive, and affirming, even reformist.[80] Such modernists were the Young Intellectuals. Nor was their modernism internationalist in the strongest sense of the term, dissolving place and nation. While they eagerly attended to and celebrated international cultural movements, they remained cultural nationalists. They could be at once "unashamedly declarative of our national identity yet equally cosmopolitan."[81]

The official culture of New York, the culture of Brownell and Gilder, was, they felt, too Anglo-Saxon and too far from the experience of modern and metropolitan life. It was, in the epithet of Malcolm Cowley, merely a "veneer." It had no organic relation to actual life as it was being lived in America; if anything, it obfuscated contemporary American reality. The Young Intellectuals wanted an art and literature that would, as Floyd Dell put it, offer "an interpretation of our own time."[82]

No one better expressed the cultural ideal of the rebellion than Randolph Bourne. Reviewing the autobiography of Brander Matthews, he complained that for the older generation "literature was a gesture of gentility and not a comprehension of life." Acknowledging considerable critical talent among his elders, he nonetheless dismissed their work, bluntly asking, "What on earth can the younger generation of today do with the remains of this gentility?" The problem, Bourne wrote elsewhere, is that the "tyranny" of the best, with its implications of universalism, made it more difficult to grasp the "distinctive" and "vital" cultural possibilities—and problems—of America. Training the intellect "to learn and appreciate the best that has been thought and done in the world" had not, so far, prepared it to "discriminate between the significant and the irrelevant that the experience of everyday is flinging up in our face." Culture for Bourne had to be living, contemporary; it had to extend and enrich experience, not deny it. The clearest evidence of "the futility of the Arnold ideal," he insisted, was the "mere callousness of our responses to our rag-bag city streets." "To have learned to appreciate a Mantegna and a Japanese print, and Dante and Debussy, and not to have learned nausea at Main Street, means an art education which is not merely worthless but destructive."[83]

More than any of his contemporaries, Bourne represented in the public mind the revolt of the Young Intellectuals. While still an undergraduate at Columbia in 1912, he had, after all, won immediate national recognition by publishing "Two Generations" in the *Atlantic*, an essay that defended youth and which was in the view of *The Nation* "amazingly disrespectful" of the older generation.[84] In the few years that remained to him—he died, tragically and far too young at thirty-two, in the influenza epidemic of 1918—Bourne was acknowledged as the "literary voice of Young America." What made him so important at the time, indeed what still makes him the founder of the modern tradition of the New York literary intellectual, was, as Waldo Frank pointed out soon after his death, Bourne's success "in the joining, through his work, of the political and cultural currents of advance."[85]

Bourne was an essayist. It would be fair, in fact, to credit him as well with establishing the essay as the favored genre of the New York intellectual. Even as an undergraduate he had developed the essay style that would later, in the era of the *Partisan Review,* be identified as characteristic of the New York intellectual. Upon receiving Bourne's first article, Ellery Sedgwick, editor of the *Atlantic,* praised his gift for combining "a philosophical breadth of view with a deep note of personal conviction."[86]

Randolph Silliman Bourne was born in Bloomfield, New Jersey, a New York suburb, in 1886, in the month of the Haymarket Riot. On his mother's side, his family was well-to-do and could trace its ancestry to the first generation of New England's settlers. His father, however, was a victim of Gilded Age America, a failure who was encouraged by Randolph's mother's family to quietly go away. He was reared, therefore, in the bourgeois atmosphere of his mother's family.

The larger context of Bourne's coming of age was later recalled and evoked in the powerful and lyrical prose of his friend the brilliant music critic Paul Rosenfeld. Bourne, Rosenfeld wrote, "had come into the dead becalmment of American life." There was much activity, "meaningless, endless, directionless," the building of cities and suburbs, commuters moving back and forth from Manhattan and New Jersey, the getting of jobs and the begetting of children, but still, "strangely, the air was motionless." For whatever reason, Bourne developed a strong sense of "his own center," and this allowed him to resist, to survive, "in a land terrorized by the conventions; bourgeois conventions giving themselves out for the laws of the universe." He challenged these conventions in the name of "reason and the adventure of beauty." Of the world, he asked not for "external symbols of power and dominion, but emotion, the beauty of a rich, fecund, mature personality, the growth of the power to receive high aristocratic pleasure from the simplest common stuff of existence."[87]

Theodore Dreiser once characterized Bourne as a "major mind encased in a minor body." Bourne himself referred to his "terribly messy birth"; a careless doctor's forceps left his face misshapen and one of his ears badly mutilated. Then, at the age of four, he contracted spinal tuberculosis, which left him dwarflike and a hunchback, something he partially masked in public by wearing a cape. Yet what is most striking about the testimony of those who knew him is how quickly one's initial, involuntary impulse to shrink back dissolved. Instead one noticed the sense of aliveness, the endlessly active eyes, the brilliant conversation, and the hands, especially if they were, as Bourne so much liked to do, playing Brahms on the piano.*[88]

Nonetheless, Bourne always felt cut off from much of life, particularly sexual life.[89] For this reason, he craved friendship, devoting the greater part of his time and energy to the cultivation of friends, particularly among women.[90] One of his early articles was on "The Excitement of Friendship," where he revealed that "I really live only when I am with my friends." Privately, he acknowledged that he needed friends because only with them could he fight off his "dreadful pessimism." Though he wished that he could achieve Whitman's "wonderful mood of serene democratic wisdom," he could not. For all of his efforts to overcome his feeling of isolation and peculiarity, he "always carried with him," one of his friends later recalled, "a sense of aloneness."[91] This sense unquestionably brought him considerable personal pain, but it may also have been the source of his peculiar strength in public. His sense of distance and distinctiveness may have made him wary of the "illusion" of power and control.[92] When the war came, some of his fellow intellectuals, particularly those at *The New Republic,* were, as we shall see, seduced by the lure of power and influence, but Bourne seems not even to have been tempted. The burden of isolation, painful though it was, provided a firm personal foundation for the intellectual disinterestedness that he maintained in public. It sustained his independence and enabled him to be the severest and most honest critic of some of the very movements he most strongly advocated.[93]

Admitted to Princeton in 1903, Bourne was prevented from entering because of financial reverses suffered by his mother's family. He worked for six years, in a variety of factory jobs and as a vaudeville piano player. Then, relying upon a combination of savings and scholarships, he entered Columbia University in 1909. Few of the Young Intellectuals went to Columbia; most had attended Harvard or Yale. But Bourne encountered at Columbia a wider world than he had ever imagined. He came into contact with a cosmopolitan outlook and with a number of Columbia professors who were pioneering the development of the exciting new social sciences, particularly Charles A. Beard, Franklin H. Giddings, James Harvey Robinson, James T. Shotwell, and, of course, John Dewey. Out of his cosmopolitan social experience, he concluded that educated or, as he put it, "acclimatized" immigrants were the "true friends" of

* It would be a mistake, however, to associate Bourne's deformities with invalidism. He was an active man, especially relishing city walks and country hikes.

those, like himself, who grew up "provincially" in a "tight little" Anglo-Saxon society.* [94]

Stirred by the intellectual excitement of the social science faculty, he rejected "deadening" literature professors, looking instead to "philosophy and history and sociology as the true nourishment of the soul."† [96] Under this impulse, Bourne opened the literary mind out to the social sciences and, through them, to society. He was not, of course, the only one to do this. Max Eastman, also under Dewey's influence, was moving in the same direction, and some years later he would publish an important discussion, *The Literary Mind* (1931). And Lewis Mumford, always aware of Bourne's example, sought also to fuse humanism and science, becoming a sort of literary sociologist in the 1920s. [98] But Bourne did it first, and did it the most gracefully.

Upon his graduation, Columbia offered Bourne a Gilder Travelling Fellowship, allowing him to spend 1913–14 in Europe. His letters—and his report to the Columbia trustees—show him to have been a close and enthusiastic student of European culture and intellectual life. [99] His hostility to Anglo-Saxonism was reinforced, and he came to appreciate Paris as the center of intellectual seriousness and human expressiveness. "Paris, of course, is the capital of the world." He found there an intellectual life that was, as Brownell had earlier recognized, essentially "public."‡ It was at once national and international, and he felt he was "breathing a freer, more congenial air" in the French capital. [101] After comparing England and France, he concluded that the good things about America were not English, President Butler notwithstanding, "but are the fruit of our far superior cosmopolitanism." [102] Most portentous of all, his trip ended as Europe rushed toward war. Writing from Dresden, two weeks before he left Europe, and less than a week before German troops entered Belgium, Bourne was "very blue" about the lack of resistance to the crazy war enthusiasm. [103] Bourne's year in Europe was crucial to his development: he had, moreover, begun to identify the themes that would be the focus of his finest writing during the war years—the only years left to him—cultural cosmopolitanism and the culture of war.

* Lewis Mumford had this same experience when he confronted the academically talented sons of the Jewish Lower East Side at New York's highly competitive Stuyvesant High School, and a few years later, Joseph Freeman, who, along with his friends Matthew Josephson, Louis Hacker, and Benjamin Ginzburg, was one of the first Russian-Jewish intellectuals from the Lower East Side and Brooklyn to make the long journey to Columbia, returned the compliment to Bourne, noting in his autobiography that he and his friends admired Bourne as a model intellectual. [95]

† Indeed, his contempt for conventional academic literary scholarship seems to have precluded an academic career for him. [97]

‡ Bourne reported to the Columbia trustees that the only American book to penetrate the "intense emotional and intellectual differences of foreign cultures," that takes a country "with entire seriousness and judges it"—and therefore to be useful—was Brownell's *French Traits*. [100]

. . .

After returning from Europe, Bourne found a place to live in Greenwich
Village and began his career in what Lewis Mumford called the "journalism of ideas." He continued to write for the *Atlantic,* and on the recom-
mendation of Charles Beard, Herbert Croly hired him to write on
literature, education, and city planning for the newly founded *New Republic.*[104] He became a regular at the Milligan Place salon of his friend
Alyse Gregory, a feminist, social worker, and, later, editor.

Bourne urged youth to reject the prudential culture of the older generation. Life and reason, all of which were comprehended in his broad
notion of experience, ought to be one's guide, and mere convention
rejected. Speaking *to* as well as *for* the Young Intellectuals, he staked out
the territory and the responsibility of the critic. The target in his famous
anti-war essays, as we shall see, was neither the politicians nor the masses.
Rather, he was concerned with the responsibility of the intellectuals in
the war. What, he always asked, were intellectuals doing to advance
American national and democratic culture?

Bourne encouraged his fellow intellectuals to sever their ties with the
dominant classes, to assume the position of "a spiritual vagabond, a de-
classed mind." The critic must stop trying to impose ready-made European culture on Americans, and upper-class culture on lower-class
Americans.[105] The new culture must have native roots, and it must have
standards. Rather than extending one class's culture to another class, he
demanded that the American cultural nationalist work toward a serious
culture made up of the multifarious experiences of all and accessible to
all, something he had a glimpse of in the theaters of Paris and in the
lecture halls of the Collège libre. Unwilling to embrace what would later
be called proletarian literature, disturbed by the first manifestations of
the movies and other forms of mass culture, he called upon the intellectual to "resist the stale culture of the masses as we resist the stale culture
of the aristocrat."[106]

The task of the critic, then, was quite obviously both large and difficult.
But Bourne at least knew where to begin—just where, incidentally, Edmund Wilson would begin in the next generation. The critic, in Bourne's
view, properly started with the particulars of contemporary life and art.
From there he worked outward, seeking in each work to "supply interpretation of things larger" than the work itself, illuminating in the process "the course of individual lives and the great tides of society."[107]

The older generation, of course, struck back. Brownell's *Standards*
(1917) was an attempt to defend the older generation from the attacks of
Bourne and his cohorts. Bourne, like Wilson after him, was always respectful of Brownell, whom he characterized as "vigorous and gentlemanly" but "quaintly irrelevant."[108] The aggressive attacks of Paul Elmer

More, the learned editor of *The Nation*, demanded a fuller and stronger response. Along with Harvard's Irving Babbitt, More had become a spokesman for the frankly reactionary New Humanism.[109] In *Aristocracy and Justice* (1915), he attacked the "nouveau *intellectual*" who failed to acknowledge the "majestic claims" of the eternal laws and truths that are the inheritance of the past. More, like Godkin before him at *The Nation*, pleaded for "the common recognition," by which he meant the acceptance by all classes, "of the law of just subordination."[110] Unlike Godkin, however, More had little interest in economics. He based his position on humanist learning and moral absolutism rather than upon laissez-faire economics. But it came to the same thing: neither humanism nor economics had room for humanitarianism.

Reviewing More's book in *The New Republic*, Bourne denied the author's absolutism and rejected out of hand his assumption that there was a single "moral imagination working in all classes of society." This "pleasing" illusion may make "power gentle," the reviewer acknowledged, but even the "calm" of More's style "cannot keep the claws of class exploitation from showing through." More, obsessed with control of the will, offered the "ethics of a parsimonious world." He failed to understand, Bourne explained, that the twentieth century is an age of surplus, and the problem—political, moral, intellectual—is how to use it.*[111]

Bourne combined in his intellectual style a strong artistic commitment to the truth of the imagination with a welcome hospitality to the philosophical pragmatism ("science") that was revolutionizing social theory in America. Part of his achievement, as I have already suggested, was to hold together these two elements of his generation's intellectual culture. In the crisis of war, Bourne and others discovered how much tension in fact there was between these two sides of the cultural commitments of the Young Intellectuals. It will be easier to grasp the intellectual consequences of the war if we first consider, however briefly, the ideas of Van Wyck Brooks and Walter Lippmann, the first of whom represented in purer form than Bourne the artistic side, the other of whom leaned more to the scientific side.

Walter Lippmann was born into one of New York's wealthy and cosmopolitan German-Jewish families. If Bourne had to wait until the award of a Gilder fellowship to get to Europe, Lippmann, in the words of his biographer, "knew his way around Paris and London, Carlsbad and St. Moritz, St. Petersburg and Berlin, before he ever saw Philadelphia or

* Bourne had no more sympathy for the anti-democratic nihilism of Mencken, suggesting at one point that the only thing to do about Mencken and the genteel critics "is to persuade them to kill each other off."[112]

Coney Island."[113] He was born in 1889, on New York's Brownstone East Side. He was sent to the best private schools, culminating with a brilliant career at Harvard. After graduation he was schooled in journalism by Lincoln Steffens, then wrote two major books, *A Preface to Politics* (1913) and *Drift and Mastery* (1914), before he was twenty-five, when he was chosen by Croly to be one of the original editors of *The New Republic*.

Although Lippmann is identified with some of the more romantic dimensions of the cultural rebellion—Mabel Dodge's salon, for example—his investment in it was not so personal. He was, paradoxically, modern but not in revolt. While his counterparts rebelled against the Victorian family, Lippmann continued to live at home, commuting to the Village, until he married in 1917. Yet he felt strongly that he was of the generation of Brooks and Bourne, and that, as he told Brooks in 1913, they were "trying to see into the same fog."[114] In his *Preface to Politics*, Lippmann articulated the generational belief that "it is out of culture that the substance of real revolutions is made." The Young Intellectuals would, therefore, have a central role, for the work ahead belongs not to politicians; rather, "it is the work of publicists and educators, scientists, preachers and artists."[115]

Drift and Mastery, Lippmann's second book, deeply impressed Bourne: "There is a book one would have given one's soul to have written—to know what to do with your emancipation after you have got it." Such praise is apt to make one think that Bourne and Lippmann shared the same cultural vision, and at one level this is true. But Lippmann's rejection of the Arnoldian tradition and his sense of democratic culture is based rather differently than Bourne's and Brooks's. Lippmann, as David Hollinger has brilliantly shown, embraced science—in its pragmatic formulation of his time—as the solution to the loss of cultural authority and as a solution to the problem of a democratic culture and politics.[116]

Like Bourne, Lippmann rejected provincialism and tradition. In fact, he argued that the old authorities were already gone; there was no longer even a need to rebel. The choice, as Lippmann phrased it, was that of going back, with Babbitt and More, or ahead with the science of William James and John Dewey. Such a culture would not be "something given," but rather "something to be shaped." If the discipline at the core of the Arnoldian tradition seemed tied to class difference, the discipline of science, Lippmann asserted, was peculiarly democratic. Even in the cosmopolitan world of complexity and difference, the method of science would facilitate "modern communion" and democratic consensus.[117]

The pragmatist in Bourne was drawn to Lippmann's vision, but Bourne, unlike Lippmann, was an artist as well as a pragmatist. When pragmatism allowed Lippmann and Dewey to support American entry into the war, Bourne grasped that something important had been elided in Lippmann's brilliant book. Although the importance of purpose was clear in the method of pragmatism, the source of the values that created purpose was not so apparent. By the time of his essays in *Seven Arts* attacking Dewey and *The New Republic*, Bourne, under the acknowledged influence of Brooks, had come to locate those values firmly and unambiguously in the realm of art, spirit, imagination, not in science.

Van Wyck Brooks is one of those intellectuals whose work divides itself dramatically and clearly into two phases. For those who know him only by his later work, particularly his undiscriminating, fact-laden, and intellectually vacant multivolume celebration of American literary culture, the power and critical edge of his early criticism may come as a surprise.* Edmund Wilson, for example, testified that the early Brooks was "the principal source of ideas on the cultural life of the United States," and even F. W. Dupee and Dwight Macdonald, the severest of his later critics, acknowledged this earlier role.[118] What Brooks offered to the Young Intellectuals was historical perspective on what went wrong and on what resources were available to them. Insisting that the past served up by literature professors was useless, "sterile for the living mind," Brooks sought, in a famous phrase, to "discover, invent a usable past." He would look, not for masterpieces, but rather "for tendencies," for evidence that predecessors "desired the things we desire."[119]

Brooks, like his friend Randolph Bourne, was born in the Haymarket year of 1886. He grew up in Plainfield, New Jersey, a place he characterized as a "Wall Street suburb." Like Bourne, too, his was an old American family, with deep New England roots. When he went to Harvard, he assumed that New England represented culture, but by the time he graduated he had come to view Boston as "narrow, conceited, provincial." Like Irving Babbitt, one of his professors, Brooks believed deeply that literature was real and important in the world. Unlike Babbitt, he was drawn to Whitman. A man full of contradictions, Brooks wanted to embrace culture as fully as Whitman did, but at the same time to give it the kind of elite and centralized direction he found in London and Oxbridge.[120] Whatever its institutional form, however, Brooks never doubted that literature, not politics, would be the basis of a regenerated America.

Brooks began his inquiry into the problem of American culture with

---

* I refer to his "Makers and Finders" series: *The World of Washington Irving* (1944), *The Flowering of New England* (1936), *The Times of Melville and Whitman* (1947), *New England: Indian Summer* (1940), and *The Confident Years* (1952).

The Wine of the Puritans (1908), where he complained that puritanism had evolved into a transcendentalism that "begs the whole question of life" and a commercialism untouched by higher values.[121] *America's Coming of Age* (1915) more fully developed this idea, introducing into American cultural discourse the notions of "highbrow" and "lowbrow" culture. Written in England, revised, ironically, while Brooks worked at *The Century* as a copy editor, *America's Coming of Age* was offered first to Scribner's —by Maxwell Perkins, Brooks's boyhood friend from Plainfield and Harvard classmate—where Brownell rejected it.[122]

Immediately upon its publication by B. W. Huebsch, one of the publishers of the rebellion, it was embraced by the Young Intellectuals. Like Bourne, Brooks complained about the separation of literature from life; there was, he complained, no middle ground between high culture and low practicality, between, as he put it, Jonathan Edwards and Benjamin Franklin. By elevating "literature" too high, the custodians of culture had "relieved" it from "responsibility" for the present. "Between university ethics and business ethics . . . between academic pedantry and pavement slang, there is no community, no genial middle ground." In Whitman, however, Brooks detected the beginnings upon which Young America might build. Here was a poet, Brooks declared, who "experienced life on a truly grand scale" and had become a "man of the world." But, while Whitman supplied "a certain focal center" for American culture, he was able to achieve it "only in an emotional form." The Young Intellectuals must give America the form of an idea, an "animating" social ideal.[123]

Three years later, in *Letters and Leadership* (1918), a book greatly admired by Bourne, Brooks continued the attack. Here, however, criticism of science as well as of politics that had been muted in the earlier work was given full expression. According to Brooks, the pragmatism of Dewey, Lippmann, and other "awakeners" had misled the rebellion. "Pragmatism has failed us," he claimed, "because it has attempted to fill the place that only a national poetry can adequately fill." Pragmatism and political realism dissolved values, making social efficiency an end in itself. "Imagination," he insisted, not "intelligence," is the only source of values. There would be "no true social revolution" until artists brought Americans "face to face" with "experience and set working in that experience the leaven of the highest culture."[124]

Bourne was profoundly affected by this attack on pragmatism and politics in the name of art. But Brooks misrepresented Bourne when— in collecting his papers for posthumous publication as *The History of a Literary Radical* (1919)—he suggested that Bourne's work pointed in this direction and would have followed it had he lived. In fact, at the time of his death Bourne was struggling mightily with a sprawling manuscript on

"The State,"* a work Brooks did not reprint, thus prompting another friend, disturbed by Brooks's depoliticization of Bourne, to print it in another collection of Bourne's writings.[125]

WAR

If any magazine represented the "pure distilled essence" of the Young Intellectuals, it was *Seven Arts*.[126] It was also in *Seven Arts* that Randolph Bourne published his powerful essays against the war, essays that caused the magazine's angel to withdraw support, ending its brilliant career after little more than a year.[127] Because of these essays, most memories of the magazine associate it with Bourne, but he did not appear until the second of its two volumes, in April 1917, with "The Puritan's Will to Power."

The founding editors were James Oppenheim and Waldo Frank, both of New York German-Jewish backgrounds.[128] Oppenheim, a poet who secured financial support for the magazine, had attended Columbia for two years before working at a settlement and becoming head of the Hebrew Technical School for Girls. His early writing was about the Lower East Side he knew so well. Frank was raised in wealth, and he came to Greenwich Village after Yale. Both believed, in Oppenheim's words, that America could be "regenerated by art." When they saw Van Wyck Brooks's *America's Coming of Age*, they recognized in it, as they told him, the "prolegomena to our future *Seven Arts* magazine." They persuaded Brooks to join them as an associate editor, "thus relieving us," Oppenheim remembered, "of the onus of being non-Anglo-Saxon."[129]

Thus, of the five major editors and contributors identified with the magazine—Oppenheim, Frank, Brooks, Bourne, and the Yale-educated music critic Paul Rosenfeld—all were raised in New York or its suburbs, and three were Jewish.† It was, then, a New York magazine, and it was the first example of an ethnic collaboration, Christian and Jew, that sought to speak for an American national culture embracing "different national strains." Long before the *Partisan Review*, Jews who were, in the words of Frank, "bitter, ironic, passionately logical" critics of the arts had assumed a significant place in the shaping of American intellectual life.[130]

Seven Arts was not to be a "little magazine"; it proposed to speak broadly for an American cultural renaissance.[131] "In all such periods," the editors wrote in the second issue, "the arts cease to be private matters; they become not only the expression of the national life but a means of its enhancement." *Seven Arts*, they declared, "is not a magazine for artists,

---

* It is in this manuscript that one of Bourne's most famous sentences appears: "War is the health of the State."

† Oppenheim was born in Minneapolis, but he was brought to New York at a fairly early age.

but an expression of artists for the community." Located around the corner from the "291" gallery of Rosenfeld's friend Stieglitz, *Seven Arts* was an intensely national magazine, promoting a new American culture, while at the same time self-consciously cosmopolitan in outlook and attentive to modern developments on the Continent.[132] Whitman was the magazine's patron saint; he was invoked in nearly every article in the first issue. Like Whitman, like a metropolitan magazine, it reached out to America. And in Chicago, to give one notable example, the magazine's Whitmanesque first issue stirred the young Sherwood Anderson. He wrote to Frank, telling him of the stories he was writing after work. Perhaps he should send some; they seemed to be what *Seven Arts* was calling for. He sent them, and then, an ambitious but unsure provincial, he, too, came to New York. Some of these stories were published in *Seven Arts,* and the whole group became *Winesburg, Ohio* (1919).[133]

The May 1917 issue of *Seven Arts* carried John Dewey's essay "In a Time of National Hesitation." Written just before the United States joined the war, the essay justified a good deal of American hesitation before entering World War I. We should take part, Dewey argued, only in the unlikely circumstance that American notions of democracy and civilization were certain to be advanced. Two months later, Dewey, the idol of the Young Intellectuals, crumbled. He began publishing an influential series of articles in *The New Republic* defending American entry into the hostilities. Even before Dewey's reversal exposed to Bourne the inadequacy of pragmatism, Bourne had begun to attack the pro-war realism of *The New Republic.* In "War and the Intellectuals," published in *Seven Arts* in June, he expressed his outrage at the proud claim of an unsigned editorial in *The New Republic* that "effective and decisive work on behalf of war has been accomplished by . . . a class which must be comprehensively but loosely described as the 'intellectuals.' " The boast was incredible. How could it be? Bourne asked. "A war deliberately made by the intellectuals!" Jane Addams praised his "masterly" reply to the "preposterous editorial," and after the war—and after Bourne's death—Waldo Frank had all of this in mind when he wrote that "the war, which drove all the world including Dewey mad, drove Bourne sane."[134]

The war's impact on intellectual life was enormous and widely ramifying. *The Masses* was closed down by the government, while *Seven Arts* lost its sponsor and it, too, stopped publication. Less directly a result of the war, but not unrelated, was Alfred Stieglitz's closing of his "291" gallery. The specifically cultural ambitions that Croly had for *The New Republic* were severely, even fatally, compromised by the war atmosphere into which the magazine was born. The grand dreams of the Young Intellectuals turned into "a nightmare." Bourne spoke for his once hopeful but now despairing generation when he wrote in *Seven Arts* (October 1917) that "one has a sense of having come to a sudden, short stop at the end of an intellectual era."[135]

It is important to understand the precise target of Bourne's war essays. He wrote little of the war's violence or its conduct. What concerned him was the relation of war to culture, what the war revealed about the intellectual culture of New York. He feared, like Julien Benda, whose slightly later *La Trahison des clercs* (1927) made the same point, that for the intellectuals politics in a fairly narrow sense had swallowed up all cultural concerns. "The war," Bourne wrote to Brooks in 1918, "has brought an immense and terrifying inflation to the political sphere, so that for most people non-governmentalized activity has ceased almost to have significance." Even before the war, he now realized, "the cult of politics" had been "inherent in the liberal intellectual's point of view," something most evident "in the pages of the 'New Republic.' "[136]

During the war the intellectuals at *The New Republic* detached themselves from the aspirations of the Young Intellectuals. They envisioned instead a privileged elite, an intelligentsia, that would interact with the governmental elite in the making of policy. The role of the publicist had changed. It was not so much a matter of giving expression to the inchoate desires of the public; rather, as Brooks put it, the new intelligentsia formulated "only its own desires" and imposed them on the public as the "deliberate choice" of a limited and knowledgeable class.[137] What was happening—at least from the vantage of our modern pattern of intellectual life—was that *The New Republic* led an important segment of American intellect onto "the road to class power," to use a phrase first devised to describe developments in Eastern Europe. In the less provocative language of Edward Shils, the war marked the first step in the long process of the incorporation of American intellectuals into the "center."[138]

This aspiring intelligentsia represents most clearly Walter Lippmann's passion for the influence of an "insider" and his desire, more to be expected in a manager than in a journalist, to make things work better.[139] The publicist in this version of intellectual life becomes the presidential confidant and adviser, and during the war the editors of *The New Republic* met weekly with high officials in the Wilson administration.[140] They thought they had acquired power, but in fact they had become public relations agents. Seeking direct influence and the experience of action, the *New Republic* intelligentsia allowed themselves to be seduced by the illusion that they "could control events," exemplifying what Harold Stearns after the war called the "technique of liberal failure." Bourne could not resist remarking "how soon their 'mastery' becomes 'drift.' "[141]

The impulse to become an intelligentsia holds two inherent dangers for any group of intellectuals. First, there is a possible, even likely, loss of independence, and, second, there is a subtle encouragement to concern oneself with technique at the expense of values, to collapse means and ends. Such was the thrust of Bourne's attack on Lippmann, Dewey, and *The New Republic* generally. In his most powerful essay, the one that finally brought the brief *Seven Arts* adventure to an end, he noted a "peculiar congeniality" between the war and the pragmatic intellectuals at *The New Republic*. "What is significant," he reflected, "is that it is the technical side of the war that appeals to them, not the interpretive or political side." Dewey's pragmatic ideas, at least in the hands of his disciples, lacked a commanding democratic vision. "The war has revealed a younger intelligentsia trained up in the pragmatic dispensation, immensely ready for the executive ordering of events, pitifully unprepared for the intellectual interpretation or the idealistic focussing of ends." In the midst of war and with the acknowledged influence of Brooks, Bourne saw clearly what he had not seen before the war. "Unless you start with the vividest kind of poetic vision," your instrumentalism is likely to land you "happily and busily engaged in the national enterprise of war." Pragmatism contains "no provision for thought or experience getting beyond itself." Defending the Young Intellectuals against the new intelligentsia, he claimed that "it is the creative desire more than the creative intelligence that we shall need if we are ever to fly."[142]

Too many of the war generation, it seems, had found it impossible to confront the evil of the war. Unable to summon the necessary spiritual resources, they escaped into technique. Bourne stood apart, if not absolutely alone, surely magnificently, demanding that intellectuals not "spiritually accept" the war. They should stand "outside the war," refusing to allow it to shape their choices, and they must maintain a commitment to themselves and to the "American promise." Bourne had never asked the "young radical" to be a "martyr," but he always insisted that he or she be "fiercely and concentratedly intellectual."[143] Bourne was almost alone among his generation in having enough faith in the worth of mind to resist the lure of power, influence, action.[144]

It is perhaps ironic that Willard Straight, who with his wife Dorothy funded *The New Republic*, died, also in his thirties, in the same 1918 epidemic that killed Bourne. Important as well as ironic was Croly's course after the war. He came to feel much like Bourne, becoming in the 1920s a spiritual seeker. By the end of the war, he was chastened, and he realized that the war had undermined and transformed the original cultural promise of *The New Republic*.[145] In 1920, he argued in *The New Republic* that while there was still a case for pro-war liberalism, it was a "precarious case," more difficult to make than it had seemed four years earlier. Always a bit skeptical about pragmatism, he pointed out now that the problem was essentially spiritual, a "lack of integrity in the authoritative moral standards of modern civilization." What was needed—and this is surely the work of intellectuals—was the building up "within nations centres of moral self-possession."[146] Croly by this time "despaired of politics," and those who knew him observed that he "never really took them seriously again." He was so disillusioned in the 1920s that, as Malcolm Cowley remembers it, he considered turning *The New Republic* into a "journal of literature, arts, and moral philosophy."[147]

Lippmann, in contrast, never acknowledged *The New Republic*'s failure. If anything, he moved in an opposite direction from Croly. During the 1920s he defended the intelligentsia, the expert, the insider, against the claims of a democratic public. Abandoning after the war the faith in public culture evident in *A Preface to Politics* and *Drift and Mastery*, Lippmann wrote two powerful books that essentially argued the public out of existence. The important point about *Public Opinion* (1922) and *The Phantom Public* (1925) is not that they pointed out the real difficulties of public opinion and its formation, but rather the ease with which he abandoned any notion of democracy in seeking a solution. What he offered was decisions by "men inside." The outsider, he declared, is "necessarily ignorant, usually irrelevant, and often meddlesome."[148] John Dewey, not nearly so ready to retreat from the democratic challenge, was disturbed by Lippmann's argument in *Public Opinion*. Dewey called it "perhaps the most effective indictment of democracy as currently conceived ever penned," and Charles Beard sardonically commented a few years later that Lippmann had somewhat more faith in the public than did Lenin and Mussolini.[149]

Two other legacies of the war bear discussion. First, there was the Russian Revolution. The success of Lenin and his fellow Bolsheviks in 1917 and the subsequent reality of the Soviet Union became a momentous fact of modern life. And it immediately became a fact of a peculiar sort, capable of extension through space, becoming an almost tangible part of intellectual life in New York. Second, nationalism, inflamed as usual by war, not only brought intolerance, repression, and Americanization programs; it also stimulated in response the formulation of a cosmopolitan ideal, sustaining an urban, ethnically diverse, and anti-provincial notion of intellect that became, as a number of historians have recently shown, a beacon for the *Partisan Review* generations of New York intellectuals.[150]

After the Russian Revolution the sort of innocent, non-doctrinaire, eclectic "revolution" represented by *The Masses* (1911–17) was no longer possible, as its reincarnation as the *Liberator* (1918–24) and the later *New Masses* (1926–48) clearly reveals. One cannot page through these magazines without sensing that something profound had happened to intellect in New York between the first magazine and the second two. Joseph Freeman, a Russian-born son of Jewish immigrants who as a sixteen-year-old youth had avidly read *The Masses* at a local socialist club in Brooklyn, who later wrote for *The Liberator,* and who still later was a founder of *New Masses,* fully understood this. The Russian Revolution, he observed, "tightened certain trends of thought, dissipated others."[151] Only after the cultural shock waves precipitated by the revolution reached New York was literary Communism introduced into American life. In 1923, the Communist Party took over *The Liberator* and, for the first time in America, art began to be judged overtly and directly by political criteria.[152] Here one thinks immediately of the proletarian literary standards of Mike Gold, the most consistent and most gifted of the literary Communists. It was a case, as Philip Rahv later observed, of the "literature of a party disguised as the literature of a class."[153]

Once the Soviet Union existed, a great deal of free speculation became difficult. Concrete positions on its policies seemed to be demanded. With the availability of such a litmus test, the tyranny of ideological correctness was encouraged. Thus the battles over Stalinism in the 1930s and 1940s were not *de novo*; they were the product of and continuous with the tragic —and ultimately vicious—division of the intellectual culture of New York that first imprinted itself in 1917. It is fitting, perhaps, that the United States government closed down *The Masses* in New York almost on the day Lenin's triumph in Moscow made the radicalism of that magazine impossible. What happened a generation later—involving a much larger intellectual community—was presaged, at least in its broad outlines, in the more immediate aftermath of World War I.[154]

Always wary of the irrational nationalism he saw in Europe at the beginning of the war and in America during the war, Bourne had called upon the young intellectuals to go beyond nationalism. If the older generation had most obviously failed in its incapacity to imagine a national culture that embraced the immigrants who were transforming New York, Bourne saw in the city's newcomers a grand opportunity for youth to liberate itself from the Anglo-Saxon parochialism they inherited. Raising his generation's feelings and dispositions to the level of cultural theory, he proposed a "trans-national" American culture. His starting point was Horace Kallen's criticism of the homogenizing and Americanizing idea of the "melting pot," but Bourne carried this farther and in a slightly different direction, elaborating a pluralistic vision of intellectual culture.

Bourne's essay "Trans-National America," published in the *Atlantic*, amounted, in the words of Paul Rosenfeld, to a "new statement of the democratic ideal."[155] It was a conception of culture that combined an acceptance of persistent particularism with a sense of a common and public discourse.

Bourne urged intellectuals to accept the distinctive character of American life; they should stop longing for European models of national and centralized social and intellectual elites.* He rejoiced in America as a "unique sociological fabric," and he asserted that "it bespeaks a poverty of imagination not to be thrilled at the incalculable potentialities of so novel a union of men." Think instead, he demanded of his generation, of a cosmopolitan culture that recognizes diversity and a certain disorder. He envisioned America in the image of New York—a federation of cultures. Rejecting the legitimacy of Anglo-Saxon dominance, he declared that American culture "lies in the future," it shall be "what the immigrant will have a hand in making it."[156]

Like Kallen, Bourne welcomed the preservation of ethnic difference, but he was particularly concerned with a unity that could embrace such permanent diversity. He was moved, as David Hollinger has written, "by the idea of a community of intellectuals, a complex, yet unified, single discourse to which a variety of contingent particularisms would make their distinctive contributions." It was a vision of urbanity and cosmopolitanism that proved itself congenial both to Anglo-Saxon radicals and to the emerging Jewish intellectuals—represented most notably, when Bourne wrote, by Morris Cohen, the philosopher who later became a legendary professor at City College.[157]

Ellery Sedgwick, editor of the *Atlantic*, who had admired Bourne's work since his first undergraduate essay, "The Two Generations," was shocked by the article Bourne had sent him. Because of his respect for Bourne and because it was so well written, he accepted it for publication. But, speaking in the tones of Boston to New York as well as of an older New York gentility, he informed Bourne: "I profoundly disagree with your paper." The United States, at least from where Sedgwick sat in the *Atlantic*'s Boston offices, was "created by English instinct and dedicated to the Anglo-Saxon ideal." "You speak," he rather incredulously retorted, "as though the last immigrant should have as great an effect upon the determination of our history as the first band of Englishmen." Insisting that the United States had neither political nor literary lessons to learn from Eastern Europe, he bridled at Bourne's equation of an old New Englander and a recent Czech as "equally characteristic of America." He was surprised a few months later at the "commendation" the essay received

---

* In this he differs from Brooks, who never escaped the European ideal.

on publication, more than he would ever have expected for what he called a "radical and 'unpatriotic' paper."[158] Even at the time and in Boston, the Harvard Menorah Society responded by inviting Bourne to address them on the theme. Bourne's talk, "The Jews and Trans-National America," was published in the *Menorah Journal,* where, it is worth recalling, Lionel Trilling began his career as a writer.[159]

It is interesting in this connection, moreover, to compare the observations of Trilling in the famous *Partisan Review* symposium "Our Country and Our Culture" (1952). Criticizing literary intellectuals for their fascination with "certain foreign traditions," Trilling complained that they did not look closely enough at American culture. "If we are to maintain the organic pluralism we have come to value more highly than ever before, it is not enough to think of it in its abstract totality—we must be aware of it in its multifarious, tendentious, competitive details."[160]

Bourne's ideal was new and profound in its implications, yet it was also deeply rooted in the city's social and literary history. Whitman, of course, would recognize it, but so, too, might Henry James. Back in the 1860s, when he was still in important ways a New York intellectual, though he lived in Cambridge, James wrote to Thomas Sargeant Perry, a Bostonian then in Europe. He proposed that perhaps America had some advantages over European nations as a home for literary advance. "We can," he observed, "deal freely with forms of civilization not our own." If the absence of a "national stamp" had in the past been "a regret and a drawback," James speculated, "it [was] not unlikely that American writers may yet indicate that a vast intellectual fusion and synthesis of the various national tendencies of the world is the condition of more important achievements than any we have seen." There must, of course, be something distinctive to give form to this fusion, and James assumed "that we shall find it in our moral consciousness." He did not, he acknowledged, expect anything "great" in his own time, but his "instincts" led him to look for "something original and beautiful" to emerge in time from "our ceaseless fermentation and turmoil."

James had not, of course, recognized Whitman in the 1860s, but by the time of his famous return to New York in 1904, he had come to regard the poet of the city as a "very great genius." His reaction to the city of immigrants he found at that time is also more complex and interesting than is usually recognized. While he felt disinherited by the destructiveness of the city's growth since his youth and displaced by newcomers for whom English was an alien sound, the experience was not shattering. Like Tocqueville with his stoic yet deeply interested acknowledgment of the inevitability of democracy, James, less disposed than Bourne to the dispossession of the language and culture of his Anglo-American forebears, acquiesced. He even grasped and responded to its possibilities. An evening of dining and conversation on the Jewish Lower East Side suggested to him a "waiting spring of intelligence." Although its present and likely forms were both profoundly different from what he knew, he recognized the "germ of a 'public,' " a social and intellectual life containing a "promise of its own consciousness." Nervously acknowledging that this new public culture would surely sacrifice the English language and culture he loved, he contemplated an "ethnic" synthesis—using this word, I think, for the first time in America—that might even become "the very music of humanity." [161] Few at the time could grasp it, but the possibilities Bourne and, more hesitantly, James saw in the city of immigrants, not the dominant and narrow Anglo-Saxonism of the time, was to become the basis for the internationalist and cosmopolitan center of art, music, dance, and literature that New York has become in our own time.

SHRINKAGE AND FRAGMENTATION

The metropolitan and cosmopolitan ideal articulated by Randolph Bourne implied a proliferation of vital subcultures—ethnic, but also aesthetic, geographical, and political. Although he celebrated diversity and difference, he felt that the geographical contiguousness of the metropolis would deny each group the privilege of provinciality. All must be tolerant of others, and they must engage in conversation with each other. What one most notices in the decade of the 1920s, however, is a striking shrinkage of the literary imagination and a diffusion of literary life into particular locales and coteries.

To make this point first in the most obvious way, we might notice that the rich interweaving of politics and culture represented by the Young Intellectuals did not survive the war, nor did their confident assumption that radical or progressive and advanced or "modern" art were natural partners.* [162] For example, *The Dial*, which had been moved from Chicago to New York in 1918 with the intention of publishing both Dewey and Bourne, was nearly torn apart by politics, and in 1920, under the direction of Schofield Thayer, it turned severely, if impressively, to aestheticism and modernism. [164] *The Freeman*, established in 1920 with aims that seemed to welcome the Young Intellectuals (now getting older), turned out to be, except for Van Wyck Brooks's regular column, "A Reviewer's Note-book," a fundamentally political magazine. To the extent any discussions of modernism in the arts appeared in *The Liberator* and *New*

---

* To the extent that it did survive, it was as a form of nearly instant nostalgia, evident in the writings, for example, of the young Lewis Mumford. [163]

Masses, it was to condemn it, usually from the perspective of proletarian art.*

We can obtain another vantage on the shrinkage of the intellectual terrain in New York by considering the fate of psychoanalysis, the major new idea entering the city's intellectual life in the 1920s. The curious course of this powerful idea, quite different from its European career, reveals something of the constraints of intellectual life in the city. Psychoanalysis was either vulgarized in the sophisticated and fashionable culture of *Vanity Fair* or *The New Yorker,* or it was medicalized and localized on Central Park West. In contrast to what happened in Vienna, Berlin, London, or, later, Paris, psychoanalysis in New York did not elicit convergence; it did not bring together intellectuals in a variety of humanistic fields.[165]

The broad outline of the configuration of intellectual life in the 1920s was anticipated in a revealing exchange between Randolph Bourne and Harriet Monroe, editor of the influential modernist magazine *Poetry.* Writing in *The Dial,* Bourne had observed that the real danger for the young artist was not the philistine, nor was it Brownell, but rather the "undiscriminating" public for the new and experimental. "The current popularity of verse, the vogue of the little theatre, and the little magazines, reveal a public that is almost pathetically receptive to anything which has the flavor or pretension of literary art." Writers needed protection from a "public too easy to please." Bourne called for a new critic who would "intervene between public and writer with an insistence on clearer and sharper outlines of appreciation by the one, and the attainment of a richer artistry by the other." Monroe responded with a charge that Bourne was making too much of the critic and not enough of the art itself. Acknowledging that the critic may be important to the public, she insisted that the artist had no need for the critic. The artist simply needed to "get himself expressed in his art and to get his art before the public." Bourne's rejoinder, with help from Brooks, distinguished his broader cultural concerns from the aestheticism that would characterize the twenties. "You can," he allowed, "discuss poetry and a poetry movement solely as poetry—as a fine art, shut up in its own world, subject to its own rules and values; or you can examine it in relation to the larger movement of ideas and social movements." He was fearful, however, that to "treat poetry entirely in terms of itself is the surest way to drive it into futility and empty verbalism."[166]

. . .

---

* Here we get some perspective on the significance in the 1930s of the *Partisan Review,* committed as it was to progressive politics *and* the modernist literary developments of the 1920s.

The tendencies Bourne distrusted were encouraged by American participation in the movement of international modernism in the 1920s. After
the war, the outcome of which had been decisively affected by United
States power, and after greater familiarity with Paris, American writers
began to feel more confident, less provincial. They were increasingly at
home in international culture, less defensive about their own, always
buoyed up, even if surprised, when French intellectuals praised the
skyscraper, jazz, and other emblems of America so congenial to the
international modernist movement.[167] As they were drawn into avant-
gardism, however, they acquired certain artistic values and modes
that worked against the possibility of a coherent metropolitanism in New
York.

The international modern movement was powerfully corrosive of
place, particularly the public quality of place. This was especially evident
in modern poetry, but one can see it in the novel as well. Even if preoccupied with a specific place, as in James Joyce's *Ulysses,* the modernist
impulse was to interiorize. This move inward was concerned, as Lionel
Trilling pointed out, with the self, not with culture. There was little in
this modernism to prompt the imagination to reflect upon the civic realm.
In fact, to the degree that the poetic imagination of the 1920s was assumed to represent an "other order of intelligence," there was not even
a continuity of language between art and the world.[168] It was difficult
to reach out and touch the social world at all. Delmore Schwartz, the
young poet and critic associated with the *Partisan Review* in the 1940s,
grasped this at the outset of his career. Modern poetry, he told an
audience of literature professors in 1939, "has fed upon itself increasingly and has created its own autonomous satisfactions, removing
itself farther all the time from any essential part of the organic life of
society."[169]

Literature's public dimension was contracting. It was becoming the
artist's expression of his or her private self. The reader of modern literature sought in reading it to identify or clarify his or her private experience, without the mediation of public culture. Perhaps the first American
novel read this way was F. Scott Fitzgerald's *This Side of Paradise* (1920).[170]
There were, of course, exceptions, but for the most part modernism did
not have a way, in the words of theologian Nathan A. Scott, Jr., to engage
the "unexclusive mutuality which belongs to the true life of the city."[171]
Imagination sought unity and completion within the confines of a work
of art. The territory of art had shrunk, from the public world of the city
and culture to the single text. This dissolution of the city, I would suggest,
helped prepare the way for the emergence of the New Criticism in the
universities.

. . .

A more down-to-earth, literal mapping of the topography of the city's intellect offers another sort of insight into the shrinkage and fragmentation of the 1920s. At first view, there seems to be a perhaps unprecedented metropolitan conjuncture of the various worlds of intellect. Within the bounds of a single two-block radius centering on Thirteenth Street, between Sixth and Seventh avenues, there was a remarkable collection of magazines in the late 1920s. The Dial's offices were at 152 West Thirteenth Street; a few doors away were The Freeman and New Masses and the Menorah Journal. A block east and around the corner on Fifth Avenue, W. E. B. Du Bois was editing Crisis, while a few blocks north, in nearby Chelsea, Croly's New Republic had its home.* Margaret Anderson's The Little Review, with its important ties to Ezra Pound in Paris, seemed to have a new address every year, but it was seldom more than three blocks from the corner of Thirteenth Street and Fifth Avenue.

Here on Thirteenth Street, one might expect, were the conditions for that enforced deprovincialization of intellectual life that Bourne had envisioned under metropolitan conditions. Members of various literary coteries and movements must have actually bumped into each other on the street. But they seem not to have opened a metropolitan conversation. The city's literary life, as Edmund Wilson remarked, was like vaudeville, a series of individual acts. "Opinions," he complained in 1928, "do not really circulate." "It is astonishing," he observed, "to what extent the literary atmosphere is a non-conductor of criticism. What actually happens is that each leader or group of leaders is allowed to intimidate his disciples, either ignoring all the other leaders or taking cognizance of their existence only by distant and contemptuous sneers."[172] No doubt it is from this era and experience that our intellectual life acquired that group sense represented by a linguistic peculiarity of New York intellectuals, the omnipresent "we." Perhaps, too, we see here the beginning of that characteristic tendency of New York coteries to translate their own parochialism into a putative universalism.

Contemporaneous with the editorial concentration on Thirteenth Street, there was an opposite geographical symbolization of the fragmentation of New York's intellectual life. Never before—or since—have the parts of the city's culture been so identified with distinctive geographical locales. Some of these, in this era of internationalism, were foreign—Paris or Moscow. Others were near or distant suburbs of Greenwich Village, whether Taos, New Mexico, or a series of country towns up the Hudson, especially Croton; in New Jersey; and in Connecticut. Within the bounds of Manhattan, the Lower East Side represented one kind of

* The Nation, which is now in this neighborhood (Fifth Avenue and Thirteenth Street), was located downtown at Vesey Street in the 1920s.

intellectual and artistic life, some of which, at this time, was finding itself welcomed in the "Uptown Bohemia" of Times Square, where Tin Pan Alley, theater, and journalism (both newspapers and such magazines as *The Smart Set, The American Mercury, Vanity Fair,* and *The New Yorker*) formed what Harold Stearns at the time called a world of "Dorothy Parkeresque smartness and briskness." [173]

Far from the center of things, despite their intentions and self-perceptions, were the honored members of the National Institute of Arts and Letters and the American Academy of Arts and Letters, located, since 1923, in two Italian Renaissance buildings facing each other across Audubon Terrace at Broadway and 155th Street. If to Robert Underwood Johnson the location and architecture might have symbolized the resistance of the academicians to modernism and their commitment to "unchangeable principles," others might have noticed the alternative symbolism suggested by Trinity Cemetery, across the street from Audubon Terrace. A decade earlier, in fact, without the prompting of this accident of urban land use, the idea had already suggested itself to Max Eastman, who wrote in *The Masses:* "Some time ago Congress passed a law making 100 American men of letters and artists immortal. It was an emergency bill, for most of them would soon have been dead otherwise." [174]

Just to the east and south of Audubon Terrace lay Harlem. Here, in this "black city, located in the heart of white Manhattan," a very special place, not a "slum," not a "fringe" area, but a district of apartment houses and new-law tenements, a small group of educated blacks—Alain Locke, Charles S. Johnson, James Weldon Johnson, Jessie Fauset, Walter White, and Casper Holstein—orchestrated a cultural movement remembered today as the Harlem Renaissance. [175] Harlem, they hoped, would not only become the "capital of the Negro World," but from a base in Harlem the black artist would, in Alain Locke's words, become a "collaborator and a participant in American civilization." [176]

In one sense, the program succeeded. The Harlem Renaissance brought black art and literature nearer to the center of American literary and artistic life than it had ever been—nearer, in fact, than the Academicians, at least in the early 1920s. But if black art was incorporated into the city's intellectual life, the terms of that incorporation must be attended to. When one looks closely, as Harold Cruse, Nathan Huggins, and David Levering Lewis have done, one sees a pattern of domination and subordination. [177]

The Harlem Renaissance was, as Nathan Huggins insists, "as much a white creation as it was black," and white interests in Harlem were different from those of the Renaissance's leaders. The exoticism of Harlem fit all too well into a history of white/black imagery in America, and in the

1920s, when the reputation of civilization and puritanism was so low, Harlem was embraced by such critics as Carl Van Vechten and H. L. Mencken, not for its own sake, but as a weapon in their somewhat different battles against gentility and, if Huggins is right, their own inner selves.[178] Such white attention, whatever its motivation, brought essential patronage, publication opportunities, and critical notice. But the price was heavy. Black art would in most cases be pressed to conform to white notions of black authenticity; such art, moreover, would not be likely to root itself in the actual life of the Harlem community. The leaders of the Renaissance took a chance, thinking they could exploit these white patrons for their own purposes. It was a dangerous game, and they lost.

The plan was to achieve through art what had eluded blacks so far by other means. Art was to redeem the standing of Afro-Americans; it would be the means to the higher end of racial acceptance. When blacks showed they could create great art, then, it was assumed, racial discrimination, at least against educated blacks, would dissolve.[179] At the base of the strategy was a belief that in the world of intellect the vicious cage of racism was more easily escaped. In retrospect, however, it is clear that intellectuals have been no more successful in overcoming the structure of American racism—cultural, political, economic—than other New Yorkers. The cosmopolitan ideal may have opened New York intellectual culture to ethnic diversity (or was it in the end only to WASPs and Jews?), but, as Harold Cruse has forcefully pointed out, it certainly did not open up the world of the New York intellectual to blacks.[180] The acceptance of a few blacks—one thinks of Jean Toomer by the *Seven Arts* group, perhaps, and Claude McKay's association with *The Liberator*—does not constitute a counter-argument, nor does the later representation of James Baldwin and Ralph Ellison as "cousins" in the *Partisan Review* "family."[181]

The Harlem Renaissance throws into relief not only a long pattern of tangled black/white relations in America, but also certain more general characteristics of literary life in the 1920s. The literature of the Renaissance had no organic relation to everyday life in Harlem. With the exception of Langston Hughes, the work it sponsored did not illuminate the actual black experience in "the city within a city."[182] Too often it limited itself to the problems of black intellectuals themselves living in two worlds, or it became a literature of romantic images of rural black life. Neither did the writers of the Renaissance have a social or economic base. Refusing to associate itself with the black masses, the Renaissance did not have a sufficiently developed middle class in Harlem to sustain it. Without such a local base, without a strong middle class to pay the bills and read the books, black writers could not meet white culture on any but white culture's terms. The Renaissance, artificially stimulated by well-directed and mostly white patronage, took place, as David Levering Lewis puts it, "in rented space—in a Harlem they did not own." Unlike the Jewish writers who emerged at about the same time—and whose experience was noted by black leaders—Harlem did not first establish the economic foundations for the cultural ambitions of its leaders.[183] In an exploitative, even colonial, situation that should have suggested the impossibility of separating art, politics, and economics, the Harlem Renaissance was relentlessly and single-mindedly artistic. It represented an attempt to invert the order of economics and art, and to substitute art for politics.

MAN OF LETTERS

It was in the context of the ideals of the Young Intellectuals and against the background of the shrinkage of the imagination in the 1920s that Edmund Wilson established his vocation as a "free man of letters."[184] Wilson's literary career is identified with two themes that would capture the attention of the city's intellectuals between the wars and after: modernism and Marxism. With these concerns, Wilson represented the Europeanization of American intellectual life that accompanied the rise of New York's stature in international political and cultural affairs, but this intellectual cosmopolitanism never compromised his striking and essential Americanism. Wilson was unmistakably American, and he was deeply interested in the American literary and historical past. He maintained a delicate balance between his insatiable interest in the ideas of the wider world and his fascination with the details of American life and with the major and minor writers who comprised for him an American literary tradition.

Wilson was generously aware of his New York predecessors, and he built his own career on the achievements of Brownell, Huneker, Brooks, Bourne, and Mencken. He wove their various legacies into a sense of vocation that came to epitomize the man of letters in New York City. He became the "gold standard" of literary journalism in New York and the "authority figure" for later New York intellectuals.[185] In his autobiographical *Starting Out in the Thirties* (1965), Alfred Kazin reveals that Brooks, Bourne, and Wilson formed for him a composite model of the New York literary intellectual. They also supplied him with a sense of the promise of the city and of American literature. For Lionel Trilling, who first met Wilson in 1929 and who at that time declared his intellectual ambition by taking an apartment in Greenwich Village (across the street from Wilson's), the older critic seemed "in his own person . . . to propose and to realize the idea of the literary life."[186]

Born into an old American family in 1895, Wilson was raised in Red Bank, New Jersey. His father, Edmund Sr., was a lawyer, an old-fashioned sort of man who had never accepted the sordid commercialism of his time. Active in New Jersey politics, the elder Wilson nonetheless made independence and rectitude his standard. Through his father, Wilson developed a sense—which he shared with the somewhat older Bourne and Brooks—that the Gilded Age represented a great and terrible shift in American life. After the Civil War, it seemed, materialism nearly overwhelmed all idealism and moral grandeur in the country. The task of literature, then, was to penetrate the cover of gentility and comprehend that transformation and its legacy. It was this persistent concern, rooted in part in his own family's history, that prompted and sustained Wilson's interest in American local history and in the Civil War, resulting, particularly, in *Upstate* (1971) and *Patriotic Gore* (1962).

Edmund Jr. followed his father to Princeton University, where, along with classmates F. Scott Fitzgerald and John Peale Bishop, he found a literary mentor in Professor Christian Gauss. When he graduated in 1916, Wilson had determined to pursue a literary career in New York. He began with a brief job as a reporter on the New York *Evening Sun,* but he soon enlisted in the hospital service and went to France. After the war, he returned to New York, writing free-lance until he became managing editor of *Vanity Fair* in 1920. A year later, he moved to a similar job on *The New Republic.*

The making of Edmund Wilson was, of course, a complex affair, shaped by Wilson's special gifts as much as it was by his social and intellectual environment. It is important to recognize, however, that the milieu of New York in the 1920s was profoundly influential in presenting him with the materials out of which he fashioned himself into a man of letters. Much like Bourne before him, Wilson sought to define the boundaries of his own critical intelligence by probing the outlines of life and culture in America.[187] He started with the *Seven Arts* program, with its concern for the relation of art and politics and with its combination of cosmopolitanism and faith in native expression. From there, he reached out to the aestheticism of *The Dial* and *The Little Review*; the experimentalism of the Provincetown Players; the humanistic learning of Paul Elmer More; and, increasingly, the radical politics of Michael Gold's *Liberator* and *New Masses.*

Like his contemporary Lewis Mumford, Wilson refused to be enclosed by any of these partial worlds of intellect. Both men rejected any "restricted form of intelligence," and this insistence lay at the base of their criticism of the shrinkage of intellectual life, whether this was manifested in the orthodoxies of literary Communism or academic specialization.[188] To the extent that intellectual life was contained in these or other more or less self-contained enclaves of thought, public culture was impoverished. Wilson's vision of himself as a man of letters impelled him to reach out to the diffused and fragmented elements of intellectual and political life, bringing them to the center, creating in the process, perhaps even in his own person, a locus for public culture. Such was the responsibility Wilson sought as he defined his literary vocation.

Wilson always insisted that literature was in the world. As he picked his way through the shards of the city's intellectual culture in the 1920s, Wilson was intensely aware that art had become increasingly private, at the expense of its responsibility to the public world, to history, to the relation of thought and action.[189] The contemporary American poet, he feared, was cutting himself off from society—or was being cut off by that society. Acknowledging that it would be worse if poets were to succumb to society, he insisted that surely one "wants them, at least, to have relations with it. If the relation is an uncomfortable or a quarrelsome one, so much, perhaps, the better."[190]

His generation's struggle to find a viable orientation to American society supplied the theme of his book *I Thought of Daisy* (1930). The book offers a series of narratives, each representing, as Wilson made clear in a preface to a later edition, a way of being an intellectual in America.[191] None worked until the last, in which intellect finally made connection with the common life of America. When he began *Daisy* in 1928, it represented a rearticulation of the ideals of the *Seven Arts* program (as well as a vehicle for expressing his near-obsession with the poet Edna St. Vincent Millay). By the time it was published, however, the Great Crash had, or so it seemed, ended the "Big Business era," leaving writers exhilarated at the "sudden unexpected collapse of that stupid gigantic fraud."[192] *Daisy* now had a new context, and its conclusion pointed toward the multi-formed discovery of the people that gave new energy to American writing in the 1930s and made possible both the great gestures of literary solidarity and the literary battles of the decade.

But Wilson moved only gradually toward the political concerns that would occupy him in the 1930s. When he first established himself in the city's literary culture in the early 1920s, he was drawn to the problem of literary modernism. Realizing, as he later recalled, that the battle against puritanism and the genteel tradition had already been largely won, he was free to address the "most recent literary events in the larger international world." The classic works of modernism needed to be understood, and his first major book, *Axel's Castle* (1931), explored their implications for American intellectual life. During the thirties, he took up his second theme, "the most recent developments of Marxism in connection with the

Russian Revolution," and this supplied the subject for his important book *To the Finland Station* (1940).[193] These two books, with their themes of modernism and Marxism, crystallized a program not only for Wilson but also for succeeding generations of intellectuals in New York, including those whose autobiographies are today proliferating. For both Wilson and his successors, the relation of Marxism to modernism was the way in which the problem of art and politics presented itself. It was Wilson who first asked the question that so preoccupied the *Partisan Review* intellectuals: How, on what terms, might one admire Eliot's poetry and still be a political progressive, even a "radical"?

Wilson was drawn to the aesthetic achievements of the European modernists, particularly those descendants of Poe and Baudelaire whom he called symbolists. Although he admired the technical innovations of Mallarmé, Valéry, Eliot, Pound, Joyce, and others, he worried about the philosophy of life that seemed to be implicit in the whole literary movement that they represented. He was concerned that the intense introspection of symbolist poetry pointed toward an aesthetically precious social isolation and political quietism. It was a literal shrinkage of the imagination.

Axel's Castle, the title he chose for his study of the symbolists, represented, he told Maxwell Perkins, his editor, the imagination, which Axel did not "get out of to participate in reality." In another, earlier letter announcing the plan of the book, Wilson told Perkins that he was convinced that any literary movement has a "serious weakness" if, as symbolism did, it had a tendency to "paralyze the will, to discourage literature from entering into action." These European developments had, he acknowledged, been embraced by young American writers in the 1920s, but Wilson told Perkins that "the time has now about come for a reaction against" such European imports. American writers were especially well situated, he thought, to lead the reaction. The "disillusion and resignation" characteristic of postwar Europe have "absolutely nothing to do with the present realities of American life" and are "largely inappropriate for us." *Axel's Castle* was his attempt to appreciate the technical accomplishments of recent European literature and, at the same time, to insist upon an American literature that was more fully in the world, more concrete, factual, and less "atmospheric."[194]

Such is the case Wilson made in *Axel's Castle.* Wilson's message was threaded through the book, but one grasps Wilson's concerns most clearly in those pages, among the most evocative and deeply felt in the book, dealing with Paul Valéry's succession to the chair of Anatole France in the Académie Française. Although Wilson acknowledged Valéry's superior gifts as a writer, his sympathies were clearly with France, whose memory and significance Valéry slighted in the customary speech he delivered on his election to France's chair in the Académie in 1925. France, who had begun as a writer of light satires, was transformed by the Dreyfus affair in the 1890s. He was one of those writers, newly called *les intellectuels,* who stood with Zola in that controversy. In the years that followed, he remained a writer in the public realm, attacking narrowness, bigotry, and injustice wherever he found it. With his commitment to the public role of the writer, France had been an early opponent of the symbolist movement. He had argued that he would "never believe in the success of a literary school which expressed difficult thoughts in obscure language." [195]

Valéry, a man of extraordinary genius, was an intensely, even pathologically, private writer. He published much, even though he largely refrained from writing for publication for twenty-five years, writing instead mostly for himself, in 257 unpublished notebooks. Insisting that one cannot be at once profound and lucid, he was a leader of the French symbolists. When Valéry appeared at the Académie Française to honor France, his every gesture—of manner, dress, and word—was disrespectful. In his speech he remarked, condescendingly, on the ordinary class origins of France (whose father had been a Paris bookseller), and he showed disdain for the common reader for whom France had written. In the process of establishing these distinctions between the two men, Wilson revealed his preference for France, not as a man of genius, which he was not, but as a literary man in the world. France, Wilson pointed out, had a public, while Valéry had a circle. What France represented for Wilson (and what Wilson himself strove for) was "a wide knowledge of human affairs, a sympathetic interest in human beings, direct contact with public opinion and participation in public life through literature." Valéry, by contrast, represented "solitary labor" and "earnest introspection." [196] Valid, of course, and with a man of genius productive of works of great beauty, but not, Wilson thought, the model he had in mind for the metropolitan literary intellectual.

When, in the 1930s, Wilson turned to the left and became overtly political in his interests, he did so as an intellectual. He did not become a practical politician. He explored the country and he reported on its condition, its hopes, and its fears, but he joined no parties and he declined to pretend that he was other than an intellectual. Echoing Bourne's declaration of 1917, he insisted that the intellectual was responsible for ideas, and for Wilson, as for Bourne (whom, as Daniel Aaron remarks, one cannot imagine as a Communist), the intellectual must be free, independent of

any party discipline or orthodoxy.[197] Wilson often supported positions of
the Communist Party, including the essential point of the inflammatory
"economic interpretation" of Thornton Wilder that Michael Gold published in *The New Republic* in 1930.[198] Wilson, however, never fell for the
Communist program of proletarian literature, always imagining, like
Leon Trotsky, that the ideal was not the literature of a class, and especially not that of a party, but rather a literature of humanity. Yet he did
insist that art and literature must "grow out of the actual present substance of life to meet life's immediate needs." Both humanism and Marxism, he feared, avoided the literary present, the one retreating to a
nonexistent past and the other leaping forward to an imaginary future.[199]

Wilson's reach as a man of letters encompassed both art and politics.
But, unlike some of his successors at the *Partisan Review* and some still
later academic literary theorists, he never conflated or confused the two.
Nor did he ever pretend that the courage to confront the difficult texts
of modern literature amounted to a form of political radicalism. He knew
that for the intellectual art and politics were related, but distinct. What
one finds in Wilson's work, as Edward Said has aptly observed, is a deep
awareness of literature as literature (not merely as an ideological construct), but also general intellect, scholarship, political sophistication, and
historical engagement.[200] It is not particularly to the point to praise Wilson as one of the great thinkers or writers of our century, for he was not.
Nor was he, in fact, an absolutely reliable critic. Our debt to him is of a
different order, but it is immense. He is our twentieth-century exemplar
of the vocation of the literary intellectual, the critic who keeps alive the
general conversation of citizens, of humanity, that makes public culture
possible and, indeed, constitutes it.

Yet even in our gratitude, we must not miss certain limitations. Although
he was formed in the multiplicity of the city, Wilson never became a
genuinely metropolitan intellectual. He never added metropolitanism to
his other M's, Marxism and modernism. In the 1920s, he often wrote
about the city, its architecture and its ways, but the city as a place gradually dissolved in his writings. Eventually, as is well known, he left the city
for Talcottville in upstate New York and Wellfleet, Massachusetts. Unfortunately, this pattern was not unique to Wilson in his generation. Lewis
Mumford, who did make metropolitanism one of the core themes of his
life work, eventually turned from the city, leaving it in the 1930s for a
rural and Spartan life at Amenia, New York. The exciting metropolitan
milieu that he had once associated with the achievements of Stieglitz,
Bourne, and others of the generation that preceded him was gradually

transformed, as the hopefulness of *The Culture of Cities* (1938) was replaced by the unrelieved pessimism of *The City in History* (1961).[201]

Wilson's relation to the academy bears some comment as well. He was always contemptuous of a university teaching career, and his famous attack in the 1960s on the Modern Language Association's critical editions and academic literary study in general is probably still part of contemporary memory. Much of what he said about the academy was, unfortunately, all too true. But the academy at its best had more to offer him than he acknowledged.

One can see in Wilson's intellectual style, for that matter, his distance from the academy, and to say this is not entirely a compliment. If the academy overreaches itself in its pursuit of universalizing abstraction, Wilson focused too much on the local, the concrete. His best and most mature writing, *Patriotic Gore*, for example, lacks even as much analytical frame as he had offered in the introductory chapter of *Axel's Castle*. It is a series of quote-laden biographies, enormously illuminating to be sure, but limited in interpretive reach. The point, here, is not to make an argument for the intellectual as academic. On the contrary, it is to suggest the value to both literary intellectuals and academic intellectuals of somewhat more sympathetic interaction.

Certainly, one of the great cultural losses of the postwar years has been the decline of the Wilson type of literary intellectual. As early as 1943, he recognized that he was on his way to becoming an anachronism. The practice of letters, he suggested, was once "a common craft," but it is now becoming "extinct" and its practitioners were becoming "a legend." The journalism of ideas that he had practiced was vanishing: journalism was abandoning literature for straight political commentary, and men and women of ideas were being drawn into the academy.[202]

A few years later, in 1949, the English poet and critic Stephen Spender was struck by the impoverishment of the "community of literature" in New York. The universities, not the cities, it seemed, were increasingly becoming the home of literary life in the United States. Recognizing that the universities provided essential financial support to American writers, Spender nonetheless feared that the withdrawal of writers from the market of literary commerce would isolate them from their proper public. Such conditions, he thought, would encourage a hermetic literary culture in which writers wrote for other writers.[203]

But it need not, of course, be an either/or matter. Cities and universities might be symbiotic as well as adversarial sponsors of intellectual life. In the later 1930s, in fact, Wilson had noticed a telling change in the usage of the word "intellectual." The word, which had originally referred to non-academic writers for New York magazines, was now understood to embrace academics as well, or at least the academics who also wrote for certain magazines, like the *Partisan Review, The New Republic,* and *The Nation.* It was possible, perhaps, to be at once a part of the academy and at home in the world of the city. Immediately after the war, a group of Columbia University academics, most notably Richard Hofstadter, Meyer Schapiro, Lionel Trilling, and C. Wright Mills, suggested the possibilities of this new New York intellectual.

PART III

ACADEMIC CULTURE

CHAPTER 7

A Metropolitan
University

In the 1860s, neither New York University, with its Gothic pile on the east side of Washington Square, nor City College, with the more restrained Gothic building James Renwick had designed on Twenty-third Street, nor Columbia College, recently moved from the neighborhood of City Hall to the discarded buildings of the Deaf and Dumb Asylum on Madison Avenue between Forty-ninth and Fiftieth streets, loomed very large either in the iconography of the city or in its practical social life. George Templeton Strong, for many years a Columbia trustee, exaggerated, but not without truth, when he wrote in his diary that Columbia "is an obscure fact; it is among the 'things not generally known.' "[1]

Collegiate institutions in mid-nineteenth-century New York had few students; Columbia's class of 1871 graduated thirty-one. Higher education offered an optional finishing course for young gentlemen, whether they aspired to lives in business or in the traditional professions. It was required in neither case. In a very important sense, the colleges were marginal to the life of the city, even its intellectual culture. Although John W. Draper at New York University and Wolcott Gibbs at City College (until 1863) were distinguished scientists, no one associated their personal accomplishments with their respective institutions. In fact, William C. Redfield and Lewis Morris Rutherford, amateurs rather than professors, were equally notable. No one would mistake New York's academic institutions for centers of creative intellect. Nor were they understood to be the foundations of social achievement and power.

If all three of these institutions of higher learning had somehow disappeared in the 1860s, the city at large hardly would have noticed. A half century later, however, universities had assumed a new and central role in New York and in American society generally. The university had become a fundamental institution of modern social and intellectual life. Knowledge and power were associated in the newly created universities, and the path to professional authority, so highly valued (and rewarded) in the modern, complex, urban society that had emerged, ran through them.

This transformation in the social and intellectual significance of higher education was represented in a new architecture. Within a decade, between 1895 and 1905, each of New York's major academic institutions built new campuses that gave them greater visibility. New York University moved first, going to University Heights, where Stanford White designed a strongly neoclassical campus for its undergraduate college; at about the same time, his partner, Charles F. McKim, began to lay out Columbia's formal Beaux Arts campus at Morningside Heights. A few years later and twenty blocks north at St. Nicholas Heights, George B. Post, whose Western Union Building (1876) on lower Broadway had been the first New York skyscraper to top the Trinity Church spire and whose most recent project had been the New York Stock Exchange (1903) on Wall Street, designed an English Gothic campus for City College. These campuses, all located in a large irregular triangle in the northern reaches of the metropolis, were major and innovative works of public architecture in the city. Earlier academic architecture in the city had concerned itself with special buildings on city streets, but these new campuses, all on prominent heights, distinguished the academy from the street pattern and from the ordinary life of the city, thus giving higher education an uncommon visibility and emphasizing its special importance in the life of the city. One could no longer imagine the city, either in visual terms or in social terms, without these institutions of higher learning.

If these new campuses stood for a changed relation between society and education, they also demanded and advanced a broader public responsibility for higher education. William F. Ware, the architect who inaugurated architectural training at Columbia, captured this change in his epigrammatic remark that Columbia's new campus would "transform Columbia from a private into a public institution."[2] What these new campuses implied and required, as Ware understood so well, was a new and unprecedented infusion of money. These vastly larger sums would come from the public, whether from city government in the case of City College or from philanthropy in the cases of New York and Columbia universities. Whatever the source of the funds, the institutions would have to justify themselves in terms of public accomplishment.

CULTURAL REFORM AND THE UNIVERSITY

The movement to transform higher learning, to create a modern university in New York, had its roots in the city, not in the academy. Urban cultural reformers, worried that intellectual life in New York threatened to dissolve into chaos, turned to the academy, particularly to Columbia College, for the solution to their problem: the justification of elite cultural authority in a democratic society.[3] More broadly, the city's elite asked Columbia to play its role in the consolidation of New York's metropolitan standing. These larger concerns, not the logic of academic development, shaped the initial discussions of university reform.

Over the course of the nineteenth century in both Europe and America there was a growing tendency, as Asa Briggs has noticed, to associate universities and cities in a way that was novel. If Paris's university was an ancient foundation, neither London, Berlin, nor Vienna had universities until the nineteenth century. Beginning with the University of Berlin, founded in 1809, in the wake of Germany's defeat by Napoleon, the world of learning and national cultural invigoration (or reinvigoration, as the case might be) came to be identified with universities, particularly those in capital cities. By midcentury, it was assumed that a great university must be located in a great city, while a city could not claim greatness without a university.[4] When in 1860, for example, George Templeton Strong projected—in the privacy of his diary—a vision of a reformed city culture in the next generation, he linked together Central Park, the Astor Library, and "a developed Columbia University" as the agents that would make New York "a real center of culture and civilization."[5]

Such assumptions set the terms of discourse, and would-be university reformers appealed to them. Lecturing before the New York Geographical Society on the subject of the "Growth of Cities" in 1855, Henry P. Tappan insisted that "a great city requires in its bosom, or in its proximity, a University." "Nothing," he added, "can take the place of a great University." A generation later, in his inaugural address as professor of philosophy at New York University in 1884, Henry N. McCracken, soon to become the university's greatest chancellor, the leader who consolidated the professional schools and formalized graduate training, insisted —in an intentional and strategic misreading of history—that from Herodotus's first use of "metropolis" in reference to Athens it had been associated with the idea of a university. Identifying the university with Alexandria and Rome, London and Edinburgh, as well as with Athens, he reiterated the wisdom of his time: "every metropolis will include a university taking up its own characteristics."[6]

No university president in New York's history was more successful than Nicholas Murray Butler in using this rhetoric to appeal to the pride and the pocketbooks of elite New York. Celebrating the mutual interests of the city and the university in his inaugural address as president of Columbia University in 1901, Butler explained that "every city which, because of its size or wealth or position, aims to be a center of enlightenment and a true world-capital must be the home of a great university." If the city's "higher life," as Butler put it, stood to gain from the influence of the university, the university would profit from the political and economic stature of the city. To the extent that New York achieved national and international standing, so would its university. This, too, Butler understood. "The metropolitan city of New York," he wrote in his autobiography, "will in all likelihood become the effective and influential capital of the thought and conduct of the world for the next few hundred years." If this indeed happens, "then surely the authority of Columbia University and its great company of productive scholars would be of the highest importance in the history of the human race."[7]

There is, of course, something rather soft in this self-serving civic boosterism. By contrast, the cultural worries of E. L. Godkin and his ilk were more hard-edged. Elite cultural reformers in the city of his day wanted a metropolitan university to solve a specific cultural problem. Godkin worried that "a large body of persons has arisen," taught by common schools, newspapers, lyceum lectures, small colleges, magazines, and the like, "who firmly believe that they have reached, in the matter of social, mental, and moral culture, all that is attainable or desirable by anybody, and who, therefore, tackle all the problems of the day." The result, he declared, "is a kind of mental and moral chaos."[8] His magazine, *The Nation*, was intended, of course, to combat such cultural tendencies, but he felt that more was needed.

Lamenting the "disintegration of opinion" in modern, urban society, he called in 1870 for "greater concentration of instructed opinion." The American Social Science Association, which he strongly supported, was established, after all, precisely to sustain the sort of authority Godkin desired. But Godkin looked as well to other possible structures of authority. He strongly commended "professional associations," urging architects, for example, not to "pander to uninstructed judgment." He also favored a proposal to create in New York a National Institute of Letters, Arts, and Sciences in the hope that it would give "organization" to "the chaotic mass of persons" who were—or should be—concerned with "mental culture." He doubted whether it could ever achieve the authority and the "standards of excellence" of the Institut de France in Paris, but he thought it might succeed in taming the "spirit of mob" and "infusing . . . discipline and order" into American intellectual life. George Templeton Strong, who also attended the organizational meetings chaired by

William Cullen Bryant in June 1868, agreed. But he acknowledged that "the chances are 100 to 1 against its success."[9]

Godkin and other cultural reformers turned to the university idea as part of a general search for authoritative cultural institutions; indeed, the embrace of the university came only after other options seemed unlikely to accomplish the cultural reform they sought. Godkin, for example, gradually shifted his attention to the academy as a defense against what he called—in a letter to Daniel Coit Gilman, who would soon be the founding president of The Johns Hopkins University, America's first real university—"quacks, charlatans and pretenders in fields of literature and science." In 1890, George William Curtis, at the annual dinner of the Columbia Alumni, spoke for the metropolitan gentry at the end of their era when he asked the college, which would officially become a university six years later, to "stimulate the intellectual and moral forces of this community."[10]

Such a transformation of Columbia was not to be an easy task. The trustees of the college, with a couple of exceptions, did not see Columbia as a public institution, and they certainly did not envision for it the role Godkin and Curtis had in mind. Neither did they notice—or at least they did not care to emulate—the way the Union Theological Seminary set out to exploit the metropolitan opportunities offered by New York. Founded by New York merchants in 1835, Union in the 1850s and 1860s resolved, with great success, to associate itself financially and intellectually with the city. By the 1870s, Union had secured an adequate endowment and an intellectually exciting faculty, enabling it to become a national, non-denominational, and cosmopolitan center of theological instruction and scholarship. This transformation, so much a part of its embrace of its metropolitan setting, enabled Union to surpass the older denominational and provincial seminaries at Andover and Princeton.[11]

One could justly say that Columbia College in 1870 had failed as a classical college, and that the majority of the trustees, unwilling to aspire to a modern university, were self-satisfied with that circumstance. Its own inquiry into "the condition of the institution" in 1858 is damning almost beyond belief. Most appalling of all is the lack of standards or, rather, the defense of standards that would not "exclude students of dull or slow minds."* Brander Matthews, who graduated in 1871, remembered Co-

---

* That is not all: there are suggestions in the report that even *this standard* was not being enforced!

lumbia of his student days as "a lazy little college, almost asleep, and almost devoid of any ambition to make itself worthy of the great city in which it was placed." In fact, Columbia was a closed corporation, more of a real estate investment trust watching the growth of the city increase its assets, rather than an educational body. Its resources were sufficient to eschew benefactors and still pay its professors twice what Harvard paid its professors. The trustees were so comfortably situated that they disdained not only the public but their own alumni as well.[12]

Godkin and the metropolitan gentry he represented challenged Columbia in 1883, after Hamilton Fish, as president of the trustees, blamed the city, not Columbia, for its invisibility and ineffectiveness. Columbia, he suggested, "is lost sight of" because New York is such a "centre of business, fashion, and pleasure." Harvard, Yale, and Princeton seem to be important because there is nothing else worthy of attention in their respective towns. While granting something of Fish's point, Godkin insisted that in fact the problem was that Columbia was too "secluded, conservative, mediocre." If it is to be a "city college," Godkin asserted, it must "endeavor to increase in every way possible the number of points at which it can come in contact with the life . . . of the city." With a commitment to "high standards," Columbia could advance "literature, science, and art" and train up a *corps d'élite* in New York. Intellect, he acknowledged, has a hard time in New York. But, he insisted, "the more difficult it is to form an intellectual centre in New York, the greater the responsibility which rests on its old and rich university."[13]

Richard Watson Gilder, too, joined the fray, telling James Bryce, the English historian, that he and his friends were trying "to stir up Columbia College and make a genuine university of it." More publicly, he published an article in *The Century* pleading that the "feeling is very general" in New York that a great university is necessary. To achieve such a university, New York must stop accepting "mediocrity in learning." He was not really certain that Columbia had the "progressive vitality" to serve even as a "nucleus for the future university." Still, he called upon Columbia to try: give up an isolated self-sufficiency and associate with the city, become the great "Metropolitan University" that New York deserves and needs.[14] In 1889, Godkin called upon Columbia again to "exert a great civilizing and enlightening force in the metropolis and in the country." Reminding his fellow gentry that only in a "community which sets a high value on culture, and has a strong sense of its political and social importance," might a great university emerge, he frankly despaired of both the city and Columbia. But with the presidency of Columbia just become vacant, he had one hope: perhaps a new-style, German-trained academic would be appointed president.[15]

. . .

When, some months later, the trustees announced the election of Seth Low, graduate of the class of 1870, merchant, and former mayor of Brooklyn, Godkin's hope might seem to have been dashed. But Godkin knew Low was no ordinary merchant and politician, and he had the wit to realize that Low could put Columbia "definitely on the footing of a university." Low's election was, in Godkin's phrase, "a new move" for Columbia, and it was a genuine endorsement of the idea of a metropolitan university.[16] Yet if Low's appointment and presidency were indeed an affirmation of Columbia as a metropolitan university, Low's sense of the university's relation to the culture of the city was not framed by Godkin's program. Low had a broader vision of the university than Godkin; he sought more than to bolster the cultural authority of traditional elites and the metropolitan gentry.

THE BEGINNINGS OF COLUMBIA UNIVERSITY

New York elites have always preferred to keep their disagreements private, fearing that a crack in their united front might stimulate the *demos*. Occasionally, however, these gentlemanly protocols have been breached. Two notable instances relate to crucial moments in the history of Columbia, or, more precisely, the historical debate about the proper place of an institution of higher learning in the general culture and social history of the city. Both times the result was a brilliant and passionate statement of the kind of institution of higher learning Columbia ought to be to adapt itself to the special circumstances of cosmopolitan New York. The polemics of William Livingston surrounding the founding of Columbia provide the first instance; the second came almost exactly a century later. In fact, Samuel Ruggles's pamphlet *The Duty of Columbia College to the Community* (1854) so upset the complacent calm of the institution that it was unable to get its trustees together to celebrate the college's centennial.

The occasion of Ruggles's pamphlet was the determination of a majority of Columbia's trustees to pass over the candidacy of Wolcott Gibbs for a vacant professorship of chemistry and natural and experimental philosophy. Neither Ruggles at the time nor historians since have had any doubt about the issue: Gibbs was denied the appointment because of his Unitarian religious beliefs. Against the majority, Ruggles argued that it was not within their province to "inquire into the religious creed" of a professional candidate. The only legitimate question was the professional competence of Gibbs, something "eminent men of science at home and abroad" were "entitled to decide" in the character of "experts."[17]

It was a strong and strikingly modern argument, and it has often been cited by historians of academic freedom.[18] But Ruggles embedded it in an equally interesting and important interpretation of Columbia's "distinct relations to the community." The whole affair, in other words, provided Ruggles with an opportunity to present to the public both a searching criticism of Columbia as it was and a vision of what it might be as a self-consciously public and metropolitan university. His insistence on the public quality of Columbia's "definite duty" to the city underlay his vision and justified his bringing the conflict out of doors.[19]

To telescope his argument and put it in rather abstract terms, he proposed that in a modern, democratic society, a public institution had particular responsibilities. It must appoint professors on the principle of what we would today call strict professional merit, and it must embrace the most advanced intellectual currents of the times—in this case, science. Excellence and scholarship are in his argument being assimilated into the principle of the academy's responsibility to the public. With the acceptance of this idea, one has a key principle of the university. Ruggles went further, however. He recognized a social as well as an intellectual obligation. A public institution, he asserted, cannot be discriminatory, especially not in a city and a nation long marked by cultural and religious diversity. Not only all Christians but Jews and even, if Chinese immigration to the West Coast were to continue, Confucians should be eligible for university offices. If, he argued, Columbia belongs "wholly to the world around us," then "we are bound by every principle of law, equity, and honor to render equal and exact justice to every part and portion, every sect and section alike."[20]

Ruggles pointed out—and this must have especially rankled his fellow trustees—that the newly founded Free Academy (later City College, where Gibbs currently held an appointment) was advancing faster than Columbia. This new institution, governed by "popular vote," may well "take the splendid and beneficient position we were meant to occupy." In a few years, if Columbia remains "stationary," the matter will be settled. Leadership will belong to a "so-called democratic school, founded avowedly because we did not satisfy the just demands of the community." Columbia must become more than "a place for the sons of gentlemen," where they might acquire "culture, refinement, and elegant taste." Let it aspire for more. Let it do its educational work in such a "mode, and with such vigor and intelligence, as to advance the moral and intellectual dignity of the community itself—to become an element in our social system, felt in all its workings, modifying the culture and elevating the character of all around us."[21]

Such hopes, he contended, were not "any idle fancy." He asked his readers to consider the founding of the University of Berlin, which he deemed the great event in "the moral and intellectual history of modern times." In the wake of defeat and demoralization, this great university "revived and rekindled" the spirit of the nation. He concluded with a plea that New Yorkers take as their "best and highest ambition" the development of a "comprehensive and liberal seat of learning" that would do the same for "our rich Metropolis, our powerful State, our rapidly expanding Empire."[22]

Ruggles did not secure the appointment of Gibbs,* and a subsequent investigation by the state of New York effectively legitimated the narrowest possible definition of the college's responsibility to the public.[23] But if he lost the Gibbs case, Ruggles lived to win the battle for the university. There is no question, as Richard Hofstadter has written of the controversy, but that "Columbia University arose out of the case."[24] Ruggles had the satisfaction in the eighty-first and last year of his life of introducing before the Columbia trustees the resolution that, favorably acted upon, inaugurated genuine university work in 1880.

To know Samuel Ruggles is to know much about how profoundly the beginnings of the university were grounded in the city and its civic life. He is one of those New Yorkers who are mostly forgotten, but who should not be.[25] Ruggles, in the only language we have available in our day, was a real estate developer.† His most notable accomplishment was the transformation of five hundred building lots into the Gramercy Park neighborhood, creating in the process not only the park but also two streets not contemplated in the 1811 plan, Irving Place and Lexington Avenue. Strongly committed to the value of public space in cities, Ruggles also contributed to the planning of Union Square, where he lived at 24 Union Place. One of his last writings was a protest against plans to build an armory in Washington Square Park.[26] But he engaged in many other enterprises as well. Ruggles was a founder of the Bank of Commerce and a builder of the Erie Railroad, and he was responsible for the extension of the Erie Canal in the 1840s. He was also an internationally recognized authority on financial statistics and coinage, serving as the United States representative at the International Monetary Conference of 1867. He retired from active business in 1851, when a bad investment in a commercial development project on the Brooklyn waterfront forced him into

---

* In 1863, Gibbs left the Free Academy to take the Rumford Professorship in Chemistry at Harvard, where he had a distinguished scientific career. In 1873, he was awarded an honorary degree by Columbia, by unanimous vote of the trustees.

† Ruggles was born in New Milford, Connecticut, in 1800, of an old New England family. He went to Yale, where he studied science with Benjamin Silliman, graduating in 1814. He then studied law, and he was licensed to practice when he arrived in New York City in 1821 or 1822. He soon married Mary Rathbone, whose father was a substantial merchant, and he began his career in real estate.

bankruptcy. For the remainder of his life, he devoted himself to civic affairs, particularly as one of the original trustees of the Astor Library and as a Columbia trustee for forty-five years.

In his own day Ruggles was often identified with an improving spirit—in economic and intellectual life—reminiscent of De Witt Clinton. We have here, then, a conjuncture between the older civic culture and the emergent academic culture. But even more of our story comes together in this man. He was a strong supporter of the cultural reforms we have already noted, endorsing the scheme of the scientific Lazzaroni for a national university, Tappan's plans for a great metropolitan university in New York, the American Social Science Association, and the effort that so appealed to Godkin to create a National Institute of Letters, Arts, and Sciences. It is difficult, in other words, to determine whether his university would represent civic culture, literary culture, or a culture of its own. The modern university has in the twentieth century sought to define its own intellectual charter. That this charter represents a narrowing of its original possibilities becomes evident when we attend to the complexity of its metropolitan beginnings.

With the informed and consistent support of his son-in-law and fellow trustee, George Templeton Strong, Ruggles continued to press for change at Columbia. In 1857, there was a halfhearted effort to respond to Ruggles and Strong by establishing schools of Letters, of Science, and of Jurisprudence for the advancement of "higher culture in learning and science." The trustees seem to have called Ruggles's bluff. "If there be really that demand for the acquisition of knowledge which has been supposed," they resolved, "it may here be satisfied. If there be in fact no such demand . . . time will soon develop the truth."[27] The School of Letters utterly failed, while the Law School succeeded, but under the essentially proprietary leadership of Professor Theodore Dwight it was severely practical and vocational, not a place of scholarship or broad learning. A School of Mines was also established. Although it was not a genuine faculty of science in the German sense, it did provide the basis for later expansion of scientific studies. University reform had little to show.

In the 1850s, American society was not ready for the modern university. The social complexity and scale of administration that required its kind of knowledge and expertise were not yet sufficiently developed. The process by which the university and society became modern was interactive. The university was at once a contributor to the transformation that made a place for it and a product of that transformation.[28] Ruggles, who was not quite sure what function in society the university would play—

or, to be more precise, uncertain about *how* it would play it—was premature at midcentury. By the 1880s and 1890s, as the rapid growth of Columbia and other universities in the United States and abroad reveals, social and intellectual life without the university had suddenly become impossible. Because Columbia was in the largest city, one increasingly assuming genuinely metropolitan functions, it had the opportunity, which it grasped, to become the largest and most powerful of these new American universities.

In January 1876, Ruggles found the instrument of his eventual success. When John W. Burgess, a German-trained political scientist, gave the last in a series of lectures at the Law School, Ruggles, who had attended every lecture, introduced himself with the words: "You are the man we have been looking for. . . . You must come to Columbia."[29]

Burgess, who descended from old Massachusetts families, was born in middle Tennessee in 1844. Raised in a slaveholding but strongly pro-Union family, he escaped conscription into the Confederate army, and with the encouragement of his father went North to enlist in the Union forces. Witnessing the terrors of war as a seventeen-year-old, he got his "first suggestion" of a life work. He vowed in those Civil War trenches to "devote my life to teaching men how to live by reason and compromise instead of by bloodshed and destruction." Having thus early "lost faith in the wisdom and goodness of the mass of men," he envisioned, in a Nietzschien phrase he later adopted, a few "supermen" who would make the "ideas and ideals of civilization."[30]

Graduating from Amherst College in 1867, he studied law (gaining admission to the Massachusetts Bar in 1869) and taught before going to Germany in 1871 for advanced training in political science. Impressed at Berlin by the intellectual honesty of the great historian Theodor Mommsen, he acquired a sense of the power and calling of the professor. Mommsen was to Burgess a "superman." Burgess sought to emulate him, determining, as he put it in the first issue of the *Political Science Quarterly* (1886), to encourage "the spirit of independent research in politics." Burgess learned another lesson, as well, at Berlin. He witnessed the role of the University of Berlin and its professorate in the making of the new German state after the Franco-Prussian War.[31] These two ideals of independence and power guided his vision of a great metropolitan university, but, as the development of the social sciences at Columbia would show, they were not so uncomplicated in their relationship as Burgess and others assumed.

After completing his studies in the fields of history, political science, and public law, Burgess returned in 1873 to Amherst. His efforts to introduce advanced studies were resisted by his faculty colleagues, and he was, therefore, in a mood of discouragement when he met Ruggles, "one of the most extraordinary men whom it has ever been my privilege to know." Ruggles, then seventy-five years old, and Burgess, only thirty-one, "flew together like steel and magnet." When Burgess shared his dream for a university, thinking that Ruggles would reject it as visionary, the young professor instead found enthusiastic agreement. Columbia, the older man informed the younger, had "one hundred thousand dollars more of income than of outgo," and it ought to be spent to establish advanced training in law and political science. "We want you to tell us how best to expend it."[32]

Ruggles persuaded the trustees to offer Burgess a professorship of history, political science, and international law. Burgess was hesitant; he was, he later wrote in his autobiography, "never a lover of metropolitan life." The "din and crowds and murky atmosphere" of New York did not appeal to him. But he realized that Amherst was "not the place for the university such as I had in mind." The "natural home" for such a university was in the city, "with its libraries, museums, laboratories, courts, operas, theatres, concerts, zoological gardens, and its large wealth." All of these he had known in Berlin. Here a metropolitan intellect could be formed. With this realization, he accepted the offer in June 1876. When he arrived, however, he again had doubts. He found that Columbia was in reality a "small old-fashioned college," with a library that was open only one and one-half hours per day. The Law School was only nominally a part of the college, located downtown in the former Peter Schermerhorn residence on Great Jones Street, and it was a mere trade school, not receptive to the sort of work he had in mind.[33]

Ruggles, however, urged patience. If advanced training could not find a place within the existing structure of Columbia, it would be necessary to create a separate graduate school of political science. When Burgess in exasperation went to Ruggles at his home in April 1880, he found that the older man had not only anticipated his proposal for a separate school but even had a model for it, Paris's Ecole libre des sciences politiques. Established as an independent institution in 1872, in response to the French defeat in the Franco-Prussian War, the Ecole libre offered a curriculum that was modern, not classical. It sought to provide cultural studies at the university level to prepare men for government service and as makers of opinion. The Ecole libre, in other words, seemed an apt model for the metropolitan ambitions of Burgess, Ruggles, and, for that matter, Godkin and Curtis.[34] In New York, the center of political opinion, the trained intellect of such a school's graduates might find a special role in American democracy.

As the model of the Ecole libre suggests, the Faculty of Political Science was at the outset as much a civic as an academic institution. It was rooted in the ideals of civic responsibility and the reform movements associated with the American Social Science Association and the Civil Service Reform Association.[35] Its graduate, its product, was conceived at first to be the politician or journalist as much as, or even more than, the academic. In this respect it had much in common with Herbert Baxter Adams's contemporary seminar at the newly founded Johns Hopkins University, which, after all, produced journalists, reformers, and politicians as well as academic historians and social scientists. Theodore Roosevelt, who in 1880–82 studied with Burgess in the School of Political Science as well as in the Law School, was precisely the type of graduate envisioned by Ruggles and Burgess.[36] Their primary aim was to train metropolitan and national leaders, not to make academics.*

Frederick A. P. Barnard, who was Columbia's president when Burgess and Ruggles pressed their reforms upon the school, fully shared their sense of advanced learning as a civic matter. In advocating university work, for example, he referred to "mental culture," a phrase more natural to Godkin or Curtis than to later disciplinary professionals, and in his annual report for 1881–82 he explained that the newly founded School of Political Science was designed to train men for the "civil service." The school's graduates would be prepared for the "duties of public life" or for work "as public journalists."[37]

This initial vision did not, however, turn out to be controlling. The problem, something suspected—perhaps for the wrong reasons—by skeptical trustees, most of whom felt profoundly alienated from political life in New York and the nation, was that such scholarly training would give little advantage in public life and that few, therefore, would seek it. They were correct; five years after the school was established it enrolled only twenty students.[38] But by the late 1880s another development, one not predicted by the trustees or anyone else, drew the school in a different direction, one that offered remarkable opportunities and which stimulated a gradual redefinition of the school's work.

In the 1890s, higher education in the United States began to expand rather dramatically. Total college and university enrollment doubled between 1880 and 1900, from just under 50,000 to about 100,000.[39] At the same time (and not unrelated) curricular changes created a large demand

* In the 1912 presidential campaign, Woodrow Wilson, an alumnus of Adams's Hopkins seminar, was pitted against Roosevelt, one of Burgess's favorite students.

for just the type of professor the School of Political Science was equipped to train. As the classical curriculum gave way in the 1890s to more modern subjects, colleges were beginning to seek scholars trained in the new social sciences.

In 1887, one begins to see signs of the shift at Columbia. Talk about civil service became muted, and for the first time an explicit concern about the training of students for academic careers became evident.[40] By the early 1890s, Burgess recognized that his program had gradually but definitely shifted from preparation for public service careers to academic careers. At the twenty-fifth anniversary of the school in 1905, Burgess, who was by then fully committed to the change, measured the school's achievements by the numbers of professors it had trained and placed.[41] This capacity to reproduce itself, to multiply its own type, the product of a specific historical moment, enabled the universities, as Edward Shils has observed, to achieve primacy in the "order of learning" in the United States.[42] Columbia, in the nation's largest and wealthiest city and able to offer to graduate students the excitement of the city, quickly became the largest and most influential center of graduate training. Columbia had achieved academic primacy as befitted a metropolitan university, but in the process it put at risk many of the metropolitan and civic ideals that had sparked its transformation in the 1880s and 1890s.

For the new academics, the older American Social Science Association and the Civil Service Reform Association held little appeal; they simply were not appropriate or relevant to a primarily academic outlook. They represented the ideals of the old metropolitan gentry. The academics increasingly looked toward new, disciplinary organizations. Between 1876 and 1905, thirteen major scholarly societies were established in the United States.* With their specialized, authoritative, and legitimating discourses, these associations were not much attached to a particular place, and this translocal pattern of intellectual community threatened to undermine metropolitan culture. If university work began in New York within the context of civic and literary culture, by the turn of the century it was well on its way toward consolidating a distinctive culture of its own, one that went far toward redrawing the map of intellectual life in New York and America, countering the metropolis with a national *system* of universities.

---

* American Chemical Society (1876), Modern Language Association (1883), American Historical Association (1884), American Economic Association (1885), Geological Society of America (1888), American Mathematical Society (1888), American Psychological Association (1892), American Astronomical Society (1899), American Physical Society (1899), American Society of Zoologists (1902), American Anthropological Association (1902), American Political Science Association (1903), American Sociological Association (1905).

CIVIC CULTURE AND ACADEMIC CULTURE

The consolidation and definition of academic culture at Columbia occurred between 1890 and 1920. There were two distinct phases in the school's development from an inferior college into a great metropolitan university. Each phase was based upon a different understanding of the relations of the university to the city, of academic culture to civic culture. These two conceptions of a metropolitan university, moreover, were each identified with a particular president: Seth Low (1890–1901) and Nicholas Murray Butler (1901–45).

In the first phase Columbia tried to engage the social diversity and cultural richness of the city in an open way, seeking a multi-voiced conversation among the many elements of the United States' unique metropolis. Later developments, however, sought to empower the university in ways that weakened its connections to metropolitan life, establishing instead the authority of university expertise in the city and nation. The university, born of the civic and literary culture as well as the wealth of New York City, became under Butler less and less a New York institution. Still Columbia University in the city of New York, it was uncertain in the 1910s and 1920s, as in our own time, whether it wanted also to be *of* the city. The history of the formative years of Columbia University is, then, a contest between, on the one hand, dialogue and conversation and, on the other hand, autonomy and authority. Both orientations are part of the inheritance of today's academics in New York. Only academics in New York among Americans have this rich and complex—genuinely metropolitan—legacy available to them.

Seth Low's role in the development of Columbia University has not been as well remembered as it deserves to be. The reasons for this relative invisibility are various, but two stand out. First, there was the jealousy of his successor. Nicholas Murray Butler, except for an acknowledgment of his predecessor in his inaugural address and first annual report, generally declined to mention the man who preceded him and who had arranged for his succession as president. Second, those historians who have studied Low himself have treated him as a political figure, presenting his Columbia presidency as an interlude between his terms as mayor of Brooklyn and his election as mayor of Greater New York and president of the National Civic Federation. But such an approach, while it fairly represents Low's intense political interests, is basically a distortion. Whether as president of Columbia or in political life, Low was acting out a life of civic responsibility. He did not distinguish so sharply as historians since between the roles. He moved comfortably between the academy and the city in the tradition of civic improvement that runs from William Livingston to De Witt Clinton and to Samuel B. Ruggles.

It was well understood at the time that in selecting Low to succeed F. A. P. Barnard the Columbia trustees were making a statement. They wanted Columbia to become more visible in the city's life.[43] Low welcomed the challenge, announcing in his first annual report that Columbia "ought to have no less an aim than to give a distinctly intellectual tone to life in the great city." It was what the institution owed "New York and the country."[44]

Low, like his near-contemporary, Charles W. Eliot of Harvard, made the position of university president into a public office. Carrying his own civic standing into the academy, he made the president a spokesman for civic life. No one else of his generation, according to George McAneny, a notable civic leader and onetime Manhattan borough president, has "been so closely in touch with the growth and development of the city," nor has anyone else's "thought . . . been so closely interwoven with what might be called the city's own thought about itself."[45]

Low had worried that he would be of "small service" to Columbia on the "academic side," but in fact he deserved full credit for transforming Columbia into a university. "Your twelve years at the helm," Burgess wrote in 1912, upon his own retirement, "was the great turning point in Columbia's history. . . . You made it a university and gave it organic wholeness."[46]

Two themes stand out in Low's presidency, one inspirational and promotional, the other organizational. He called upon Columbia to "show herself worthy" of the city's "pride" and generosity. At the same time, he reorganized the university internally so that it "operated as a whole instead of as so many parts," solving in the process the complicated and distinctively American tension between undergraduate and graduate education, organizing the several faculties, establishing a role for the faculty in university governance, and bringing the Law and Medical schools, heretofore only nominally associated, fully into the university.[47] Within three years of assuming the presidency, he had "created a new Columbia," making it, in Burgess's words, "a genuine university."[48]

It was Seth Low who moved Columbia to Morningside Heights, and with this act he transformed Columbia's relationship to the city. If Columbia had not been in the habit of going to the public for funds in the nineteenth century, relying rather upon the income from its city lands, it began under Low to receive, and to require, large private contributions. But even Low could not have raised the necessary money for the new campus and the expansion of university work without a key change in New York law relating to bequests and charitable trusts. In comparison with New Jersey, Massachusetts, and Connecticut, the laws of New York did not give much protection to the intentions of donors and, in addition, they limited the size of endowments and the proportion of estates that could be designated for charitable purposes. All of this became a public issue in the early 1890s, when the heirs of Samuel Tilden successfully challenged his bequest of five million dollars to establish a public library in New York City.* In 1893, the New York laws were changed. If too late for the Tilden trust, the change made possible the consolidation and expansion of several metropolitan cultural institutions, including Columbia. Had the law not been changed, it is possible that Columbia would not have been able—in spite of the city's wealth—to compete with Princeton, Harvard, and Yale, all of which were substantial recipients of New York philanthropy. Columbia would not have had the resources to assume, as it did, a leading role in scholarship and in the training of a national elite.[49] The economic foundations for a metropolitan university had been laid; the way for Butler's prodigious fund raising and expansion had been paved. But Low's vision was not that of the university Butler later made.

It is worth the effort to pay close attention to Low's life and work, for we will see in that way how he situated Columbia within the city: different from what Godkin hoped for and from what Butler made. Seth Low was born in Brooklyn in 1850, growing up in a mansion at 3 Pierrepont Street, from which he could see his father's clipper ships docked before the A. A. Low Company building, which still stands near South Street. Descended from New England Puritan stock, he was always intensely aware of that heritage. He was a man who, in the words of Lincoln Steffens, "always gave more than he took."[50]

After graduating from Columbia in 1870 and touring Europe, he entered his father's business, becoming a partner in 1875. After 1879, he reduced his involvement in the business; in 1887, he liquidated it, realizing by some reports as much as ten million dollars. Like his father, he had involved himself early on in the civic life of Brooklyn, then the third-largest city in the United States, in Civil Service Reform, and in Columbia affairs, becoming a trustee in 1881, one day before he was elected mayor of Brooklyn. Reelected in 1883, for four years he fought corruption, expanded social services, raised the property taxes of the wealthy, integrated the public school system, and established the "rule of common sense" regarding the Sunday closing of saloons in immigrant neighborhoods.[51]

During these years he also wrote on urban affairs, authoring a fine and

* Because of the generosity of one heir in particular, the library trust received in the end two million dollars. It was not enough for the great library envisioned, and for this reason a merger with the Astor Library and the Lenox Library was negotiated.

still useful chapter on municipal government in James Bryce's *The American Commonwealth* (1888). While most of Bryce's American circle, especially Godkin, believed that democracy and immigrants constituted the problem, Low strongly defended both, looking instead to structural problems in the machinery of government. He also pointed out the magnitude of the task at hand. Democracy, he maintained, was a part of the solution, not the problem. He never abandoned his faith in the democratic political process or in the immigrants.[52]

His term as mayor of Greater New York, 1901–4, continued and expanded upon these themes. He sought to modernize the city, making it better able to serve all classes of people. He strengthened the machinery of government, and he allocated more resources to education and housing, recognizing that the Tammany machine could be replaced only by the expansion of municipal services. A founder of University Settlement, he maintained close ties to the social workers on the Lower East Side. More important, he reached out to immigrants themselves, appointing, in the judgment of historian Martin Schiesl, "large numbers of Italians, Jews, and Negroes" to administrative posts. Lincoln Steffens, no mean judge of municipal administrations, wrote that Low in his one term as mayor had demonstrated in "New York what a city might be under our economic system."[53]

After leaving the mayoralty, Low devoted himself to the question of labor and capital, developing an approach to modern industrial conditions as president of the National Civic Federation similar to the "New Nationalism" identified with his friend Theodore Roosevelt. He insisted upon the rights of organized labor, a position that made him a close friend and collaborator of AF of L leader Samuel Gompers but an enemy of conservative businessmen and socialists. He also concerned himself with the fate of immigrants, opposing immigration restriction, and he increasingly directed his attention to the problem of race relations, becoming in 1907 chairman of the board of trustees of Tuskegee Institute.

The civic and democratic themes that marked his life in politics are evident in his particular vision for Columbia. It was his aim, as he indicated in his inaugural, that "the city may be made to a considerable extent, a part of the university."[54] And the university was to be part of the city, but on democratic terms. He approached the city with a willingness to enter into dialogue, even debate, with the various groups and interests in the city. Declining to claim the privilege of authoritative knowledge, he was willing to engage the city—which is different from providing it with expertise.

Recalling Tappan's dreams of the 1850s for a metropolitan university at the center of the city's learned institutions, Low supported the alliance of the city's scientific societies, and he forged formal links between Columbia and the Union Theological Seminary, the Jewish Theological Seminary, Cooper Union, the Metropolitan Museum of Art, the American Museum of Natural History, and the Bronx Botanical Garden. At all of these places, as well as at Morningside Heights, he initiated public lectures dealing with both academic and public issues. Wanting as well to bring the university into closer relations with the city's contemporary literary and artistic life, he recruited, without worrying about German Ph.D.s, Brander Matthews, the drama critic, and Edward MacDowell, the composer, for the Columbia faculty.

Not only the unique cultural life of New York but its social life as well called for academic initiative and innovation. Out of his own pocket, Low created the nation's first chair in sociology at Columbia, "to take advantage, so far as possible, of the special opportunities for sociological study incident to our location in the City of New York."[55] Such a scholarly project may not be, of course, entirely benign. It could result in labeling social groups as "problems," thus denying the worth of working-class and immigrant self-perceptions and, by implication, politics. Such a criticism is to the point in this instance and in respect to the emergence of the social sciences generally. But in Low's case there is more to be said. He always welcomed both dialogue and politics. He had already indicated, in an article, "The University and the Workingman," that he "should be glad to have it known by the workingmen of America that at Columbia College . . . the disposition exists to teach the truth . . . without fear or favor, and *we ask their aid to enable us to see the truth as it appears to them.*"[56]

Low sought to extend the influence of Columbia's university-level work by opening graduate courses to those "persons residing in the city who might wish to attend regular lectures of the university and who might be competent to profit by them." In a memorandum to the deans he pointed out that they must "understand that the public includes both men and women."[57] Dean Burgess of the Faculty of Political Science worried that opening courses to the public might compromise their "scientific" character, and he absolutely resisted making courses available to women. They would "distract" male students, while the women's own "physical affirmities" rendered them incapable of the "evenness of scholarship and constancy of attendance" required for serious work. But it was another argument, as Burgess proudly tells it in his autobiography, that "took like wildfire" among his colleagues and caused Low to be "beaten badly." "Coeducation," Burgess explained, would drive away boys. It would tend "to make the college a female seminary, and a Hebrew female seminary, in the character of the student body, at that."[58] Low never forgave Burgess. Neither did he give up, and by 1904, 14 percent of the candidates for higher degrees in the Faculty of Political Science were women.[59]

At Low's Columbia the ideal of the German university was fused with the tradition of civic learning and responsibility. In a notable address of 1895, "A City University," he expressed, as clearly as he ever did in one place, his conception. The highest ideal for Columbia—or any American university—must be the model of the German university where the "profoundest scholars [pursue] research in all directions of study." But simple imitation would be a mistake; the task he set for Columbia in New York City was to "realize" this model "under the conditions natural to American life." Without the power and resources of the state and without control over access to the professions and the civil service, the American university, unlike its German forebear, must win a place for itself in "the midst of a democratic community." It must demonstrate that advanced studies by "the few is, without doubt, of the utmost service to the multitude." In accomplishing this an urban university must and will "absorb that which is characteristic in the life of the city in which it does its work." Not above the city, but a part of it was Low's aim. "When I dream of Columbia and its possibilities, I always think of a university not only great enough to influence the life of New York, but a university able to influence the life of New York because it is itself a part of it."[60]

History was not kind to Low's magnificent dream. Columbia in the twentieth century would be in the city, but not of it. The terms of Columbia's relationship would be that of authoritative, expert service, rather than democratic dialogue, and it would resist a student body representative of the city's population. While it is true that Columbia remained ready, even eager, to serve New York, Nicholas Murray Butler phrased this promise very differently. Instead of Low's language of collaboration, we have Butler's offer of "guidance," of "leadership," of "expert knowledge."[61] The different language with which they referred to the Morningside Heights campus makes the same point. Low used the image of a city upon a hill, the same Puritan metaphor he had earlier used to describe his experiment in governing Brooklyn. In good Puritan fashion, it suggested the exemplary and observed behavior of men trying to live good lives in the midst of ordinary experience. Butler, by contrast, immediately seized upon the image of an "acropolis," with its suggestion of a "protected" sacred district under the control of a priestly class.[62]

If Low came to the university from civic life and politics, Butler approached the city with the far more limited status and experience that Columbia gave him, that of an educator, or educational expert. The give-and-take of ordinary civic life and politics had far less appeal to him than did the authority of expertise.[63]

Butler, who was born into a middle-class family in Paterson, New Jersey, and graduated from Columbia in 1882, was only a dozen years younger than Low. Yet his New York was profoundly different, a new era in the city's history. Low was one of the last representatives of mercantile New York. The type of economic and cultural leadership he stood for found its appropriate image in the harbor, and Low's decision to liquidate the family business in 1887, closing the era of clipper ships, symbolizes a turning point in the city's history. Butler's New York was the center of finance capital, the city of skyscrapers (by 1908 there were 550 buildings over ten stories downtown). His city was an administrative hub, relying upon a wide range of professionals in the public and private sectors to manage a national industrial economy. Such a society was unimaginable without the university, which insists, in Butler's words, "that its methods and ideals" penetrate all aspects of life. It would be, Butler thought, by "constantly creating new professions" that the university would extend its influence.[64]

Butler, unlike Low, was trained as a scholar, having earned a Ph.D. at Columbia in 1884. He completely identified his life with the academy, spending sixty-seven years at Columbia as student, professor, and president. Yet he was not a man of academic distinction; his dissertation in philosophy, in fact, was never made public. While William James and John Dewey were revolutionizing philosophy, Butler, as Randolph Bourne put it, continued to preach the "absolute idealism" of the Good, the True, and the Beautiful.[65]

During the first decade or two of the twentieth century, the university, which only a few years earlier had seemed so promising a home for intellect, lost much of its appeal. As we have already noted, young men who a generation before might have become professors became the Young Intellectuals in Greenwich Village. The academy in general, not simply Columbia, was in crisis.[66] But nowhere else was the crisis more deeply felt: the quality and number of professors who left Columbia between 1904 and 1918, whether by resignation or by dismissal, is striking.* The problem, according to one of those fired, Joel Spingarn, was a growing sense of "an inner emptiness" at Morningside Heights, while the attractions and possibilities of a literary or artistic career beyond the walls of academe in the city became, for several of Columbia's best, irresistible.[67]

Butler did not acknowledge that any problem existed. Rather, he turned to soothing affirmation, seeking more money, more growth, more influence. This response betrays Butler's banality, but there is more to it. Butler knew—as did his critics—that his prestige in public life, something

---

* The most important: Harry Thurston Peck (literature), Joel Spingarn (literature), George Woodberry (literature), Edward MacDowell (music), James McKeen Cattell (psychology), Charles Beard (politics), James Harvey Robinson (history), Henry Mussey (history), Henry Wadsworth Longfellow Dana (literature).

very important to him, was grounded in the growth and visibility of the university.[68] Unlike Low, he could not afford critical reflection: he would lose everything. Like other modern university presidents, for which he is the archetype, his commitment at Columbia was to growth and development, not to intellect. With Butler the university president and the corporate executive become indistinguishable. It is hardly a surprise (or a compliment to the academy) that Butler was offered railroad presidencies by both J. P. Morgan and E. H. Harriman. The assimilation was, however, broader than the mere matter of technical administration. Like the captains of industry, Butler, the captain of erudition, grasped the strategic opportunity offered by the metropolis to facilitate educational as well as corporate consolidation and to extend national power and influence.

Laurence Veysey, in *The Emergence of the American University*, remarks that for all Butler wrote about higher learning, he "simply was not a figure in the intellectual history of higher education." Indeed, "no other prominent academic executive said less of significance." While Butler "applauded the fact that ideals existed," he was a man of platitudes, not ideas.[69] It is hard for anyone who has read Butler's voluminous and vaporous writings to disagree.

Yet the judgment does not fully do justice to the man. He expressed himself, including his ideas, in a different medium. His special gift was organization, management. By looking closely at his management of Columbia, it is possible to see that he had a clear idea of Columbia's relation to the city, its population, and the class structure. Sooner and more clearly than anyone else Butler understood the way knowledge under modern conditions was transformed into power. He further grasped the essential point that this made the university constitutive of the class system. If the old college had reflected the class structure, Butler early appreciated a central fact of modern society, as pointed out by Daniel Bell, among others: that the university helps create the class structure.[70]

ETHNICITY AND CLASS

Once it is incorporated into the structure of society, a metropolitan university cannot evade the implications of its relations to the various groups who constitute the city.[71] Any pattern of social exclusion qualifies the ideal of cultural democracy. Not to seek and gather in the cultural richness of the metropolis in an affirmative way is to fail to realize the possibilities for intellect inherent in metropolitan life. Whether a university is to be of as well as in a democratic metropolis is to be discovered, at least in part, by examining its admissions policies. Did it open itself to receive the talent offered by the city, or did it try to protect itself from identifiable social groups in the city? Located in the midst of the variety of metropolitan life, the New York institutions of higher learning had the opportunity to associate themselves with this life and transmute it into a cosmopolitan and democratic cultural ideal for the city and the nation. To some extent this happened at City College and at NYU's Washington Square College, but after initial efforts in this direction—undertaken by Seth Low—at Columbia it did not. The rise of Columbia under Butler's leadership was largely at the expense of this metropolitan possibility.

By 1920 Columbia had clearly established itself at the top of a newly defined hierarchy of institutions in the city. Much as urban geographers speak of a rank-ordered distribution of functions among cities in an urban system, so higher learning had (and has) its ranked differentiation of function. What makes this metropolitan process of hierarchical sorting so interesting and important is its relationship to the distinctive class structure and ethnic composition of New York City. To the extent that segments of the population identified by class and ethnicity were channeled to different levels in the local system of higher learning, the promise of cultural democracy in the city was seriously compromised. The reorganization of higher learning in New York promoted by Butler in the first two decades of the twentieth century made the always strained association of democracy and higher learning even more tenuous.

Columbia, whose future and role were so uncertain in the 1870s, had by 1910 situated itself to train a metropolitan and national elite. Next in the metropolitan hierarchy was New York University, striving to be an elite institution with a similar function, but, characteristically, not quite making it, though stumbling into another pattern of distinction. Finally, there was a revitalized and expanding City College that served a broad spectrum of students, increasingly from immigrant backgrounds, who were prepared, mostly, for middle-level professional and business careers. Off to the side, a historical result of the bruising conflict between Protestant educational leaders and the Catholic hierarchy, was Fordham, established by Bishop John J. Hughes in 1841. It served an exclusively Catholic constituency, and it did not much participate in the revolution of higher education that we have been discussing.[72]

In the 1890s Seth Low aimed to have a student body at Columbia that represented, if it did not precisely reflect, the social composition of the city. He even adjusted admissions requirements to make Columbia more accessible to graduates of the city's new public high schools, and he worried about geographical accessibility.[73] Had the move to Morningside Heights, he wondered, "materially affected" the enrollment of students from downtown or Brooklyn neighborhoods?[74] Such worries were relieved in 1904, when the city's first subway, the IRT line running from City Hall along the East Side until Forty-second Street and then west and up Broadway, made Columbia easily accessible to students from downtown. Later, in 1917, the subway link was extended to Brooklyn. But by the 1910s the problem, as understood by Low's successor, Butler, had become inverted. With 40 percent of the public high school graduates in the city Jewish, mostly the children of Eastern European immigrants, he began to worry that Columbia was too accessible.*[75]

The emergence of the ambitious, talented Jewish student reshaped the local matrix of higher learning. Butler played a key role not only at Columbia but in the city at large in bringing about this transformation. For example, he strongly supported the expansion of City College, hoping to divert immigrant students there. In the 1920s, when the threat seemed to be coming from Brooklyn, he urged the creation of a City College campus there, a hope realized with the founding of Brooklyn College in 1932.[76] Columbia, meanwhile, sought to dissociate itself from the city's immigrant population by favoring students from outside of the city who were, not merely incidentally, non-Jewish.[77]

It was under Low in the 1890s that Columbia made the changes, particularly those strengthening the tie between undergraduate and professional training, that made the college the gatekeeper of the professions and, more generally, of the upper middle class, which is, perhaps, a creation of the university. Low did not fully grasp the implications of this new role for Columbia, but Butler did. He instinctively understood, perhaps because of his own life experience, that the university system was a new social force that would regulate both social mobility and professional standards. Different universities, he realized, would feed different levels in the structure of the professions. He wanted Columbia with its potentially decisive metropolitan location to be the premier national academic influence. Other, lesser colleges and universities could facilitate more modest levels of social mobility and more intermediate levels of professional authority. If Columbia, for example, educated Wall Street lawyers and city and state school administrators, NYU and CCNY could supply neighborhood lawyers and public school teachers.[78]

Training a metropolitan and national elite involved more than professional competence; such men must also be "gentlemen," a quality to be acquired through a liberal arts baccalaureate.[79] This meant that undergraduate education at elite schools, not elite professional training, was the point of entry to the upper middle classes.[80] To the degree that Butler successfully associated liberal education with professional advancement, ambitious students, including Jewish students, were drawn to Columbia College, as well as to the professional schools. But with this development,

---

* Catholics would not have been more welcome at Columbia, but, as has just been noted, they were largely isolated in a separate parochial educational system.

background suddenly seemed as important as liberal studies in the making of gentlemen. It was becoming a general problem among elite institutions, but Columbia's location in a city of immigrants made the "problem" of the Jewish student more pressing there. And Butler devised a brilliant administrative solution, one that had the effect of transforming the whole notion of what marked a leading institution of higher education.

As late as 1909, Butler, like all educational leaders up to that time, had believed that no qualified student of serious purpose should be turned away. The more such students a college attracted, it was assumed, the more prestigious it was. But as the numbers of Jewish students increased, Columbia, in concert with other leading private universities, redefined academic prestige. Butler developed the notion of "selective admission," a concept that turned the old basis of prestige on its head. Now the sign of leadership was the number of *qualified* students *turned away*. It was never openly acknowledged at Columbia, as it was at Harvard, that the new admissions policies were designed to limit Jewish enrollment, but within four years of its introduction in 1917, the proportion of Jewish students at Columbia declined from 40 percent to 22 percent.[81]

Columbia now inquired more deeply into the individual's family history on application forms and, along with several other schools, including NYU, turned to the scientifically dubious Army Intelligence Tests that were reborn after the war as the Scholastic Aptitude Tests. Under this new system, Butler explained in 1917, the academically qualified students constituted only "an eligible list." By "an affirmative process of selection" —really exclusion—Columbia would choose those "upon whom it wishes to expend its funds and its energies." Butler realized that such a "policy could not be followed without public damage" were Columbia the only college in the United States. Fortunately, however, academically qualified but rejected students could go elsewhere. He proposed, in other words, to exclude Jewish students from an elite college, but not from all colleges.[82]

The simultaneous homogenization and nationalization of the student body of Columbia College was part of a more general development in which, as E. Digby Baltzell has shown, Eastern elite schools, emphasizing shared values and social experience as well as professional skills, participated in the making of a national elite.[83] The whole phenomenon, Protestant at its core, was at once forward-looking in its commitment to professional standards and reactionary in its fears of immigration as subversive of the values of Anglo-American civilization.

The problem with the children of Eastern European Jews, according to the deans of Columbia College, was that, lacking "social advantages," they were "not particularly pleasant companions" for Columbia's "natural constituency."*[84] They were, moreover, a bit too "enthusiastic" about "accomplishment," and this made their commingling with Columbia's preferred students, those whose college experience was more social, difficult. Still, Columbia was hesitant to exclude Jewish students completely. The solution was reduction of numbers and the creation of a "residential college" for Columbia's most valued students. John Jay Hall, constructed to advance this policy of separating the day students from a wealthier class of residential students, quite fittingly closed off the south campus view of the city. After this fashion Columbia managed to meet its obligation to a limited number of Jewish students from the city without "endangering the solidarity and homogeneity of the group . . . that must meet the tremendous problems of the future."[85] The leadership class being created at Columbia must not, in other words, be contaminated by social contact or intellectual combat with the children of the Lower East Side.

This program of selective admissions was put into place during a short span of years punctuated by World War I, the Red Scare of 1919, and the racist immigration legislation of 1921 and 1924. These external facts were very important in allowing such a thing to happen, just as the recognition of the Holocaust a generation later worked powerfully against these policies and helped open up elite institutions. But there was nothing inevitable about what happened at Columbia; indeed, it was adopted as a conscious strategy designed to enhance the power and prestige of the university.

New York University, at its University Heights campus, tried to use the same mechanism to achieve elite standing. Its Heights campus had from the beginning a strong collegiate and Protestant atmosphere, but after 1913, when an attractive pre-professional program was established, Jewish enrollment soared, reaching 50 percent by 1919. Student leaders petitioned the chancellor, complaining of the "excessive" number of Jews. They threatened to withdraw from the university unless something was done. NYU responded by developing its own selective admissions policy. With fewer Jewish students, it would be possible, in the words of the dean, for "Americanizing influences to work more freely and efficiently." The problem, Chancellor Elmer E. Brown informed Charles W. Eliot, now retired and himself a critic of Harvard's Jewish quota, was that the school was "deluged with applicants for admission who were able to satisfy our scholastic requirements but whose whole cultural background

* Children of more prosperous and assimilated German-Jewish families made "satisfactory companions."

was dismally un-American. They came from the newest and least assimi-lated East-Side immigrant population."

The policy, however, did not last as long at NYU as it did at Columbia. By the late 1920s, NYU, with mortgages on the new campus buildings falling due, needed the tuition income that an increase in Jewish students would bring. New York University could no longer aspire to the role Columbia had won, and by 1929, 54 percent of the students in the college at University Heights were Jewish, after having been reduced to 30 per-cent in 1922.[86] Downtown at Washington Square the story was different and far more edifying. NYU's smaller and less prestigious undergraduate college there never tried to escape the city, never discriminated on the basis of ethnicity. Its extraordinary dean, James B. Munn, welcomed and supported ambitious students from "newer social strata."[87]

Butler's conception of the hierarchy of higher education in the city, which he used his substantial influence to promote in the city at large, helped to redefine the mission of City College, making the new campus the place where many immigrant dreams were fulfilled. City College's new president, John H. Finley, a reform journalist and sometime profes-sor who had studied with Herbert Baxter Adams at Johns Hopkins, had been strongly endorsed for the job by Butler, and the two were in regular communication during the whole selection process. Finley secularized and liberalized the school, abolishing compulsory chapel, in an effort to make the school more attractive to the children of immigrant New York. He used the new campus to enhance the school's visibility and prestige in the city, and with help from Butler he linked City College to the rapidly expanding public school system, taking students from its high schools and sending back graduates as teachers. He embraced the ethnic hetero-geneity of New York, and he developed a great respect for his students, occasionally walking all the way to the Lower East Side to visit them in their tenement neighborhoods. He tried to make City College a place where "rich and poor shall strive and study together" and where "new and old Americans shall come to know the worth that is in the other."[88] What Finley managed to do was to bring the intellectual vitality and social ambition of the Jewish Lower East Side under the watchful and nourish-ing care of City College, transforming the lives of thousands while laying the foundations that made CCNY one of the nation's most exciting col-leges in the 1920s and 1930s.[89]

Developments at NYU and CCNY had the effect, as Butler saw it in the early 1930s, of freeing Columbia from responsibility for other than a narrow spectrum of potential students in the city. Complaining that Co-lumbia's "metropolitan condition" was a "nuisance," Butler assured his deans and admissions officers that they should not hesitate to exclude students of "the undesireable type," regardless of "their record in the very unimportant matter of A's and B's." Since such students had "New York University and the College of the City of New York as an alternative, we should not be depriving young men of an opportunity for a college education."[90] With this pluralistic image of the higher learning in the metropolis, Butler is at his most disingenuous. The options Butler offered to immigrant students were, by his own understanding of higher education and society, inferior to the one he so self-righteously closed off to them. NYU and CCNY offered far less access to power and prestige. Once the university was integrated into the social system and once a hierarchy of universities was established, admissions policies became central to any notion of a democratic society and culture. What is finally most disturbing about all of this is that Columbia's bigoted irresponsibility was a significant factor in Butler's successful effort to consolidate Columbia's position as a national elite institution.

Columbia in the 1920s had developed beyond the most extravagant hopes of Samuel B. Ruggles. It had, as he envisioned it someday would, become a part of the social order. Yet its admissions policy, with all its implications for justice and democracy, certainly qualified Ruggles's dream of a great metropolitan university. Seth Low, who shared and expanded that dream, died in 1916, so he did not live to see the advent of selective admissions. Yet he had seen it coming, and he had warned Butler and the trustees against cutting themselves off from the city as a whole.

When Butler proposed to invite the General Convention of the Protestant Episcopal Church to use the Columbia Chapel and Earl Hall for three weeks in the spring of 1911, Low, who had been increasingly uncomfortable with his successor's policies, asked rather pointedly whether Columbia's facilities would be equally available to Jewish groups. Butler's response, reflecting the attitudes of the trustees as well, was negative. Low, who resolved to resign over the issue, reminded Butler—in words reminiscent of Ruggles—that the university had a public responsibility to a city that included a million Jews within its population. A metropolitan university, he explained, must avoid any policy "that may compel us to discriminate . . . between large bodies of our fellow-citizens."[91]

If the university is to be a "Christian foundation," Low insisted, then let it say so and have the honor to refuse "gifts from people whom it proposes to discriminate against." But such withdrawal, even if honest, offended Low's deepest civic beliefs. Restating the argument of William Livingston in the eighteenth century, at the time of Columbia's founding, Low defended the ideal of a metropolitan university. "From the beginning of its history, New York has been cosmopolitan in character, and any university that hopes to command the sympathy and support of the city, as a whole, must be equally cosmopolitan. That, in my judgment, is Columbia's true role."[92]

Failing to win over Butler or the trustees, Low asked that his name be stricken from the mailing list. He never again attended a meeting of the trustees, and he quietly resigned in 1914.[93] Always the gentleman, Low declined to disagree in public. Few then or since have realized the depths of his opposition to his successor. Had he followed the example of Ruggles, both Columbia and the city might have benefited. Had he more publicly articulated the cosmopolitan and metropolitan vision that he shared with Livingston and Ruggles, Columbia's consolidation as a great university might not have been so substantially built upon a denial of the city of immigrants that surrounded it.

CHAPTER 8

Professors as Intellectuals

Morris R. Cohen was the first New York academic intellectual to have grown up on the Lower East Side. It is striking that Cohen—born in the Russian city of Minsk in 1880, brought to New York City by his parents at the age of twelve, drawn into and under the wing of German-Jewish philanthropic uplift, and graduated from CCNY in 1900—should in his view of the city's intellectual culture so closely resemble that wealthy descendant of the Puritans, Seth Low. If Low sought to welcome the talent of the burgeoning Lower East Side to Columbia, Cohen, by precept, by example, and by practice as a teacher at CCNY, became a pivotal figure in the accommodation of Eastern European Jewry to the city's intellectual culture, helping to establish in the process the cosmopolitan ideal later associated with those writers and academics connected to the *Partisan Review* in the 1940s.[1] It is this accomplishment, the product of a particular moment in the city's history—not his philosophical or political ideas, which have not worn well and are not seriously studied any longer —that compels us to attend to Cohen.

It was in a class at the Educational Alliance that Cohen was "discovered" by a teacher, Thomas Davidson, a friend of William James and Felix Adler, who encouraged the young man's ambition. At the settlement house at East Broadway and Jefferson Street, founded by wealthy German Jews in 1891 with the intention of raising their Eastern European religious brethren to respectability, and at the home of Davidson at Stuyvesant Square, near the apartment where Howells had written *A Hazard of New Fortunes* only a few years before, Cohen learned his lessons well, well enough for Adler to arrange for the Ethical Culture Society to finance his graduate training at Harvard. After completing a Ph.D. in philosophy in 1906, Cohen returned to CCNY as an instructor in mathematics. It would be five years before Harry Overstreet, the new chairman of the Philosophy Department, was able to persuade his colleagues and the administration to permit a Jew to profess philosophy at the college. Philosophy, like English literature, was at most academic institutions, even in New York, the exclusive domain of Anglo-Saxons well into the 1930s. Cohen's success—as an academic philosopher and as a public moralist, mostly in the pages of *The New Republic*—helped to break down this academic provincialism. If his proposed appointment to the Columbia faculty was blocked in the 1920s on account of his Jewishness, several of his Jewish students at CCNY would become distinguished professors at Columbia and elsewhere.[2]

Having rather quickly won for himself a considerable reputation as a spokesman for intellectual values and liberalism, Cohen contributed an article, "Intellectual Leadership in America," to the second issue of *The New Republic* in 1914. With unconcealed enthusiasm he explained that the clergy and the legal profession had deservedly lost their claims to intellectual leadership. His appreciation for—and identification with— the "growing influence of the university professor" was equally clear. Yet he worried that, given the American university's lack of respect for the intellectual independence of professors, who were treated as "hired help" in a "factory," there was not much room left for teaching to "develop into a truly liberal profession." Just at this point, however, when one might expect him to demand the conditions necessary for professional hegemony, he backed off. Much after the fashion of Seth Low twenty years before, he suggested instead many complementary sources of intellectual leadership, all characteristic of metropolitan civic life: journalists, experts (whom he distinguished from professors), and even businessmen.[3]

The article illuminates the fluidity of the intellectual culture of the city at the beginning of the European war. Many lines of definition and division that would soon be taken for granted were not yet drawn for Cohen, as they had not been for Low. If the shock of war divided literary culture, so it shattered the tense calm of academic culture, submerging Low's essentially eighteenth-century civic ideals in the process. Out of the crucible of war two models of intellect crystallized within the city and the academy. Although this development was national in scale, it was most dramatic and intense at Columbia University in the city of New York. Only in New York were both of the developing intellectual roles fully realizable. Because New York was both a center of national administration and national opinion, academics in the course of the decade following the war found themselves with an increasingly sharply defined choice between associating themselves with administrative power as experts or embracing the literary culture of the city as intellectuals. These choices had begun to define themselves in the city as early as the 1880s, particularly in the division of intellect during the Henry George mayoral campaign of 1886 and during the academic freedom battles of the 1890s, but it was the war and its aftermath that in New York defined the range and choices of the academic intellect.[4]

WAR ON CAMPUS

At a general assembly of the faculty and students of Columbia University in February 1917, when the drift toward American entry into the war was taking on a quality of inevitability, Professor John Erskine of the English Department, a man consigned to the genteel tradition by Bourne, called upon his colleagues to make Morningside Heights "a shelter for rational ideas." The university had the opportunity to "illustrate within its own intimate community that intelligent understanding of the other man's hopes and needs without which no peace will ever be in the world." The special obligation of the university, he pleaded, is to "do something to keep the mind of the nation open, even in circumstances that tend most to close it."

Such was not, however, Nicholas Murray Butler's vision of university service in time of war. After the meeting he wired President Wilson, pledging Columbia "to the service of the nation whenever the call shall come."[5] Three weeks later, still before any declaration of war, Butler distributed a remarkable document, *The Organization of Columbia University for National Service,* outlining the "mobilization of Columbia University." It replaced the existing structure of schools, divisions, and departments with military corps. The president's office became the Staff Corps, while the various faculties were reorganized as the Medical Corps, the Legal Corps, the Technical Corps, the Economic and Social Service Corps, the Home Instruction and Organization Corps, the Language Corps, and the Military Training Corps. Within the Economic and Social Service Corps, Charles A. Beard was designated to head the Civics Division.[6] It was a supremely ironic designation. Beard, as we shall see, would indeed give Columbia a lesson in civics, but certainly not the one Butler intended or wanted.

If in some respects the service role of the university was enhanced and consolidated, the war also brought to a head long-simmering opposition to Butler's definition of the university and his manner of administration. If before the war it had seemed difficult, for some at least, to specify the distinction between the professor as intellectual and the professor as expert, the war clarified the difference. The intrusion of war into affairs at Columbia tended to impress upon the academics the necessity of a choice; either they must assert themselves as free intellectuals or they must become servants of power. Neither a middle ground nor ambiguity fared well in the crisis of war. The postwar resolution of these issues was not absolutely clear, but certainly the general thrust of events at Columbia was to favor institutional loyalty and service to established power over independent and critical intellect.

There had been a certain uneasiness and restiveness among the faculty at Columbia ever since Butler had replaced Low. The large number of resignations and dismissals already noted were but the most visible sign of this tension. In the immediate prewar years, however, Columbia's troubles found focus in one man, James McKeen Cattell. One of Columbia's most distinguished social scientists, Cattell was also a difficult and fiercely independent man. He joined the Columbia faculty in 1891, as professor of experimental psychology. A year later he helped found the American Psychological Association, whose president he became in 1895. He edited and published the important journal *Science,* and he was the founding editor of the *Psychological Review.* At Columbia he was an effective teacher, directing more than fifty doctoral dissertations. The first psychologist elected to the National Academy of Science, he was, historian Dorothy Ross notes, "second only to William James in the esteem of his colleagues."[7] A final but important point: although Cattell was a committed academic, he refused to be dependent on the academy. He was not afraid of pursuing the life of the mind outside of the academy.[8]

Although Cattell had flourished under Low's leadership, later, under Butler, as he told a friend, he had "not been comfortable." With the publication of *University Control* in 1913, he made public his opposition to the "autocratic system" of university administration.[9] Neither as acerbic nor as brilliant as Thorstein Veblen's "memorandum on the conduct of universities by businessmen," Cattell's book was, nonetheless, intelligent and telling in its criticism. His favored image of the university was that of a free association of intellect, "unhierarchical, democratic, anarchic, in its organization." Linking the rise of universities in America with the rise of the trusts, he identified both the "trust promoter" and the university president as "utterly subversive of a true democracy." The modern university president was "not a leader, but a boss." The problem was one of governance; the university was not keeping up with the progress of democracy. "No one," he pointed out, "believes that a city should be owned by a small self-perpetuating board of trustees who would appoint a dictator to run it, to decide what people could live there, what work they must do and what incomes they should have. Why should a university be conducted in that way?" He proposed that university governance be radically revised. The governing body ought to be made up in equal parts of the faculty, alumni, and the members of the community, while deans and the president should be elected by the faculty. Only then, he thought, would the university itself be democratic and thus able to serve "the larger democracy of which it is a part." [10]

Butler did not take well to these suggestions; in fact, he proposed that the trustees "retire" Cattell, who was then fifty-three years old and the father of seven children. A number of faculty leaders, however, came to Cattell's defense, including John Dewey and Franz Boas, and Butler abandoned this attempt. But there was another conflict in January 1917, and then a final one in August 1917. In late August, Cattell wrote to several congressmen—on stationery that identified him as a Columbia professor—asking them to "support a measure against sending conscripts to Europe against their will." [11] When Butler learned of this, he invoked his June 6, 1917, general warning to the faculty: with the declaration of war, he had announced, the period of debate had ended. "What had been tolerated before became intolerable now. . . . What had been folly was now treason." Anyone who failed to adhere to these principles, he warned, would be summarily dismissed. And now Butler proposed to fire Cattell, as well as Henry Wadsworth Longfellow Dana, a young professor of English, likewise for his alleged anti-war activities. [12]

At this point, by now early October and after the fall term had begun, Charles A. Beard offered his civics lesson. It was a dramatic one. He announced to his classes that the day's lecture would be his last. His resignation, effective immediately, had been submitted to President Butler. Beard's announcement surprised and shocked students and faculty, but it was not a sudden decision. He had been disturbed by affairs at Columbia for some time. But the firing of Cattell and Dana moved Beard, who in fact strongly supported the war, finally to a public act. [13] If Butler defended the firings in terms of the obligation of professors to consider the "reputation" of the university in their "public conduct," Beard responded to higher values. [14] He stood absolutely for the principle of free speech and the free intellectual.

The New York Times, in an editorial on Beard's resignation, declared that "Columbia University was better" for it, but the resignation was, as John Dewey immediately realized, an enormous, irreplaceable loss for Columbia and for academic life. [15] Dewey, who had been a member of a faculty committee that had tried, in his words, to "smooth over" the real problems at Columbia in 1917, now realized that the faculty should have acted more strongly to defend the integrity of intellect. If they had, he wrote to another member of the committee, "Beard would be our colleague today," for they had left him "in a position where he felt isolated, and without the support of his colleagues." [16] Dewey did not follow

Beard's example—he did not resign his professorship, nor does he seem to have been tempted to do so. But he did withdraw substantially from the affairs of the university; increasingly he made the city rather than the university the habitat of his mind and work.[17]

Beard's resignation—as a simple fact—rocked the literary and academic worlds. But we must attend to the words that surrounded the act. Beard's letter of resignation was a reasoned and stinging criticism of the academic intellect of his time. He pointed out that his own early and consistent support of the war was a matter of public record. But, and this was the nub of it all, the opinion of an intellectual, he explained, can be trusted by the public only if its "disinterestedness is above all suspicion," if its "independence is beyond all doubt." The public must have reason to believe in the intellectual's "devotion to the whole country, as distinguished from any single class or group." At the present time, with the university apparently under the control of a small group of "reactionary and visionless" trustees, the public cannot have that faith in a Columbia professor. "I am convinced that while I remain in the pay of the Trustees of Columbia University I cannot do effectively my humble part in sustaining public opinion."[18]

Responding to Beard—though not naming him—in his annual report, Butler made explicit Beard's distinction between the obligations of a Columbia professor and those of an intellectual. Butler, not surprisingly, inverted Beard's valuation of their respective duties. Since professors benefit from the prestige of the university, Butler argued, they have "a distinct, constant, and compelling obligation" to protect that prestige. One cannot, he insisted, be loyal to "humanity" rather than to the institution. Such expressions reveal "muddled thinking," what one has come to expect from "those who, for lack of a more accurate term, call themselves intellectuals." These intellectuals, he reported to the Columbia trustees, "know so many things which are not so that they make ignorance appear to be not only interesting but positively important." Yet it was true, he ruefully acknowledged, that they "abound just now" in the city's lesser literary circles and that even in the academy they "are not without representation." But he pledged himself and the university to stand firmly against the "rule of the literary and academic Bolsheviki."[19]

Farther from the actual events at Columbia, from the distance of Newport, Rhode Island, John W. Burgess, now in retirement, observed it all. He knew something had gone wrong, his understanding perhaps prompted by his pro-German sympathies. He would not say so publicly, but privately he worried that his grand hope for Columbia's Faculty of Political Science was being destroyed. With Columbia fallen to such a "sad state," how could it serve as the foundation of "reason" in public life? "Freedom of thought and speech," he urgently wrote his former student E. R. A. Seligman—the economist who headed the faculty committee that had failed to protect Cattell and Dana—"is the life of a university." A year later, when James Harvey Robinson, too, resigned to join Beard in founding the New School for Social Research, Burgess was "grieved." It saddened him that Beard, Robinson, and "the younger men" would abandon the Faculty of Political Science "in order to construct a rival to it." Yet Burgess, whose political and intellectual outlook was so different from those now fleeing Columbia, could understand that their effort was in fact a rekindling of his own original dream. And he did not begrudge them their attempt. "I can understand their point of view," he confided to Seligman.[20]

The effort to establish the New School for Social Research, originally to be called the Free School of Political Science, after the same French model that had inspired Burgess, arose directly from the perceived constraints on intellect inherent in the service ideal's alliance of the university with the dominant classes.[21] Although this particular effort was sparked by problems at Columbia, it is important to understand that it was only the most ambitious of several contemporary efforts to free the social sciences from this alliance or to forge a new alliance with the subordinated classes.

The Rand School of Social Science, founded in 1906, for example, was inspired by Beard's earlier work as co-organizer of Ruskin Hall (later College) for workers, which he had done while a student at Oxford in 1899–1901. Funded initially by Carrie Rand Herron, the Rand School later received increased support from socialist trade unions. By 1918, recently moved to its new quarters at 7 East Fifteenth Street, it provided a social science curriculum for 1,500 students, nearly all of whom were socialist workers. Beard, who was already a member of the three-person advisory board, began lecturing there in 1918.[22] A few years later, in 1921, Brookwood Labor College opened in Katonah, New York, forty-two miles north of Grand Central Terminal. Under the inspiring leadership of A. J. Muste and others, this two-year residential college devoted itself to teaching and research on behalf of peace and social justice for labor. Workers selected by labor unions received training in the social sciences as preparation for working-class leadership.[23] Brookwood, the Rand School, and the New School for Social Research were all involved in different ways, moreover, with the Workers Education Bureau of America, which Charles and Mary Beard helped to found in 1921.[24] It was, indeed, a moment of unusual ferment in the city.

The prime mover behind the New School experiment was James

Harvey Robinson, characterized by economist Wesley Clair Mitchell "as a man of ideas, which is not orthodox in an historian."[25] Robinson, an enormously popular teacher of both graduate and undergraduate students, was absolutely committed to independence of thought.[26] He quit Columbia both in protest and in sympathy for his friend and sometime co-author Beard. Beard and Robinson were soon joined by two other Columbia colleagues, both distinguished: Dewey, who did not resign, and Mitchell, who did. Herbert Croly of *The New Republic,* who brought with him economist Alvin Johnson, one of his editors, joined the Columbians. That the early meetings were mostly held at the offices of *The New Republic* and that the school was organized in a group of three townhouses near the magazine's own house in Chelsea makes an important point about this moment of crisis and ferment in New York: academic and literary cultures were interacting and sustaining each other. Infusing the whole effort was the assumpion that New York, which was not only the "greatest social science laboratory in the world" but which "of its own force attracts scholars," was a place that could become "the center of the best thought in America."[27]

There was considerable agreement on what the founders did not want, less on what they did want. Probably, however, they all agreed with Robinson that it was to be an "independent school of social science," with neither trustees, presidents, nor degrees. The students would be adults who did not need to be persuaded to learn, who would attend in order to learn, not to earn degrees.[28] The overall design, as Croly put it, was to free social knowledge from the constraints of "individual, national, and class particularism," and it would avoid the limitations of "excessive specialization."[29]

Within this broad area of consensus, there was room for considerable disagreement. Robinson envisioned an intellectual center, a sort of club where social ideas were discussed by men and women of intellectual distinction. Beard tended more toward the idea of a research institution, but he was also attracted to the notion of a place for free and conversational intellect to find itself in the city. Mitchell looked toward it as a research institution committed to the free pursuit of objective fact, while Croly advocated what we would today call applied social research, with a particular emphasis on the training of experts in labor relations.[30]

Even with these unresolved differences, the opening of the school in 1919 was an intellectual event in the city. The faculty was brilliant: Robinson, Beard, Dewey, and Mitchell were joined in the first year by Elsie Clews Parsons, Thorstein Veblen, Emily James Putnam, Graham Wallas, and Harold Laski—a roster of distinguished scholars unmatched by any university in the country. They offered competition enough from the start to prompt President Butler to condemn the New School as "a little bunch of disgruntled liberals setting up a tiny fly-by-night radical counterfeit of education."[31]

Butler's blast—and others from established leaders—made fundraising commensurate with the school's intellectual standing impossible.[32] But the experiment suffered from internal problems as well. A school without an administration could not, as it turned out, avoid internal chaos, and the founders soon parted ways. Croly left first, in the spring of 1921, while Beard and Robinson resigned soon after, at the first signs of incipient bureaucratization. Alvin Johnson, who suddenly found himself in charge, was enormously creative and resourceful in transforming the institution in the 1920s and 1930s and keeping it alive. But the attempt to create an independent school of social science in New York had failed.

Beard, who had gone into the experiment with such enthusiasm, was chastened by the failure. After trying to devise a way for adults freely to associate under academic auspices "in the pursuit of wisdom and knowledge," he concluded that it was a noble but impossible dream. Writing in *The Freeman* in 1921, he asked whether the "modern university" is really the place "where men with an intellectual mission" can "best deliver their message." Has not the printing press, he asked, "made the university obsolete for all except those engaged in cramming candidates for degrees?" For the "true teacher, the restless searcher-out of all things," there is, he decided, "a greater forum than the narrow school room," the printed word.[33] The professor in rebellion against the academy had become a writer, the social scientist had become a critic.

POWER AND INTELLECT

Wesley Clair Mitchell, by contrast, became even more the social scientist, the academic expert. Until the failure of the New School project, Mitchell's and Beard's lives were remarkably parallel. Born in small Midwestern towns in 1874, as adults they both embraced the social and intellectual excitement of New York without ever quite relinquishing a characteristically Midwestern faith in the land.[34] Mitchell, who studied at the University of Chicago, with Veblen and Dewey, joined the Columbia faculty in 1913, after having taught at Berkeley. Beard, who began his graduate studies at Columbia in 1902, after an undergraduate education at DePauw University in Indiana and after two years at Oxford, during which he wrote his first book, *The Industrial Revolution* (1901), joined the Columbia faculty in 1904. In 1913, each published the book that established their respective reputations. *An Economic Interpretation of the Constitution* transformed the study of American history and politics, while Mitchell's

Business Cycles is a landmark in twentieth-century economic thought, a book that ranks—in elegance of conception, grace and precision of expression, and significance to the discipline—with John Maynard Keynes's *General Theory of Employment, Interest and Money* (1936).

Both men assumed that objective social data, collected in an organized and scientific manner, translated rather directly into social betterment. Although Beard later changed his thinking on this point, judging it naïve and proposing a broader and more critical role for intellect in public life, the two men were in agreement when they joined together in the New School experiment. Beard shared Mitchell's faith that by collecting "social facts" and putting that "knowledge at the disposal of responsible officials," essentially without interpretation, social scientists played a "crucially important part toward achieving the gravest task that confronts mankind today—the task of developing a method by which we may make cumulative progress in social organization." [35] Toward this end, each combined with his teaching at Columbia a position with an independent research institution. After 1909, Beard spent as much as three afternoons a week downtown at 261 Broadway at the Bureau of Municipal Research, while Mitchell in the 1920s did most of his work at the National Bureau of Economic Research, on Washington Square, near his West Twelfth Street home.

Mitchell left the New School in 1922, returning to his professorship at Columbia. He went back, according to Lucy Sprague Mitchell, his wife and biographer, because "he came to feel that the graduate students there who expected to become professional economists would have more influence than students at the New School on the development of economics as a science." [36] The move and the logic behind it were revealing of his notion of intellect in society, and it was not a unique view by any means. During the 1920s Mitchell was probably the most distinguished and respected American academic social scientist. He was far too brilliant to be called typical; rather he was the 1920s academic writ large, at his best. In observing Mitchell, we can watch the dominant impulse of the social sciences of his time.

Mitchell was an effective, even outstanding, teacher of graduate students at Columbia, but research was his true passion. The National Bureau of Economic Research, which mixed academic economists with those of the unique New York financial community, provided him with his preferred context for work. During the war he had been exhilarated by the possibilities open to social science, but he had also been disturbed by his wartime experiences: too often he had been asked to make decisions without adequate data. The National Bureau of Economic Research, which he helped to found, was intended to remedy that situation, and he served as its director of research for twenty-five years. Its object, in the phrasing of its charter, was to make "exact and impartial investigations in the field of economic, social, and industrial science, and to this end to cooperate with governments, universities, learned societies, and individuals."[37] Under the auspices of the National Bureau, economists embarked on quantitative studies of price index numbers, national income, capital formation and flows, consumer credit, and economic indicators. Mitchell's faith in objective fact was so great that no study was published until it had been reviewed for impartiality by the bureau's board of directors, which included businessmen as well as academics.

In its special, but very vital, field, the National Bureau of Economic Research was a microcosm of social science research in the 1920s. Social scientists were engaged in public affairs, but it was as advisers and consultants to government and business, rather than as participants in a general political or cultural discourse. The National Bureau of Economic Research was an early and influential example of a scholarly organization that linked individual researchers, universities, and the government, all in the interest of addressing major social problems.[38] They staked their reputations upon the ideal of objectivity, which tended to give priority to quantitative social science.

During the interwar years Mitchell extended this model, stressing interdisciplinary work, and he became a major champion of the coordination of disciplinary specialties around a common problem and research program. This movement for cross-disciplinary cooperation was sponsored by the foundations, new agents in the intellectual life of the city and nation. Fearing that they could not compete with universities for ideas and men on the accepted terms of academic social science research, the foundations asserted themselves by calling for and becoming the principal sponsors of problem-oriented, interdisciplinary research, something difficult for universities, plagued by departmental jealousies. Under the leadership of Beardsley Ruml, who represented the involvement of the Rockefeller philanthropies in social science, Professor Charles Merriam of the University of Chicago, and Mitchell, such work assumed a dominant position in the academic culture of the 1920s and 1930s. This reorientation of social research was accomplished under the auspices of the Social Science Research Council.[39]

The Social Science Research Council, which had been organized somewhat informally in 1922, was incorporated in New York in 1924, with substantial financial support from Ruml, then directing the Laura Spelman Rockefeller Memorial, with its assets of $80 million. The first president of the SSRC was Charles Merriam (1923–26), and its second was Mitchell (1927–30). Founded to enhance the influence and increase the resources available to the social sciences, the SSRC sought to do so by emphasizing the study of "real" social life, which, they argued, demanded overcoming the "excessive departmentalization" of the academic disciplines.[40]

At first the powerful new New York foundations and institutes, with their interdisciplinary capacities, seemed a threat to university hegemony. But the universities, especially Chicago and Columbia, responded rather quickly, establishing their own coordinating and research planning bodies, like the Council for Research in the Social Sciences established at Columbia in 1925. The academic social sciences, thus reformed, were in part a creation of the foundations. But even better, they were the beneficiaries of a new and transforming largess. Between 1921 and 1927, the amount of money expended on research in history and the social sciences by foundations increased from $180,000 to $8 million.[41] What emerged was a novel pattern of cooperation among foundations, institutes, universities, and the government that gave form to social research and policy formation in the 1920s and 1930s. That configuration of partners remains, as Barry Karl has observed, one of "the essential methods of generating American intellectual life."[42]

Their problem-focus and their emphasis on what Ruml called functional knowledge made social scientists better able to offer their expertise to business and government. But academic social scientists, who were typically, as Joseph Schumpeter quaintly described his friend Mitchell, men of "warm and elevated social sympathies," would have been uncomfortable so openly serving power—save for their faith in scientific objectivity. However naïve it may now seem to us, their belief in a value-neutral social science stilled their qualms. "If their findings were morally neutral, objective descriptions of institutional and human functions," historian Edward A. Purcell, Jr., has written, "then they were obviously neither being used nor being partisan."[43] They were happily freed from all the difficult questions about the class affiliation of intellect, and they could without reservation assume a practical role in advancing modern instrumentalities of social control. They reflected little on the implications of their quest for a neutral and comprehensive social knowledge that denied politics and public life as a way of generating social knowledge and policy.[44]

The drive—and to a considerable degree the achievement—of Mitchell's generation of academic experts was to academicize social knowledge.[45] These academic ways of perceiving and interpreting experience were institutionalized in the tight matrix of government, universities, and foundations. This privileged and significantly empowered academics and their ideas.[46] A good deal of the public's political business was in the process withdrawn from the sphere of public discourse.

The paradigmatic example of this reformed social science is the monumental report of the President's Research Committee on Social Trends, a study commissioned by Herbert Hoover, sponsored by the SSRC, funded by the Rockefeller Foundation, and directed by Wesley Clair Mitchell. The task of the committee was to accomplish for the whole of social life what Mitchell's National Bureau of Economic Research had achieved with its report on *Recent Economic Changes in the United States* (1929). Here, however, the breadth of coverage required a more complex approach. It was necessary "to interrelate the disjointed factors and elements in the social life of America, in the attempt to view the situation as a whole." All of this, of course, would be presented scientifically and impartially, and the facts would, it was assumed, translate rather directly into social improvement. Underlying the whole report was an assumed division of labor; facts and social action could be separated. The report presented "knowledge" that would be the "basis for intelligent action" by others, unnamed, but presumably the government.[47] The implicit but unmistakable claim being made by both Hoover and the committee was that social science offered a better guide to an improved society than the observations of citizens or their political representatives.[48]

When *Recent Social Trends* was published in 1933, its 1,500 pages of text, charts, and tables seemed, in the view of Charles A. Beard, to reveal both the problem and the promise of social science in America. Its manifest commitment to value-free and non-political social research in the interest of a neutral state drew his particular attention. Such scholarship and service was not, he had come to believe, the necessary task of intellect in a democracy. If the intellectual culture of the metropolis could sustain the individual writer as publicist as well as the conjuncture of foundation, government, and university, with its social scientific expertise, he took a stand for the ideas of the former against the data of the latter.

The report, Beard observed, reflected "the coming crisis in the empirical method to which American social science has long been in bondage." If it was assumed that the assembly of "data" by social scientists would produce "conclusions," Beard challenged this social scientific and political naïveté with two questions. First, he asked: What was an important fact, one worth collecting? And important to whom, for what purpose? He pressed the point further with his second query: "What do hopes, aspirations, and values come from? From exhaustive surveys of facts?" "Soon," he pronounced in the Olympian manner he sometimes affected, "that issue will have to be faced in the intellectual life of the United States."

If Beard thus questioned the formal assumptions of the report, he saw promise in the actual result. "The excellence of this study, apart from the accumulation of significant social materials, lies in the very fact that its . . . investigators generally depart from the terms of their Presidential commission and proclaim or assume that values do not flow . . . from their 'data' or 'trends.' " To the considerable extent that they discuss "problems," the social scientists violate their professed method. "Problems," he explained, "do not come out of the facts. They are tensions that arise in the human mind when facts are observed. They come from the realm of the human spirit . . . ever evolving in relation to facts. The committee has found problems because it has brought to the consideration of the findings minds charged with ideas, ideals, values, and aspirations." Without acknowledging it—indeed, without realizing it—the report pointed toward a revolution in social science, one Beard would have welcomed: "the subjection of science to ethical and esthetic purpose."[49]

Beard had profoundly altered his views in the decade since resigning from Columbia. Earlier, he had shared Mitchell's assumptions about the power of facts, and he had devoted himself to budgetary and administrative studies under the auspices of the Bureau of Municipal Research from 1909 to 1921, when he resigned. He left the Bureau of Municipal Research because he felt constrained in his work there. This restraint took different forms. He was convinced, as were his colleagues, that Nicholas Murray Butler had persuaded donors, Andrew Carnegie in particular, to withhold funds from the bureau because of Beard's alleged "radicalism." Faced with the choice of bowing to the politics of his sponsors or of resignation, he preferred the latter.[50] He also came to understand, in a rather insightful way, that the institutionalization of research and reform tended intrinsically to limit one's intellectual ken and freedom to act.[51] He feared that social research and reform were being sucked into a rather confined world of technical concerns, all at the expense of vision, imagination, courage, the qualities Bourne had emphasized in his attack on technique.[52]

While scholars like Mitchell flourished in a dense matrix of institutions such as a metropolis could offer, Beard's vision of himself, after resigning from Columbia, the New School, and the Bureau of Municipal Research, was that of a lonely publicist, something also sustained by a metropolitan milieu. Instead of seeking influence through the orchestration of academic, governmental, and philanthropic institutions, instead of seeking a role, after the fashion of Lippmann, as an expert, an insider, Beard's mode of influence would be the book, the article, the public lecture. Wary of any institution that threatened to enclose and capture him, Beard embraced the whole public as his habitat as Emerson's man thinking.[53]

Beard's reservations about *Recent Social Trends* and the mainstream of social science in the 1920s were based on a major philosophic shift in his thinking about social research, the emergence of his so-called historical relativism. Although this reorientation in his thought is often discussed (and dismissed) as a matter of technical philosophy, we can also approach it as a phase in Beard's thinking about the relation of intellect to society, of the intellectual and the public.

From the beginning of his career as a scholar, Beard had been concerned to associate his work with public life and social reform. But in the decade following the war, he reconsidered his strategy, partly, I think, because of the alternatives provided by the rather fully developed literary culture of the city. Earlier, during the period of his involvement with the Bureau of Municipal Research, he thought objective facts had immediate political consequence in political life and public affairs. By the late 1920s, however, he had lost that faith. Social facts, he came to believe, had meaning—political and moral significance—only if interpreted through a prior and necessarily subjective frame of reference. Accordingly, a commitment to values (as Bourne had insisted during the war) was essential to scholarship and to the public role of the man of ideas. The intellectual must choose values, must give expression to them in his work, even while knowing and acknowledging that there was no certain justification for them.[54] Such commitments made the scholar *ipso facto* a man of affairs. He became, as Beard once put it, "a statesman, without portfolio to be sure, but with a kindred sense of responsibility" to the public. All of this returned the intellectual to the swirl of politics and public culture, and it made the life of the mind a moral and public act.[55]

No longer interested in influencing history through administrative intervention as an expert, Beard, now more the historian than the social scientist, increasingly sought to gain influence by providing interpretive contexts, by providing compelling myths about how the society works. Such was the task of the intellectual; such was his opportunity in New York in the midst of the national center of communications.[56]

Beard, whose books sold more than eleven million copies, eschewed the influence of the expert for the opportunity to address the educated public directly and without encumbrance. Always generous in his acknowledgment of his dependence upon the research of ordinary academic scholarship, he asked more of himself and of those who would be intellectuals. The responsibility of intellect in a democratic society was to enrich politics and culture by proposing in public powerful ideas that invited, even demanded, response. "The older I grow," he reflected in a letter to Abraham Flexner, who had asked Beard's advice as he planned the Institute for Advanced Study in Princeton, "the more I feel the urgency of more thinking at the top, more bold, free, imaginative, integrating thinking."[57]

DEMOCRACY'S INTELLECT

If New York ever had an academic who was a genuinely independent and democratic intellectual, it was John Dewey during the interwar years. Dewey became America's great public philosopher only after coming to New York. It is a point seldom noticed, but it is important. In the American metropolis, the Vermont Yankee became a cosmopolitan intellectual, finding a place for himself that bridged the academic and literary worlds. Using *The New Republic* as his principal platform, he spoke for civic values with compelling honesty.

When John Dewey moved from the University of Chicago to Columbia in 1904, he was forty-five years old. He was an academic of considerable distinction, with a Ph.D. from Johns Hopkins and previous appointments at the universities of Michigan and Minnesota. He had already served as president of the American Psychological Association (1899), and a year after arriving at Columbia he was elected president of the American Philosophical Association.[58] But he was not yet the Dewey we tend to remember. Except for some of his writing on education, his work was confined to difficult technical issues and was published in academic journals. As late as 1915, it was possible for Randolph Bourne to introduce his former teacher to the readers of *The New Republic* as a major thinker whose work was not generally available to the public. "Where the neatly uniform works of William James are to be found in every public library," Bourne wrote, "you must hunt long and far for the best things of the man who, since the other's death, is the most significant thinker in America."[59] Only a year later, however, one could say that Dewey's career as a public philosopher had been launched. In 1916, he published *Democracy and Education*, the quite accessible and widely read culmination of his thinking on education, and he began contributing regularly to *The New Republic*, writing on a wide range of subjects. After the war, he was paid a weekly stipend by the magazine, with the understanding that he would contribute articles whenever he had something to say.[60]

The ten years Dewey had spent at the University of Chicago had been important for his development as a technical philosopher; it enabled him to establish a distinct school of philosophy that won the notice and praise of William James. The city of Chicago, too, had been important for him. For the young professor reared in Burlington, Vermont, Chicago in general and Hull-House in particular had widened his social experience and perceptions. When he moved to New York, this pattern continued. New colleagues at Columbia, especially Frederick Woodbridge, an Aristotelian of considerable gifts, challenged Dewey and contributed to his maturation as a philosopher. In New York, Dewey replicated his urban involvements, transferring his Hull-House concerns to Greenwich House and taking an interest in many of the same sorts of movements for educational and social reform. But something else happened in New York that had not happened in Chicago. The density of the metropolitan community of literary and political intelllectuals emboldened Dewey and nudged him into becoming a wide-ranging and cosmopolitan intellectual. Max Eastman, a graduate student Dewey early befriended, introduced his distinguished professor to the artistic and cultural life of Greenwich Village, and Charles Beard brought him into the "X" Club, a small but diverse group including journalist Lincoln Steffens, socialist leader Morris Hillquit, editor Norman Hapgood, and others, who met every two weeks from 1903 to 1917 in an Italian restaurant to discuss politics, science, and art.[61]

The milieu of the metropolis and his associations in it did not *cause* Dewey's transformation. That would be putting it too strongly and, perhaps, too crudely. All the relevant impulses were evident earlier, but his experiences and opportunities in New York enormously broadened his intellectual range and cultural sensibilities. The man who wrote *Experience and Nature* (1925) and *Art as Experience* (1934) was not simply a more mature scholar but, as is revealed in the very prose of these works, a more worldly man; he had even taken up smoking and appreciated a drink. By the time of the war, moreover, Dewey, like New York intellectuals before and after him, had discovered the way New York worked as an intellectual center. In the century since New York became the center of magazine editing and publishing, the talk of intellectuals has typically been transmuted into print. Editors have coaxed talk into type. Much of what has been published in the intellectual magazines of New York is talk put to paper, and Dewey in New York learned to put his talk on general social, cultural, and political issues into print for the educated and liberal readers of *The New Republic*. New York in its character as an intellectual center thus enabled Dewey to realize and extend the ambition that even in the 1890s had helped move him from Hegelian idealism to pragmatism. His aim, he had told his students at Michigan in 1891, was to translate "philosophical truth into common terms."[62]

Dewey's program for his discipline went against the developing pattern of academic philosophy, which, as Bruce Kuklick has shown in *The Rise of American Philosophy,* became in the twentieth century a highly technical discipline, quite esoteric and isolated from general social, political, or cultural concerns.[63] Worried always by these larger trends in the field, Dewey insisted in 1917 that philosophy would recover itself "when it ceases to be a device for dealing with the problems of philosophers and becomes a method, cultivated by philosophers, for dealing with the problems of men."[64]

To say this was not, however, to dismiss the study of technical problems in philosophy. What the current project of publishing Dewey's complete writings makes abundantly and impressively clear in the volumes thus far published is the way Dewey in the 1920s tacked back and forth between technical issues pursued in the philosophical journals and public issues. Far more than Beard, Dewey remained deeply involved in the trench work of his discipline while he addressed himself increasingly to the larger world on larger issues. For Dewey it was important that his general discourse be grounded in a technically coherent philosophical position. His conception of philosophy's role in the world, in fact, depended upon his conclusion, fully clarified in his early Columbia years, that the whole project of epistemology had been a wrong turn for philosophy. Like Richard Rorty in our own time, Dewey rejected the epistemological search for the representation of reality. In exchanging epistemology for history, Dewey forced philosophy into the world, into the pursuit of pragmatic and provisional understandings and ethics based upon experience, not Kantian universal categories.[65] But if he thus dispatched absolutes, moral responsibility remained. Academic philosophy, Dewey increasingly worried, was avoiding that responsibility.

When he reviewed *Recent Social Trends* in 1933, Dewey was less critical than Beard had been. He was pleased by the simple fact that social scientists—knowingly, he assumed—had presented facts in a way that made "problems stand out." He seemed more interested, however, in using the report as an occasion to make a larger point about philosophy. He observed that in the crisis of the Depression "literary folk" were busy talking about social problems, no longer restricting themselves, as they had in the 1920s, to questions of "literary form." While there was, he thought, some danger of converting literature into "social propaganda," he was less worried about that potential problem than the nearly complete absence of academic philosophers in the discussion of the "general problems" pressed to the fore by the Depression. They are, "to judge from their public output," preoccupied with "merely technical and formal questions so that we are threatened with a new kind of scholasticism."[66]

Neither the Depression nor Dewey effectively countered this twentieth-century trend in philosophy, a trend that partially accounts for Dewey's diminished reputation among philosophers in our own time. But until Dewey's retirement in 1930, Columbia stood apart from this dominant development. Or, to state it more properly and accurately, it was resisted into the 1930s in New York City, where, besides Dewey, Morris Cohen at CCNY, Sidney Hook at NYU, Horace Kallen at the New School, and J. H. Randall at Columbia kept philosophy in the world. One senses that in New York's universities—as opposed to Harvard in Boston, where these trends were most advanced—it was simply impossible, even within the high walls and tight discourse of the academy, to avoid the experience of the world in such a turbulent era.* In the later 1930s and 1940s, however, the academic incorporation of Anglo-American analytical philosophy, aided by a selective immigration of European philosophers escaping Fascism, particularly the Vienna group, made the discourse of philosophy in New York and elsewhere even more technical and self-contained. But until that time there was a distinctively public and urban philosophy pursued by New York's academic philosophers.

World War I and its aftermath helped Dewey to define his intellectual stance during the interwar years. It brought Dewey difficult challenges from the two sides of his pragmatic legacy. Bourne had complained that values had been subordinated to technique during the war, while Walter Lippmann, a symbol of just that tendency, seemed in his writing on the public all too willing to sacrifice democratic values to efficient administration by experts and insiders. In a series of papers in the *Journal of Philosophy* and in *Experience and Nature*, a great book that constituted the core of his philosophy, Dewey largely accepted and accommodated Bourne's criticisms, finding a larger significance for art, value, and free contemplation. *The Public and Its Problems* (1927), prompted by Lippmann's *Phantom Public* (1925), sought to reclaim a fundamental role for the democratic public in specifically modern times.

To make a point that is, perhaps, a trifle too neat, but true, one might say that Dewey met the different challenges of Bourne and Lippmann with the same answer. Bourne's query had concerned the source and role of values. Dewey, too anxious to keep philosophy constructive during the war, had collapsed means and ends in 1917. After the war, however, he worked to clarify his thinking. Then, as before, he talked about science and inquiry as the source of values, but this does not mean, as some then and since have thought, that Dewey proposed to establish an objective basis for values. His impulse was in fact quite otherwise. He sought through science and inquiry to free values from established interests and customs. The implication of that move was not, however, the dissolution of social interests in the making and defining of values. Rather his aim was to open up the process. His purpose was to facilitate the fresh construction of values in a public and a political way, a way that acknowledged a variety of interests and emotional commitments contending to

---

* Philosophy at Chicago, led by T. V. Smith, tended to follow the New York, not the Harvard, model.

establish the public meaning of values. Such had been his aim before the war, when he talked about hearing "all interests, however humble," in the making of "public opinion."[67]

Under the stimulus of Bourne's stinging attack, however, he became clearer and more careful, more sensitive to a wider range of sources of ideas and commitments. Dewey never fully resolved the problem of how values were created. No one, in fact, who both resists relativism and eschews appeal to some transcendent and absolute source of values can avoid some difficulty on this point. Yet the solution he proposed did have the very important effect of bringing the intellectual into the world in a way that enriched public culture. For Dewey, politics in public constituted the proper source of values, purposes, and social knowledge in a democracy. From this perspective, as James T. Kloppenberg has explained, "politics is an endless search for better truths."[68] All of this, of course, implies a vital and open public politics and culture, itself a fundamental democratic goal. It was with his ideas thus grounded in a democratic commitment and in this philosophical principle that Dewey set out to meet the challenge of Lippmann's corrosive book.

If Lippmann proposed a polity marked by active insiders and a passive public, Dewey inverted the image and elaborated the implications of that inversion for the role of the intellectual. Dewey was quick to acknowledge the difficulty of his position. Modern technology and social forms, most notably the functional organization of society, had indeed, as Lippmann argued, undermined the capacity of the public to form opinions and to act. But Dewey's argument, not unlike that of Lewis Mumford in the 1930s, was that modern technology, communication, and scientific inquiry could be mastered and used to re-create the public.

For our purposes, the most interesting line of argument in *The Public and Its Problems* concerns the relation of intellect to democracy. Although Dewey called for social inquiry by intellectuals, he denied them the authority to prescribe solutions. They must instead bring their intelligence and findings into the public realm. Social policies, which are to Dewey the reconciliation of interests, are not for him the simple product of social science or of expert intervention in state administration. Rather they should be developed by a process of discussion and persuasion, by public politics. No result is absolute or final; reconciliation is always contextual, specific to time and place, and experimental.*

Neither of the two tendencies characteristic of academic social science was, according to Dewey, adequate to the democratic challenge. The academy could not be justified as a "refuge" for "specialism" and "scho-

---

* The notion of the "public sphere" developed in our time by Jürgen Habermas, with explicit awareness of Dewey, differs on this point of contextualism. Habermas's still-developing conception points toward a universal pragmatics.

lasticism," nor should social science be assimilated to administration. Scientific social inquiry belonged in public, providing a model of method and willing to engage ordinary culture and politics. If democracy had its "seer in Walt Whitman," then, Dewey believed, "it will have its consummation when free social inquiry is indissolubly wedded to the art of full and moving communication." Rule by experts, Dewey insisted, was not only the wrong dream, it was impossible as well. To acquire power, social scientists must either "become the willing tools of big economic interests" or "ally themselves with the masses." Either way, however, they are agents, not principals. Let them forget the dream of expert authority. "A class of experts is inevitably so removed from common interests as to become a class with private interests and private knowledge, which in social matters is not knowledge at all."[69]

When Dewey offered the alternative of democracy, he meant something more than the mere counting of heads. While they were fundamental to democracy, electoral majorities were not the essential virtue of democracy. The value of democracy, as Dewey put it, derived from what the power of the ballot compelled: "recourse to methods of discussion, consultation, and persuasion."[70] Instead of seeking ways to avoid or circumvent the power of the ballot, intellectuals ought to engage the larger process.[71]

Dewey was particularly anxious to refute the characteristic claim of intellectuals that the masses were too stupid and, somehow, too dangerous for active involvement in public life. "The world," Dewey reflected, "has suffered more from leaders and authorities than from the masses." He had no doubt that educated intelligence, a product of social experience, was easily adequate to the demands of democracy. What he called "effective" intelligence is not innate; it is made by society. It is this process and this intelligence that allows the ordinary citizen in the twentieth century to know more about electricity than Newton did. And it is such effective intelligence that is relevant in public life. For those who promoted the "notion that intelligence is a personal endowment or personal attainment," Dewey had no patience. It is, he rather sharply remarked, "the great conceit of the intellectual classes, as that of the commercial class is that wealth is something which they personally have wrought and possess."[72]

The effective intelligence and open discourse that he proposed could be nourished, at least in the first instance, only in the "give-and-take" of the personal politics and cultural life characteristic of local life, in particular cities and towns, rather than in the nation as a whole. Fully aware that such a civic definition of politics and culture was being undercut by modern social structures that were "functional" or "occupational" rather than local, Dewey nonetheless associated the promise of a democratic public with the vigilant maintenance of a local orientation as part of modern social life. "Unless local community life can be restored, the public cannot adequately resolve its most urgent problem: to find and identify itself."[73]

It has been said with considerable truth that there is more than a trace of nostalgia for the New England town of fond memory in all of this. Yet in its concern for the relation of history, place, and ordinary human speech to civic life, there is an important point that transcends whatever nostalgia may have prompted and informed it. The language of modern social science is increasingly, as Alvin Gouldner has pointed out, "situation-free," dissociated from time and place, from context. Its tendency is to lose contact with everyday life and its language, and further, to devalue the "context-limited" meanings that characterize actual local culture and politics.[74] This universalizing impulse seeks not only to purify and distinguish the discourse of intellectuals but also to privilege it in social life and politics. By respecting the actual speech of local politics and culture, Dewey challenged this aspiration, already apparent in the 1920s. While privileged and legislated languages are, of course, quite indispensable in many fields of pure research, in other contexts caution is in order. When they become associated with power, problems arise. The choice, as Dewey would have it, is between the discourse of expertise and that of democracy.

Dewey's emphasis on discussion and experimental resolutions in particular times and places stands, as well, in sharp contrast to the recently and widely acclaimed work of the Harvard moral philosophers John Rawls and Robert Nozick.[75] From the perspective of Dewey, what is most striking about their work is not the difference, that one is liberal, the other conservative, but that they both present absolute and ahistorical theories of value and politics, neither of which allows a formative role for democratic intelligence. *The Public and Its Problems* is hardly adequate to the problem it addresses, yet one cannot but appreciate the direction Dewey took and the aspiration that drove him in that direction. One can only regret its eclipse.

Dewey's contextualism, finally, had a broader implication for his thinking about a pattern of culture and politics that was as American as it was democratic. His strong sense of context prompted his resistance to capture by European ideals of culture. Willing to learn from Europe, but not willing to bow to it, Dewey did not long for a model of cultural practice and authority that was the product of another time and place. He was not afraid to be an American, a New Yorker. In a certain way he was a representative American democrat, in the succession of Thomas Jefferson, the eighteenth-century farmer, and Abraham Lincoln, the nineteenth-century lawyer. In common with them, John Dewey, the twentieth-century urban academic, was appreciative but not intimidated by Europe. Like his student Randolph Bourne, Dewey identified distinctively American nationalism with cosmopolitanism, with a culture, as Jefferson and Lincoln would have it, of world importance, but evolving out of the particular, diverse, and complex American experience.

The uncritical importation of European cultural standards would, Dewey worried, produce at best a veneer, at worst the basis of class authority, the possession only, but rather easily, of those with the privilege of time, the resources for travel, and "a reasonably apt memory for some phrases." Looking toward Europe would, he feared, direct American intellectuals to a defensive action, protecting a "shrinking classicism." He preferred a more constructive approach: he wanted American intellectuals to take responsibility for their own distinctive culture. American democratic culture was something "to achieve, to create." Dewey called upon intellectuals to "transmute a society built on industry which is not yet humanized into a society which wields its knowledge and its industrial power in behalf of a democratic culture." Success would require "the courage of an inspired imagination," and Dewey offered no guaranteed result. But he warned that certain failure awaited the denial of the facts of American life in pursuit of European standards of culture and models of intellectual life.[76]

SUCCESSION

The 1940s were hard on Dewey and Beard—and the Progressive liberalism they had come to represent. Their faith in progress could not survive Hitler, Stalin, and the Bomb. Dewey's educational theories were rejected in a new wave of school reform, and his scholarship was pushed aside by philosophers pursuing a different order of problems. New directions in historiography, emphasizing "consensus," undermined Beard's economic interpretation of the Constitution, as well as his general emphasis on conflict in American history.

The generation of Columbia academics who came of age in the forties found the liberalism of Beard and Dewey wanting, but they continued to embrace the model of the critical academic intellect that their predecessors had defined. For Lionel Trilling, Richard Hofstadter, and C. Wright Mills, the mandarin conservative, the cosmopolitan moderate, and the radical populist, the social role that Dewey and Beard had defined for the scholar was a valued inheritance, one that released them from the threat of enclosure by Butler's Columbia. The achievements of their New York intellectual forebears made it easier for the generation of the forties to take advantage of the city, to feel equally at home on Morningside Heights and downtown in the literary world of *The Nation, The New Re-*

public, and the *Partisan Review.* The clarity of this generational emulation and succession is made all the more emphatic when we recognize the nostalgia it still evokes among the present generation of academics, who are not certain how or even whether to try to recover and renew this tradition of academic intellectuals.[77]

If Trilling, Hofstadter, and Mills found Dewey's philosophy shallow and Beard's interpretation of American history too simple, they did not on that account dismiss them. They respected them enough to argue with them. Hofstadter's first professional article, published in 1938, addressed itself to the Beardian interpretation of the Civil War, and his last major book, *The Progressive Historians* (1968), which he likened to a "parricidal foray," was his final effort to reckon with Beard.[78] Mills wrote his dissertation on Dewey, pragmatism, and higher education. He learned his American history from *The Rise of American Civilization* (1927), by Charles and Mary Beard. But in *White Collar* (1951), his most widely read book, he argued that the "liberal ethos" as developed by Beard and Dewey "is now often irrelevant."[79] Trilling aimed, of course, to make the same point in *The Liberal Imagination* (1950).

These three Columbia luminaries did not, of course, agree among themselves. It is important to acknowledge their differences and the tensions between them, even as we emphasize what they shared. Trilling seems to have been particularly disturbed by Mills's style and his increasing radicalism, and the earlier, apparently close, friendship between Hofstadter and Mills cooled as the 1950s wore on.[80] Yet they formed an intellectual generation. Trilling, who was Jewish and the first Jew to receive a regular appointment (in 1939) in Columbia's English Department; Hofstadter, who was half Jewish; and Mills, a WASP from Texas by way of Wisconsin, were able to establish themselves in New York's self-consciously cosmopolitan intellectual culture that was heralded a generation before by Randolph Bourne and Morris Cohen. Most important of all—and most directly the legacy of Dewey and Beard—they shared a sense of the public significance of the academic mind. Such was their belief in ideas that commitment to them was vocation enough; none of the three men succumbed to the temptation of expertise. Intensely conscious of the responsibility of intellect, even at the risk, particularly in the cases of Trilling and Mills, of some pretension, they believed, as well, in the power of ideas.[81] The precedent of Dewey and Beard assured them that such a critical intellect was a natural extension of the university and that the university, with the vigor of its disciplines, could be, at least in a metropolitan city, a base for forays into the larger world of culture and politics.

However important this academic triptych—and one could add others easily enough, Meyer Schapiro or NYU's Sidney Hook, for example—

they never assumed the mantle of public philosopher in the way Dewey had. For Dewey's successor we must look elsewhere, to the Union Theological Seminary. Reinhold Niebuhr Place on Morningside Heights today commemorates the man who made Union his academic base in the city while he gradually but definitely assumed Dewey's public role. Most commentators on Niebuhr's ideas—and Niebuhr himself—have made much of his disagreements with Dewey. The differences between the two men are important, particularly the secularism of the one and the religiosity of the other, but in the longer view of the city's intellectual life succession and continuity of role seem more important. If Niebuhr's neo-orthodoxy better explained the evil that was too large to avoid at midcentury, if words like "irony," "pathos," "complexity," and "tragedy" appear more frequently and "progress" less in Niebuhr, still *Moral Man and Immoral Society* (1932), *The Children of Light and the Children of Darkness* (1944), and *The Irony of American History* (1952) sought to deepen American public philosophy and strengthen American democratic ideals.

Niebuhr, who moved to New York in 1928, when he became professor of social ethics at the Union Theological Seminary, found in the metropolis the means to incorporate more and wider experience—moral, intellectual, political—and to transmute it into a public philosophy.[82] If Union sustained the religious core of his thought and work, the city was continually broadening for someone who, like the earlier Morris Cohen, had grown up within a rather tight ethnic (German), religious (Lutheran), and provincial (Midwestern) world. In New York, like Dewey, Niebuhr became more worldly, deeper in his appreciation of moral complexity, choosing, for example, the liberal reformism of Al Smith at the cost of the "provincial" commitment to prohibition he had brought with him to New York.

Being in New York had consequences for Niebuhr. He was able in New York to be more worldly without becoming secular. The metropolis provided him with an ideology of cosmopolitanism (the legacy of Bourne and Cohen) and an experience of cosmopolitanism that did not wash out or challenge the religious core of his life and work. Had he left New York, to accept a Harvard non-departmental or university-wide professorship, as he contemplated but declined to do in 1943, he would have lost both the academic foundations of his religious identity and the social basis of his cosmopolitanism. New York did not cause Niebuhr to become a public philosopher, reaching far beyond his co-religionists, any more than it made Dewey one. But for both of them the city made the transformation a possibility. It may well have contributed, moreover, as much to Niebuhr's sense of human complexity and the ambiguity of virtue as did his theological studies. Such is the gift of New York, for those who are ready for it.

PART IV

AN INTERNATIONAL
CAPITAL OF CULTURE

CHAPTER 9

Refiguration

Our sense of the thirties—fortified by the ever-increasing volumes of memoirs written by the postwar "New York Intellectuals" who started out then—is that of a political decade. And so it was. Yet this widely shared and well-cultivated memory distorts the meaning of the period, and its contribution to our own time. To give canonical status to politics and the intellectual axes that connected the *New Republic, The Nation,* and, especially, the *Partisan Review* to academics at Washington Square, Morningside Heights, and St. Nicholas Terrace, is to narrow our vision of the decade unduly.

If we are to understand the full contribution of the 1930s to the translation of New York City from province to international metropolis, we need a wider sense of the decade's intellectual culture, one that embraces more than politics and ideology. It was not through the making of ideology, after all, that New York ceased being provincial. Who can name a work of ideology of international significance identified with New York in the 1930s? The *Partisan Review* achieved its position in American cultural and intellectual life as a consumer of European political ideology, and it was a provincial importer of European literary modernism, coming rather late to that movement and celebrating the heroes of the previous generation.[1]

The journal and its academic collaborators after the war prefigured neither the present elaboration of art, intellect, and society nor the cultural ascendancy of New York as an international metropolis. Rather, the *Partisan Review* circle was a brilliant afterglow of an older vision of intellect that was undercut and bypassed during the 1930s and 1940s by a series of cultural initiatives in both elite and popular culture which valued the image and the sound at least as much as the word.[2]

New York's postwar ascendancy had its roots in the painting, sculpture, photography, architecture, music, and, especially, dance, both modern and ballet, of the 1930s and 1940s. This cultural flowering represented more than an isolated episode of unprecedented invention and quality in the arts; it was firmly embedded in an aesthetic and a theory of culture formulated during those years that was at once American, grounded in the life of the metropolis, and international. For the most part, the great critics who defined and promoted this achievement in dance, music, and architecture rarely appeared in the canonical journals, publishing rather in magazines mostly unknown to "New York Intellectuals" of either the past or the present.[3] Painting was the exception: it was Clement Greenberg, writing chiefly in *The Nation* in the 1940s, who defined the modernity, the Americanness, and the international significance of the work of the Abstract Expressionists.*

Much of the critical discussion that underlay the creation of a culture of the eye and ear that was modern, American, democratic, and international was the work of intellectuals and artists associated with such magazines as *Modern Music* (1924–1946), *New Theatre* (1933–37), *Dance Index* (1942–49), and the cultural pages of the New York *Herald Tribune*. Here, in their regular columns, Virgil Thomson and Edwin Denby wrote on music and dance, the one brilliantly following new musical developments, the other explicating, better than anyone else would ever do, the genius of George Balanchine and the implications of his distinctive way of making ballets for broader questions of culture and intellect in America.

Modern Music—inspired in part by Paul Rosenfeld, who provided a link with the earlier generation of modernists, particularly Bourne and Steiglitz—was edited by Minna Lederman. Sponsored by the League of Composers, the magazine was intended to advance both the performance of modern music and critical writing about that music. Its range was broad, incorporating dance and set design, and its visual material was of high quality: the first issue, for example, carried drawings by Picasso. Lederman published Aaron Copland, Virgil Thomson, Roger Sessions, and Elliot Carter, helping them to become writers as well as composers, encouraging them to write both technical articles that analyzed concepts such as harmony and more reflective ones that probed the relations of culture, society, and nationalism. She gave Edwin Denby and Lincoln Kirstein space to write about dance and musical theatre.

Dance Index was edited and funded by Kirstein. It was monographic in

---

* Interestingly, Greenberg remarks that during the two years when he was an editor of the *Partisan Review* (1941–43), he was "almost entirely out of touch with art life."[4]

spirit, but visually brilliant, documenting and thus creating a dance tradition upon which Americans might build. But it was not exclusively historical. A remarkable article by Lederman on Stravinsky and the theater appeared in it, as well as Balanchine's "Notes on Choreography," a summary of his choreographic principles. *Dance Index* was, in the words of Arlene Croce, "perhaps the single most lavish contribution to dance scholarship made in the United States."[5]

Music, dance, and drama were covered by *New Theatre*. A self-consciously radical magazine, it called for a "new theater," not simply (or more narrowly) a workers' theater to succeed the bourgeois theater. It carried articles by a wide variety of intellectuals—from Lincoln Kirstein to Robert Edmond Jones to Paul Robeson to quite obscure coterie and pseudonymous writers—addressing questions about the relation of art and politics that we usually associate with the thirties. But here these issues were argued in the context of dance, music, and drama, not literature or painting. No artist invited so much discussion as Martha Graham. Her modernism and apparently liberal politics were appreciated, but her *Primitive Mysteries* (1931), for example, seemed to bear distressingly little relation to the world, to politics. The precise relationship between her art and her politics eluded easy description or, for that matter, prescription. But the attempt to define it provided a rich focus for discussion that lasted as long as the magazine.

Once one realizes how vital and pervasive was the interest in visual and aural culture in the intellectual life of the thirties, our sense of the configuration of the decade's literary culture is affected as well. Thus, as Warren Susman has pointed out, *Let Us Now Praise Famous Men* (1941), by James Agee and Walker Evans—a book that began as an assignment from the picture-conscious Luce *Time-Life* empire—can be clearly seen as a "classic" of the decade. That seemingly idiosyncratic book represents, as Susman observed, "much of what was characteristic of the Thirties' finest contributions." Lionel Trilling, the first critic to recognize its greatness, hailed the book as "the most realistic and important moral effort of our generation."[6] For Trilling as for Agee by 1941, ideology was less important to politics than was moral intensity.

But *Let Us Now Praise Famous Men* is emblematic of the thirties and prophetic of the postwar era in another way. On the advice of Lincoln Kirstein, Agee decided to give equal weight to both text and photographs.[7] The photographs, all printed together at the beginning of the volume, constitute Book I; the text is Book II. "The photographs," Agee wrote in the introduction, "are not illustrative. They, and the text, are co-equal, mutually independent, and fully collaborative." The images were as important as the words, and the words were composed by Agee with "reading aloud in mind."[8] This consciously avant-garde literary work thus invites comparison with the ballets of George Balanchine. At the same time—and with Kirstein looking over his shoulder—Balanchine was creating a radically new aesthetics for ballet that was described by Igor Stravinsky, his friend and collaborator, as "visual hearing."*[9]

UPTOWN BOHEMIA

Except for some painting, very little of this reorientation, clarification, and acceleration of the cultural and intellectual life of the city was noticed by the "New York Intellectuals" at the time or, later, in their autobiographies. Irving Howe stands alone as a partial exception: in 1971, admittedly twenty years late, he "blundered," as he put it, "onto a great artistic enterprise," discovering the New York City Ballet and the genius of George Balanchine.[10] No one else among the New York Intellectuals had noticed, or if they did, they did not grasp the opportunity for themselves, as intellectuals, to write about it.

Diana Trilling and Virgil Thomson recently addressed this matter directly. Discussing New York's intellectual life in the 1930s and 1940s, they agreed that there was remarkably little contact between her literary/political intellectual group and Thomson's more broadly artistic circle. The visual and aural sensibilities of the *Partisan Review* intellectuals were not, she admitted, much developed.[11] These writers, it seems, shared an almost puritanical fear of the seductiveness of the aesthetic pleasures of the ear and the eye.[12]

Indeed, the more one looks at the period, the more one is struck by this existence of two worlds of art and intellect, one focused on the word, the other concerned with images and sounds, especially when combined as in dance and opera. With the exception, perhaps, of W. H. Auden and of a joint interest in some painters and sculptors, most notably the Abstract Expressionists, these worlds were sealed off from each other. Our historical sense of the thirties has been formed by allowing one of these to constitute the whole of the thirties, while we ignore the other. Only by recovering this other side of the thirties, the world of those Virgil Thomson called the "eye people and ear people," will we be able to orient ourselves to the decade in a way that allows us to understand its profoundly important role in making New York what it has become in our own time.[13]

The group more familiar to us—the political "New York Intellectuals," as they have come to call themselves and be called—represented a collab-

---

* Another classic, if a minor one, of the period is Constance Rourke's *The Roots of American Culture* (1942), which bears remark here because it identified those roots in cultural forms that do not depend centrally upon the printed word.

oration of WASPs and upwardly mobile Eastern European Jews who united under the aegis of the cosmopolitan ideal articulated by Randolph Bourne during the First World War. It is because we have so completely let these once-left-of-center (and now mostly right-of-center) political intellectuals define the domain of intellect that we have largely overlooked another, equally coherent group, equally cosmopolitan and generally liberal, if less overtly political.* Much more passionate about the arts, this group also represented an ethnic alliance, but the match was made much higher up the economic ladder—a collaboration of rich WASPs with wealthy German Jews. If one group was passionate about politics and intelligent about aesthetics, the other was passionate about aesthetics and intelligent about politics.[14]

But it is wealth, more than politics, that differentiates the two groups. The "New York Intellectuals" had a downtown quality, while the "Civic Intellectuals," as I shall call the second group, were distinctly "uptown." Like their eighteenth-century predecessors in New York's civic culture, they were at once patrons and intellectuals. While the future "New York Intellectuals" were debating politics in the cafeteria of City College, the "Civic Intellectuals" were discussing art at Harvard. They met in the university's Liberal Club, where they founded and edited a major literary magazine, *Hound and Horn,* which covered the visual arts as well as writing. In addition, as members of their own Harvard Society for Contemporary Art, they put on exhibitions that very much anticipated the direction MOMA took in the 1930s.

Who were these rich and talented young men? At the center of the group was the multitalented but erratic Lincoln Kirstein, son of a Boston department store magnate. The Liberal Club's walls were covered by murals he drew, his money funded the *Hound and Horn* and he was its most influential editor, and his energies gave extraordinary vitality to the exhibition program of the Harvard Society for Contemporary Art. Others in the group included Virgil Thomson, from Kansas City on his way to Paris to study with Nadia Boulanger; Philip Johnson, the rich son of a Cleveland industrialist; Henry-Russell Hitchcock, the architectural historian, Johnson's friend and later collaborator in the celebration of the modern movement in architecture; Edward M. M. Warburg, whose family home on Fifth Avenue now houses the Jewish Museum; A. Everett "Chick" Austin, who, as director of the Wadsworth Atheneum in Hartford, which he made into a cultural outpost of New York City, provided a first—if very brief—home for Balanchine in America and gave Thomson's first opera its premiere; and Kirk Askew, like Thomson from Kan-

---

* Philip Johnson, who was drawn to Huey Long's crusade and Hitler's Nazis in the 1930s, provides the major exception to this statement.

sas City, who later became a New York art dealer and, along with his wife, Constance, presided over an exciting and influential "bohemian" salon in their East 61st Street brownstone. All of these men, as well as Alfred H. Barr, a Harvard graduate student then, later to become founding director of the Museum of Modern Art, found a common guide to matters artistic in the Harvard art historian Paul Sachs, scion of New York's Goldman Sachs banking family.

Once the members of the group came to New York, usually after a sojourn in Paris, their associations were broadened. The Askew salon drew in the worlds of art, drama, dance, and music. Through Barr, they were introduced into the world of vast wealth, mostly WASP, that sustained the Museum of Modern Art. (In 1931, MOMA established an "advisory committee," chaired by Nelson Rockefeller, and including Edward Warburg, Philip Johnson, Lincoln Kirstein, and art critic James Johnson Sweeney.)

And there was Carl Van Vechten. Although not properly one of the "Civic Intellectuals," he was close to many of them, playing the role of cultural broker in New York City much as his friend Gertrude Stein did in Paris. In 1926, Kirstein, still a Harvard undergraduate, visited New York with Muriel Draper and met Van Vechten, who encouraged his interests in dance—and a wide variety of arts. In 1930 Van Vechten stopped writing books and took up photography.* His enthusiasm was shared by Kirstein, who helped bring photography into the Museum of Modern Art, even curating an exhibit in 1938 of the photographs of his friend Walker Evans.

Philip Johnson had already created the museum's Architecture Department in 1931, serving as both its curator and its patron. Modern architecture—given the name "International Style" in the department's first exhibition, organized by Johnson and Henry-Russell Hitchcock in 1932—was realized in a public way by the museum in 1939, when Edward Durell Stone designed its new building. When the building opened, a film department had been organized by Jay Leyda and Lincoln Kirstein, and in 1940 Kirstein even established a dance archive.†

Modern music was welcomed into the museum, and in 1943 John Cage presented in concert there what Thomson considered to be the most advanced music being composed anywhere.[15] Always, the effort was to extend the domain of art, seeking to incorporate the various expressions of modern culture while maintaining high aesthetic standards.

* One of Van Vechten's first serious photographs was of Lincoln Kirstein (1933), as was his last (1964).

† It was later transferred to the Dance Collection of the New York Public Library at Lincoln Center.

As he had done for others, Van Vechten introduced the group to Harlem and black culture. Not only were there occasional forays north from the Askews' salon, but, more seriously, Virgil Thomson determined that his first opera, *Four Saints in Three Acts,* directed by John Houseman (whom he first met at the Askews'), with sets by Van Vechten's friend Florine Stettheimer, should be sung by black singers. Later, Thomson, Houseman, and Orson Welles (then only eighteen years old) produced, under WPA auspices, the famous all-black *Macbeth,* set in Haiti.

Remarkable resources were available to these "Civic Intellectuals." When Kirstein, who, after admiring Balanchine in Paris, actually met him in the Askews' London home, it was to his friend Edward Warburg that he turned for the financial means to promise Balanchine both a company and a school in America. And "Chick" Austin was there ready to offer the Wadsworth Atheneum as a home for both.* Later, Nelson Rockefeller, as Coordinator of Inter-American Affairs under Roosevelt, responding to the suggestion of his friend Kirstein that dance was a "universal language," arranged the first international tour for Balanchine's ballet company, sending them to Latin America under State Department auspices. For the government, it was part of the program to maintain inter-American unity against Fascism; for Balanchine, it was the occasion to create two of his greatest plotless ballets, *Concerto Barocco* and *Ballet Imperial* (both 1941), the latter since reworked as the *Tchaikovsky Concerto.*[17]

The "Civic Intellectuals" lived in a world of talent and resources. Almost impossible to describe in brief, this world was, however, evoked in the paintings of Florine Stettheimer, daughter of a wealthy German-Jewish family living at Alwyn Court on 58th Street, a block from Carnegie Hall.† Her work manifests a play between public life, the world of skyscrapers and major institutions of the city, and private life, the world of elegance and grace that was so much a part of the atmosphere of uptown bohemia. A particular group of four paintings done in the 1930s—collectively the *Cathedrals of New York,* all today in the collection of the Metropolitan Museum of Art—constitutes an iconography of this world. *Cathedrals of Broadway* (1929) represents the world of theater and film, *Cathedrals of Fifth Avenue* (1931) celebrates fashion and society, *Cathedrals of Wall Street* (1939) recognizes the wealth and power of Wall Street but

* Stunned to find himself in provincial Hartford, Balanchine demanded that Kirstein move operations to New York, or he would return to Paris. Kirstein (1973): "I had never questioned that Balanchine would be anything but content in a provincial American landscape."[16]

† If one takes note of the people represented in the doll house made by Florine's sister Ettie, now at the Museum of the City of New York, one discovers another evocation of this world.

also endorses Roosevelt's New Deal liberalism, and *Cathedrals of Art* (dated 1942 but unfinished at her death in 1944) concerned itself, in her words, with "Our Dawn of Art."

There is about these paintings, as art historian Linda Nochlin has observed, an "airy and mobile" quality. They are "energized by a weightless breezy sort of dynamism." Of course, this quality represents an individual artistic style and personality, but it is not inaccurate as a representation of the life and culture of her world. Her bohemia was, like her, at once "serious and lightheartedly outrageous." The social criticism of Stettheimer, like that of her bohemian circle, was real, but it took the form of quietly subversive allusions by people who were at home in a world of prosperity and aesthetic sensuality.[18]

Cathedrals of Art, the panel most pertinent to our discussion, represents the relation of networks of friends to the larger institutionalization of art and culture in the city. At the center of her painting is the arched stairway of the Metropolitan Museum of Art, home of the great tradition of art. On the left is the Museum of Modern Art ("Art in America"), and on the right the Whitney Museum ("American Art"). But the painting shows more than institutions; it also includes the friends who ran them, as well as dealers and art promoters, some of whom were much too noisy and disruptive of both the seriousness and the pleasures of art.*

PRECEDENTS AND CONTEXTS

The cultural reorientation of the thirties was not without historical precedent in New York City. Founded by seventeenth-century Dutch merchants whose own culture was, as Svetlana Alpers has brilliantly demonstrated, profoundly and distinctively visual as well as commercial, New York City had always been uncommonly receptive to visual, musical, and performance arts.[20] The history of painting, opera, music, theater, and dance in New York was, except for some competition in painting from Philadelphia early and late in the nineteenth century, always much fuller than in any other city. More important: the leading men and women of intellect in New York were closely associated with this wider culture. Can one imagine Emerson being so deeply committed to the opera and popular theater and so indebted to it for the genesis of his work as was Whitman? Where else in America, in the era of Morse and Bryant, were writers and artists so closely associated? Where else was an artist, Frederick Law Olmsted, a central civic and national intellectual

---

* Those who can be identified in the painting include Alfred Steiglitz, Kirk Askew, A. Everett Austin, Alfred H. Barr, Juliana Force (director of the Whitney), Francis Henry Taylor (director of the Metropolitan), Henry McBride (art critic for the New York *Sun*), and Virgil Thomson.[19]

figure? What city could match the generous representation of the arts and letters found weekly in the salon of Helena de Kay and Richard Watson Gilder? Think, too, of *The Masses*, that remarkable collaboration of writers and artists. Finally, in a much abbreviated list, where else in America would radical intellectuals produce a work of theater, the Paterson Strike Pageant at Madison Square Garden (June 7, 1913), to advance a political cause?

The roots of the achievements of the 1930s reach back—in ways that are rather easily specified—to the beginning of the century. Direct lines of influence and continuity link the era of the Greenwich Village rebellion with the uptown consolidation of the 1930s. Paul Rosenfeld, whose dreams for an American musical modernism dated from the days of *Seven Arts*, encouraged Minna Lederman to establish *Modern Music*, to which he also contributed. Peggy Guggenheim, whose Art of This Century gallery (1942–47) gave Jackson Pollock, Mark Rothko, Robert Motherwell, and other Abstract Expressionists their first uptown visibility, had been first shown an abstract painting by Alfred Steiglitz. Arthur B. Davies, one of the organizers of the Armory Show (1913), inspired Lilly Bliss, an established patron of music, to interest herself in modern art. Later, with her friends Mary Quinn Sullivan and Abigail Aldrich Rockefeller, she set in motion the project that in 1929 began the Museum of Modern Art.

The Paris–New York axis that ran between Gertrude Stein in Paris and Carl Van Vechten in New York promoted many intellectual and artistic careers in New York, most notably, perhaps, that of Virgil Thomson, whose first opera had a libretto by Stein and found patronage in New York in part through Van Vechten's efforts. Although she only passed through New York, as she did many other places, Isadora Duncan, who once performed before Mayor John Purroy Mitchell in Mabel Dodge Luhan's living room, also left her mark, awakening serious interest in modern dance in the city and giving American dance an international existence.

During the 1920s, *Vanity Fair*, which had been established in 1913, carried the message of modernism in the arts to an emerging upper-middle-class audience. These readers were treated to visual delight, in the advertisements as well as in the editorial graphics and illustrations. They could peruse regular columns on fashion, art, music, theater, and current events, but they would learn little of book culture—except for the brief period when Edmund Wilson was managing editor early in the twenties, *Vanity Fair* never published regular critical coverage of literature. With its proliferating images and its celebration of performance, Frank Crowninshield's magazine submerged the book and the word under a new kind of urban sophistication.

Crowninshield and his magazine declined to accept the distinction that Clement Greenberg would make in 1939 between "avant garde" and "kitsch."[21] For *Vanity Fair,* as for the Museum of Modern Art, of which Crowninshield would be one of the original trustees, art was not confined to the work of the individual creator. It was defined more broadly to include objects produced under commercial and industrial conditions: industrial design, poster and advertising art, film, and photography all found a place in *Vanity Fair* and MOMA. Perhaps this convergence of the aesthetics of the magazine and of the museum was to be expected: it was his reading of *Vanity Fair,* along with *The Dial,* as a Princeton undergraduate (1918–1922) that first interested Alfred H. Barr in modern art.[22]

Much that is visual, that is commercial, and that is popular in American culture is not serious art. But some is. With some misguidance from Greenberg and, perhaps, from the social theorists of the Frankfurt School then sojourning in New York, with some help from their own ambitious cultural elitism, the "New York Intellectuals" found it increasingly difficult to respond to the visual and aural culture, the images and sounds, that surged past them in the 1940s and 1950s. They missed the circularity and reciprocal relations of levels and genres of culture, something Balanchine understood and exploited in dance, as did Thomson in music. If *Vanity Fair,* which stopped publication in 1936, could not adapt itself to the politics and the political crisis of the thirties, the self-consciously political intellectuals were unable to orient themselves to the new domains of art nurtured in the 1930s and which define advanced and serious culture in New York to this day.

If literary culture, as we usually remember it, contributed little to the reorientation of culture in New York, neither did the academy. While John Dewey, the city's most distinguished academic intellectual, did address the question of aesthetics in his *Art as Experience* (1934), and Martha Hill, professor of Physical Education at NYU, offered the first course in modern dance and created the important Bennington Summer Festival of Modern Dance (1934), neither Columbia nor NYU—as institutions— did much to advance the arts. Columbia contemplated the organization of a school of the arts in the 1920s, but produced only some internal memos.

More was done at NYU. It provided a home in the University Building on Washington Square for A. E. Gallatin's fine collection of modern painting, his Gallery of Living Art, established in 1927 and until the opening of MOMA the only public gallery in the city devoted to new trends in painting. It offered many New Yorkers, including some who later became significant in the New York art world, their first chance to view the modern masters. NYU's Institute of Fine Arts, augmented by refugee scholars, established itself in the 1930s as the nation's premier center of art-historical scholarship, but the university's short-lived School of the Arts, established on the eve of the Depression and seeking a more contemporary relation to art, became an early, almost immediate, casualty of the Depression.

For constructive academic involvement with the arts during this period, one must look to the New School for Social Research. After the departures of Beard, Robinson, Dewey, Mitchell, and Veblen, Alvin Johnson was left with the difficult task of keeping the school afloat. Luckily, he recognized the possibilities inherent in sponsoring modernism in the arts. Those with money, he supposed, might take courses from those with more talent than money. Hard-pressed artists in the city would thus find support, while at the same time a new audience for artistic modernism would be nourished in the city.[23]

In the late 1920s and early 1930s, the New School became a major center of modernist experimentation. Not the least of its contributions was its new and self-consciously modern building on West 12th Street, completed in 1931. It was designed to provide studio and performance spaces for the arts, where some of the most important experimental modern music and dance of the period were performed, as well as at the municipally supported Hunter College. At the New School, Paul Rosenfeld taught the first course in an American college on modern composition, while Waldo Frank taught the first on modern art. Lewis Mumford taught what was probably the first on modern architecture. During the 1930s, Roger Sessions, Aaron Copland, and Henry Cowell (John Cage's teacher) presented courses on modern music and concerts featuring new music. There were also courses on photography by Berenice Abbott; on modern dance by John Martin, Doris Humphrey, and Martha Graham; and on art by Leo Stein (Gertrude's brother) and Meyer Schapiro. It was at the New School—and not at Columbia—that the young artists of radical inclinations who later became Abstract Expressionists came into contact with Schapiro, who helped them legitimate abstract art in both art-historical and political terms.*[24]

While the creation of the University in Exile at the New School in 1933 reinvigorated the original social scientific thrust of the institution, it is striking that much of the most significant social science being done there in the 1930s bore an important relation to the visual culture being supported by the school's art program. One thinks, for example, of the development of the field of Gestalt psychology and the brilliantly

* Robert Motherwell, who studied formally with Schapiro at Columbia, is a notable exception to this statement.

innovative studies of Rudolph Arnheim in the psychology of visual perception.

Government patronage, returning to the city's cultural life for the first time since the collapse a century before of the New York Institution for Scientific and Learned Societies, helped shape the institutional context of art and intellect. If the earlier experiment in patronage had failed to stimulate the development of a democratic and metropolitan culture in New York, the 1930s witnessed far more success. Government policy demonstrably democratized and significantly enhanced culture, thus contributing to the making of New York into an international capital of culture.

We easily recall that various postwar notables, particularly among painters, were indebted to their WPA experience for their later success, but it has been harder to appraise and assimilate the democratic implications of the government cultural policies of the 1930s. Still one encounters, as one has throughout the city's intellectual history, a persistent motif: the impulse to democratize or popularize art is assumed to be at the expense of excellence. Certainly art in the thirties was at times corrupted by both Popular Fronters and government patrons, to say nothing of private patrons and ordinary commercial values. But there is more to be said, and the establishment of City Center, which became the home of the New York City Ballet, offers one way to say it. If we acknowledge the degree to which this preeminent postwar cultural institution originated in the visions of cultural democracy of the LaGuardia years, we better understand both the thirties and the New York City Ballet.

The WPA music program suggested to Mayor Fiorello LaGuardia that there was a popular audience for good music, if ticket prices were kept low. Hence his dream of a municipally sponsored City Center of Music and Drama. He envisioned a "cultural reawakening" that would sustain a "civic" and "artistic life" similar to that of "cities on the continent." But his scheme was distinctively American and aggressively democratic: "good music and popular prices."[25] In pursuit of this ideal, theaters, sometimes commercial houses, sometimes high school auditoriums, were rented by the city for such performances.

In the early 1940s, however, Newbold Morris, president of the City Council and a political confidante of LaGuardia's, recognized a unique opportunity to institutionalize the idea. In 1941, the city had foreclosed on the Mecca Temple on 55th Street for tax arrears. While some of his colleagues on the Board of Estimate were anxious to convert it into a parking lot, Morris conceived the idea of turning the building over to a non-profit cultural organization created by the city. Except for the building, the proposed City Center would be self-supporting. Understanding that for the center to be truly civic, it would have to rest on a broader base than conventional philanthropy, LaGuardia and Morris looked to the city's workers as well as to its elite. While a few wealthy patrons, particularly Mrs. Lytle Hull, Gerald Warburg, and Edward Guggenheim, gave generously, the financial support of the city's trade unions, through the purchase of subscriptions for their members, was equally important: David Dubinsky's International Ladies Garment Workers, Sidney Hillman's Amalgamated Clothing Workers, and Adolph Held's Workingmen's Circle.[26]

City Center opened December 11, 1943, with Leopold Stokowsky conducting, at LaGuardia's personal request and without compensation. Before it opened, LaGuardia had committed the Center to both "high standards" and special 5:30 p.m. performances that would be more convenient for "working people," and on opening night he reiterated that City Center offered New Yorkers the "opportunity of hearing the best at prices they can afford." As Lincoln Kirstein later phrased it, City Center combined "populist service and aristocratic quality."[27]

LaGuardia, who prompted the creation of the New York City Opera by asking the whereabouts of "opera for the people," had died a few months before the Ballet Society was brought under the protective umbrella of the City Center in 1948, and renamed the New York City Ballet. Had he still been mayor, this might not have happened. He had little appreciation of ballet; he did not like to see, as he put it, "American young men leaping around the stage in those white tights exhibiting their crotches."[28] But Morton Baum, the amateur musician, former alderman, and LaGuardia tax counsel appointed by the mayor to run City Center, saw, essentially by accident, a performance of Balanchine's and Kirstein's Ballet Society, and he immediately recognized that he was "in the presence of greatness."[29] He sought out Kirstein, proposing that the Ballet Society be made a public institution, with its home at City Center. In return for the stability this institutional base promised, Kirstein told Baum, the populist with, in Kirstein's words, a "ferocity for excellence," that he would develop for him and for New York the finest ballet company in the country. When Baum died in 1968, he knew that at City Center Kirstein and Balanchine had created the best ballet company in the world, and that through his own remarkable efforts prices were maintained at popular levels, even after the move to Lincoln Center in 1964.[30]

INTERNATIONAL MODERNISM

Before New York could become a world cultural capital, the issue that framed Florine Stettheimer's *Cathedrals of Art* had to be resolved: American art or art in America. All provincial cultures are presented with the problem of choice between metropolitan domination and parochialism. The great cultural accomplishment of the 1930s and 1940s was, finally, to transcend this dilemma that had haunted American culture from the beginning. What happened was partly accomplished in the realm of thought, art, and criticism, but it was also the result of a new configuration of power in the world, both political and economic. The collapse of European political, economic, and cultural life provided both an opportunity and, as many of New York's intellectuals saw it, a responsibility for international cultural leadership. "The conclusion forces itself," Clement Greenberg observed in 1948, much to his own surprise, "that the main premises of Western art have at last migrated to the United States, along with the center of gravity of industrial production and political power." [31]

When New York City became the most powerful and important city in the world in the 1940s, new cultural possibilities presented themselves. Older forms of nationalism in the arts now seemed unduly parochial, acceptable, perhaps, for the regional backwaters of America, but not for New York, the center of American internationalist political opinion since the failure of the League of Nations. [32]

The arrival of European artists and intellectuals—some, like Balanchine, coming before Fascism forced them from Europe, but most arriving in the late 1930s and early 1940s, after the fall of Paris to the Nazis —made New York the center of things in a way it had never been before. Europe was no longer over there; it was on Manhattan. Just as Paris had earlier become the world's capital by being "an accepting center of cosmopolitans," so "polyglot New York," as Thomas Hess observed in 1951, welcomed the internationalization of its cultural life "with enthusiasm." [33] With the political symbol of the city's new status, the modern United Nations building, rising on the East River, the novel experience of being at the center of world politics, economics, and culture emboldened the city's artists and intellectuals.

As early as 1941, John Peale Bishop declared that "without waiting for the outcome" of the war, "it is possible even now to say that the center of western culture is no longer in Europe. . . . Its immense responsibilities are ours." The task for American artists and intellectuals, he urged, was to locate themselves in the larger international world. Jackson Pollock, once the student of regionalist Thomas Hart Benton, had come by 1943 to take it for granted, as Clement Greenberg put it, "that any kind of American art that could not compete on equal terms with European art was not worth bothering with." Regionalism, a group of the city's self-consciously modern artists declared in the New York Times, cannot serve as the basis for New York's emergence as the "cultural center of the world." And a year later, in 1944, Pollock wrote:

The idea of an isolated American painting, so popular in this country during the thirties, seems absurd to me, just as the idea of creating a purely American mathematics or physics would seem absurd. . . . An American is an American and his painting would naturally be qualified by that fact, whether he wills it or not. But the basic problems of contemporary painting are independent of any one country.

It was, as Arthur Danto has recently recalled, "as though one could no longer simply be an American painter: one painted to the world or not at all."[34]

Speaking in 1945, on the subject of Europe's collapse and the immigration of many notable European composers to the United States, Roger Sessions argued that the old contrast between "native American" art and "European" art had been rendered moot by events. Americans, he urged, must dispense with both of these crutches; they will have to orient their work to an international scale that they will themselves largely make.[35]

Lincoln Kirstein's Ballet Caravan (1936–1940) had created such nationalist works as *Pocahontas, Yankee Clipper, Filling Station,* and *Billy the Kid* during Balanchine's sojourn in Hollywood. But in 1946, in the founding announcement of the Ballet Society, which he organized with Balanchine, he declared that it was appropriate neither to revive classic European ballets in America nor to create "works based on national themes." "Now, with the close of the second world war, broader directions are possible and desirable."[36] Two years later, when the New York City Ballet was formed, Kirstein associated this new international aesthetic particularly with New York City. Summing up the aspirations of Balanchine, Baum, and himself, he reflected that the new ballet company represented "one city in its immediacy rather than remotely personifying a nation." We were, he remarked, "not Americans in general, but specifically New Yorkers." At about the same time, Clement Greenberg insisted that the American achievement of Pollock was in fact an urban achievement, expressing "the kind of life we live in our cities," specifically that district of New York "downtown, below 34th Street," where young artists living in "cold-water flats" were making the "future of American art." A decade before, Martha Graham had made the same point: "Modern Dance is couched in the rhythm of our time; it is urban and not pastoral."[37] Out of the experience of life in New York City emerged a new and modern aesthetic that belonged to the world as much as—even more than—to its host nation.

Instead of being a province of Paris, or even an imitator of Paris, New York in the 1940s became Paris. And the assimilation of the culture of Paris was crucially important for what happened in New York. The music, art, and dance that had been created in Paris from 1900 to the mid-1930s—unlike the increasingly nationalistic music of Germany or the intensely Russian Imperial Ballet at St. Petersburg—was of a mobile character, capable of extension and vernacular expression.

The most influential American musical modernists—a whole generation of leading composers, including Copland, Thomson, Carter, and Sessions—studied with the great Paris teacher of composition Nadia Boulanger. Boulanger made them into modernists without making them cease to be Americans. Whether North Americans, Latin Americans, or Asians, aspiring composers all flocked to her apartment at 36, rue Ballus, where she sought, as she said, to teach them "to be themselves," to be American or Japanese, but at the same time "to conform to the limits" of the international discipline.[38]

The rising and suffocating nationalism of the 1920s and 1930s, whether in politics or culture, worried Boulanger's students, who had a refreshingly generous understanding of the relation of modernism and nationalism. Roger Sessions, who worried the most about nationalism, wrote frequently of its dangers in *Modern Music* and elsewhere. Beginning with a strong attack on the Nazi cultural policies announced by Hitler's Minister of Propaganda, Joseph Goebbels, in 1933, Sessions also lamented the degeneration of German music, from "the voice of Europe's soul," in Nietzsche's phrase, to "mere *Vaterländerei.*" The lesson for Americans was quite clear, as he explained in an address to the American Musicological Society in 1937: "American leadership in music, therefore, can only grow on the basis of an attitude not dissimilar to that of the 'good European' of a century ago. It is a little strange that our cultural isolationists should not have thought their position through to the point of seeing that it is precisely cultural isolationism—the loss of the universal principle and the overglorification of, so to speak, the accident of locality —that has . . . come very near to destroying Europe." The music he called for would not begin with nationalist criteria; rather it would be generative. It would "reveal America to us, not as the mirror of things already discovered, but as a constantly renewed and fresh experience of the realities which music alone can reveal."[39]

Ballet at the beginning of this century was Russian, but Paris and, especially, New York de-Russified it. By the middle of the century, Balanchine, a Russian-trained choreographer working with American bodies and observing the ways Americans moved on the streets of New York as well as in the studio, internationalized ballet and made New York its world center.[40] An interlude in Paris, with its special freedom, helped make this possible. There, in Serge Diaghilev's Ballets Russes, the Romantic tradition of Russian ballet was loosened, if not revolutionized, allowing the young Balanchine to initiate the cycle of invention that would last for half a century.

Even before he left Russia, Balanchine had realized that modern ballet needed, as Kirstein later put it, "its own tempi, which were jazzy and syncopated." He grasped, too, that "asymmetrical rhythm was deep in the motor dynamism" of the twentieth century. Already in Paris in the summer of 1933, when Kirstein saw him, the young Russian was, as Elizabeth Kendall has written, melding "classical steps . . . with the flagrantly vernacular gestures and behavior of the Jazz Age." But New York was where twentieth-century modernity most fully expressed itself in streets, buildings, and social life, and immediately upon Balanchine's arrival in late 1933 *Modern Music* predicted that he would make a modern ballet out of "our rich disorganized stuff" of life.

By 1947, Edwin Denby could declare that "ballet in America has developed a standard of technique internationally valid and a [classical] style founded on characteristics by nature our own." Such "classicism" with an "American flavor" independent of "literary content," Denby concluded, possessed "novel and unique qualities which just now we are contributing to international ballet."[41] In dance and music, as in art, New York's modernist achievement dissolved, or seemed to dissolve, not only American provincialism but, as the other side of the same coin, the parochial and dangerous nationalism that had come to represent unacceptable limits on political and cultural freedom.

Architecture fits less comfortably into this discussion than do the other arts. Very little modern architecture was built during these decades of depression and war. There was very important American commentary, but it tended to reduce rather than enrich the international movement.* The MOMA show on "Modern Architecture" in 1932 was one of the most important architectural events of the century. In defining and popularizing the International Style, a phrase coined by Alfred Barr for the exhibition, MOMA achieved what was perhaps the most effective museum exhibit, as an educational venture, ever organized in New York. That show, and the book that resulted from it, Johnson's and Hitchcock's *The International Style* (1932), created the language of modern architecture. While much of that language is compatible with that of other arts, there are differences. They had less praise for freedom, particularly qualifying the asymmetrical and jazzy qualities so common in other arts. Much taken by the cool (and static) elegance of the work of Ludwig Mies Van der Rohe, making it their prescriptive standard, they were, particularly Johnson, quite patronizing to the rougher, more vital and freewheeling work of the only New York modernist represented in the show, Raymond Hood. They worried that his work was too commercial, failing

* Lewis Mumford's modernism provides an exception, but it was increasingly marginalized by the American modernists and, as we shall see, he stopped writing in the field with a blast at the much narrowed ideology of modernism.

to recognize that his commercial buildings, vertical rather than horizontal like the work they praised, gave a peculiarly American energy and rhythm to the international form and structure, with an emphasis on the exhibition of freedom and inventiveness.[42]

In all the arts, abstraction eclipsed narrative. Although it is true that Martha Graham produced a series of thematic modern dances, from *Frontier* (1935) to *Appalachian Spring* (1944), the thrust of her work was against story-telling, and her student Merce Cunningham reasserted this logic in the 1940s, rejecting story-lines and representation, becoming simply "a person moving in space."[43] Graham, too, later abandoned story dances, returning to her ideal of the 1930s: "My dancing is just dancing. It is not an attempt to interpret life in a literary sense. It is the affirmation of life through movement."[44] Others, too, tacked between stories and abstractions, but the general drift was clear. One thinks, for example, of Kirstein during the Ballet Caravan years, and of Copland, Carter, and Thomson, who composed music for Graham's and Kirstein's thematic ballets. But in general, the emphasis of the emerging international modernism, as Meyer Schapiro observed in connection with abstract painting, was on communion, not communication.[45]

It was a time of peculiar inarticulateness. Not only narrative and story, but the word itself, even the conventional public symbolism of architecture, were all devalued. Perhaps the horrors of Nazi and Stalinist ideology and the awful indescribability of the bomb account, in part, for this development. The appeal of Balanchine's plotless ballets may have been, as Denby suggested, their mute civility at a time when it had become hard to believe in the rhetoric of civilization.[46] At any event, the arts that did not require words flourished, while writing did not.[47]

Plotless ballets, as Balanchine explained, expressed with peculiar "intensity" the "accumulated results" of all the choreographer had "felt, thought, seen and done" and resulted in a "visual spectacle." There was no "story" to be apprehended, and it required no "verbal introduction or explanation." Or, as Arlene Croce has observed of Graham's performances of the 1940s: "movement expressed what no words could."[48] Similarly, for Mark Rothko and other Abstract Expressionists, the very inarticulateness of the canvas produced a communion, a mutual comprehension of something that could be neither spoken, nor named, nor represented.

In the criticism of the 1940s, whether one reads Edwin Denby and Lincoln Kirstein on dance, Virgil Thomson and Aaron Copland on music, or Clement Greenberg on art, certain key words, unrelated to theme or subject matter, repeat themselves: athleticism, rhythm, energy;

openness and clarity; freshness, nervousness, even coltishness.[49] All of these qualities (identified as American) emerge and are exploited within the international disciplines of music, dance, and painting. Here, not in the theme or story, was the living, contingent culture of America, or, more precisely, New York City. It was possible for this abstract internationalism to be American without self-consciousness, without referring to parochial American themes and places.

The masterword in the critical discourse of the era was freedom. This omnipresence deserves some explication, for it brings these art forms into the politics of the time. Reference to freedom ranged from discussions of the "graceful freedom" of Balanchine's ballerinas to the spontaneity of Pollock's paintings and Cage's musical compositions.[50] Whether or not artists or critics were themselves political, the critical discourse, both sophisticated and popular, emphasized freedom as the basic quality of American life and art. While there is a certain truth, of course, to this claim, especially in light of the contemporary world's experience with Fascism, the whole rhetoric of freedom made this postwar American international art and its creators—whether knowingly or not, whether willingly or not—collaborators in the making of the U.S. interpretation of the Cold War.

Much of the local and international appeal of American art was based on its identification with the ideology of freedom. One must be cautious and precise here. The achievements of American international modernism in music, dance, and painting were of the highest order and deserve to be counted among the major artistic achievements of the century. Yet there was another aspect to their postwar international ascendancy. American art, as the representative art of the "Free World," had an ideological as well as an aesthetic appeal. French art could not compete on either ground. The more "finished" paintings of French Abstract Expressionists had less appeal than the freer, rougher, more dynamic American examples, while the "games of chance" that were central to John Cage's method of composition were inevitably contrasted with the highly determined *sérialisme intégral* of Paris's Pierre Boulez.[51] When Meyer Schapiro commented on the interiorization of art, the tendency of modern painters (but also, incidentally, Martha Graham) to cultivate the "surest realms of freedom—the interior world of their fancies, sensations, and feelings, and the medium itself," he was surely being critical of modern society, even American society; but his rhetoric, with its apparent celebration of freedom as represented by American art, tended, in the context of the culture and politics of the time, to sustain the ideology of the Cold War.[52] Such understandings of American art tended to enhance and advance appreciation of American international modernism at home and abroad.

Because the political intellectuals ignored most of the visual and aural arts does not mean, then, that there was no politics in them. It is true that there was little overt political ideology, for which we can, I think, be thankful. It is the case, moreover, that artists and intellectuals associated with music, dance, and painting followed the same path from political commitment to political independence that was trod by the "New York Intellectuals." Yet there was more political significance in this new artistic achievement in the city than met the eye of the "New York Intellectuals." If dance, for example, seemed too far from ideology for Irving Howe and made him nervous about both his politics and his aesthetics, it was because the "New York Intellectuals" of his generation were so terribly inexperienced with the culture of the eye and the ear.[53] None but Howe and Kazin, and even they very little at best, dared to approach this wider world of the city's culture. Perhaps it is time for intellectuals in New York to bring the word, the image, and the sound into a common discourse of culture and politics.

Surely there are political implications to the way dance (or other non-verbal arts) heightens our respect for the human condition and its fate. It is politically important, if not, of course, sufficient, to clarify notions of pleasure, sensuousness, civility, and order, and to distinguish between that which is beautiful and that which is not. Because art is never independent of the historical conditions of its making, asking questions about the making of art and the making of audiences for art is certainly a primary task of intellectuals, a task of considerable political significance. It would be tragic if a large segment of New York's intellectuals continued to be mute before the rich aural and visual culture around them.

Here it is the example of the youngest of the "New York Intellectuals" that bears notice. However erratic her judgments of both politics and art, Susan Sontag has been attentive to the full spectrum of the city's culture in a way that distinguishes her from her elders. Or, among contemporary academics, we would do well to attend to the example of Arthur C. Danto, Johnsonian Professor of Philosophy at Columbia and, recently, the regular art critic at *The Nation*. What is important about Danto is that his fine aesthetic sense is broadened and deepened by his philosophical learning, thus giving a larger significance to his art criticism, particularly in its relation to public culture.

Yet Sontag and Danto are today anomalies; the worlds of the book and the image still remain largely isolated from each other. The best criticism for a general audience published in New York over the past decade or so has been neither political nor literary in nature; rather, it has concerned the cultures of the eye and ear—Arlene Croce in dance, Ada Louise Huxtable in architecture, and Janet Malcolm in photography. And yet, though often scintillating and always important, this criticism has failed to engage the world. It has not brought to these arts the broad humanistic and political perspective that Lewis Mumford, most notably, brought to art and architectural criticism in the 1930s, 1940s, and 1950s.[54]

Mumford, however, was not able to continue or to pass on the torch. He found himself at odds with both the "New York Intellectuals" and the "Civic Intellectuals"—and essentially for the same reason: he retained the notions of cultural nationalism of the *Seven Arts* circle long after they had been rejected both by the *Partisan Review*'s literary intellectuals, themselves so anxiously modernist and Europe-struck, and by the international modernists of dance, music, art, and architecture. By the time he achieved his greatest fame, in the early 1960s, Mumford had become increasingly uneasy with international modernism and had lapsed into almost pathological pessimism in the aftermath of the war and, especially, the bomb. He stood alone, with no successor.* Distressed by the architectural developments he had to cover, he gave up his column in *The New Yorker* in December 1963; since then the territory of both political and cultural criticism has shrunk terribly.[55] Such is the legacy of the great schism of the 1930s—not that between Trotskyists and Stalinists, about which we have heard so much, but between the book people and the eye-and-ear people.

EPILOGUE

It is unclear at present whether New York will be able to sustain itself as a metropolis and remain central as a city to American intellectual and artistic life. Political discourse in the city has been reduced to a mayoral monologue, while the emphasis in the city's cultural life has shifted away from the production of art and ideas to their consumption as fashion. Such an elevation of cultural consumption has profound implications for the meaning of the city as a center of intellectual and artistic life. It threatens to turn the metropolis into a museum of its own culture.

The social foundation for such a transformation of metropolitanism might plausibly be identified as the highly (if not necessarily well) educated and well-paid young men and women, specialists in finance, communications, and the law, who are migrating to the city. Innocent of the diversity and chaos of artistic production in a metropolis, they appreciate instead certified artistic products. They thus provide support for those corporate and public policies that privilege opportunities for the consumption of culture, reducing it to fashion. All of this today is at the

---

* Compare the concluding section of *The Culture of Cities* (1938), where Mumford exudes an almost utopian optimism, with the closing part of *The City in History*, where he elaborates on our contemporary and future city life as "Necropolis."

expense of a serious concern for the conditions (e.g., affordable rents) that make a community of intellectual and artistic producers possible.

The metropolitan ideal suffers in our time in yet another important respect. It was deeply damaged in the 1960s, when, as Saul Bellow has complained, the universities, flush with money, bought up not only intellectuals and writers, but painters, choreographers, and composers as well.[56] This national development not only decentralized and provided regular salaries for literary and artistic talent but also academicized their work in subtle and insidious ways that weakened its association with the more open culture of cities. The principal categories of our intellectual and artistic life became academic rather than urban, something most clearly evident in literary criticism, but apparent as well in much self-consciously post-modernist writing, painting, dance, and architecture.

A persistently worrisome tendency in our intellectual life has become, it seems, the dominant mode. A fruitful tension between academic and civic or literary culture has been largely abolished by rich, arrogant, and deadening universities that have since become poorer, but no less problematical.

A few briefly recounted examples may illuminate this academic enclosure and diminution of intellectual life in the city. During the 1940s, to take a key case, Lionel Trilling thrived at the intersection of the university and the city's literary culture. His friend William Barrett, the NYU philosopher, remarked to Trilling in 1948 that it was possible for him to devote himself to "university teaching without academicism" because he was "living in N.Y."[57] The cosmopolitan and metropolitan sensibility that Barrett thus praised is manifest in *The Liberal Imagination* (1950). In the 1960s, however, Trilling seems to have retreated to the academy. No longer reaching out from literature to society, his most notable essays in *Beyond Culture* (1965) increasingly substituted psychology for society and, more revealing yet, worried about the problems of teaching modern literature in the university, not about the conditions of its making, past or present. At the same time, Diana Trilling, who in the 1940s had been a regular and wonderfully wide-ranging reviewer of books for *The Nation*, seemed also to privilege the university, though she was not herself an academic. In her *Claremont Essays* (1964), most notably in her account of Allen Ginsberg's reading at Columbia in 1958, she reduced the intellectual life of the city, even the nation, to the culture of Morningside Heights. "The Other Night at Columbia: A Report from the Academy" is remarkable for its sense of the stakes involved: the academy, not the independent intellectual life of the city, had won the authority to bestow cultural standing upon an avant-garde poet. Finally, for a somewhat different but equally important case, Meyer Schapiro, the Columbia art historian who lived in the Village and was a colleague of the downtown artists in the 1930s and 1940s, became in the 1950s and 1960s a distinctively academic presence in the artistic life of New York. Revered for his awesome learning, he was increasingly identified with the academy rather than with the neighborhood he still shared with the city's artists.[58]

The encroaching and, ultimately, fatal parochialism of the city's academics combined with larger processes of intellectual decentralization to enhance the role of universities in our intellectual life, even while isolating them and undermining their historical—and fruitful—association with metropolitan culture. "The sad fact," remarks Lionel Abel in his recent autobiography, "is that New York City . . . is today almost as bankrupt intellectually as are the provincial cities of this country, for ideas no longer hit the center of city life, but go directly to the campuses, where they are academicized."[59]

This academicization of intellectual and artistic life has terribly reduced the range and significance of art and ideas, if not of technical knowledge and artistic technique, in our society. The promise of metropolitan culture, the natural locale of general cultural and political ideas, has been a victim of these developments. If cities need universities, so the academy, if it is to avoid the fate of the dinosaur, desperately needs the intellectual, artistic, and political provocations of a vibrant metropolitan culture.

The city's cultural resources today are vastly greater than they were in 1750, when William Livingston and his friends made the first concerted effort to create city culture in New York. Yet, as then, the promise remains unfulfilled. If one can demonstrate the existence of an intellectual tradition of unsuspected richness and significance in New York City, it is hardly an unambiguous story of triumph. Achievements there surely are, but one cannot miss the persistent pattern of retreat and the chronic pattern of movements falling short of democratic aspiration. What has eluded New York City—and still eludes it—is the creation of a vital public culture, harmoniously integrating civic, literary, and academic elements.

If the metropolitan intellect of our time and beyond is to engage the full possibilities of the city and culture, it must embrace the image and the sound as well as the word. And it must be broad in its social foundations. In a city that has always been a receiver of peoples and cultures, we surely want a public culture that is at once democratic, inclusive, and committed to forms of excellence in principle and in practice.

NOTES

PREFACE

1. Thomas Bender, "The Cultures of Intellectual Life: The City and the Professions," in John Higham and Paul K. Conkin, eds., *New Directions in American Intellectual History* (Baltimore: The Johns Hopkins University Press, 1979), pp. 181–95.

2. Thomas Bender, "The End of the City?" *democracy*, 3 (January 1983), 8–20.

3. See my various formulations of the historian's relation to civic renovation: "Making History Whole Again," *New York Times Book Review* (October 6, 1985), 1, 42–43; "The New History—Then and Now," *Reviews in American History*, 12 (1984), 612–22; "Wholes and Parts: The Need for Synthesis in American History," *Journal of American History*, 73 (June 1986), 120–36; "The Historian and Public Life: The Case of Charles A. Beard and the City," in my *History and Public Culture*, forthcoming.

PROLOGUE

1. Adam Ferguson, *An Essay on the History of Civil Society* (3rd ed.; London: A. Millar and T. Cadell, 1768), pp. 304–05, 306–12, 296, 362.

2. The first two examples require no specific citation. For the third, see Colin Campbell, "Tenure Denial of Noted Sociologist Stirs Troubling Queries at Harvard," *New York Times*, April 21, 1985.

3. In developing the notion of the sort of conversation described here, I have been influenced by Clifford Geertz, *Local Knowledge* (New York: Basic Books, 1983), pp. 147–63; Michael Oakeshott, "The Voice of Poetry in the Conversation of Mankind," in his *Rationalism in Politics* (London: Methuen, 1962), pp. 197–247; Richard Rorty, *Philosophy and the Mirror of Nature* (Princeton: Princeton University Press, 1979).

CHAPTER 1

1. Peter Gay, *The Enlightenment: The Rise of Modern Paganism* (New York: Vintage, 1966), p. 14. For the connection between towns and Enlightenment thought in eigh-

teenth-century France, see the excellent study by Daniel Roche, *Le Siècle des lumière en province académies et académiciens provinciaux, 1680–1789* (2 vols.; Paris and The Hague: Mouton). For a comment almost identical to Gay's, see *ibid.*, I, 75.

2. J. J. Rousseau, *A Discourse* [1751] (London: G. Burnet, 1760).

3. David Hume, *The Life of David Hume* (London: W. Strahan, 1777), p. 16.

4. William Dunlap, *The Diary of William Dunlap*, ed. Dorothy Barck (3 vols.; New York: New-York Historical Society, 1930), I, 336.

5. See Roche, *Le Siècle des lumière en province.* For the earlier period, see Robert Mandrou, *From Humanism to Science, 1480–1700* (New York: Penguin, 1978).

6. Margaret Jacob, *The Radical Enlightenment* (London: Allen & Unwin, 1981).

7. On London, see Dorothy Marshall, *Dr. Johnson's London* (New York: Wiley, 1968), chap. 6; Lewis Coser, *Men of Ideas* (New York: Free Press, 1965), chap. 3. On Edinburgh, see N. T. Phillipson and Rosalind Mitchison, eds., *Scotland in the Age of Improvement* (Edinburgh: Edinburgh University Press, 1970), especially the essay by John Clive, "The Social Background of the Scottish Renaissance," pp. 225–44; N. T. Phillipson, "Culture and Society in the 18th Century Province: The Case of Edinburgh and the Scottish Enlightenment," in Lawrence Stone, ed., *The University in Society* (2 vols.; Princeton: Princeton University Press, 1974), II, 407–48; Henry G. Graham, *Scottish Men of Letters in the Eighteenth Century* (London: Adam and Charles Black, 1901). For Scottish-American comparisons and linkages, see John Clive and Bernard Bailyn, "England's Cultural Provinces: Scotland and America," *William and Mary Quarterly*, 11 (1954), 200–13.

8. See Peter Borsay, "The English Urban Renaissance: the Development of Provincial Urban Culture, c. 1680–c. 1760," *Social History*, 5 (May 1977), 581–603. See also Roche, *Le Siècle des lumière en province;* and Phillipson and Mitchison, eds., *Scotland in the Age of Improvement.*

9. G. C. D. Odell, *Annals of the New York Stage* (14 vols.; New York: Columbia University Press, 1927–49), I, 50.

10. On Trinity, see Norval White and Elliot Willensky, *AIA Guide to New York City* (New York: Collier, 1978), p. 18; on St. Paul's, see John Tauranac, *Essential New York* (New York: Holt, Rinehart and Winston, 1979), p. 1.

11. Quoted in Austin Keep, *History of the New York Society Library* (New York: De Vinne Press, 1908), p. 54.

12. William Smith, Jr., *The History of the Province of New-York*, ed. Michael Kammen (2 vols.; Cambridge: Harvard University Press, 1972), I, 227.

13. *New York Weekly Journal*, February 12, 1748/49, quoted in David C. Humphrey, *From King's College to Columbia, 1746–1800* (New York: Columbia University Press, 1976), p. 38.

14. Brooke Hindle, *The Pursuit of Science in Revolutionary America, 1735–1789* (Chapel Hill: University of North Carolina Press, 1956), pp. 40–48; Raymond P. Stearns, *Science in the British Colonies* (Urbana: University of Illinois Press, 1970), pp. 560–75. Stearns is less sure than is Hindle of the negative or limiting influence of New York City.

15. For Colden's suggestion, see *Letters and Papers of Cadwallader Colden, Collections of the New-York Historical Society*, 50 (1918), 272.

16. Quoted in Michael Kammen, *Colonial New York: A History* (New York: Scribner's, 1975), p. 242.

17. Andrew Burnaby, *Travels Through the Middle Settlements in North America in the Years 1759 and 1760* (New York: A. Wessels, 1904), p. 116.

18. Unless otherwise noted, brief quotes and the information upon which this interpretation is based are taken from Milton M. Klein, "The American

Whig: William Livingston of New York" (Ph.D. dissertation, Columbia University, 1954).

19. William Livingston to Noah Welles, November 14, 1743, Johnson Family Papers, Yale University, microfilm copies at Columbia University (hereafter cited as Livingston-Welles Correspondence); [William Livingston,] *Some Serious Thoughts on the Design of Erecting a College in the Province of New York . . . by Happonates Mithridate* (New York, 1749), p. 3.

20. William Livingston to Noah Welles, December 7, 1754, Livingston-Welles Correspondence.

21. Quoted in Klein, "The American Whig," p. 293.

22. [Livingston,] *Some Serious Thoughts*, p. 3.

23. William Livingston to Noah Welles, October 6, 1745, Livingston-Welles Correspondence. Those aware of his very youthful fatherhood and secret marriage may ask whether he too was one of the libertines he criticizes. One can make this claim only if one cannot distinguish between what seems to have been romantic love and libertinism.

24. [Livingston,] *Some Serious Thoughts*, p. 1.

25. See Milton M. Klein, "The Rise of the New York Bar: William Livingston," *William and Mary Quarterly*, 15 (1958), 334 ff.

26. Quoted in Clive and Bailyn, "England's Cultural Provinces," p. 204.

27. Milton M. Klein, *Politics of Diversity: Essays in the History of Colonial New York* (Port Washington: Kennikat Press, 1974), p. 100.

28. Smith, *History*, I, 226.

29. John W. Francis, *Old New York* (New York: Samuel Francis, 1858, reprint, 1866), p. 288.

30. William Livingston to Noah Welles, January 5, 1749/50, Livingston-Welles Correspondence.

31. Klein, "The American Whig," p. 117.

32. William Livingston to Noah Welles, February 18, 1748/49, Livingston-Welles Correspondence. For Addison in London, see Terry Eagleton, *The Function of Criticism* (London: Verso, 1984), esp. pp. 9–27.

33. Phrase "liberal Education" quoted in Klein, *Politics of Diversity*, p. 100; [Livingston,] *Some Serious Thoughts*, p. 2.

34. *Independent Reflector*, ed. Milton Klein (Cambridge: Harvard University Press, 1963), p. 193.

35. [Livingston,] *Some Serious Thoughts*, pp. 2–3.

36. *Independent Reflector*, ed. Klein, p. 172.

37. For informative histories, see Keep, *History of the New York Society Library;* Humphreys, *From King's College to Columbia*.

38. Smith, *History*, II, 150.

39. Keep, *History of the New York Society Library*, pp. 145–46.

40. Carl Bridenbaugh, *Cities in Revolt: Urban Life in America, 1743–1776* (New York: Capricorn Books, 1964), p. 182.

41. Smith, *History*, II, 150.

42. Klein, "The American Whig," pp. 219–20.

43. Keep, *History of the New York Society Library*, pp. 161–62.

44. Quoted in Lawrence Cremin, *American Education: The Colonial Experience* (New York: Harper & Row, 1970), p. 405.

45. *New York Evening Post*, November 28, 1748.

46. See Samuel Johnson to Cadwallader Colden, April 15, 1757, quoted in I. N. P. Stokes, *The Iconography of Manhattan Island, 1498–1909* (6 vols.; New York: Robert H. Dodd, 1915–28; reprint edition, New York: Arno Press, 1967), IV, 602.

47. Cadwallader Colden to Benjamin Franklin, November 1749, in Leonard W. Larrabee, ed., *The Papers of Benjamin Franklin* (New Haven: Yale University Press, 1959–), III, 431. For other arguments for a non-urban location, with proposals for suburban Oyster Bay and Rye as sites, see *New York Evening Post*, May 18, 1747; August 17, 1747; January 9, 1748/49.

48. William Smith, *Some Thoughts on Education: with Reasons for Erecting a College in this Province, and Fixing the Same at the City of New-York . . .* (New York: James Parker, 1752), pp. 8–11.

49. *Independent Reflector*, ed. Klein, p. 171.

50. Quoted in Stokes, *Iconography*, IV, 655.

51. William Livingston to Noah Welles, February 1753, Livingston-Welles Correspondence.

52. *Independent Reflector*, ed. Klein, pp. 182, 176.

53. See Thomas J. Wertenbaker, *The Golden Age of Colonial Culture* (New York: New York University Press, 1942), p. 60.

54. See Joseph Ellis, *The New England Mind in Transition: Samuel Johnson of Connecticut, 1696–1772* (New Haven: Yale University Press, 1973), p. 198; Donald Gerardi, "The King's College Controversy, 1753–1756, and the Ideological Origins of Toryism in New York," *Perspectives in American History*, 11 (1977–78), 164.

55. See Stokes, *Iconography*, IV, 631, 649.

56. Gerardi, "The King's College Controversy," p. 168.

57. William Livingston to Noah Welles, December 7, 1754, Livingston-Welles Correspondence.

58. William Livingston to Noah Welles, February 1753, *ibid.*

59. *Independent Reflector*, ed. Klein, pp. 194–95.

60. [Benjamin Nicoll,] *A Brief Vindication of the Proceedings of the Trustees Relating to the College* (New York: H. Gaine, 1754), p. 5.

61. Quoted in Ellis, *New England Mind in Transition*, p. 195.

62. William Livingston to Noah Welles, December 7, 1754, Livingston-Welles Correspondence. On the charter they proposed, see Jürgen Herbst; *From Crisis to Crisis: American College Government, 1636–1819* (Cambridge: Harvard University Press, 1982), pp. 108–09.

63. Brander Matthews, ed., *A History of Columbia University, 1754–1904* (New York: Columbia University Press, 1904), pp. 9–10.

64. Later, between 1770 and 1820, King's/Columbia turned severely inward, becoming an isolated island of Episcopalianism in the city.

65. See Humphrey, *From King's College to Columbia*, chap. 5.

66. *Ibid.*, p. 91.

67. *Independent Reflector*, ed. Klein, p. 172.

68. See Cremin, *American Education*, p. 407; Louis B. Wright, *The Cultural Life of the American Colonies, 1607–1783* (New York: Harper, 1957), p. 123. On the architectural points, see Paul V. Turner, *Campus* (Cambridge: MIT Press, 1984), p. 2.

69. Samuel L. Mitchill, *A Discourse on the Life and Character of Samuel Bard* (New York: D. Fanshaw, 1821), p. 20.

70. Samuel Bard, *A Discourse upon the Duties of a Physician* [1769] (New York: C. S. Van Winkle, 1819), p. 16.

71. Eric Larrabee, *The Benevolent and Necessary Institution: The New York Hospital, 1771–1971* (Garden City, N.Y.: Doubleday, 1971), p. 2.

72. For more on this, see Thomas Bender, "The Cultures of Intellectual Life: The City and the Professions," in John Higham and Paul Conkin, eds., *New Directions in*

American Intellectual History (Baltimore: Johns Hopkins University Press, 1979), pp. 183–84.

73. See, for example, David Hosack, *Memoir of De Witt Clinton* (New York: J. Seymour, 1829), p. 510; Mitchill, *Bard,* p. 20.

74. For a judgment, a rather high one, on the quality of doctors and lawyers, see Noah Webster, "General Description of the City of New York," *American Magazine,* 1 (March 1788), 227.

75. J. P. Brissot de Warville, *New Travels in the United States of America* [1788], trans. Durand Echeverria and Mara Soceanu Vamos (Cambridge: Harvard University Press, 1964), p. 146.

76. Humphrey, *From King's College to Columbia,* p. 38.

77. Webster, "General Description of New York," p. 227.

78. See Ralph Taft Heymsfeld, "Literary Societies and Associations in New York City, 1790–1830," unpublished essay, 1926, Misc. Mss. Prize Essays, Box 2, New-York Historical Society; G. Adolph Koch, "Literary Societies in the City of New York, from 1770–1830," unpublished prize essay, Misc. Mss. Prize Essays, Box 2, New-York Historical Society.

79. Henry F. May, *The Enlightenment in America* (New York: Oxford University Press, 1976), pp. 233-34. See also George G. Raddin, Jr., *Hocquet Caritat and the Early New York Literary Scene* (Dover, N.J.: The Dover Advance Press, 1953), p. 4.

80. William Dunlap, *History of the Rise and Progress of the Arts of Design in the United States* (2 vols.; New York: Dover Press, 1969, orig. 1834), I, 267.

81. Henry Adams, *The United States in 1800* (Ithaca: Cornell University Press, 1955, orig. 1889), p. 79.

82. James E. Cronin, ed., *The Diary of Elihu Hubbard Smith (1771–1798)* (Philadelphia: American Philosophical Society, 1973), p. 55.

83. James Cronin, "Elihu Hubbard Smith and the New York Friendly Club, 1795–1798," *Publications of the Modern Language Association,* 64 (June 1949), 472.

84. Cronin, ed., *Smith Diary,* pp. 154, 158, 160.

85. Quoted in Raddin, *Hocquet Caritat,* p. 52.

86. Cronin, ed., *Smith Diary,* p. 326.

87. *Ibid.,* p. 355.

88. On Webster's editorship, see William A. Duer, *New York as It Was During the Latter Part of the Last Century* (New York: Stamford & Swords, 1849), p. 46.

89. Frank Luther Mott, *A History of American Magazines, 1741–1850* (Cambridge: Harvard University Press, 1966), I, 194, 200. On subscribers, see David Nord, "A Republican Literature: A Study of Magazine Reading and Readers in Late Eighteenth Century New York (unpub. ms., Indiana University, 1986).

90. *New York Magazine* (April 1790), 195, 197.

91. Cronin, ed., *Smith Diary,* p. 359.

92. On this matter, see the fine study by Joseph Ellis, *After the Revolution: Profiles of Early American Culture* (New York: Norton, 1979).

93. Cronin, ed., *Smith Diary,* p. 77.

94. *Ibid.,* p. 78.

95. *Ibid.,* pp. 126–27.

96. *Ibid.,* p. 299.

97. Jedidiah Morse, *The American Geography* (2nd ed.; London: John Stockdale, 1792), pp. 252, 257.

98. Cronin, ed., *Smith Diary,* p. 230.

99. Gilbert Chinard, "A Landmark in American Intellectual History: Samuel Mill-

er's A Brief Retrospect of the Eighteenth Century," *Princeton University Library Chronicle*, 14 (1953), 59.

100. Cronin, ed., *Smith Diary*, p. 353.

101. *Ibid.*, p. 438.

102. Raddin, *Hocquet Caritat*, pp. 41–47.

103. Merle Curti, *American Paradox* (New Brunswick: Rutgers University Press, 1956), p. 11. On other provincial cities, see Robert Emerson, "The Enlightenment and Social Structures," in Paul Fritz and David Williams, eds., *City & Society in the 18th Century* (Toronto: Hakkert, 1973), pp. 99–124.

104. Quoted in Mott, *History of American Magazines*, I, 193.

105. Maria Morelove, Letter to Editor, *New York Magazine*, 1 (1790), 9.

106. See Linda Kerber, *Women of the Republic: Intellect and Ideology in Revolutionary America* (Chapel Hill: University of North Carolina Press, 1980), p. 241.

107. See Carolyn C. Lougee, *Le Paradis des Femmes: Women, Salons, and Social Stratification in Seventeenth Century France* (Princeton: Princeton University Press, 1976).

108. William Smith, *A General Idea of the College of Mirania . . .* (New York: J. Parker & W. Weyman, 1753), p. 19.

109. *Independent Reflector*, ed. Klein, p. 172.

110. *Ibid.*, p. 194.

111. Cadwallader Colden, "An Introduction to the Study of Phylosophy wrote in America for the use of a young Gentleman," reprinted in Joseph Blau, ed., *American Philosophic Addresses, 1700–1900* (New York: Columbia University Press, 1946), p. 311.

112. Ellis, *After the Revolution*, p. xiv.

113. "Introductory Essay," *New York Magazine* (April 1790), 198.

114. "Preface," *New York Magazine* (December 1795).

115. Dunlap, *Diary*, I, 43.

116. Much the same point is made in respect to Dunlap by Ellis, *After the Revolution*, chap. 5.

117. M., "On the State of American Literature," *Monthly Magazine*, 1 (1799), 15–19.

118. Chinard, "Landmark," 55.

119. *Ibid.*, p. 58.

120. Samuel Miller, *The Life of Samuel Miller* (2 vols.; Philadelphia: Remsen & Haffelfinger, 1869), I, 128.

121. May, *The Enlightenment in America*, part IV.

122. Samuel Miller, *A Brief Retrospect of the Eighteenth Century . . . containing a Sketch of the Revolutions and Improvements in Science, Arts and Literature During that Period* (2 vols.; New York: T. & J. Swords, 1803), II, 295–97. Italics in original.

123. *Ibid.*, II, 256–59.

124. *Ibid.*, II, 357–58, 385.

125. *Ibid.*, II, 404–9.

CHAPTER 2

1. Edwin P. Kilroe, *Saint Tammany and the Origins of the Society of Tammany* (New York: n.p., 1913), pp. 119, 118, 132.

2. Alfred F. Young, *The Democratic-Republicans of New York: The Origins, 1763–1797* (Chapel Hill: University of North Carolina Press, 1967), pp. 398–99.

3. Kilroe, *Saint Tammany*, pp. 136, 138, 141.

4. Young, *Democratic-Republicans*, p. 203.

5. Quoted in Pamela Smit, "The New-York Historical Society Library: A History, 1804–1978" (Ph.D. dissertation, Columbia University, 1978), p. 1 n.

6. Quoted in *ibid.*, p. 7.

7. *New York Journal*, May 24, 1791.

8. Charles C. Sellers, *Mr. Peale's Museum: Charles Willson Peale and the First Popular Museum of Natural Science and Art* (New York: Norton, 1980), pp. 20, 52–53; Kilroe, *Saint Tammany*, p. 136.

9. Quoted in David L. Sterling, "New York Patriarch: A Life of John Pintard, 1759–1844" (Ph.D. dissertation, New York University, 1958), p. 121. Italics in original.

10. For insightful observations on this point, see Joseph Ellis, *After the Revolution: Profiles of Early American Culture* (New York: Norton, 1979), pp. 6–7 and *passim*.

11. Quoted in Sterling, "New York Patriarch," p. 94.

12. For the best brief biographical treatment, see Richard Harrison, *Princetonians, 1776–1783* (Princeton: Princeton University Press, 1981). For a full-length account, see Sterling, "New York Patriarch."

13. Dorothy Barck, ed., *Letters from John Pintard to His Daughter* (4 vols.; New York: New-York Historical Society, 1937–40), I, 47.

14. George W. Johnston, "John Pintard," typescript, New-York Historical Society, p. 6.

15. Barck, ed., *Pintard Letters*, I, 7.

16. *Ibid.*, I, 94; [Joseph Scoville,] *Old Merchants of New York* [1862] (4 vols.; New York: Thomas R. Knox, 1885), II, 237.

17. Barck, ed., *Pintard Letters*, IV, 26.

18. Quoted in Sterling, "New York Patriarch," p. 308.

19. Robert W. July, *The Essential New Yorker: Gulian Crommelin Verplanck* (Durham: Duke University Press, 1951), p. 43.

20. The standard biography of De Witt Clinton is Dorothy Bobbé, *De Witt Clinton* (New York: Minton, Balch, 1933). For his cultural activities, see Kenneth R. Nodyne, "The Role of De Witt Clinton and the Municipal Government in the Development of Cultural Organizations in New York City, 1803–1817" (Ph.D. dissertation, New York University, 1969).

21. See Richard B. Morris, *The Encyclopedia of American History* (rev. and updated; New York: Harper, 1965), p. 688.

22. Theodore Roosevelt, *New York* (London: Longmans, Green, 1891), p. 177.

23. [De Witt Clinton,] *An Account of Abimelech Coody and Other Celebrated Writers of New York* (New York: n.p., 1815), pp. 15–16.

24. Dixon Ryan Fox, *The Decline of Aristocracy in the Politics of New York* [1919] (New York: Harper Torchbook, 1965), p. 203.

25. David Hosack, *Memoir of De Witt Clinton* (New York: J. Seymour, 1829), pp. 34–35; James Renwick, *Discourse on the Character and Public Services of De Witt Clinton* (New York: G. & C. & H. Carvill, 1829), p. 24.

26. See Hosack, *Clinton*, p. x.

27. Gulian C. Verplanck, *An Address Delivered Before the Philolexian and Peithologian Societies . . . of Columbia College* (New York: G. & C. & H. Carvill, 1830), pp. 25–26; John W. Francis, *A Discourse Delivered Upon the Opening of the New Hall of the New-York Lyceum of Natural History* (New York: H. Ludwig, 1841), pp. 82–84.

28. This "Dinner and Supper List" is reproduced in Dixon Wecter, *The Saga of American Society* (New York: Charles Scribner's Sons, 1937), pp. 199–204.

29. Henry Adams, *The United States in 1800* [1889] (Ithaca: Cornell University Press, 1955), p. 83.

30. Stephen Elliott, *An Address to the Literary and Philosophical Society of South Carolina* (Charleston: W. P. Young, 1814), p. 3.

31. Albert O. Hirschman, *The Passions and the Interests* (Princeton: Princeton University Press, 1977), pp. 72ff.

32. Hosack, *Clinton*, pp. 87–89.

33. [Samuel L. Mitchill,] *The Picture of New York* (New York: I. Riley, 1807), p. vi.

34. See Robert G. Albion, *The Rise of New York Port, 1815–1860* (New York: Charles Scribner's Sons, 1939).

35. De Witt Clinton, Committee of Citizens, De Witt Clinton Papers, New-York Historical Society. For similar ideas from Pintard, see Johnston, "Pintard," p. 17.

36. De Witt Clinton, *Address to Columbia College Alumni* (New York: n.p., 1828), p. 15. For a similar statement by Pintard, see Barck, ed., *Pintard Letters*, III, 240.

37. Edward Lind Morse, ed., *Samuel F. B. Morse: His Letters and Journals* (2 vols.; Boston: Houghton Mifflin, 1914), I, 248–49.

38. See Eugene Exman, *The Brothers Harper* (New York: Harper & Row, 1965).

39. Federal Writers Project, *New York Panorama* (New York: Random House, 1938), p. 178.

40. John Bach McMaster, *History of the People of the United States* (New York: D. Appleton, 1883–1913), V, 269.

41. See Carter Goodrich, *Government Promotion of American Canals and Railroads, 1800–1890* (New York: Columbia University Press, 1960).

42. Bernard Fäy, "Learned Societies in Europe and America in the Eighteenth Century," *American Historical Review,* 37 (1932), 259; Margaret C. Jacob, *The Radical Enlightenment: Pantheists, Freemasons, and Republicans* (London: Allen & Unwin, 1981); and Dorothy Ann Lipson, *Freemasonry in Federalist Connecticut* (Princeton: Princeton University Press, 1977).

43. William Preston, *Illustrations of Masonry* [1772] (new ed.; London: G. & T. Wilkie, 1788), p. 11.

44. See Lipson, *Freemasonry;* Jacob, *Radical Enlightenment;* William Hutchinson, *The Spirit of Masonry* [1775] (New York: Bell Publishing Co., 1982). I have also benefited from several discussions with Dr. Allan Boudreau, Curator, Grand Lodge Library, New York City, August 1982.

45. James Hardie, *The New Free-Mason's Monitor; or Masonic Guide* (New York: George Long, 1818), p. 131. See also p. 187.

46. Ossian Lang, *History of Freemasonry in the State of New York* (New York: Grand Lodge, 1922), p. 91.

47. Hardie, *New Free-Mason's Monitor,* pp. vii, 127. See also Preston, *Illustrations of Masonry,* pp. 28, 17.

48. On the economy and this spirit, see Michael Kammen, " 'The Promised Sunshine of the Future': Reflections on Economic Growth and Social Change in Post-Revolutionary New York," in Manfred Jonas and Robert Wells, eds., *New Opportunities in a New Nation: The Development of New York After the Revolution* (Schenectady, N.Y.: Union College Press, 1982), pp. 111–12.

49. De Witt Clinton, *Address Delivered Before Holland Lodge* (New York: Francis Childs and John Swaine, 1794), p. 4.

50. *Ibid.,* p. 13.

51. Samuel L. Knapp, *A Discourse on the Life and Character of De Witt Clinton* (Washington: William Green, 1828), p. 26.

52. Samuel Miller, *A Discourse Delivered in the New Presbyterian Church, New York: Before the Grand Lodge of the State of New York* (New York: F. Childs, 1795), pp. 24–25. On these pedagogical assumptions, see Preston, *Illustrations of Masonry,* pp. 14–15.

53. For New York City, the strongest statement of this thesis is Raymond Mohl, *Poverty in New York, 1783–1825* (New York: Oxford University Press, 1971). The most sophisticated is David Rothman, *The Discovery of the Asylum* (Boston: Little, Brown, 1971), though for him, and this is important in connection with what I will argue, the social-control aspect becomes important only in the late 1820s.

54. For the earliest statement, see Clifford Griffin, *Their Brothers' Keepers: Moral Stewardship in the United States, 1800–1860* (New Brunswick: 1960). For the most sophisticated statement of these themes, see Lois Banner, "Religious Benevolence as Social Control: A Critique of an Interpretation," *Journal of American History*, 60 (1973), 23–41.

55. Generally, see Herbert G. Gutman, *Work, Culture and Society in Industrializing America* (New York: Knopf, 1976). For New York City, see the fine studies by Christine Stansell, *City of Women: Sex and Class in New York, 1789–1860* (New York: Knopf, 1986); and Sean Wilentz, *Chants Democratic: New York City and the Rise of the American Working Class* (New York: Oxford University Press, 1984).

56. Barck, ed., *Letters of Pintard*, I, 25–26.

57. *Ibid.*, II, 198–99.

58. George Templeton Strong, *Diary*, ed., Allan Nevins and Milton Halsey Thomas (4 vols.; New York: Macmillan Company, 1952), I, 56–57.

59. John Pintard to De Witt Clinton, August 28, 1812, American Academy of Fine Arts Papers, New-York Historical Society. Other historians have read Clinton's key word as "impudent." Admittedly, it is difficult to make out the crucial letters, but I think the word is *imprudent*. For another statement at this time on the need to concentrate the city's intellectual resources, see John Bristed, *An Oration on the Utility of Literary Establishments* (New York: Eastburn, Kirk, 1814).

60. New York City, *Minutes of the Common Council*, VII, 269–70.

61. *Ibid.*, VIII, 177–78.

62. *Ibid.*, VIII, 232–33.

63. *Ibid.*, VIII, 236; [Fitz-Greene Halleck,] *Fanny* [1821] (New York: Harper & Bros., 1839), stanza 68, p. 28.

64. New York City, *Minutes of the Common Council*, VIII, 515, 686; IX, 80; VIII, 681; IX, 615; X, 442; XIII, 4.

65. See, for example, Barck, ed., *Letters of Pintard*, I, 107; and, of course, the City Council Report already cited.

66. "Address of the New-York Historical Society to the Public [1805]," reprinted in R. W. G. Vail, *Knickerbocker Birthday: A Sesquicentennial History of the New-York Historical Society, 1804–1954* (New York: New-York Historical Society, 1954), pp. 452–56.

67. John Pintard to De Witt Clinton, August 28, 1812, American Academy of Fine Arts Papers, New-York Historical Society.

68. Brooke Hindle, "The Underside of the Learned Society in New York, 1754–1854," in Alexandra Oleson and Sanborn C. Brown, eds., *The Pursuit of Knowledge in the Early American Republic* (Baltimore: Johns Hopkins University Press, 1976), p. 101.

69. Printed circular, New York, January 26, 1814, interleaved in the Literary and Philosophical Society records, New-York Historical Society.

70. Literary and Philosophical Society, Minutes, February 13, 1814, New-York Historical Society.

71. *Ibid.*, February 27, 1814; April 13, 1830.

72. This is a summary of data in Nodyne, *De Witt Clinton*, p. 74.

73. De Witt Clinton, *Introductory Discourse Delivered Before the Literary and Philosophical Society of New-York* (New York: David Longworth, 1815), pp. 3–8.

74. *Ibid.*, pp. 19, 17.

75. *Ibid.*, pp. 14, 22, 13.

76. *Ibid.*, p. 20.

77. See *New York American*, December 22, 1819.

78. William Cullen Bryant, *A Discourse on the life, character, and writings of Gulian Crommelin Verplanck* (New York: New-York Historical Society, 1870), p. 13.

79. [Gulian Verplanck,] *The State Triumvirate* (New York: J. Seymour, 1819), pp. 120–22, 125.

80. See Herman L. Fairchild, *A History of the New York Academy of Sciences* (New York: by the author, 1887), p. 17; Bobbé, *Clinton*; July, *Essential New Yorker*.

81. *The Trial of Gulian C. Verplanck, Hugh Maxwell, and others for a Riot in Trinity Church . . . 1811* (New York: n.p., 1821), p. 27.

82. Clinton, *Account of . . . Coody*, pp. 13, 16. Italics in original.

83. Hosack, *Clinton*, p. 151.

84. Clinton, *Account of . . . Coody*, p. 12.

85. Quoted in Fox, *Decline of Aristocracy*, p. 204 n.

86. Fairchild, *History of the New York Academy of Sciences*, pp. 23–27.

87. Barck, ed., *Letters from John Pintard to His Daughter*, I, 66.

88. K., "New York Institution," *American Monthly Magazine*, 1 (1817), 272.

89. Christine C. Robbins, "John Torrey (1796–1873): His Life and Times," *Bulletin of the Torrey Botanical Club*, 95 (1968), 561.

90. John W. Francis, *Old New York; or, Reminiscences of the Past Sixty Years* [1858] (New York: Samuel Francis, 1866), p. 372.

91. See New York Lyceum, *Index of the Library* (1830); Nathan Reingold, "Definitions and Speculations: The Professionalization of Science in America in the Nineteenth Century," in Oleson and Brown, eds., *The Pursuit of Knowledge in the Early American Republic*, pp. 40–41.

92. See Nodyne, "Clinton," pp. 185–87; Jonathan Harris, "New York's First Scientific Body: The Literary and Philosophical Society, 1814–1834," *Annals of the New York Academy of Sciences*, 196 (1972), 329–37.

93. Quoted in Bobbé, *De Witt Clinton*, p. 220.

94. John Pintard to De Witt Clinton, August 28, 1812, American Academy of Fine Arts Papers, New-York Historical Society.

95. R. T. Heymsfeld, "The New York Atheneum," *New-York Historical Society Quarterly*, 11 (1927), 3.

96. "Report of William Gracie relating to the establishment of an Atheneum" (1824), New York City, Box 23, New-York Historical Society.

97. George W. Pierson, *Tocqueville and Beaumont in America* (New York: Oxford University Press, 1938), p. 84.

98. Henry Wheaton, *Address Pronounced at the Opening of the New York Atheneum* (New York: J. W. Palmer, 1825), pp. 24–25.

99. Robert Taft Heymsfeld, "Literary Societies and Associations in New York City, 1790–1830," pp. 98–99, unpublished prize essay, 1926, Misc. Mss., Prize Essays, New-York Historical Society.

100. New York Atheneum, Records, 1824–28, New-York Historical Society.

101. Quoted in Austin Keep, *History of the New York Society Library* (New York: De Vinne Press, 1908), p. 326.

102. Edward Pessen, *Riches, Class, and Power Before the Civil War* (Lexington, Mass.: D. C. Heath, 1973), esp. chap. 9; James Grant Wilson, ed., *The Memorial History of the City of New York* (4 vols.; New York: New-York History Company, 1892–93), III, 327; Thomas Bender, "Washington Square in the Growing City," in *Around the Square*, ed. Mindy Cantor (New York: New York University, 1982), pp. 30–39.

103. See Keep, *History of the New York Society Library*, p. 362.

104. See Martin Green, *The Problem of Boston* (New York: Norton, 1967); Peter Dobkin Hall, *The Organization of American Culture 1700–1900* (New York: New York University Press, 1982); Ronald Story, *The Forging of an Aristocracy: Harvard and the Boston Upper Class, 1800–1870* (Middletown, Conn.: Wesleyan University Press, 1980); E. Digby Baltzell, *Puritan Boston and Quaker Philadelphia* (New York: Free Press, 1979).

105. *Edinburgh Review* (January 1820), pp. 79–80.

106. John W. Francis, *An Inaugural Address Delivered Before the Academy of Medicine* (1848), p. 13.

107. Milton Halsey Thomas, "Mid-Nineteenth Century Life in New York: More Revelations from the Diary of George Templeton Strong," *New-York Historical Society Quarterly*, 37 (January 1953), 19.

108. See Arnold Thackray, "Natural Knowledge in Cultural Context: The Manchester Model," *American Historical Review*, 79 (1974), 672–709; Robert Kargon, *Science in Victorian Manchester* (Baltimore: Johns Hopkins University Press, 1977). For another intriguing comparison, it is worth considering the relative success of the Albany Institute and Albany Academy at this period (in 1820, Albany was the nation's fourth-largest city). For some discussion of this, see Thomas Bender, "Science and the Culture of American Communities: The Nineteenth Century," *History of Education Quarterly*, 16 (1976), 63–77.

109. *National Advocate*, March 2, 1818.

110. New York City, *Minutes of the Common Council*, XIX, 78.

111. See "A Mechanic," *New York American*, January 22, 1830.

112. William Charvat, *The Origins of American Critical Thought, 1810–1830* (Philadelphia: University of Pennsylvania Press, 1936), pp. 1, 2, 5.

113. On political and class relations, see Edward Countryman, *A People in Revolution* (Baltimore: Johns Hopkins University Press, 1981); Gary B. Nash, *The Urban Crucible* (Cambridge: Harvard University Press, 1979).

114. Howard B. Rock, *Artisans of the New Republic: The Tradesmen of New York in the Age of Jefferson* (New York: New York University Press, 1979), pp. 22–24. See also Young, *Democratic-Republicans*.

115. Thomas Earle and Charles T. Congdon, eds., *Annals of the General Society of Mechanics and Tradesmen* (New York: by the Society, 1882), pp. 10–11.

116. Rock, *Artisans of the New Republic*, p. 145 n.

117. *Ibid.*, p. 130.

118. [Scoville,] *Old Merchants of New York*, II, 235.

119. Rock, *Artisans of the New Republic*, pp. 165–68. Data on Mercein, Edmund Willis, "Social Origins of Political Leadership in New York City from the Revolution to 1815" (Ph.D. dissertation, University of California, Berkeley, 1967), p. 346.

120. Dan Schiller, *Objectivity and the News: The Public and the Rise of Commercial Journalism* (Philadelphia: University of Pennsylvania Press, 1981), chap. 1 and *passim*.

121. Sean Wilentz, "Artisan Republican Ritual and the Rise of Class Conflict in New York City, 1788–1837," in Michael Frisch and Daniel J. Walkowitz, eds., *Working Class America* (Urbana: University of Illinois Press, 1982), pp. 48, 53–65. See also Wilentz, *Chants Democratic*, pp. 35–42.

122. Barck, ed., *Pintard Letters*, I, 271.

123. I. N. P. Stokes, *The Iconography of Manhattan Island, 1498–1909* (6 vols.; New York: Robert H. Dodd, 1915–28; reprint edition, New York: Arno Press, 1967), V, 1637.

124. General Society of Mechanics and Tradesmen, *Charter* (1823), p. 12; General Society of Mechanics and Tradesmen, *Charter* (1839), p. 39.

125. Thomas R. Mercein, "An Address Delivered on the Opening of the Institution," in *Catalogue of the Apprentices' Library* . . . (New York: William A. Mercein, 1820), pp. 3, 4, 9.

126. *Ibid.*, p. 22; *Mechanic's Gazette*, May 17, 1823.

127. Thomas R. Mercein, *Remarks Made at the Request of the Mechanics Society, on Laying the Corner Stone of That Edifice* (New York: William A. Mercein, 1822), p. 24.

128. New York Mechanic and Scientific Institution, *Charter, Constitution & By-Laws* (1823), pp. 3, 4, 5–6.

129. Bruce Sinclair, *Philadelphia's Philosopher Mechanics: A History of the Franklin Institute, 1824–1865* (Baltimore: Johns Hopkins University Press, 1974), pp. 12–13.

130. *Report on a Plan for Extending & More Perfectly Establishing the Mechanic and Scientific Institution of New York* (New York: Daniel Fanshaw, 1824), p. 14.

131. Fairchild, *History of the New York Academy of Sciences*, pp. 29–30.

132. John H. Griscom, *Memoir of John Griscom* (New York: Robert Carter & Bros., 1859), pp. 52–55, 89, 98, 322.

133. John H. Griscom, *Discourse on the Importance of Character and Education in the United States* (New York: Mahlon Day, 1823), pp. 5, 6, 13, 8, 18.

134. M. M. Noah, *An Address Delivered Before the General Society of Mechanics and Tradesmen* (New York: William A. Mercein, 1822), p. 16.

135. The names of incorporators have been taken from the published constitution and bylaws of 1823 for the Mechanic and Scientific Institution, while the occupations are taken from *Longworth's City Directory* for the years 1816–17, 1822–23, 1832–33. The information on Lorillard is taken from Rock, *Artisans of the New Republic*, p. 104.

136. Stephen Allen, "The Memoirs of Stephen Allen, 1767–1852," ed. by James C. Travis (New York: typescript transcription, 1927), pp. 88, 111. At the New-York Historical Society.

137. See Wilentz, "Artisan Republican Ritual and the Rise of Class Conflict in New York City, 1788–1837," and Wilentz, *Chants Democratic*.

CHAPTER 3

1. *Journal of the Proceedings of a Convention of Literary and Scientific Gentlemen, held in the Common Council of the City of New York, October, 1830* (New York: G. & C. & H. Carvill, 1831), pp. 14, 140.

2. James M. Mathews, *Recollections of Persons and Events* (New York: Sheldon and Co., 1865), pp. 199–200.

3. [Jonathan Mayhew Wainwright,] *Considerations Upon the Expediency and Means of Establishing a University in the City of New York* (New York: Grattan, Printer, 1830), p. 13.

4. Paul O. Weinbaum, *Mobs and Demogogues: The New York Response to Collective Violence in the Early Nineteenth Century* (Ann Arbor: UMI Research Press, 1979), p. 13. More generally, see Sean Wilentz, *Chants Democratic: New York City and the Rise of the American Working Class* (New York: Oxford University Press, 1984).

5. Mathews, *Recollections*, p. 217; Dorothy Barck, ed., *Letters from John Pintard to His Daughter* (4 vols.; New York: New-York Historical Society, 1937–40), III, 240.

6. *Ibid.*, IV, 176. Joseph Green Cogswell, "On the Means of Education and the State of Learning in the United States of America," *Blackwood's Magazine*, 4 (1819), 550; John S. Whitehead, *The Separation of the College and State: Columbia, Dartmouth, Harvard, and Yale, 1776–1876* (New Haven: Yale University Press, 1973), pp. 30–31, 170. See also David C. Humphrey, *From King's College to Columbia, 1746–1800* (New York: Columbia University Press, 1976), p. 313.

7. Whitehead, *The Separation of the College and the State*, pp. 100–101.

8. *New York American*, March 24, 1819.

9. The minutes of this and other preliminary meetings held before the actual organization of the university are preserved in typescript in the NYU Archives.

10. [Wainwright,] *Considerations Upon the Expediency and Means of Establishing a University*, preface.

11. On his authorship, see Theodore F. Jones, *New York University, 1832–1932* (New York: New York University, 1933), p. 12. One crucial idea raised for the first time at the public meeting—use of the old Almshouse for the university—was incorporated into the pamphlet. See minutes of the meeting, NYU Archives.

12. [Wainwright,] *Considerations Upon the Expediency and Means of Establishing a University*, pp. 15, 7, 21, 6, 10–11, 7.

13. *Ibid.*, p. 14.

14. On the influence of Edinburgh, see J. B. Morrell, "Individualism and the Structure of British Science in 1830," in *Historical Studies in the Physical Sciences*, 3 (1971), 198–99. More generally, see H. H. Bellot, *The University College, London, 1826–1926* (London: University of London Press, 1929). On Edinburgh and its Genevan antecedents, see Sir Alexander Grant, *The Story of the University of Edinburgh* (2 vols.; London: Longmans, Green, 1884), I, 99–100, 126–27, 263.

15. [Wainwright,] *Considerations Upon the Expediency and Means of Establishing a University*, pp. 21, 9.

16. *Ibid.*, pp. 27, 24, 21.

17. Austin Keep, *History of the New York Society Library* (New York: De Vinne Press, 1908), pp. 376–77.

18. "A Mechanic," in *New York American*, January 22, 1830.

19. Thomas Earle and Charles T. Congdon, eds., *Annals of the General Society of Mechanics and Tradesmen* (New York: by order of the Society, 1882), pp. 85, 77. William C. Bryant II and T. G. Voss, eds., *The Letters of William Cullen Bryant* (New York: Fordham University Press, 1975), I, 287. See also *Mechanics Magazine*, I (1833), iv.

20. See, for example, Ely Moore, "Address Delivered Before the General Trade Union of the City of New York . . . 1833," reprinted in Joseph Blau, ed., *Social Theories of Jacksonian Democracy* (Indianapolis: Bobbs-Merrill, 1954), pp. 289–300. On working-class movements and education, see Rush Welter, *Popular Education and Democratic Thought in America* (New York: Columbia University Press, 1962), part II.

21. See the fine study by Dan Schiller, *Objectivity and the News: The Public and the Rise of Commercial Journalism* (Philadelphia: University of Pennsylvania Press, 1981), esp. chap. 2.

22. Transcript of a newspaper clipping in minutes of preliminary meetings, February 1830, Archives, New York University; Brander Matthews, ed., *A History of Columbia University, 1754–1904* (New York: Columbia University Press, 1904), pp. 115–16.

23. Columbia College, *Report . . . for Extending the Scheme of Instruction* (New York: n.p., 1830), pp. 1–3; *New York American*, February 15, 1830.

24. Columbia College, *Address to the Citizens of New York on the Claims of Columbia College and the New University, to Their Patronage* (New York, 1830), pp. 3, 8.

25. *Ibid.*, p. 9.

26. See the communications and addresses in the *Journal of the Proceedings of a Convention of Scientific and Literary Gentlemen, held in the Common Council of the City of New York*.

27. See *New York American*, February 16, 1830.

28. Yale College, *Reports on the Course of Instruction* (New Haven: Hezekiah Howe, 1828), pp. 25, 27.

29. *Ibid.*, pp. 24, 42.

30. For a brief account of the founding of the Smithsonian, see A. Hunter Dupree, *Science in the Federal Government* (Cambridge: Harvard University Press, 1957), chap. 4.

31. Henry Adams, *The Life of Albert Gallatin* (Philadelphia: Lippincott, 1879), pp. 643–44.

32. Jones, *New York University*, pp. 21–22.

33. Albert Gallatin to Josiah Quincy, December 9, 1830, in Henry Adams, ed., *The Writings of Albert Gallatin* (3 vols.; Philadelphia: Lippincott, 1879), II, 445.

34. *Proceedings of a Convention of Scientific and Literary Gentlemen, held in New York City*, pp. 170–79.

35. Albert Gallatin to Josiah Quincy, December 9, 1830, in Adams, ed., *Writings of Albert Gallatin*, II, 446.

36. Samuel Bard, *A Discourse on Medical Education* (New York: C. S. Van Winkle, 1819), p. 9.

37. This is true in the otherwise quite generous proposal of William Smith, *A General Idea of the College of Mirania . . .* (New York: J. Parker & W. Weyman, 1753).

38. Albert Gallatin to John Badollet, February 7, 1833, quoted in Adams, *Gallatin*, p. 648.

39. Earle and Congdon, *Annals of the General Society of Mechanics and Tradesmen*, pp. 99–100.

40. For two sensitive, though quite different, explorations of this issue in contemporary America, see Richard Sennett and Jonathan Cobb, *The Hidden Injuries of Class* (New York: Knopf, 1972); and Richard Rodriguez, *Hunger of Memory: The Education of Richard Rodriguez* (Boston: David R. Godine, 1982).

41. Bruce Sinclair, *Philadelphia's Philosopher Mechanics: A History of the Franklin Institute, 1824–1865* (Baltimore: Johns Hopkins University Press, 1974), pp. 67–68.

42. "To the Honourable the Legislature of the State of New York in Senate and Assembly Convened," January 28, 1831, Archives, New York University. Gallatin was the chairman of the committee that drafted the petition, but it is not certain that this —or any other language in it—is his. The typescript in the NYU Archives designates Morgan Lewis as probable author.

43. His resignation is recorded in the Minutes of the Council, October 22, 1831, Archives, New York University. For his private feelings, see Adams, *Gallatin*, p. 648.

44. Reprinted in Mathews, *Recollections*, pp. 209–10.

45. Jones, *New York University*, p. 36.

46. *Letter to the Councillors of the University of the City of New-York, from the Professors of the Faculty of Science and Letters* (New York: University Press, 1838), p. 38. See also S. Willis Rudy, *The College of the City of New York* (New York: City College Press, 1949), p. 8.

47. Allan S. Horlick, *Country Boys and Merchant Princes: The Social Control of Young Men in New York* (Lewisburg, Pa.: Bucknell University Press, 1975), p. 175.

48. Rudy, *College of the City of New York*, pp. 18, 13; Townsend Harris to James Kent, July 23, 1847, James Kent Papers, Library of Congress. On Harris generally, see William Elliot Griffis, *Townsend Harris* (Boston: Houghton Mifflin, 1895).

49. Carl F. Kaestle, *The Evolution of an Urban School System: New York City, 1750–1850* (Cambridge: Harvard University Press, 1973), p. 105; Sherry Gorelick, *City College and the Jewish Poor* (New Brunswick: Rutgers University Press, 1981).

50. Kaestle, *The Evolution of an Urban School System*, p. 109.

51. Rudy, *College of the City of New York*, pp. 68–69, 92.

52. John W. Draper, *The Indebtedness of the City of New-York to Its University* (New York: Alumni Association, 1853), p. 17.

53. Draper, *Indebtedness of the City*, pp. 27, 28, 24; Stow Persons, *The Decline of American Gentility* (New York: Columbia University Press, 1973), p. 185.

54. Draper, *Indebtedness of the City*, pp. 28–29.

55. James Bryce, *The American Commonwealth* (2nd ed., rev.; 2 vols.; London: Macmillan, 1889), II, 660.

56. Samuel L. Knapp, *The Great American Metropolis* (New York: A. Neal & Co., 1837), p. 9.

57. Joseph Green Cogswell, "University Education," *New York Review*, 7 (1840), 132–36.

58. Printed in Milton Halsey Thomas, "Mid-Nineteenth Century Life in New York: More Revelations from the Diary of George Templeton Strong," *New-York Historical Society Quarterly*, 37 (1953), 24–25.

59. Andrew Dickson White credits Tappan at Michigan for the real beginning of the American university. See White's *Autobiography* (2 vols.; New York: Century Company, 1905), I, 292.

60. Charles M. Perry, *Henry Philip Tappan* (Ann Arbor: University of Michigan Press, 1933), pp. 84, 139.

61. *Ibid.*, p. 151.

62. Henry P. Tappan, "Letter from Berlin to Graduating Class, 1853," in Henry P. Tappan Papers, Michigan Historical Collection, Bentley Historical Library, University of Michigan.

63. Henry P. Tappan, *The Growth of Cities* (New York: R. Craighead, 1855), pp. 7–8, 31–35.

64. Henry P. Tappan, *University Education* (New York: G. P. Putnam, 1851), pp. 88–89.

65. Tappan, *The Growth of Cities*, p. 45.

66. *Ibid.*

67. Tappan, *University Education*, pp. 89, 60, 68, 60, 89–90.

68. *Ibid.*, pp. 95, 92, 93.

69. Alexander Dallas Bache, *Anniversary Address Before the American Institute of the City of New York* (New York: Pudney & Russel, 1857), pp. 44, 59. See also Benjamin Peirce, *Working Plan for the Foundation of a University* [Cambridge, 1856]. For evidence that all of these plans were part of a single campaign, see Henry P. Tappan to Samuel Ruggles, March 3, 1856, March 17, 1856, Henry P. Tappan Papers, Michigan Historical Collection.

70. See Fernando Wood's "Communication relative to the establishment of a large university of learning in this city," July 7, 1856, in Board of Aldermen, *Documents*, No. 31, 1856; Henry P. Tappan to Samuel B. Ruggles, February 11, 1856, Henry P. Tappan Papers, Michigan Historical Collection.

71. Henry P. Tappan to William B. Astor, February 18, 1856, Henry P. Tappan Papers, Michigan Historical Collection.

72. The best account of these efforts is Richard J. Storr, *The Beginnings of Graduate Education in America* (Chicago: University of Chicago Press, 1953), chaps. 8–9. Storr treats the matter in the context of the evolution of the research university in America rather than in terms of the conjuncture with the city.

73. Information on Cooper and his institution is taken from Edward Clarence Mack, *Peter Cooper: Citizen of New York* (New York: Duell, Sloan & Pearce, 1949); Allan Nevins, *Abram Hewitt, with Some Account of Peter Cooper* (New York: Harper & Row, 1935), pp. 175–82; and Lawrence Cremin, *American Education: The National Experience* (New York: Harper & Row, 1980), p. 446. There is no history of the Cooper Union, though there certainly should be one.

74. Mack, *Peter Cooper*, pp. 13, 253, 265–66.

75. Frederick Law Olmsted to Charles Loring Brace, December 1, 1853, in Charles McLaughlin, ed., *The Papers of Frederick Law Olmsted*, II (Baltimore: Johns Hopkins University Press, 1981), 234, 235.

76. Nevins, *Abram Hewitt*, p. 177; Rossiter Raymond, *Peter Cooper* [1901] (Freeport, N.Y.: Books for Libraries, 1972), p. 75.

CHAPTER 4

1. Quoted in Edward K. Spann, *Ideals and Politics: New York Intellectuals and Liberal Democracy, 1820–1880* (Albany: State University of New York Press, 1972), p. 14.

2. Edward Lind Morse, ed., *Samuel F. B. Morse: His Letters and Journals* (2 vols; Boston: Houghton Mifflin, 1914), I, 248–49.

3. Samuel F. B. Morse to J. L. Morton, April 18, 1831, quoted in Paul J. Staiti, "Ideology and Politics in Samuel F. B. Morse's Agenda for a National Art," in *Samuel F. B. Morse: Educator and Champion of the Arts in America* (New York: National Academy of Design, 1982), p. 9.

4. Quoted in Spann, *Ideals and Politics*, p. 21.

5. Quoted in Staiti, "Ideology and Politics," pp. 47, 46.

6. Paul O. Kristeller, " 'Creativity' and 'Tradition,' " *Journal of the History of Ideas*, 44 (1983), 105–13, makes a different point but is illuminating here. On the emergence of the public as discussed here, see T. J. Clark, *Image of the People: Gustave Courbet and the 1848 Revolution* (Princeton: Princeton University Press, 1982), pp. 9–15.

7. Levin L. Schücking, *The Sociology of Literary Taste* (rev. ed.; London: Routledge and Kegan Paul, 1966), pp. 62–63. See also Peter Hohendahl, *The Institution of Criticism* (Ithaca: Cornell University Press, 1983), chap. 1.

8. On Morse's biography, see Carlton Mabie, *The American Leonardo: A Life of Samuel F. B. Morse* (New York: Knopf, 1943); and Samuel I. Prime, *The Life of Samuel F. B. Morse* (New York: Appleton, 1875).

9. Morse, ed., *Samuel F. B. Morse: His Letters*, I, 282.

10. James Grant Wilson, *The Memorial History of the City of New-York* (4 vols.; New York: New-York History Company, 1892–93), III, 356–57.

11. Thomas Cole to Luman Reed, September 18, 1833, in L. L. Noble, *The Life and Works of Thomas Cole*, ed. Elliott S. Versell (Cambridge: Harvard University Press, 1964), pp. 129–31.

12. Prime, *Morse*, p. 173.

13. William Cullen Bryant II, "Bryant: The Middle Years. A Study in Cultural Fellowship" (Ph.D. dissertation, Columbia University, 1954), pp. 14–47.

14. This point is importantly elucidated by Nicolai Cikovsky, Jr., "Samuel Morse as Writer and Lecturer," in *Samuel F. B. Morse: Educator and Champion of the Arts in America*, esp. pp. 68–70. The lectures have recently been published for the first time: Samuel F. B. Morse, *Lectures on the Affinity of Painting With the Other Fine Arts*, ed. N. Cikovsky, Jr. (Columbia: University of Missouri Press, 1983).

15. Prime, *Morse*, p. 281.

16. On Morse's invention of the telegraph, see the brilliant analysis by Brooke Hindle, *Emulation and Invention* (New York: New York University Press, 1981), chap. 4.

17. Compare the later Victorian scientists discussed in David Hollinger, "Inquiry and Uplift: The Expansion of Scientific Practice and the Elaboration of the Scientific Ethos in Late-Nineteenth-Century America," in Thomas Haskell, ed., *The Authority of Experts* (Bloomington: Indiana University Press, 1984), pp. 142–56. See also, more generally, Burton Bledstein, *The Culture of Professionalism* (New York: Norton, 1976).

18. See Nathan Reingold, "Definitions and Speculations: The Professionalization of Science in America in the Nineteenth Century," in Alexandra Oleson and Sanborn C. Brown, eds., *The Pursuit of Knowledge in the Early American Republic* (Baltimore: Johns Hopkins University Press, 1976), pp. 40–41.

19. Brooke Hindle, "The Underside of the Learned Society in New York, 1754–1854," in *ibid.*, pp. 112–13.

20. Nathan Reingold, ed., *The Papers of Joseph Henry* (Washington: Smithsonian Institution Press, 1972), I, 349.

21. Nathan Reingold, ed., *Science in Nineteenth Century America* (New York: Hill and Wang, 1964), p. 88.

22. Quoted in Michael Hall and David Van Tassell, eds., *Science and Society in the United States* (Homewood, Ill.: Dorsey Press, 1966), p. 195.

23. On Henry, see Thomas Bender, "Science and the Culture of American Communities: The Nineteenth Century," *History of Education Quarterly,* 16 (1976), 63–77.

24. See Carl Diehl, *Americans and German Scholarship, 1770–1870* (New Haven: Yale University Press, 1978), esp. chap. 2.

25. *National Advocate,* March 21, 1818.

26. William Dunlap, *History of the Rise and Progress of the Arts of Design in the United States* [1834] (2 vols.; New York: Dover Press, 1964), II, 278, 280.

27. *Ibid.,* II, 280.

28. *Ibid.,* I, 419.

29. Quoted in Thomas S. Cummings, *Historic Annals of the National Academy of Design* (Philadelphia: George W. Childs, 1865), p. 34. My italics.

30. Prime, *Morse,* p. 153.

31. Samuel F. B. Morse, *Academies of Art* (New York: G. & C. Carvill, 1827). For context, Nikolaus Pevsner, *Academies of Art* (Cambridge, Eng.: At the University Press, 1940), chap. 5.

32. Samuel F. B. Morse to J. F. Cooper, February 21, 1833, Morse, ed., *Morse,* II, 23.

33. Quoted in Cummings, *National Academy of Design,* p. 29.

34. Quoted in Eliot Clark, *History of the National Academy of Design, 1825–1853* (New York: Columbia University Press, 1954), p. 31.

35. Alexis de Tocqueville, *Democracy in America,* ed. Thomas Bender (New York: Random House, Modern Library, 1981), p. 296.

36. James F. Cooper to Horatio Greenough, June 14, 1836, *Letters and Journals of James Fenimore Cooper,* ed. James F. Beard (6 vols.; Cambridge: Harvard University Press, 1960–68), III, 220.

37. James Fenimore Cooper to William Gilmore Simms, January 5, 1844, *Letters and Journals of James Fenimore Cooper,* IV, 438–39.

38. Robert A. Ferguson, *Law and Letters in American Culture* (Cambridge: Harvard University Press, 1984).

39. Nelson F. Adkins, *Fitz-Greene Halleck* (New Haven: Yale University Press, 1930), p. 152.

40. Pierre Irving, *The Life and Letters of Washington Irving* (2 vols.; New York: G. P. Putnam, 1865), I, 165.

41. Martin Green, *Cities of Light and Sons of the Morning* (Boston: Little, Brown, 1972), pp. 185–89; John Clive, *The Scotch Reviewers: The Edinburgh Review, 1802–1815* (Cambridge: Harvard University Press, 1957); David Daiches, *Edinburgh* (London: Granada, 1980), chap. 10.

42. Irving, *Life and Letters of Washington Irving,* I, 258.

43. *Salmagundi,* No. 1, p. 70; Irving, *Life and Letters of Washington Irving,* I, 145.

Whatever he said, Irving and his group were receiving money for *Salmagundi* and seeking it for other projects. See R. Jackson Wilson, "Washington Irving" (unpublished manuscript, 1976), pp. 28–29.

44. Beard, ed., *The Letters and Journals of James Fenimore Cooper,* I, 209.

45. Green, *Cities of Light,* pp. 221, 223.

46. Bryant II, *Bryant,* p. 85; James Fenimore Cooper to William Dunlap, November 14, 1832, in William Dunlap, *Diary,* ed. Dorothy Barck (3 vols.; New York: New-York Historical Society, 1930), III, 645.

47. See esp. James Fenimore Cooper, *The American Democrat* [1838] (New York: Funk & Wagnalls, 1969), as well as his so-called social novels.

48. Ferguson, *Law and Letters,* chap. 7.

49. Allan Nevins, *The Evening Post: A Century of Journalism* (New York: Boni & Liveright, 1922), p. 338.

50. See Thomas Bender, "James Fenimore Cooper and the City," *New York History,* 51 (1970), 287–305.

51. Any discussion of the Bread and Cheese must begin with Albert H. Marckwordt, "The Chronology and Personnel of the Bread and Cheese Club," *American Literature,* 6 (1935), 389–99.

52. John W. Francis, *Old New York* (New York: Samuel Francis, 1866), p. 291.

53. Quoted in Adkins, *Halleck,* p. 152. On Kent and scholarship, see Perry Miller, *The Life of the Mind in America* (New York: Harcourt, Brace, 1964), pp. 134–43.

54. Prime, *Morse,* p. 241.

55. There is no serious history of the Century. On the origins, see John H. Gourlie, *The Origin and History of "The Century"* (New York: William C. Bryant, 1856); John Durand, *Prehistoric Notes of the Century Club* (New York: n.p., 1882). For an overview, see the collaborative book by several members, some of them distinguished historians: Century Association, *The Century, 1847–1946* (New York: Century Association, 1957).

56. The best biography is Robert W. July, *The Essential New Yorker: Gulian Crommelin Verplanck* (Durham: Duke University Press, 1951).

57. Spann, *Ideals and Politics,* p. 192.

58. William Cullen Bryant, *A Discourse on the Life, Character, and Writings of Gulian Crommelin Verplanck* (New York: New-York Historical Society, 1870), p. 5.

59. Century Association, *Proceedings . . . in Honor of Gulian C. Verplanck* (New York: Appleton, 1870), p. 91.

60. This oration is most accessible in Joseph Blau, ed., *American Philosophic Addresses, 1700–1900* (New York: Columbia University Press, 1946), pp. 115–50. See also G. C. Verplanck, *An Address Delivered before the Philolexian and Peithologian Society . . . of Columbia College* (New York: G. & C. & H. Carvill, 1830), esp. pp. 34–35; idem, *The Right Moral Influence of and Use of Liberal Studies* (New York: Harper, 1833), esp. pp. 31–33; idem, *A Lecture Introductory to the Use of Scientific Lectures Before the Mechanic's Institute of the City of New York* (New York: G. P. Scott, 1833), pp. 5–6, 20–22.

61. Edgar Allan Poe, "The Literati of New York City," *Complete Works of Edgar Allan Poe,* ed. James A. Harrison (New York: AMS Press, 1965), XV, 39; Bryant, *Discourse on . . . Verplanck,* p. 34; July, *Essential New Yorker,* p. 245.

62. Durand, *Prehistoric Notes,* p. 19.

63. Gourlie, *Origin and History,* p. 31.

64. Century Association, *The Century,* p. 36.

65. Durand, *Prehistoric Notes,* pp. 12–13.

66. Walt Whitman, "Democratic Vistas," in Laurence Buell, ed., *Leaves of Grass and Selected Prose* (New York: Modern Library, 1981), p. 491; George Santayana, "The Genteel Tradition in American Philosophy," in D. L. Wilson, *The Genteel Tradition:*

Nine Essays by George Santayana (Cambridge: Harvard University Press, 1976), pp. 37–64.

67. See Richard Cary, *The Genteel Circle: Bayard Taylor and His New York Friends* (Ithaca: Cornell University Press, 1952); John Tomsich, *A Genteel Endeavor: American Culture and Politics in the Gilded Age* (Stanford: Stanford University Press, 1971).

68. Century Association, *The Century*, pp. 55–56.

69. See Perry Miller, *The Raven and the Whale* (New York: Harcourt, Brace, 1956).

70. Frank Luther Mott, *A History of American Magazines, 1741–1850* (Cambridge: Harvard University Press, 1966), I, 345–46, 607.

71. Poe, "The Literati of New York City," p. 115.

72. On the literary movement of the 1840s, see John Stafford, *The Literary Criticism of 'Young America': A Study in the Relationship of Politics and Literature, 1837–1850* (Berkeley: University of California Press, 1952); and, of course, Miller, *The Raven and the Whale*. In the 1850s, after the literary movement exhausted itself, Young America, with a different cast of characters, was associated with a different mission. See Merle E. Curti, "Young America," *American Historical Review*, 32 (1926), 34–35. On the sociological category here being noticed, see Karl Mannheim, *Essays on the Sociology of Culture* (London: Routledge and Kegan Paul, 1956), p. 117.

73. For Duyckinck's biography, see William A. Butler, *Evert Augustus Duyckinck* (New York: Trow's, 1879); Samuel A. Osgood, *Evert A. Duyckinck* (Boston: David Clapp & Son, 1879); and George E. Mize, "The Contribution of Evert A. Duyckinck to the Cultural Development of Nineteenth Century America" (Ph.D. dissertation, New York University, 1955).

74. Herman Melville to Evert A. Duyckinck, March 3, 1849, in Merrill R. Davis and William H. Gilman, eds., *The Letters of Herman Melville* (New Haven: Yale University Press, 1960), p. 80.

75. Osgood, *Duyckinck*, p. 9.

76. Butler, *Duyckinck*, p. 15; Nathaniel Hawthorne to Evert Duyckinck, April 8, 1851, Duyckinck Family Papers, New York Public Library.

77. Jedidiah Auld to William A. Jones, March 3, 1841, Duyckinck Family Papers, New York Public Library.

78. Miller, *The Raven and the Whale*, p. 71.

79. Quoted in *ibid.*, p. 76.

80. *Ibid.*, p. 93. Less explicit but similar are the essays in the first number of *Arcturus* (December 1840) on Bryant, Dana, and public lectures, as well as Mathews's lead article on politics.

81. George T. Strong to Evert Duyckinck, February 14, 1848, Duyckinck Family Papers, New York Public Library; George Templeton Strong, *Diary*, eds. Allan Nevins and Milton Halsey Thomas (4 vols.; New York: Macmillan, 1952), I, 312. I do not know why Duyckinck sent a volume of *Arcturus* to Strong in 1848, six years after its demise. He may have been seeking Strong's support for another venture; it is during the period just before he regained (through purchase) control of the *Literary World*.

82. Quoted in Stafford, *Young America*, p. 7.

83. Quoted in Benjamin T. Spencer, *The Quest for Nationality* (Syracuse: Syracuse University Press, 1957), p. 126.

84. Arthur M. Schlesinger, Jr., *The Age of Jackson* (Boston: Little, Brown, 1945), p. 371 n.

85. The best account is Julius W. Pratt, "John L. O'Sullivan and Manifest Destiny," *New York History*, 14 (1933), 213–34.

86. John L. O'Sullivan to Samuel J. Tilden, May 17, 1850, Samuel J. Tilden Papers, New York Public Library.

87. Quoted in Pratt, "O'Sullivan," p. 218.

88. Miller, *The Raven and the Whale*, p. 110.

89. Quoted in Pratt, "O'Sullivan," p. 218.

90. Schlesinger, *Age of Jackson*, p. 372.

91. Pratt, "O'Sullivan," p. 217.

92. William A. Jones, "Criticism in America," *Democratic Review*, 15 (1844), 248.

93. Godwin lists his articles for O'Sullivan in Parke Godwin to Evert A. Duyckinck, July 11, 1854, Duyckinck Family Papers, New York Public Library. On his writing of the Republican platform, see George Haven Putnam, *Memoirs of a Publisher, 1865–1915* (New York: Putnam's, 1916), pp. 12–13.

94. See Stafford, *Young America*, p. 12; James T. Callow, *Kindred Spirits: Knickerbocker Writers and American Artists, 1807–1855* (Chapel Hill: University of North Carolina Press, 1967), p. 6.

95. "Mr. Forrest's Oration," *Democratic Review*, 3 (1838), 52. See also "Preface," *Democratic Review*, 7 (1840), iii–iv.

96. William Cullen Bryant, "William Leggett," *Democratic Review*, 6 (1839), 430.

97. *Democratic Review*, 7 (1840), 3. See also [Parke Godwin,] "Democracy," *ibid.*, pp. 215–29.

98. For biographical information see Page S. Procter, Jr., "William Leggett (1801–1839): Journalist and Literater," *Papers of the Bibliographic Society of America*, 44 (1950), 239–53; Richard Hofstadter, "William Leggett: Spokesman of Jacksonian Democracy," *Political Science Quarterly*, 58 (1943), 581–94; Schlesinger, *Age of Jackson*, pp. 186–89, 260, 314–17; Nevins, *The Evening Post*, chap. 6.

99. *New York Evening Post*, March 20, 1834.

100. [Parke Godwin,] "The Course of Civilization," *Democratic Review*, 6 (1839), 208–17; "Democracy and Literature," *ibid.*, 11 (1842), 196.

101. "American Aristocracy," *ibid.*, 8 (1840), 116; "On the Elevation of the Labouring Portion of Society," *ibid.*, pp. 53–54; "On the Intelligence of the People," *ibid.*, pp. 360–64.

102. Quoted in Stafford, *Young America*, p. 57.

103. Martin Duberman, *James Russell Lowell* (Boston: Beacon Press, 1966), p. 51.

104. Stafford, *Young America*, pp. 20–21.

105. On the relation of personal associations to literary reputation, see Poe's brilliant introduction to his "Literati of New York City," pp. 2–3.

106. See Merle E. Curti, "George N. Sanders: American Patriot of the Fifties," *South Atlantic Quarterly*, 27 (1928), 79–87.

107. William A. Jones, "Poetry for the People," *Democratic Review*, 13 (1843), 266–79.

108. John O'Sullivan to Evert Duyckinck, March 3, 1843, Duyckinck Family Papers, New York Public Library; John O'Sullivan to Evert Duyckinck, July 3, 1845, *ibid.*; John O'Sullivan to Samuel J. Tilden, April 4, 1844, Samuel J. Tilden Papers, New York Public Library.

109. Parke Godwin to Evert A. Duyckinck [December 6, 1844], Duyckinck Family Papers, New York Public Library.

110. John O'Sullivan to Samuel J. Tilden, June 1, 1845, Samuel J. Tilden Papers, New York Public Library.

111. Ferguson, *Law and Letters*, pp. 204, 240, 271. Whitman quotes are from Buell, ed., *Leaves of Grass and Selected Prose*, p. 497.

112. Herman Melville to Evert Duyckinck, March 3, 1849, in Davis and Gilman, eds., *Letters of Herman Melville*, pp. 79–80.

113. *Literary World*, 14 (April 21, 1849), 352.

114. Emerson quote in Buell, ed., *Leaves of Grass and Selected Prose*, p. lviii. I refer to Floyd Stoval, *The Foreground of Leaves of Grass* (Charlottesville: University Press of Virginia, 1974); and Paul Zweig, *Walt Whitman: The Making of a Poet* (New York: Basic Books, 1984).

115. Quoted in Gay Wilson Allen, *The Solitary Singer: A Critical Biography of Walt Whitman* (New York: New York University Press, 1967), pp. 41, 128.

116. Stafford, *Young America*, p. 126; and Horace Traubel, *With Walt Whitman in Camden* (Carbondale: Southern Illinois University Press, 1982), VI, 379.

117. Allen, *Solitary Singer*, pp. 127–28. See also Stafford, *Young America*, p. 126; Justin Kaplan, *Walt Whitman* (New York: Simon & Shuster, 1980), p. 100.

118. Allen, *Solitary Singer*, p. 134.

119. Quoted in Walter Benjamin, *Charles Baudelaire* (London: Verso, 1983), p. 69.

120. Walt Whitman, *The Gathering of Forces*, ed. Cleveland Rodgers and John Bleck (2 vols.; New York: Putnam's, 1920), vol. II.

121. "Prospects of American Poetry," *Knickerbocker*, 7 (1836), 593.

122. Strong, *Diary*, II, 210–11.

123. Quoted in Kaplan, *Whitman*, p. 213. Thoreau was also impressed by this quality. See Zweig, *Whitman*, pp. 16, 134.

124. Quoted in Allen, *Solitary Singer*, p. 111.

125. See Edward Grier, "Walt Whitman, the Galaxy, and Democratic Vistas," *American Literature*, 23 (1951), 333–50. Carlyle's essay: "Shooting Niagaras: And After?," *Macmillan's Magazine*, 16 (1867), 319–36. See Walt Whitman, "Democracy," *Galaxy*, 4 (1867), 919–33.

126. Walt Whitman to Edward Dowden, January 18, 1872, in Edwin H. Miller, ed., *Collected Writings of Walt Whitman* (New York: New York University Press, 1961), I, 154; Allen, *Solitary Singer*, p. 156.

127. Buell, ed., *Leaves of Grass and Selected Prose*, pp. 470–72, 496–97.

128. This was noticed by very acute observers. See the novel by Charles F. Briggs, *The Adventures of Harry Franco* (New York: Saunders, 1839), pp. 62–63.

129. Diane Lindstrom, "The Economy of Antebellum New York City," paper prepared for Conference of New York City, Social Science Research Council, November 18, 1983, p. 15.

130. Mott, *History of American Magazines*, I, 375; II, 103.

131. *Literary World*, 2 (August 1847), 5.

132. "Cooper's Last Works," *New York Review*, 4 (January 1839), 213–14.

133. "Journalism," *Democratic Review*, 10 (1842), 52, 57–59, 61.

134. Edgar Allan Poe, "Marginal Notes . . . No. II. A Sequel to the 'Marginalia' of the *Democratic Review*," *Godey's Lady's Book*, September 1845, in Harrison, ed., *Complete Works of Edgar Allan Poe*, XVI, 82. He describes himself as a "magazinist" and makes the same point in a letter: Edgar Allan Poe to Charles Anthon, November 2, 1844, in John Ostrom, ed., *The Letters of Edgar Allan Poe* (2 vols.; Cambridge: Harvard University Press, 1948), I, 266–71.

135. Frederick Law Olmsted to John Olmsted, December 9, 1855, Frederick Law Olmsted Papers, Library of Congress. Olmsted claimed the endorsement of Washington Irving was decisive. See Frederick Law Olmsted, Jr., and Theodora Kimball, *Frederick Law Olmsted* (2 vols. in one; New York: Benjamin Blom, 1970), II, 38.

136. Nevins, *The Evening Post*, p. 216.

137. The closeness of this fit between the 1840s and the 1940s is remarkable. On the later period, see the fine appraisal by Grant Webster, *The Republic of Letters: A History of Postwar American Literary Opinion* (Baltimore: Johns Hopkins University Press, 1979).

138. Perry Miller, ed., *Margaret Fuller* (Garden City; N.Y.: Doubleday, Anchor, 1963), p. xi.

139. Margaret Fuller, *Memoirs* (2 vols.; Boston: Phillips, Sampson, 1852), II, 151; Mason Wade, *Margaret Fuller* (New York: Viking Press, 1940), p. 143; Fuller, *Memoirs*, II, 149.

140. On the increase in time, see Margaret Fuller, *Papers on Literature and Art* (London: Wiley & Putnam, 1846), p. vi. For a discussion of her engagement with history as a New York writer, see Ann Douglas, *The Feminization of American Culture* (New York: Knopf, 1977). I am, however, far less pessimistic than is Douglas about her prospects had she safely returned to New York.

141. Fuller, *Memoirs*, II, 131.

142. *New York Tribune*, May 29, 1845. Fuller is here quoting the translator of Goethe's *Essays on Art*.

3. Margaret Fuller, "Philosophy of Criticism," in Miller, ed., *Margaret Fuller*, pp. 215–18.

144. Fuller, *Papers on Literature and Art*, p. vii. There is also an interesting statement by Fuller quoted in Susan Conrad, *Perish the Thought: Intellectual Women in Romantic America, 1830–1860* (New York: Oxford University Press, 1976), p. 85. Unfortunately, the quote does not appear in the source she cites.

145. Fuller, *Papers on Literature and Art*, pp. 139–40.

146. Edgar Allan Poe to James Russell Lowell, July 2, 1844, Ostrom, ed., *Letters of Edgar Allan Poe*, I, 256.

147. See Lewis P. Simpson, "Poe's Vision of His Ideal Magazine," in his *The Man of Letters in New England and the South* (Baton Rouge: Louisana State University Press, 1973), pp. 131–49.

148. *Broadway Journal*, 1 (1845), 281–82.

149. Robert D. Jacobs, *Poe: Journalist and Critic* (Baton Rouge: Louisiana State University Press, 1969), chap. 11. All quotes from p. 278.

150. *Broadway Journal*, 1 (January 4, 1845), 1. On Maria White Lowell's remark, see Miller, *The Raven and the Whale*, p. 49.

151. Miller, *The Raven and the Whale*, p. 356. Miller did inspire a dissertation which tells us more, perhaps all we'll ever know, but still not enough. See Bette S. Weidman, "Charles Frederick Briggs: A Critical Biography" (Ph.D. dissertation, Columbia University, 1968).

152. James Russell Lowell, *Fable for Critics* in *The Political Works of James Russell Lowell* (4 vols.; Boston: Houghton Mifflin, 1890), vol. 3, 71–72.

153. Charles F. Briggs, *The Trippings of Tom Pepper* (New York: Burgess & Stringer, 1847), pp. 70–77, 156–72.

154. Quoted in Miller, *The Raven and the Whale*, p. 175.

155. James Russell Lowell to Charles F. Briggs, March 6, 1844, in *Letters of James Russell Lowell*, ed. Charles Eliot Norton (2 vols.; New York: Harper, 1894), I, 77.

156. Weidman, "Charles Frederick Briggs," p. 15.

157. Quoted in *ibid.*, p. 23 n.

158. *Ibid.*, pp. 119, 90.

159. Mott, *History of American Magazines*, II, 32; Laura Wood Roper, "Mr. Law and Putnam's Monthly Magazine," *American Literature*, 26 (1954), 92.

160. Quoted in Miller, *The Raven and the Whale*, p. 48.

161. Weidman, "Charles Frederick Briggs," pp. 245–47; "The Old and the New: A Retrospect and a Prospect," *Putnam's Magazine*, 1 (January 1868), 5.

162. George H. Putnam, *George P. Putnam: A Memoir* (New York: Putnam's, 1912), pp. 208, 209.

163. Parke Godwin to Evert Duyckinck, July 11, 1854, Duyckinck Family Papers, New York Public Library.

164. For a brief biography, see Carlos Baker, "Parke Godwin: Pathfinder in Politics and Journalism," in Willard Thorp, ed., *The Lives of Eighteen from Princeton* (Princeton: Princeton University Press, 1946), pp. 212–31.

165. George Putnam to Evert Duyckinck, October 1, 1852, Duyckinck Family Papers, New York Public Library.

166. *Putnam's Monthly*, 1 (1853), 1.

167. *Ibid.*

168. "New York Daguerreotyped," *ibid.*, p. 122.

169. On the Melville story, see Jay Leyda, *The Melville Log* (2 vols.; New York: Harcourt, Brace, 1951), I, 487.

170. [Parke Godwin,] "American Despotism," *Putnam's Monthly*, 4 (1854), 524–32, reprinted in Parke Godwin, *Political Essays* (New York: Dix & Edwards, 1856), pp. 85–87. See also "Editorial Notes," *Putnam's Monthly*, 8 (1856), 442; and Parke Godwin, *George William Curtis* (New York: Harper, 1893), pp. 27–34.

171. "World of New York," *Putnam's Monthly*, 4 (1854), 108. See also "New York Daguerreotyped," *ibid.*, 36 (1854), 243.

172. Putnam, *G. P. Putnam*, p. 173.

173. Miriam Kotzin, "Putnam's Monthly and Its Place in American Literature" (Ph.D. dissertation, New York University, 1969), p. 4.

174. *Ibid.*, and Roper, "Mr. Law and Putnam's Monthly Magazine."

CHAPTER 5

1. Diane Lindstrom, "The Growth of the New York City Economy," paper presented to SSRC conference, November 1983. Also her comments at SSRC workshop, September 14, 1984.

2. Raymond Williams, *Keywords* (New York: Oxford University Press, 1976).

3. On Coleridge and culture, see Raymond Williams, *Culture and Society, 1780–1950* (New York: Harper & Row, 1966), part I, chap. 3.

4. For Emerson and Arnold, see John H. Raleigh, *Matthew Arnold and American Culture* (Berkeley: University of California Press, 1957), pp. 1–13.

5. Emerson quotes from *ibid.*, p. 10. Peter G. Buckley, in "To the Opera House: Culture and Society in New York City, 1820–1860" (Ph.D. dissertation, SUNY–Stony Brook, 1984), p. 292, sees this redefinition emerging in the 1850s, in the wake of the Astor Place Riot of 1849.

6. On Norton, see Kermit Vanderbilt, *Charles Eliot Norton* (Cambridge: Harvard University Press, 1959).

7. George M. Fredrickson, *The Inner Civil War* (New York: Harper & Row, 1965), p. 32.

8. T. W. Higginson, "A Plea for Culture," *Atlantic Monthly*, 19 (1867), 29–37; Charles Dudley Warner, "What Is Your Culture to Me," *Scribner's Monthly*, 4 (1872), 470–78.

9. On the importance of the large electorate in defining the political culture of American cities, see Amy Bridges, *A City in the Republic* (New York: Cambridge University Press, 1984).

10. See T. W. Heyck, *The Transformation of Intellectual Life in Victorian England* (New York: St. Martin's, 1982), p. 36.

11. Fredrickson, *Inner Civil War*, pp. 108–9.

12. See "A Word About Museums," *The Nation* (July 27, 1865), 113–14. Even

more revealing, see the letter from P. T. Barnum printed in *ibid.* (August 10, 1865), 171–72.

13. See Thomas Bender, "The Erosion of Public Culture: Cities, Discourses, and Professional Disciplines," in Thomas L. Haskell, ed. *The Authority of Experts* (Bloomington: Indiana University Press, 1984), 84–106.

14. Frederick Law Olmsted to Oliver Wolcott Gibbs, November 5, 1862, Union League Club Archives, to be published in Charles Capen McLaughlin, ed., *The Papers of Frederick Law Olmsted,* vol. IV (hereafter cited as *FLO Papers*). See also *Historical Sketch of the Union League Club of New York* (New York: privately printed, 1879), pp. 11–16.

15. William Dean Howells, *Literature and Life* (New York: Harper & Row, 1902), p. 7: On Olmsted, see Thomas Bender, *Toward an Urban Vision* (Baltimore: Johns Hopkins University Press, 1982), pp. 164–74.

16. Edmund Wilson, *Patriotic Gore* (New York: Oxford University Press, 1966); Fredrickson, *Inner Civil War.*

17. Fredrickson, *Inner Civil War,* chap. 7; Bender, *Toward an Urban Vision,* pp. 189–91.

18. Besides Fredrickson, *Inner Civil War,* see Thomas L. Haskell, *The Emergence of Professional Social Science* (Urbana: University of Illinois Press, 1977); and Robert Wiebe, *The Search for Order, 1877–1920* (New York: Hill and Wang, 1967).

19. On the link between Northern cities and the South in constitutional thought and on *Gelpcke* v. *Dubuque,* I have been instructed by Harold M. Hyman, *A More Perfect Union* (New York: Knopf, 1973); and Hyman's lectures at the NYU School of Law on American Cities and Constitutionalism in November 1983. See also, more especially, Frederick Law Olmsted to Henry W. Bellows, October 3, 1862, Henry W. Bellows Papers, Massachusetts Historical Society.

20. See, for example. E. L. Godkin, "The Growth and Expression of Public Opinion," *Atlantic Monthly,* 81 (1898), 1–15.

21. Frank Luther Mott, *A History of American Magazines, 1865–1885* (Cambridge: Harvard University Press, 1938), p. 18.

22. Charles Eliot Norton, ed., *Orations and Addresses of George William Curtis* (3 vols.; New York: Harper, 1894), I, 1–35.

23. John Tomsich, *A Genteel Endeavor* (Stanford: Stanford University Press, 1971), p. 8.

24. William M. Armstrong, ed., *The Gilded Age Letters of E. L. Godkin* (Albany: State University of New York Press, 1974), p. 186.

25. Vernon Parrington, *The Beginnings of Critical Realism in America* (New York: Harbinger, 1930), p. 148; "A Great Citizen," *The Century,* 45 (November 1892), 149.

26. See "Blacks and the Ballot" (May 20, 1865), 306; "Our Duty of Reorganization" (June 24, 1865), 387; "The United States and Suffrage" (October 14, 1865), 642; "Freedom to Work and Enjoy" (October 28, 1865), 674–75; "The Freedman" (March 9, 1867), 146; "Equal Suffrage" (April 27, 1867), 257.

27. For the specific linkage of Tweed and the South, see "Mr. Tweed's Nomination," *Harper's Weekly* (October 8, 1870), 642.

28. "The Imperial Ring," *ibid.* (February 11, 1871), 122.

29. Frank Luther Mott, *History of American Magazines, 1850–1865* (Cambridge: Harvard University Press, 1957), p. 278; Morton Keller, *The Art and Politics of Thomas Nast* (New York: Oxford University Press, 1968), p. 181.

30. "The Victory of the People," *Harper's Weekly* (November 25, 1871), 1098.

31. Brander Matthews, *These Many Years* (New York: Scribner's, 1917), p. 171.

32. Keller, *Art of Nast,* p. 77.

33. *Ibid.,* p. 181.

34. Norton, ed., *Orations of Curtis*, II, 149.

35. Morton Keller, *Affairs of State* (Cambridge: Harvard University Press, 1977), p. 272.

36. "The Civil Service Bill," *Harper's Weekly* (June 27, 1868), 403; "A Vital Reform," *ibid.* (November 28, 1868), 754.

37. Stephen Skowronek, *Building a New American State* (New York: Cambridge University Press, 1982), chap. 3, quotes from p. 55.

38. Norton, ed., *Orations of Curtis*, II, 117–41, quotes from pp. 123, 131. See also Edward Cary, *George William Curtis* (Boston: Houghton Mifflin, 1895), p. 299.

39. Theodore Roosevelt, *An Autobiography* (New York: Scribner's, 1925), p. 176.

40. George Templeton Strong, *Diary*, ed. Allan Nevins and Milton Halsey Thomas (4 vols.; New York: Macmillan, 1952), III, 325.

41. Armstrong, ed., *Godkin Letters*, p. 21; Rollo Ogden, ed., *Life and Letters of Edwin Lawrence Godkin* (2 vols.; New York: Macmillan, 1907), II, 63, 114; Diana Klebanow, "E. L. Godkin and the American City" (Ph.D. dissertation, New York University, 1965), p. 50.

42. Mott, *History of American Magazines, 1865–1885*, p. 26.

43. On Godkin, see William Armstrong, *E. L. Godkin* (Albany: State University of New York Press, 1978).

44. *Ibid.*, 76.

45. *The Nation* (July 6, 1865), 1.

46. For this complicated and not very edifying episode, see Armstrong, *Godkin*, pp. 75–92; the letters reprinted in Armstrong, ed., *Godkin Letters*, pp. 29–86; and Laura Wood Roper, *FLO* (Baltimore: Johns Hopkins University Press, 1973), pp. 294–98.

47. Armstrong, ed., *Godkin Letters*, p. 31.

48. *Ibid.*, p. 28.

49. *Ibid.*, pp. 11, 91.

50. *Ibid.*, p. 70; Henry Holt, *Garrulities of an Octogenerian Editor* (Boston: Houghton Mifflin, 1923), p. 293.

51. Armstrong, ed., *Godkin Letters*, p. 170.

52. John G. Sproat, *"The Best Men": Liberal Reformers in the Gilded Age* (New York: Oxford University Press, 1968), p. 8.

53. Quoted in Richard Hofstadter, *Anti-intellectualism in American Life* (New York: Knopf, 1963), p. 174.

54. Henry James, *Autobiography*, ed. F. W. Dupee (Princeton: Princeton University Press, 1983), p. 488; Ogden, *Life of Godkin*, I, 221.

55. For the best example of this, see his reflections on the Henry Ward Beecher adultery scandal, "Chromo-Civilization," in his *Reflections and Comments, 1865–1895* (New York: Scribner's, 1895).

56. Matthews, *These Many Years*, p. 173.

57. "Democratic Nationality," *The Nation* (July 13, 1865), 38. See also "Blacks and the Ballot," *Harper's Weekly* (May 20, 1865), 306; "Our Duty of Reorganization," *ibid.* (June 24, 1865), 387; "The United States and State Suffrage," *ibid.* (October 14, 1865), 642; "Freedom to Work and Enjoy," *ibid.* (October 28, 1865), 674–75; "Political Equality," *The Nation* (July 20, 1865), 72–74; "National Protection for Whites and Blacks," *ibid.* (December 7, 1865), 710–11.

58. For a notable exception, see David Montgomery, *Beyond Equality* (New York: Vintage, 1967).

59. Armstrong, ed., *Godkin Letters*, pp. 21–23, 27, 16. See also E. L. Godkin, "Democratic View of Democracy," *North American Review*, 101 (1865), 103–33; "Mr. Sumner on 'White Washing,' " *The Nation* (October 28, 1865), 806–7.

60. "The Eight Hour Movement," *The Nation* (October 26, 1865), 517–18.

61. "The Eight Hour Movement," *ibid.* (November 16, 1865), 616.

62. *Harper's Weekly* (December 9, 1865), 770. See also "The Labor Convention," *ibid.* (September 15, 1886), 579.

63. "Municipal Government," *The Nation* (May 30, 1867), 434–36; and "The Rights of 'the People,' " *ibid.* (June 6, 1867), 475–76. See also "City Government," *Harper's Weekly* (May 25, 1867), 322; and "The Government of the City of New York," *ibid.* (October 26, 1867), 674.

64. "Classes in Politics," *The Nation* (June 27, 1867), 519–20. See also "The Political Decline of the Perfect Gentleman," *ibid.* (August 22, 1867), 153–54.

65. On these groups, see Montgomery, *Beyond Equality*, chap. 10; and Irwin Unger, *The Greenback Era: A Social and Political History of American Finance, 1865–1879* (Princeton: Princeton University Press, 1964), pp. 94–114.

66. For Stanton on ignorant men, see *The Revolution* (January 29, 1869), 50. For changes in feminism, see Ellen DuBois, *Feminism and Suffrage* (Ithaca: Cornell University Press, 1978), chaps. 5–6. For Curtis's worries that feminism was getting mixed up in too many other reforms he opposed, see "The Cleveland Convention," *Harper's Weekly* (December 4, 1869), 771.

67. "Municipal Caesarism", *The Nation* (September 28, 1871), 205–6; "The Problem at the South," *ibid.* (March 23, 1871), 192–93.

68. "The Bottom of the Great City Difficulty," *ibid.* (September 7, 1871), 157–59; "Municipal Government," *ibid.* (September 21, 1871), 188–90. On municipal law and local democracy, see Hendrick Hartog, *Public Property and Private Power: The Corporation of the City of New York in American Law, 1730–1870* (Chapel Hill: University of North Carolina Press, 1983), pp. 1–10, 227, 261–64; Michael H. Frisch, " 'The Hope of Democracy': Urban Theorists, Urban Reform, and American Political Culture in the Progressive Period," *Political Science Quarterly*, 97 (1982), 295–315.

69. This paragraph and the two that follow it are dependent upon Herbert G. Gutman's articles: "The Tompkins Square 'Riot' in New York City on January 13, 1874: A Re-examination of Its Causes and Its Aftermath," *Labor History*, 6 (1965), 44–70; and "The Failure of the Movement of the Unemployed for Public Works in 1873," *Political Science Quarterly*, 80 (1965), 254–76.

70. *Harper's Weekly* (January 31, 1874), 98.

71. "The Real Nature of the Coming Struggle," *The Nation* (April 9, 1874), 230–31; *ibid.* (September 5, 1872), 148.

72. Alan P. Grimes, *The Political Liberalism of the New York Nation, 1865–1932* (Chapel Hill: University of North Carolina Press, 1953), p. 11.

73. Quoted in Unger, *Greenback Era*, p. 139.

74. William Leach, *True Love and Perfect Union: The Feminist Reform of Sex and Society* (New York: Basic Books, 1980), effectively shows the feminist and reform side of the ASSA, but he errs in thinking that to be the whole of the organization. It was an important but distinctly minority position. For the best analysis of the ASSA, see Haskell, *Emergence of Professional Social Science*.

75. Roosevelt, *Autobiography*, pp. 69–76; Theodore Roosevelt, "The College Graduate and Public Life" [1894], in his *American Ideals* (New York: Putnam's, 1906), p. 103.

76. "Social Science," *The Nation* (November 4, 1869), 381.

77. Unger, *Greenback Era*, p. 137.

78. Haskell, *Emergence of Professional Social Science*, p. 101.

79. See Thomas Bender, "The End of the City?" *democracy*, 3 (1983), 8–20.

80. My understanding of this was advanced by a conversation with Herbert G.

Gutman (September 30, 1984) conveying his findings on the formation of the middle class in the third quarter of the nineteenth century, and by Ira Katznelson, *City Trenches* (New York: Pantheon, 1981).

81. "The Real Objection to the Candidacy of Henry George," *The Nation* (September 30, 1886), 264–65.

82. Sproat, *"The Best Men,"* pp. 232–34.

83. On Curtis's lecture and Howells, see Rodney Olsen, "Identity and Doubt: The Youth of William Dean Howells" (Ph.D. dissertation, University of Missouri, 1981), pp. 317–19.

84. William Dean Howells, *Selected Letters* (6 vols.; Boston: Twayne, 1983), III, 208, 201. His italics.

85. Everett Carter, *Howells and the Age of Realism* (Philadelphia: Lippincott, 1954), p. 177.

86. On the New York literary business, see Howells, *Literature and Life,* which includes his essay "The Literary Man as a Man of Business." More generally, see Lewis Simpson, *The Man of Letters in New England and the South* (Baton Rouge: Louisiana State University Press, 1973), pp. 32–61, 85–128.

87. Howells, *Letters,* III, 195, 321.

88. William Dean Howells, *A Hazard of New Fortunes* (New York: Dutton, 1952), p. 339.

89. Howells, *Letters,* III, 232, 223.

90. Clara Kirk and Rudolf Kirk, "William Dean Howells, George William Curtis, and the Haymarket Affair," *American Literature,* 40 (1969), 487–98.

91. Howells, *Letters,* III, 208.

92. Howells, *Hazard,* pp. xxi–xxii.

93. *Ibid.,* p. xxii.

94. Howells, *Letters,* III, 231.

95. Larzer Ziff, *The American 1890s* (New York: Viking, 1966), p. 39. On Howells and New York, see also Alfred Kazin, *On Native Ground* (Garden City, N.Y.: Doubleday Anchor, 1956), chap. 1.

96. Howells, *Hazard,* pp. 339, 67–68; Howells, *Literature and Life,* pp. 36–44, esp. 43–44. On Howells's notion of complicity, see Robert L. Hough, *The Quiet Rebel* (Lincoln: University of Nebraska Press, 1959), p. 33.

97. William Dean Howells, "The Nature of Liberty," *Forum,* 20 (1895), 408. See also "An East Side Ramble," in his *Impressions and Experiences* (New York: Harper, 1896), pp. 127–49; and "Are We a Plutocracy?," *North American Review,* 158 (1894), 185–96.

98. William Dean Howells, *The Altrurian Romances,* ed. Clara Kirk and Rudolf Kirk (Bloomington: Indiana University Press, 1968), p. xxix.

99. Van Wyck Brooks, *The Confident Years, 1885–1915* (London: J. M. Dent, 1952), p. 81.

100. Franklin B. Sanborn, *Recollections of Seventy Years* (2 vols.; Boston: Richard Badger, 1909), II, 317.

101. The first quote is from Brace, in a letter to Olmsted, in Emma Brace, ed., *Charles Loring Brace* (New York: Scribner's, 1894), p. 111; the second is from a letter from Olmsted to Brace, quoted in Broadus Mitchell, *Frederick Law Olmsted* (Baltimore: Johns Hopkins University Press, 1924), p. 39. Italics in original.

102. See Vincenzo Botta, *Memoirs of Anne C. L. Botta* (New York: Tait, 1894); and Anne Marie Dolan, "The Literary Salon in New York, 1830–1860" (Ph.D. dissertation, Columbia University Press, 1957), pp. 82–100.

103. Parke Godwin to Vincenzo Botta, December 20, 1892, Goddard-Roslyn Collection, New York Public Library.

104. *FLO Papers,* II, 274 n; Roper, *FLO,* p. 84.

105. Eric Foner, *Free Soil, Free Labor, Free Men* (New York: Oxford University Press, 1970), pp. 42–43.

106. Frederick Law Olmsted to father, June 13, 1853, Olmsted Papers, Library of Congress.

107. Frederick Law Olmsted to Parke Godwin, January 29, 1856, Bryant-Godwin Collection, New York Public Library.

108. *FLO Papers,* II, 376.

109. Frederick Law Olmsted, Jr., and Theodora Kimball, eds., *Frederick Law Olmsted* (2 vols. in one; New York: Benjamin Blom, 1970), II, 36–37; *FLO Papers,* III, 80.

110. See, for example, Frederick Law Olmsted to Charles Eliot Norton, October 19, 1881, Charles Eliot Norton Papers, Houghton Library, Harvard University. See also letters to R. G. White, Parke Godwin, and James Fields in *FLO Papers,* vol. III.

111. Brace, ed., *Brace,* pp. 58–59, 76–77. Italics in original.

112. *Ibid.,* pp. 99–100, 153. See also *ibid.,* pp. 115–20.

113. Charles L. Brace to William Colt, December 22, 1845, copy supplied by the late Gerald Brace; Brace, ed., *Brace,* pp. 75–76.

114. Charles L. Brace to George Bushnell, May 21, 1852, Blake Family Papers, Yale University.

115. Brace, ed., *Brace,* p. 160.

116. Paul Boyer, *Urban Masses and Moral Order in America, 1820–1920* (Cambridge: Harvard University Press, 1978), pp. 94, 102.

117. Charles Loring Brace, *The Dangerous Classes of New York* (New York: Wynkoop & Hallenbeck, 1872), p. 29.

118. Children's Aid Society, *Second Annual Report* (1855), p. 4. Italics mine.

119. Brace, *Dangerous Classes,* pp. i–ii.

120. *Ibid.,* p. 95.

121. *Ibid.,* p. iii; Children's Aid Society, *Second Annual Report* (1855), p. 11.

122. Brace, *Dangerous Classes,* pp. 80–81.

123. Charles L. Brace, *Address on Industrial Schools* (New York: Wynkoop & Hallenbeck, 1868), p. 4. For more on this, see Bender, *Toward an Urban Vision,* pp. 136–38.

124. Jacob Riis, *How the Other Half Lives* [1890] (New York: Dover Press, 1971), pp. 140, 157–63.

125. *FLO Papers,* I, 242–44.

126. *Ibid.,* p. 377.

127. *Ibid.,* II, 232–36.

128. *Ibid.,* III, 201.

129. *Ibid.,* III, 303–4. There are deep psychological meanings here that do not concern me in this book, but for a fine exploration of them, see the dissertation in progress at NYU by Melvin Kalfus.

130. Frederick Law Olmsted, "Public Parks and the Enlargement of Towns," *Journal of Social Science,* III (1871), 34.

131. Albert Fein, ed., *Landscape into Cityscape: Frederick Law Olmsted's Plans for a Greater New York City* (Ithaca: Cornell University Press, 1967), p. 101.

132. *FLO Papers,* III, 272, 272 n.–273 n., 213. See also *ibid.,* pp. 280–83.

133. Olmsted, "Public Parks," pp. 18–19.

134. Frederick Law Olmsted, "Of the Villagizing Tendency," undated ms., Olmsted Papers, Library of Congress, Box 41. See also Frederick Law Olmsted, "The Future of New-York," *New York Daily Tribune,* December 28, 1879.

135. Jacob Riis, *The Making of an American* [1901] (New York: Macmillan, 1925), p. 280.

136. Josephine Shaw Lowell to Charles Fairchild, July 7, 1877, Fairchild Papers, New-York Historical Society.

137. See Leach, *True Love.*

138. William Rhinelander Stewart, ed., *The Philanthropic Work of Josephine Shaw Lowell* (New York: Macmillan, 1911), pp. 358, 130.

139. *Ibid.,* pp. 377–78.

140. *Ibid.,* p. 338.

141. Quoted in Lloyd C. Taylor, "Josephine Shaw Lowell and American Philanthropy," *New York History,* 44 (1963), 353.

142. Dedication Program, New York Public Library.

<h2 style="text-align:center">CHAPTER 6</h2>

1. Henry F. May, *The End of American Innocence* (Chicago: Quadrangle, 1964), part I.

2. See, here, Ann Douglas, *The Feminization of American Culture* (New York: Knopf, 1977), but see also Mary Kelley, *Private Woman, Public Stage* (New York: Oxford University Press, 1984).

3. Lincoln Steffens, *Autobiography* (New York: Harcourt, Brace, 1931), pp. 180–81; F. O. Matthiessen, *Theodore Dreiser* (n.p.: William Sloane, 1951), pp. 45–46; Joseph Freeman, *An American Testament* (New York: Farrar & Rinehart, 1936), p. 7.

4. For a similar point in respect to England, see T. W. Heyck, *The Transformation of Intellectual Life in Victorian England* (New York: St. Martin's, 1982), p. 190.

5. Edith Wharton in *W. C. Brownell: Tributes and Appreciations* (New York: Scribner's, 1929), p. 3; Edmund Wilson, *The Shores of Light* (New York: Farrar, Straus & Giroux, 1952), p. 245.

6. Emerson quoted in Henry Blumenthal, *American and French Culture, 1800–1900* (Baton Rouge: Louisiana State University Press, 1975), p. 204; W. C. Brownell, "New York After Paris," *New Princeton Review,* 6 (1888), 83.

7. May, *American Innocence,* p. 65.

8. W. C. Brownell, *French Traits* (New York: Scribner's, 1890), pp. 6, 12, 93–94, 165, 252–53, 266, 86, 85, 94, 85. On Durkheim, see his *Rules of Sociological Method* [1894] (New York: Free Press, 1938), chap. 1.

9. Brownell, *French Traits,* pp. 380, 381, 383.

10. *Ibid.,* pp. 384, 388, 393, 395–96.

11. W. C. Brownell, *Standards* (New York: Scribner's, 1917), p. 2.

12. John Henry Raleigh, *Matthew Arnold in American Culture* (Berkeley: University of California Press, 1957), p. 107; Matthew Arnold, "The Literary Influence of Academies," in *Poetry and Criticism of Matthew Arnold,* ed. A. D. Culler (Boston: Houghton Mifflin, 1961), pp. 259–79.

13. Brownell, *French Traits,* pp. 317–19.

14. Brownell, *Standards,* pp. 37–38; Brownell, *French Traits,* pp. 317–23.

15. Raleigh, *Arnold in America,* p. 117; W. C. Brownell, *Democratic Distinction in America* (New York: Scribner's, 1927), p. 204.

16. *Ibid.,* pp. 59, 64; Matthew Arnold, *Culture and Anarchy* in *Poetry and Criticism,* ed. Culler, p. 427. Italics in original.

17. Raymond Williams, *Culture and Society, 1780–1950* (New York: Harper Torchbook, 1958), p. 126.

18. On this error, see Richard Ruland, *The Rediscovery of American Literature: Premises of Critical Taste, 1900–1940* (Cambridge: Harvard University Press, 1967), pp. 11–23; Raleigh, *Arnold in America,* p. 114.

19. John Tomisch, *A Genteel Endeavor: American Culture and Politics in the Gilded Age* (Stanford: Stanford University Press, 1971), p. 24.

20. Alfred Kazin, *On Native Grounds* (Garden City, N.Y.: Doubleday Anchor, 1956), p. 41.

21. Rosamond Gilder, ed., *Letters of Richard Watson Gilder* (Boston: Houghton Mifflin, 1916), pp. 66, 408–10.

22. On Huckleberry Finn, see Gilder, ed., *Letters,* p. 399; and Arthur John, *The Best Years of the Century* (Urbana: University of Illinois Press, 1981), p. 156. On Eastman, see Max Eastman, *Enjoyment of Living* (New York: Harper, 1948), p. 301. For an early defense of *The Century* as a family magazine, see *The Century,* 30 (May 1885), 164–65.

23. "A New Volume of the Century," *The Century,* 30 (May 1885), 164–65; *The Nation* (September 28, 1882), 265.

24. "A New Volume of the Century," pp. 164–65; "To the Readers of the Century," *The Century,* 35 (November 1887), 160.

25. On Melville, see Brander Matthews, *These Many Years* (New York: Scribner's, 1917), p. 221.

26. Gilder, ed., *Letters,* pp. 273, 188. See also pp. 326–27.

27. Quoted in John, *Best Years,* p. 207.

28. On Howells and the custodians of traditional culture, see May, *American Innocence,* chap. 1.

29. Gilder, ed., *Letters,* p. 63.

30. On Union Square, see John W. Frick, Jr., "The Rialto: A Study of Union Square, the Center of New York's First Theatre District, 1870–1900" (Ph.D. dissertation, New York University, 1983).

31. Brownell, *Democratic Distinction,* p. 259.

32. Charles C. Alexander, *Here the Country Lies: Nationalism in the Arts in Twentieth Century America* (Bloomington: Indiana University Press, 1980), p. 128. On the fascinating history of several generations of Damrosches, see George Martin, *The Damrosch Dynasty* (Boston: Houghton Mifflin, 1983).

33. For an excellent account of the place of music in the life of Jewish immigrants, the largest group on the Lower East Side, see Mark Slobin, *Tenement Songs* (Urbana: University of Illinois Press, 1982).

34. Lucy P. and Richard P. Stebbins, *Frank Damrosch* (Durham: Duke University Press, 1945), p. 138.

35. *Ibid.,* p. 140.

36. *Ibid.,* chap. 8. On Adler, see Horace Friess, *Felix Adler and Ethical Culture* (New York: Columbia University Press, 1981), p. 99.

37. Stebbins, *Damrosch,* pp. 154–55.

38. *Ibid.,* p. 160.

39. I have relied upon Charles Fenton, "The Founding of the National Institute of Arts and Letters in 1898," *New England Quarterly,* 32 (1959), 435–54; Charles Fenton, "The American Academy of Arts and Letters vs. All Comers," *South Atlantic Quarterly,* 58 (1959), 572–86; Malcolm Cowley, *And I Worked at the Writer's Trade* (New York: Penguin, 1979), chap. 11; Geoffrey T. Hellman, "Some Splendid and Admirable People," *The New Yorker* (February 23, 1976), 43–81.

40. Laura Stedman and George Gould, eds., *Life and Letters of Edmund Clarence Stedman* (2 vols; New York: Moffat, Yard, 1910), II, 443.

41. Robert U. Johnson, *Remembered Yesterdays* (Boston: Little, Brown, 1923), pp. 145–46.

42. Ellen Glasgow, *The Woman Within* (New York: Harcourt, Brace, 1954), pp. 139, 141.

43. Quoted in Hellman, "Splendid," p. 52.

44. For biographical information, see Arnold T. Schwab, *James Gibbons Huneker* (Stanford: Stanford University Press, 1963).

45. *M'lle New York* is not paginated; the quotes come from the first three numbers (1895).

46. Schwab, *Huneker*, p. vii; Kazin, *Native Grounds*, p. 47.

47. Charles Forcey, *Crossroads of Liberalism* (New York: Oxford University Press, 1961), pp. 11–21. For an exhaustively researched biography of Croly, see David W. Levy, *Herbert Croly and the New Republic* (Princeton: Princeton University Press, 1984).

48. Wilson, *Shores of Light*, p. 477.

49. Matthews, *These Many Years*, p. 451. See also Herbert Croly, "Civic Improvement: The Case of New York," *Architectural Record*, 21 (May 1907), 347–52; *The American Renaissance* (New York: Pantheon Books, for the Brooklyn Museum, 1979); Thomas Bender and William R. Taylor, "Culture and Architecture: Some Aesthetic Tensions in the Shaping of Modern New York City," in William Sharpe and Leonard Wallock, eds., *Visions of the Modern City*, Proceedings of the Columbia University Society of Fellows in the Humanities (New York: Columbia University Press, 1983), pp. 185–215; and Eric Sandeen, ed., *The Letters of Randolph Bourne* (Troy, N.Y.: Whitson, 1981), p. 167.

50. Herbert Croly, "The New World and the New Art," *Architectural Record*, 12 (June 1902), 134–53. See also Herbert Croly, "Why I Wrote My Latest Book," *The World's Work*, 20 (June 1910), 13086.

51. Herbert Croly, "American Architects and Their Public," *Architectural Record*, 10 (February 1901), 256–62.

52. Croly, "New World and New Art," p. 153.

53. Herbert Croly, "New York as the American Metropolis," *Architectural Record*, 13 (March 1903), 193–206.

54. Croly, "Why I Wrote My Latest Book."

55. Herbert Croly, *The Promise of American Life* [1909] (New York: Bobbs-Merrill, 1965), p.150.

56. Herbert Croly, "The Architect in Recent Fiction," *Architectural Record*, 17 (February 1905), 137–39. See also Herbert Croly, "What Is Civic Art?" *ibid.*, 16 (July 1904), 49; Croly, "New World and New Art"; and Steven Kesselman, *The Modernization of American Reform* (New York: Garland, 1979), pp. 274–77.

57. Croly, *Promise*, pp. 5, 17, 22–23.

58. *Ibid.*, p. 140.

59. *Ibid.*, pp. 411, 421, 439.

60. *Ibid.*, p. 443.

61. *Ibid.*, p. 447.

62. *Ibid.*, pp. 4, 50–52.

63. Forcey, *Crossroads*, p. 183.

64. Quoted in Kesselman, *Modernization of Reform*, p. 307.

65. *The New Republic* (November 7, 1914), 3, 7.

66. Herbert Croly to Randolph Bourne, September 15, 1915, Randolph S. Bourne Papers, Columbia University.

67. Waldo Frank, *The Re-Discovery of America* (New York: Scribner's, 1929), p. 314 and dedication page.

68. William James, "The Social Value of the College-Bred," *McClure's*, 30 (1908), 419–22. Lewis Feuer, "The Political Linguistics of 'Intellectual,' 1898–1909," *Survey*, 78 (1971), esp. 156–57, 159, 163.

69. See Robert Wohl, *The Generation of 1914* (Cambridge: Harvard University Press,

1979): Carl E. Schorske, "Generational Tension and Cultural Change: Reflections on the Case of Vienna," *Daedalus,* 107 (Fall 1978), 111–22; and Annie Kriegel, "Generational Difference: The History of an Idea," *ibid.,* pp. 23–38.

70. Walter Lippmann, *Drift and Mastery* (Westport: Greenwood Press, 1978), p. 16.

71. Floyd Dell, *Homecoming* (New York: Farrar & Rinehart, 1933), p. 272.

72. See her essay in Harold Stearns, ed., *Civilization in the United States* (New York: Harcourt, Brace, 1922). There are some very perceptive comments on her in Rosalind Rosenberg, *Beyond Separate Spheres: Intellectual Roots of Modern Feminism* (New Haven: Yale University Press, 1982), chap. 6.

73. Lewis Mumford, *Sketches from Life* (New York: Dial, 1982), p. 366.

74. Eastman, *Enjoyment of Living,* p. 399.

75. Christopher Lasch, *The New Radicalism in America* (New York: Knopf, 1965), chap. 3; Leslie Fishbein, *Rebels in Bohemia* (Chapel Hill: University of North Carolina Press, 1982).

76. Van Wyck Brooks, Introduction to Randolph Bourne, *The History of a Literary Radical* (New York: S. A. Russell, 1956), p. 18.

77. James Gilbert makes this point in his *Writers and Partisans: A History of Literary Radicalism in America* (New York: Wiley, 1968).

78. May, *American Innocence,* p. 281. See also Bernard Duffey, *The Chicago Renaissance in American Letters* (East Lansing: Michigan State College Press, 1954).

79. May, *American Innocence,* p. 281.

80. Compare Lionel Trilling, *Beyond Culture* (New York: Viking, 1965), esp. pp. 3–30, 209–33, with Peter Gay, *Freud, Jews and Other Germans* (New York: Oxford University Press, 1978), pp. 22–26. See also Daniel Singal, *The War Within* (Chapel Hill: University of North Carolina Press, 1982), chap. 1.

81. Mumford, *Sketches,* p. 357. See also Warren Susman, "A Second Country: The Expatriate Image," *Texas Studies in Literature and Languages,* 3 (Summer 1961), 171–83.

82. Malcolm Cowley, *Exile's Return* (New York: Viking, 1956), p. 33; Floyd Dell, *Intellectual Vagabondage* (New York: George H. Doran, 1926), p. 107.

83. Randolph Bourne, "A Vanishing World of Gentility," *The Dial,* 64 (March 14, 1918), 234–35; Randolph Bourne, *The Radical Will: Selected Writings,* ed. Olaf Hansen (New York: Urizen Books, 1977), pp. 194–95.

84. *The Nation* (May 20, 1913), 551.

85. Waldo Frank, *Our America* (New York: Boni & Liveright, 1919), p. 199. See also Lewis Mumford, "The Image of Randolph Bourne," *The New Republic,* 64 (September 24, 1930), 151–52.

86. Ellery Sedgwick to Randolph S. Bourne, March 15, 1911, Bourne Papers.

87. Paul Rosenfeld, *Port of New York* [1924] (Urbana: University of Illinois Press, 1966), pp. 215–18. Bruce Clayton, *Forgotten Prophet: The Life of Randolph Bourne* (Baton Rouge: Louisiana State University Press, 1984) is the best biography.

88. See Rosenfeld, *Port of New York,* p. 217; Waldo Frank, *Memoirs,* ed. A. Trachtenberg (Amherst: University of Massachusetts Press, 1973), p. 92; Max Eastman, *Love and Revolution* (New York: Random House, 1964), p. 28.

89. This is apparent in his letters, especially those to women during his college years. See Sandeen, ed., *Letters.*

90. Alyse Gregory, *The Day Is Gone* (New York: Dutton, 1948), p. 135.

91. Randolph Bourne, *Youth and Life* (Boston: Houghton Mifflin, 1913), p. 135; Sandeen, ed., *Letters,* p. 89; Beulah Amidon to Alyse Gregory, October 4, 1948, Bourne Papers.

92. Bourne, *Youth and Life,* p. 228.

93. On the public qualities, see Daniel Aaron, "American Prophet," *New York Review of Books* (November 23, 1978), 36–40.

94. Quotes from David Hollinger, "Ethnic Diversity, Cosmopolitanism, and the Emergence of the American Liberal Intelligentsia," *American Quarterly*, 27 (1975), 135.

95. Lewis Mumford, *My Works and Days* (New York: Harcourt Brace Jovanovich, 1979), pp. 44–46; Freeman, *American Testament*, p. 104.

96. Sandeen, ed., *Letters*, p. 163.

97. See Harry Dana to Randolph S. Bourne, March 21, 1914, Bourne Papers.

98. Robert Spiller, ed., *The Van Wyck Brooks–Lewis Mumford Letters* (New York: Dutton, 1970), p. 30; Thomas Bender, "Lewis Mumford," *Skyline* (December 1982), 12–14.

99. His report is reprinted in Bourne, *The History of a Literary Radical*, pp. 75–102.

100. *Ibid.*, p. 80.

101. Sandeen, ed., *Letters*, pp. 196, 182, 185.

102. *Ibid.*, p. 196. On his identification of Anglo-Saxonism with Butler, see *ibid.*, p. 179.

103. *Ibid.*, p. 263. See also the way the war issue frames his report to the trustees of Columbia University, in Bourne, *Literary Radical*, pp. 75–102.

104. Mumford, "Images," p. 152; Herbert Croly to Randolph S. Bourne, June 3, 1914, Bourne Papers; Charles A. Beard to Randolph S. Bourne, May 15, 1914, *ibid.*

105. Randolph Bourne, *War and the Intellectuals*, ed. Carl Resek (New York: Harper Torchbook, 1964), p. 182; Randolph Bourne, "Our Cultural Humility," *Atlantic Monthly* (October 1914), 503–7; Sandeen, ed., *Letters*, pp. 233–34; Beulah Amidon to Alyse Gregory, October 4, 1948, Bourne Papers.

106. Randolph Bourne, "The Heart of the People," *The New Republic* (July 3, 1915), 233.

107. Bourne, *War and the Intellectuals*, p. 192.

108. Bourne, *Radical Will*, p. 480.

109. For a sympathetic treatment of the New Humanists, see J. David Hoeveler, *The New Humanism* (Charlottesville: University Press of Virginia, 1977).

110. Paul Elmer More, *Aristocracy and Justice* [1915] (New York: Phaeton Press, 1967), pp. 37, 31.

111. Bourne, *Radical Will*, pp. 467–70.

112. *Ibid.*, p. 480.

113. Ronald Steel, *Walter Lippmann and the American Century* (Boston: Atlantic–Little, Brown, 1980), p. 3.

114. Quoted in *ibid.*, p. 58.

115. Walter Lippmann, *A Preface to Politics* [1913] (New York: Macmillan, 1933), pp. 306–7.

116. Sandeen, ed., *Letters*, p. 303; David A. Hollinger, "Science and Anarchy: Walter Lippmann's *Drift and Mastery*," *American Quarterly*, 29 (1977), 463–75.

117. Lippmann, *Drift and Mastery*, pp. 151, 155. See also pp. 16–17.

118. Edmund Wilson, *Classics and Commercials* (New York: Farrar, Straus & Giroux, 1950), p. 11; F. W. Dupee, "The Americanism of Van Wyck Brooks," *Partisan Review*, 6 (1939), 69–85; Dwight Macdonald, *Memoirs of a Revolutionist* (New York: Farrar, Straus & Cudahy, 1957), pp. 203–14.

119. Claire Sprague, ed., *Van Wyck Brooks: The Early Years, A Selection from His Works, 1908–1921* (New York: Harper Torchbook, 1968), pp. 219–26.

120. James Hoopes, *Van Wyck Brooks* (Amherst: University of Massachusetts Press, 1977), pp. 32, 94, 106. This is the best biography of Brooks.

121. Van Wyck Brooks, *The Wine of the Puritans* [1908] (Folcroft, Pa.: Folcroft Press, 1969), pp. 17–18.

122. On Brooks at *The Century*, see Hoopes, *Brooks*, p. 108. On Brownell, see John Wheelock, ed., *Editor to Author* (New York: Scribner's, 1950), p. 10.

123. Van Wyck Brooks, *America's Coming of Age* (New York: B. W. Huebsch, 1915), pp. 5–6, 7, 113, 119, 121, 150.

124. Van Wyck Brooks, *Three Essays on America* (New York: Dutton, 1934), pp. 169–70, 173, 170, 189. On Bourne's admiration, see Sandeen, ed., *Letters*, p. 410.

125. See Randolph Bourne, *Untimely Papers*, ed. James Oppenheim (New York: B. W. Huebsch, 1919), p. 141. See also Hoopes, *Brooks*, p. 132.

126. May, *American Innocence*, p. 322.

127. It should be noted that other money probably could have been found to continue had not the editors fallen into a quarrel about who should be number one, and whether Bourne should be added to the editorial group. See Frank, *Memoirs*, pp. 93–94; and Clayton, *Forgotten Prophet*, p. 229.

128. The best information on Oppenheim is to be found in Stanley Kunitz and Howard Haycraft, eds., *Twentieth Century Authors* (New York: H. W. Wilson, 1942), pp. 1053–54; on Frank, the best source is his *Memoirs*.

129. James Oppenheim, "The Story of the Seven Arts," *The American Mercury*, 20 (1930), 156, 158; Hoopes, *Brooks*, p. 110.

130. Oppenheim, "The Story of Seven Arts," p. 158; Frank, *Our America*, p. 89. Cf. Irving Howe, *A Margin of Hope* (New York: Harcourt Brace Jovanovich, 1982), pp. 137–38.

131. Oppenheim, "The Story of Seven Arts," p. 157.

132. *Seven Arts*, 1 (November 1916), 52–53; Van Wyck Brooks, "A Reviewer's Notebook," *The Freeman*, 2 (November 3, 1920), 190–91.

133. Howard Mumford Jones and Walter B. Rideout, eds., *Letters of Sherwood Anderson* (Boston: Little, Brown, 1953), pp. 4, 29–31, 84.

134. "Who Willed American Participation," *The New Republic* (April 14, 1917) 308–10; Bourne, *War and the Intellectuals*, p. 3; Jane Addams to Randolph S. Bourne, June 30, 1917, Bourne Papers; Frank, *Our America*, p. 198.

135. Sandeen, ed., *Letters*, p. 425; Bourne, *War and the Intellectuals*, p. 59.

136. Sandeen, ed., *Letters*, p. 412. Cf. Bourne, *Youth and Life*, p. 50.

137. Sprague, ed., *Brooks Writings*, p. 213.

138. George Konrad and Ivan Szelenyi, *The Intellectuals on the Road to Class Power* (New York: Harcourt Brace Jovanovich, 1979); Edward Shils, *The Constitution of Society* (Chicago: University of Chicago Press, 1982), chap. 10.

139. Steel, *Lippmann*, p. xv and *passim*.

140. Forcey, *Crossroads*, pp. 265–66; Steel, *Lippmann*, p. 109; Levy, *Croly*, pp. 245–46.

141. Harold Stearns, *Liberalism in America* (New York: Boni & Liveright, 1919), p. 112; Bourne, *War and the Intellectuals*, p. 47.

142. *Ibid.*, pp. 59–64.

143. *Ibid.*, pp. 41, 43, 46, 140.

144. Harold Stearns, *America and the Young Intellectual* (New York: George H. Doran, 1921), pp. 49–50; Lewis Mumford, "In Sackcloth and Ashes," *The Freeman*, 2 (December 1, 1920), 282–83.

145. Forcey, *Crossroads*, pp. 285, 204, 279.

146. Herbert Croly, "Liberalism vs. War," *The New Republic* (December 8, 1920), 35–39. On Croly's "superiority" to uncreative pragmatists, see Waldo Frank's undated memorandum in Bourne Papers.

147. Wilson, *Shores of Light*, p. 482; Malcolm Cowley, *The Dream of the Golden Mountains* (New York: Viking, 1980), p. 9.

148. Walter Lippmann, *Public Opinion* [1922] (New York: Macmillan, 1954), p. 400; Walter Lippmann, *The Phantom Public* (New York: Harcourt, Brace, 1925), p. 150.

149. John Dewey, "Public Opinion," *The New Republic* (May 3, 1922), 286–88; Charles A. Beard and William Beard, *American Leviathan: The Republic in the Machine Age* (New York: Macmillan Co., 1930), pp. 103–8.

150. Hollinger, "Ethnic Diversity"; Terry A. Cooney, "Cosmopolitan Values and the Identification of Reaction: The *Partisan Review* in the 1930s," *Journal of American History*, 68 (1981), 580–98; Daniel J. Singal, "Beyond Consensus: Richard Hofstadter and American Historiography," *American Historical Review*, 89 (1984), 976–1004. On intolerance, see William Preston, Jr., *Aliens and Dissenters* (Cambridge: Harvard University Press, 1963).

151. Freeman, *American Testament*, pp. 49, 339 (quote).

152. *Ibid.*, p. 310.

153. Philip Rahv, *Essays on Literature and Politics* (Boston: Houghton Mifflin, 1978), pp. 299–300.

154. For a thorough discussion, see Daniel Aaron, *Writers on the Left* (New York: Harcourt, Brace & World, 1961).

155. Rosenfeld, *Port of New York*, p. 212. For the article that stimulated Bourne, see Horace M. Kallen, "Democracy Versus the Melting Pot," *The Nation* (1915), 219–20.

156. Bourne, *War and the Intellectuals*, pp. 108, 114, 108, 115, 119.

157. Hollinger, "Ethnic Diversity," p. 142. On Cohen, see David Hollinger, *Morris Cohen and the Scientific Ideal* (Cambridge: MIT Press, 1975).

158. Ellery Sedgwick to Randolph S. Bourne, March 30, 1916; Ellery Sedgwick to Randolph S. Bourne, July 27, 1916, Bourne Papers.

159. Bourne, *War and the Intellectuals*, pp. 124–33.

160. *Partisan Review*, 19 (1952), 324.

161. Leon Edel, ed., *Henry James Letters*, I (Cambridge: Harvard University Press, 1974), p. 77; Leon Edel, *Henry James* (5 vols.; Philadelphia: Lippincott, 1953–72), V, 255; Henry James, *The American Scene* (Bloomington: Indiana University Press, 1968), pp 138–39.

162. For a fine history of this relation, see Gilbert, *Writers and Partisans*.

163. Lewis Mumford, "The American Intelligentsia," *World Tomorrow*, 8 (July 1925), 200–201; Mumford, "Image of Randolph Bourne."

164. Nicholas Joost, "Culture Versus Power: Randolph Bourne, John Dewey, and *The Dial*," *Midwest Quarterly*, 9 (1968), 245–59; Nicholas Joost, *Schofield Thayer and the Dial* (Carbondale: Southern Illinois University Press, 1964).

165. Nathan G. Hale, "From Berggasse XIX to Central Park West: The Americanization of Psychoanalysis, 1919–1940," *Journal of the History of the Behavioral Sciences*, 14 (1978), 299–315.

166. Bourne, *War and the Intellectuals*, pp. 179–83; Harriet Monroe, "Mr. Bourne on Traps," *Poetry*, 12 (May 1918), 90–94; Randolph Bourne and Van Wyck Brooks, "The Retort Courteous," *Poetry*, 12 (September 1918), 341–44.

167. Cowley, *Exiles*, p. 95. See also Dickran Tashjian, *Skyscraper Primitives* (Middleton, Conn.: Wesleyan University Press, 1975).

168. Trilling, *Beyond Culture*, p. 8; Max Eastman, *The Literary Mind* (New York: Scribner's, 1931), p. 21.

169. Quoted in James Atlas, *Delmore Schwartz* (New York: Avon, 1977), pp. 149–50.

170. See the suggestive remark in John Chamberlain, *Farewell to Reform* (New York: Liveright, 1932), p. 304.

171. Nathan A. Scott, Jr., *The Poetry of Civic Virtue* (Philadelphia: Fortress Press, 1976), p. x.

172. Wilson, *Shores of Light*, pp. 247, 369.

173. Harold Stearns, *Confessions of a Harvard Man* [1935] (Santa Barbara, Calif.: Paget, 1984), p. 176. The phrase "Uptown Bohemia" is from Eastman, *Love and Revolution*, p. 252.

174. Johnson, *Remembered Yesterdays*, p. 440; Eastman, *Enjoyment of Living*, p. 580.

175. Quotes from James Weldon Johnson, *Black Manhattan* [1930] (New York: Atheneum, 1972), pp. 4, 146. On the six leaders, see David Levering Lewis, *When Harlem Was in Vogue* (New York: Knopf, 1981), chap. 5.

176. Alain Locke, ed., *The New Negro* (New York: Albert and Charles Boni, 1925), p. 15.

177. Harold Cruse, *The Crisis of the Negro Intellectual* (New York: Morrow, 1967); Nathan Huggins, *Harlem Renaissance* (New York: Oxford University Press, 1971); Lewis, *When Harlem Was in Vogue.*

178. Huggins, *Harlem Renaissance*, p. 85. See also Charles Scruggs, *The Sage in Harlem: H. L. Mencken and the Black Writers of the 1920s* (Baltimore: Johns Hopkins University Press, 1984).

179. W. E. B. Du Bois, "Criteria of Negro Art," *Crisis*, 32 (October 1926), 290–97; Lewis, *When Harlem Was in Vogue*, esp. chap. 5.

180. Cruse, *Crisis*, pp. 451–97.

181. Daniel Bell, *The Winding Passage* (New York: Basic Books, 1980), p. 128.

182. Quote from Johnson, *Black Manhattan*, p. 147.

183. David Levering Lewis, "Parallels and Divergences: Assimilationist Strategies of Afro-American and Jewish Elites from 1910 to the Early 1930s," *Journal of American History*, 71 (1984), 563.

184. Sherman Paul, *Edmund Wilson: A Study of Literary Vocation in Our Time* (Urbana: University of Illinois Press, 1965), p. 1.

185. Grant Webster, *The Republic of Letters: A History of Postwar American Literary Opinion* (Baltimore: Johns Hopkins University Press, 1979). pp. 292, 268.

186. Alfred Kazin, *Starting Out in the Thirties* (Boston: Little, Brown, 1965), pp. 5, 136–37; Lionel Trilling, *A Gathering of Fugitives* (Boston: Beacon Press, 1956), p. 50.

187. Leonard Kriegel, *Edmund Wilson* (Carbondale: Southern Illinois University Press, 1971), p. 3.

188. Paul, *Wilson*, p. 191. On Mumford, see Bender, "Lewis Mumford."

189. Paul, *Wilson*, p. 34.

190. Edmund Wilson, "The Muses Out of Work," *The New Republic* (May 11, 1927), 321.

191. Edmund Wilson, *I Thought of Daisy* (New York: Farrar, Straus, & Young, 1953), preface.

192. Wilson, *Shores of Light*, p. 498.

193. Wilson, *Classics and Commercials*, pp. 114–15.

194. Edmund Wilson, *Letters on Literature and Politics*, ed. Elena Wilson (New York: Farrar, Straus & Giroux, 1977), pp. 201, 151, 211. See also Edmund Wilson, *Axel's Castle* (New York: Scribner's, 1931), pp. 21, 25.

195. Wilson, *Axel's Castle*, p. 85.

196. *Ibid.*, pp. 87–92.

197. Aaron, "American Prophet," p. 39.

198. Wilson, *Shores of Light*, pp. 500–03.

199. Quoted in Aaron, *Writers on the Left*, p. 251.

200. Edward Said, *The World, the Text and the Critic* (Cambridge: Harvard University Press, 1983), p. 161.

201. Cf. Lewis Mumford, "The Metropolitan Milieu," in Waldo Frank, ed., *America and Alfred Stieglitz* (New York: Doubleday, Doran, 1934), pp. 33–58.

202. Wilson, *Classics and Commercials*, p. 109.

203. Stephen Spender, "Writers in America," *The Nation* (1949), reprinted in Henry M. Christman, ed., *One Hundred Years of The Nation* (New York: Capricorn, 1965), pp. 269–73.

CHAPTER 7

1. Quoted in "Mid-Nineteenth Century Life in New York: More Revelations from the Diary of George Templeton Strong," *New-York Historical Society Quarterly*, 37 (1953), 19.

2. Brander Matthews, *A History of Columbia University* (New York: Columbia University Press, 1904), p. 263.

3. The point is developed more fully in my "Erosion of Public Culture: Cities, Discourses, and Professional Disciplines," in Thomas L. Haskell, ed., *The Authority of Experts* (Bloomington: Indiana University Press, 1984), pp. 84–106.

4. Asa Briggs, "University, City, Community: A Historical Perspective," Lecture at Columbia University, September 30, 1981. See also Paul Farmer, "Nineteenth Century Ideas of the University: Continental Europe," in Margaret Clapp, ed., *The Modern University* (Ithaca: Cornell University Press, 1950), pp. 4, 9.

5. George Templeton Strong, *Diary*, ed. Allan Nevins and M. H. Thomas (4 vols.; New York: Macmillan, 1952), III, 30.

6. Henry P. Tappan, *The Growth of Cities* (New York: R. Craighead, 1855), pp. 35, 45. Henry N. McCracken, "The Relation of Metropolis and the University," *University Quarterly*, 8 (1880), 65. See also *idem*, "Universities in Great Cities," ms., no date, Henry N. McCracken Papers, University Archives, New York University.

7. Nicholas Murray Butler, "Inaugural Address," *Columbia University Quarterly*, 4 (Inauguration Supp., 1901), 57; N. M. Butler, *Across the Busy Years* (2 vols.; New York: Scribner's, 1939–40), I, 172–73. See also N. M. Butler, memorandum, 1908–1910, N. M. Butler Files, Central Filing, Columbia University. More modestly, Low, too, understood how New York's stature affected Columbia. See his *Annual Report* (1895), p. 5.

8. E. L. Godkin, *Reflections and Comments, 1865–1895* (New York: Scribner's, 1895), pp. 203–4.

9. E. L. Godkin, "Professional Guildes," *American Institute of Architects, Proceedings* (1870), 192; E. L. Godkin, "The Organization of Culture," *The Nation* (June 18, 1868), 486–88; Strong, *Diary*, IV, 216–17.

10. William Armstrong, ed., *The Gilded Age Letters of E. L. Godkin* (Albany: State University of New York Press, 1974), p. 111; Columbia College, Alumni Association, *Annual Dinner of 1890* (New York: printed by order of the Association, 1890), p. 34.

11. George L. Prentice, *The Union Theological Seminary in the City of New York* (New York: Randolph & Co., 1889), esp. pp. 53–57, 66, 78–79; Charles A. Briggs, "The Ideal Study of Theology," in Union Theological Seminary, *Dedication of the New Building* (New York: n.p., 1910), pp. 115–36; William Adams Brown, "A Century in Retrospect," in Union Theological Seminary, *One Hundredth Anniversary, 1836–1936* (New York: n.p., 1936), pp. 25–38; William Adams Brown in *Dedication of the New Building*, pp. 51–62.

12. Columbia College, *Report of a Committee of the Trustees of Columbia College Appointed to Inquire into the Condition of the Institution* (New York: John W. Amerman, 1858), p. 17; Brander Matthews, *These Many Years* (New York: Scribner's, 1917), p. 395; John S. Whitehead, *The Separation of the College and the State: Columbia, Dartmouth, Harvard, and Yale, 1776–1876* (New Haven: Yale University Press, 1973), p. 220.

13. E. L. Godkin, "Columbia College and the Public," *The Nation* (March 15, 1883), 226–27. For Fish's report, see Columbia College, *The Financial Condition and Present Needs of the College* (New York: printed for the College, 1883).

14. Rosamond Gilder, ed., *Letters of Richard Watson Gilder* (Boston: Houghton Mifflin, 1916), p. 118; "A Great Metropolitan University," *The Century*, 25 (April 1883), 951–53.

15. E. L. Godkin, "New York and Her University," *The Nation* (January 10, 1889), 24–25. See also A. D. White, "The Need for Another University," *The Forum*, 6 (January 1889), 465–73.

16. E. L. Godkin, "A New Move in Columbia College," *The Nation* (May 8, 1890), 369–70.

17. Samuel B. Ruggles, *The Duty of Columbia College to the Community* (New York: John E. Trow, 1854), pp. 3–5.

18. Richard Hofstadter, *Academic Freedom in the Age of the College* (New York: Columbia University Press, 1955), pp. 269–74.

19. Ruggles, *Duty of Columbia*, pp. 13, 4.

20. *Ibid.*, pp. 29, 30, 39, 14.

21. *Ibid.*, pp. 19, 14.

22. *Ibid.*, pp. 16, 54.

23. New York State, Legislature, Senate, *Select Committee Appointed to Examine into the Affairs of Columbia College* (1855); Whitehead, *College and the State*, pp. 220–22.

24. Hofstadter, *Academic Freedom*, p. 273.

25. There are two basic sources on Ruggles, a biography by Daniel G. B. Thompson, *Ruggles of New York* (New York: Columbia University Press, 1946), p. 82; and the diary of his son-in-law, George Templeton Strong.

26. Samuel B. Ruggles, *Memorial . . . on the Social and Fiscal Importance of Open Squares in the City of New York . . .* (New York: Bessey, 1878).

27. Matthews, *A History of Columbia*, p. 214.

28. See Konrad H. Jarausch, "Higher Education and Social Change: Some Comparative Perspectives," in Jarausch, ed., *The Transformation of Higher Learning, 1860–1930* (Chicago: University of Chicago Press, 1983), p. 9. See also Thomas L. Haskell, *The Emergence of Professional Social Science* (Urbana: University of Illinois Press, 1977).

29. John W. Burgess, *Reminiscences of an American Scholar* (New York: Columbia University Press, 1934), p. 151.

30. *Ibid.*, pp. 28, 29, 12.

31. *Ibid.*, pp. 123–24; John W. Burgess, "The American Commonwealth in Its Relation to the Nation," *Political Science Quarterly*, 1 (1886), 35; Burgess, *Reminiscences*, p. 131.

32. *Ibid.*, pp. 151, 178. See also John W. Burgess, "The Founding of the School of Political Science," *Columbia University Quarterly*, 22 (1930), 361.

33. Burgess, *Reminiscences*, pp. 135, 151, 161.

34. See Brander Matthews, "Columbia College: The Development of a Great University," *Harper's Weekly* (November 3, 1894), 1042. On the *Ecole libre*, see Theodore Zeldin, *France, 1848–1945* (2 vols.; Oxford University Press, 1973–77), II, 343.

35. See, for example, Samuel Eliot, "An American University," *Journal of Social*

Science, 5 (1873), 162–77; E. L. Godkin, "Legislation and Social Science," *ibid.,* 3 (1871), 120.

36. Burgess, *Reminiscences,* pp. 212–13.

37. Columbia College, *Outline of a Plan for the Instruction of Graduate Classes . . . and for the Creation of a School of Preparation for the Civil Service* (New York: MacGowan & Slipper, 1880), pp. 4, 11. See also William F. Russell and Edward Elliott, eds., *The Rise of a University* (2 vols.; New York: Columbia University Press, 1932), I, 358; Columbia College, *Outline,* pp. 12, 15.

38. Columbia College, *Report of the Committee on the Statutes and Courses of Instruction . . . May 3, 1880* (New York: MacGowan & Slipper, 1880), p. 6; Harold S. Wechsler, *The Qualified Student: A History of Selective Admissions in America* (New York: Wiley, 1977), p. 70.

39. Jarausch, "Higher Education and Social Change," p. 13.

40. Hoxie, *Faculty of Political Science,* pp. 55, 29; Matthews, *A History of Columbia,* pp. 273–77.

41. See John W. Burgess to E. R. A. Seligman, September 29, 1894, Seligman Collection, Butler Library, Columbia University; Matthews, *A History of Columbia,* pp. 293–95; Hoxie, *Faculty of Political Science,* p. 80.

42. Edward Shils, "The Order of Learning in the United States from 1865 to 1920: The Ascendancy of the University," *Minerva,* 16 (1978), 166.

43. Columbia College, *Proceedings at the Installation of Seth Low as President . . .* (New York: printed for the College, 1890), pp. 17–22, 33. See also George W. Curtis, "A Great Day for Columbia," *Harper's Weekly* (February 15, 1890), 118.

44. Seth Low, *Annual Report* (1890), p. 8.

45. *Columbia Alumni News,* 8 (October 20, 1916), 77–79.

46. Seth Low to A. A. Low, May 7, 1889, Seth Low Papers, Butler Library, Columbia University; John W. Burgess to Seth Low, July 20, 1912, *ibid.*

47. Low, *Annual Report* (1890), pp. 5, 8.

48. First quote from the resolution of the trustees accepting Low's resignation in October 1901, Seth Low Files, Central Filing, Columbia University; second quote from Burgess, *Reminiscences,* p. 332.

49. See Peter Dobkin Hall, *The Organization of American Culture, 1700–1900* (New York: New York University Press, 1982), chap. 3; Phyllis Dain, *The New York Public Library* (New York: New York Public Library, 1972).

50. Lincoln Steffens, *Autobiography* (New York: Harcourt, Brace, 1931), p. 431.

51. Gerald Kurland, *Seth Low* (New York: Twayne, 1971), chap. 2.

52. Seth Low, "An American View of Municipal Government in the United States," in James Bryce, *The American Commonwealth* (2 vols.; London: Macmillan, 1889), I, 620–35; Kurland, *Seth Low,* esp. chaps. 4–7.

53. Martin Schiesl, *The Politics of Efficiency: Municipal Administration and Reform in America, 1880–1920* (Berkeley: University of California Press, 1977), p. 78; Steffens, *Autobiography,* p. 431.

54. Seth Low, in *Proceedings at the Installation of Seth Low,* p. 55. See also James M. Keating, "Seth Low and the Development of Columbia University" (Teachers College, Columbia University, unpublished Ed.D. dissertation, 1973), p. 168.

55. Seth Low, *Annual Report* (1894), p. 19.

56. Seth Low, "The University and the Workingman," *The Social Economist* (May 1891), 7–9. My italics.

57. Hoxie, *Faculty of Political Science,* p. 65; Seth Low to Faculty of Political Science and Philosophy, December 8, 1891, Butler Files, Central Filing, Columbia University.

58. Burgess, *Reminiscences,* pp. 241–42.

59. Hoxie, *Faculty of Political Science,* p. 67.

60. Seth Low, "A City University" [1895], in *State Aid to Higher Education* (Baltimore: Johns Hopkins University Press, 1898), pp. 45–63.

61. N. M. Butler, *Scholarship and Service* (New York: Scribner's, 1921), p. 11.

62. For Low's imagery as mayor, see Kurland, *Seth Low,* p. 41; For Columbia, see Seth Low, "Address," in Columbia University, *Dedication of the New Site* (1896), p. 53; for Butler see his "Columbia University and the City of New York," *Harper's Weekly* (May 16, 1896), 485–86.

63. See David Hammack, *Power and Society: Greater New York at the Turn of the Century* (New York: Russell Sage, 1982), chap. 9; Diane Ravitch, *The Great School Wars* (New York: Basic Books, 1974), chap. 14.

64. Nicholas Murray Butler, "The University and Modern Life," *Educational Review,* 29 (1905), 396–97. See also N. M. Butler, *Annual Report* (1919), pp. 26–27.

65. Randolph Bourne, *The Radical Will: Selected Writings,* ed. Olaf Hansen (New York: Urizen Books, 1977), p. 219.

66. On the whole phenomenon, see Laurence R. Veysey, *The Emergence of the American University* (Chicago: University of Chicago Press, 1965), chap. 7.

67. Quote from Joel Spingarn, "Scholarship and Criticism," in Harold Stearns, ed., *Civilization in the United States* (New York: Harcourt, Brace, 1922), p. 98.

68. See James McKeen Cattell, *University Control* (New York: Science Press, 1913), p. 33; William Summerscales, *Affirmation and Dissent: Columbia's Response to the Crisis of World War I* (New York: Teachers College Press, 1970), p. 14; Upton Sinclair, *The Goose-Step* [1923] (New York: AMS Press, 1970), esp. pp. 29–30. On Butler and public life, see his autobiography, *Across the Busy Years,* noting in particular the remarkable nineteen-page apologia at the beginning.

69. Veysey, *Emergence of the American University,* p. 366.

70. See Daniel Bell, *The Reforming of General Education* (New York: Columbia University Press, 1966), p. 96.

71. My thinking on this whole section has been importantly stimulated by the work of Wechsler, *Qualified Student;* Sherry Gorelick, *City College and the Jewish Poor* (New Brunswick: Rutgers University Press, 1981); and Robert Shaffer, "Jews, Reds, and Violets: Anti-Semitism and Anti-Radicalism at New York University, 1916–1933" (New York University, Master's Seminar Essay, January 1985).

72. See Robert I. Gannon, *Up to the Present: The Story of Fordham* (Garden City, N.Y.: Doubleday, 1967). Catholic education was similarly isolated in Chicago. See Steven J. Diner, *A City and Its Universities* (Chapel Hill: University of North Carolina Press, 1980), pp. 24–25.

73. Butler in the 1890s supported this policy. See N. M. Butler to Seth Low, August 7, 1897, Butler Files, Central Filing, Columbia University. See also Matthews, *A History of Columbia,* p. 170.

74. Seth Low to J. F. Plummer, July 18, 1898, Low Files, Central Filing, Columbia University.

75. On the percentage of Jewish students in high schools, see Wechsler, *Qualified Student,* p. 134.

76. S. Willis Rudy, *The College of the City of New York* (New York: City College Press, 1949), p. 382; and Wechsler, *Qualified Student,* pp. 192–93.

77. This trend toward national recruitment began with Low's academic improvements of the 1890s. See Low's *Annual Reports* (1895), p. 4; (1898), p. 12; (1899), p. 23; (1901), p. 31.

78. Wechsler, *Qualified Student,* pp. 187, 192–93.

79. N. M. Butler, Annual Report (1912), pp. 25–26. See also Dwight Miner, ed., *A*

History of Columbia College on Morningside (New York: Columbia University Press, 1954), pp. 19, 31–32.

80. Wechsler, *Qualified Student,* p. 82.

81. *Ibid.,* p. 163.

82. N. M. Butler, *Annual Report* (1917), pp. 13–15. See also *ibid.* (1920), pp. 36–39; and Wechsler, *Qualified Student.* On the low performance of Jews, Italians, and blacks on these tests (and the reason for it), see Allen Chase, *The Legacy of Malthus* (New York: Knopf, 1977), p. 262 and *passim.*

83. E. Digby Baltzell, *The Protestant Establishment* (New York: Vintage, 1966). See also Hall, *Organization of American Culture.*

84. Wechsler, *Qualified Student,* p. 135.

85. Herbert Hawkes, "Memorandum regarding the establishment of a Residential College," Herbert Hawkes File, Central Filing, Columbia University. See also Herbert Hawkes to Prof. E. B. Wilson, June 16, 1922, *ibid.*; Herbert Hawkes to N. M. Butler, October 29, 1919, *ibid.*; N. M. Butler to Herbert Hawkes, October 30, 1919, *ibid.*

86. Quotes and statistics in this and the preceding paragraph are from Shaffer, "Jews, Reds, and Violets," pp. 28, 1, 21, 31, 33. See also Theodore F. Jones, *New York University 1832–1932* (New York: New York University Press, 1933), pp. 226, 234.

87. *Ibid.,* p. 198.

88. Quoted in Marvin Gettleman, *An Elusive Presence: John H. Finley and His America* (Chicago: Nelson-Hall, 1979), p. 182.

89. Generally, see Marvin Gettleman, "John H. Finley at CCNY," *History of Education Quarterly,* 10 (1970), 423–39; Gorelick, *City College and the Jewish Poor;* and Rudy, *College of the City of New York,* esp. pp. 252, 269, 275.

90. Quoted in Wechsler, *Qualified Student,* p. 166.

91. Seth Low to N. M. Butler, January 11, 1911, Low Files, Central Filing, Columbia University; N. M. Butler to Seth Low, January 12, 1911, *ibid.*; Seth Low to N. M. Butler, January 17, 1911, *ibid.*

92. Seth Low to Trustees Committee on Education, January 31, 1911, *ibid.*

93. Seth Low to George L. Rives, September 14, 1911, *ibid.*; George L. Rives to John B. Pine, September 17, 1911, *ibid.*; Seth Low to George L. Rives, January 29, 1914, *ibid.*

CHAPTER 8

1. On Cohen and his significance, see David A. Hollinger, *Morris R. Cohen and the Scientific Ideal* (Cambridge: MIT Press, 1975); and *idem, In the American Province* (Bloomington: Indiana University Press, 1985), chap. 4.

2. On anti-Semitism in the discipline, see Hollinger, *Morris Cohen,* pp. 63 n.–64 n. Hollinger reports that Sidney Hook told him Cohen's appointment to Columbia was blocked on anti-Semitic grounds. Hollinger to author, September 24, 1985.

3. *The New Republic* (November 14, 1914), 16–17.

4. On these earlier episodes, see Thomas Bender, *History and Public Culture* (Baltimore: Johns Hopkins University Press, forthcoming), chap. 5.

5. Quotes from William Summerscales, *Affirmation and Dissent: Columbia's Response to the Crisis of World War I* (New York: Teachers College Press, 1970), pp. 51, 141, 52.

6. A copy of this pamphlet is in the Columbiana Room, Low Library.

7. Ross's characterization appears in her sketch of Cattell for the *Dictionary of American Biography.*

8. See James McK. Cattell to John Dewey, May 14, 1913, and May 15, 1913, James McKeen Cattell Papers, Butler Library, Columbia University.

9. James McK. Cattell to John Dewey, May 14, 1913, *ibid.;* James McKeen Cattell, *University Control* (New York: Science Press, 1913), p. v. The best account of the whole affair is Carol Cruber, "Academic Freedom at Columbia University, 1917–1918: The Case of James McKeen Cattell," *AAUP Bulletin,* 58 (1972), 297–305.

10. Cattell, *University Control,* pp. 5, 14, 32, 35, 18, 62.

11. James McK. Cattell to Honorable Julius Kahn, August 23, 1917, Cattell Papers.

12. Columbia University, *Report of the Special Committee Appointed March 5, 1917, to Inquire into the State of Teaching in the University* (1917), p. 2.

13. For Beard's explanation, see his statement, first published in *The New Republic* and conveniently available in Richard Hofstadter and Wilson Smith, eds., *American Higher Education: A Documentary History* (2 vols.; Chicago: University of Chicago Press, 1961), II, 887–92.

14. N. M. Butler, *Annual Report* (1918), p. 42.

15. *New York Times,* October 10, 1917. For Dewey's public response, see *New York American,* October 10, 1917.

16. John Dewey to E. R. A. Seligman, October 10, 1917, Seligman Papers, Butler Library, Columbia University.

17. Jacques Barzun, ed., *A History of the Faculty of Philosophy* (New York: Columbia University Press, 1957), pp. 126–27. The only communications after this date to or from John Dewey that I was able to locate in the official university files concerned his pension and retirement plans.

18. Reprinted in Hofstadter and Smith, eds, *American Higher Education,* II, 883–84.

19. N. M. Butler, *Annual Report* (1917), pp. 49–50. See also his *Annual Report* (1918), pp. 42, 48.

20. John W. Burgess to E. R. A. Seligman, February 17, 1917, and August 29, 1918, Seligman Papers.

21. This motivated even Wesley Clair Mitchell, the least "radical" of the founders. See Lucy Sprague Mitchell, *Two Lives: The Story of Wesley Clair Mitchell and Myself* (New York: Simon & Shuster, 1953), p. 340. On the original name, see *ibid.,* p. 333. On the *Ecole libre* model, see Herbert Croly, "A School of Social Research," *The New Republic* (June 8, 1918), 167.

22. Bertha Mailly, "The Rand School of Social Science," *Report of Proceedings, First National Conference on Workers Education in the United States* (New York: Workers Education Bureau, 1921), pp. 25–27; Margaret Hodgen, *Workers' Education in England and the United States* (New York: Dutton, 1925), pp. 216–17; Morris Hillquit, *Loose Leaves from a Busy Life* (New York: Macmillan, 1934), p. 66.

23. Charles F. Howlett, "More than Business Unionism: Brookwood Labor College and Worker Commitment to Peace and Social Justice, 1919–1937" (Master's thesis, Teachers College, Columbia University, 1983).

24. Ellen Nore, *Charles A. Beard: An Intellectual Biography* (Carbondale: Southern Illinois University, 1983), p. 94.

25. Quoted in Mitchell, *Two Lives,* p. 333.

26. James T. Shotwell, *Autobiography* (Indianapolis: Bobbs-Merrill, 1961), p. 42; James Harvey Robinson, "A Journal of Opinion," *The New Republic* (May 8, 1915), 9–11.

27. Peter Rutkoff and William B. Scott, *New School: A History of the New School for Social Research* (New York: Free Press, 1986), pp. 11–12.

28. Luther V. Hendricks, "James Harvey Robinson and the New School for Social Research," *Journal of Higher Education,* 20 (1949), 5; James Harvey Robinson, "The New School," *School and Society,* 11 (January 31, 1920), 130–31.

29. Croly, "A School of Social Research," p. 168.

30. Alvin Johnson, *Pioneer's Progress: An Autobiography* (New York: Viking, 1952), p. 273.

31. Quoted in Nore, *Beard*, p. 89.

32. On other attacks, see David Levy, *Herbert Croly and the New Republic* (Princeton: Princeton University Press, 1985), p. 271; Hendricks, "James Harvey Robinson and the New School for Social Research," pp. 9–10.

33. Charles A. Beard, "A Suggestion from Professor Beard," *The Freeman*, 3 (July 20, 1921), 450–51.

34. The best biographical source on Mitchell is Mitchell, *Two Lives*, and on Beard, see Nore, *Beard*.

35. W. C. Mitchell, "Statistics and Government" (1917), excerpted in Mitchell, *Two Lives*, p. 304.

36. *Ibid.*, pp. 342–43.

37. *Ibid.*, p. 351.

38. On the general trend, see Merle Curti, ed., *American Scholarship in the Twentieth Century* (Cambridge: Harvard University Press, 1953), pp. 7–8.

39. Robert Kohler, "A Policy for the Advancement of Science: The Rockefeller Foundation, 1924–1929," *Minerva*, 16 (1978), 480–515; Beardsley Ruml, "Recent Trends in Social Science," in Leonard White, ed., *The New Social Science* (Chicago: University of Chicago Press, 1930), esp. p. 105; Wesley Clair Mitchell, "Research in the Social Sciences," *ibid.*, pp. 4–15; Barry Karl, *Charles E. Merriam and the Study of Politics* (Chicago: University of Chicago Press, 1974); Frederick A. Ogg, *Research in the Humanities and Social Sciences* (New York: Century Company, 1928), pp. 155–63; Martin Bulmer, "The Early Institutional Establishment of Social Science Research: The Local Community Research Committee at the University of Chicago, 1923–1930," *Minerva*, 18 (1980), 51–110; Guy Alchon, *The Invisible Hand of Planning: Capitalism, Social Science, and the State in the 1920s* (Princeton: Princeton University Press, 1985), esp. pp. 117–23.

40. Social Science Research Council, *Decennial Report, 1923–1933* (1934), pp. 1–2, 6.

41. Edward A. Purcell, Jr., *The Crisis of Democratic Theory* (Lexington: University Press of Kentucky, 1973), p. 28.

42. Karl, *Merriam*, p. ix.

43. Joseph Schumpeter, "The General Economist," in Arthur Burns, ed., *Wesley Clair Mitchell* (New York: National Bureau of Economic Research, 1952), p. 321; Purcell, *Crisis of Democratic Theory*, p. 26.

44. On this profoundly important issue, see the honest, refreshing, and illuminating work of Charles Lindblom and David K. Cohen, *Usable Knowledge: Social Science and Social Problem Solving* (New Haven: Yale University Press, 1979).

45. See, for example, Luther H. Gulick, "Educational Adjustment to Modern Governmental Needs," in Henry Pratt Fairchild, ed., *The Obligation of Universities to the Social Order* (New York: New York University Press, 1933), p. 279.

46. On this notion of institutionalization, see Edward Shils, "Tradition, Ecology, and Institution in the History of Sociology," in his *The Constitution of Society* (Chicago: University of Chicago Press, 1982), esp. pp. 275–84.

47. President's Research Committee on Social Trends, *Recent Social Trends in the United States* (2 vols.; New York: McGraw-Hill, 1933), pp. xiii, xciv.

48. Barry Karl, "Presidential Planning and Social Science Research: Mr. Hoover's Experts," *Perspectives in American History*, 3 (1969), 348.

49. Charles A. Beard, review of *Recent Social Trends,* in *Yale Review,* 22 (1933), 595–97; Charles A. Beard, "Limits to the Application of Social Science Implied in *Recent Social Trends,*" *Social Forces,* 11 (1933), 510.

50. Jane S. Dahlberg, *The New York Bureau of Municipal Research* (New York: New York University Press, 1966), pp. 30, 41 n.

51. John Braeman, "Charles A. Beard, Historian and Progressive," in Martin C. Swanson, ed., *Charles A. Beard: An Observance of the Centennial of His Birth* (Greencastle, Ind.: DePauw University, 1976), p. 57. For an example of such constraint, a rather bald one, see A. Fulton Cutting to E. R. A. Seligman, July 24, 1907; E. R. A. Seligman to George Sikes, July 24, 1907; and Charles Merriam to E. R. A. Seligman, May 6, 1907, all in Seligman Papers.

52. Charles A. Beard, *Government Research* (New York: Municipal Administration Service, 1926), p. 4.

53. Matthew Josephson, "Charles A. Beard: A Memoir," *Virginia Quarterly Review,* 25 (1949), 585.

54. See Purcell, *Crisis of Democratic Theory,* pp. 191–92.

55. Charles A. Beard, *The Open Door at Home* (New York: Macmillan, 1934), p. 138.

56. For a fuller discussion of all these themes, see my essays "The New History—Then and Now," *Reviews in American History,* 12 (1984), 612–22; "The Historian and Public Life: Charles A. Beard and the City," in my *History and Public Culture,* forthcoming.

57. Charles A. Beard to Abraham Flexner, December 21, 1930, Beard Letters, Microfilm, Butler Library, Columbia University.

58. The basic biographical work on Dewey is George Dykhuizen, *The Life and Mind of John Dewey* (Carbondale: Southern Illinois University Press, 1973).

59. Randolph Bourne, "John Dewey's Philosophy," *The New Republic* (March 13, 1915), 154. See also C. Wright Mills, *Sociology and Pragmatism* (New York: Oxford University Press, 1964), p. 312.

60. Dykhuizen, *Dewey,* p. 180.

61. Neil Coughlin, *Young John Dewey* (Chicago: University of Chicago Press, 1975), p. 155; Hillquit, *Loose Leaves,* pp. 68–70.

62. Quoted in Coughlin, *Young John Dewey,* p. 136.

63. Bruce Kuklick, *The Rise of American Philosophy: Cambridge, Massachusetts, 1860–1930* (New Haven: Yale University Press, 1977); Robert Westbrook, "Dewey's Truth," *History of Education Quarterly,* 20 (1980), 346.

64. John Dewey, "The Need for a Recovery of Philosophy," in John Dewey et al., *Creative Intelligence* (New York: Holt, 1917), p. 65.

65. See Westbrook, "Dewey's Truth"; James T. Kloppenberg, "Independent Intellectuals and Democratic Theory in America, 1880–1920" (paper presented to Hungarian-American Historians Conference, Princeton, April 1985), pp. 3, 4, 7. See also James T. Kloppenberg, *Uncertain Victory: Social Democracy and Progressivism in European and American Thought, 1870–1920* (New York: Oxford University Press, 1985); and Robert Westbrook, *John Dewey and Democracy* (forthcoming). More generally, see Richard Rorty, *Philosophy and the Mirror of Nature* (Princeton: Princeton University Press, 1979).

66. John Dewey, "Social Stresses and Strains," *International Journal of Ethics,* 43 (1933), 344–45. The presentation of "problems" by social scientists was not so knowingly done as Dewey assumed. See Karl, "Presidential Planning," p. 401.

67. John Dewey, *The Middle Works, 1899–1924,* ed. Jo Ann Boydston (14 vols.; Carbondale: Southern Illinois University Press, 1976), VIII, 100. See also Westbrook, "Dewey's Truth," p. 350.

68. Kloppenberg, "Independent Intellectuals and Democratic Theory in America," p. 29.

69. Citations to *The Public and Its Problems* (1927) are to the printing in John Dewey, *The Later Works, 1925–1953*, ed. Jo Ann Boydston, Vol. II (Carbondale: Southern Illinois Univ. Press, 1984), pp. 341, 350, 364.

70. *Ibid.*, p. 365.

71. See also John Dewey, *Liberalism and Social Action* (New York: G. P. Putnam's, 1935), pp. 44, 79. More generally, see John Dewey, *Freedom and Culture* [1939] (New York: Capricorn Books, 1963).

72. Dewey, *The Public and Its Problems*, pp. 365, 367.

73. *Ibid.*, pp. 371, 367–68, 370.

74. Alvin Gouldner, *The Future of the Intellectuals and the Rise of the New Class* (New York: Seabury Press, 1979), pp. 3–4, 28–29.

75. John Rawls, *A Theory of Justice* (Cambridge: Harvard Univ. Press, 1971); Robert Nozick, *Anarchy, State and Utopia* (New York: Basic Books, 1974).

76. John Dewey, "American Education and Culture," *New Republic* (July 1, 1916), 215–17.

77. For their appreciation of this legacy, see Trilling's chapter in Miner, ed. *A History of Columbia College,* p. 29; Richard Hofstadter, *The Progressive Historians* (New York: Knopf, 1968), p. 184; Richard Hofstadter, "The Revolution in Higher Education," in Arthur Schlesinger and Morton White, eds. *Paths of American Thought* (Boston: Houghton Mifflin, 1963), p. 287; Mills, *Sociology and Pragmatism*, esp. chaps. 16–17. See also Rexford Tugwell, *To the Lesser Heights of Morningside: A Memoir* (Philadelphia: University of Pennsylvania Press, 1982), p. 151.

78. Hofstadter, *Progressive Historians*, p. xiv. His first article: "The Tariff Issue on the Eve of the Civil War," *American Historical Review*, 44 (1938), 50–55.

79. C. Wright Mills, *White Collar* (New York: Oxford University Press, 1956), p. xx. His dissertation was published as *Sociology and Pragmatism*.

80. On all of this, see Richard Gillam, "Richard Hofstadter and C. Wright Mills and the 'Critical Ideal,' " *American Scholar*, 47 (1977–78), 69–85. His larger study, an intellectual biography of Mills, will further illuminate these matters.

81. This was especially true of Hofstadter. See H. Stuart Hughes, interview, Richard Hofstadter Project, p. 4, Oral History Collection, Columbia University.

82. For biographical information, I have relied upon Richard W. Fox, *Reinhold Niebuhr: A Biography* (New York: Pantheon, 1985).

CHAPTER 9

1. On this matter of lateness, see Irving Howe, *A Margin of Hope: An Intellectual Autobiography* (New York: Harcourt Brace Jovanovich, 1982), p. 151.

2. On this general shift, see Warren Susman, *Culture as History* (New York: Pantheon, 1984), chap. 9. For the best telling of the traditional story, see James B. Gilbert, *Writers and Partisans* (New York: Wiley, 1968).

3. This is not the place for a full evaluation of the cultural coverage of the *Partisan Review, The Nation,* and *The New Republic* in the 1930s and 1940s, but a few generalizations are possible, based upon a survey of the magazines. *Partisan Review* took the least notice of the fields of architecture, music, and dance (practically none), while it regularly reported on developments in art in the 1940s (George L. K. Morris, Clement Greenberg, James Johnson Sweeney, and Robert Goldwater, with occasional pieces, usually book reviews, by Meyer Schapiro). During the late 1940s there was some coverage of music, and two articles on architecture by Frederick Kiesler.

Coverage in *The Nation* was better than in *The New Republic*. During the 1930s Paul Rosenfeld wrote on music in *The New Republic*, while Horace Gregory, Stark Young, and James Johnson Sweeney wrote on art, with Rosenfeld sometimes contributing as well. Lewis Mumford, Douglas Haskell, and Catherine Bauer wrote regularly on architecture. As the thirties wore on, coverage declined. *The Nation,* by contrast, extended its coverage as the thirties passed into the forties. Margaret Marshall, as editor of the "back of the book," made the cultural pages an exciting cultural forum, with Clement Greenberg writing on art, B. H. Haggin on music and dance, Diana Trilling on books, James Agee on films. Earlier, in the thirties, Paul Rosenfeld wrote on art, Douglas Haskell on architecture, and Lincoln Kirstein on dance.

4. Clement Greenberg, *Art and Culture* (Boston: Beacon Press, 1961), p. 230.

5. Arlene Croce, "Dance Books in My Life," *Dance Magazine* (March 1969), 39.

6. Susman, *Culture as History,* p. 182; Trilling quoted in Laurence Bergreen, *James Agee* (New York: Penguin, 1985), p. 260.

7. Bergreen, *James Agee,* p. 214.

8. James Agee and Walker Evans, *Let Us Now Praise Famous Men* (Boston: Houghton Mifflin, 1941, 1980), p. xv.

9. Bernard Taper, *Balanchine* (rev. ed.; New York: Macmillan, 1974), p. 268.

10. Irving Howe, "Ballet for the Man Who Enjoys Wallace Stevens," *Harper's* (May 1971), 102. Denby had unequivocally called Balanchine "the greatest choreographer of our time" in 1944. Denby, *Looking at the Dance* (New York: Horizon, 1968), p. 70.

11. Virgil Thomson, *A Virgil Thomson Reader* (Boston: Houghton Mifflin, 1981), pp. 542–55.

12. Howe is both honest and revealing on this point. See his "Ballet for the Man Who Enjoys Wallace Stevens" and his *A Margin of Hope,* pp. 336–37.

13. Thomson, *A Virgil Thomson Reader,* p. 553.

14. This phrasing comes from Thomson, who was describing the shift from the 1930s to the 1940s in New York, but I think that in a relative way it also well characterizes the difference between the two groups. See Virgil Thomson, *Virgil Thomson* (London: Weidenfeld & Nicholson, 1967), p. 313.

15. Thomson, *A Virgil Thomson Reader,*p. 263.

16. Lincoln Kirstein, *Thirty Years* (New York: Knopf, 1978), p. 33.

17. *Ibid.,* p. 82.

18. Quotes from Linda Nochlin, "Florine Stettheimer: Rococo Subversive," *Art in America* (September 1980), 73.

19. For identifications, see Parker Tyler, *Florine Stettheimer: A Life in Art* (New York: Farrar, Straus, 1963), pp. 73–78.

20. Svetlana Alpers, *The Art of Describing: Dutch Art in the Seventeenth Century* (Chicago: University of Chicago Press, 1983).

21. Reprinted in his *Art and Culture,* pp. 3–21. See also Robert Warshow, "The Legacy of the 30s," in his *The Immediate Experience* (Garden City, N.Y.: Doubleday, 1962).

22. Dwight Macdonald, "Action on West 53rd Street," *The New Yorker* (December 12, 1953), 79.

23. Peter M. Rutkoff and William B. Scott, *New School: A History of the New School for Social Research* (New York: Free Press, 1986), chap. 3.

24. Thomas B. Hess, "Sketch for a Portrait of the Art Historian Among Artists," *Social Research,* 45 (1978), 6–14. For Schapiro's most important service of this sort, see his article "Nature of Abstract Art," originally published in the *Marxist Quarterly* (1937), but since reprinted, without reference to its origins, in his *Modern Art* (New York: Braziller, 1978), pp. 185–211.

25. *New York Times*, January 7, 16, 1935.

26. Newbold Morris, *Let the Chips Fall: My Battles Against Corruption* (New York: Appleton-Century-Crofts, 1955), pp. 161, 164.

27. *New York Times*, November 30, December 12, 1943; Kirstein, *Thirty Years*, p. 105.

28. August Heckscher, *When La Guardia Was Mayor* (New York: Norton, 1978), p. 368.

29. Taper, *Balanchine*, p. 229.

30. *New York Times*, February 18, 1968. See also the ephemeral obituary material in the Baum clipping file, Dance Collection, New York Public Library, Lincoln Center.

31. Quoted in Serge Guilbaut, *How New York Stole the Idea of Modern Art*, trans. Arthur Goldhammer (Chicago: University of Chicago Press, 1983), p. 172.

32. On internationalism between the wars, see Robert A. Divine, *Second Chance: The Triumph of Internationalism During World War II* (New York: Atheneum, 1967).

33. Thomas B. Hess, *Abstract Painting* (New York: Viking, 1951), pp. 97, 98.

34. John Peale Bishop, "The Arts," *Kenyon Review*, 3 (1941), 183–84; Greenberg, *Art and Culture*, p. 234; *New York Times*, January 19, 1943; Pollock is reprinted in Barbara Rose, ed., *Readings in American Art Since 1900* (New York: Praeger, 1968), p. 152; Arthur Danto, "Ralston Crawford," *The Nation* (December 7, 1985), 626.

35. Roger Sessions, *Roger Sessions on Music* (Princeton: Princeton University Press, 1979), pp. 320–22. See also Aaron Copland, *Copland on Music* (Garden City, N.Y.: Doubleday, 1960), pp. 55, 58; and John Rockwell, *All American Music* (New York: Vintage, 1984), p. 45.

36. Quoted in Walter Terry, *I Was There* (New York: Marcel Dekker, 1978), p. 171.

37. Kirstein, *Thirty Years*, pp. 106, 119; Greenberg, "The Present Prospects of American Painting and Sculpture," *Horizon*, 16 (October 1947), 25, 29; Merle Armitage, ed., *Martha Graham* [1937] (Brooklyn: Dance Horizons, 1966), p. 102.

38. Quotes from Aaron Copland and Vivian Perlis, *Copland: 1900 through 1942* (New York: St. Martin's, 1984), pp. 68–69. On Boulanger in this context, see Barbara Tischler, *An American Music: The Search for an American Musical Identity* (New York: Oxford University Press, 1986).

39. Sessions, *Roger Sessions on Music*, pp. 29, 135, 293.

40. On streets and Balanchine's ballets, see Edwin Denby, *Dancers, Buildings and People in the Streets* (New York: Popular Library, 1965), esp. pp. 58, 61.

41. Kirstein, *Thirty Years*, p. 130; Elizabeth Kendall, *Dancing* (New York: Ford Foundation, 1983), p. 10; Marc Blitzstein, "Talk, Music, Dance: New York, 1933," *Modern Music*, 11 (1933), 35–36; Edwin Denby, *Looking at the Dance*, pp. 45, 44.

42. Henry-Russell Hitchcock and Philip Johnson, *The International Style* [1932] (New York: Norton, 1966), esp. pp. 65–67. See, more generally, William Jordy, "The Aftermath of the Bauhaus in America: Gropius, Mies, and Breuer," *Perspectives in American History*, 2 (1968), 485–541.

43. Don McDonagh, *Martha Graham* (New York: Popular Library, 1975), p. 185.

44. Armitage, ed., *Graham*, pp. 102–3.

45. Schapiro, *Modern Art*, p. 224.

46. Denby, *Looking at the Dance*, p. 36.

47. It may be worth making three points here about the limited international visibility of literature in New York. First, émigré writers had less impact on the culture of New York than did artists, composers, and choreographers simply because lack of facility in the local language hampered their work in a way it did not the work of nonliterary artists. Second, it is harder to internationalize writing at any event. Words, perhaps because of the greater complexity of language, less easily transcend the local and experiential roots of their meanings than do sounds and images. Third, if there

was, as I have suggested, some difficulty about describing the world, abstraction was not an option for writers, though in the early 1950s there was talk in New York about creating an Abstract Expressionist theater, and earlier Gertrude Stein had largely reduced the subject to non-existence, making a literature of nearly pure sound and syntax, but she had few successors. Words could not be separated from meaning, and this left only the silence of refusal. If one writer chooses silence, as Beckett did, literature, on an international scale, can advance. But there are limits. If more do the same, not only does boredom result, but the whole enterprise of literature itself is endangered.

48. George Balanchine, "Notes of Choreography," *Dance Index*, 4 (February–March 1945), 30, 20, 21; Arlene Croce, *Afterimages* (New York: Knopf, 1978), p. 55.

49. Kirstein, *Thirty Years;* Kirstein, "The Popular Style in American Dancing," *The Nation* (April 16, 1938), 450–51; Denby, *Looking at the Dance;* Denby, *Dancers;* Virgil Thomson, *A Virgil Thomson Reader;* Thomson, *American Music Since 1910* (New York: Holt, Rinehart and Winston, 1971); Aaron Copland, *Copland on Music;* Copland, *The New Music, 1900–1960* (New York: Norton, 1968); Greenberg, *Art and Culture.* The works of the younger Harold Rosenberg are worth noting. See his *The De-definition of Art* (Chicago: University of Chicago Press, 1983); and *Discovering the Present* (Chicago: University of Chicago Press, 1973).

50. Quote from Denby, *Looking at the Dance,* p. 402.

51. See Greenberg, *Art and Culture,* pp. 124–26; Thomson, *American Music,* pp. 72–73.

52. Schapiro, *Modern Art,* p. 176. Note how often freedom and its cognates appear in *ibid.,* pp. 185–232. More generally, see Guilbaut, *How New York Stole the Idea of Modern Art.*

53. Howe, *A Margin of Hope,* pp. 336–37.

54. See Martin Filler, "Tall Stories," *New York Review of Books* (December 5, 1985), 11–18, on Huxtable and Mumford.

55. Lewis Mumford, "The Case Against 'Modern Architecture,' " in his *The Highway and the City* (New York: Harvest, 1963), pp. 162–75. On his reasons for resigning the *New Yorker* column, I rely on Sophia Mumford to author, December, 19, 1985.

56. Saul Bellow, "Literature and Culture: An Interview with Saul Bellow," *Salmagundi,* no. 30 (1975), 12.

57. "From the Notebooks of Lionel Trilling," *Partisan Review,* 51 (1984), 509.

58. Hess, "Sketch for a Portrait of the Art Historian Among Artists," pp. 6–14.

59. Lionel Abel, *The Intellectual Follies* (New York: Norton, 1984), p. 210.

INDEX

NOTE: All institutions, organizations, and buildings cited in this index without geographical identification are located in New York City.

"Duty of the American Scholar to
Politics and the Times, The," 178
and Godkin, 177–8
and *Nation*, 185–6, 190–1
and *Putnam's Monthly*, 164, 168, 178
"Saturday Sermon, A," 185–6

Damrosch, Frank, 217–19
Damrosch, Leopold, 217
Damrosch, Walter, 217
Dana, Charles Anderson, 165 *n.*
Dana, Henry Wadsworth Longfellow,
298
Dana, James Freeman, 124 and *n.*
Dance Index, 322–3
dance in NYC (20th century), 322–3,
327–40 *passim*
Danto, Arthur C., 335, 340
Darwin, Charles, 198
Davidson, Thomas, 294
Davies, Arthur B., 329
Davis, Charles A., 135
Defence of Poetry, A (Shelley), 155 *n.*
de Kay, Helena, 213, 214, 329
Delafield, John, 92, 93
Delafield, Joseph, 92, 93
Delafield, William, 58
De Lancey family, 11
Dell, Floyd, 230, 232
Democracy and Education (Dewey), 309
democracy and literature, 149, 151, 152,
153–5
democratic culture, xvi–xvii
Bourne on, 246–8
Brownell and Arnold on, 212–13
James (H.) on, 248–9
Olmsted on, 199–202 *passim*
university and, 96, 97–107; *see also*
universities and colleges:
admissions policies; universities and
colleges: and immigrant students
see also knowledge, diffusion of
Democratic Party, Locofoco faction
and Free University, 104–5
Leggett and, 147–8
Longfellow on, 149
and Young America, 141

Democratic Review, 144–52
circulation, 144 *n.*
contributors, 146, 150, 165
and *Knickerbocker Magazine*,
contrasted, 140
and Melville, 151–2
and *New Republic*, compared, 227
and *Putnam's Monthly*, contrasted, 167
and Whitman, 151, 152–4
Democratic Society, 46
Demorest's Illustrated Monthly, 222
Denby, Edwin, 322, 337, 338
Depression (1930s), 311, 331
Dewey, John, 234, 235, 238, 242, 245,
285, 298–9, 309–16
Art as Experience, 310, 330
and Beard, rejected by successors,
316–17
Democracy and Education, 309
Experience and Nature, 310, 312
and *New Republic*, 309, 310
Public and Its Problems, The, 312, 313–15
and World War I, 242
Dial, The, 158, 249, 250, 252, 256
Dickens, Charles, 3
diversity (social) of NYC, xvi, 5–6,
201–2, 247–9, 334
economic, 171, 198–9
see also immigrants in NYC
doctors, *see* medical profession in NYC
Dodge, Mabel, 228, 230 *n.*, 238
Douglas, Stephen A., 167
Draft Riots (1864), 188
Drake, Joseph Rodman, 130, 214
drama, *see* theater and drama in NYC
Draper, John W., 106–7 and *n.*, 113,
265
at Cooper Union inauguration, 116
Draper, Muriel, 326
Dreiser, Theodore, 208, 233
Dreyfus affair, 228, 259
Drift and Mastery (Lippmann), 238,
245
Drone Club, *see* Friendly Club
Duberman, Martin, 149
Dubinsky, David, 333
Du Bois, W. E. B., 252
Duer, John, 135
Duer, William, 49, 135
Duncan, Isadora, 228, 329

on centralizing NYC's cultural
    institutions, 268–9
and Columbia, 265, 267, 274
on New-York Historical Society, 76
and philanthropy, 109
on poetry of NYC, 154 *n.*
Strong, George Washington, 30
Sturges, Jonathan, 123
subways, 287–8
Sullivan, Mary Quinn, 329
Sumner, Charles, 178
Susman, Warren, 323
Sweeney, James Johnson, 326
Swords, Thomas and James, 32, 42
symbolists (French), 258–9

Talisman, The (annual), 136
Tallmadge, James, 103–4 and *n.*
Tammany Museum, 47
Tammany Society (Tammany Hall),
    46–8
  Clinton and, 52
  and General Society of Mechanics and
    Tradesmen, 79
  Miller (S.) and, 42
  as national improvement society,
    46–7, 55
  as political power, 170–1, 179, 215,
    230, 282
Tappan, Arthur, 61
Tappan, Henry P., 108–14, 267
  University Education, 110, 111
Taylor, Bayard, 139
telegraph, 106, 119, 124 and *n.*, 125 *n.*
tenement buildings, 171, 206
Tetracty's Club, 142
Thackeray, William Makepeace, 164
Thayer, Schofield, 249
theater and drama in NYC, 328
  City Center for, 332–3
  Dunlap and (18th century), 30, 37–8
  1930s, 323, 326
  vaudeville, 216
Thompson, Vance, 220–1
Thomson, Virgil, 322, 324, 325, 326,
    329, 330, 338
  Four Saints in Three Acts, 327
Thoreau, Henry David, 154, 165 *n.*

Tilden, Samuel J., 145, 281
Times Square, 156, 253
Tin Pan Alley, 216, 253
Tocqueville, Alexis de, xiv, 3, 248
  and Atheneum, 73
  on egalitarian impulse in America,
    129
  on Hosack, 66
Tompkins Square Riot (1874), 187–8
Toomer, Jean, 254
Torrey, John, 72
"Tradition and the Individual Talent"
    (Eliot), 212 *n.*
Trahison des clercs, La (Benda), 243
Traubel, Horace, 153
Triangle Shirtwaist Factory fire (1911),
    230
Trilling, Diana, 324
  Claremont Essays, 342
Trilling, Lionel, 231, 248, 251, 255,
    262, 316–17, 323
  Beyond Culture, 342
  Liberal Imagination, The, 317, 342
Trinity Cemetery, 253
Trinity Church, 11, 27
  and King's College, 21, 22
  as slumlord, 215
Trow's City Directory, 163
Trumbull, John, 127
Tuesday Club (Philadelphia), 32
Twain, Mark, 140, 214
Tweed, William Marcy ("Boss Tweed"),
    170, 174
  Curtis and Godkin and, 186, 187,
    189
  Curtis and Nast and, 179, 180

Ulysses (Joyce), 251
Uncle Tom's Cabin (Stowe), 197
Union College, Schenectady, N.Y., 103
    n., 137
Union League Club, 175, 181, 216
Union Square and environs, 216, 273
Union Theological Seminary, 43, 269,
    283, 318
United Nations building, 334
United Society of Journeymen
    Shipwrights and Caulkers, 65